Theory of Modeling and Simulation

Integrating Discrete Event and Continuous Complex Dynamic Systems

Theory of Modeling and Simulation

Integrating Discrete Event and Continuous Complex Dynamic Systems

Second Edition

BERNARD P. ZEIGLER
Electrical and Computer Engineering Department
University of Arizona
Tucson, Arizona

HERBERT PRAEHOFER
Institute of Systems Science
Johannes Kepler University
Linz, Austria

TAG GON KIM
Department of Electrical Engineering
Korea Advanced Institute of Science and Technology
Taejon, Korea

ELSEVIER

AMSTERDAM • BOSTON • HEIDELBERG • LONDON
NEW DELHI • NEW YORK • OXFORD • PARIS • SAN DIEGO
SAN FRANCISCO • SINGAPORE • SYDNEY • TOKYO
Academic Press is an imprint of Elsevier

Theory of Modeling and Simulation, 2/e
Zeigler, Praehofer and Kim

Original ISBN: 978-0-12-778455-7

Reprinted 2007, 2012, 2013

Indian Reprint ISBN: 978-81-312-0740-6

Published by Elsevier, a division of Reed Elsevier India Private Limited

Registered Office: 305, Rohit House, 3 Tolstoy Marg, New Delhi - 110 001
Corporate Office: 14th Floor, Tower 10B, DLF Cyber City, Phase-II, Gurgaon - 122 002, Haryana

Printed and bound in India at Sheel Print-N-Pack
D-132, Hosiery Complex, Phase II, NOIDA 201 305.

To parents: Maurice and Sylvia Zeigler and Stanley and Helen Dymek

B.P.Z.

To my father, Karl Praehofer, and my mother-in-law, Friederike Bell

H.P.

To my wife, Hyun Sook, and my daughter, Bo Young

T.G.K.

Contents

Preface to the First Edition

A Theory of Modeling and Simulation—Why?

The field of modeling and simulation is as diverse as the concerns of man. Every discipline has developed, or is developing, its own models and its own approach and tools for studying these models. Why then is an overall theory of modeling and simulation necessary?

Why should a college senior or first-year graduate student majoring in biology, aeronautical engineering or business management be introduced to the general theory of modeling and simulation—yet another discipline not specific to his own? The answer relies on the same reasoning that determined that the student should have acquired at least some grounding in mathematics. Nobody questions the role of arithmetic in the sciences, engineering, and management. Arithmetic is all pervasive, yet it is a mathematical discipline having its own axioms and logical structure. Its content is not specific to any other disciplines but is directly applicable to them all. Thus students of biology and engineering are not taught how to add differently—the different training comes in what to add, when to do it, and why.

The practice of modeling and simulation too is all pervasive. However, it has its own concepts of model description, simplification, validation, simulation, and exploration, which are not specific to any particular discipline. These statements would be agreed to by all. Not everyone, however, would say that the concepts named could be isolated and abstracted in a generally useful form.

In response, this book attempts to provide a framework in which the concepts can be sketched in their clear abstract forms; embodying the concepts in concrete modeling situations further serves to illuminate them. Of what use is such a framework for the specializing student, or the one who later will specialize? It can fulfill the following purposes:

1. Introduce the student to the full range of concepts and tools available in the field, rather than just those currently employed in his discipline.
2. Provide a perspective on the modeling activity of his own discipline, permitting the creative employment of insights and approaches stemming from other disciplines.
3. Provide an understanding of why we model and simulate, what can be achieved, and what cannot be achieved.
4. Provide a universal language for communicating the structure and behavior of models to others, regardless of whether they are conversant with the interpretive frameworks of their respective disciplines.

We have been talking about the theory of modeling and simulation relative to the noncomputer sciences. However, the book is also addressed to those who are interested in general and mathematical systems theory or in the more specialized computer and information sciences. Indeed, the framework developed here reflects several related influences:

- General systems theory, with its belief in an underlaying and exploitable unity in all systems, diverse though they may seem.
- Mathematical systems theory, with its attempts to formalize the concepts of system structure and behavior.
- Automata theory, with its formal, logical, and algebraic analysis of the behavior and interrelations of computer-related models.

In this context this book marshals the available approaches and formalisms in order to deal with the particular issues raised by modeling and simulation. Thus the theory presented should introduce the student of systems and computer science to the many open problems in the area needing conceptual and/or mathematical development, as well as furnish a basis for attacking them.

For the veteran practitioner of modeling and simulation, the book will fill an important gap in the literature between the material that is very abstract and that which is very applied. The reader who has had little formal mathematics may find the going rough. Still, my hope is that he will be led to more clearly perceive the issues faced daily in his modeling efforts.

B.P.Z.
Ann Arbor, 1976

Preface to the Second Edition

This is the second edition of *Theory of Modeling and Simulation* originally published by Wiley Interscience in 1976 and reissued by Krieger Publishers in 1984. The first edition made the case that a theory was necessary to help bring some coherence and unity to the ubiquitous field of modeling and simulation. Although nearly a quarter of a century later there have been many advances in the field, we believe that a widely accepted framework and theoretical foundation are even more necessary today. Modeling and simulation lore is still fragmented across the disciplines making it difficult to share in the advances, reuse other discipline's ideas, and work collaboratively in multidisciplinary teams. As a consequence of the growing specialization of knowledge, there is even more fragmentation in the field now than ever. The need for "knowledge workers" who can synthesize disciplinary fragments into cohesive wholes is increasingly recognized. Modeling and simulation—as a generic, non-discipline-specific, set of activities—can provide a framework of concepts and tools for such knowledge work.

In the years since the first edition, there has been much significant progress in modeling and simulation, but the progress has not been uniform across the board. Generally, model building and simulation execution have been made easier and faster by riding piggyback on the technology advances in software (e.g., object-oriented programming) and hardware (e.g., faster processors). However, hard, fundamental issues such as model credibility (e.g., validation, verification, and model family consistency) and interoperation (e.g., repositories, reuse of components, and resolution matching) have received a lot less attention. But these issues are now moving to the front and center under the impetus of the High Level Architecture (HLA) standard mandated by the United States Department of Defense for all its contractors and agencies.

In this edition, two major contributors to the theory of modeling and simulation join with the original author to completely revise the original text. As suggested by its subtitle, the current book concentrates on the integration of the continuous and discrete paradigms for modeling and simulation. A second major theme is that of distributed simulation and its potential to support the coexistence of multiple formalisms in multiple model components.

Although the material is mostly new, the presentation format remains the same. There are three major sections. Part I introduces a framework for modeling and simulation and the primary continuous and discrete approaches to making models and simulating them on computers. This part offers a unified view of the field that most books lack and, written in an informal manner, it can be used as instructional material for undergraduate and graduate courses.

Part II revisits the introductory material but with a rigorous, multi-layered systems theoretic basis. It then goes on to provide an in-depth account of models as systems specifications, the major systems specification formalisms and their integration, and simulators for such formalisms, in sequential, parallel, and distributed forms.

The fundamental role of systems mosphisms is taken up in Part III—any claim relating systems, models and simulators to each other ultimately must be phrased with an equivalence or morphism of such kinds. Both perfect and approximate morphisms are discussed and applied to model abstraction and system representation. Especially, in the latter vein, we focus on the ability of the DEVS (Discrete Event System Specification) formalism to represent arbitrary systems, including those specified in other discrete event and continuous formalisms. The importance of this discussion derives from two sources—the burgeoning use of discrete event approaches in high technology design (e.g., manufacturing control systems, communication, computers) and the HLA-stimulated growth of distributed simulation, for which discrete events match the discreteness of message exchange.

Part IV continues with the theme of DEVS-based modeling and simulation as a foundation for a high-technology systems design methodology. We include integration with other formalisms for analysis and the system entity structure/model base concepts for investigating design alternatives and reusing good designs. Thoughts on future support of collaborative modeling and simulation close the book.

Although the book is primarily intended as a reference, its structure makes it appropriate for use as a textbook in graduate courses on modeling and simulation. As a textbook, the book affords the advantage of providing an open systems view that mitigates the closed-box trust-on-faith approach of many commercial domain-specific simulation packages. If nothing else, the student will have a more sophisticated skepticism about the model reliability and simulator correctness inside such boxes. For hands-on experience, the book needs to be supplemented with an instructional modeling and simulation environment such as DEVSJAVA (available from the Web site: arizona.edu). Other books on statistical aspects of simulation and application to particular domains should be part of the background as well.

We suggest that Part IV might be a good place to start reading, or teaching, since most of the concepts developed earlier in the book are put into use in the last chapters. In this strategy, the learner soon realizes that new concepts are needed to achieve successful designs and is motivated to fill in the gaps by turning to the chapters that supply the requisite knowledge. More likely, a good teacher will guide the student back and forth between the later and earlier material.

Space limitations have prevented us from including all the material in the first edition. The decision on what to leave out was based on relevance to the current theme, whether significant progress had been made in an area, and whether this could be reduced to the requirements of a book. Thus, for example, a major omission is the discussion of structural inference in Chapters 14 and 15 of the original. We hope that a next revision would be able to include much more on developments in these important directions.

B.P.Z.
H.P.
T.G.K.

Acknowledgments

The authors have, when combined, way too many mentors, colleagues, students, and sponsors to acknowledge individually. Our mentors have provided the right word at the right time, and their colleagues have collaborated to develop concepts and software that are beyond the individual capacities to achieve. Our graduate students have struggled with the theories and the recalcitrant software tools to implement prototypes that demonstrated key principles. And of course our sponsors have made it all possible, often with only faith as collateral. The relationship of the authors to each other illustrates the student-mediated intergenerational transmission process. One of the book's authors, Tag Gon Kim, now a full professor at KAIST (Korea Advanced Institute of Science and Technology), obtained his Ph.D. degree under supervision of the senior author (BPZ) at the University of Arizona. Herbert Praehofer, the third author, is now a member of the Systems Science Institute at the University of Linz, Austria, where he also obtained his Ph.D. degree under Franz Pichler, a colleague of Zeigler's. HP especially thanks Prof. Pichler for initiating his interest in systems theory and for the continuing promotion of his work.

Starting near the beginning, Tunçer Ören of Turkey and Canada, and Maurice Elzas of the Netherlands, initiated a series of meetings that were critical to the development of modeling and simulation methodology. Along the way Art Burks, John Holland, George Klir, Ghi Vansteenkiste, Richard Nance, Francois Cellier, Larry Ho, Andrew Sage, Alex Sisti, Paul Davis, and Judith Dahmann provided encouragement at critical turning points. Colleagues Roger Weinberg, Kyetu Ho Park, Paul Fishwick, George Ball, and Steve Hall played important roles in theory and software developments. Of all the students that have contributed important advances, Jerzy Rozenblit, Hessam Sarjoughian, and Adelinde Uhrmacher, now noted researchers in their own right, deserve special mention. Among the many other graduates that dragged us, sometimes hesitantly, in new directions, space allows us to mention David Belogus, Art Concepcion, Doo Kwan Baik, Joon Sung Hong, Ki Hyung Kim, Hyu Chan Park, Kyung Pyo Hong, Yound Jae Kim, Wan Bok Lee, Yi Won Kwon, Alex Chow, Maria Vasconselos, Doo Hwan Kim, Yoonkeon Moon, Gernot Reisinger, Sung-Do Chi, Jerry Couretas, and Hyup Jae Cho. From his varied roles in the United States Department of Defense, Dell Lunceford was the mover and shaker behind the Advanced Simulation Technology Thrust, a DARPA initiative that funded advanced work on DEVS, some of which is described in Chapter 16.

Finally, we want to thank our parents, wives, and children for their love, patience, and understanding.

B.P.Z.
H.P.
T.G.K.

I

Basics

1

Introduction to Systems Modeling Concepts

This chapter introduces some key concepts that underlie the framework and methodology for modeling and simulation (M&S) originally presented in *Theory of Modeling and Simulation* published in 1976—referred to hereafter as TMS76 to distinguish it from the current revised edition TMS99. Perhaps the most basic concept is that of mathematical systems theory. First developed in the 1960s, this theory provides a fundamental, rigorous mathematical formalism for representing dynamical systems. There are two main, and orthogonal, aspects to the theory:

- **Levels of system specification**—These are the levels at which we can describe how systems behave and the mechanisms that make them work the way they do.
- **Systems specification formalisms**—These are the types of modeling styles, such continuous or discrete, that modelers can use to build system models.

Although the theory is quite intuitive, it does present an abstract way of thinking about the world that you will probably find unfamiliar. So we introduce the concepts in a spiral development consisting of easy-to-grasp stages—with each spiral revolution returning to a more faithful version of the full story.

In this chapter we first introduce some basic systems concepts, then motivate the systems specification formalisms by describing their evolution over time. This also provides a way to point out the differences between TMS99 and its predecessor. Finally, we discuss the levels of system specification, illustrating them with familiar examples. In this ground stage of our spiral development, the presentation is informal and prepares the way for the framework for M&S that comes in the next chapter. Later, in the second part of the book, we return to a more rigorous development of the concepts to lay a sound basis for the developments to come in the third part.

1.1 Systems Specification Formalisms

System theory distinguishes between system *structure* (the inner constitution of a system) and *behavior* (its outer manifestation). Viewed as a

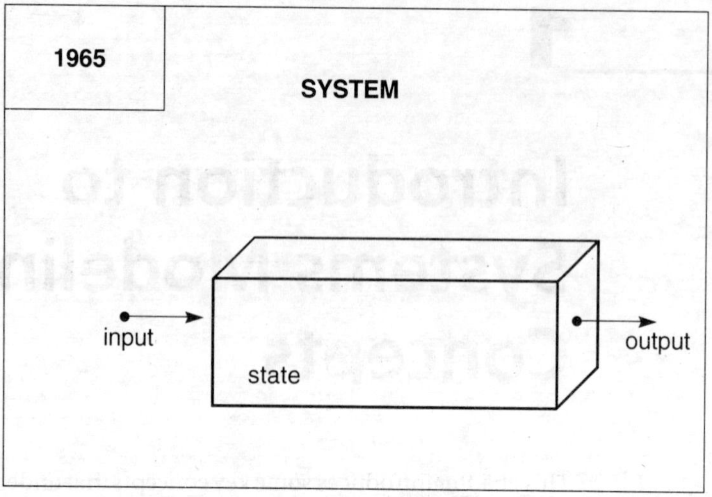

Figure 1 Basic system concepts.

black box (Fig. 1) the external *behavior* of a system is the relationship it imposes between its input time histories and output time histories. The system's input/output behavior consists of the pairs of data records (input time segments paired with output time segments) gathered from a real system or model. The internal *structure* of a system includes its state and state transition mechanism (dictating how inputs transform current states into successor states) as well as the state-to-output mapping. Knowing the system structure allows us to deduce (analyze, simulate) its behavior. Usually, the other direction (inferring structure from behavior) is not univalent—indeed, discovering a valid representation of an observed behavior is one of the key concerns of the M&S enterprise.

An important structure concept is that of *decomposition,* namely, how a system may be broken down into component systems (Fig. 2). A second concept is that of *composition,* i.e., how component systems may be coupled together to form a larger system. Systems theory is *closed under composition* in that the structure and behavior of a composition of systems can be expressed in the original system theory terms. The ability to continue to compose larger and larger systems from previously constructed components leads to *hierarchical construction.* Closure under composition guarantees that such a composition results in a system, called its *resultant,* with well-defined structure and behavior. *Modular* systems have recognized input and output ports through which all interaction with the environment occurs. They can be *coupled* together by coupling output ports to input ports and can have hierarchical structure in which component systems are coupled together to form larger ones.

The difference between decomposed systems, as in Fig. 2, and undecomposed systems, as in Fig. 1, provides our first introduction to *levels* of systems specification. We'll say later that the former are at a higher level of specification than the latter since they provide more information about the structure of the system.

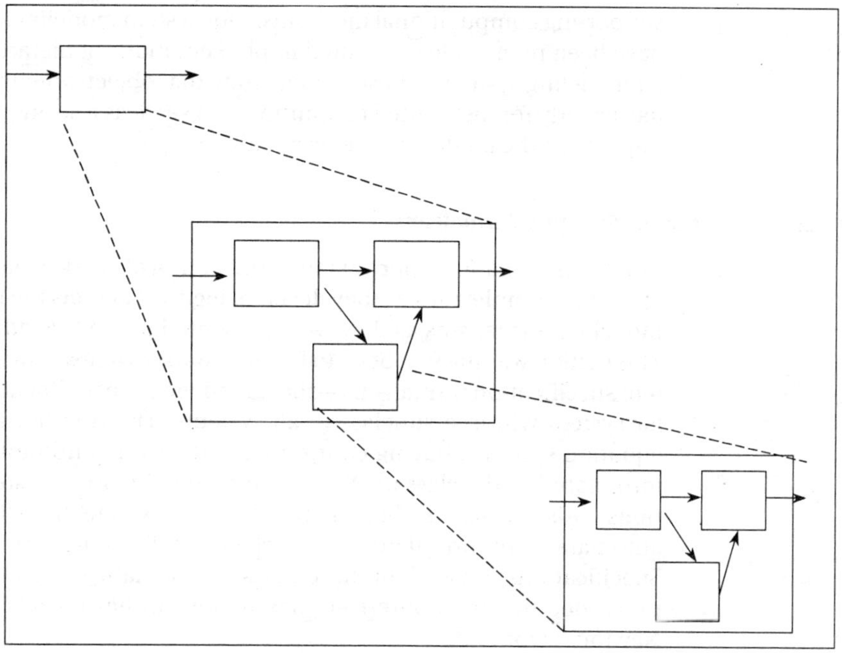

Figure 2 Hierarchical system decomposition.

1.1.1 Relation to Object Orientation

Models developed in a system theory paradigm bear a resemblance to concepts of object-oriented programming. Both objects and system models share a concept of internal state. However, mathematical systems are formal structures that operate on a time base, whereas programming objects typically do not have an associated temporal semantics. Objects in typical object-oriented paradigms are not hierarchical or modular in the sense just described. The coupling concept in modular systems provides a level of delayed binding—a system model can place a value on one of its ports, but the actual destination of this output is not determined until the model becomes a component in a larger system and a coupling scheme is specified. It can therefore (a) be developed and tested as a stand-alone unit, (b) be placed in a model repository and reactivated at will, and (c) be reused in any applications context in which its behavior is appropriate and coupling to other components makes sense.

Although coupling establishes output-to-input pathways, the systems modeler is completely free to specify how data flows along such channels. Information flow is one of many interactions that may be represented. Other interactions include physical forces and fields, material flows, monetary flows, and social transactions. The systems concept is broad enough to include the representation of any of these and supports the development of M&S environments that can include many within the same large-scale model.

Although systems models have formal temporal and coupling features not shared by conventional objects, object orientation does provide a supporting computational mechanism for system modeling. Indeed, there have been many object-oriented implementations of hierarchical, modular modeling systems. These demonstrate that object-oriented paradigms, particularly for distributed computing, can serve as a strong foundation to implement the modular systems paradigm.

1.1.2 Evolution of Systems Formalisms

As in many situations, portraying the evolution of an idea may help understand the complexities as they develop. Figure 3 depicts the basic systems modeling formalisms as they were presented in the first edition, TMS76. This edition was the first book to formulate approaches to modeling as system specification formalisms—shorthand means of delineating a particular system within a subclass of all systems. The traditional differential equation systems, having continuous states and continuous time, were formulated as the class of DESS (Differential Equation System Specifications). Also, systems that operated on a discrete time base such as automata were formulated as the class of DTSS (Discrete Time System Specifications). In each of these cases, mathematical representation had preceeded their computerized incarnations (it has been 300 years since Newton–Leibnitz!).

However, the reverse was true for the third class, the Discrete Event System Specifications (DEVS). Discrete event models were largely prisoners of their simulation language implementations or algorithmic code expressions. Indeed, there was a prevalent belief that discrete event "world views" constituted new mutant forms of simulation, unrelated to the traditional mainstream paradigms. Fortunately, that situation has begun to change as the benefits of abstractions in control and design became clear. Witness the variety of discrete event dynamic system formalisms that have emerged [3].

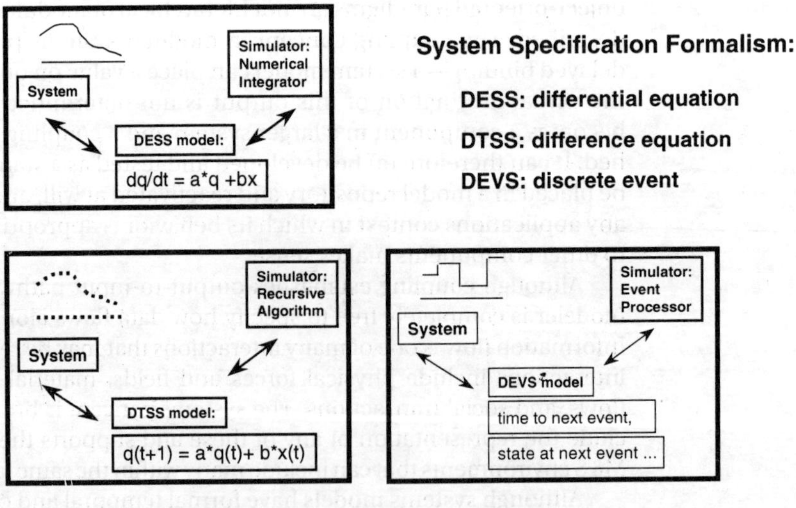

Figure 3 Basic systems specification formalisms.

While each one—examples are Petri nets, min-max algebra, and GSMP (generalized semi-Markov processes)—has its application area, none were developed deliberately as subclasses of the systems theory formalism. Thus to include such a formalism into an organized system-theory-based framework requires "embedding" it into DEVS.

"Embedding." What could such a concept mean? The arrows in Fig. 4 indicate *subclass* relationships; for example, they suggest that DTSS is a "subclass of" DEVS. However, it is not literally true that any discrete time system is also discrete event system (their time bases are distinct, for example). So we need a concept of *simulation* that allows us to say when one system can do the essential work of another. One formalism can be *embedded* in another if any system in the first can be simulated by some system in the second. Actually, more than one such relationship, or *morphism,* may be useful, since, as already mentioned, there are various levels of structure and behavior at which equivalence of systems could be required. As a case in point, the TMS76 edition established that any DTSS could be simulated by a DEVS by constraining the time advance to be constant. However, this is not as useful as it could be until we can see how it applies to *decomposed* systems. Until that is true, we either must reconstitute a decomposed discrete time system to its resultant before representing it as a DEVS or we can represent each DTSS component as a DEVS but we can't network the DEVS together to simulate the resultant. The current edition, TMS99, establishes this stronger simulation relation (Chapter 15).

1.1.3 Combining Continuous and Discrete Formalisms

Skipping many years of accumulating developments, the next major advance in systems formalisms was the combination of discrete event and differential equation formalisms into one, the DEV&DESS. As shown in Fig. 5,

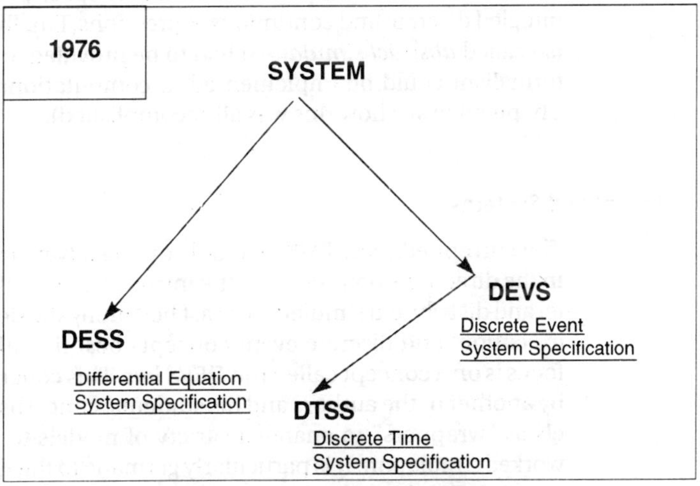

Figure 4 The dynamics of basic system classes.

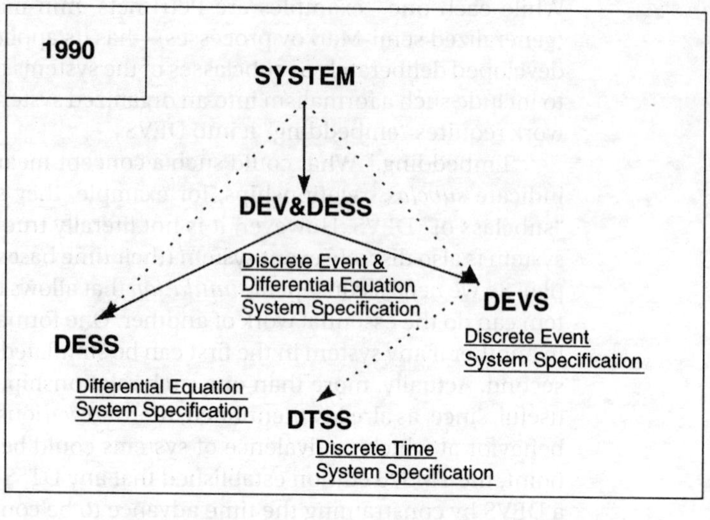

Figure 5 Introducing the DEV&DESS formalism.

this formalism subsumes both the DESS and the DEVS (hence also the DTSS) and thus supports the development of coupled systems whose components are expressed in any of the basic formalisms. Such *multiformalism* modeling capability is important since the world does not usually lend itself to using one form of abstraction at a time. For example, a chemical plant is usually modeled with differential equations while its control logic is best designed with discrete event formalisms. In 1990, one of the authors of this book showed that DEV&DESS was closed under coupling and in order to do so, had to deal with the pairs of input–output interfaces between the different types of systems. Closure under coupling also required that the DEV&DESS formalism provide a means to specify components with intermingled discrete and continuous expressions. Finally, simulator algorithms (so called *abstract simulators*) had to be provided to establish that the new formalism could be implemented in computational form (look ahead to Chapter 9 to see how this was all accomplished).

1.1.4 Quantized Systems

The current edition, TMS99, builds on the advances since 1976 especially in the directions pointed to by the introduction of DEV&DESS. Since parallel and distributed simulation is fast becoming the dominant form of model execution, and discrete event concepts best fit with this technology, our focus is on a concept called the *DEVS bus*. This concept, introduced in 1996 by another of the authors and his students, concerns the use of DEVS models as "wrappers" to enable a variety of models to interoperate in a networked simulation. It is particularly germane to the High Level Architecture (HLA) defined by the United States Department of Defense. One way of looking at this idea is that we want to embed any formalism, including, for example, the DEV&DESS, into DEVS. Another way is to introduce a new class of systems, called quantized system, as illustrated in Fig. 6. In such systems, both the input and output are quantized. As an example, an analog-to-digital converter does such quantization by mapping a real number into a finite string of digits. In general, quantization forms equivalence classes of outputs that then become indistinguishable for downstream input receivers, requiring less data network bandwidth, but also possibly incurring error.

Quantization provides a process for representing and simulating continuous systems that is an alternative to the more conventional discretization of the time axis. While discretization leads to discrete time systems, quantization leads to discrete event systems. The beginnings of a theory of quantized systems are presented in Chapter 16 of this book. When we restrict quantization to differential equation systems, we can express the resulting class, Quantized DESS, within DEV&DESS and study its properties, especially from the point of view of the DEVS bus. We can then study the approximation capability and simulation efficiency of DEVS in distributed simulation in comparison with classical time stepped integration and simulation approaches. Particularly with respect to reduction of message passing and network bandwidth (a major concern in distributed simulation), promising results are being obtained.

1.1.5 Extensions of DEVS

Various extensions of DEVS have been developed as illustrated in Fig. 7. They will be discussed in Chapter 10. These developments expand the classes of system models that can be represented in DEVS, and hence, integrated within both the DEVS bus and the parent systems theory formalism.

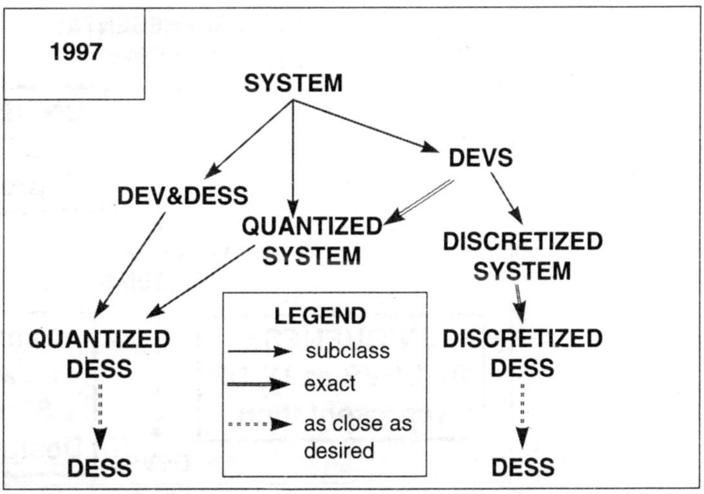

Figure 6 Introducing quantized systems.

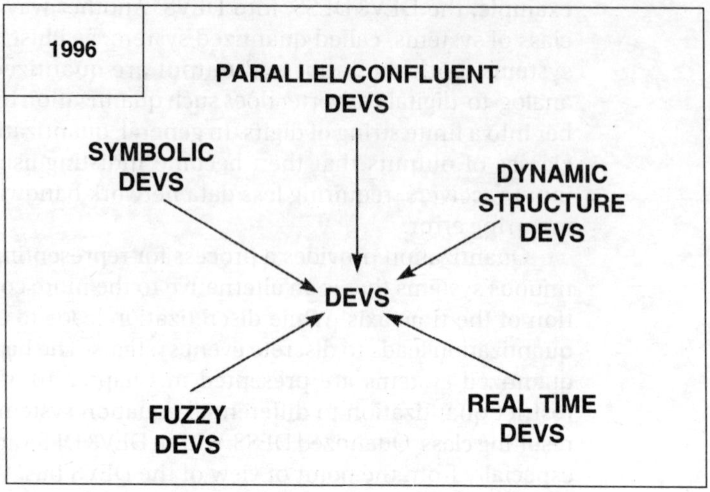

Figure 7 Extensions of the DEVS formalism.

These developments lend credence to the claim that DEVS is a promising computational basis for analysis and design of systems, particularly when simulation is the ultimate environment for development and testing (Fig. 8). The claim rests on the *universality* of the DEVS representation, namely the ability of DEVS bus to support the basic system formalisms. This edition goes some distance toward substantiating the claim that DEVS is the unique form of representation that underlies any system with discrete event behavior. This *uniqueness* claim of DEVS, discussed in Chapter 15, offers the promise that the profusion of discrete event formalisms under development

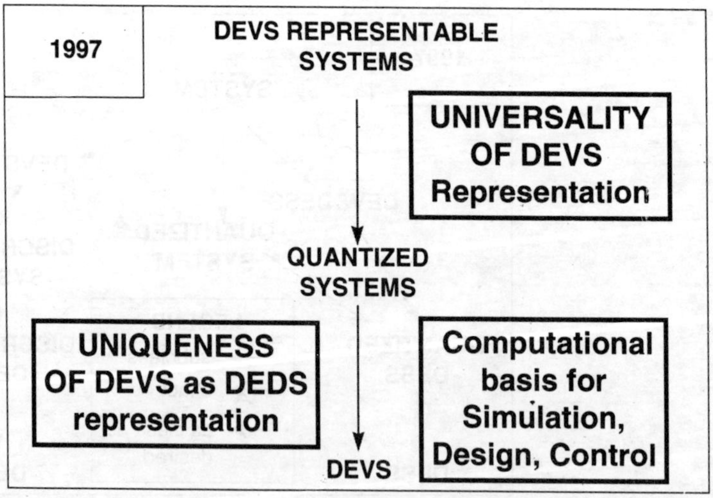

Figure 8 DEVS as a computational basis for simulation, design, and control.

for control and management of systems can be embedded as subformalisms of DEVS in the DEVS bus and thus made accessible in an integrated distributed simulation environment.

1.2 Levels of System Knowledge

As already mentioned, the systems specification hierarchy is the basis for a framework for M&S which sets forth the fundamental entities and relationships in the M&S enterprise. The hierarchy is first presented in an informal manner and later, in Chapter 5, in its full mathematical rigor. Our presentation starts with a review of George Klir's [4] systems framework.

Table 1 identifies four basic levels of knowledge about a system recognized by Klir. At each level we know some important things about a system that we didn't know at lower levels. At the lowest level, the *source level* identifies a portion of the real world that we wish to model and the means by which we are going to observe it. As the next level, the *data level* is a data base of measurements and observations made for the source system. When we get to Level 2, we have the ability to recreate this data using a more compact representation, such as a formula. Since, typically, there are many formulas or other means to generate the same data, the *generative level,* or particular means or formula we have settled on, constitutes knowledge we didn't have at the data system level. When people talk about models in the context of simulation studies they are usually referring to the concepts identified at this level. That is, to them a model means a program to generate data. At the last level, the *structure level,* we have a very specific kind of generative system. In other words, we know how to generate the data observed at Level 1 in a more specific manner—in terms of component systems that are interconnected together and whose interaction accounts for the observations made. When people talk about systems, they are often referring to this level of knowledge. They think of reality as being made up of interacting parts—so that the whole is the sum (or as sometimes claimed, more or less than the sum) of its parts. Although some people use the term "subsystems" for these parts, we call them **component** systems (and reserve the term subsystem for another meaning).

As we have suggested, Klir's terms are by no means universally known, understood, or accepted in the M&S community. However, his framework is a useful starting point since it provides a unified perspective on what are

Table 1 Levels of System Knowledge

Level	Name	What we know at this level
0	Source	What variables to measure and how to observe them
1	Data	Data collected from a source system
2	Generative	Means to generate data in a data system
3	Structure	Components (at lower levels) coupled together to form a generative system

usually considered to be distinct concepts. From this perspective, there are only three basic kinds of problems dealing with systems and they involve moving between the levels of system knowledge (Table 2). In *systems analysis,* we are trying to understand the behavior of an existing or hypothetical system based on its known structure. *Systems inference* is done when we don't know what this structure is—so we try to guess this structure from observations that we can make. Finally, in *systems design,* we are investigating the alternative structures for a completely new system or the redesign of an existing one.

The central idea is that when we move to a lower level, we don't generate any really new knowledge—we are only making explicit what is implicit in the description we already have. One could argue that making something explicit can lead to insight, or understanding, which is a form of new knowledge, but Klir is not considering this kind of subjective (or modeler-dependent) knowledge. In the M&S context, one major form of *systems analysis* is computer simulation which generates data under the instructions provided by a model. Although no new knowledge (in Klir's sense) is generated, interesting properties may come to light of which we were not aware before the analysis. On the other hand, *systems inference* and *systems design* are problems that involve **climbing up** the levels. In both cases we have a low level system description and wish to come up with an equivalent higher level one. For systems inference, the lower level system is typically at the data system level, being data that we have observed from some existing source system. We are trying to find a generative system, or even a structure system, that can recreate the observed data. In the M&S context, this is usually called *model construction.* In the case of systems design, the source system typically does not yet exist and our objective is to build one that has a desired functionality. By functionality we mean what we want the system to do; typically, we want to come up with a structure system, whose components are technological, i.e.,

Table 2 Fundamental Systems Problems

Systems problems	Does source of the data exist? What are we trying to learn about it?	Which level transition is involved?
Systems analysis	The system being analyzed may exist or may be planned. In either case we are trying to understand its behavioral characteristics.	Moving from higher to lower levels, e.g., using generative information to generate the data in a data system.
Systems inference	The system exists. We are trying to infer how it works from observations of its behavior.	Moving from lower to higher levels, e.g., having data, finding a means to generate it.
Systems design	The system being designed does not yet exist in the form that is being contemplated. We are trying to come up with a good design for it.	Moving from lower to higher levels, e.g., having a means to generate observed data, synthesizing it with components taken off the shelf.

can be obtained off-the-shelf, or built from scratch from existing technologies. When these components are interconnected, as specified by a structure system's coupling relation, the result should be a real system that behaves as desired.

It is interesting to note that the process called *reverse engineering* has elements of both inference and design. To reverse engineer an existing system, such as was done in the case of the cloning of IBM compatible PCs, an extensive set of observations is first made. From these observations, the behavior of the system is inferred and an alternative structure to realize this behavior is designed—thus bypassing patent rights to the original system design!

1.3 Introduction to the Hierarchy of Systems Specifications

At about the same time (in the early 1970s) that Klir introduced his epistemological (knowledge) levels, TMS76 formulated a similar hierarchy that is more oriented toward the M&S context. This framework employs a general concept of *dynamical system* and identifies useful ways in which such a system can be specified. These ways of describing a system can be ordered in levels as in Table 3.

The major difference between the two frameworks is that the System Specification Hierarchy recognizes that simulation deals with **dynamics,** the way in which systems behave over time. Therefore, *time* is the base upon

Table 3 System Specification Hierarchy

Level	Specification name	Corresponds to Klir's	What we know at this level
0	Observation frame	Source system	How to stimulate the system with inputs; what variables to measure and how to observe them over a time base;
1	I/O behavior	Data system	Time-indexed data collected from a source system; consists of input/output pairs.
2	I/O function		Knowledge of initial state; given an initial state, every input stimulus produces a unique output.
3	State transition	Generative system	How states are affected by inputs; given a state and an input what is the state after the input stimulus is over; what output event is generated by a state.
4	Coupled component	Structure system	Components and how they are coupled together. The components can be specified at lower levels or can even be structure systems themselves – leading to hierarchical structure.

which all events are ordered. We also view systems as having *input* and *output* interfaces through which they can interact with other systems. As illustrated in Fig. 9, systems receive stimuli ordered in time through their *input ports,* and respond on their *output ports.* The term "port" signifies a specific means of interacting with the system, whether by stimulating it (input) or observing it (output). The time-indexed inputs to systems are called *input trajectories;* likewise, their time-indexed outputs are called *output trajectories.* Ports are the only channels through which one can interact with the system. This means that system are *modular.* Although Klir's framework can include dynamics, input/output ports and modularity, it is not dedicated to these concepts. However, understanding these concepts is critical to effectively solving the problems that arise in M&S.

Before discussing each level of the specification hierarchy in some detail, let's observe that we could have the very same real-world object specified simultaneously at each of the levels. Thus there should be a way to associate the next lower level specification with any given one. This association concept is illustrated in Fig. 10. For example, if we have know the detailed structure at the Coupled Component level, then we ought to be able to construct the corresponding specification at the State Transition level. The hierarchy is set up to provide such an *association mapping* at each (other than the lowest) level. Since the association mapping is not necessarily one-to-one, many upper-level specifications may map to the same lower level one. This is the underlying reason why climbing up the levels is much harder than climbing down the levels. Indeed, when we select one of the associated upper level specifications for a given lower level one, we are gaining knowledge we didn't have at the lower level.

1.4 The Specification Levels Informally Presented

1.4.1 Observation Frame

The Observation Frame specifies how to stimulate the system with inputs: what variables to measure and how to observe them over a time base.

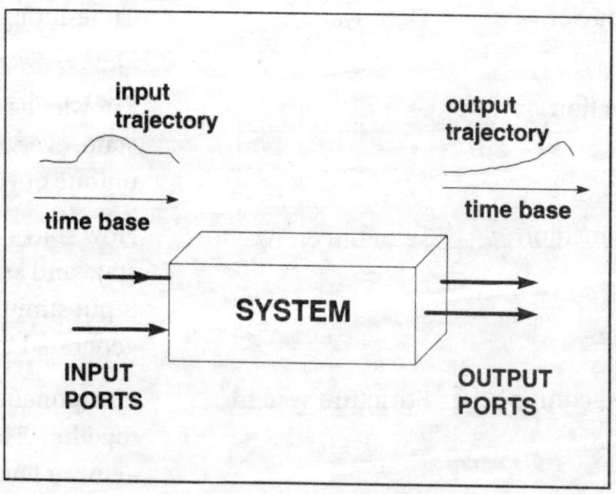

Figure 9 Input/output system.

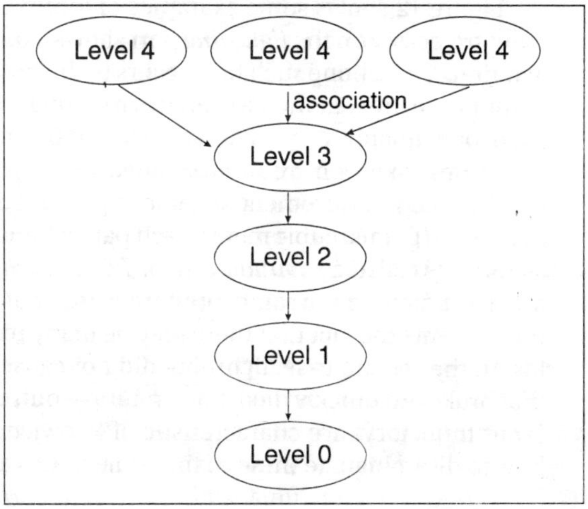

Figure 10 Association between levels of the System Specification Hierarchy.

As an example, Fig. 11 shows a forest subject to *lightning, rain,* and *wind,* modeled as input ports and *smoke* produced from fire, represented as an output port. This is a level 0 or Observation Frame specification. Note the choice of variables we included as ports and their *orientation* (i.e., whether they are input or output ports). We could have chosen differently. For example, we could have included an output port to represent heat radiation. Moreover, rather than being represented by a single value, each variable can be distributed over space, i.e., represented by an array of values. Such choices depend on our modeling objectives and are specified through *experimental frames,* a concept we discuss in Chapter 2.

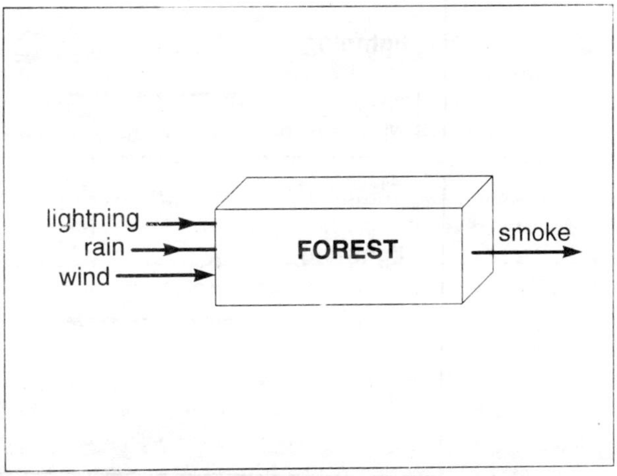

Figure 11 A forest specified as a system in the Observation Frame (Level 0).

Figure 12 shows some examples of input and output trajectories. The input trajectory on the *lightning* port shows a bolt occurring at some particular time t_0. Only one such bolt occurs in the time period shown. The *smoke* output trajectory, at the top, depicts a gradual buildup of smoke starting at t_0 (so, presumably, caused by a fire started by the lightning bolt). The possible values taken on by *smoke,* called its *range,* would result from some appropriate measurement scheme, e.g., measuring density of particulate material in grams/cubic meter. Each pair of input and associated output trajectories is called a *input/output (or I/O) pair.* Figure 12 also displays a second I/O pair with the same input trajectory but different output trajectory. It represents the fact that there may be many responses to the same stimulus. In the second case, lightning did not cause a major fire, since the one that broke out quickly died. Such multiple output trajectories (for the same input trajectory) are characteristic of knowledge at Level 1. We will learn how to disambiguate these output trajectories at the next level.

1.4.2 I/O Behavior and I/O Function

The collection of all I/O pairs gathered by observation is called the *I/O Behavior* of a system. Returning to Table 3, this represents a system specification at Level 1. Now suppose that we are able to uniquely predict the response of the smoke output to a lightning bolt. For example, suppose we know that if the vegetation is dry, then a major fire will ignite, but if the vegetation is moist, then any fire will quickly die. Having such a factor represents knowledge at Level 2, that of the *I/O Function.* Here, in addition to lower level information, we add *initial states* to the specification—when the initial state is known, there is a functional relationship between input and output trajectories, i.e., the initial state determines the **unique** response to any input (Fig. 13a).

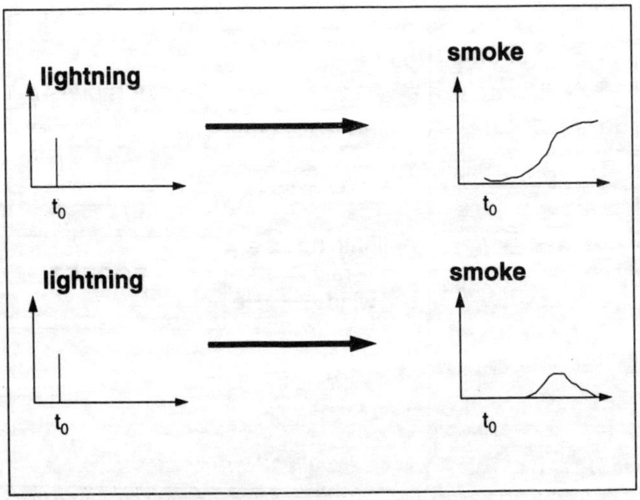

Figure 12 Some input–output pairs for the forest system frame of Fig. 11.

1.4.3 State Transition System Specification

At the next level (3) of system specification, we can specify not only initial state information, but also how the *state changes* as the system responds to its input trajectory. Figures 13b and 13c illustrate this important concept. Figure 13b presents the situation where the forest is in state (dry vegetation, unburned) when a lightning bolt occurs at time t_0. The state that the forest is in at time t_1 when a second bolt occurs is (dry vegetation, burnt), reflecting the fact that a fire has ignited. Since the forest is in a different state, the effect of this second bolt is different from that of the first. Indeed, since there is little left to burn, there is no effect of the second bolt.

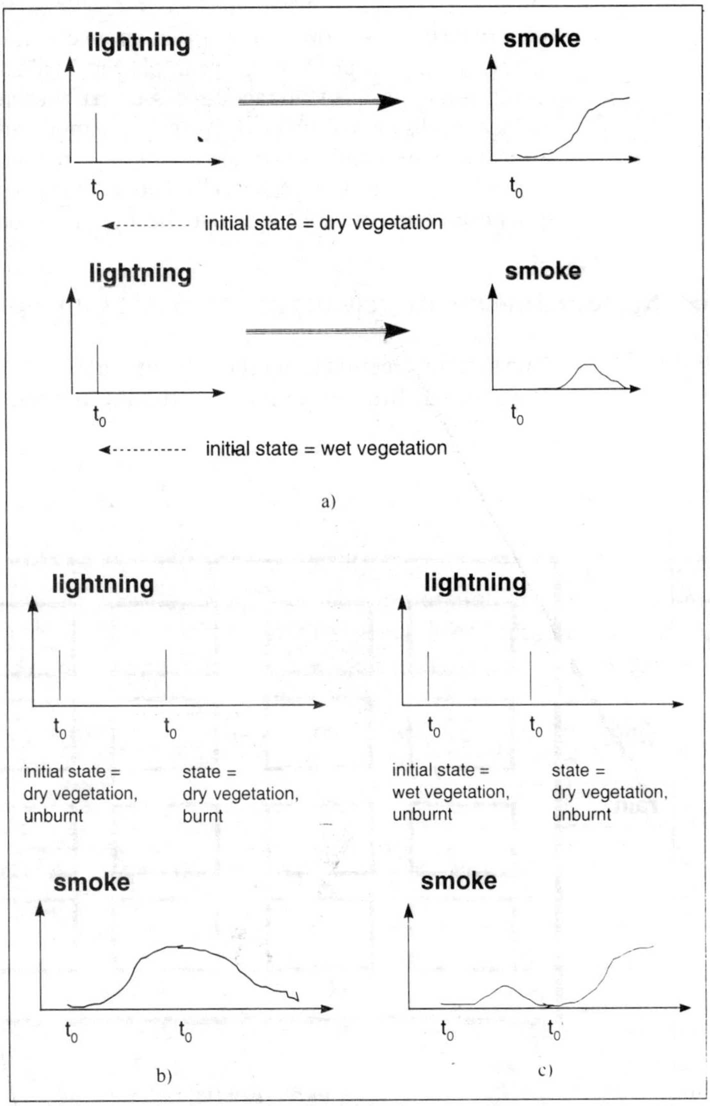

Figure 13 Initial State Concept: a specification at Level 3 (I/O Function) in which we have initial state knowledge about the forest.

In contrast, Fig. 13c illustrates the situation where the forest is wet and unburned when the first bolt occurs. It does not cause a major fire, but it does dry out the vegetation so the resulting state is (dry, unburned). Now the second bolt produces a major fire, just as the first bolt did in Figure 13b—since both the state and subsequent input trajectory are the same, the response of the system is the same.

1.4.4 Coupled Component System Specification

At the highest level of system specification, we can describe more about the internals of the system. Until now, it was a black box, at first observable only through I/O ports. Subsequently, we were able to peer inside to the extent of observing its state. Now, at level 4, we can specify how the system is composed of interacting components. For example, Fig. 14 illustrates how a forest system could be composed of interacting cells, each representing a spatial region, with adjacent cells interconnected. The cells are modeled at level 3, i.e., their state transition and output generation definitions are used to act upon inputs from, and generate outputs to, other cells. The cells are coupled using ports. The output ports of one cell are coupled to the input ports of its neighbors.

1.5 System Specification Morphisms: Basic Concepts

The system specification hierarchy provides a stratification for constructing models. But, although constructing models is the basic activity in

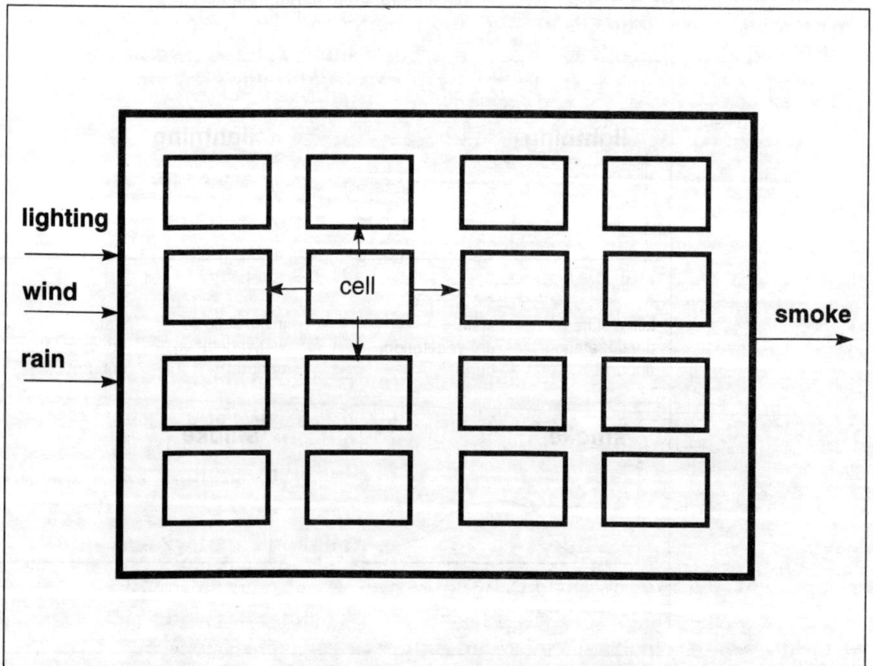

Figure 14 Component Structure System Specification for the forest system.

M&S, much of the real work involves establishing relationships between system descriptions. The system specification hierarchy also provides an orderly way of presenting and working with such relationships. Figure 15 illustrates the idea that pairs of system can be related by morphism relations at each level of the hierarchy. A morphism is a relation that places elements of system descriptions into correspondence as outlined in Table 3.

For example, at the lowest level, two Observation Frames are *morphic* if we can place their defining elements—inputs, outputs, and time bases—into correspondence. Such Frames are *isomorphic* if their inputs, outputs, and time bases, respectively, are identical. In general, the concept of morphism tries to capture similarity between pairs of systems at the same level of specification. Such similarity concepts have to be consistent between levels. When we associate lower level specifications with their respective upper level ones, a morphism holding at the upper level must imply the existence of one at the lower level. The morphisms defined in Table 4 are set up to satisfy these constraints.

The most important morphism, called **homomorphism,** resides at the State Transition level and is illustrated in Fig. 16. Consider two systems specified at level 3, S and S′, where S may be bigger than S′ in the sense of having more states. Later, we'll see that S could represent a complex model and S′ a simplification of it. Or S could represent a simulator and S′ a model it is executing. When S′ goes through a state sequence such as *a,b,c,d,* then S should go through a corresponding state sequence, say, *A,B,C,D.* Typically, a simulator has a lot of apparatus, represented in its states, necessary to accommodate the whole class of models rather than a single one. Thus we don't assume

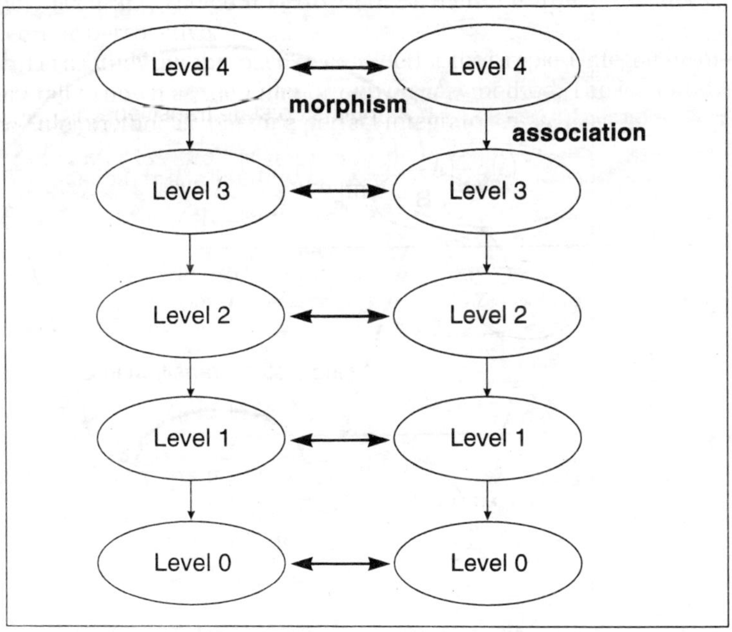

Figure 15 Morphism concepts for system specification hierarchy.

Table 4 Morphism Relations Between Systems in System Specification Hierarchy

Level	Specification name	Two systems are morphical at this level if
0	Observation frame	Their inputs, outputs and time bases can be put into correspondence
1	I/O behavior	They are morphic at level 0 and the time-indexed input/output pairs constituting their I/O behaviors also match up in one-one fashion
2	I/O function	They are morphic at level 0 and their initial states can be placed into correspondence so that the I/O functions associated with corresponding states are the same
3	State transition	The systems are homomorphic (explained below)
4	Coupled component	Components of the systems can be placed into correspondence so that corresponding components are morphic; in addition, the couplings among corresponding components are equal

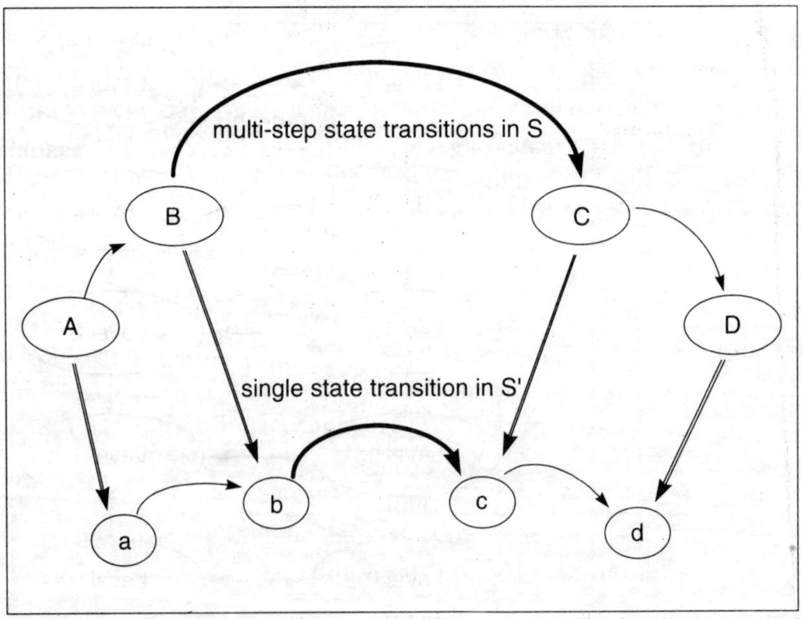

Figure 16 Homomorphism concept. This figure illustrates the preservation of state transitions that a homomorphism requires.

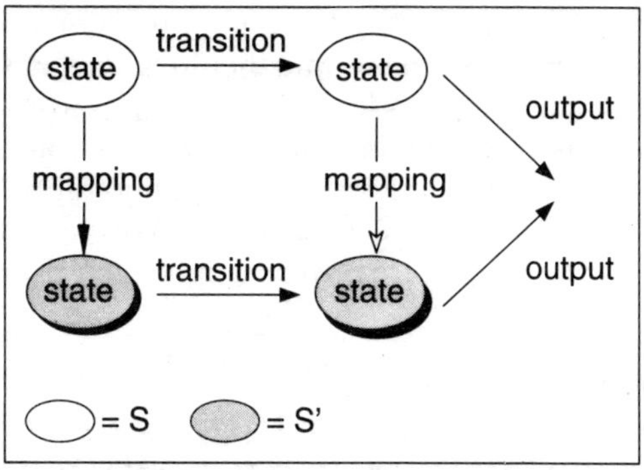

Figure 17 Homomorphism: a mapping preserving step-by-step state transition and output.

that states of S ánd S′ are identical—only that there is a predefined correspondence between them illustrated by the shaded connecting lines in the figure. Now to establish that this correspondence is a homomorphism requires that whenever S′ specifies a transition, such as from state *b* to state *c*, then S actually makes the transition involving corresponding states *B* and *C*. Typically, the simulator is designed to take a number of *microstate* transitions to make the *macrostate* transition from *B* to *C*. These are computation steps necessary to achieve the desired end result. It is not hard to see that if such a homomorphism holds for all states of S′, then any state trajectory in the S′ will be properly reproduced in S.

Often, we require that the correspondence hold in a step-by-step fashion—in other words, that the transition from *a* to *b* is mirrored by a one-step transition from *A* to *B*. Also, as just indicated, we want the I/O behaviors of homomorphic models specified at the I/O System level to be the same. Thus, as in Fig. 17, we require that the outputs produced from corresponding states be the same. In this type of homomorphism, the values and timing of the transitions and outputs of the base model are preserved in the lumped model. Thus, in this case, the state and output trajectories of the two models, when started in corresponding states, are the same.

1.6 Summary

We have outlined the basic concepts of systems theory: structure, behavior, levels of system specification, and their associated morphisms. We have brought out the important distinctions that justify having different levels of specification. However, we have not considered all the possible distinctions and levels. For example, the important distinction between modular and nonmodular systems has not been recognized with distinct levels. A more complete hierarchy will emerge as revisit the concepts introduced here in a more formal and rigorous manner in Chapter 5. We also have introduced the basic system specification formalisms and outlined the advances in the development of such formalisms that characterize this second edition, TMS99.

We now turn to a framework for modeling and simulation that identifies the key elements and their relationships. The systems specification hierarchy will provide the basis for presenting this framework. For example, we use specifications at different levels to characterize the different elements. The various system specification formalisms and their simulators provide the operational means to employ the framework in real-world applications. We focus on real-world application in the last part of the book.

1.7 Sources

The basic concepts of systems theory were developed by pioneers such as Arbib [2], Zadeh [14] (later known more for his fuzzy sets theories), Klir [4], Mesarovic [5], and Wymore [12].

Since the first edition of this book [15] there have been several trends—toward deepening the theory [6, 13], extending its range of applicability with computerized tools [8], and going on to new more abstract formulations [11]. Also, somewhat independently, a new recognition of systems concepts within discrete event systems was fostered by Ho [3]. The DEV&DESS formalism was introduced by Praehofer in his doctoral dissertation [9]. The DEVS Bus originated in the research group of Tag Gon Kim [10]. Quantized system theory was first presented in Ref. [16]. A recent collection of systems concepts in computer science is given in Ref. [1].

1. Allbrecht, R., Ed., *Systems: Theory and Practice.* Springer, Vienna, 1998.
2. Arbib, M. A., *Theories of Abstract Automata.* Prentice-Hall, 1967.
3. Ho, Y. C., *Discrete Event Dynamic Systems: Analyzing Complexity and Performance in the Modern World.* IEEE Press, 1994.
4. Klir, G. J., *Architecture of Systems Complexity.* Sauders, New York, 1985.
5. Mesarovic, M. D., and Y. Takahara, *General Systems Theory: Mathematical Foundations.* Academic Press, New York, 1975.
6. Mesarovic, M. D., and Y. Takahara, *Abstract Systems Theory.* Springer-Verlag, New York, 1989.
7. Padulo, L., *System Theory: A Unified State-Space Approach to Continuous and Discrete Systems.* W. B. Saunders Co., 1972.
8. Pichler, F., and H. Schwaertzel, Eds., *CAST (Computer Aided System Theory) Methods in Modelling.* Springer-Verlag, Berlin, 1992.
9. Praehofer, H., "System Theoretic Foundations for Combined Discrete–Continuous System Simulation," Doctoral dissertations Johannes Kepler University of Linz, Linz, Austria (1991).
10. Seong, M. Cho, and T. G. Kim, "Real-time DEVS Simulation: Concurrent, Time-Selective Execution of Combined RT-DEVS Model and Interactive Environment," Proc. of SCSC-98, July 19–22, 1998, Reno, NV, pp. 410–415.
11. Takahashi, S., and Y. Takahara, *Logical Approach to Systems Theory.* Springer-Verlag, London, 1995.
12. Wymore, W., *Mathematical Theory of Systems Engineering: The Elements.* Krieger Publishing Company, 1977.

13. Wymore, A. W., *Model-Based Systems Engineering: An Introduction to the Mathematical Theory of Discrete Systems and to the Tricotyledon Theory of System Design.* CRC Press, 1993.

14. Zadeh, L. A., and C. A. Desoer, *Linear System Theory.* Krieger Publishing Co., 1979.

15. Zeigler B. P., *Theory of Modeling and Simulation.* Wiley Interscience, 1976.

16. Zeigler, B. P., and J. S. Lee. Theory of Quantized Systems: Formal Basis for DEVS/HLA Distributed Simulation Environment. Enabling Technology for Simulation Science(II), SPIE AeoroSense 98. Orlando, FL, 1998.

Definitions, Acronyms, Abbreviations

DEDS, Discrete Event Dynamic Systems
DESS, Differential Equation System Specification
DEVS, Discrete Event System Specification
DTSS, Discrete Time System Specification
DEV&DESS, Discrete Event and Differential Equation System Specification
M&S, Modeling and Simulation
TMS76, 1976 edition of *Theory of Modeling and Simulation*

2

Framework for Modeling and Simulation

This chapter is devoted to establishing a *framework for modeling and simulation (M&S)*. The framework defines *entities* and their *relationships* that are central to the M&S enterprise. Understanding these concepts will help everyone involved in a simulation modeling project—analysts, programmers, managers, users—to better carry out their tasks and communicate with each other. Terms such as "model" and "simulator" are often loosely used in current practice but have very sharp meanings in the framework we will discuss. Therefore, it is important to understand what is included and excluded by the definitions. [This is especially true if you have some experience in M&S and are likely to associate (or prefer) meanings that are different from those developed here.] As illustrated in Fig. 1, the basic entities of the framework are *source system, model, simulator,* and *experimental frame*. The basic interrelationships among entities are the *modeling* and the *simulation* relationships. The entities are defined in Table 1.) This table also characterizes the level of system specification that typically describes the entities. The level of specification is an important feature for distinguishing between the entities, which is often confounded in the literature. You can return to Fig. 1 and Table 1 to keep an overall view of the framework as we describe each of the components in the following presentation.

Based on this framework, the basic issues and problems encountered in performing M&S activities can be better understood and coherent solutions developed.

2.1 The Entities of the Framework

2.1.1 Source System

The *source system* (we will omit the "source" qualifier, when the context is clear) is the real or virtual environment that we are interested in modeling. It is viewed as a *source of observable data,* in the form of time-indexed trajectories of variables. The data that has been gathered from observing or

Material in this chapter adapted from D. Cloud and L. Rainey, Eds. *Applied Modeling & Simulation: An Integrated Approach to Development and Operation.* McGraw-Hill, New York, 1998, with permission.

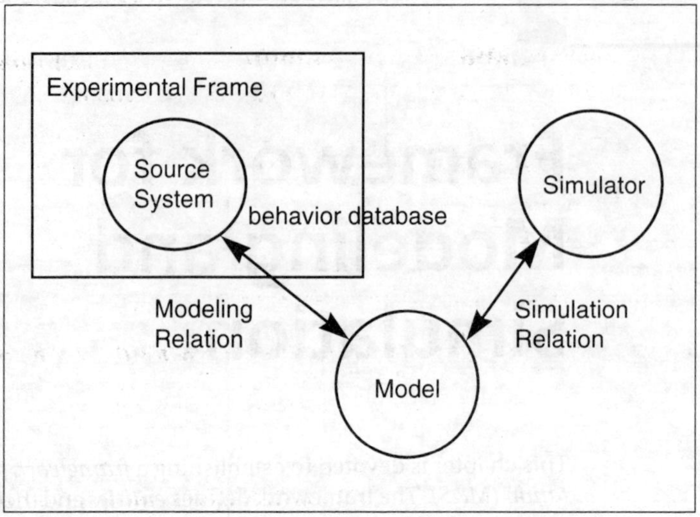

Figure 1 The basic entities in M&S and their relationships.

otherwise experimenting with a system is called the *system behavior database.* As indicated in Table 1, this concept of system is a specification at level 0 (or equivalently, Klir's source system) and its database is a specification at level 1 (or equivalently, Klir's data system). This data is viewed or acquired through experimental frames of interest to the modeler.

Applications of M&S differ with regard to how much data is available to populate the system database. In *data-rich* environments, such data is abundant from prior experimentation or can easily be obtained from measurements. In contrast, *data-poor* environments offer meager amounts of historical data or low-quality data (whose representativeness of the system of interest is questionable). In some cases it is impossible to acquire better data (for example, of combat in real warfare); in others, it is expensive to do so (for example, topography and vegetation of a forest). In the latter case, the modeling process can direct the acquisition of data to those areas that have the highest impact on the final outcome.

Table 1 Defining the Basic Entities in M&S and Their Usual Levels of Specification

Basic entity	Definition	Related system specification levels
Source system	Real or artificial source of data	Known at level 0
Behavior database	Collection of gathered data	Observed at level 1
Experimental frame	Specifies the conditions under which system is observed or experimented with	Constructed at levels 3 and 4
Model	Instructions for generating data	Constructed at levels 3 and 4
Simulator	Computational device for generating behavior of the model	Constructed at level 4

2.1.2 Experimental Frame

An *experimental frame* is a specification of the conditions under which the system is observed or experimented with. As such, an experimental frame is the operational formulation of the objectives that motivate a modeling and simulation project. For example, out of the multitude of variables that relate to a forest, the set {lightning, rain, wind, smoke} represents one particular choice. Such an experimental frame is motivated by the interest in modeling the way lightning ignites a forest fire. A more refined experimental frame would add the moisture content of the vegetation and the amount of unburned material as variables. Thus, many experimental frames can be formulated for the same system (both source system and model) and the same experimental frame may apply to many systems. Why would we want to define many frames for the same system? Or apply the same frame to many systems? For the same reason that we might have different objectives in modeling the same system, or have the same objective in modeling different systems. More of this in a moment.

There are two equally valid views of an experimental frame. One views a frame as a definition of the type of data elements that will go into the database. The second views a frame as a system that interacts with the system of interest to obtain the data of interest under specified conditions. In this view, the frame is characterized by its implementation as a measurement system or observer. In this implementation, a frame typically has three types of components (as shown in Fig. 2): *generator,* which generates input segments to the system; *acceptor,* which monitors an experiment to see the desired experimental conditions are met; and *transducer,* which observes and analyzes the system output segments.

Objectives and Experimental Frames

Objectives for modeling relate to the role of the model in systems design, management, or control. The statement of objectives serves to focus model construction on particular issues. It is crucial to formulate such a statement as early as possible in the development process. A firmly agreed-upon state-

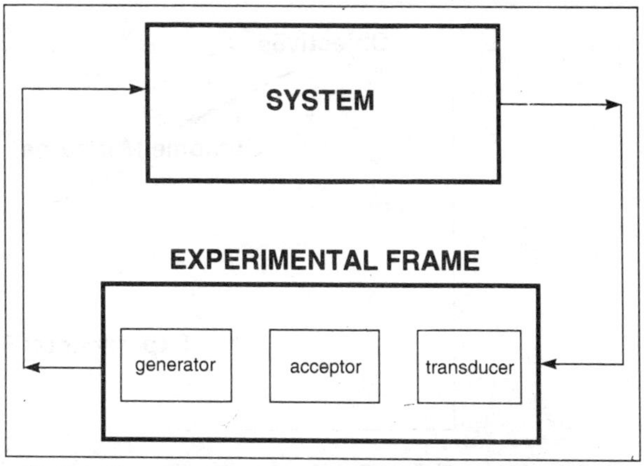

Figure 2 Experimental frame and its components.

ment of objectives enables project leaders to maintain control on the efforts of the team. Once the objectives are known, suitable experimental frames can be developed. Remember that such frames translate the objectives into more precise experimentation conditions for the source system or its models. A model is expected to be valid for the system in each such frame. Having stated our objectives, there is presumably a best level of resolution to answer the questions raised. The more demanding the questions, the greater the resolution likely to be needed to answer it. Thus, the choice of appropriate levels of abstraction also hinges on the objectives and their experimental frame counterparts.

Figure 3 depicts the process of transforming objectives into experimental frames. Typically, modeling objectives concern system design. Here measures of the effectiveness of a system in accomplishing its goal are required to evaluate the design alternatives. We call such measures *outcome measures.* In order to compute such measures, the model must include variables, which we'll call *output variables,* whose values are computed during execution runs of the model. The mapping of the output variables into outcome measures is performed by the transducer component of the experimental frame. Often there may be more than one layer of variables intervening between output variables and outcome measures. For example, in military simulations, *measures of performance* are output variables that typically judge how well parts of a system are operating. For example, the success of a missile in hitting its target is a performance measure. Such measures enter as factors into outcome measures, often called *measures of effectiveness,* that measure how well the overall system goals are being achieved, e.g., how many battles are actually won by a particular combination of weapons, platforms, personnel, etc. The implication is that high-performing components are necessary, but not sufficient, for highly effective systems, in which they must be coordinated together to achieve the overall goals.

Forest fire management is an interesting application domain. There are two quite different uses of M&S in this area: (1) that of fighting fires when

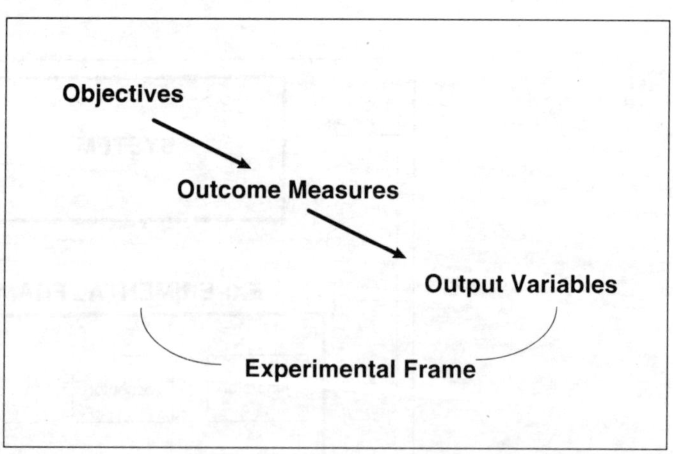

Figure 3 Transforming objectives into experimental frames.

they break out, and (2) that of trying to prevent them from breaking out in the first place, or at least minimizing the damage when they do. Formulated as objectives for modeling, these purposes lead to quite different experimental frames. Let's look at each of these frames.

In the first frame, real-time interdiction, which refers to on-the-spot fire fighting, we require accurate prediction of where the fire will spread within a matter of hours. These predictions are used to allocate resources in the right places for maximum effectiveness. Because humans may be placed in great danger, highly reliable short-term predictions are required. A typical question asked here would be: Is it safe to put a team of fire fighters on a particular ridge within reach of the current fire front for the next several hours? To improve the ability to make accurate predictions, the model state may be updated with satellite data to improve its correspondence with the real fire situation as it develops.

In fire prevention and mitigation the emphasis is less on short-term prediction of spread than on answering "what-if" questions for planning purposes. For example, land use planners might ask what should be the width of a fire break (area cleared of trees) around a residential area bordering a forest so that there is a less than 0.1% chance of houses catching fire. Here the model needs to be capable of working with a larger area of the landscape, but the resolution it needs may be considerably less in order for useful comparisons of different planning alternatives to result. Indeed, a model might be capable of rank ordering alternatives without necessarily producing fire spread behavior with high accuracy.

As suggested, the experimental frames that are developed for these contrasting objectives, interdiction and prevention, are quite different. The first (interdiction) calls for experimenting with a model in which all known prevailing fuel, wind, and topographic conditions are entered to establish its initial state. The output desired is a detailed map of fire spread after, say, 5 hours within the region of interest.

The second experimental frame (prevention) calls for a wider scope, lower resolution representation of the landscape in which a range of expected lightning, wind, rain, and temperature regimes may be injected as input trajectories. The model may then be placed into different states corresponding to different prevention alternatives, e.g., different fire break spatial regions might be investigated. The output for a particular run might be as simple as a binary variable indicating whether or not the residential area was engulfed by fire. The output, summarized over all runs, might be presented as a rank ordering of alternatives according to their effectiveness in preventing fire spreading to the residential area (e.g., the percent of experiments in which the residential area was not engulfed by flame).

2.1.3 Model

In its most general guise, a *model* is a system specification at any of the levels discussed in Chapter 1. However, in the traditional context of M&S, the system specification is usually done at levels 3 and 4, corresponding to Klir's generative and structure levels. Thus, the most common concept of a simulation model is that it is a *set of instructions, rules, equations, or constraints for generating I/O behavior.* In other words, we write a model with a state transition and output generation mechanisms (level 3) to accept input trajectories and generate output trajectories depending on its initial state setting. Such models form the basic components in more complex models that are constructed by coupling them together to form a level 4 specification.

There are many meanings that are ascribed to the word "model." For example, a model is conceived as any physical, mathematical, or logical representation of a system, entity, phenomenon, or process. The definition in terms of system specifications has the advantages that it has a sound mathematical foundation and is has a definite semantics that everyone can understand in unambiguous fashion. Like other formal definitions, it cannot capture all meanings in the dictionary. However, it is intended to capture the most useful concepts in the M&S context.

2.1.4 Simulator

As a set of instructions, a model needs some agent capable of actually obeying the instructions and generating behavior. We call such an agent a *simulator.*[1] Thus, a simulator is any computation system (such as a single processor, a processor network, the human mind, or more abstractly an algorithm) capable of executing a model to generate its behavior. A simulator is typically specified at a high level, since it is a system that we design intentionally to be synthesized from components that are off-the-shelf and well understood. Separating the model and simulator concepts provides a number of benefits for the framework:

- The same model, expressed in a formalism, may be executed by different simulators, thus opening the way for portability and interoperability at a high level of abstraction.
- Simulator algorithms for the various formalisms may be formulated and their correctness rigorously established.
- The resources required to correctly simulate a model afford a measure of its complexity.

2.2 Primary Relations Among Entities

The entities—*system, experimental frame, model, simulator*—become truly significant only when properly related to each other. For example, we build a model of a particular system for some objective—only some models, and not others, are suitable. Thus, it is critical to the success of a simulation modeling effort that certain relationships hold. The two most fundamental are the *modeling* and the *simulation* relations (Table 2).

2.2.1 Modeling Relation: Validity

The basic modeling relation, *validity,* refers to the relation between a *model,* a *system,* and an *experimental frame.* Validity is often thought of as

[1] TMS76 referred to the generic "computer" instead of the more specific "simulator."

Table 2 Primary Relationships Among Entities

Basic relationship	Definition	Related system specification Levels
Modeling relation	Concerned with how well model-generated behavior agrees with observed system behavior	
Replicative validity		Comparison is at level 1
Predictive validity		Comparison is at level 2
Structural validity		Comparison is at levels 3 and 4
Simulation relation	Concerned with ensuring that the simulator carries out the model instructions correctly	Basic comparison is at level 2; involves homomorphism at levels 3 or 4
Correctness		

the degree to which a model faithfully represents its system counterpart. However, it makes much more practical sense to require that the model faithfully capture the system behavior only to the extent demanded by the objectives of the simulation study. In our formulation, the concept of validity answers the question of whether it is impossible to distinguish the model and system **in the experimental frame of interest**. The most basic concept, *replicative validity*, is affirmed if, for all the experiments possible within the experimental frame, the behavior of the model and system agree within acceptable tolerance. Thus, replicative validity requires that the model and system agree at the I/O relation level 1 of the system specification hierarchy.

Stronger forms of validity are *predictive validity* and *structural validity*. In predictive validity we require not only replicative validity, but also the ability to predict as yet unseen system behavior. To do this the model needs to be set in a state corresponding to that of the system. Thus, predictive validity requires agreement at the next level of the system hierarchy, that of the I/O function level 2. Finally, structural validity requires agreement at level 3 (state transition) or higher (coupled component). This means that the model not only is capable of replicating the data observed from the system, but also mimics in step-by-step, component-by-component fashion the way in which the system does its transitions.

The term *accuracy* is often used in place of validity. Another term, *fidelity*, is often used for a combination of both validity and detail. Thus, a high-fidelity model may refer to a model that is high both in detail and in validity (in some understood experimental frame). However, when using the term this way, beware that there may be a tacit assumption that high detail alone is needed for high fidelity, as if validity were a necessary consequence of high detail. In fact, it is possible to have a very detailed model that is nevertheless very much in error, simply because some of the highly resolved components function in a different manner than their real system counterparts.

2.2.2 Simulation Relation: Simulator Correctness

The basic simulation relation, simulator correctness, is a relation between a *simulator* and a *model*. A *simulator correctly simulates a model* if it is guaranteed to faithfully generate the model's output trajectory given its initial state and its input trajectory. Thus, simulator correctness requires agreement at the I/O function level (2). In practice, simulators are constructed to execute not just one model, but a family of possible models. This flexibility is necessary if the simulator is to be applicable to a range of applications. In such cases, we must establish that a simulator will correctly execute a particular class of models. Since the structures of both the simulator and the model are at hand, it may be possible to prove correctness by showing that a *homomorphism* relation holds. Recall from Chapter 1 that a homomorphism is a correspondence between simulator and model states that is preserved under transitions and outputs.

2.3 Other Important Relationships

Besides the two fundamental relationships, there are others that are important for understanding modeling and simulation work. These relations have to do with the interplay and orderings of models and experimental frames.

2.3.1 Modeling As Valid Simplification

The inescapable fact about modeling is that it is severely constrained by complexity limitations. Complexity, is at heart, an intuitive concept—the feeling of frustration or awe that we all sense when things get too numerous, diverse, or intricately related to discern a pattern, to see all at once—in a word, to comprehend. Generalizing from the boggled human mind to the overstressed simulator suggests that the complexity of a model can be measured by the resources required by a particular simulator to correctly interpret it. As such, complexity is measured relative to a particular simulator, or class of simulators. However, as we will see in Chapter 13, properties intrinsic to the model are often strongly correlated with complexity independently of the underlying simulator. Although computers continue to get faster and possess more memory, they will always lag behind our ambitions to capture reality in our models. Successful modeling can then be seen as *valid simplification*. We need to *simplify*, or reduce the complexity, to enable our models to be executed on our resource-limited simulators. But the simplified model must also be *valid*, at some level, and within some experimental frame of interest. As in Fig. 4, there is always a pair of models involved—call them the *base* and *lumped* models. Here, the base model is typically "more capable" and requires more resources for interpretation than the lumped model. By the term "more capable," we mean that the base model is valid within a larger set of experimental frames (with respect to a real system) than the lumped model. However, the important point is that within **a particular frame of interest** the lumped model might be just as valid as the base model. The concept of morphism introduced in Chapter 1 affords criteria for judging the equivalence of base and lumped models with

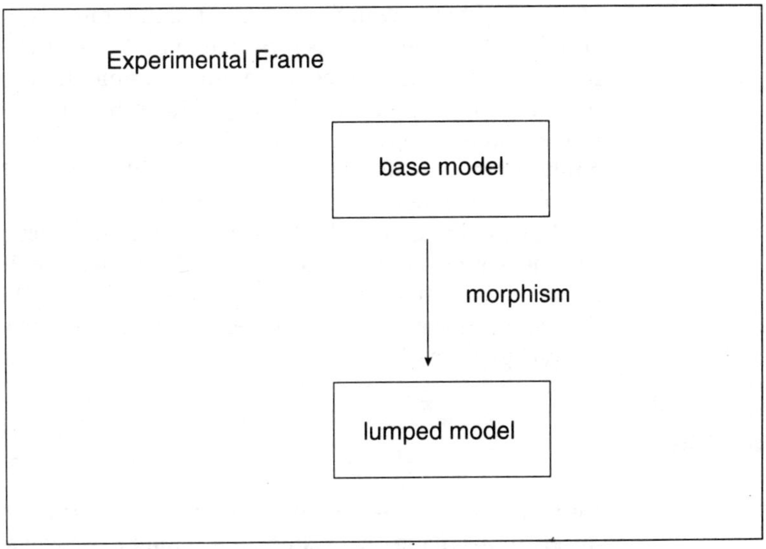

Figure 4 Base/lumped model equivalence in experimental frame.

respect to an experimental frame. In Chapter 13, we will discuss methods for constructing such morphisms.

2.3.2 Experimental Frame: Model Relationships

Assume that we have a whole repository of models and experimental frames that have been built up over years of experience. Then it is critical to have an ability to ask whether there are any experimental frames that meet our current objectives and whether there are models that can work within this frame—only those models have a chance of providing valid answers to our current questions. The relation that determines if a frame can logically be applied to a model is called *applicability,* and its converse is called *accommodation* (Table 3). Notice that validity of a model in a particular experimental frame, requires, as a precondition, that the model accommodates the frame.

Table 3 Other M&S Relationships Important When Dealing With a Model Repository

Relationship	Definition
Experimental frame applies to a model (or "is applicable to")	The conditions on experimentation required by the frame can be enforced in the model
Model accommodates experimental frame	Frame is applicable to the model
Experimental frame 1 is derivable from experimental frame 2	Any model that accommodates experimental frame 2 also accommodates experimental frame 1

The degree to which one experimental frame is more restrictive in its conditions than another is formulated in the *derivability* relation. A more restrictive frame leaves less room for experimentation or observation than one from which it is derivable. So, as illustrated in Fig. 5, it is easier to find a model that is valid in a restrictive frame for a given system. It turns out that applicability may be reduced to derivability. To see this, define the *scope* frame of the model to represent the most relaxed conditions under which it can be experimented with (this is clearly a characteristic of the model). Then a frame is applicable to a model if it is derivable from the scope frame of the model. This means that a repository need not support both applicability and derivability queries. Only the latter is sufficient if each model has an associated scope frame.

2.4 Time

Implicitly, until now, we have assumed that time is a way of ordering observations made on a system. In Chapter 3, we will formally characterize a *time base* as an ordered set for indexing events that models the flow of actual time. If the interpretation of such a time base is left abstract in this manner, we refer to it as *logical* time. In contrast, when we consider events happening in the real world, in real time, we refer to a time variable as measured by an actual clock. Thus, *physical* time, also called metric time or wall-clock time, is measured by ticks of physical clocks, while logical time is measured by ticks of a clock somehow embedded in a model. Also, as relativity theory made clear, time as perceived by observers at different locations may be different. Based on this distinction, time can be either *local* or *global*. The former is valid only within a component of a system; the latter is valid in the whole system. Thus, there are at least two dimensions for classifying time: one along the logical/physical axis and the other along the local/global axis.

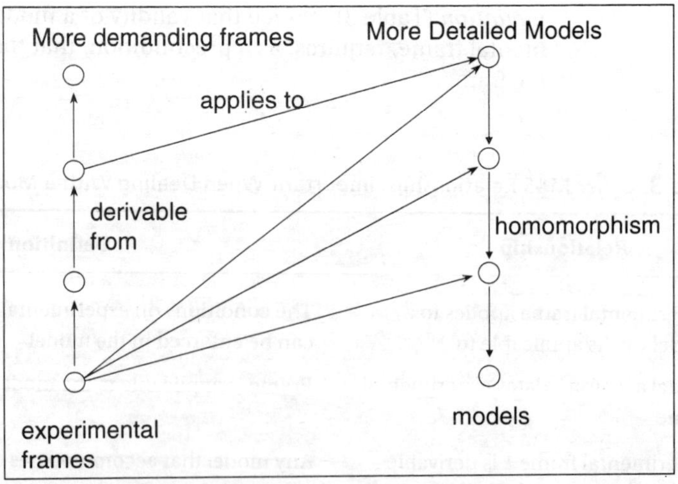

Figure 5 Illustrating important M&S relations relevant to model repositories.

Table 4 A Time Taxonomy

		Logical/physical	
		Logical time	**Physical time**
Local/global	**Global time**	Global, logical: All components operate on the same abstract time base.	Global, physical: All components operate on the same system clock.
	Local time	Local, logical: A component operates on its own abstract time base.	Local, physical: A component operates on its own system clock.

Consequently, a time base can be interpreted as falling in any one of the four combinations shown in Table 4.

Traditionally, modeling and simulation has considered mainly the first (global, logical) combination. That is, we assume all components of a modeled system have the same time frame of reference and we consider time as an abstract quantity. However, when a model is executing in a simulator, which may be distributed among computer nodes in a network and may also be interacting with the real world, it is hard to maintain this fiction. We will discuss such real-time and distributed simulation approaches later starting with Chapters 10 and 11. For now, we note that synchronization between time bases requires maintaining a correspondence between the two. For example, a distributed simulation protocol synchronizes the local, logical times maintained by the individual simulator nodes. Another example of synchronization occurs in real-time, human-in-the-loop simulation-based training. Here the simulator employs a physical time base (e.g., computer system clock) to synchronize between a pilot's physically perceived time base and the logical time of a model of the aircraft being simulated.

2.5 Summary

With this introductory exposition of the framework and the systems foundation in Chapter 1, the pattern of development underlying the book's table of contents should be readily apparent. The next two chapters of Part I continue, in an informal manner, to present the basic modeling formalisms and their simulation algorithms. Part II returns, in a spiral manner, to present the levels of system specification and introduce the modeling formalisms and their simulators in a rigorous, but readable, manner. Part III takes the same approach to the system specification morphisms and goes on to tackle the issues of modeling as valid simplification. A theme that is strongly emphasized in this edition (one that could only be dimly perceived in TMS76) is that of representing systems, whatever their native formalism, in discrete event form. Part IV starts the process of examining the implications of the framework and its theory for the methodology of modeling and simulation and the computer environments to support it. Indeed, we leave the reader at a superhighway exit ramp with many country roads to explore, guidebook in hand, concepts and theory providing the compass.

2.6 Sources

The framework discussed here derives from the one in TMS76. It was subsequently elaborated and extended in Ref. [1], which contains much more in-depth development than can be provided here. The framework was presented in its current form in the book edited by Cloud and Rainey [2]. Readers may consult the latter book for an integrated approach to the development and operation of models. The development of modeling and simulation methodology is chronicled in [3–6].

1. Zeigler, B. P., *Multifaceted Modeling and Discrete Event Simulation.* Academic Press, London, 1984.
2. Zeigler, B. P. "A Framework for Modeling & Simulation," in *Applied Modeling & Simulation: An Integrated Approach to Development & Operation,* D. Cloud and L. Rainey, Eds. McGraw-Hill, New York, 1997.
3. Methodology is Systems Modeling and Simulation. B. P. Zeigler, M. S. Elzas, G. Klir, and T. I. Oren, Eds. Elsevier North Holland Press: Amsterdam, 1979.
4. Simulation and Model-Based Methodologies: An Integrative View. T. I. Oren, M. S. Elzas, and B. P. Zeigler, Eds. Springler-Verlag: Berlin, 1984.
5. Modeling and Simulation Methodology in the Artificial Intelligence Era. M. S. Elzas, T. I. Oren, and B. P. Zeigler, Eds. Elsevier North Holland Press: Amsterdam, 1986.
6. Modeling and Simulation Methodology: Knowledge Systems Paradigms. M. S. Elzas, T. I. Oren, and B. P. Zeigler, Eds. Elsevier North Holland Press: Amsterdam, 1989.

3

Modeling Formalisms and Their Simulators

3.1 Introduction

This chapter presents, in an informal manner, the basic modeling formalisms for discrete time, continuous, and discrete event systems. It is intended to provide a taste of each of the major types of models, how we express behavior in them, and what kinds of behavior we can expect to see. Each modeling approach is also accompanied by its prototypical simulation algorithms. The presentation employs commonly accepted ways of presenting the modeling formalisms. It does not presume any knowledge of formal systems theory and therefore serves as an independent basis for understanding the basic modeling formalisms that will be cast as basic system specifications (DESS, DTSS, and DEVS) after the system theory foundation has been laid.

3.2 Discrete Time Models and Their Simulators

Discrete time models are usually the most intuitive to grasp of all forms of dynamic models. As illustrated in Fig. 1, this formalism assumes a stepwise mode of execution. At a particular time instant the model is in a particular state and it defines how this state changes—what the state at the next time instant will be. The next state usually depends on the current state and also what the environment's influences currently are.

Discrete time systems have numerous applications. The most popular are in digital systems where the clock defines the discrete time steps. But discrete time systems are also frequently used as approximations of continuous systems. Here a time unit is chosen, e.g., 1 second, 1 minute, or 1 year, to define an artificial clock, and the system is represented as the state changes from one "observation" instant to the next. Therefore, to build a discrete time model, we have to define how the current state and the input from the environment determine the next state of the model.

The simplest way to define the way states change in a model is to provide a table such as Table 1. Here we assume there are a finite number of states and inputs. We write down all combinations of states and inputs and next states and outputs for each. For example, let the first column stand for the current state of the model and the second column for the input it is currently receiving. The table gives the next state of the model in column 3 and the output it produces in column 4. In Table 1, we have two states (0 and 1) and two inputs (also 0 and 1). There are four combinations, and each one has an asso-

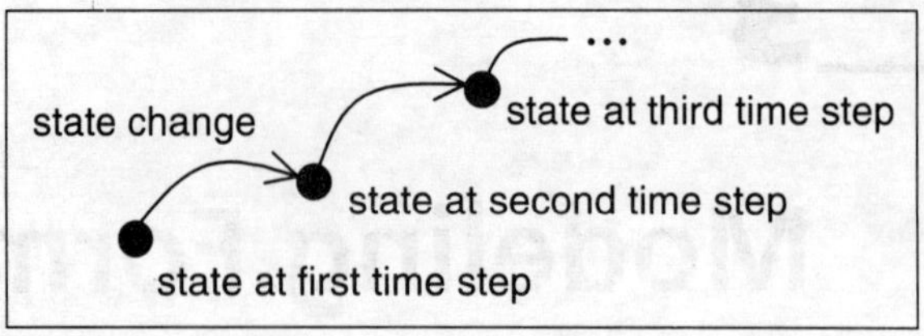

Figure 1 Stepwise execution of discrete time systems.

ciated state and output. The first row says that if the current state is 0 and the input is 0, then the next state will be 0 and the output will be 0. The other three rows give similar information for the remaining state/input combinations.

In discrete time models, time advances in discrete steps, which we assume are integer multiples of some basic period such as 1 second, 1 day or 1 year. The transition/output table just discussed would then be interpreted as specifying state changes over time, as in the following:

> If the state at time t is q and the input time t is x, then the state at time $t+1$ will be $\delta(q,x)$ and the output y at time t will be $\lambda(q,x)$.

Here δ is called the *state transition* function and is the more abstract concept for the first three columns of the table. λ is called the *output function* and corresponds to the first two and last columns. The more abstract forms, δ and λ, constitute a more general way of giving the transition and output information. For example, Table 1 can be summarized more compactly as

$$\delta(q,x) = x \text{ and}$$
$$\lambda(q,x) = x,$$

which say that the next state and current output are both given by the current input. The functions δ and λ are also much more general than the table.

Table 1 Transition/Output Table for a Delay System

Current state	Current input	Next state	Current output
0	0	0	0
0	1	1	1
1	0	0	0
1	1	1	1

They can be thought about and described even when it is tedious to write a table for all combinations of states or inputs—or indeed, when they are not finite and writing a table is not possible at all.

A sequence of states, $q(0), q(1), q(2), \ldots$ is called a *state trajectory.* Having an arbitrary initial state $q(0)$, subsequent states in the sequence are determined by

$$q(t+1) = \delta(q(t), x(t)).$$

Similarly, a corresponding *output trajectory* is given by

$$y(t) = \lambda(q(t), x(t)).$$

Table 2 illustrates state and output trajectories (third and fourth rows, respectively) that are determined by the input trajectory in the second row.

3.2.1 Discrete Time Simulation

We can write a little algorithm to compute the state and output trajectories of a discrete time model given its input trajectory and its initial state. Such an algorithm is an example of a simulator (as defined in Chapter 2).

Note that the input data for the algorithm corresponds to the entries in Table 3.

```
Ti = 0, Tf = 9 the starting and ending times, here 0 and 9
x(0) = 1, . . ., x(9) = 0 the input trajectory
q(0) = 0 the initial state

t = Ti
while (t <= Tf) {
  y(t) = λ(q(t), x(t))
  q(t+1) = δ(q(t), x(t))
}
```

Executing the algorithm fills in the blanks in Table 3 (except for those checked).

Exercise: Execute the algorithm by hand to fill in Table 3. Why are the marked squares not filled in?◆

Table 2 State and Output Trajectories

Time	0	1	2	3	4	5	6	7	8	9	
Input trajectory	1	0	1	0	1	0	1	0	1	0	
State trajectory	0	1	0	1	0	1	0	1	0	1	0
Output trajectory	1	0	1	0	1	0	1	0	1	0	

Table 3 Computing State and Output Trajectories

Time	0	1	2	3	4	5	6	7	8	9	
Input trajectory	1	0	1	0	1	0	1	0	1	0	√
State trajectory	0										
Output trajectory											√

Exercise: Table 4 is for a model called a binary counter. Hand simulate the model in the table for various input sequences and initial states. Explain why it is called a binary counter.◆

3.2.2 Cellular Automata

Although the algorithm just discussed seems very simple indeed, the abstract nature of the transition and output functions hides a wealth of potentially interesting complexities. For example, what if we connected together systems (as in Chapter 1) in a row with each system connected to its left and right neighbors, as shown in Fig. 2?

Imagine that each system has two states and gets the states of its neighbors as inputs. Then there are eight combinations of states and inputs as listed in Table 5. We have left the next state column blank. Each complete assignment of a 0 or 1 to the eight rows results in a new transition function. There are $2^8 = 256$ such functions. Suppose we chose any one such function, started

Table 4 State and Output Trajectories

Current state	Current input	Next state	Current output
0	0	0	0
0	1	1	0
1	0	1	0
1	1	0	1

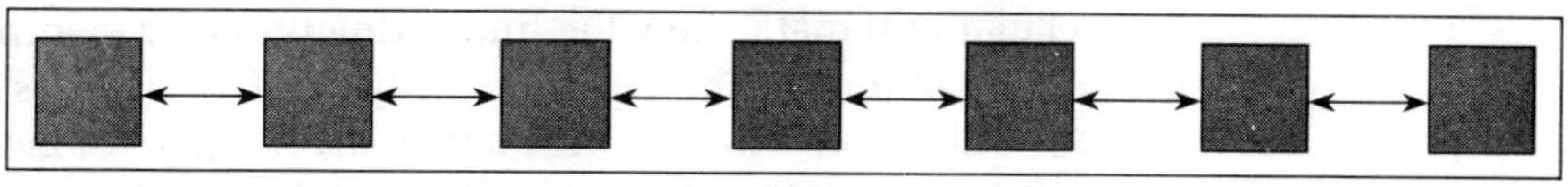

Figure 2 One-dimensional cell space.

each of the components in Fig. 2 in one of its states, and applied an appropriate version of the preceding simulation algorithm. What would we observe?

The answer to such questions is the concern of the field of *cellular automata.* A cellular automaton is an idealization of a physical phenomenon in which space and time are discretized and the state sets are discrete and finite. Cellular automata have components, called *cells,* which are all identical with identical computational apparatus. They are geometrically located on a one-, two-, or multidimensional grid and connected in a uniform way. The cells influencing a particular cell, called the *neighborhood* of the cell, are often chosen to be the cells located nearest in the geometrical sense. Cellular automata were originally introduced by von Neumann and Ulam [7] as idealization of biological self-production.

Table 5 A Two-Input Transition Function

Current state	Current left input	Current right input	Next state
0	0	0	?
0	0	1	?
0	1	0	?
0	1	1	?
1	0	0	?
1	0	1	?
1	1	0	?
1	1	1	?

Cellular automata show the interesting property that they yield quite diverse and interesting behavior. Actually, Wolfram [18] systematically investigated all possible transition functions of one-dimensional cellular automata. He found out that there exist four types of cellular automata that differ significantly in their behavior; (1) automata where any dynamic soon dies out, (2) automata that soon come to periodic behavior, (3) automata that show chaotic behavior, and (4), the most interesting ones, automata whose behaviors are unpredictable and nonperiodic but that show interesting, regular patterns.

Conway's Game of Life in its original representation in *Scientific American* [10] can serve as a fascinating introduction to the ideas involved. The game is framed within a two-dimensional cell space structure, possibly of infinite size. Each cell is coupled to its nearest physical neighbors both laterally and diagonally. This means for a cell located at point (0, 0) its lateral neighbors are at (0, 1), (1, 0), (0, –1), and (–1, 0) and its diagonal neighbors are at (1, 1), (1,–1), (–1, 1) and (–1, –1), as shown in Fig. 3. The neighbors of an arbitrary cell at (i, j) are the cells at $(i, j+1)$, $(i+1, j)$, $(i, j-1)$, $(i-1, j)$, $(i+1, j+1)$, $(i+1, j-1)$, $(i-1, j+1)$, and $(i-1, j-1)$, which can be computed from the neighbors at (0,0) by a simple translation. The *state* set of a cell consists of one variable, which can take on only two values, 0 (*dead*) and 1 (*alive*). Individual cells survive (are alive and stay alive), are born (go from 0 to 1), or die (go from 1 to 0) as the game progresses. The rules as defined by Conway are as follows:

1. A live cell remains alive if it has between 2 and 3 live cells in its neighborhood.
2. A live cell will die because of overcrowding if it has more than 3 live cells in its neighborhood.
3. A live cell will die because of isolation if it has fewer than 2 live neighbors.
4. A dead cell will become alive if it has exactly 3 alive neighbors.

When started from certain configurations of alive cells, the Game of Life shows interesting behavior over time. As a state trajectory evolves, live cells form varied and dynamically changing clusters. The idea of the game is to find new patterns and study their behavior. Figure 4 shows some interesting patterns.

The Game of Life exemplifies some of the concepts introduced earlier. It evolves on a *discrete time base* (time advances in steps 0,1,2,. . .) and is a *multi-component system* [it is composed of *components* (cells) that are coupled

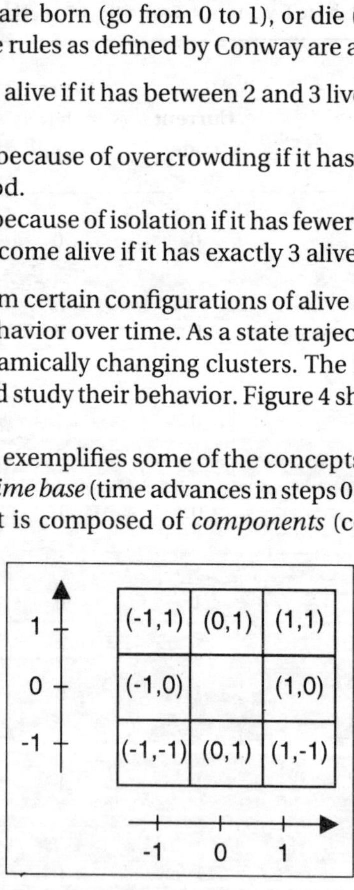

Figure 3 Cellular coupling structure for Game of Life.

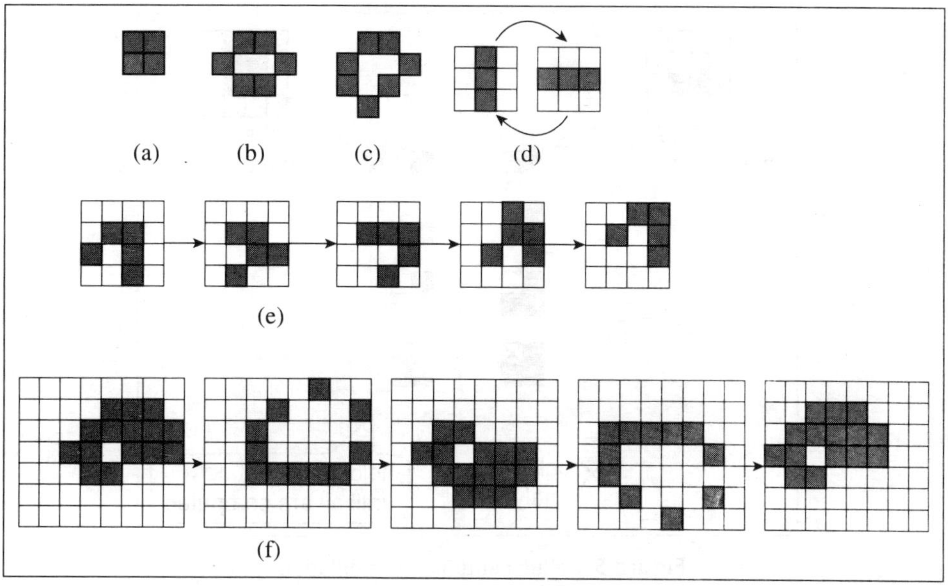

Figure 4 Patterns from Conway's Game of Life: Patterns (a) to (c) are stable—they don't change; (d) is an oscillating patterns; (e) and (f) are cycles of patterns that move.

together]. In contrast to the *local* state (the state of a cell), the *global state* refers to the collection of states of all cells at any time. In the Game of Life, this is a finite pattern, or configuration, of alive cells with all the rest being dead. Every such state starts a *state trajectory* (sequence of global states indexed by time) that either ends up in a cycle or continues to evolve forever.

Exercise: If an initial state is a finite configuration of alive cells, why are all subsequent states also finite configurations?◆

3.2.3 Cellular Automaton Simulation Algorithms

The basic procedure for simulating a cellular automaton follows the discrete time simulation algorithm introduced earlier. That is, at every time step we scan all cells, applying the state transition function to each, and saving the next state in a second copy of the global state data structure. When all next states have been computed, they constitute the next global state and the clock advances to the next step. For example, let's start with the three live cells in a triangle shown in the upper left of Fig. 5. Analyzing the neighborhood of the lower corner cell, we see it is alive and has 2 alive neighbors; thus, it survives to the next generation. As shown, the other alive cells also survive. However, only one new cell is born. This is the upper right corner cell, which has exactly three neighbors.

Of course, as stated, the cell space is an infinite and we can't possibly scan all the cells in a finite amount of time. To overcome this problem, the examined part of the space is limited to a finite region. In many case, this region is fixed throughout the simulation. For example, a two-dimensional space might be represented by a square array of size N (= 1,2,. . .). In this case, the basic algorithm scans all N^2 cells at every time step. Something

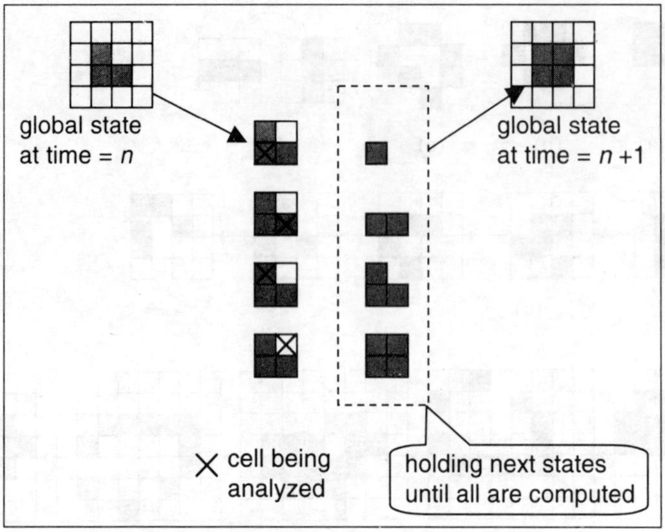

Figure 5 Cellular automaton simulation cycle.

must be done to take care of the fact that cells at the boundary lack their full complement of neighbors. One solution is to assume fixed values for all boundary cells (for example, all dead). Another is to wrap the space in toroidal fashion (done by letting the index N also be interpreted as 0). But there is a smarter approach that can handle a potentially infinite space by limiting the scanning to only those cells that can potentially change states at any time. This is the discrete event approach discussed next.

3.2.4 Discrete Event Approach to Cellular Automaton Simulation

In discrete time systems, at every time step each component undergoes a "state transition"; this occurs whether or not its state actually changes. Often, only a small number of components really change. For example, in the Game of Life, the dead state is called a *quiescent* state—if the cell and all its neighbors are in the quiescent state, its next state is also quiescent. Since most cells in an infinite space are in the quiescent state, relatively few actually change state. Put another way, if *events* are defined as changes in state (e.g., births and deaths in the Game of Life), then often there are relatively few events in the system. Scanning all cells in an infinite space is impossible, but even in a finite space, scanning all cells for events at every time step is clearly inefficient. A discrete event simulation algorithm **concentrates on processing events** rather than cells and is inherently more efficient.

The basic idea is to try to predict whether a cell will possibly change state or will definitely be left unchanged in a next global state transition. Suppose we have a set of potentially changing cells. Then we only examine those cells in the set. Some or all of these cells are observed to change their states. Then, in the new circumstances, we collect the cells that can possibly change state in the next step. The criterion under which cells can change is simple to define. *A cell will not change state at the next state transition time, if none of its neighboring cells changed state at the current state transition time.* The event-based simulation procedure follows from this logic:

In a state transition mark those cells which actually changed state. From those, collect the cells that are their neighbors. The set collected contains all cells that can possibly change at the next step. All other cells will definitely be left unchanged.

For example, Fig. 6 continues the simulation just discussed. Since only the black cell changed state, only its eight neighbors can possibly change state in the next simulation cycle. In other words, if we start with cells at which events have occurred, then we can readily predict where the next events can occur.

Note that although we can limit the scanning to those cells that are candidates for events, we cannot *predict which cells will actually have events* without actually applying the transition function to their neighborhood states.

Exercise: Identify a cell that is in the can-possibly-change set but that does not actually change state.◆

Exercise: Write a simulator for one-dimensional cellular automata such as in Table 5 and Fig. 2. Compare the direct approach that scans all cells all the time with the discrete event approach in terms of execution time. Under what circumstances would it not pay to use the discrete event approach? (See later discussion in Chapter 16.)◆

Exercise: Until now we have assumed a neighborhood of eight cells adjacent to the center cell. However, in general, a neighborhood for the cell at the origin is defined as any finite subset of cells. This neighborhood is translated to every cell. Such a neighborhood is called reflection symmetric if whenever cell (i,j) belongs to it then so does (j,i). For neighborhoods that are not reflection symmetric, define the appropriate set of influences required for the discrete event simulation approach.◆

3.2.5 Switching Automata/Sequential Machines

Cellular automata are uniform both in their composition and interconnection patterns. If we drop these requirements but still consider connecting finite state components together, we get another useful class of discrete time models.

Switching automata (also called digital circuits) are constructed from flip-flop components and logical gates. The flip-flops are systems with

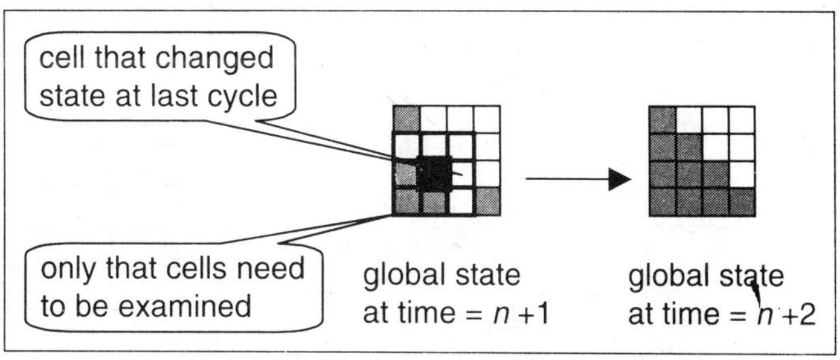

Figure 6 Collecting cells with possible events.

Table 6 State and Output Trajectories of a Delay Flip-Flop

Time	0	1	2	3	4	5	6	7	8	9	
Input trajectory	1	0	1	0	1	0	1	0	1	0	
State trajectory	0	1	0	1	0	1	0	1	0	1	0
Output trajectory	0	1	0	1	0	1	0	1	0	1	

binary states, the most straightforward example of which we have already met. This has the transition function shown in Table 1. However, instead of allowing the input to propagate straight through to the output, we will let the output be the current state (as in cellular automata). Table 6 shows how the output trajectory now lags the input trajectory by one time step. The difference, we'll see later, is between so-called Mealy and Moore models of sequential machines. In Mealy networks the effects of an input can propagate throughout space in zero time—even cycling back on themselves, causing "vicious circles" or ill-behaved systems.

To construct networks we can not only couple flip-flop outputs to inputs, but also connect them through so-called *gates,* which realize elementary Boolean functions. As we shall see later, these are instantaneous or memoryless systems. As shown in Fig. 7, their outputs are directly deter-

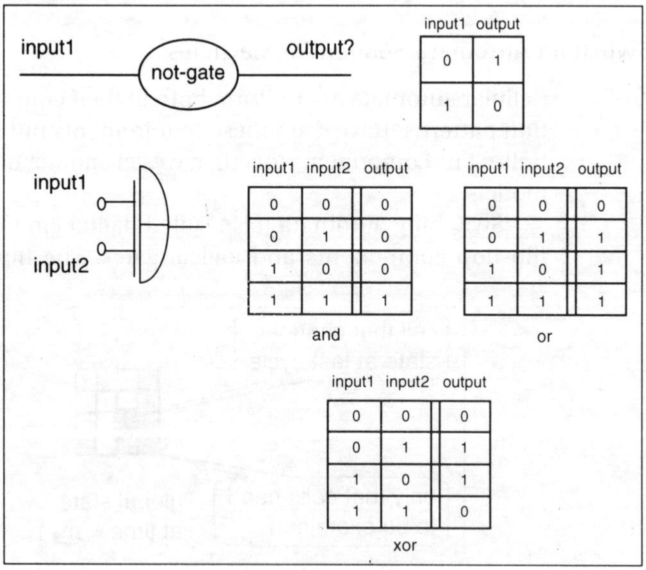

Figure 7 Gates realizing elementary boolean functions.

mined by their inputs with no help from an internal state. The clock usually used in synchronous machines determines a constant time advance. This enables transistor circuits to be adequately represented by discrete time models, at least for their functional behavior.

The switching automaton in Fig. 8 is made up of several flip-flop components coupled in series and a feedback function defined by a coupling of XOR gates. Each flip-flop is an elementary memory component as before. Flip-flops q_1 to q_7 are coupled in series, that is, the state of flip-flop *i* defines the input and hence the next state of flip-flop *i*–1. This linear sequence of flip-flops is called a *shift register,* since it shifts the input at the first component to the right each time step. The latter input may be computed using gates. For example, the input to flip-flop 8 is defined by an XOR-connection of memory values q_i and input value x: $x \oplus q_8 \oplus q_6 \oplus q_5 \oplus q_3 \oplus q_1$. (An XOR, $q_1 \oplus q_2$ outputs the exclusive-or operation on its inputs, i.e., the output is 0 if, and only if, both inputs are the same, otherwise 1.)

In Chapter 8 we will discuss simulators for such combinations of memoryless and memory-based systems.

3.2.6 Linear Discrete Time Networks and Their State Behavior

Fig. 9 illustrates a Moore network with two delay elements and two memoryless elements. However, in distinction to the switching automaton above, this network now is defined over the reals. The structure of the network can be represented by the matrix

$$\begin{bmatrix} 0 & g \\ -g & 0 \end{bmatrix},$$

where g and $-g$ are the gain factors of the memoryless elements. Started in a state represented by the vector [1,1], (each delay is in state 1), the next state $[q_1, q_2]$ of the network is $[-g, g]$, which can be computed by the matrix multiplication

$$\begin{bmatrix} g \\ -g \end{bmatrix} = \begin{bmatrix} 0 & g \\ -g & 0 \end{bmatrix}\begin{bmatrix} 1 \\ 1 \end{bmatrix}.$$

The reason that a matrix representation and multiplication can be used is that the network has a *linear* structure. This means that all components produce outputs or states that are linear combinations of their inputs and states. A delay is a very simple linear component—its next state is identical to its input. A memoryless element with a gain factor is called

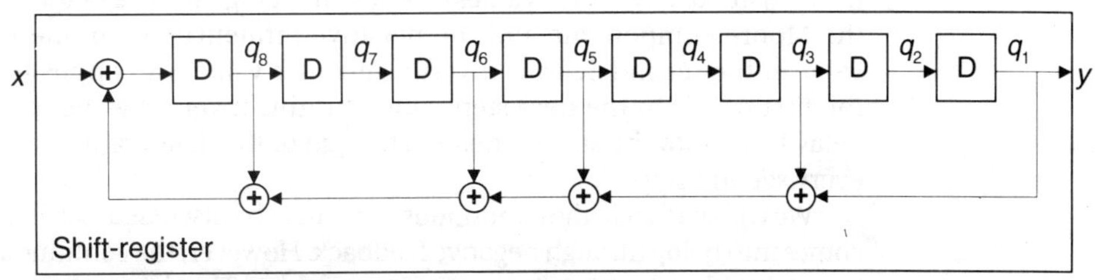

Figure 8 Shift register coupling flip-flop elements and logical gates.

a *coefficient* element and it multiplies its current input by the gain to produce its output. Both of these are simple examples of linearity. A summer, that is a memoryless function that adds its inputs to obtain its output, is also a linear element.

A Moore discrete time system is in *linear matrix* form if its transition and output functions can be represented by matrices $\{A,B,C\}$. This means that its transition function can be expressed as

$$\delta(q,x) = Aq + Bx.$$

Here q is a real n-dimensional state vector, and A is an n by n matrix. Similarly, x is a real m-dimensional input vector, and B has dimension m by n. Also, the output function is

$$\lambda(q) = Cq,$$

where, if the output y is a p-dimensional vector, then C is an n by p-dimensional matrix. A similar definition holds for Mealy discrete time system.

Exercise: Any discrete time network with linear structure can be represented by a linear system in matrix form. Conversely, any linear discrete time system in matrix form can be realized by a discrete time network with linear structure. Develop procedures to convert one into the other.◆

The state trajectory behavior of the linear system in Fig. 9 is obtained by interatively multiplying the matrix A into successive states. Thus, if $[g,-g]$ is the state following $[1,1]$, then the next state is

$$\begin{bmatrix} -g^2 \\ g^2 \end{bmatrix} = \begin{bmatrix} 0 & g \\ -g & 0 \end{bmatrix} \begin{bmatrix} g \\ -g \end{bmatrix}$$

Thus, the state trajectory starts out as

$$\begin{bmatrix} 1 \\ 1 \end{bmatrix} \ldots \begin{bmatrix} g \\ -g \end{bmatrix} \ldots \begin{bmatrix} -g^2 \\ g^2 \end{bmatrix}.$$

Exercise: Characterize the remainder of the state trajectory.◆

There are three distinguishable types of trajectories as illustrated in Fig. 9. When $g = 1$, we have a steady alternation between + 1 and –1. When $g < 1$, the envelope of values decays exponentially; and finally, when $g > 1$, the envelope increases exponentially.

Actually the model just given is a discrete form of an oscillating system. In the following sections we will learn to understand its better-known continuous system counterpart. In the discrete form, oscillations (switching from positive to negative values) come into being because of the delays in the Moore components and the negative influence $-g$. In one step the value of the second delay is inverted, giving a value with opposite sign to the first delay. In the next step, however, this inverted value in the first delay is fed into the second delay. The sign of the delay values is inverted every second step.

We will see that in the continuous domain to be discussed, oscillation also comes into being through negative feedback. However, the continuous models work with derivatives instead of input values. The delays in the discrete domain correspond to integrators in the continuous domain. But let us first

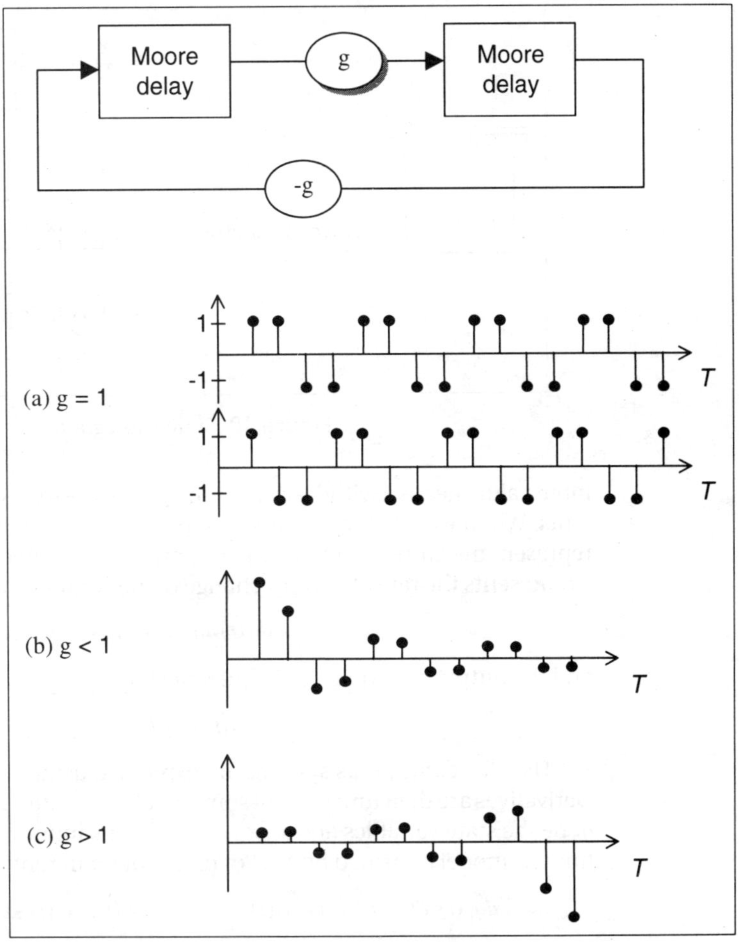

Figure 9 Simple linear Moore network and its behavior.

discuss the basics of modeling and simulation of continuous systems, and then come back to compare the two forms of oscillating systems thereafter.

3.3 Differential Equation Models and Their Simulators

In discrete time modeling we had a state transition function that gave us the information of the state at the next time instant given the current state and input. In the classical modeling approach of differential equations, the state transition relation is quite different. For differential equation models we do not specify a next state directly, but use a *derivative function* to specify the rate of change of the state variables. At any particular time instant on the time axis, given a state and an input value, we only know the rate of change of the state. From this information, the state at any point in the future has to be computed.

To discuss this issue, let us consider the most elementary continuous system—the simple integrator (Fig. 10). The integrator has one input variable x and one output variable y. One can imagine it as a reservoir with infinite capacity. Whatever is put into the reservoir is accumulated—but a negative

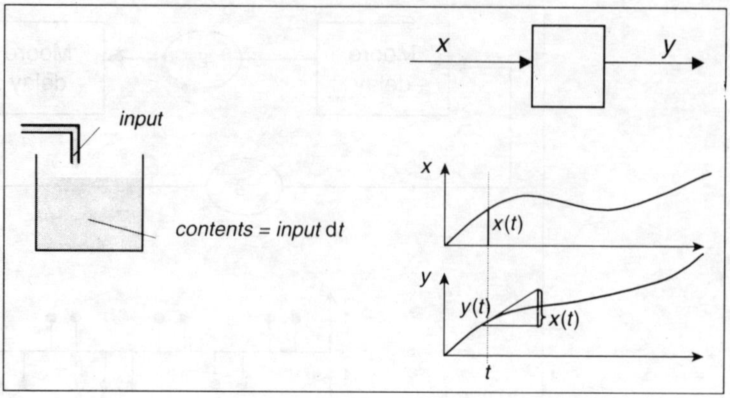

Figure 10 Simple integrator.

input value means a withdrawal. The output of the reservoir is its current contents. When we want to express this in equation form we need a variable to represent the current contents. This is our state variable q. The current input x represents the rate of current change of the contents, which we express by

$$dq(t)/dt = x(t),$$

and the output y is equal to the current state

$$y(t) = q(t).$$

Usually, continuous systems are expressed using several state variables. Derivatives are then functions of some, or all, the state variables. Let $q_1, q_2, \ldots, q_n$ be the state variables and $x_1, x_2, \ldots, x_m$ be the input variables. Then a continuous model is formed by a set of first-order differential equations,

$$dq_1(t)/dt = f_1(q_1(t), q_2(t), \ldots, q_n(t),\ x_1(t),\ x_2(t), \ldots, x_m(t))$$
$$dq_2(t)/dt = f_2(q_1(t), q_2(t), \ldots, q_n(t),\ x_1(t),\ x_2(t), \ldots, x_m(t))$$
$$\ldots$$
$$dq_n(t)/dt = f_n(q_1(t), q_2(t), \ldots, q_n(t),\ x_1(t),\ x_2(t), \ldots, x_m(t)).$$

Note that the derivatives of the state variables q_i are computed, respectively, by functions f_i that have the state and input vectors as arguments. This can be shown in diagrammatic form as in Fig. 11. The state and input vector are input to the rate of change functions f_i. Those provide as output the derivatives dq_i/dt of the state variables q_i, which are forwarded to integrator blocks. The outputs of the integrator blocks are the state variables q_i.

3.3.1 Continuous System Simulation

Figure 11 reveals the fundamental problem that occurs when a continuous system is simulated on a digital computer. In the diagram we see that given a state vector q and an input vector x for a particular time instant t_i we only obtain the derivatives dq_i/dt. But how do we obtain the dynamic behavior of the system over time? In other words, how do we obtain the state values after this time? This problem is depicted in Fig. 12. In digital simulation, there is

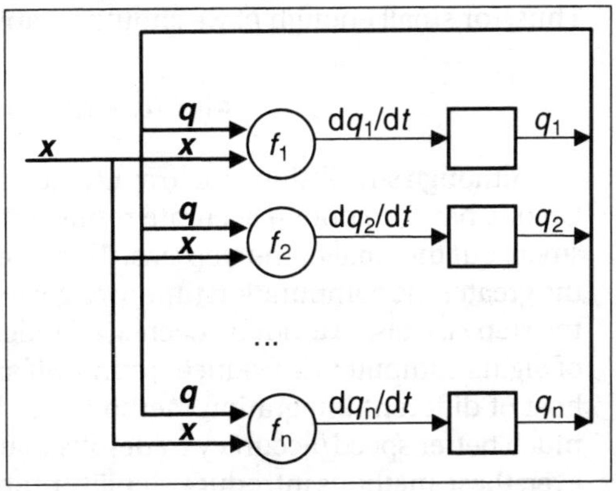

Figure 11 Structure of differential equation specified systems.

necessarily a next computation instant t_{i+1} and a nonzero interval $[t_i, t_{i+1}]$. The model is supposed to be operating in continuous time over this interval, and the input, state, and output variables change continuously during this period. The computer program has available only the values at t_i and from those it must estimate the values at t_{i+1} *without* knowledge of what is happening in the gaps between t_i and t_{i+1}. This means it must do the calculation without having computed the input, state, and output trajectories associated with the interval (t_i, t_{i+1}).

Schemes for solving this problem are generally known as *numerical integration methods.* A whole literature deals with design and analysis of such methods [6,16]. Here we try only to provide some insight into the operation, accuracy, and complexity of these methods from a broader systems theoretic perspective.

Let us study the approach by considering the simplest integration method, generally known as the *Euler* or *rectangular* method. The idea underlying the Euler method is that for a perfect integrator

$$\frac{dq(t)}{dt} = \lim_{h \to 0} \frac{q(t+h) - q(t)}{h}.$$

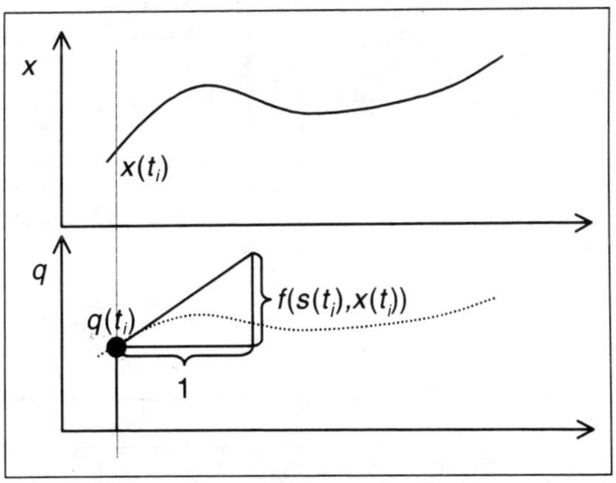

Figure 12 Continuous system simulation problem.

Thus, for small enough h, we should be able to use the approximation

$$q(t+h) = q(t) + h \cdot \frac{dq(t)}{dt}.$$

Although straightforward to apply, Euler integration has some drawbacks. On one hand, to obtain accurate results the step size h has to be sufficiently small. But the smaller the step size, the more iterations are needed, and hence the greater the computation time for a given length of run. On the other hand, the step size also cannot be decreased indefinitely, since the finite word size of digital computers introduces round-off and truncation errors. Therefore, a host of different integration method have been developed that often show much better speed/accuracy trade-offs than the simple Euler method. However, these methods introduce stability problems, as we discuss in a moment.

Exercise: Show that the number of iterations varies inversely to the step size in Euler integration. How does reducing the step size an order of magnitude affect the number of iterations?◆

The basic idea of numerical integration is easily stated—an integration method employs estimated past and/or future values of states, inputs, and derivatives in an effort to better estimate a value for the present time (Fig. 13). Thus, computing a state value $q(t_i)$ for a present time instance t_i may involve computed values of states, inputs, and derivatives at prior computation times $t_{i-1}, t_{i-2}, \ldots$ and/or predicted values for the current time t_i and subsequent time instants $t_{i+1}, t_{i+2}, \ldots,$

$$q(t_i) = integration\_method(\ldots, q(t_{i-2}), f(q(t_{i-2}), x(t_{i-2})),$$
$$q(t_{i-1}), f(q(t_{i-1}), x(t_{i-1})), q'(t_i), f(q'(t_i), x'(t_i)), q'(t_{i+1}),$$
$$f(q'(t_{i+1}), x'(t_{i+1})), \ldots)$$

where q' and x' are the state and input estimates.

Notice that the values of the states and the derivatives are mutually interdependent—the integrator itself causes a dependence of the states on the derivatives and through the derivative functions f_i the derivatives are

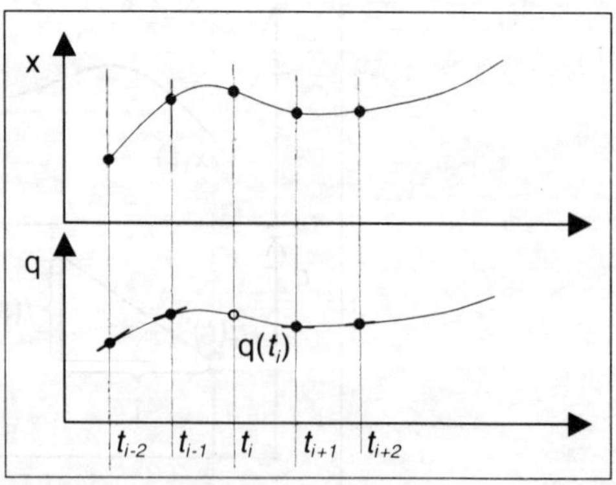

Figure 13 Computing state values at time t_i based on estimated values at time instants prior and past time t_i.

dependent on the states. This situation sets up an inherent difficulty that must be faced by every approximation method—the propagation of errors.

We now describe briefly the principles of some frequently employed integration methods. We can distinguish methods according to whether or not they use estimated future values of variables to compute the present values. We call a method *causal* if it only employs values at prior computation instants. A method is called *non-causal* if in addition to prior values it also employs estimated values at time instants at and after the present time. The order of a method is the number of pairs of derivative/state values it employs to compute the value of the state at time t_i. For example, a method employing the values of q and its derivative at times t_{i-2}, t_{i-1}, t_i, and t_{i+1} is of order 4.

Causal Methods

A causal method of order m is often a linear combination of the state and derivative values at time instants t_{i-m} to t_{i-1} with coefficients chosen to minimize the error from the computed estimate to the real value. Usually the basis of the derivation of the coefficients is the assumption that the state trajectories and the output trajectories are smooth enough to be approximated by the dth-order polynomial. Of course, often it is not known beforehand whether the requisite smoothness indeed obtains.

Example: The Adams method is a simple causal method of order 2 and can be described by

$$q(t_i) = q(t_{i-1}) + h(3f(q(t_{i-1}), x(t_{i-1})) - f(q(t_{i-2}), x(t_{i-2}))).$$

A general problem in causal integration methods is the startup, namely, the determination of the state, derivative, and output values for the times t_{1-m} to t_0 at the initial simulation time t_1. This is generally referred to as the *startup problem.* A solution to this problem is to use causal methods of lower orders in the startup phase. That is, in the first cycle, where only the initial state is available, a method of order 1 is used and subsequently the order of the method is increased to its final order m. Another, more reliable solution is to change the method completely for the startup phase—for example, to use a noncausal method (see next section) in the startup phase when past values are not available but future values can be estimated.

Noncausal Methods

As we have indicated, the noncausal integration methods make use of "future" values of states, derivatives, and inputs. Clearly, the only way of obtaining "future" values is to run the simulation out past the present model time, calculate and store the needed values, and use these data to estimate the present values. Thus, the values at the present time may be computed twice—tentatively, during the initial "predictor" phase when the future is simulated, and once again during the "corrector" phase when the final value is computed. A simulator program with a noncausal method, therefore, has to work in several phases. At first there may be several predictor phases, and finally there is usually one corrector phase.

Example: A simple predictor–corrector method generally known as the *Heun* method is

$$q'(t_i) = q(t_{i-1}) + hf(q(t_{i-1}), x(t_{i-1}))$$

$$q(t_i) = q(t_{i-1}) + h/2(f(q'(t_i), x'(t_i)) + f(q(t_{i-1}), x(t_{i-1}))),$$

where $q'(t_i)$ is the predicted value and $q(t_i)$ is the final corrected value.

In some methods, called *variable stepsize* methods, the difference between two computed values is compared with a criterion level; if the estimated error is too large, the step size is decreased and the predictor–corrector cycle repeated until a step size is found for which the difference is below the criterion level. Of course, if the state trajectory is not sufficiently smooth, no finite step size may be found for which the divergence is sufficiently small, and the simulation will drive to an expensive halt.

Many noncausal methods, among them the most popular *Runge–Kutta* methods, do not use past values but only use the current state and input value to make the predictions of future values. For those methods, the startup phase is not a problem. Such methods therefore are also good alternatives to employ in the startup phase of causal methods.

To Euler or Not: That Is The Question

Error arises from two sources: Some error is introduced in each step by the approximation method, and some accumulates through the effect of prior error propagating through the system. In case of integration methods, the first source of error exists even if the values of state and derivative are correct. The second source of error is due to the mutual dependence of states and derivatives just mentioned. An error in state is transmitted to the derivative functions, where it may further affect the state values. An integration method may tend to amplify or dampen the effect of error feedback. All other things being equal, a so-called *stable* method (one that dampens error propagation) is preferable to one that amplifies the error propagation. But the error propagation does not only depend on the method, it also depends on the nature of the model—whether it tends to amplify or dampen deviations (e.g., whether trajectories emerging from initial states close together tend to remain close together). From this we can see that the choice of integration method, or for that matter any simulation algorithm, for a given model is not an easy one.

We have suggested that multipoint methods can be faster than direct Euler integration while preserving accuracy. However, these methods also have their drawbacks. They introduce stability and startup problems that Euler doesn't suffer from. They make assumptions about the analytic nature of the trajectories that can easily be violated in hybrid models with state events (see Chapter 9). Also, with modern high-speed computers, the use of Euler and other direct integration methods is becoming more practical.

Fortunately, modern environments and packages for continuous simulation shield the modeler from many of these considerations. Indeed, in principle, users should be able to work with models independently of the underlying integration method. Unfortunately, however, today's environments are not perfect and the user has to be on the lookout for signs that the simulator is not faithfully generating the model trajectories. For example, puzzling results may be due to the integration becoming unstable rather than an interesting model behavior. Or more perniciously, innocent-looking simulated trajectories may hide unsuspected integration errors. Table 7 summarizes the pros and cons of integration methods.

The problems of error introduction and error propagation are endemic to simulator and model construction throughout the whole M&S enterprise. We will take up these issues later in Chapters 13 and 14.

3.3.2 Feedback in Continuous Systems

After acquiring a basic understanding of differential equation models and how they are simulated on digital computers, let us now try to get some insight into the nature of continuous system behavior. By considering several elementary systems we will demonstrate that the reason for the emergence of quite complex behavior is *feedback*. In a system model embodying feedback loops, state variables are fed back to influence their own rates of change. Feeding back a state variable to its own derivative can be direct or also involve several other state variables. Figure 14 shows a feedback loop where a state variable q_1, influences the derivative of q_2, which again influences q_3, and so on. Finally, a state variable q_n is used to define the derivative of q_1, closing the feedback loop.

Qualitative analysis of the feedback loops in a system can give insights into its possible behaviors. Most important is whether a feedback loop is positive or negative. When traversing the feedback loop, we can count the signs of the direct influences between the state variables. When the sign of a function f_i is positive, we speak of a positive influence from q_{i-1} to q_i, which means that a positive value of q_{i-1} will make q_i increase. Conversely, when the sign of a function f_i is negative, a positive value of q_{i-1} will cause a decrease of q_i. A positive feedback loop is one with a even number of negative influences. A negative feedback loop is one with an odd number of negative influences.

How do they differ? Let us consider as an example a positive feedback loop with zero negative influences and a negative feedback loop with one negative influence. In the positive feedback loop a greater value of a state variable will cause all influenced variables in the feedback loop to increase.

Table 7 Summary of Integration Method Speed–Accuracy Trade-Offs

Integration method	Efficiency	Startup problems	Stability problems	Robustness
Euler	Low	None	Not for sufficiently small step sizes	High
Causal methods	High	Yes	Yes	Low
Noncausal methods	High	No, if only future values used	Yes	Low

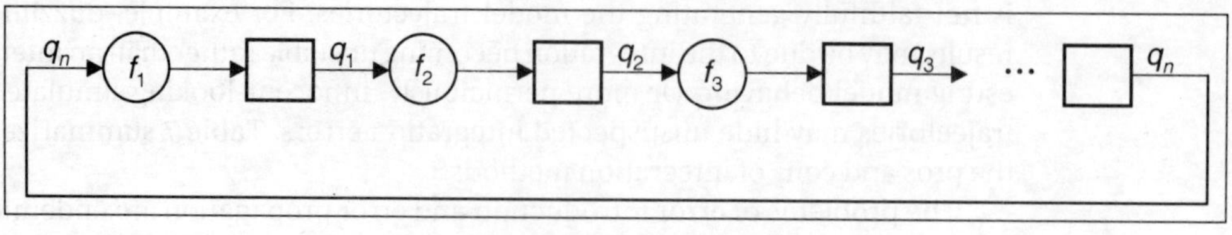

Figure 14 Feedback loop.

In turn, this will cause its own derivative to increase and the variable will get even greater. This feedback loop causes the variable to grow indefinitely. In some contexts, this is called unstable behavior and is undesirable. However, in other contexts, such as biological and economic growth, this is very desirable (at least for some part of the trajectory). For negative feedback loops, however, the negative influence will tend to stabilize a system. Growth of the state variable will tend to be turned into negative influence on its derivative, which would cause the state variable to decrease (we say "tend" because, the situation is actually more complex; see Ref. [13]).

Exercise: Argue why a feedback loop with an even number of negative influences works like one with no negative influence and one with an odd number of negative influences is the same as one with one negative influence.◆

3.3.3 Elementary Linear Systems

After this general discussion of feedback in continuous systems, let us introduce some well-known basic continuous systems and study their behavior. These often appear as elementary substructures in models of complex real phenomena independently of the application domain at hand (the feedback takes different forms in the different structures). As we will see, simple continuous systems can show quite interesting behavior, despite their simple-looking structure. The reason for this is feedback.

First of all, let us discuss a system with one state variable with a direct feedback loop to itself. The derivative of the state variable is computed by the state variable multiplied with a linear factor c. When the factor c is positive, we have a positive feedback. In this case, the system will grow exponentially and we speak of an *exponential growth.* Conversely, when the factor c is negative, we have a negative feedback and the variable will shrink approaching zero exponentially. We have a *exponential decay.* When the factor is zero, the state remains constant. Figure 15 shows the system structure and several different behaviors for different values for factor c. The larger c is in magnitude, the steeper the curve, whether increasing or decreasing.

As illustrated in Fig. 16, when we apply an input to an exponential decay, we have the so-called *exponential delay of first order.* This type of continuous system plays an important role in many real-world phenomena. In abstract terms, this is the right type of model to use for system with a driving force and a linear damping. The input to the system represents the driving force and the feedback through negative factor c models the damping. These two are added, defining the derivative for the state variable. The characteristic of the system is that the system reaches an equilibrium state when the damping through the

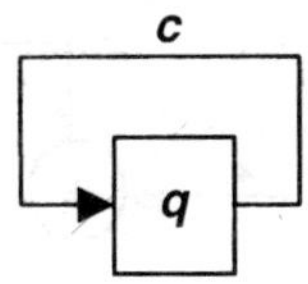

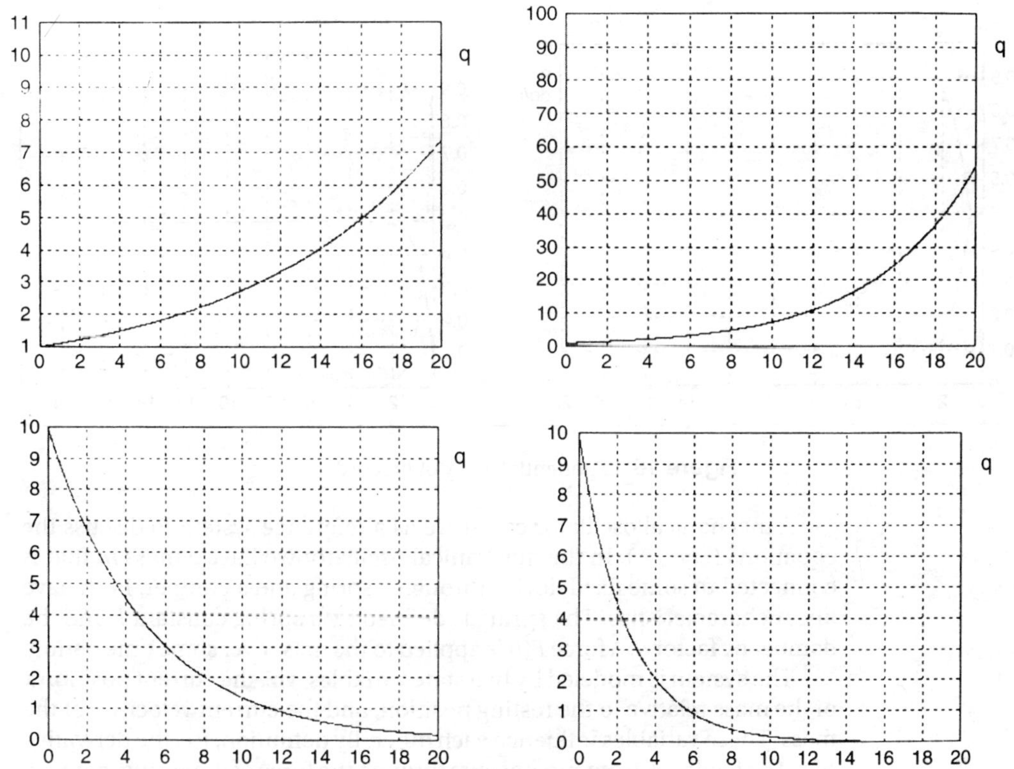

Figure 15 Exponential growth and decay.

feedback $-c * q$ equals the driving input. Figure 16 shows this for a constant input force x_1 and different damping factors c. The greater the damping factor, the smaller the equilibrium state.

There are many real-world phenomena that can be modeled by an exponential delay of first order. Examples range from heating systems where the input is the heat supply and the damping represents the heat losses to the environment, to mechanical systems where the input is the force supplied and the damping represents the friction that should be counteracted, to input of pollution into a natural system and its reduction through an absorption process.

The examples just given are systems with one state variable with a direct feedback loop to itself. Let us now consider a system in two variables. The *linear (or harmonic) oscillator of second order* is the best known example where the effect of feedback can easily be studied.

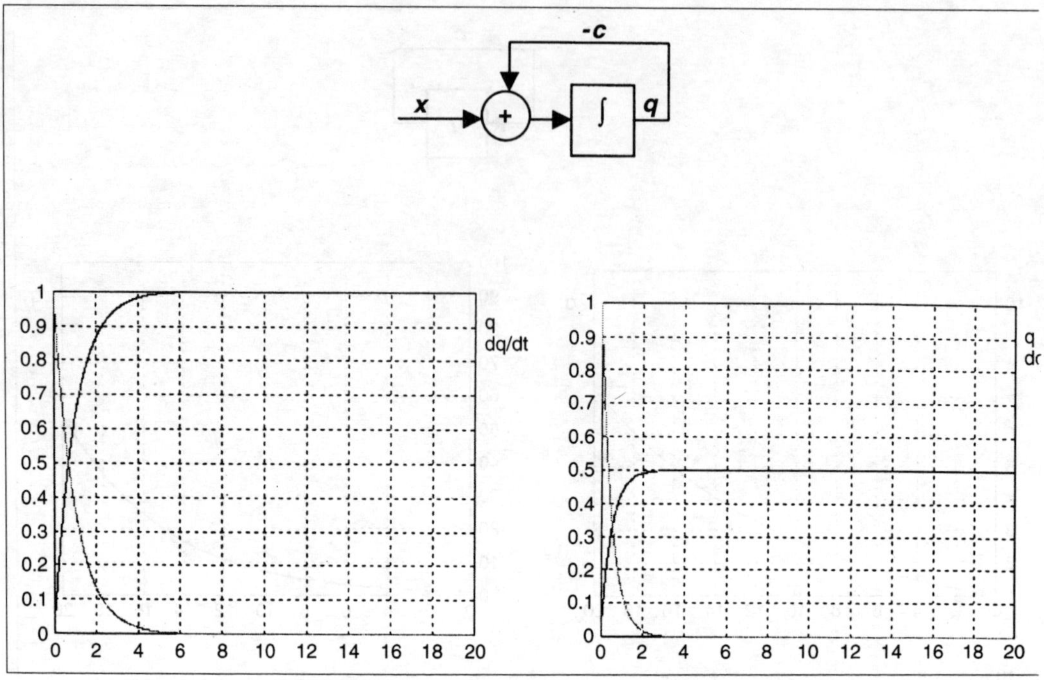

Figure 16 Exponential delay of first order.

A mechanical oscillator can serve as a reference system to discuss the equations (Fig. 17). In the mechanical oscillator we have a mass m that is connected to some fixed device through a spring and a damper. Both have linear characteristics. The spring is defined by a spring constant k and the damper by factor d. A force $F(t)$ is applied to the mass over some time period.

The system is modeled by two state variables, viz. the current position x of the mass relative to the resting position, and the current velocity v of the mass. These variables influence each other. By definition, v is the derivative of x. The feedback from x to v occurs through the force of the spring, namely, depending on the current deflection x of the mass, the spring will counteract and influence the velocity v by $-k * x$. Also, damping exerts a direct negative feedback from the velocity to itself $(d * v)$. The greater the velocity, the greater the damping gets.

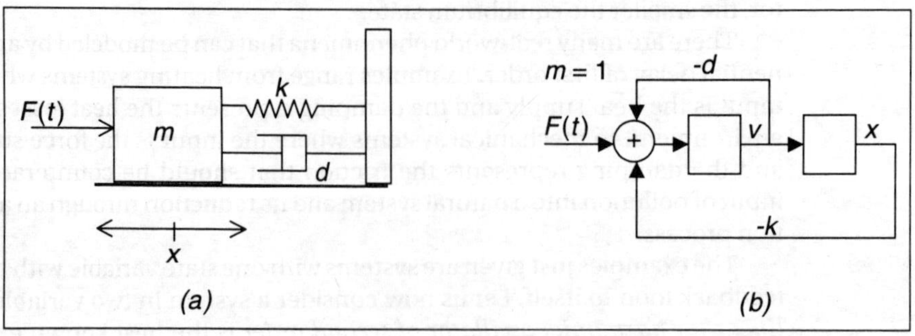

Figure 17 Damped linear oscillator of second order.

Most interesting for the behavior of the system is the negative feedback loop from the position x to the velocity v due to the spring force. Rather than cause growth or decay, this feedback actually causes the system to oscillate. Let us analyze the situation in a little more detail. In Fig. 18, we start with the mass at position 1 with velocity being 0. Now we let the mass loose. The effect will be that the spring force will accelerate the mass toward its resting position. When the mass has reached the zero position, the mass has acquired its maximum velocity and the kinetic energy will move the mass into the opposite direction. On the other side, however, the spring will act in the opposite direction, decelerating the mass until it comes to a rest and finally accelerating the mass back to its resting position again. Therefore, the system oscillates. If the damping factor is strong, the amplitude of the oscillation will rapidly decrease, bringing the system to a halt.

In some situations, the "damping" can be positive. In this case, it adds rather than removes energy from the system.

Exercise: Show that a system with positive damping oscillates with exponentially increasing amplitude (until something stops it—such as exploding into another system!).◆

If we remove damping altogether, we get a pure oscillator, as shown in Fig. 19. Here the spring or other system such as an electronic circuit with no resistance keeps "ringing" forever. In the figure, each integrator has the same gain, ω (although the signs differ), and the oscillation has frequency ω (with period $2\pi/\omega$). It is described by the familiar $\sin \omega t$ and $\cos \omega t$ curves shown. Such a system is called *neutrally* stable since it is neither damped nor undamped. If we add a small value to the state of an integrator, it will incorporate this change into the magnitude of its oscillation. We will see later (Chapter 16) that this is really the worst environment in which a simulator or approximation procedure has to operate, since every error accumulates in both an absolute and relative sense.

Exercise: Relate ω to k in Fig. 17 and thereby provide an expression for the frequency of oscillation in the damped spring shown there.◆

Now that we have also gained a general understanding of continuous modeling and simulation, let us come back to the comparison of the linear

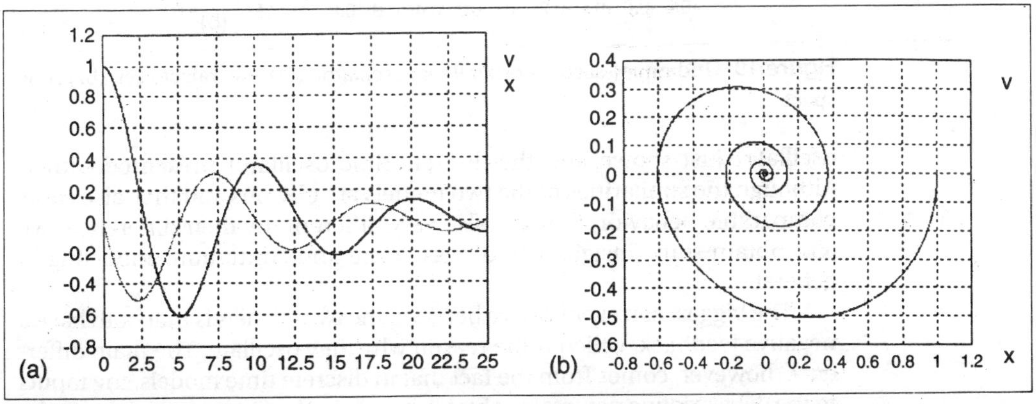

Figure 18 Damped linear oscillator: (a) position and velocity trajectories, (b) phase space.

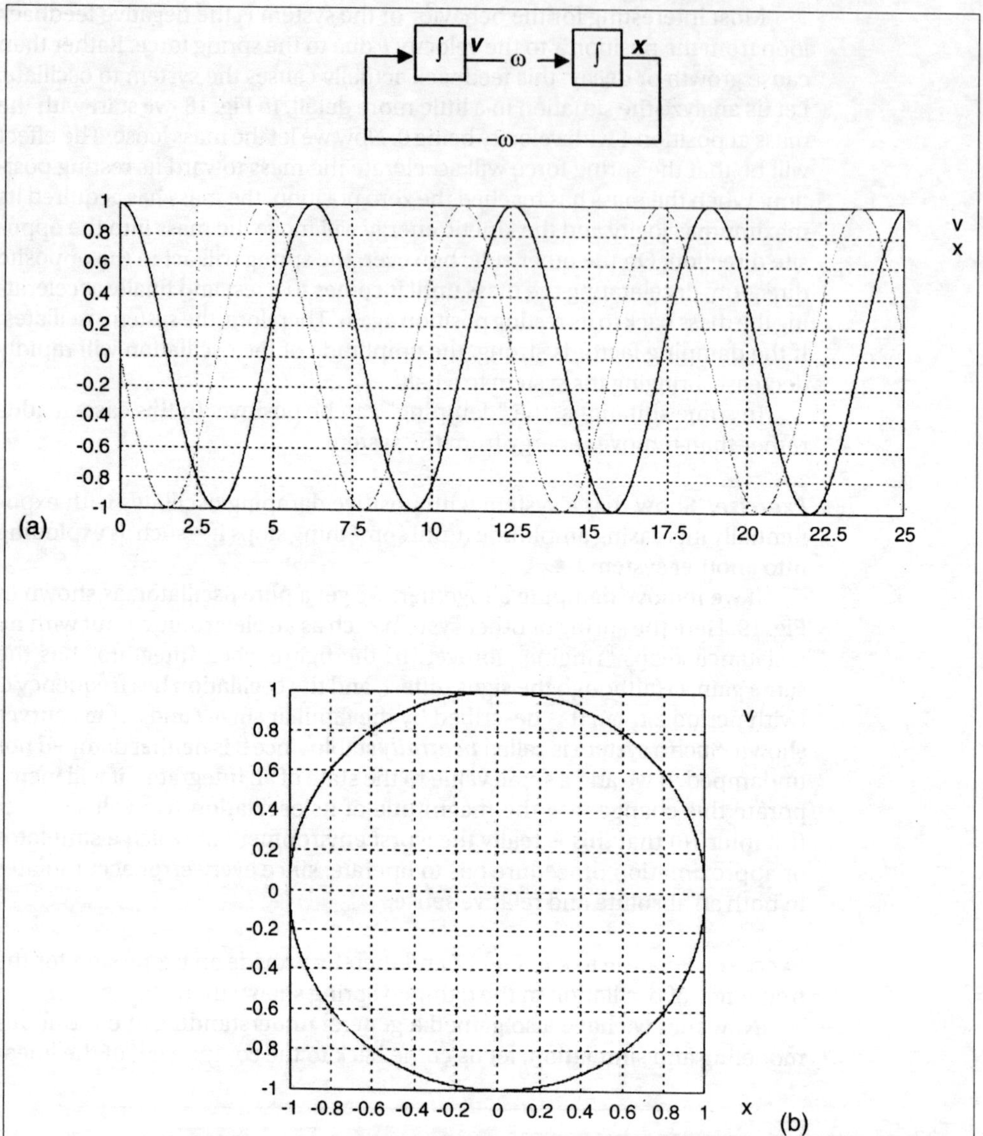

Figure 19 Undamped second-order linear oscillator: (a) time trajectories, (b) phase space.

oscillator just shown and the discrete time oscillator presented earlier. Although the similarities of the two models are obvious and they also show comparable behavior, they are also very different. By their differences we also obtain some insight into discrete time and continuous modeling in general.

The biggest correspondence between the two models is that both have a negative feedback, which is the reason why they oscillate. The main difference, however, comes from the fact that in discrete time models, the inputs to the delays define new state values, whereas in the continuous domain the inputs represent rate of change values for the state variables. Let us consider the gains in the continuous and the discrete oscillators. In the discrete oscillator, the gain determines the amplification or decay of the value of one delay as it is fed to the other. In the continuous oscillator, the gain amplifies the rate of change of the influenced variable and thereby defines how *fast* the change of the state occurs. It determines the frequency of the oscillation. How is the frequency defined in the discrete domain? Actually by two things—namely, by the clock rate and by the number of delays in the feedback loop. Recall that in the discrete oscillator, we had two delays, and the sign of the values changed every two clock ticks. If we introduce a further delay, it will take another tick for a change in sign due to the negative feedback to propagate through all the delays. An oscillation frequency of three clock ticks results. Thus, the mechanism underlying the oscillation is quite different in the discrete and continuous cases.

3.3.4 Nonlinear Oscillators: Limit Cycles and Chaotic Behaviors

The systems we have considered so far were all linear. Now we discuss a nonlinear system—the so-called Van der Pol system, which comes into being when a nonlinear feedback is added to the linear oscillator. Instead of the linear damping factor $-d$, a nonlinear feedback is introduced that is dependent on the value of x—namely, the feedback is equal to $(1 - x^2) * v$. Figure 20a shows the model structure.

Through this nonlinear modification, the system acquires some quite astonishing properties. Independent of its initial state values, the system quickly comes into a stable oscillation. The reason for this is that for small values of x, the factor $(1 - x^2)$ is positive, thus leading to an amplification of the value v, whereas for large values of x, the factor $(1 - x^2)$ rapidly becomes negative, which leads to fast damping of v. The effect is that for small values of x, the feedback drives the values out of the region around zero, but as soon as the value is above 1 or −1, the factor becomes negative and drives the value of x back. The result is a stable oscillation, as shown in Fig. 21. Because the trajectory of the system always returns to a closed loop in state space, the latter is called a *limit cycle*.

Exercise: Compare cyclic behavior of the Van der Pol system with that of the second-order linear oscillator.◆

Lotka–Volterra predatory–prey systems form an interesting class of nonlinear models that exhibit oscillatory behavior—although not as limit cycles.

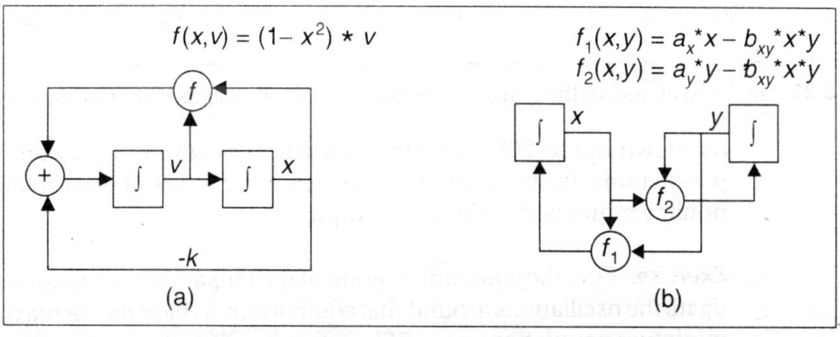

Figure 20 (a) Van der Pol and (b) Lotka–Volterra systems.

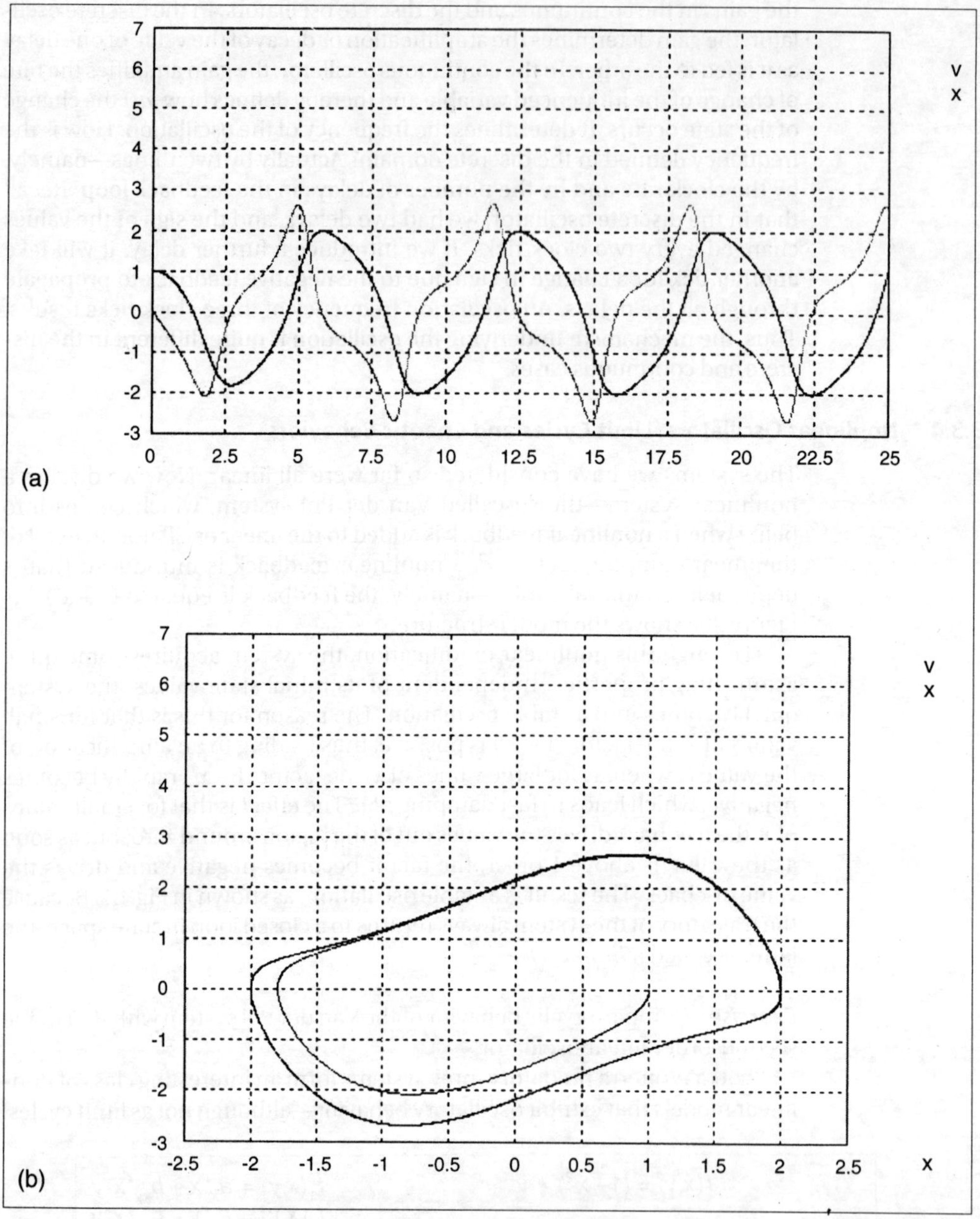

Figure 21 Stable oscillation of the Van der Pol system: (a) time trajectory, (b) state space portrait.

As shown in Fig. 20b, the integrator outputs represent prey and predator populations. In this case, the feedback parameters of each integrator is a nonlinear function of the other output.

Exercise: Find the equilibrium point of the Lotka–Volterra model and investigate the oscillations around this equilibrium. Where do the maximum and minimum populations occur? Show that small oscillations around the equilibrium are approximated by the second-order linear oscillator.◆

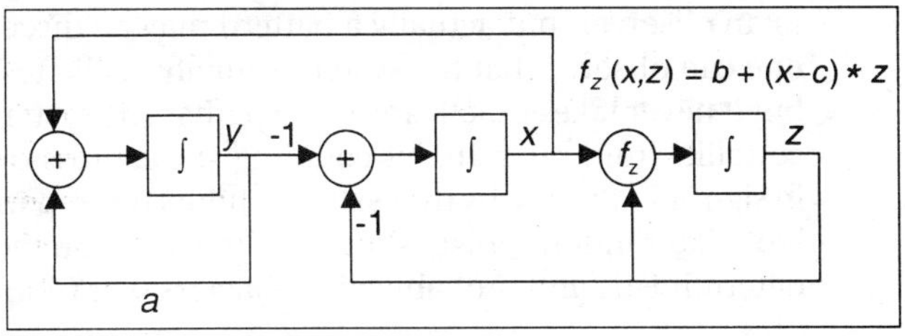

Figure 22 Rössler system.

Although nonlinear systems can show remarkable stability properties, they can also exhibit highly unstable behaviors that appear chaotic. Indeed, the term *chaos* is used by mathematicians for the patterns underlying such "strange" behaviors [1]. Chaotic behavior can come into existence by simple nonlinear feedback. The so-called Rössler attractor is a modified linear oscillator in three variables (Fig. 22). Its typical characteristic is that, independently of the initial condition, the system will come neither to rest nor to some periodic behavior (Fig. 23). The behavior appears to be unpredictable

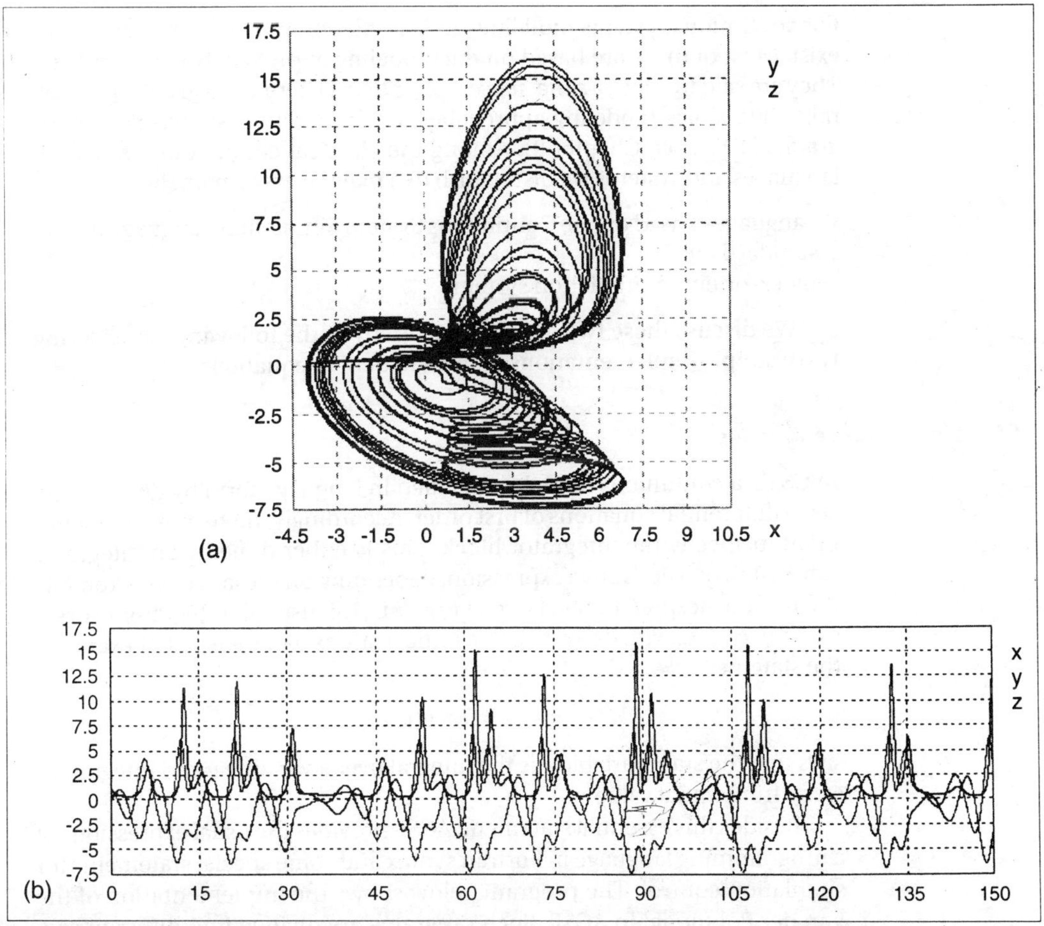

Figure 23 Chaotic behavior of Rössler system: (a) state plane v and z to x, (b) time trajectories.

to an observer, but actually a pattern may be discerned. In the state space one can observe that the system actually oscillates around the zero point, but it never takes exactly the same paths. The system is linear except for the coupling from x to z. In this coupling, the expression $(x-c)$ causes a change in sign, and this is why the system exhibits nonrepetitive fluctuations. These look like random noise, showing the close connection between complex deterministic and probabilistic behaviors (see Chapter 10).

Exercise: Compare cyclic behaviors of the Rössler, Van der Pol, and second-order linear oscillator.◆

Exercise: As with randomness, chaotic behavior can have useful "statistical" properties. For example, the manufacturer of a mobile swimming pool vacuum cleaner certifies that it will cover every inch of the surface every 12 hours. Yet the cleaner never exactly repeats its trajectory through the pool. How might a model exhibiting chaotic behavior justify the manufacturer's claim?◆

3.3.5 Continuous System Simulation Languages and Systems

For continuous systems modeling and simulation many diverse languages exist. Most of these are based on the modeling approach discussed earlier. They are said to adopt a *state-space description.* (There are also newer causal, non-state-space modeling approaches to continuous systems, e.g., Bond-graphs [4,17]; see Chapter 9). Among the classical continuous simulation languages and systems we distinguish two major classes, namely,

- Languages based on the Continuous System Simulation Language (CSSL) standard [2]
- Block-oriented simulation systems

We discuss these two approaches briefly in the following, considering two example implementations of the Van der Pol equations.

CSSL Simulation Languages

In CSSL, a continuous model is specified in language form by defining the set of differential equations of first order. Accordingly, there must be a statement to specify the integrator block. This is either done by an integrator expression or a derivative expression, depending on the language. Probably the most widespread CSSL language, ACSL [15], uses an integrator expression $integ\,(d,q_0)$ with derivative and initial state as parameters. For example, the statement

$$x = integ(v, x_0)$$

says that the state variable x is the integral over a variable v and integration starts from initial value x_0.

Besides this essential statement, ACSL provides the usual expressions of a programming language in Fortran syntax and some special statements for simulation control. The program below shows the implementation of the Van der Pol model in ACSL. Such programs are divided into different sections. In the example, the first section is the initialization section where some constants are defined. The main part is the DYNAMIC section and within it the DERIVATIVE section, where the derivative equations are defined by the *integ* expression just discussed. Note that CCSL model texts are not programs in the standard sense. The model statements are not executed sequentially, instead, they represent equations that are sorted and translated into an imperative, sequentially executable program.

```
PROGRAM Van der Pol
  INITIAL
    constant
      k = -1, x0 = 1, v0 = 0,
      tf = 20
  END
  DYNAMIC
    DERIVATIVE
      x = integ(v, x0)
      v = integ((1 - x**2)*v - k*x, v0)
    END
    termt (t.ge.tf)
  END
END
```

Algorithm 1 CSSL simulation model of Van der Pol equation.

Block-Oriented Simulation Systems

Block-oriented simulation tools work similarly to the programming of analog computers and are primarily used by control engineers. Modeling is done by coupling together primitive components and elementary functional building blocks. In a graphical user interface, blocks can be "dragged and dropped" into a model to form components in a network. The modeler then provides the interconnection information by drawing lines from output ports to input ports. Thus, here system specification is at the coupled model level as opposed to the state level represented by ACSL. Figure 24 shows some elementary building blocks from *Simulink* [14], a superset of the popular *Matlab* calculation package. Besides the blocks shown, the

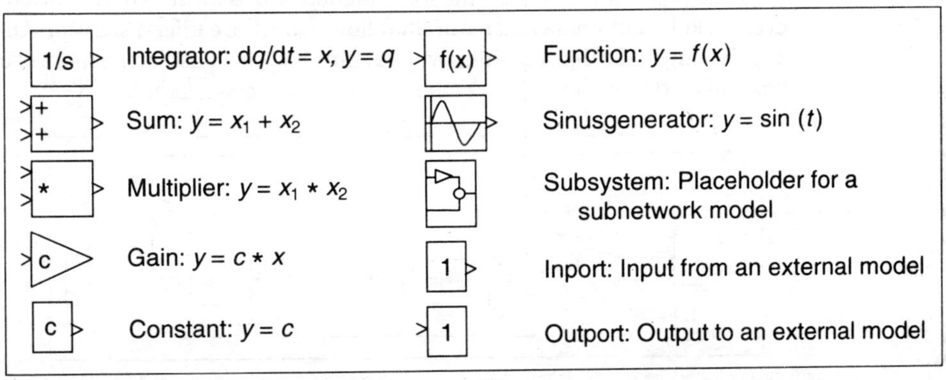

Figure 24 Some building blocks from the Simulink block-oriented simulation package.

Simulink system provides many other blocks that also realize modeling concepts going beyond pure continuous modeling—in particular, building blocks for difference equations and blocks to realize discrete control systems. Our purpose here, however, is to discuss continuous network modeling by means of the Simulink system.

Once more, the most basic block is the *integrator.* It receives one real-valued input and outputs the integral of the input trajectory starting from a particular initial state (a real value which is the first output—initial states are often called initial conditions in the differential equation literature). The integrator therefore realizes a memory element with a single state variable. Besides the integrator, a set of algebraic functions are provided. In Fig. 24 we see building blocks for the sum of two inputs, the multiplication of two inputs, and the gain element that amplifies the input by a constant *c.* There is also a function element that can be programmed in a C-like language. *Sources* are provided to generate test signals (e.g., Constant and Sinus generator).

Simulink allows hierarchical modeling by providing the *subsystem* block as a placeholder for a coupled component and the *inport* and *outport* blocks to model input and output of coupled systems.

Figure 25 shows a block model specification of the Van der Pol equation. The inputs to the integrators are the outputs of a network of algebraic functions. These define the equations for the derivatives of state variables. The network generates the values of state variable *x* as its output.

3.4 Discrete Event Models and Their Simulators

3.4.1 Introduction

We have already seen how a discrete event approach can be taken to obtain more efficient simulation of cellular automata. In this section, we will consider discrete event modeling as a paradigm in its own right. However, the basic motivation remains that discrete event modeling is an attractive formalism because it is intrinsically tuned to the capabilities and limitations of digital computers. Being the "new guy on the block," it still has not achieved the status that differential equations, with a 300, year history, have. But it is likely to play more and more of a role in all kinds of modeling in the future. In keeping with this prediction, we start the introduction with a formulation of discrete event cellular automata that naturally follows from the earlier discussion. Only after having made this transition will we come back to consider the more usual types of workflow models associated with discrete event simulation.

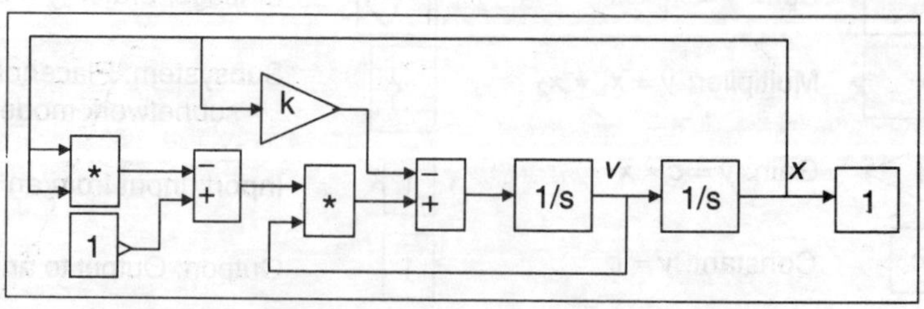

Figure 25 Block model of Van der Pol equations.

3.4.2 Discrete Event Cellular Automata

The original version of the Game of Life assumes that all births and deaths take the same time (equal to a time step). A more accurate representation of a cell's life cycle assumes that birth and death are dependent on a quantity that represents the ability of the cell to fit into its environment, called its *fitness*. A cell attains positive fitness when its neighborhood is supportive, that is, when it has exactly 3 neighbors, and the fitness will diminish rapidly when its environment is hostile. Whenever the fitness then reaches 0, the cell will die. On the other hand, a dead cell will have a negative initial fitness, let's say –2. When the environment is supportive and the fitness crosses the zero level, the cell will be born.

Figure 26 shows an example behavior of such a cell model dependent on its environment (the sum of alive neighbors). The initial sum of alive neighbors being 3 causes the fitness of the dead cell to increase linearly until it crosses zero and a birth occurs. The fitness increases further until it reaches a saturation level (here 6). When the sum of alive neighbors changes from 3 to 4, the environment gets hostile, the fitness will decrease, and the cell will die. The death is accompanied by a discontinuous drop of the fitness level to a minimum fitness of –2.

What is needed to model such a process? One way would be to compute the trajectories of the fitness parameter and see when zero crossings and hence death and birth events occur. This would be the approach of combined discrete event and continuous simulation, which we discuss in detail in Chapter 9. However, this approach is computationally inefficient since we have to compute each continuous trajectory at every point along its path. A much more efficient way is to adopt a pure event-based approach where we concentrate on the interesting events only, namely births and deaths, as well as the changes in the neighborhood. The event-based approach jumps from one interesting event to the next, omitting the uninteresting behavior in between.

The prerequisite of discrete event modeling therefore is to have a means to determine when interesting things happen. Events can be caused by the enviroment, such as the changes of the sum of alive neighbors. The occur-

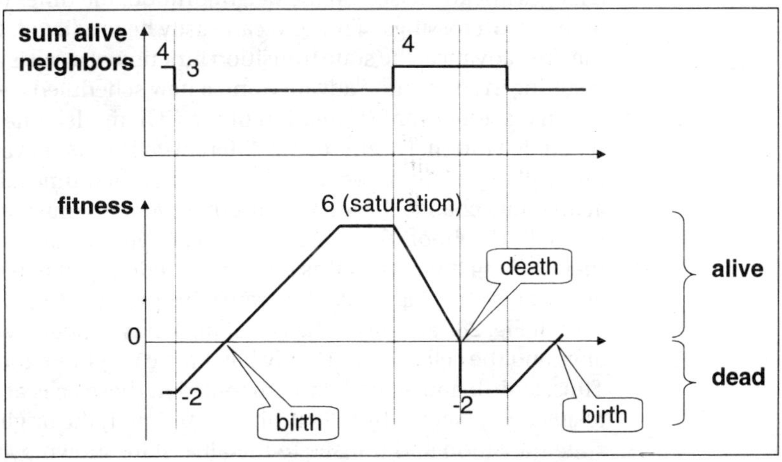

Figure 26 Behavior of GOL model with fitness.

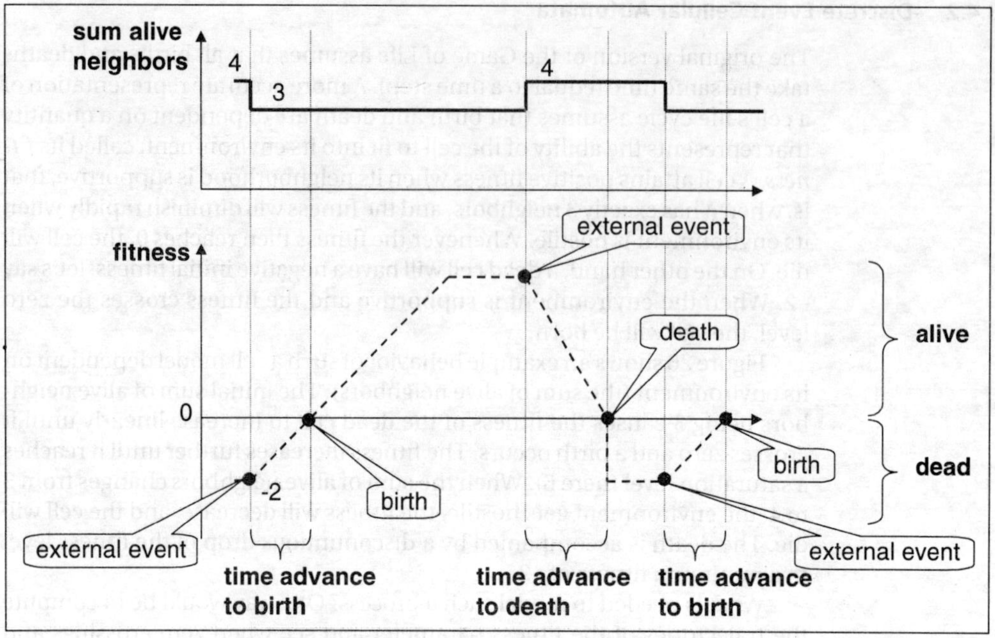

Figure 27 Behavior of the eventistic GOL model.

rences of such *external* events are not under the control of the model component itself. On the other side, the component may schedule events to occur. Those are called *internal* events and the component itself determines their time of occurrence. Given a particular state, e.g., a particular fitness of the cell, a time advance is specified as the time it takes until the next internal event occurs, supposing that no *external event* happens in the meantime. In our event-based GOL model the time advance is used to schedule the times when a birth or a death is supposed to happen (Fig. 27). As fitness changes linearly based on the neighborhood, the times of the events (times of the zero-crossings of fitness) can easily be predicted. Upon expiration of the time advance, the state transition function of a cell is applied, eventually resulting in a new time advance and a new scheduled event.

In discrete event simulation of the GOL model, one has to execute the scheduled internal events of the different cells at their event times. And since now cells are waiting, we must see to it that their time advances. Moreover, at any state change through an internal event we must take care to examine the cell's neighbors for possible state changes. A change in state may affect their waiting times as well as result in scheduling of new events and cancellation of events. Figure 28 illustrates this process. Consider that all shaded cells in Fig. 28a are alive. The cell at (0, 0) has enough neighbors to become alive and the cell at (–1, –1) only has 1 alive neighbor and therefore will die. Thus, a birth and a death are scheduled in these cells at times, say 1 and 2, respectively (shown by the numbers). At time 1, the origin cell undergoes its state transition and transits to the alive state shown by the thunderbolt in Fig. 28b. What effect does this have on the neighboring cells? Figure 28b shows that as a result of the birth, cells at (0, 1), (0, –1), and (1, 1) have three

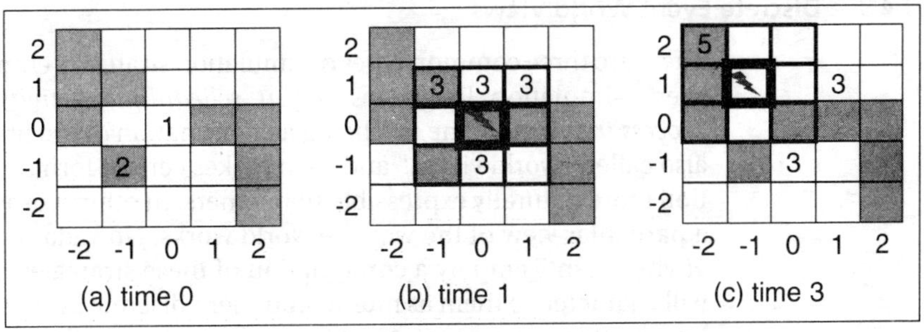

Figure 28 Event processing in Game of Life event model.

neighbors and must be scheduled for births at time 3. Cell (−1, 1) has 4 alive neighbors now and a death will be scheduled for it at time 3. Cell (−1, −1) has had a death scheduled before. However, because of the birth it has two neighbors now, and the conditions for dying do not apply any more. Hence, the death at time 2 must be canceled. We see that *the effect of a state transition may not only be to schedule new events, but also to cancel events that were scheduled in the past.*

Now in Fig. 28 (b), the next earliest scheduled event is at time 3. Therefore, the system can jump from the current time, 1, to the next event time, 3, without considering the times in-between. This illustrates an important *efficiency advantage in discrete event simulation*—during times when no events are scheduled, no components need be scanned. Contrast this with discrete time simulation, in which scanning must be performed at each time step (and involves all cells in the worst case).

The situation at time 3 also illustrates a problem that arises in discrete event simulation—that of *simultaneous events.* From Fig. 28 (b) we see that there are several cells scheduled for time 3, namely a birth at (0, 1), (1, 1) and (0, −1) and a death at (−1, 1). The question is who goes first and what is the result. Note that if (−1, 1) goes first, the condition that (0, 1) has three live neighbors will not apply any more and the birth event just scheduled will be canceled again (Fig. 28c). However, if (0, 1) would go first, the birth in (0, 1) is actually carried out. Therefore, the results *will be different for different orderings of activation.* There are several approaches to the problem of simultaneous events. One solution is to let all simultaneous events undergo their state transitions together. This is the approach of parallel DEVS, to be discussed in Chapter 6. The approach employed by most simulation packages and classic DEVS is to define a priority among the components. Components with high priority go first. To adopt this approach we employ a *tie-breaking* procedure, which selects one event to process out of a set of contending simultaneous events.

We'll return to show how to formulate the Game of Life as a well-defined discrete event model in Chapter 7 after we have introduced the necessary concepts for DEVS representation. In the next section, we show how discrete event models can be simulated using the most common method, called event scheduling. This method can also be used to simulate the Game of Life, and we'll leave that as an exercise at the end of the section.

3.4.3 Discrete Event World Views

There are three common types of simulation strategies employed in discrete event simulation languages—*event scheduling, activity scanning,* and *process interaction,* the last being a combination of the first two. These are also called "world views," and each makes certain forms of model description more naturally expressible than others. In other words, each is best for a particular view of the way the world works. Nowadays, most simulation environments employ a combination of these strategies. In Chapter 7, we will characterize them as multicomponent discrete event systems and analyze them in some detail. As an introduction to workflow modeling, here we will now discuss only the simplest strategy, event scheduling.

Event Scheduling World View

Event oriented models *preschedule* all events—there is no provision for conditional events that can be activated by tests on the global state. Scheduling an event is straightforward when all the conditions necessary for its occurrence can be known in advance. However, this is not always the case, as we have seen in the Game of Life. Nevertheless, understanding pure event scheduling in the following simple example of workflow modeling will help to understand how to employ more complex world views later.

Figure 29 depicts a discrete event model with three components. The generator *Gen* generates jobs for processing by a server component *SS.* Jobs are queued in a buffer called *Queue* when the server is busy. Component *Gen* continually reschedules a job output with a time advance equal to *inter-gen-time.* If the server is idle when a job comes in, then it is activated immediately to begin processing the job. Otherwise, the number of waiting jobs in the queue is increased by one. When processing starts, the server is scheduled to complete work in a time that represents the job's *service-time.* When this time expires, the server starts to process the next job in the queue, if there is one. If not, it *passivates* in phase *idle.* To passivate means to set your time advance to infinity. The queue is a *passive* component (its time advance is always infinity) with a variable to store the number of jobs waiting currently.

Two event routines and a tie-breaking function express the interaction between these components:

```
Event: Generate_Job
  nr-waiting = nr-waiting + 1
  schedule a Generate_Job in inter-gen-time
```

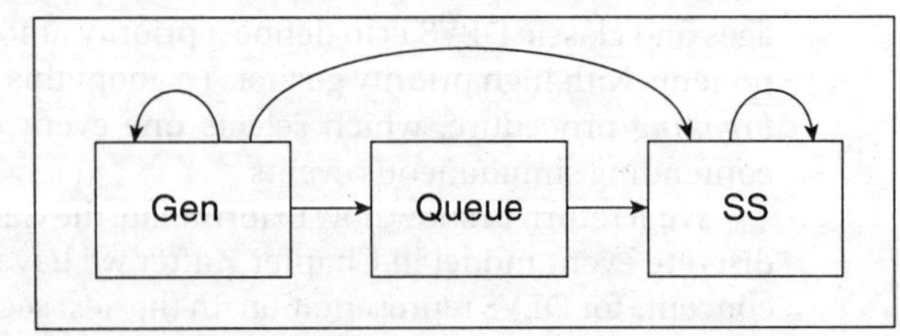

Figure 29 Generator, queue, and server event scheduling model. The arrows indicate the effects of the event routines.

```
  if nr-waiting = 1 then
     schedule a Process_Job in service-time
Event: Process_Job
  nr-waiting = nr-waiting - 1
  if nr-waiting > 0 then
     schedule a Process_Job in service-time
Note that the phrase "schedule an event in T" means the same
as "schedule an event at time = clock time + T".
Break-Ties by: Process_Job then Generate_Job
```

As shown in Fig. 30, the event scheduling simulation algorithm employs a *list of events* that are ordered by increasing scheduling times. The event with the earliest scheduled time (*e*1 in Fig. 30) is removed from the list and the clock is advanced to the time of this imminent event (3). The routine associated with the imminent event is executed. A tie-breaking procedure is employed if there is more than one such imminent events (recall the select function). Execution of the event routine may cause new events to be added in the proper place on the list. For example, *e*4 is scheduled at time 6. Also, existing events may be rescheduled or even canceled (as we have seen).

The next cycle now begins with the clock advance to the earliest scheduled time (5), and so on. Each time an event routine is executed, one or more state variables may get new values.

Let's see how this works in our simple workflow example. Initially, the clock is set to 0 and a *Generate_Job* event is placed on the list with time 0. The state of the system is represented by *nr-waiting,* which is initially 0. Since this event is clearly imminent, it is executed. This causes two events to be scheduled: a *Generate_Job* at time *inter-gen-time* and (since *nr-waiting* becomes 1) a *Process_Job* at time *service-time.* What happens next depends on which of the scheduled times is earliest. Let's assume that *inter-*

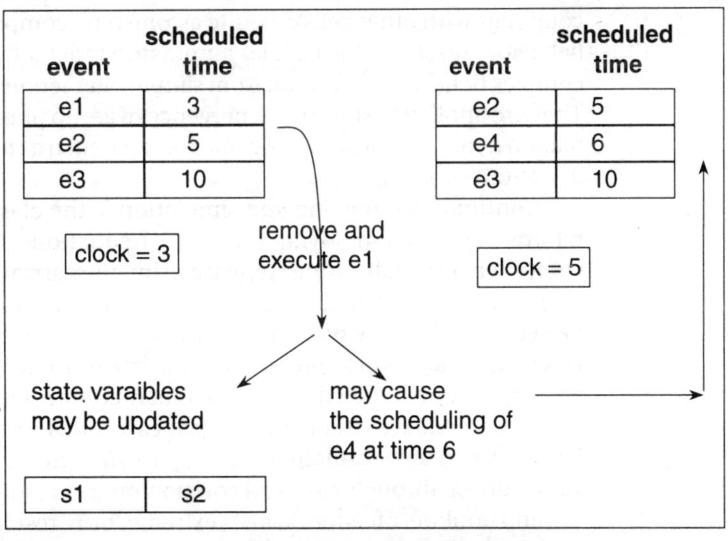

Figure 30 Event list scheduling.

gen-time is smaller than *service-time*. Then time is advanced to *inter-gen-time* and *Generate_Job* is executed. However, now only a new *Generate_Job* is scheduled — since the *nr-waiting* is 2, the *Process_Job* is not scheduled. Let's suppose that *service-time* < 2 ∗ *inter-gen-time* (the next event time for *Generate_Job*). Then the next event is a *Process_Job* and simulation continues in this manner.

Exercise: Hand execute the simulation algorithm for several cases. For example, (*1*) *inter-gen-time* > *service-time*, (*2*) *inter-gen-time* = *service-time*, (*3*) *inter-gen-time* < *service-time* < 2 ∗ *inter-gen-time, etc.*◆

Exercise: Use the event scheduling approach to simulate the eventistic Game of Life introduced earlier in the section.◆

3.5 Summary

In this chapter we have discussed the fundamental modeling formalisms that we will introduce in depth in the second part of the book. Here we gained some insight into the intrinsic nature of the different modeling approaches. But the presentation can give us also some insight into the nature of dynamical systems in general. Let us summarize the modeling approaches in this sense.

The discrete time modeling approach, which subsumes the popular finite state automaton formalism as well as the difference equation formalism, stands out through its simple simulation algorithm. It adopts a stepwise execution mode where all the components states are updated based on the state of the previous time step and the inputs.

The simplest form of this model type is the cellular automaton. In a cellular automaton a real system is reduced to basic coupling and communication between components. A cell on its own is quite boring. Only through couplings with other cells do quite astonishing complex and unpredictable behaviors result. So the cellular automaton is actually a model to study the complex behaviors that result from simple interactions among components. They are applied to study the emergence of group phenomena, such as population dynamics, or spreading phenomena, such as forest fires, avalanches, or excitable media.

Continuous modeling and simulation is the classical approach of the natural sciences employing differential equations. Simulation on digital computers is usually done stepwise using numerical integration methods. From a general perspective, continuous modeling and simulation also can be seen as the study of feedback phenomena, a form of system coupling where the changes of a component state circle around to affect itself through a feedback loop. When discussing elementary continuous systems, we have seen that feedback results in different categories of behavior. Direct linear feedback can only result in quite simple exponential behavior; indirect linear feedback through a second component can result in oscillatory behavior; and nonlinear feedback, in its extreme form, results in chaotic behavior. Positive feedback in real world systems is the cause of exponential growth, which sometimes needs to be avoided. Negative feedback loops, on the other hand, tend to be stabilizing. In any case, the study of feedback lies at the heart of the study of dynamical systems.

Finally, the event-based version of the Game of Life model gave us insight into the intrinsic nature of discrete event modeling and simulation. We have seen that considering only the interesting points in time—the events—is the basis of this modeling approach. To be able to find and schedule the events in time is the prerequisite for applying discrete event simulation. A local event is scheduled by specifying a time advance value based on the current state of a component.

In the GOL model, defining the event times was quite straightforward. Since the fitness parameter increases and decreases linearly, it is simple to compute the time when a zero crossing will occur—that is, when an event occurs. However, in general this will not always be feasible, and several different approaches to tackle this problem are known. A very common approach, which is heavily employed in workflow modeling, is to use stochastic methods and generate the time advance values from a random distribution. Another approach is to measure the time spans for different states and keep them in a table for later look-up. These approaches are discussed in Chapter 16. If none of these methods is appropriate, one has the possibility to step back to the more expensive combined simulation approach where the continuous trajectories are actually computed by continuous simulation and, additionally, events have to be detected and executed in between. This combined continuous/discrete event modeling approach is the topic of Chapter 9.

The GOL event model also showed us two important advantages of discrete event modeling and simulation compared to the traditional approaches. First, only those times, and those components, have to be considered where events actually occur. Second, only those state changes must be reported to coupled components that are actually relevant for their behavior. For example in the GOL model, only changes in the alive state but not changes in the fitness parameter are relevant for a cell's neighbors. Actually, in discrete event modeling, the strategy often is to model only those state changes as events that are actually relevant to the environment of a component. As long as nothing interesting to the environment happens, no state changes are made. These two issues give the discrete event modeling and simulation approach a great lead in computational efficiency, making it most attractive for digital computer simulation. We will come back to this issue in Chapter 16 on DEVS representation of dynamical systems.

3.6 Sources

Research on cellular automata is summarized in Ref. [18]. Good expositions of continuous modeling are found in Refs. [5,9] Books on numerical integration methods are numerous. For example, a compact introduction to the most popular algorithms is given in Ref. [6] and algorithms in C can be found in Ref. [16]. References [3] and [12] give popular introductions to discrete event simulation. A control-oriented view of discrete event systems is given in Ref. [8].

1. Alligood, K. T., T. D. Sauer, and J. A. Yorke, *Chaos: An Introduction to Dynamical Systems.* Springer Verlag, 1996.
2. Augustin, D. C., M. S. Fineberg, B. B. Johnson, R. N. Lineberger, F. J. Sansom, and J. C. Strauss, "The Sci Continuous System Simulation Language (CSSL)." *Simulation* **9,** pp. 281–303 (1967).
3. Banks, J., J. Carson, and B. L. Nelson, *Discrete-Event System Simulation.* Prentice Hall, 1995.
4. Blundell, A., *Bond Graphs for Modelling Engineering Systems.* Ellis Horwood Publishers, Chichester, UK, 1982.
5. Bossel, H., *Modeling and Simulation.* Ak Peters, Ltd., 1994.
6. Burden, R. L., and J. D. Faires, *Numerical Analysis,* 4th ed. PWS-KENT Publishing Company, 1989.
7. Burks, A. W., U. Illinois Press, Urbana, IL, 1970. Essays on Cellular Automata.
8. Cassandras, C. G., *Discrete Event Systems: Modeling and Performance Analysis.* Richard Irwin, New York, 1993.
9. Cellier, F. E., *Continuous System Modeling.* Springer-Verlag, New York, 1991.
10. Gardner, M., "The Fantastic Combinations of John Conway's New Solitaire Game of Life." *Scientific American* **23**(4), 120–123 (1970).
11. Gould, H. and J. Tobochnik, *An Introduction to Computer Simulation Methods, Parts* 1 *and* 2. Addison-Wesley, 1988.
12. Law, A. M. and W. D. Kelton, *Simulation Modeling and Analysis,* 2nd ed. McGraw hill, New York: 1991.
13. Levins, R., and C. J. Puccia, *Qualitative Modeling of Complex Systems: An Introduction to Loop Analysis and Time Averaging.* Harvard Univ. Press, 1986.
14. Mathworks, Inc., *SIMULINK, User's Guide.* Prentice Hall, Englewood Cliffs, NJ, 1996.
15. Edward E. Mitchell, E. E., and J. S. Gauthier, *ACSL: Advanced Continuous Simulation Language.* Mitchell & Gauthier Assoc., Concord, MA, 1986.
16. Press, W. H., S. A. Teukolsky, W. T. Vetterling, and B. P. Flannery, *Numerical Recipes in C,* 2nd ed. Cambridge University Press, 1992.
17. Thoma, J. U. *Simulation by Bondgraphs,* Springer-Verlag, 1990.
18. Wolfram, S., Ed., *Theory and Application of Cellular Automata.* World Scientific, Singapore, 1986.

4

Introduction to Discrete Event System Specification (DEVS)

4.1 Introduction

This chapter introduces the DEVS formalism for discrete event systems. DEVS exhibits, in particular form, the concepts of systems theory and modeling that we have introduced already. DEVS is important not only for discrete event models, but also because it affords a computational basis for implementing behaviors that are expressed in the other basic systems formalisms—discrete time and differential equations. Particular features of DEVS are also present in more general form in the systems theory that we will see in the next chapter. So starting with DEVS also serves as a good introduction to this theory and the other formalisms that it supports.

In this chapter, we start with the basic DEVS formalism and discuss a number of examples using it. We then discuss the DEVS formalism for coupled models, also giving some examples. The DEVS formalism that we start with is called Classic DEVS because after some 15 years, a revision was introduced called Parallel DEVS. As we will explain later, Parallel DEVS removes constraints that originated with the sequential operation of early computers and hindered the exploitation of parallelism, a critical element in modern computing. Finally, we discuss how DEVS is implemented in an object-oriented framework.

4.2 Classic DEVS System Specification

A *discrete event system specification* (*DEVS*) is a structure

$$M = \langle X, S, Y, \delta_{int}, \delta_{ext}, \lambda, ta \rangle$$

where

X is the set of input values
S is a set of states,
Y is the set of output values
$\delta_{int}: S \to S$ is the *internal transition* function
$\delta_{ext}: Q \times X \to S$ is the *external transition* function, where
$Q = \{(s,e) | s \in S, 0 \le e \le ta(s)\}$ is the *total state* set
e is the *time elapsed* since last transition

$\lambda: S \rightarrow Y$ is the output function

$ta: S \rightarrow R^+_{0,\infty}$ is the set positive reals with 0 and ∞

The interpretation of these elements is illustrated in Fig. 1. At any time the system is in some state, *s*. If no external event occurs, the system will stay in state *s* for time *ta*(*s*). Notice that *ta*(*s*) could be a real number as one would expect. But it can also take on the values 0 and ∞. In the first case, the stay in state *s* is so short that no external events can intervene—we say that *s* is a *transitory* state. In the second case, the system will stay in *s* forever unless an external event interrupts its slumber. We say that *s* is *a passive* state in this case. When the resting time expires, i.e., when the elapsed time, $e = ta(s)$, the system outputs the value, $\lambda(s)$, and changes to state $\delta_{int}(s)$. Note that output is only possible just before internal transitions.

If an external event $x \in X$ occurs before this expiration time, i.e., when the system is in total state (s,e) with $e \leq ta(s)$, the system changes to state $\delta_{ext}(s,e,x)$. Thus, the internal transition function dictates the system's new state when no events occurred since the last transition. The external transition function dictates the system's new state when an external event occurs—this state is determined by the input, *x*, the current state, *s*, and how long the system has been in this state, *e*. In both cases, the system is then is some new state *s′* with some new resting time, *ta*(*s′*), and the same story continues.

The preceding explanation of the semantics (or meaning) of a DEVS model suggests, but does not fully describe, the operation of a simulator that would execute such models to generate their behavior. We will delay discussion of such simulators to later chapters. However, the behavior of a DEVS is well defined and can be depicted as in Fig. 2. Here the *input trajectory* is a series of events occurring at times such as t_0 and t_2. In between these event times may be those such as t_1, which are times of internal events. The latter are noticeable on the *state trajectory*, which is a steplike series of states that change at external and internal events (second from top). The *elapsed time trajectory* is a sawtooth pattern depicting the flow of time in an elapsed time clock that is reset to 0 at every event. Finally, at the bottom, the *output tra-*

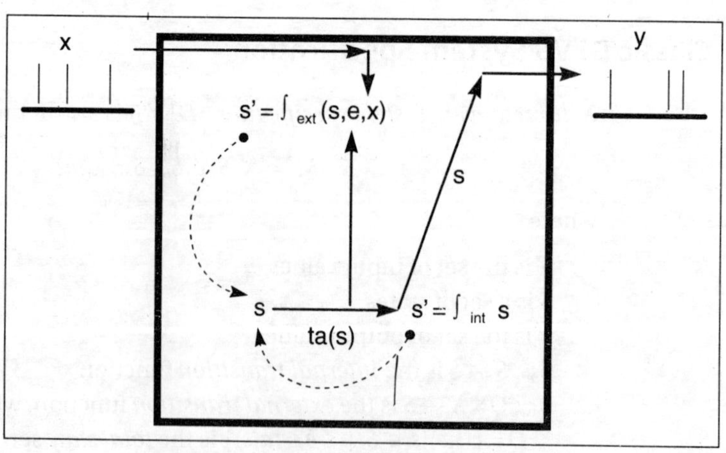

Figure 1 DEVS in action.

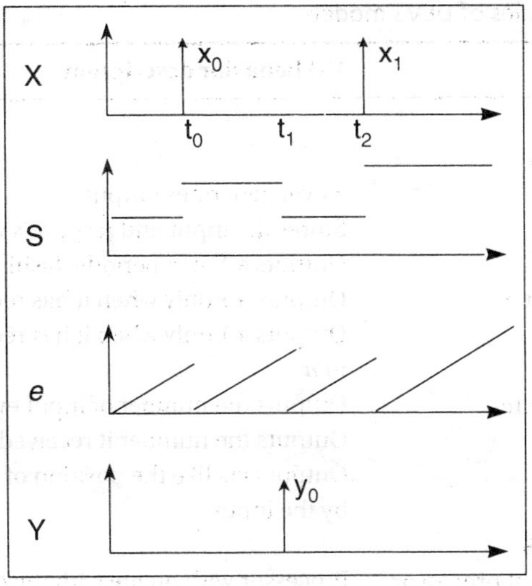

Figure 2 DEVS trajectories.

jectory depicts the output events that are produced by the output function just before applying the internal transition function at internal events. Such behaviors will be illustrated in the next examples.

4.2.1 DEVS Examples

We will present a number of models and discuss their behaviors to illustrate practical construction of DEVS models. Table 1 lists the models to be discussed. As will be detailed later, there are two classes of models in any object-oriented implementation of DEVS. *Atomic* models are expressed in the basic formalism. *Coupled* models are expressed using the coupled model specification—essentially providing component and coupling information.

We start with models that have only a single input and a single output, both expressed as real numbers.

Exercise: Write a simulator for any DEVS model that has scalar real values for its inputs, states, and outputs. Pending discussion of DEVS simulators in Chapter 8, you can use the event scheduling approach of Chapter 3 in which the external events in an input trajectory are all prescheduled on the event list. The DEVS is started in a state s and an internal event notice is placed in the event list with a time advance given by ta(s). This notice must be rescheduled appropriately every time an internal or external transition is processed.◆

Passive

The simplest DEVS to start with is one that literally does nothing. Appropriately called *passive*, it does not respond with outputs no matter what the input trajectory is. Illustrated in Fig. 3, the simplest realization of this behavior is:

$$DEVS = (X, Y, S, \delta_{ext}, \delta_{int}, \lambda, ta)$$

Table 1 Examples of DEVS models

Models	I/O behavior description
Atomic	
Classic DEVS	
passive	Never generates output
storage	Stores the input and responds with it when queried
generator	Outputs a 1 in a periodic fashion
binaryCounter	Outputs a 1 only when it has received an even number of 1's
nCounter	Outputs a 1 only when it has received a number of 1's equal to *n*
Infinite counter	Outputs the number of input events received since initialization
processor	Outputs the number it received after a processing time
ramp	Output acts like the position of a billiard ball that has been hit by the input
Parallel DEVS	
multiple input processor with queue	Processor with queue with the capability to accept multiple simultaneous inputs
Coupled	
Classic DEVS	
pipeSimple	Pipeline—processes successive inputs in assembly line fashion
netSwitch	Outputs the input it receives after a processing time (internally input is alternated between two processors)
Parallel DEVS	
pipeSimple	Same as before except for handling of event collisions
netSwitch	Revised Switch and coupled model handling simultaneous inputs on different ports
experimental frame	Generator and transducer encapsulated into a coupled model
Hierarchical DEVS	
frame-processor	Experimental frame coupled to processor (could be an port compatible model e.g., processor with buffer, netSwitch, etc)

where

$$X = R$$
$$Y = R$$
$$S = \{\text{“passive”}\}$$
$$\delta_{ext}(\text{“passive”}, e, x) = \text{“passive”}$$
$$\delta_{int}(\text{“passive”}) = \text{“passive”}$$
$$\lambda(\text{“passive”}) = \varnothing$$
$$ta(\text{“passive”}) = \infty.$$

The input and output sets are numerical. There is only one state that is "passive." In this state, the time advance given by *ta* is infinite. As already indicated, this means the system will stay passive forever unless interrupted by an input. However, in this model, even such an interruption will not awaken it, since the external transition function does disturb the state.

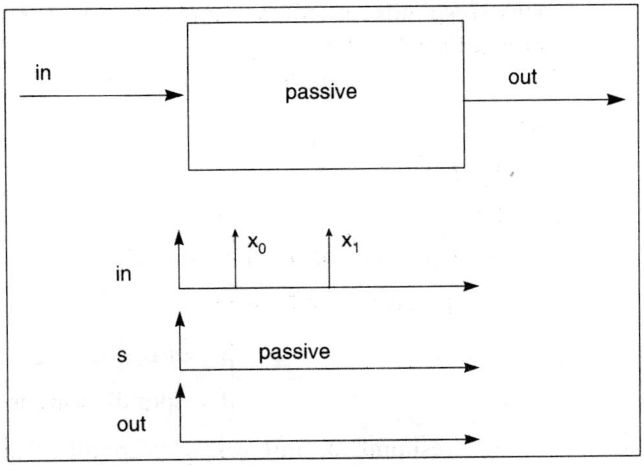

Figure 3 Passive DEVS.

The specifications of the internal transition and output functions are redundant here since they will never get a chance to be applied.

Storage

In contrast to the passive DEVS, the next system responds to its input and stores it forever, or until the next input comes along. This is not very useful unless we have a way of asking what is currently stored. So there is a second input to do such querying. Since there is only one input port in the current DEVS model, we let the input value of zero signal this query. As the first part of Fig. 4 shows, within a time, *response_time*, of the zero input arrival, the

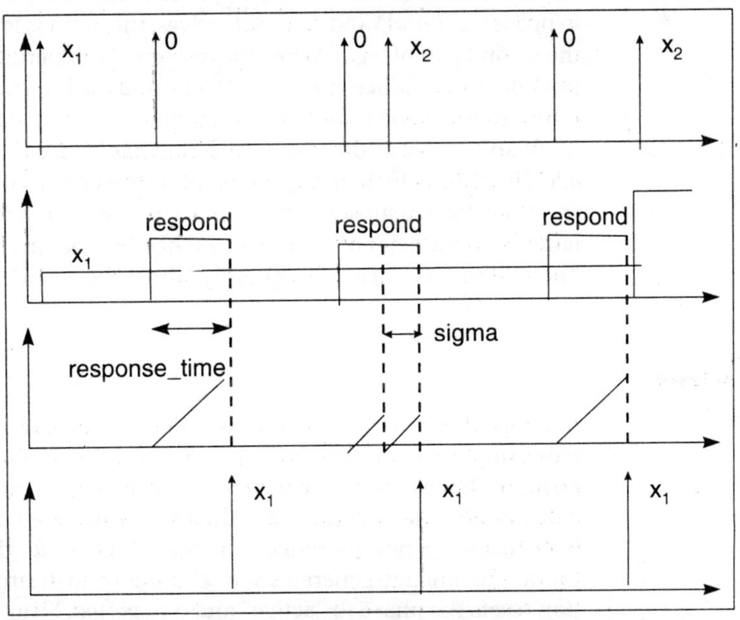

Figure 4 Trajectories for storage.

DEVS responds with the last stored nonzero input. To make this happen, the Storage is defined by:

$$DEVS_{response\_time} = (X, Y, S, \delta_{ext}, \delta_{int}, \lambda, ta)$$

where

$X = R$

$Y = R$

$S = \{\text{"passive"}, \text{respond"}\} \times R_0^+ \times R - \{0\}$

$\delta_{ext}(\text{"passive"}, \sigma, \text{store}, e, x) =$

$$\begin{cases} (\text{"passive"}, \sigma - e, x) & \text{if } x \,!\neq 0 \\ (\text{"respond"}, \text{response\_time}, \text{store}) & \text{if } x = 0 \end{cases}$$

$\delta_{ext}(\text{"respond"}, \sigma, \text{store}, e, x) = (\text{"respond"}, \sigma - e, \text{store})$

$\delta_{int}(\text{"respond"}, \sigma, \text{store}) = (\text{"passive"}, \infty, \text{store})$

$\lambda(\text{"respond"}, \sigma, \text{store}) = \text{store}$

$ta(\text{phase}, \sigma, \text{store}) = \sigma.$

There are three state variables: *phase* with values {"passive","respond"}, σ, having positive real values, and *store* having real values other than zero. We need the active "respond" phase to tell when a response is underway. As for σ, the definition of *ta* shows that it stores the time advance value. In other words, σ is the time remaining in the current state. Note that when an external event arrives after elapsed time, *e*, σ is reduced by *e* to reflect the smaller time remaining in the current state. When a zero input arrives, σ is set to *response_time* and the "respond" phase is entered. However, if the system is in phase "respond" and an input arrives, the input is ignored as illustrated in the second part of Fig. 4. When the *response_time* period has elapsed, the output function produces the stored value and the internal transition dictates a return to the passive state. What happens if, as in the third part of Fig. 4, an input arrives just as the response period has elapsed? Classic DEVS and Parallel DEVS differ in their ways of handling this collision, as we shall show later.

Note that we subscript the DEVS with *response_time*, to indicate that the latter is a parameter of the model—it needs to be specified before execution but it doesn't change subsequently, under the model's own actions.

Generator

Although the store reacts to inputs, it does not do anything on its own. A simple example of a proactive system is a *generator*. As illustrated in Fig. 5, it has no inputs but when started in phase "active," it generates outputs with a specific period. The generator has the two basic state variables, *phase* and σ. Note that the generator remains in phase "active" for the *period*, after which the output function generates a "one" output and the internal transition function resets the phase to "active" and σ to *period*. Strictly speaking, restoring

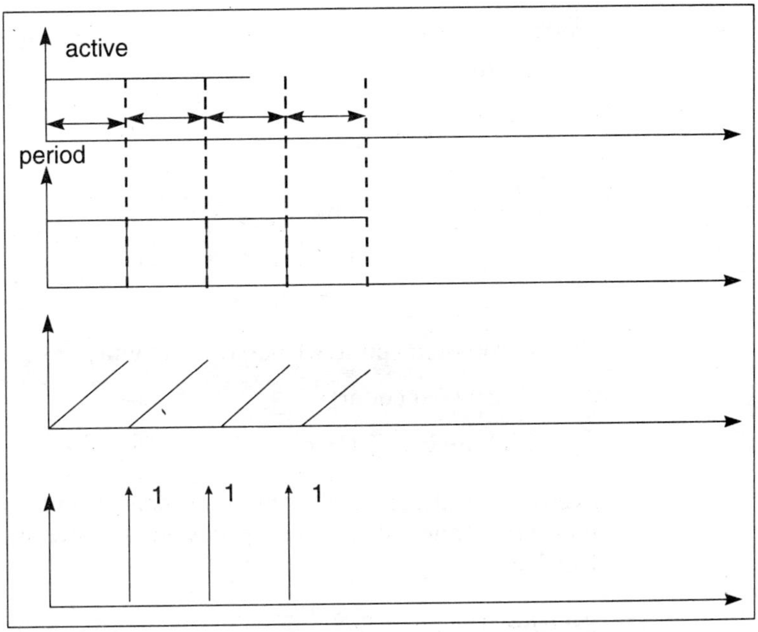

Figure 5 Generator trajectories.

these values isn't necessary unless inputs are allowed to change them (which they aren't in this model).

$$DEVS_{period} = (X, Y, S, \delta_{ext}, \delta_{int}, \lambda, ta)$$

where

$$X = \{\}$$
$$Y = \{1\}$$
$$S = \{\text{“passive”}, \text{“active”}\} \times R^{+}$$
$$\delta_{int}(\text{phase}, \sigma) = (\text{“active”}, \text{period})$$
$$\lambda(\text{“active”}, \sigma) = 1$$
$$ta(\text{phase}, \sigma) = \sigma$$

Binary Counter

In this example, the DEVS outputs a “one” for every two “one”s that it receives. To do this it maintains a count (modulo 2) of the “one”s it has received to date. When it receives a “one” that makes its count even, it goes into a transitory phase, “active,” to generate the output. This is the same as putting *response_time* := 0 in the storage DEVS.

$$DEVS = (X, Y, S, \delta_{ext}, \delta_{int}, \lambda, ta)$$

where

$$
\begin{aligned}
&X = \{0.1\}\\
&Y = \{1\}\\
&S = \{\text{“passive”},\text{“active”}\} \times R_0^+ \times \{0.1\}\\
&\delta_{ext}(\text{“passive”},\sigma,\text{count},\text{e},\text{x}) =\\
&\qquad\qquad (\text{“passive”},\sigma,-\text{e},\text{count}+\text{x}) \qquad \text{if count} + \text{x} < 2\\
&\qquad\qquad (\text{“active”},0,0) \qquad \text{otherwise}\\
&\delta_{int}(\text{phase},\sigma,\text{count}) = (\text{“passive”},\infty,\text{count})\\
&\lambda(\text{“active”},\sigma,\text{count}) = 1\\
&ta(\text{phase},\sigma,\text{count}) = \sigma
\end{aligned}
$$

Exercise: An nCounter generalizes the binary counter by generating a “one” for every *n* “one”s it receives. Specify an nCounter as an atomic model in DEVS.◆

Exercise: Define a DEVS counter that counts the number of non-zero input events received since initialization and outputs this number when queried by a zero valued input.◆

Processor

A model of a simple workflow situation is obtained by connecting a generator to a processor. The generator outputs are considered to be jobs to do and the processor takes some time to do them. In the simplest case, no real work is performed on the jobs, only the times taken to do them are represented.

$$DEVS_{processing\_time} = (X, Y, S, \delta_{ext}, \delta_{int}, \lambda, ta),$$

where

$$
\begin{aligned}
&X = \text{R}\\
&Y = \text{R}\\
&S = \{\text{“passive”},\text{“active”}\} \times R_0^+ \times \text{R}\\
&\delta_{ext}(\text{phase},\sigma,\text{job},\text{e},\text{x}) =\\
&\qquad\qquad \begin{cases} (\text{“busy”},\text{processing\_time},\text{job}) & \text{if passive} = \text{“passive”}.\\ (\text{phase},\sigma-\text{e},\text{x}) & \text{otherwise}\end{cases}\\
&\delta_{int}(\text{phase},\sigma,\text{job}) = (\text{“passive”},\text{processing\_time},\text{job})\\
&\lambda(\text{“busy”},\sigma,\text{job}) = \text{job}\\
&ta(\text{phase},\sigma,\text{job}) = \sigma
\end{aligned}
$$

Here, if the DEVS is passive (idle), when it receives a job, it stores the job and goes into phase “busy.” If it is already busy, it ignores incoming jobs. After a period, *processing_time,* it outputs the job and returns to “passive.”

Exercise: Draw typical input/state/elapsed time/output trajectories for the simple processor.◆

Ramp

As we shall see later, DEVS can model systems whose discrete event nature is not immediately apparent. Consider a billiard ball. As illustrated in Fig. 6, struck by a cue (external event), it heads off in a direction at constant speed determined by the impulsive force imparted to it by the strike. Hitting the side of the table is considered as another input that sets the ball off going in a well-defined direction. The model is described by

$$DEVS_{step\_time} = (X, Y, S, \delta_{ext}, \delta_{int}, \lambda, ta),$$

where

$$X = \mathrm{R}$$
$$Y = \mathrm{R}$$
$$S = \{\text{“passive,”“active}\} \times R_0^+ \times \mathrm{R} \times \mathrm{R}$$
$$\delta_{ext}(\text{phase}, \sigma, \text{position}, \text{input}, \text{e}, \text{x}) = (\text{“active”}, \sigma - \text{e}, \text{x}, \text{position} + \text{e} * \text{input})$$
$$\delta_{int}(\text{phase}, \sigma, \text{input}, \text{position}) = (\text{“active”}, \text{step\_time}, \text{input}, \text{position} + \sigma * \text{input})$$
$$\lambda(\text{phase}, \sigma, \text{input}, \text{position}) = \text{position} + \sigma * \text{input}$$
$$ta(\text{phase}, \sigma, \text{input}, \text{position}) = \sigma$$

The model stores its input and uses it as the value of the slope to compute the position of the ball (in a one-dimensional simplification). It outputs

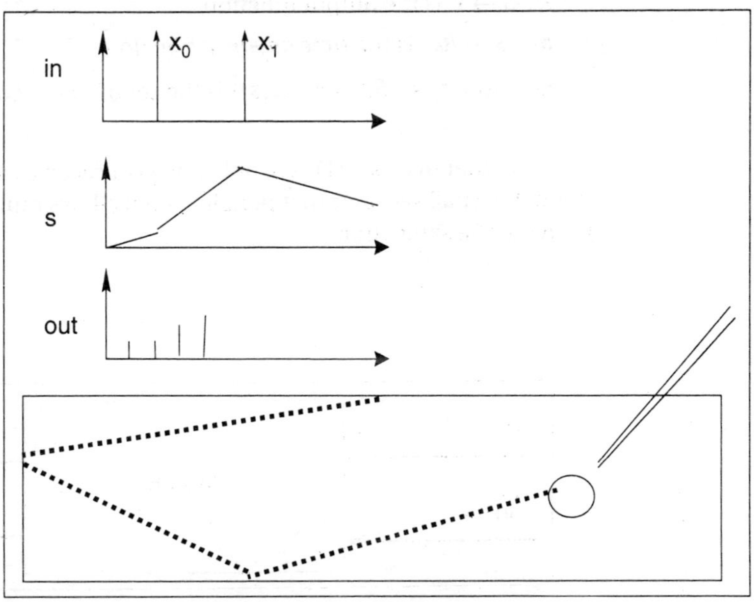

Figure 6 Ramp trajectories.

the current position every *step_time*. If it receives a new slope in the middle of a period, it updates the position to a value determined by the slope and elapsed time. Note that it outputs the position prevailing at the time of the output. This must be computed in the output function since it always called before the next internal event actually occurs. Note that we do not allow the output function to make this update permanent. The reason is that the output function is not allowed to change the state in the DEVS formalism. (A model in which this is allowed to happen may produce **unexpected and hard-to-locate** errors because DEVS simulators do not guarantee correctness for nonconforming models.)

4.2.2 Classic DEVS With Ports

Modeling is made easier with the introduction of input and output ports. For example, a DEVS model of a storage naturally has two input ports, one for storing and the other for retrieving. The more concrete DEVS formalism with port specifications is as follows:

$$DEVS = \left(X, Y, S, \delta_{ext}, \delta_{int}, \lambda, ta\right)$$

where

$X = \left\{(p,v) \mid p \in InPorts, v \in X_p\right\}$ is the set of input ports and values

$Y = \left\{(p,v) \mid p \in OutPorts, v \in Y_p\right\}$ is the set of output ports and values

S is the set of *sequential* states

δ_{ext}: $Q \times X \rightarrow S$ is the *external state transition function*

δ_{int}: $S \rightarrow S$ is the *internal state transition function*

λ: $S \rightarrow Y$ is the output function

ta : $S \rightarrow R^{+}_{0,\infty}$ is the *time advance function*

Q: $= \left\{(s,e) \mid s \in S, 0 \le e \le ta(s)\right\}$ is the set of *total states.*

Note that in classic DEVS, only one port receives a value in an external event. We shall see later that parallel DEVS allows multiple ports to receive values at the same time.

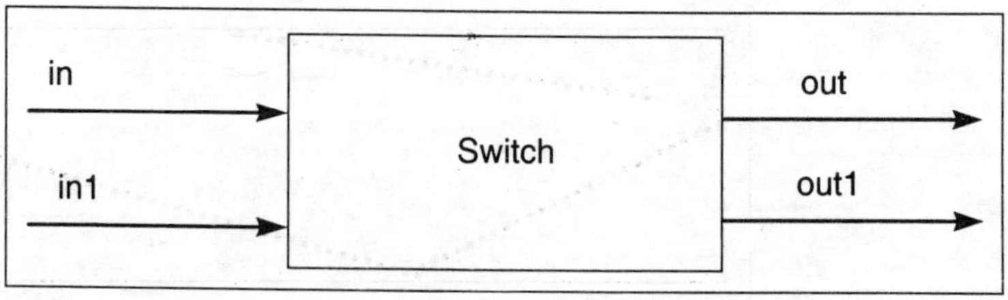

Figure 7 Switch with input and output ports.

Switch

A switch is modeled as a DEVS with pairs of input and output ports, as shown in Fig. 7. When the switch is in the standard position, jobs arriving on port "in" are sent out on port "out", and similarly for ports "in1" and "out1." When the switch is in its other setting, the input-to-output links are reversed, so that what goes in on port "in" exits at port "out1," etc.

In the following switch DEVS, in addition to the standard *phase* and σ variables, there are state variables for storing the input port of the external event, the input value, and the polarity of the switch. In this simple model, the polarity is toggled between true and false at each input.

$$DEVS = (X, Y, S, \delta_{ext}, \delta_{int}, \lambda, ta)$$

where

$$InPorts = \{\text{"}in\text{"}, \text{"}in1\text{"}\}, \text{where } X_{in} = X_{in1} = V(\text{an arbitrary set})$$

$$X = \{(p,v) \mid p \in InPorts\ v \in X_p\} \text{ is the set of input ports and values;}$$

$$\text{OutPorts} = \{\text{"out"}, \text{"out1"}\}, \text{ where } Y_{out} = Y_{out1} = V(\text{an arbitrary set}),$$

$$Y = \{(p,v) \mid p \in OutPorts, v \in Y_p\} \text{ is the set of output ports and values;}$$

$$S = \{\text{"passive"}, \text{"active"}\} \times R_0^+ \times \{in, in1\} \times V \times \{true, false\}$$

$$\delta_{ext}(\text{phase}, \sigma, \text{ inport, store, Sw}, e, (p,v))$$

$$= (\text{"busy", processing\_time}, p, v, !\text{Sw}) \quad \text{if phase} = \text{"passive" and } p \in \{in, in1\}$$

$$(\text{phase}, \sigma - e, \text{ inport, store, Sw}) \quad \text{otherwise}$$

$$\delta_{int}(\text{phase}, \sigma, \text{ inport, store, Sw}, e, (p,v)) = (\text{"passive"}, \infty, \text{ inport, store, Sw})$$

$$\lambda(\text{phase}, \sigma, \text{ inport, store, Sw})$$

$$= (\text{out}, \text{store}) \quad \text{if phase} = \text{"busy" and Sw} = true \text{ and inport} = \text{in}$$

$$= (\text{out1}, \text{store}) \quad \text{if phase} = \text{"busy" and Sw} = true \text{ and inport} = \text{in1}$$

$$= (\text{out1}, \text{store}) \quad \text{if phase} = \text{"busy" and Sw} = false \text{ and inport} = \text{in}$$

$$= (\text{out}, \text{store}) \quad \text{if phase} = \text{"busy" and Sw} = true \text{ and inport} = \text{in1}$$

$$ta(\text{phase}, \sigma, \text{ inport, store, Sw}) = \sigma$$

4.2.3 Classic DEVS Coupled Models

The DEVS formalism includes the means to build models from components. The specification in the case of DEVS with ports includes the external interface (input and output ports and values), the components (which must be DEVS models), and the coupling relations:

$$N = (X, Y, D, \{M_d \mid d \in D\}, EIC, EOC, IC, Select),$$

where

$X = \{(p,v) \mid p \in IPorts, v \in X_p\}$ is the set of input ports and values

$Y = \{(p,v) \mid p \in OPorts. v \in Y_p\}$ is the set of output ports and values

D is the set of the component names.

Component Requirements

- components are DEVS models, for each $d \in D$,

$$M_d = (X_d, Y_d, S, \delta_{ext}\ \delta_{int}, \lambda, ta) \text{ is a DEVS}$$

$$\text{with } X_d = \{(p,v) \mid p \in IPorts_d, v \in X_p\}$$

$$Y_d = \{(p,v) \mid p \in OPorts_d, v \in Y_p\}.$$

Coupling Requirements

- external input coupling connect external inputs to component inputs,

$$EIC \subseteq \{((N, ip_N), (d, ip_d)) \mid ip_N \in IPorts, d \in D, ip_d \in IPorts_d\}.$$

- external output coupling connect component outputs to external outputs,

$$EOC \subseteq \{((d, op_d), (N, op_N)) \mid op_N \in OPorts, d \in D, op_d \in OPorts_d\}.$$

- internal coupling connects component outputs to component inputs:

$$IC \subseteq \{((a, op_a), (b, ip_b)) \mid a, b \in D, op_a \in D, \in OPorts_a, ip_b \in IPorts_b\}.$$

However, *no direct feedback loops are allowed,* i.e., no output port of a component may be connected to an input port of the same component:

$$((d, opd), (e, ipd)) \in IC \text{ implies } d \neq e.$$

(We omit constraints on the interface sets, which are covered in Chapter 5.)

- *Select:* $2^D - \{\} \rightarrow D$, the tie-breaking function (used in Classic DEVS but eliminated in Parallel DEVS).

Simple Pipeline

We construct a simple coupled model by placing three processors in series to form a pipeline. As shown in Fig. 8, we couple the output port "out" of the first processor to the input port "in" of the second, and likewise for the second and third. This kind of coupling is called *internal coupling (IC)* and, as in the preceding specification, it is always of the form where an output port connects to an input port. Since coupled models are themselves usable as components in bigger models, we give them input and output ports. The pipeline has an input port "in" that we connect to the input port "in" of the first processor. This is an example of *external input coupling (EIC)*. Likewise, there is an external output port "out" that gets its values from the last processor's "out" output port. This illustrates *external output coupling (EOC)*.

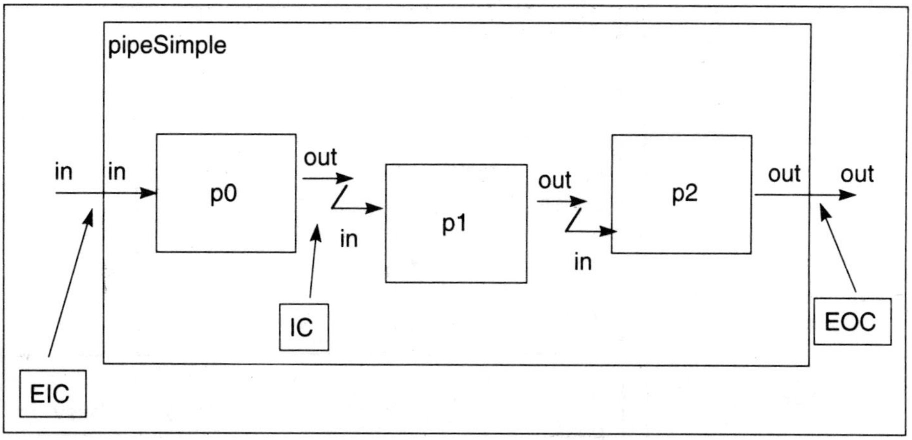

Figure 8 Pipeline coupled model.

The coupled DEVS specification of the pipeline is

$$N = \left(X, Y, D, \{M_d \mid d \in D\}, EIC, EOC, IC\right),$$

where

$$InPorts = \{\text{"}in\text{"}\},$$
$$X_{in} = V \text{ (an arbitrary)}$$
$$X = \{(\text{"}in\text{"}, v) \mid v \in V\}$$
$$OutPorts = \{\text{"}in\text{"}\}$$
$$Y_{out} = V$$
$$Y = \{(\text{"}out\text{"}, v) \mid v \in V\}$$
$$D = \{processor0, processor1, processor2\}$$
$$M_{processor\,2} = M_{processor\,1} = M_{processor\,0 = Processor}$$
$$EIC = \{((N, \text{"}in\text{"}), (processor0, \text{"}in\text{"}))\}$$
$$EOC = \{((processor2, \text{"}out\text{"}), (N, \text{"}out\text{"}))\}$$
$$IC = \{((processor0, \text{"}out\text{"}), (processor1, \text{"}in\text{"})),$$
$$((processor1, \text{"}out\text{"}), (processor2, \text{"}in\text{"}))\}$$
$$Select(D') = \text{the processor in } D' \text{ with the highest index.}$$

The interpretation of coupling specifications is illustrated in Fig. 9. An external event, x_1 arriving at the external input port of pipeSimple is transmitted to the input port "in" of the first processor. If the latter is passive at the time, it goes into phase "busy" for the processing time. Eventually, the job appears on the "out" port of processor0 and is transmitted to the "in" port of processor1 because of the internal coupling. This transmission from output port to input port continues until the job leaves the external output port of the last processor and appears at the output port of pipeSimple because of external output coupling.

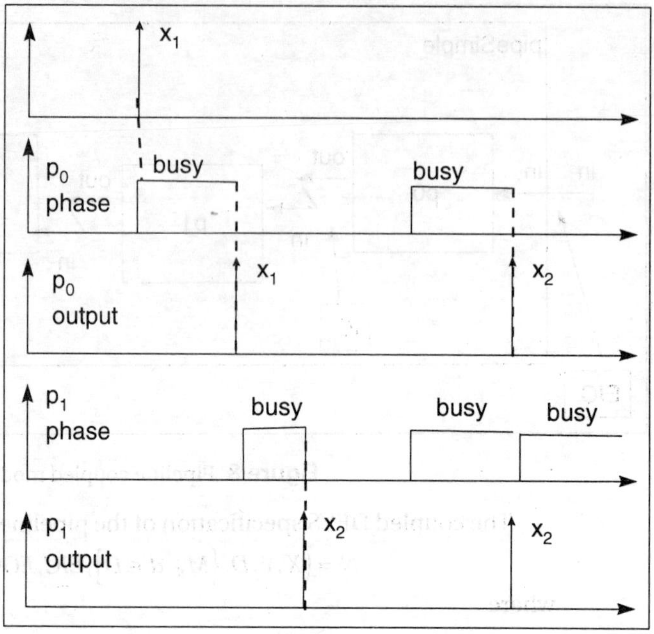

Figure 9 Message transmission and simultaneous events.

Now if the jobs arrive at the same rate that they are processed, the situation shown in the second part of Fig. 9 will arise. The outputs of processor0 and processor1 are generated at the same time with the output of processor0 appearing as the input to processor1. There are now two choices for the modeler to make: (a) should processor1 apply its *internal transition function* to return to phase "passive" in which it can accept the upstream input, or (b) should it apply its *external transition function* first, in which case it will lose the input since it is in phase "busy"? The *Select* function specifies that if both processor0 and processor1 are imminent, then processor1 is the one that generates its output and carries out its internal transition. Thus it enforces alternative (a). In parallel DEVS, we shall see that a similar solution can be achieved without serializing imminent component actions.

Switch Network

A second example of a coupled network employs the *switch DEVS* model defined before to send jobs to a pair of *processors.*

As shown in Fig. 10, the "out" and "out1" ports of the switch are coupled individually to the "in" input ports of the processors. In turn, the "out" ports of the processors are coupled to the "out" port of the network. This allows an output of either processor to appear at the output of the overall network. The coupled DEVS specification is

$$N = (X, Y, D, \{M_d \mid d \in D\}, EIC, EOC, IC),$$

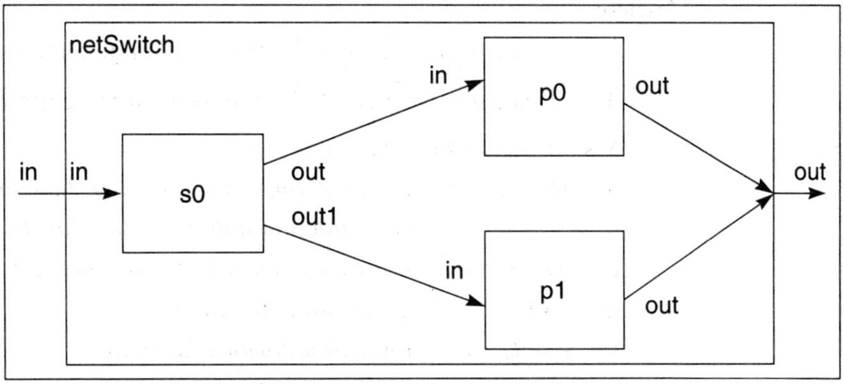

Figure 10 Switch network.

where

$$
\begin{aligned}
&InPorts = \{\text{“}in\text{”}\} \\
&X_{in} = V(\text{an arbitrary set}) \\
&X_M = \{(v) \mid v \in V\} \\
&OutPorts = \{\text{“}out\text{”}\} \\
&Y_{out} = V \\
&Y_M = \{(\text{“}out\text{”}, v) \mid v \in V\} \\
&D = \{Switch0, processor0, processor1\} \\
&M_{Switch0} = Switch;\ M_{processor1} = M_{processor0} = Processor \\
&EIC = \{((N, \text{“}in\text{”}), (Switch0, \text{“}in\text{”})\} \\
&EOC = \{((processor0, \text{“}out\text{”}), (N, \text{“}out\text{”})), \\
&\qquad ((processor1, \text{“}out\text{”}), (N, \text{“}out\text{”}))\} \\
&IC = \{((Switch0, \text{“}out\text{”}), (processor0, \text{“}in\text{”})), \\
&\qquad ((Switch0, \text{“}out1\text{”}), (processor1, \text{“}in\text{”}))\}.
\end{aligned}
$$

4.3 Parallel DEVS System Specification

Parallel DEVS differs from classic DEVS in allowing all imminent components to be activated and to send their output to other components. The receiver is responsible for examining this input and properly interpreting it. Messages, basically lists of port–value pairs, are the basic exchange medium. This section discusses Parallel DEVS and gives a variety of examples to contrast with classic DEVS.

A basic Parallel DEVS is a structure,

$$DEVS = (X_M, Y_M, S, \delta_{ext}, \delta_{int}, \delta_{con}, \lambda, ta)$$

where

$X_M = \{(p,v) | p \in IPorts, v \in X_p\}$ is the set of input ports and values

$Y_M = \{(p,v) | p \in OPorts, v \in Y_p\}$ is the set of output ports and values

S is the set of *sequential* states

$\delta_{ext}: Q \times X_M^b \rightarrow S$ is the *external state transition function*

$\delta_{int}: S \rightarrow S$ is the *internal state transition function*

$\delta_{con}: Q \times X_M^b \rightarrow S$ is the *confluent transition function*

$\lambda: S \rightarrow Y^b$ is the output function

$ta: S \rightarrow R_{0,\infty}^+$ is the *time advance function*

$Q: = \{(s,e) | s \in S, 0 \leq e \leq ta(s)\}$ is the set of *total states*.

Note that instead of having a single input, basic Parallel DEVS models have a bag of inputs. A *bag* is a set with possible multiple occurrences of its elements. A second difference is noted—this is the addition of a transition function, called *confluent*. It decides the next state in cases of collision between external and internal events. We have seen examples of such collisions earlier in examining Classic DEVS. There is also a coupled model version of parallel DEVS that matches the assumptions discussed earlier. We return to discuss it after discussing some examples.

4.3.1 Processor With Buffer

A processor that has a buffer is defined in Parallel DEVS as

$$DEVS_{processng\_time} = (X_M, Y_M, S, \delta_{ext}, \delta_{int}, \delta_{con}, \lambda, ta),$$

where

$IPorts = \{\text{“in”}\}$, where $X_{in} = V$(an arbitrary set)

$X_M = \{(p,v) | p \in IPorts, v \in X_p\}$ is the set of input ports and values

$OPorts = \{\text{“out”}\}$, where $Y_{out} = V$(an arbitrary set)

$Y_M = \{(p,v) | p \in IPorts, v \in Y_p\}$ is the set of output ports and values

$S = \{\text{“passive”}, \text{“busy”}\} \times R_0^+ \times V^+$

$\delta_{ext}(\text{“phase”}, \sigma, q, e, ((\text{“in”}, x1), (\text{“in”}, x2), \ldots, (\text{“in”}, xn)))$

$= (\text{“busy”}, \text{processing\_time}, x1, x2, \ldots, xn)$ if phase = “passive”

$= (\text{phase}, \sigma - e, q.x1, x2, \ldots, xn)$ otherwise

$\delta_{int}(\text{phase}, \sigma, q.v) = (\text{“passive”}, \text{processing\_time}, q)$

$\delta_{con}(s, ta(s), x) = \delta_{ext}(\delta_{int}(s), 0, x)$

$\lambda(\text{“busy”}, \sigma, q.v) = v$

$ta(\text{phase}, \sigma, q) = \sigma$.

Using its buffer the processor can store jobs that arrive while it is busy. The buffer, also called a queue, is represented by a sequence of jobs, x1 . . . xn in V^+ (the set of finite sequences of elements of V). In Parallel DEVS, the processor can also handle jobs that arrive simultaneously on in its input port. These are placed in its queue and it starts working on the one it has selected to be first. Note that bags, like sets, are not ordered so there is no ordering of the jobs in the input bag. For convenience we have shown the job which is last in the written order in δ_{ext} as the one selected as the one to be processed. Figure 11 illustrates the concurrent arrival of two jobs and the subsequent arrival of a third just as the first job is about to be finished. Note that the confluent function, δ_{con} specifies that the internal transition function is to be applied first. Thus, the job in process completes and exists. Then the external function adds the third job to the end of the queue and starts working on the second job. Classic DEVS has a hard time doing all this as easily!

Exercise: Write a Parallel DEVS for the storage model with separate ports for store and query inputs. Also resolve the collision between external and internal transitions when a store input occurs.◆

Exercise: Write a Parallel DEVS for a generator that has ports for starting and stopping its generation. Explore various possibilities for using the elapsed time when an stop input occurs. How does each of these choice affect the behavior of the start input.◆

4.3.2 Parallel DEVS Coupled Models

Parallel DEVS coupled models are specified in the same way as in classic DEVS except that the Select function is omitted. While this is an innocent-looking change, its semantics are much different—they differ significantly in how

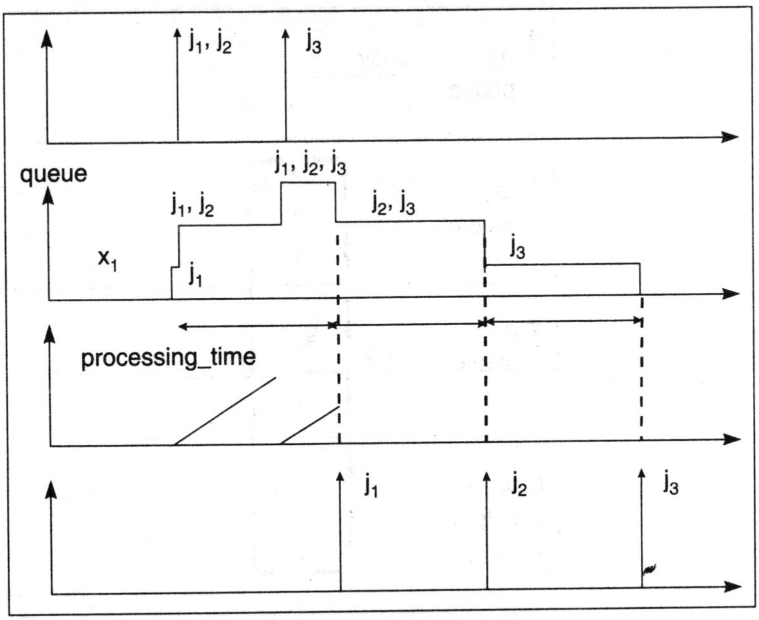

Figure 11 Parallel DEVS process with buffer.

imminent components are handled. In parallel DEVS there is no serialization of the imminent computations—all imminent components generate their outputs which are then distributed to their destinations using the coupling information. The detailed simulation algorithms for parallel DEVS will be discussed in later chapters. For now, let's revisit the simple pipeline in Fig. 8 to see how the interpretation underlying Parallel DEVS differs from that of Classic DEVS.

Simple Pipeline (Parallel DEVS)

Recall that the specification of the pipeline model is the same as in Classic DEVS except for omitting the Select function. In Fig. 12, processor0 and processor1 are imminent. In classic DEVS, only one would be chosen to execute. In contrast, in Parallel DEVS, they both generate their outputs. Processor0's output goes to processor1's input. Since now processor1 has both internal and external events, the confluent transition function is applied. As in Fig. 11, the confluent function is defined to first apply the internal transition function and then the external one. As we have seen, this causes processor1 to complete the finished job before accepting the incoming one.

Now consider a pipeline in which a downstream processor's output is fed back to an upstream processor. For example, let processor1's output be fed back to precessor1's input. In Classic DEVS, the Select function must always make the same choice among imminent components. Thus, either one or the other processor will lose its incoming job (assuming no buffers). However, in Parallel DEVS, both processors output their jobs and can handle the priorities between arriving jobs and just finished jobs in a manner specified by the confluent transition function.

Exercise: Define the coupled model for a cyclic pipeline and draw a state trajectory similar to that in Fig. 12.◆

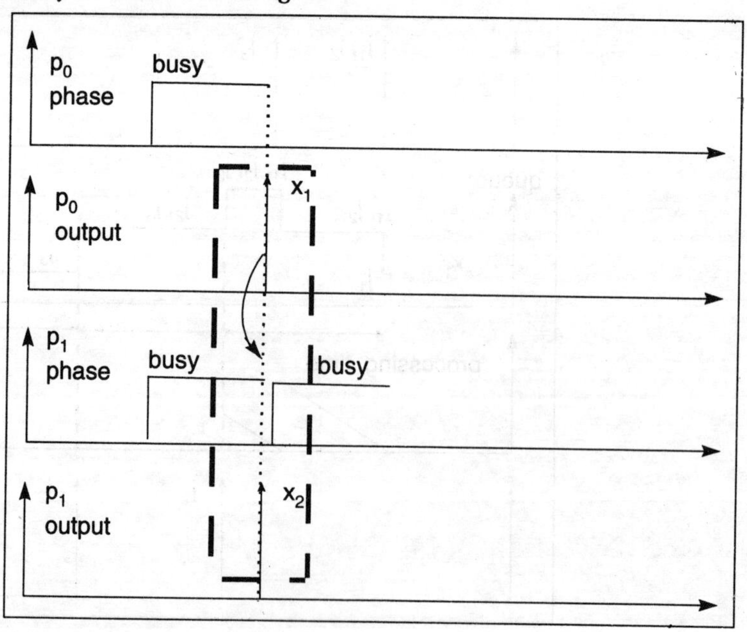

Figure 12 Illustrating handling of imminent components in Parallel DEVS.

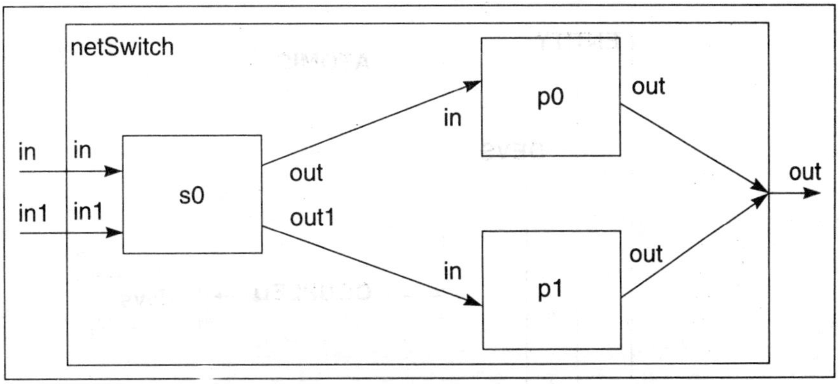

Figure 13 A switching net in Parallel DEVS.

Exercise: Write a Parallel DEVS basic model for a Switch that can accept simultaneous input on two ports as shown in Fig. 13. Write a Parallel DEVS coupled model as shown in the figure and draw its state trajectories.◆

4.4 Hierarchical Models

Hierarchical models are coupled models with components that may be atomic or coupled models. As Fig. 14 illustrates, we encapsulate a generator and a transducer into a coupled model called an experimental frame, *ef.* The experimental frame can then be coupled to a processor to provide it with a stream of inputs (from the generator) and observe the statistics of the processor's operation (the transducer). The processor can be an atomic model (as is the processor with buffer, for example) or can itself be a coupled model (the coupled model in Fig. 13).

4.5 Object-Oriented Implementations of DEVS: An Introduction

DEVS is most naturally implemented in computational form in an object-oriented framework. The basic class is *entity,* from which class *devs* is derived (Fig. 15). *Devs* in turn is specialized into classes *atomic* and *coupled. Atomic* enables models to be expressed directly in the basic DEVS formal-

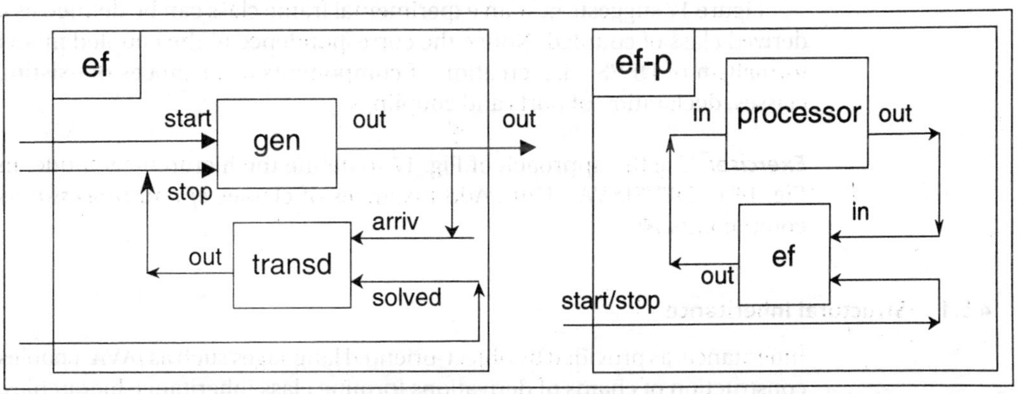

Figure 14 Hierarchical model.

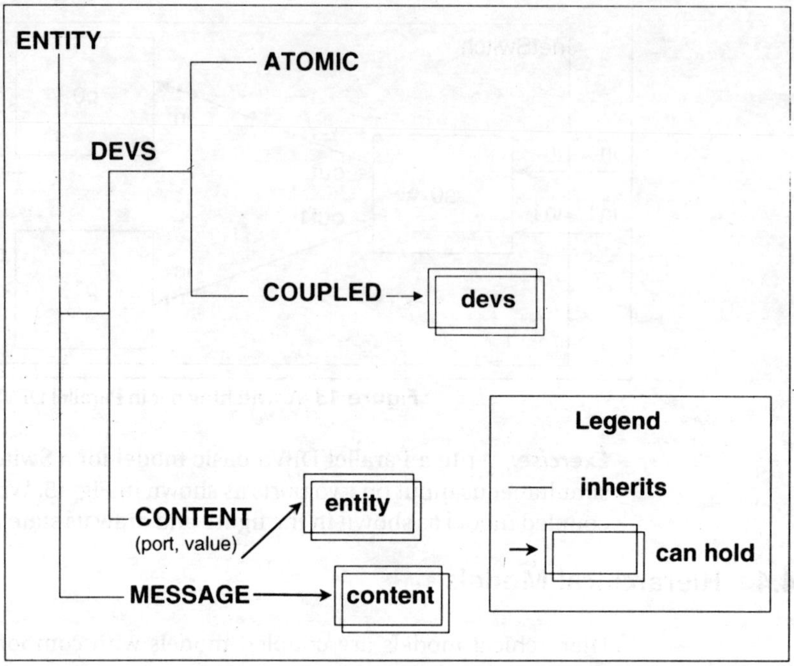

Figure 15 Basic classes in object-oriented DEVS.

ism. *Coupled* supports construction of models by coupling together components. Class *content* is derived from *entity* to carry *ports* and their *values,* where the latter can be any instance of *entity* or its derived classes. Typically a modeler defines such derived classes to structure the information being exchanged among models. In the implementation of Parallel DEVS, the outputs of component models are instances of class *message,* which are containers of *content* instances.

Figure 16 illustrates the implementation of a simple processor as a derived class of *atomic* in DEVSJAVA, a realization of Parallel DEVS. Notice the one-to-one correspondence between the formal DEVS elements, e.g., external transition function, and their direct expression as methods in DEVSJAVA.

Figure 17 suggests how an experimental frame class can be defined as a derived class of coupled. Notice the correspondence to the coupled model formalism of DEVS, viz., creation of components as instances of existing classes, declaration of ports and couplings.

Exercise: Use the approach of Fig. 17 to define the hierarchical model in Fig. 14 in DEVSJAVA. (Hint: Add instances of classes *ef* and *processor* as components.)◆

4.5.1 Structural Inheritance

Inheritance, as provided by object-oriented languages such as JAVA, enables construction of chains of derivations forming class inheritance hierarchies. This means that DEVSJAVA supports not just immediate derivation from

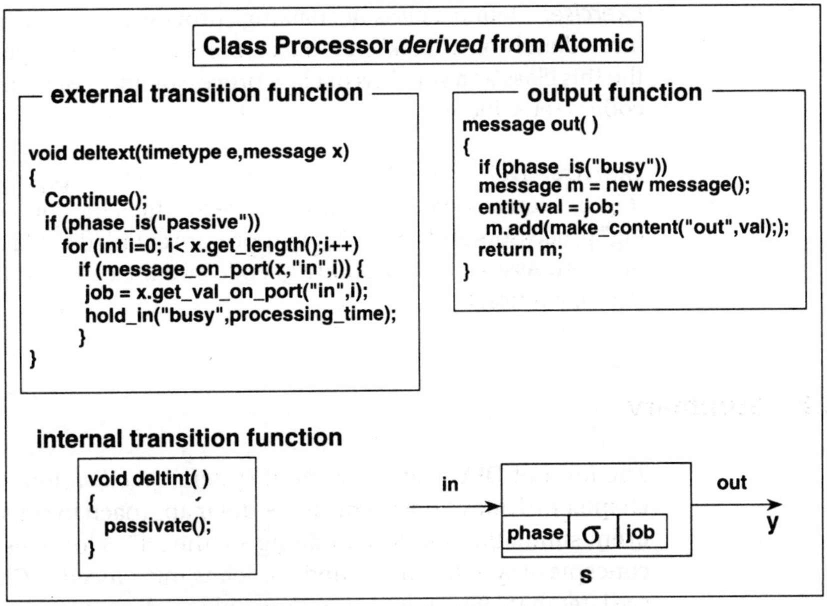

Figure 16 Processor as an atomic model in DEVSJAVA.

classes *atomic* and *coupled,* but also derivation of new model classes from those **already defined.** This is called *structural* inheritance because structure definitions, such as ports in atomic models and couplings in coupled models can be reused, and even modified, thus exploiting the polymorphism of object-orientation.

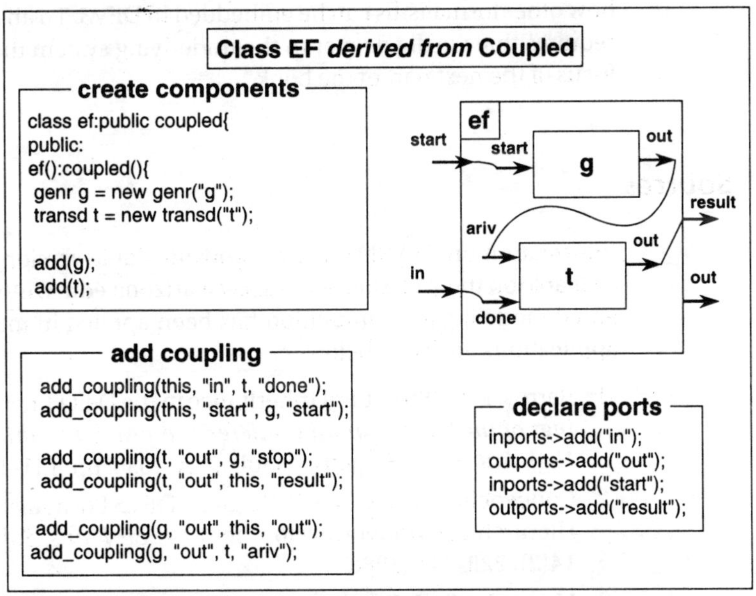

Figure 17 Experimental frame as a coupled model in DEVSJAVA.

Exercise: Define a class of "balking" processors in which a job is sent out immediately on a "balk" port if it cannot be processed upon arrival. Rewrite the this class as a subclass of class processor and assess the extent to which code is reusable.◆

Exercise: Define a class pipeSimple for a simple pipeline of processors (Fig. 8). Derive a class from pipeSimple in which the components are "balking" processors and whose "balk" ports are coupled to a "balk" external output port. Assess the reusability of code and the ease or difficulty in achieving such reuse.◆

4.6 Summary

The form of DEVS (discrete event system specification) discussed in this chapter provides a hierarchical, modular approach to constructing discrete event simulation models. In doing so, the DEVS formalism embodies the concepts of systems theory and modeling introduced in Chapters 1. We will see later that DEVS is important not only for discrete event models, but also because it affords a computational basis for implementing behaviors that are expressed in DESS and DTSS, the other basic systems formalisms. This chapter introduced both Classic DEVS and the revision oriented to parallel and distributed simulation called Parallel DEVS. We also saw the essentials of how DEVS is implemented in an object-oriented framework.

Having a good understanding of how DEVS is used to model real systems should motivate us to ask deeper questions, such as whether DEVS always specifies meaningful systems, how simulation of a DEVS model works, and how other formalisms can be embedded in DEVS. To answer such questions requires that we dig deeper in the underlying system theory, and this is the focus of the next part of the book.

4.7 Sources

Information on DEVSJAVA and a downloadable version of the software are available on the Web site: www-ais.ece.arizona.edu. DEVS-based, object-oriented modeling and simulation has been applied in many fields. Example applications are listed below.

1. Barros, F. J., "Structural Inheritance in the Delta Environment." *Proceedings of the Sixth Annual Conference on AI, Simulation and Planning in High Autonomy Systems,* La Jolla, CA, 1996, pp. 141–147.
2. Concepcion, A. I., and B. P. Zeigler, "DEVS Formalism: A Framework for Hierarchical Model Development." *IEEE Trans. Software Engineering,* **14**(2), 228–241 (1988).
3. Moon, Y., B. P. Zingler, V. L. Lopes, J. Kim. "DEVS Approximation of Infiltration Using Genetic Algorithm Optimization of a Fuzzy System." *J. Math. Comp. Model.* **23,** 215–228 (1996).

4. Nidumolu, R. N. Menon and B. P. Zeigler, "Object-Oriented Business Process Modeling and Simulation: a Discrete-Event System Specification (DEVS) Framework. *Sim. Pract. and Theory,* **6**, pp. 531–571 1998.
5. Ninios, P., *An Object Oriented DEVS Framework for Strategic Modelling and Industry Simulation.* London Business School, London, 1994.
6. Sato, R., and H. Praehofer, "A Discrete Event System Model of Business Systems." *IEEE Trans. System, Man and Cybernetics,* **27**(1), 1–22.(1997).
7. Vahie, S., "Dynamic Neuronal Ensembles: Issues in Representing Structure Change in Object-Oriented, Biologically-based Brain Models," Presented at Intl. Conf. on Semiotics and Intelligent Systems, Washington, DC, 1996.
8. Wainer, G., and N. Giambiasi, "Cell-DEVS with Transport and Inertial Delay." Presented at SCS European MultiConference, Passau, Germany, 1998.
9. Zeigler, B. P., H. Sarjoughian, and W. Au., "Object-Oriented DEVS." Presented at Enabling Technology for Simulation Science, SPIE AeoroSense 97, Orlando, FL, 1997.

5

Hierarchy of System Specifications

In this chapter we provide basic system theoretical concepts that will serve as a rigorous foundation for the simulation modeling formalisms in subsequent chapters. In particular, we will formulate the hierarchy of system specifications, first introduced in Chapter 1, using mathematical set theory. Please refer to any book on discrete mathematics for the necessary set theory background. Also, don't hesitate to refer back to corresponding parts of Chapter 1 to augment the presentation here.

5.1 Time Base

Fundamental to the notion of a dynamic system is the passage of time. Time is conceived as flowing along independently, and all dynamic changes are ordered by this flow.

A *time base* is defined to be a structure

$$time = \langle T, < \rangle,$$

where T is a set and $<$ is an *ordering relation on elements of* T. $<$ is *transitive, irreflexive,* and *antisymetric.*

An ordering is called *linear* or *total* if for every pair (t, t') either $t < t'$, $t' < t$ or $t = t'$. Otherwise an ordering is called *partial.* We usually assume the total ordering, but sometimes a partial ordering offers a better representation of system knowledge, especially when uncertainty or multiplicity of trajectories is involved, as we shall see in Chapter 8 (Extended Formalisms).

The ordering relation enables us to use terms such as *past, future,* and *present.* If t is interpreted to be the present time, then the set $T_{t)} = \{\tau \mid \tau \in T, \tau < t\}$ denotes the past and the set $T_{(t} = \{\tau \mid \tau \in T, t < \tau\}$ denotes the future. The past and the future are disjoint, as is required in a world where each moment counts and cannot be recaptured in the future once it is past. The set $T_{t]} = \{\tau \mid \tau \in T, \tau \leq t\}$ denotes the past including the present time and the set $T_{[t} = \{\tau \mid \tau \in T, t \leq \tau\}$ denotes the future including the present time. It is often not critical whether we deal with closed or open intervals. In this case, $T_{t>}$ means either $T_{t)}$ or $T_{t]}$. Similarly, $T_{<t}$ denotes $T_{(t}$ or $T_{[t}$. In like manner, the set $T_{[t_1, t_2)} = \{\tau \mid \tau \in T, t_1 \leq \tau < t_2\}$ denotes the *time interval* $[t_1, t_2)$ from starting time t_1 (included in the interval) and final time t_2 (excluded). Analogously, we define intervals $T_{(t_1, t_2)}$ or $(t_1, t_2) = \{\tau \mid \tau \in T, t_1 < \tau < t_2\}$, $T_{[t_1, t_2]}$ or $[t_1, t_2] = \{\tau \mid \tau \in T, t_1 \leq \tau \leq t_2\}$, $T_{(t_1, t_2]}$ or $(t_1, t_2] = \{\tau \mid \tau \in T, t_1 < \tau \leq t_2\}$. $T_{<t_1, t_2>}$ or $<t_1, t_2>$ refers to one of the above intervals.

For the interval $<t_1, t_2>$, t_1 is called the *initial* or *beginning* time and t_2 is called *final* or *ending* time. Note that the special interval $<t_1, t_1>$ refers either to the singleton t_1 or to the empty interval, depending on the type of interval we use.

Besides the properties just mentioned, a time base may have additional structure. The time base may enjoy the *abelian group property*, i.e., there is a binary operation + such that $(T, +)$ is an abelian group with the identity element 0 and for every element t the inverse element $-t$. The addition operation + is said to be *order preserving* if $t_1 < t_2 \Rightarrow t_1 + t_3 < t_2 + t_3$.

A time base may have a *minimal element* t_0, a *lower bound*, then all elements $t \in T$ are greater than t_0. If there is no lower bound, then $-\infty$ denotes the fictitious lower bound. If a time base has no upper bound, the fictitious upper bound is denoted by ∞. Note, that $-\infty$ and ∞ are not included in the time base. The infinity symbol satisfies $\infty + t = \infty$ for any $t \in T$.

Examples of useful time bases are the real number $\Re$, the integers $\Im$, and all sets $c * \Im$, $c \in \Re$ a constant, isomorphic to $\Im$.[1] They have the abelian group property and the + operation is order preserving. Time base $\Re$ represents the *continuous time base* and all time bases isomorphic to the integers $\Im$ are denoted to be *discrete* (Fig. 1).

5.2 Segments and Trajectories

Having a time base, we are in the position to describe how behavior occurs over time.

Let A denote a set, for example, an input, state, or output set of a model, and let T be a time base as defined previously. A function of the form

$$f : T \to A$$

is called a *time function* (also called a *trajectory* or *signal*). The value of f at time t is given by $f(t)$. Restricting f to a subset T' of T is denoted by

$$f|T' : T' \to A,$$

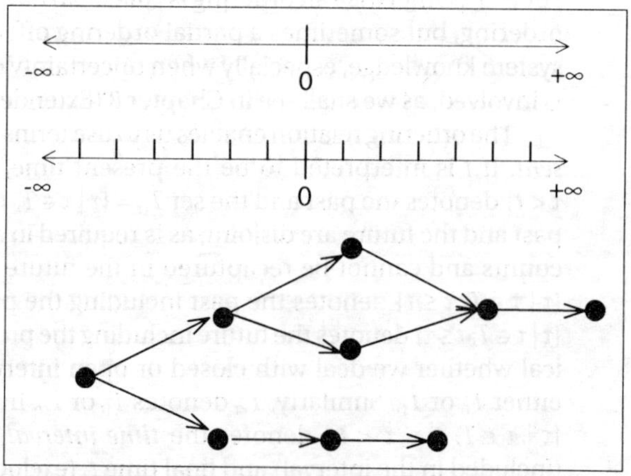

Figure 1 A continuous, a discrete, and a partial ordered time base.

[1] We also use R and I to denote these sets.

where

$$f|T'(t) := f(t) \text{ for all } t \in T'.$$

A restriction of a time function is also a time function.

Of special importance are restrictions to subsets $T_{t>}$, $T_{<t}$, and $T_{<t_1,t_2>}$. With t denoting the present time, $f|T_{t>}$, also written $f_{t>}$, is called the past of f. Similarly, $f|T_{<t}$, also written $f_{<t}$, is called the future of f. A restriction of f to a time interval $<t_1, t_2>$ is called a *segment,* and we usually write

$$\omega: <t_1, t_2> \rightarrow A \text{ or } \omega_{<t_1, t_2>}.$$

The set of all segments over A and T is denoted by (A, T).

The trajectory $\omega: <t_1, t_2> \rightarrow A$ describes a motion through the set A that begins at t_1 and ends at t_2, and at every $t \in <t_1, t_2>$ $\omega(t)$ describes where the motion is at time t. For example, if a is a variable of a program with range A, a segment ω_a: $<t_1, t_2> \rightarrow A$ would describe a sequence of values $\omega_a(t_1)$, $\omega_a(t_1+1), \ldots, \omega_a(t_2)$ assumed by the variable a during the run of the program beginning at time t_1 and ending at time t_2 (here $\Im = \Im$ and $<t_1, t_2> = [t_1, t_2]$).

For segments we define a length operator $l: \Omega \rightarrow T_0^+$ by $l(\omega) = t_2 - t_1$, where $\text{dom}(\omega) = <t_1, t_2>$ with $\text{dom}(\omega)$ denoting the domain of ω. Thus, $l(\omega)$ is the length of the observation interval on which ω is defined. The segment with empty domain $<t_1, t_1>$ is an *empty segment,* which usually is denoted by special symbol Φ. Obviously, an empty segment has length 0.

A pair of segments ω_1: $<t_1, t_2> \rightarrow A$ and ω_2: $<t_3, t_4> \rightarrow A$ are said to be *contiguous* if their domains are contiguous, i.e., $t_2 = t_3$. For contiguous segments ω_1 and ω_2 we define the *concatenation operation* •

$$\omega_1 \bullet \omega_2 : <t_1, t_4> \rightarrow A,$$

with

$$\omega_1 \bullet \omega_2(t) = \omega_1(t) \text{ for } t \in <t_1, t_2>$$
$$\omega_1 \bullet \omega_2(t) = \omega_2(t) \text{ for } t \in <t_3, t_4>.$$

(See Fig. 2.) We note that the uniqueness of the value of $\omega_1 \bullet \omega_2$ at time t_2 depends on the type of interval used. If the interval $[t_1, t_2)$ or $(t_1, t_2]$ is used, a unique value is defined and the concatenation operation is associative.

Exercise: Let $< >$ mean [ ). Show that the operation $\omega_1 \bullet \omega_2$ is associative.◆

Note that we often omit the concatenation operator and use $\omega_1\omega_2$ instead.

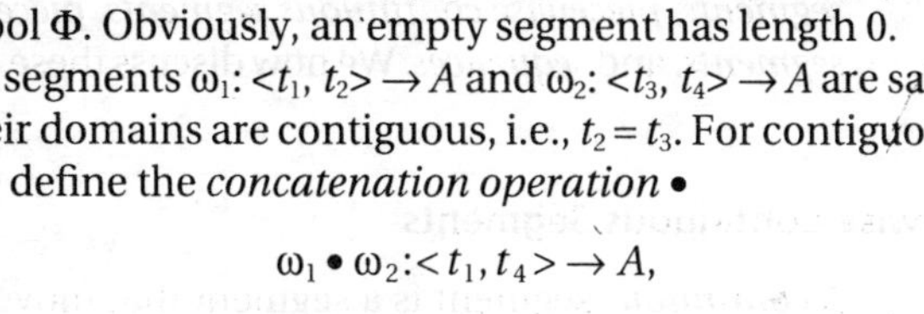

Figure 2 Concatenation of segments ω_1 and ω_2.

A set Ω of segments over A and T is said to be *closed under concatenation* if for every contiguous pair $\omega_1, \omega_2 \in \Omega$ also $\omega_1 \bullet \omega_2 \in \Omega$.

Analogous to $f_{t>}$ and $f_{<t}$, for segments we define $\omega_{t>}$ or $\omega_{<t_1,t>}$ and $\omega_{t>}$ or $\omega_{<t,t_2>}$ with $t \in <t_1, t_2>$ and call them *left segment* and *right segment* of ω (Fig. 3). We always choose the type of left segment and right segment operation in such a way that the resulting segment is of the same type as the original segment, e.g., for a segment ω defined over an interval $[t_1, t_2)$ we use left segments of the form $\omega_{t)}$ and right segments of the form $\omega_{[t}$. Similarly, for a segment defined over an interval $(t_1, t_2]$ we use $\omega_{t]}$ and $\omega_{(t}$.

It is only natural that having split a segment into parts, we should be able to put it back together again. Thus, we require that

$$\omega_{t>} \bullet \omega_{<t} = \omega.$$

A set Ω of segments over A and T is said to be *closed under left segmentation* if every left segment is also in the set, i.e., if for every $\omega: <t_1, t_2> \rightarrow A \in \Omega$ and $t \in <t_1, t_2>$ we have $\omega_{t>} \in \Omega$. Analogously, a set Ω of segments over A and T is said to be *closed under right segmentation* if for every $\omega:<t_1, t_2> \rightarrow A \in \Omega$ and $t \in <t_1, t_2>$, we have $\omega_{<t} \in \Omega$.

Depending on the type of the time base and the type of the set A, we will be dealing with the different special types of segments, such as *continuous segments, piecewise continuous segments, piecewise constant segments, event segments,* and *sequences.* We now discuss these classes and their applications.

5.2.1 Piecewise Continuous Segments

A *continuous* segment is a segment that moves smoothly through a real n-dimensional vector space $\Re^n$ for some $n = 1,2,3, \ldots$. In other words, a segment $\omega:<t_1, t_2> \rightarrow \Re^n$ over a continuous time base is a continuous segment if it is continuous at all points $t \in <t_1, t_2>$.

A *piecewise continuous segment* is continuous at all points t except a finite number of points $t' \in <t_1, t_2>$ as in Fig. 4.

Continuous and piecewise continuous segments often occur in differential equation modeling. Of special interest are here the subset of *bounded piecewise continuous* (bpc) segments, that is, a piecewise continuous segment with a finite upper bound.

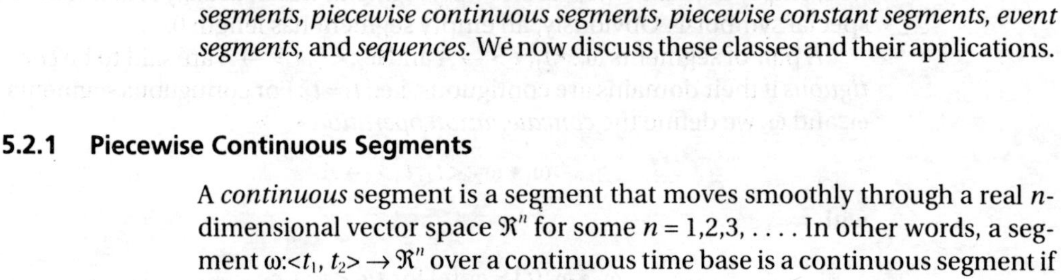

Figure 3 Segment ω, left segment $\omega_{t>}$, and right segment $\omega_{<t}$.

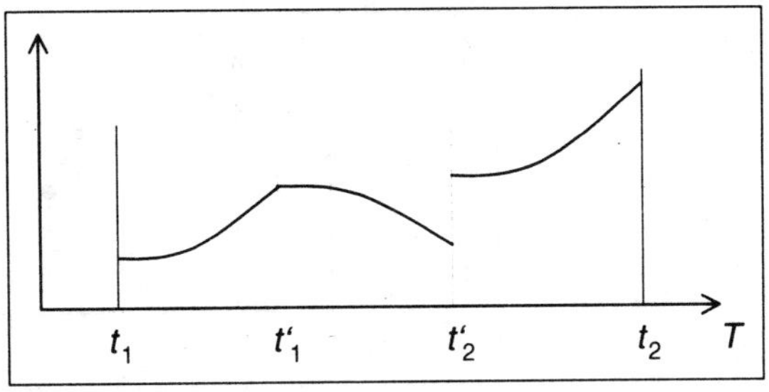

Figure 4 A piecewise continuous segment.

5.2.2 Piecewise Constant Segments

The class of *piecewise constant segments* is a subclass of piecewise continuous segments in which each subsequence is a constant segment. A piecewise constant segment ω: $<t_0, t_n> \rightarrow A$ can be characterized as follows: There exist a finite set of time points $t_1, t_2, t_3, \ldots, t_{n-1} \in <t_0, t_n>$ and values $c_1, c_2, \ldots, c_n \in A$, such that $\omega = \omega_{<t_0, t_1>} \bullet \omega_{<t_1, t_2>} \bullet \ldots \bullet \omega<t_{n-1}, t_n>$ and $\omega_{<t_{i-1}, t_i>}(t) = c_i$, for all $t \in <t_{i-1}, t_i>$ (see Fig. 5).

Piecewise constant segments occur in discrete event models as state trajectories.

5.2.3 Event Segments

An *event segment* represents a sequence of events ordered in time. Formally, let ω:$<t_0, t_n> \rightarrow$ A $\cup$ {$\varnothing$} be a segment over a continuous time base and an arbitrary set $A \cup \{\varnothing\}$. Here $\varnothing$ denotes the *nonevent* and is an element not in A. Then ω is an event segment if there exists a *finite* set of times points $t_1, t_2, t_3, \ldots, t_{n-1} \in <t_0, t_n>$ such that $\omega(t_i) = a_i \in A$ for $i = 1, \ldots, n-1$, and $\omega(t) = \varnothing$ for all other $t \in <t_0, t_n>$. In an event segment, most of the domain is mapped to the nonevent, with a finite number of events (possibly none) occurring otherwise (Fig. 6).

An event segment ω:$<t_1, t_2> \rightarrow A \cup \{\varnothing\}$ that does not contain any events is denoted by $\varnothing_{<t_1, t_2>}$.

Event segments are employed in discrete event models as input and output trajectories.

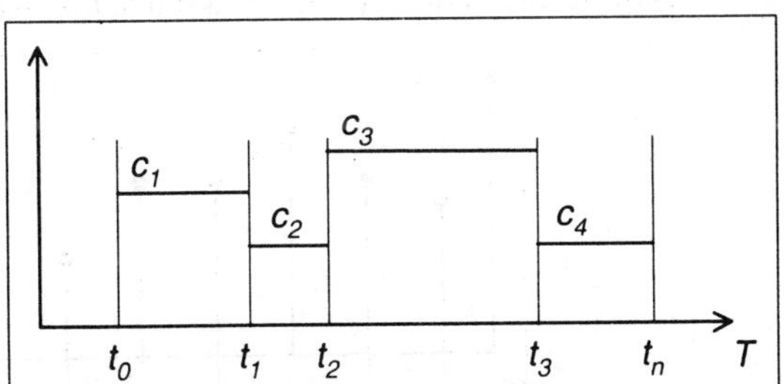

Figure 5 A piecewise constant segment.

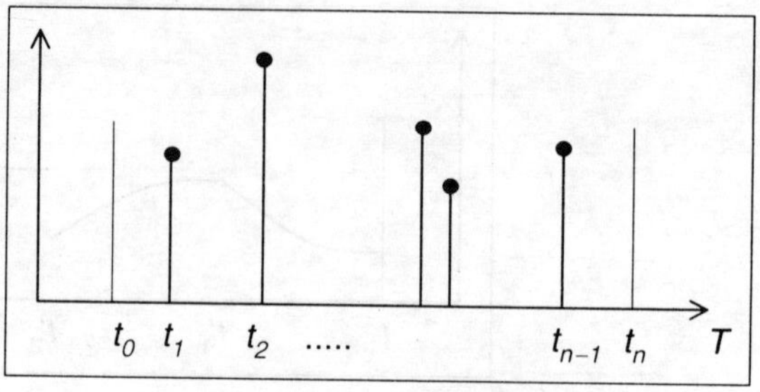

Figure 6 An event segment.

Correspondence Between Piecewise Constant and Event Segments

An event segment can be transformed into a piecewise constant segment and vice versa. Let ω:<t_0, t_n> $\rightarrow A \cup \{\varnothing\}$ be an event segment with event times $t_1, t_2, t_3, \ldots, t_{n-1} \in$ <t_0, t_n> as before. Then we define the corresponding piecewise constant segment ω':<t_0, t_n> $\rightarrow A$ by $\omega'(t) = \omega(t_x)$ with t_x being the largest time in $\{t_1, t_2, t_3, \ldots, t_{n-1}\}$ with $t_x \leq t$. If such a number t_x does not exist, then $\omega'(t) = \varnothing$.

Let ω':<t_0, t_n> $\rightarrow A$ be a piecewise constant segment with event times $t_1, t_2, t_3, \ldots, t_{n-1} \in$ <t_0, t_n> and constant values $c_1, c_2, \ldots, c_n \in A$ as defined above. Then we define the corresponding event trajectory ω:<t_0, t_n> $\rightarrow A \cup \{\varnothing\}$ by $\omega(t) = \omega'(t) = c_{i+1}$ if $t = t_i \in \{t_0, t_1, t_2, t_3, \ldots, t_{n-1}\}$ and $\omega(t) = \varnothing$ otherwise.

5.2.4 Sequences

All segments over a discrete time base are called *finite sequences,* or for short just *sequences* (Fig. 7). Sequences are employed in discrete time models as input, state, and output trajectories.

To test for the type of a segment, we introduce predicates *is-continuous-segment*(ω), *is-event-segment*(ω), and *is-sequence*(ω), which respond with true if ω is a continuous or piecewise continuous segment, an event segment, or a sequence, respectively.

5.3 I/O Observation Frame

We start our elaboration of a hierarchy of system specifications at the most basic level with a means to describe the input/output interface of a system. This description of a system as a black box will be later elaborated into the

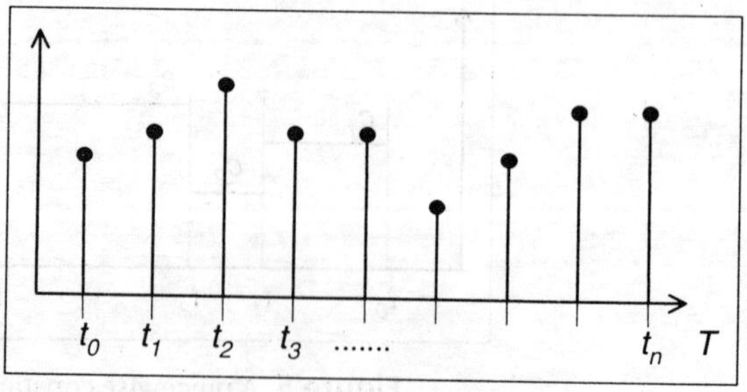

Figure 7 A sequence.

concept of experimental frame, which can characterize in more detail the observation and control constraints that can govern experimentation.

Suppose we have isolated a real system and have specified a set of input and output variables. An input variable is one we consider to influence the system but not to be directly influenced by it. An output variable is one which is controlled by the system and through which the system directly influences its environment. If $x_1, \ldots, x_n$ denote the input variables and $X_1, \ldots, X_n$ are their range sets, the cross product $X_1 \times X_2 \times \cdots \times X_n$ represents the set of all possible assignments to input variables. Let us use values coming from some subset X of this cross product to stimulate the system. We call X an *input* set. Even though we might know that X comes from some particular inputs, at the basic level of knowledge, where we are starting, we consider X to be an abstract set, independent of any particular representation as a subset of a crossproduct of input variables (in the words of Section 5.8, it is uncoordinatized or unstructured). The implication here is that in the abstract set theory we are not interested in any system properties that are tied to a particular structuring or representation of input set X. Likewise, we consider an abstract set Y as *output* set.

To capture systems at that level, we employ the I/O observation frame (IO) as

$$\text{IO} = (T, X, Y),$$

where

T is a time base
X is a set—the input values set
Y is a set—the output values set

Thus, very simply, we have set X of values that can appear at the input of the system and an abstract set Y of values that can appear at its output. The input set and output set together with a time base constitute our most basic abstraction of a system as a black box.

5.4 I/O Relation Observation

The I/O observation frame just introduced gives us a means for specifying the input/output interface of a system, and segments introduced in Section 5.3 give us a means for recording the behavior of variables over time. So equipped, we are able specify a system at the behavioral level.

We can now conduct an experiment: We apply to the input a segment from (X, T) and we observe at the output a segment from (Y, T). Thus we have a picture as in Fig. 8. A segment $\omega \in (X, T)$ is called an *input segment;* a segment $\rho \in (Y, T)$ is called an *output segment.* We adopt the reasonable convention that the output segment observed in response to an input segment is recorded over the same observation interval (other conventions are possible). Thus, if ω and ρ are to be associated, the domain of ω equals the domain of ρ. We call such a pair an *input–output* (I/O) pair.

If we continue experimenting, we will collect a set of such I/O pairs, which we call the *I/O relation.* The set of all such pairs for all possible allowable input

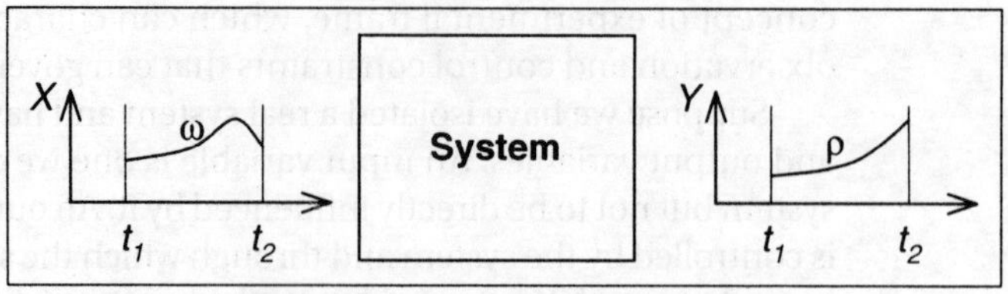

Figure 8 A system experiment.

segments Ω defines all possible input/output behaviors of a system. To render this information about a system we introduce the *I/O relation observation* as a structure,

$$\text{IORO} = (T, X, \Omega, Y, R),$$

where *T*, *X*, and *Y* are the same as for IO frame and

Ω is a set—the set of allowable input segements
R is a relation—the I/O relation,

with the constraints that *(a)* $\Omega \subseteq (X,T)$ and *(b)* $R \subseteq \Omega \times (Y,T)$ where $(\omega,\rho) \in R \Rightarrow \text{dom}(\omega) = \text{dom}(\rho)$.

Our definition does not require that *R* is finite because we want to deal with models that attempt to characterize the potential data observable from a real system. Such data are assumed to be infinite even though we can collect only a finite portion of the full amount.

Example. An IORO is often the underlying form used when the behavior of a system is described by means of a differential equation such as

$$\frac{d^3y}{dt^3} + \frac{2d^2y}{dt^2} + \frac{8dy}{dt} + 7y = x.$$

This equation implies that time is continuous and that the input and output sets are also one-dimensional continuous variables. Thus, in an explicit IORO = (*T*, *X*, Ω, *Y*, *R*), we have $T = X = Y = \Re$. Since input segment set Ω is not specified by the equation, however, we are at liberty to choose it to meet the modeling situation at hand. One natural choice is the set of bounded piecewise continuous segments (bpc).

Now it follows that

$$R = \{(\omega,\rho) \mid \omega \in \text{bpc}, \text{dom}(\omega) = \text{dom}(\rho) \text{ and}$$

$$\frac{d^3\rho(t)}{dt^3} + \frac{2d^2\rho(t)}{dt^2} + \frac{8d\rho(t)}{dt} + 7\rho(t) = \omega(t) \quad \text{for all } t \in \text{dom}(\omega)\}.$$

This means that we would pair an output segment ρ with an input segment ω over the same observation interval, if ω and ρ satisfy the differential equation at each point in time. Of course ρ would have to have derivatives up to third order at each point in the interval.

Exercise: Considering the differential equation above, argue why many output responses, ρ, will be paired with any one input segment, ω.◆

An IORO, as we have shown, summarizes what can be known about the system as a black box viewed externally. Two problems areas immediately suggest themselves. First we have the problem of *going from structure to behavior:* If we know what lies inside the box, we ought to be able to describe, in one or the other way, the behavior of the box as viewed externally. The second area relates to the reverse situation—*going from behavior to structure:* the problem of trying to infer the internal structure of a black box from external observations.

The first problem is a recurrent theme of this chapter. Each time we introduce a new, more structured level of system description, we show to convert such a description into a description at a less structured level. Hence by a number of steps one may always convert a higher level structural description into one at the I/O relation observation level. The problem in the behavior-to-structure direction is more difficult and the reader is refered to Chapter 15 of TMS76 book.

5.5 I/O Function Observation

The I/O relation observation just introduced associates a set of output segments with allowable input segments. The output segments make up the possible system responses for the possible stimuli of the system. Depending on its inner (unknown) state, the system may respond with different output segments to a particular input segment. The system response is ambiguous when observed externally, since it depends on the inner state information. In this section we develop concepts to characterize a system's initial state that will allow us to uniquely determine the transformation of input segments to output segments.

Starting with an I/O relation observation, suppose we have a means that allows us to record just as much of a system needed to uniquely associate one output segment with a particular input segment. We call this information the *initial state.* With this information we can partition the relation R into a set of functions $F = \{f_1, f_2, \ldots f_i \ldots\}$ such that for each input segment ω, each function f_i produces one unique output segment $\rho = f_i(\omega)$. In effect then, these functions represent the initial state information. Given an input segment and an initial state in the form of one of the functions, the system response is unambiguously defined.

In this sense we define an I/O function observation (IOFO) to be a structure

$$\text{IOFO} = (T, X, \Omega, Y, F),$$

where T, X, Y, Ω are the same as for IORO and F is a set of I/O functions with the constraint that

$$f \in F \Rightarrow f \subseteq \Omega \times (Y, T) \text{ is a function,}$$

and if $\rho = f(\omega)$, then $\text{dom}(\rho) = \text{dom}(\omega)$.

Note that f may be a partial function, that is, for some segments ω, $f(\omega)$ need not be defined, or equivalently, there is no pair of the form $(\omega, f(\omega))$.

Given an IOFO (T, X, Ω, Y, F), we associate with it an IORO (T, X, Ω, Y, R), where

$$R = \bigcup_{f \in F} f.$$

In other words, by collecting together all the I/O segment pairs that were formerly partitioned into functional groupings, we obtain an I/O relation. In this process we lose the information about which individual functions were so united. This is what we would expect, since the IOFO represents a higher level of knowledge than the IORO.

Example: In the case of behavior described by a differential equation such as

$$\frac{d^3y}{dt^3} + \frac{2d^2y}{dt^2} + \frac{8dy}{dt} + 7y = x$$

it is well known how to characterize an appropriate set of I/O functions. In our example, we have an IOFO (T, X, Ω, Y, F), where T, X, Ω, Y are as in the IORO, and

$$F = \{f_{a,b,c} \mid a, b, c \in \Re\},$$

where $f_{a,b,c}: \Omega \to (Y, T)$ is defined by

$$f_{a,b,c}(\omega) = \rho$$

where $\frac{d^3\rho(t)}{dt^3} + \frac{2d^2\rho(t)}{dt^2} + \frac{8d\rho(t)}{dt} + 7\rho(t) = \omega(t)$ for $t \in \text{dom}(\omega) = \text{dom}(\rho) = <t_1, t_2>$ and

$$\frac{d^2\rho(t_1)}{dt^2} = a, \; \frac{d\rho(t_1)}{dt} = b, \; \rho(t_1) = c.$$

In general, given a differential equation operator L of order n, we require n parameters to specify an I/O function, corresponding to the specification of the initial values of the derivatives

$$\frac{d^{n-1}y}{dt^{n-1}}, \ldots, \frac{dy}{dt}, y.$$

Exercise: Given a differential operator L of order n, define the corresponding IOFO.◆

5.6 I/O System

At the IOFO level of system description we have knowledge of the initial state of the system in the sense that if it is in a state represented by f, then the input segment ω will yield a unique response $f(\omega)$. Note that at this level we are able to observe the initial state of the system (before the experiment), but not its immediate and final states. This section now extends these concepts and develops *the I/O system* as our most basic concept of a "system." This will

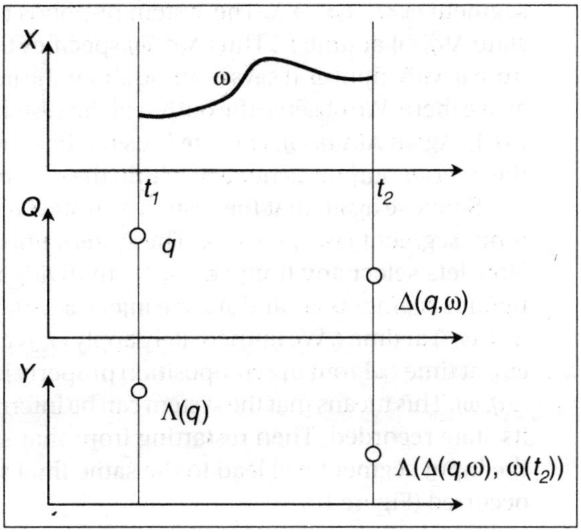

Figure 9 The basic system functions.

employ a state set and state transition function for modeling the interior of a system. The state set is fundamental, as it has to have the property to summarize the past of the system such that the future is uniquely determined by the current state and the future input. This property of the state set is called the *semigroup* or *composition property*.

The notion of concatenation of segments as defined in Section 5.2 allows us to formalize how we perform successive experiments on a system. We employ sets of segments closed under concatenation as our input segments. Thus, if we consider the injection of contiguous segments ω and ω′ separately, we can consider the concatenation ω • ω′ also.

So equipped, we are ready to formulate the input/output system as

$$S = (T, X, \Omega, Y, Q, \Delta, \Lambda)$$

where T, X, Y, and Ω are the same as before and

Q is a set, the *set of states*

$\Delta: Q \times \Omega \rightarrow Q$ is the *global state transition function*

$\Lambda: Q \times X \rightarrow Y$ (or $\Lambda: Q \rightarrow Y$) is the *output function*[2],

subject to the following constraints:

1. *Closure property.* Ω is closed under concatenation as well as under left segmentation
2. *Composition (or semigroup) property.* For every pair of contiguous input segments $\omega, \omega' \in \Omega$ $\Delta(q, \omega \bullet \omega') = \Delta((\Delta(q, \omega)), \omega')$.

The interpretation of the functions Δ and Λ is as illustrated in Fig. 9. Suppose that the system is in state $q \in Q$ at time $t_1 < t$ and we inject an input

[2] The output function Λ might be a function of state and input or only a function of state.

segment ω:$<t_1, t_2> \rightarrow X$. The system responds to this segment and finishes in state $\Delta(q, \omega)$ at time t_2. Thus $\Delta(q, \omega)$ specifies the *final* state reached starting from q with input ω. It says nothing about the intermediate states traversed to arrive there. We observe the output of the system at time t_2, which is $\Lambda(\Delta(q, \omega), \omega(t_2))$. Again $\Lambda(\Delta(q, \omega), \omega(t_2))$ tells us the final output only and nothing about the interior outputs generated within the observation interval $<t_1, t_2>$.

Suppose again that the system is in state $q \in Q$ at time t_1 and we inject an input segment ω:$<t_1, t_2> \rightarrow X$. The system finishes in state $\Delta(q, \omega)$ at time t_2. Now lets select any time $t \in <t_1, t_2>$ to divide the segment ω into two contiguous segments $\omega_{t>}$ and $\omega_{<t}$. We inject $\omega_{t>}$: $<t_1, t> \rightarrow X$ which transfers q into $\Delta(q, \omega_{t>})$ at time t. We immediately apply $\omega_{<t}$:$<t, t_2> \rightarrow X$ and reach $\Delta(\Delta(q, \omega_{t>}), \omega_{<t})$ at time t_2. From the composition property it follows that $\Delta(\Delta(q, \omega_{t>}), \omega_{<t}) = \Delta(q, \omega)$. This means that the system can be interrupted at any point in time and its state recorded. Then restarting from that state with the continuation of the input segment will lead to the same final state as if no interruption had occurred (Figure 10).

5.6.1 Going from System Structure to Behavior

Having an internal structure of a system, we ought to be able to generate its behavior. In terms of the knowledge levels, given the I/O system structure S, we ought to be able to associate with S an I/O function observation and an I/O relation observation that are complete in the sense of containing all possibly observable input/output pairs.

To do this we have to be able to describe the time course of state and output values in response to an input segment along the entire observation period. The global state transition function, however, only determines the final state after an input segment is applied and it says nothing about the intermediate states. However, since admissible input segments of I/O systems are closed under left segmentation, we are able to define a unique *state* and *output trajectory* given an input segment and an *initial state.*

For every $q \in Q$ and for every $\omega \in \Omega$, ω:$<t_1, t_2> \rightarrow X$, we define

$$\text{STRAJ}_{q,\omega}: <t_1, t_2> \rightarrow Q,$$

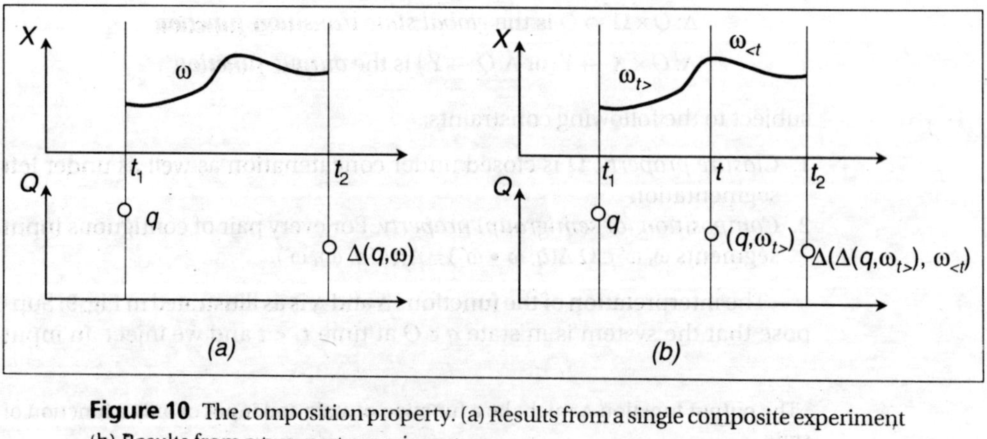

Figure 10 The composition property. (a) Results from a single composite experiment (b) Results from a two-part experiment.

with

$$\text{STRAJ}_{q,\omega}(t) = \Delta(q, \omega_{t>}) \text{ for all } t \in <t_1, t_2>,$$

and

$$\text{OTRAJ}_{q,\omega}: <t_1, t_2> \to Y,$$

with

$$\text{OTRAJ}_{q,\omega}(t) = \Lambda(\text{STRAJ}_{q,\omega}(t), \omega(t)) \text{ for all } t \in <t_1, t_2>.$$

Figure 11 demonstrates the relation between ω, $\text{STRAJ}_{q,\omega}$, and $\text{OTRAJ}_{q,\omega}$. Given an input trajectory ω that is left segmentable, we are in the position to compute the state value as it moves from initial state to final state. From the state value and input at every time point, we can directly compute the output value.

Now with each state $q \in Q$ we can associate a function $\tilde{\beta}_q: \Omega \to (Y, T)$, called *the I/O function of state q*, where for each $\omega \in \Omega$,

$$\tilde{\beta}_q(\omega) = \text{OTRAJ}_{q,\omega}.$$

The set of functions $\tilde{\beta}_S = \{\tilde{\beta}_q \mid q \in Q\}$ is called the *I/O behavior of S*. Thus, with an I/O system $S = (T, X, \Omega, Y, Q, \Delta, \Lambda)$ we associate the I/O function observation $\text{IOFO}_S = (T, X, \Omega, Y, \tilde{\beta}_S)$.

By the union of all functions $\tilde{\beta}_q \in \tilde{\beta}_S$ we derive the I/O relation observation $\text{IORO}_S = (T, X, \Omega, Y, R_S)$ associated with S, where

$$R_S = \{(\omega, \rho) \mid \omega \in \Omega,\ \rho = \text{OTRAJ}_{q,\omega}, q \in Q\}.$$

With each state $q \in Q$, we can also associate a function $\beta: \Omega \to Y$, called the *final output* function of state *q*, where for each $\omega \in \Omega$,

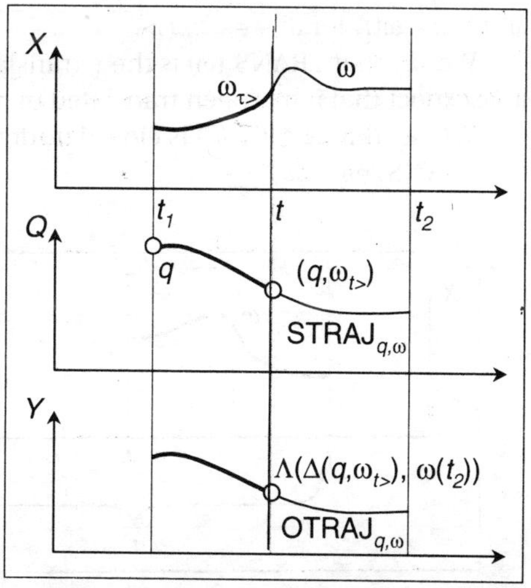

Figure 11 Generation of state and output trajectories.

$$\beta_q(\omega) = \Lambda(\Delta(q,\omega)).$$

The relationship between $\tilde{\beta}_q$ and β_q is given by

$$\beta_q(\omega_{t>}) = \tilde{\beta}_q(\omega)(t) \qquad \text{for } t \in \text{dom}(\omega).$$

Exercise: Prove this.◆

Knowing either one of the functions $\tilde{\beta}_q$ or β_q is tantamount to knowing the other one. Thus the set of functions $B_S = \{\beta_q \mid q \in Q\}$ carries the same information as the set $\tilde{B}_S$.

Exercise: Show how to define $\tilde{\beta}_q$ given β_q.◆

To summarize, given a system description $S = (T, X, \Omega, Y, Q, \Delta, \Lambda)$ we can always define the observable behavior it can produce. This behavior can be observed at two levels. If we have *no access* to the initial state of the system at the beginning of an experiment, we can collect the I/O pairs in R_S. If we *know* the initial state, we can separate the I/O pairs into functional relations, indexed by initial states, thus obtaining the set of functions $\tilde{B}_S$ or the related set B_S.

5.6.2 Time-Invariant Systems

Until now we have not automatically allowed ourselves the freedom of sliding a segment around so that if $\omega: <t_1, t_2> \to X$ is applicable at time t_1, for example, we can also apply it at some other time t_3. To formalize this idea, we consider a class of unary operators on (X, T) called "translation" operators.

For each $\tau \in T$, we define a unary operator on segments

$$\text{TRANS}_\tau: (X,T) \to (X,T),$$

where if $\omega: <t_1, t_2> \to X$ and $\text{TRANS}_\tau(\omega) = \omega'$, then $\omega': <t_1 + \tau, t_2 + \tau> \to X$ and $\omega'(t + \tau) = \omega(t)$ for all $t \in <t_1, t_2>$.

We say that $\text{TRANS}_\tau(\omega)$ is the τ-translate of ω and it has the same shape as ω expect that it has been translated by τ time units, as in Fig. 12.

We say that $\Omega \subseteq (X, T)$ is closed under translation if $\omega \in \Omega \Rightarrow$ for every $\tau \in T$, $\text{TRANS}_\tau(\omega) \in \Omega$.

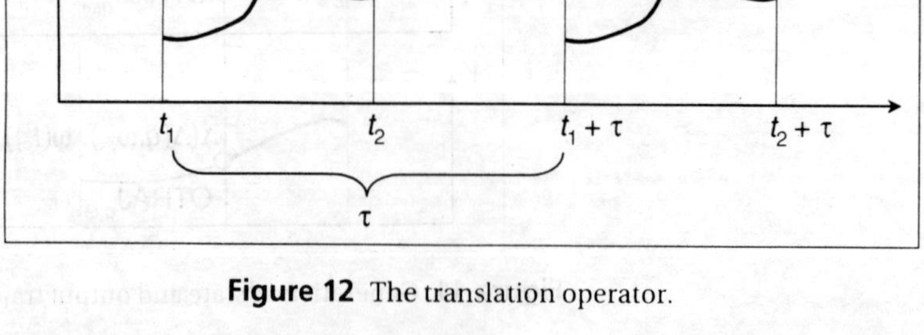

Figure 12 The translation operator.

Having the notion of translation of segments, we can now formally define time-invariant systems. A system $S = (T, X, \Omega, Y, Q, \Delta, \Lambda)$ is *time invariant* if

(a) Ω is *closed under translation*.
(b) Δ is *time independent*: For every $\tau \in T$, $\omega \in \Omega$, and $q \in Q$

$$\Delta(q,\omega) = \Delta(q, \mathrm{TRANS}_\tau(\omega)).$$

For a time-invariant system, if a segment can be applied somewhere in time, it can be applied anywhere in time. Moreover, anywhere the same-shaped segment is applied to the same initial state, the same result will be achieved.

From here on, we restrict our treatment to time-invariant systems. Most of our concepts carry through to time-varying systems, perhaps with some modification, but the time invariance enables certain simplifications in notation that make exposition more straightforward.

Since for time invariant systems S, Ω is closed under translation, all segments can be represented by those beginning at some particular time—we pick $0 \in T$.

Formally, for $\omega{:}<t_1, t_2> \rightarrow X$ let the standard translation of ω, $\mathrm{STR}(\omega) = \mathrm{TRANS}_{-t_1}(\omega)$. Then $\mathrm{STR}(\omega)$ is the translate of ω beginning at 0 ($\mathrm{STR}(\omega){:}<0, t_2 - t_1> \rightarrow X$). Let $\Omega_0 = \mathrm{STR}(\Omega) = \{\mathrm{STR}(\omega) | \omega \in \Omega\}$. Then Ω_0 is the set of all segments beginning at zero.

Exercise: Show that Ω is the translation closure of Ω_0 (i.e., the least set containing Ω_0 and closed under translation).◆

Recall the concatenation operator on segments from Section 5.2. With the concatenation operator it is possible to compose two contiguous segments. Here we define a natural extension of the concatenation operator for elements of Ω_0. When two segments beginning at zero are concatenated we translate the second so that it is contiguous to the first and then use the original concatenation operator.

Formally, we define the *concatenation operation* $\bullet_0$: $\Omega_0 \times \Omega_0 \rightarrow \Omega_0$ by

$$\omega \bullet_0 \omega' = \omega_1 \bullet_0 TRANS_{l(\omega)}(\omega')$$

for all $\omega, \omega' \in \Omega_0$, and $l(\omega)$ is the length of ω (Section 5.2). The $\bullet_0$ is illustrated in Fig. 13. Usually, for $\omega \bullet_0 \omega'$ we write $\omega \bullet \omega'$ or just $\omega\omega'$, when the context is clear.

Since Δ is time independent, it can be fully defined simply be specifying its values for all segments in Ω_0 and we can introduce a shorthand form for specifying time-invariant systems. A *time-invariant system* in short form is a structure

$$S_0 = (T, X, \Omega_0, Y, Q, \Delta_0, \Lambda),$$

where T, X, Y, Q, and Λ are the same as before but Ω_0 is the set of segments beginning at time 0 and Δ_0: $Q \times \Omega_0 \rightarrow Q$ satisfies the composition property: For all $q \in Q$, $\omega, \omega' \in \Omega_0$,

$$\Delta_0(q, \omega \bullet \omega') = \Delta_0(\Delta_0(q,\omega), \omega').$$

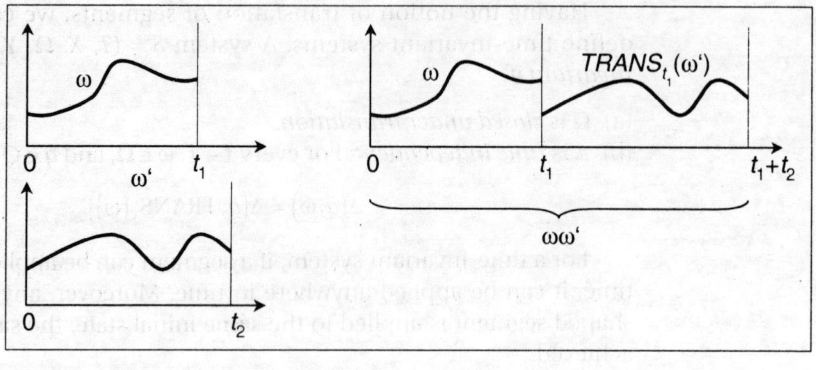

Figure 13 Composition of segments beginning at zero. The second segment is translated so that it is contiguous to the first.

The expanded form of S_0 is the structure

$$S = (T, X, \Omega, Y, Q, \Delta, \Lambda),$$

where Ω is the translation closure of Ω_0 and $\Delta: Q \times \Omega \to Q$ is defined by

$$\Delta(q, \omega) = \Delta_0(q, \mathrm{STR}(\omega)) \qquad \text{for all } q \in Q, \omega \in \Omega.$$

Example: *Linear Systems.*

Let $S^{cont}_{A,B,C} = (T, X, \Omega_0, Y, Q, \Delta_0, \Lambda)$, where X, Q, Y are finite-dimensional vector spaces over $\Re$; $T = \Re$; Ω_0 is the set of bpc segments beginning at 0; $\Delta_0: Q \times \Omega_0 \to Q$ is given by

$$\Delta_0(q, \omega) = \exp(Al(\omega))q + \int_0^{l(\omega)} \exp(A(l(\omega) - \tau))\, B\omega(\tau)d\tau;$$

and Λ: $Q \to Y$ is given by

$$\Lambda(q) = Cq,$$

where

$$A: Q \to Q$$

$$B: X \to Q$$

$$C: Q \to Y$$

are linear transformations. In addition,

$$\exp(A) = e^A = \sum_{i=0}^{\infty} A^i\ i!,$$

where $A^0 = I$, $A^{i+1} = A \cdot A^i$.

Let $S^{discr}_{A,B,C,F} = (T, X, \Omega_0, Y, Q, \Delta_0, \Lambda)$, where X, Q, Y are finite-dimensional vector spaces over a field F; $T = \Im$; $\Omega_0 = (X, T)_0$; $\Delta_0: Q \times \Omega_0 \to Q$ is given by

$$\Delta_0(q, \omega) = A^{i(\omega)}q + \sum_{i=0}^{l(\omega)-1} A^{l(\omega)-1-i} B\omega(i);$$

and $\Lambda: Q \rightarrow Y$ is given by

$$\Lambda(q) = Cq.$$

Exercise: Show that $S^{cont}_{A,B,C}$ and $S^{discr}_{A,B,C,F}$ are systems in short form and provide the corresponding expanded versions.◆

We say that $S^{cont}_{A,B,C}$ is the linear continuous time system specified by {*A, B, C*}. Similarly, $S^{discr}_{A,B,C,F}$ is the linear discrete time system specified by {*A, B, C, F*}.

Since we are restricting our attention to time-invariant systems, we henceforth work only with systems in time-invariant form. Moreover, we drop the subscript zeros in the descriptions.

5.6.3 Special Cases: Input-Free and Memoryless Systems

Defining additional constraints on the elements of a I/O system allows us to derive systems that have special properties. As we introduce system formalism in the following chapters, we will employ this procedure extensively. In the following sections, however, we discuss special types of systems that are of general interest independent from the particular formalism in hand.

Input-Free Systems

By omitting the input set, we obtain a subclass of systems that cannot respond to input segments. These *input-free* systems are sometimes called *autonomous.* Such a system has the structure

$$S = (T, Y, Q, \Delta, \Lambda),$$

with

$\Delta: Q \rightarrow Q$ is the *global state transition function*

$\Lambda: Q \rightarrow Y$ is the *output function.*

The behavior, and other properties, that are defined for dynamic systems can also be defined for input-free systems. To do this, we extend the input-free structure to a full system structure by considering the input set to be a single-element set.

Exercise: Define the trajectories and the behavior on an input-free system by specializing these concepts for a corresponding system with a single-element input set. Show that the latter system satisfies the closure and semigroup properties required to be a system.◆

Input-free systems generate a unique output segment given a unique initial state. This means that given the initial state, the response of the system is uniquely determined.

Exercise: Prove this.

Input-free systems are often used as generators for input signals of other systems, in particular for the generation of test segments in experimental frames.◆

Memoryless Systems

Instead of omitting the input set, we can also omit the state set. Such systems are static rather than dynamic. Their state set degenerates to a single element, which can be omitted entirely. Hence, we do not have a state transition function and the output function is a function of time and input only. The output is unambiguously determined by the current input. For this reason, they are often called *function specified systems.* We will use function systems together with differential equation specified and discrete time specified systems. Such specifications will be degenerated differential equation or discrete time systems.

A *function specified system* is a structure

$$\mathrm{FNSS} = (X, Y, \lambda)$$

where

X is the set of inputs

Y is the set of outputs

$\lambda: X \to Y$ is the output function.

The function specified system is extended to a full I/O system specification dependent on the context employed in the following way. The time base T of a function specified system is arbitrary and is taken to be continuous when the function specified system is employed together with a differential equation specified system and discrete when employed together with a discrete time specified system. For the state set Q we take a single element 0. With that, the state transition function degenerates to a constant function always yielding 0, i.e., $\Delta(0, \omega[t_1, t)) = 0$ for all $\omega \in (X, T)$, all $t \in \mathrm{dom}(\omega)$.

5.7 Iterative Specification of Systems

I/O systems describe system behavior with a global transition function that determines the final state given the initial state and the applied input segment. Since input segments are left segmentable and closed under composition, we are able to generate the state and output values along the entire input interval. However, such an approach is not very practical. What we need is a way to generate state and output trajectories in an iterative way going from one state along the trajectory to the next.

Iterative specification of systems is a general scheme for defining systems by iterative applications of *generator segments.* These are elementary segments from which all input segments of a system can be generated. Having such a concept we define a *generator state transition function* and iteratively apply generator segments to the generator state transition function. The results produced by the generator state transitions constitute the state trajectory for the input segment resulting from the composition of the generator segments.

The general scheme of iterative specification to be discussed here forms a basis for more specialized types of specifications of systems. System specification formalisms to be introduced in the subsequent chapters are special forms of iterative specifications with their special type of generator segments and generator state transition functions.

5.7.1 Generator Segments

Consider (Z, T) the set of all segments $\{\omega\text{: } <0, t_1> \to Z \mid t_1 \in T\}$, which is a semigroup under concatenation.

For a subset Γ of (Z, T), we designate by Γ^+ the *concatenation closure* of Γ (also called the *semigroup generated* by Γ). Then Γ^+ can be constructed as follows. Let $\Gamma^1 = \Gamma$ and let $\Gamma^{i+1} = \Gamma^i \bullet \Gamma = \{\omega\omega' \mid \omega \in \Gamma^i \text{ and } \omega' \in \Gamma\}$. Then

$$\Gamma^+ = \bigcup_{i \in \mathfrak{I}^+} \Gamma^i.$$

The proof is subject of the following exercise.

Exercise: Show that $\Gamma^i = \{\omega_1, \omega_2, \ldots, \omega_i \mid \omega_j \in \Gamma \text{ for } j = 1, \ldots, i\}$. Then show that as the least semigroup containing Γ, Γ^+ is included within $\bigcup_{i \in \mathfrak{I}^+} \Gamma^i$. On the other hand, since Γ^+ contains Γ, it also contains Γ^2; hence by induction $\Gamma^2, \Gamma^3, \ldots, \Gamma^i$ for each $i \in \mathfrak{I}^+$, and

$$\bigcup_{i \in \mathfrak{I}^+} \Gamma^i \subseteq \Gamma^+.$$

Conclude that

$$\Gamma^+ = \bigcup_{i \in \mathfrak{I}^+} \Gamma^i.$$

◆

Example: Consider the following set of segments:

1. bc = bounded continuous segments.
2. CONST = $\{a_\tau \mid \tau > 0, a_\tau(t) = a \text{ for } t \in <0,\tau>, a \in \Re\}$ (constant segments of variable length).
3. $\{\omega\}$ where ω is a segment.

Exercise: Show that bc generates bpc (bounded piecewise continuous), CONST generates the piecewise constant segments over $\Re$, and $\{\omega\}$ generates periodic segments with period $l(\omega)$.◆

Now given a set of segments Ω, we are interested in finding a set Γ with the property that $\Gamma^+ = \Omega$. If Γ has this property, we say it is a *set of generators for* Ω or that Γ *generates* Ω.

We say that $\omega_1, \omega_2, \ldots, \omega_n$ is a *decomposition of* ω by Γ if $\omega_i \in \Gamma$ for each $i = 1, \ldots, n$ and $\omega = \omega_1 \bullet \omega_2 \bullet \cdots \bullet \omega_n$.

It happens in general that if Γ generates Ω, we *cannot* expect each $\omega \in \Omega$ to have a unique decomposition by Γ; that is, there may be distinct decompositions $\omega_1, \omega_2, \ldots, \omega_n$ and $\omega_1', \omega_2', \ldots, \omega_n'$ such that $\omega_1 \bullet \omega_2 \bullet \cdots \bullet \omega_n = \omega$ and $\omega_1' \bullet \omega_2' \bullet \cdots \bullet \omega_n' = \omega$.

Exercise: Show that unique decompositions exist in case of $\{\omega\}$ but not in cases bc and CONST. Consider what properties Γ might have to ensure that each $\omega \in \Gamma^+$ has a unique decomposition.◆

Of the many possible decompositions, we are interested in selecting a single representative, or *canonical* decomposition. We go about selecting such a decomposition by a process called *maximal length segmentation.* First we find ω_1, the longest generator in Γ that is also a left segment of ω. This process is repeated with what remains of ω after ω_1 is removed, generating ω_2, and so on. If the process stops after n repetitions, then $\omega = \omega_1\omega_2 \ldots \omega_n$, and $\omega_1, \omega_2, \ldots, \omega_n$ is the decomposition sought.

We call a decomposition obtained by this process a *maximal length segment* (mls) decomposition.

More formally, a decomposition $\omega_1, \omega_2, \ldots, \omega_n$ is an *mls decomposition* of ω by Γ if for each $i = 1, \ldots, n$, $\omega' \in \Gamma$ is a left segment of $\omega_i \bullet \omega_{i+1} \ldots \omega_n$, $\Rightarrow \omega'$ is a left segment of ω_i. In other words, for each i, ω_i is the longest generator in Γ that is a left segment of $\omega_i \ldots \omega_n$.

It is not necessarily the case that mls decompositions exist (i.e., that the just-mentioned processes will stop after a finite number of repetitions). Thus, we are interested in checkable conditions on a set of generators that will guarantee that each segment generated has an mls decomposition.

Exercise: Let $\Gamma = \{a_{t_1} 0_{t_2} | t_1, t_2 > 0\} \cup \{a_{t_1}0_{t_2}a_{t_3} | t_1, t_2, t_3 > 0\}$, Show that $a_{t_1}0_{t_2}a_{t_3}0_{t_4} \in \Gamma^+$ but has no mls decomposition.◆

Fortunately, a segment can have at most one mls decomposition.

Exercise: Show that ω_1 is a left segment of ω_1' and ω_1' is a left segment of ω_1 if and only if $\omega_1 = \omega_j'$. Hence, show that if w has a mls decomposition by Γ, it is unique.◆

Let us say that Γ is an *admissible* set of generators for Ω if Γ generates Ω and for each $\omega \in \Omega$, a unique mls decomposition of ω by Γ exists. (We also say Γ admissibly generates Ω.)

We now provide a set of conditions guaranteeing that Γ is an admissible set of generators. It should be noted that these conditions are too strong in some cases—for example, when all segments have unique decompositions. We provide a weaker set of conditions in Section 5.7.2.

Exercise: Check whether conditions *a* and *b* of the following theorem hold for bc, CONST. $\{\omega\}$.◆

***Theorem 1** Sufficient Conditions for Admissibility*

If Γ satisfies the following conditions, it admissibly generates Γ^+:

(a) Existence of longest segments:

$$\omega \in \Gamma^+ \Rightarrow \max\left\{t \,\middle|\, \omega_{t>} \in \Gamma\right\} \text{ exists}$$

(b) Closure under right segmentation:

$$\omega \in \Gamma \Rightarrow \omega_{<t} \in \Gamma \qquad \text{for all } \tau \in \mathrm{dom}(\omega)$$

Proof. In our proof by induction, the parameter of the induction is the length of a decomposition—a decomposition $\omega_1, \omega_2, \ldots, \omega_n$ of ω by Γ is said to have length n, the number of generators in it. The induction statement is

$P(n) \equiv$ [ω has a decomposition by Γ of length $n \Rightarrow \omega$ has an mls decomposition by Γ of length n or less]

To establish $P(1)$, the basis case, note that "ω has a decomposition by Γ of length 1" implies $\omega \in \Gamma$ (i.e., ω is itself a generator). It follows directly that ω is an mls decomposition by Γ of itself of length 1.

Exercise: Show that ω is an mls decomposition by Γ of itself, having length 1.◆

For the inductive step, assume $P(i)$ true for all $i < n$. We must show that $P(n)$ follows. As in Fig. 14, let ω have a decomposition $\omega_1, \omega_2, \ldots, \omega_n$ by Γ of length n. We wish to resegment ω to obtain an mls decomposition $\omega'_1, \omega'_2, \omega'_3, \ldots, \omega'_m$ with $m < n$. Let us call the points $t_0, t_1, t_2, \ldots, t_n$ the breakpoints of the decomposition $\omega_1, \omega_2, \omega_3, \ldots, \omega_n$ (i.e., $\omega_1 = \omega_{t_1>}$), $\omega_2 = \omega\,|_{<t_1, t_2>}$, etc.).

Let t'_1 be the greatest value of t such that $\omega_{t>} \in \Gamma$; this exists by condition *a* of the hypothesis of Theorem 1. Then t'_1 is the first breakpoint of the mls decomposition and $\omega'_1 = \omega_{t'_1>}$ (by construction, ω'_1 is the longest generator in Γ that is a left segment of ω).

Let k be the integer such that $t_k \leq t'_1 < t_{k-1}$. Note that $k \geq 1$, since ω_1 is a generator in Γ which is a left segment of ω and as the longest such segment, ω'_1 is at least as long as ω_1 ($k = 2$ in Fig. 14).

Now ω_k is split by t'_1 into left and right segments, call these γ and μ, respectively. By condition b, μ is a generator in Γ. Now $\mu \in \Gamma$ and $\omega_{k+2}\,\omega_{k+3} \ldots \omega_n \in \Gamma^+$, which means that the right segment of ω caused by t'_1, namely $\omega_{<t'_1} = \mu \bullet \omega_{k+2} \bullet \omega_{k+3} \ldots \omega_n$ (by the postulated property of composition that composition of left and right subsegments of a segment yields the original). Thus, $\mu, \omega_{k+2}, \ldots, \omega_n$ is a decomposition of $\omega_{<t'_1}$ of length $n - (k+1) + 1 = n - k$. Since $k \geq 1$, $n - k \leq n - 1$, and we can employ $P(n-k)$ to obtain an mls decomposition by Γ of $\omega_{<t_1}$ of length $n - k$ or less; call it $\bar{\omega}_1, \bar{\omega}_2, \ldots, \bar{\omega}_{\bar{m}}$ (where $\bar{m} \leq n - k$). We now claim that $\omega'_1, \bar{\omega}_1, \bar{\omega}_2, \ldots, \bar{\omega}_{\bar{m}}$ is the desired mls decomposition of ω of length $m < n$.

First $\omega'_1 \bullet \bar{\omega}_1 \ldots \bar{\omega}_{\bar{m}} = \omega_{t'_1>} \bullet \omega_{<t'_1} = \omega$ (composition of left and right segments); thus $\omega'_1, \bar{\omega}_1, \ldots, \bar{\omega}_{\bar{m}}$ is a decomposition of ω by Γ.

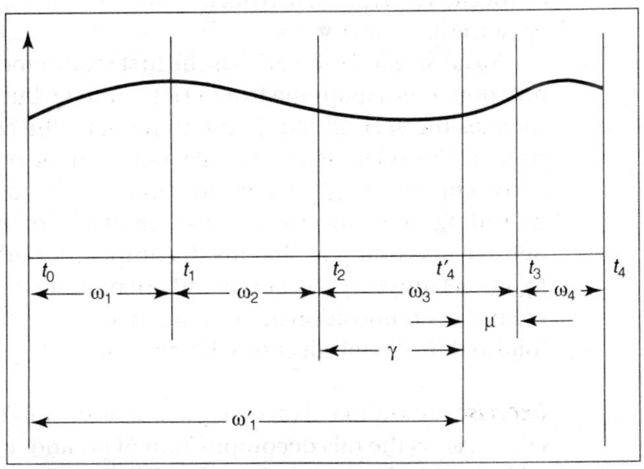

Figure 14 Initial segment of mls decomposition.

Second, ω_1' is an mls segment and $\bar{\omega}_1, \bar{\omega}_2, \ldots, \bar{\omega}_{\bar{m}}$ is an mls decomposition of $\omega_{<t_1'}$; thus $\omega_1', \bar{\omega}_1, \ldots, \bar{\omega}_{\bar{m}}$ is an mls decomposition of ω.

Third, $\omega_1', \bar{\omega}_1, \ldots, \bar{\omega}_{\bar{m}}$ has length $m = 1 + \bar{m} \leq 1 + n - k \leq n$ as required.

Having shown $P(n)$, we are entitled by the induction scheme to assert that $P(i)$ is true for all $i = 1, 2, \ldots$. But this means that every $\omega \in \Gamma^+$ has an mls decomposition, since $\omega \in \Gamma^+$ implies $\omega \in \Gamma^i$ for some $i = 1, 2, \ldots$, and then $P(i)$ applies to ω. By a previous exercise, the mls decomposition is unique and thus the theorem is established.

5.7.2 Generator State Transition Systems

Having established a terminating process for obtaining mls decompositions, we wish to use these decompositions to help us generate a transition function given only that function's action on the generators. In other words, let Ω_G be an admissible generating set for Ω and suppose we have defined a function $\delta: Q \times \Omega_G \to Q$, which we call a *single segment transition function.*

Let $\omega_1, \omega_2, \ldots, \omega_n$ be the mls decomposition of ω. Having δ defined for each segment ω_i, we wish to piece together these parts to obtain compound transition associated with ω itself. We do this by iteration: if q_0 is the initial state, $q_1 = \delta(q_0, \omega_1)$ is the state after injecting ω_1, $q_2 = \delta(q_1, \omega_2)$ is the state after injecting ω_2, and so on.

Formally, we define a function $\delta^+: Q \times \Omega_G^+ \to Q$, called the extension of δ to Ω_G^+ by

$$\begin{aligned} \delta^+(q,\omega) &= \delta(q,\omega) && \text{if } \omega \in \Omega_G \\ &= \delta^+(\delta(q,\omega_1), \omega_2 \bullet \cdots \bullet \omega_n) && \text{if } \omega \in \Omega_G^+, \end{aligned}$$

where $\omega_1 \bullet \omega_2 \bullet \cdots \bullet \omega_n$ is the mls decomposition for ω.

Exercise: Show by induction that δ^+ is well defined, that is, $\delta^+(q, \omega)$ exists and is unique for each $q \in Q, \omega \in \Omega_G^+$. Use (1) the uniqueness of mls decompositions, and (2) the fact that $\omega_1 \bullet \omega_2 \bullet \cdots \bullet \omega_n$ is the mls decomposition for ω, which implies that $\omega_i, \omega_{i+1}, \ldots, \omega_n$ is the mls decomposition for $\omega_i \bullet \omega_{i+1} \bullet \cdots \bullet \omega_n$ for each $i = 1, 2, \ldots, n$. In fact, show that $\delta^+(q, \omega_1 \bullet \omega_2 \bullet \cdots \bullet \omega_n) = \delta(\delta(\ldots\delta(\delta(q, \omega_1), \omega_2), \ldots), \omega_n)$.◆

So far so good—δ^+ satisfies the first requirement of a bona fide transition function: It is a mapping from $Q \times \Omega_G^+$ into Q. But this does not imply that it satisfies the second requirement, namely, the composition property. The reason? Consider Figure 10 once more. On the one hand, $\delta^+(q, \omega)$ is defined according to the mls decomposition of ω; $\delta^+(\delta^+(q, \omega), \omega')$ is then defined according to the mls decomposition of ω'. On the other hand $\delta^+(q, \omega\omega')$ is defined according to the mls decomposition of $\omega\omega'$. Although both $\delta^+(\delta^+(q, \omega), \omega')$ and $\delta^+(q, \omega\omega')$ exist and are unique, they need not be equal since the mls decomposition of $\omega\omega'$ is not necessarily the mls decomposition of ω followed by the mls decomposition of ω'.

Exercise: Show that if (a) $\omega_1, \omega_2, \ldots, \omega_n$ is the mls decomposition of ω, (b) $\omega_1', \omega_2', \ldots, \omega_n'$ is the mls decomposition of ω', and (c) $\omega_1, \omega_2, \ldots, \omega_n, \omega_1', \omega_2', \ldots, \omega_n'$ is the mls decomposition of $\omega\omega'$, then $\delta^+(\delta^+(q, \omega), \omega') = \delta^+(q, \omega\omega')$. In general, however, when ω is joined to ω', it may be possible to extend ω_n to a longer mls. The new mls may encompass part or all of ω′, thus displacing all its old breakpoints.◆

Thus we are led to seek conditions that will guarantee that δ^+ has the composition property. Having such conditions, we can employ Ω_G and δ as the basis for a system specification. Since other specification schemes are possible, and since iteration is the basis of the present scheme, we designate it *iterative specification.*

An *iterative specification* of a system is a structure

$$G = \langle T, X, \Omega_G, Y, Q, \delta, \lambda \rangle,$$

where *T, X, Y, Q* have the same interpretation as for I/O systems,

Ω_G is the set of input segment generators
$\delta: Q \times \Omega_G \to Q$ is the single segment state transition function
$\lambda: Q \times X \to Y$ is the output function,

with the restriction that $\Omega_G \subseteq (X, T)$ and, most important, Ω_G is an admissible set of generators and $\delta^+: Q \times \Omega_G^+ \to Q$ has the composition property.

With an iterative specification $G = \langle T, X, \Omega_G, Y, Q, \delta, \lambda \rangle$ we may associate a system $S_G = \langle T, X, \Omega_G^+, Y, Q, \delta^+, \lambda \rangle$.

We can provide a set of conditions guaranteeing that a structure is an iterative specification. Since these conditions are based on those for admissibility, they are not as weak as they might be. A weaker set of conditions can be found in the exercise following the theorem.

Theorem 2 *Sufficient Conditions for Iterative Specification*

Let $G = \langle T, X, \Omega_G, Y, Q, \delta, \lambda \rangle$ be a structure as just defined. Then if the following conditions hold, *G* is an iterative specification and S_G is a system.

(a) Existence of longest segments:

$$\omega \in \Omega_G^+ \Rightarrow \max\{t \mid \omega_{t>} \in \Omega_G\} \text{ exists}$$

(b) Closure under right segmentation:

$$\omega \in \Omega_G \Rightarrow \omega_{<t} \in \Omega_G \qquad \text{for } t \in \mathrm{dom}(\omega)$$

(c) Closure under left segmentation:

$$\omega \in \Omega_G \Rightarrow \omega_{t>} \in \Omega_G \qquad \text{for } t \in \mathrm{dom}(\omega)$$

(d) Consistency of composition:

$$\omega_1, \omega_2, \ldots, \omega_n \in \Omega_G \text{ and } \omega_1 \bullet \omega_2 \bullet \cdots \bullet \omega_n \in \Omega_G^+$$
$$\Rightarrow \quad \delta^+(q, \omega_1 \bullet \omega_2 \bullet \cdots \bullet \omega_n) = \delta(\delta(\ldots \delta(\delta(q, \omega_1), \omega_2), \ldots), \omega_n).$$

Proof. Requirements (a) and (b) were shown by the Theorem 1 in Section 5.7.1, to guarantee that Ω_G is admissible, which means that mls decompositions always exist. This in turn implies that $\delta^+: Q \times \Omega_G^+ \to Q$ is a well-defined function as required. Thus the theorem is established once we can show that δ^+ has the composition property. We do this as follows.

Let ω: $<0, \tau> \to X$ be a segment. A partition of $<0, \tau>$ is a finite subset $\{t_1, t_2, \ldots, t_n\}$ of $<0, \tau>$. A partition is said to be a *breakpoint partition* if its points form the breakpoints of a decomposition of ω by Ω_G, that is, if $t_1 < t_2 < \cdots < t_n$, for each $i = 1, \ldots, n-1$, $\omega_{<t_i, t_{i+1}>} \in \Omega_G$ (where $t_1 = 0$ and $t_n = \tau$).

A partition A refines a partition B if $B \subseteq A$ (so the intervals $<t_i, t_{i+1}>$ defined by B may be split up by A). The common refinement of partitions A and B is the partition $A \cup B$.

For breakpoint partition $\{t_1, t_2, \ldots, t_n\}$ we define $\delta^*_\omega(q, \{t_1, t_2, \ldots, t_n\}) = \delta(\ldots\delta(q, \omega_{<0,t_1>}), \ldots), \omega_{<t_n,\tau>})$, that is, the state reached starting from q and applying the successive subsegments of ω.

Lemma 1 If B is a breakpoint partition, any refinement of B is also a breakpoint partition.

Proof: Let A refine B. Then every interval $<t_i, t_{i+1}>$ due to B can be segmented further into intervals $<t_i, \tau_1>, <\tau_1, \tau_2>, \ldots, <\tau_n, t_{i+1}>$ due to A. Since B is a breakpoint partition, $\omega_{<t_i,t_{i+1}>} \in \Omega_G$, and since by hypotheses (a) and (b), Ω_G is left and right segmentable, the subsegments intervals $\omega_{<t_i,\tau_1>}, \omega_{<\tau_1,\tau_2>}, \ldots, \omega_{<\tau_n,t_{i+1}>}$ are all in Ω_G. Thus, A is a breakpoint partition.

Lemma 2 If A refines B and B is a breakpoint partition, $\delta^*_\omega(q, A) = \delta^*_\omega(q, B)$, for all $q \in Q$.

Proof: By Lemma 1, A is also a breakpoint partition. Moreover, from the requirement of composition consistency (part c), we have

$$\delta(q, \omega_{<ti,ti+1>}) = \delta(\ldots(\delta(q, \omega_{<t_i,\tau_1>}), \ldots), \omega_{<\tau_n,t_{i+1}>})$$

for any interval $<t_i, t_{i+1}>$ due to B and the fine intervals $<t_i, \tau_1>, <\tau_1, \tau_2>, \ldots, <\tau_n, t_{i+1}>$ due to A. By induction, it follows that $\delta^*_\omega(q, A) = \delta^*_\omega(q, B)$ for all $q \in Q$.

Exercise: Show that the equation in δ^*_ω is true.◆

Having these lemmas, we can complete the proof of Theorem 2. Let $\bar{A}$ be the breakpoint partition defined by the mls decomposition of $\omega\omega'$. Now notice that if $\omega_1, \omega_2, \ldots, \omega_n$ and $\omega'_1, \omega'_2, \ldots, \omega'_n$ are mls decompositions of ω and ω', respectively, then $\omega_1, \omega_2, \ldots, \omega_n, \omega'_1, \omega'_2, \ldots, \omega'_n$ is a decomposition (although not necessarily an mls decomposition!) of $\omega\omega'$. Let $\bar{B} = B_\omega \cup B_{\omega'}$ be the breakpoint partition defined by this decomposition, where B_ω and $B_{\omega'}$ are points in the domains of ω and ω', respectively. Then we have

$$\begin{aligned}
\delta^+(\delta^+(q,\omega), \omega') &= \delta^*_\omega(\delta^*_\omega(q, B_\omega), B_{\omega'}) && \text{(by definition)}\\
&= \delta^*_\omega(q, \bar{B}) && \text{(by an easy induction)}\\
&= \delta^*_\omega(q, \bar{A} \cup \bar{B}) && \text{(by Lemma 1)}\\
&= \delta^*_\omega(q, \bar{A}) && \text{(by Lemma 2)}\\
&= \delta^+(q, \omega\omega') && \text{(by definition)}
\end{aligned}$$

Exercise: Conditions (b) and (c), requiring left and right segementability in the definition of iterative specification, can be weakened while still enabling the theorem to be true. Replace (b) and (c) by

For $\omega \in \Omega_G^+$, if $\max t^\bullet = \max \{t | \omega_{t>} \in \Omega_G\}$ and $t_k < t^* < t_{k+1}$, then $\omega_{<t_k, t^*>} \in \Omega_G$ and $\omega_{<t^*, t_{k+1}>} \Omega_G^+$ (see Fig. 15).

Show that G is an iterative specification.◆

To summarize, an iterative specification G specifies a time invariant system S_G. Since we have already seen in Section 5.6.1 how to associate an I/O function set and an I/O relation with a system such as S_G, we can associate these objects with the specification G.

5.8 Multivariable Sets and Structured Systems

An I/O system as introduced in Section 5.6 specifies the sets and functions as abstract entities without any information about how these sets and functions are structured and realized. The I/O system is a general concept that allows us to represent and compare system specifications independently of any particular application and realization. We now show how additional knowledge can be introduced by recording not only the sets and functions, but also how these sets and functions arise from more primitive sets and functions. Each of the sets and functions can be made more concrete by being represented as crossproducts of more primitive sets and functions. This procedure takes a step toward a more concrete system representation, toward concrete structure. It is often used when a system has to be constructed out of an available set of primitive elements and elementary operators.

To discuss the idea, let us take a system S at the abstract I/O system level. Let's suppose we want the same system to be represented with sets being crossproducts of some primitive sets, e.g., Boolean set, and functions being crossproducts of some primitive functions, e.g., Boolean functions. This new system specification is at a higher level of specification since we not only know the abstract sets and behavior but also the structure of the sets and functions and how they arise from more primitive sets and functions. We call this a *multivariable* or *structured system.* Structured sets and functions are the system theoretic mechanism for representing the use of variables in modeling and simulation practice. To formally deal with multivariable systems, we introduce multivariable sets and functions in the following.

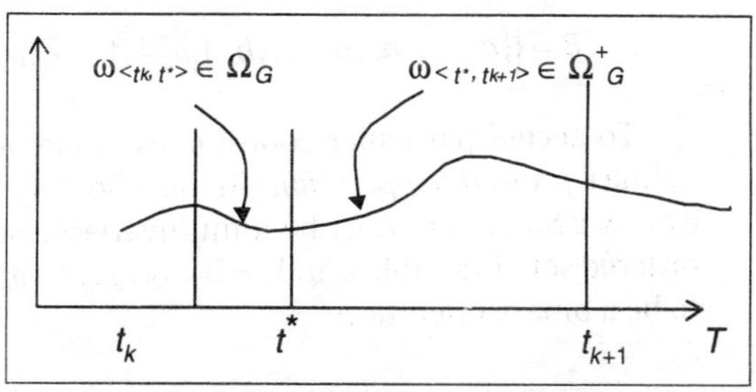

Figure 15 Relaxed conditions for Theorem 2.

The *crossproduct* S of sets $S_1, S_2, \ldots, S_n$ is given by

$$S = S_1 \times S_2 \times \cdots \times S_n = \{(s_1, s_2, \ldots, s_n) \mid s_1 \in S_1, s_2 \in S_2, \ldots, s_n \in S_n\}.$$

Furthermore, let V be an ordered set of n variables $V = (v_1, v_2, \ldots, v_n)$ and $S_1, S_2, \ldots, S_n$ n arbitrary sets. Then we define a *multi-variable* or *structured set*

$$S = (V, S_1 \times S_2 \times \cdots \times S_n)$$

to be a pair consisting of ordered set V of n variables and the crossproduct of sets $S_1, S_2, \ldots, S_n$ where each coordinate i is denoted by variable $v_i \in V$, i.e., for an element $s \in S$, $s = (s_1, s_2, \ldots, s_n)$, the value of v_i is equal to s_i. For notational convenience we usually will present multivariable sets by writing

$$S = \{(v_1, v_2, \ldots, v_n) \mid v_1 \in S_1, v_2 \in S_2, \ldots, v_n \in S_n\}.$$

The elements $(v_1, v_2, \ldots, v_n)$ are denoted *variables, coordinates,* or *ports,* depending on the set used (for input and output sets we will preferably speak of input and output ports while in connection with state sets we will speak of state variables). We use the operation *variables(S)* to retrieve the set of variables, i.e., *variables(S)* $= (v_1, v_2, \ldots, v_n)$. The set S_i is denoted the *range* of v_i and we also write $range_{vi}(S) = S_i$.

Example: Let V = (make, type, cost). Let $range_{make}$ = {*IBM, Apple, Sun, HP*}, $range_{type}$ = {*Home, PC, Workstation, Mainframe*} and $range_{cost} = \Im^+$ respectively. Then we define the multi-variable set *Computer* by

$$Computer = \{(make, type, cost) \mid make \in \{IBM, Apple, Sun, HP\},$$
$$type \in \{Home, PC, Workstation, Mainframe\}, cost \in \Im^+\}$$

with typical element (*IBM, PC, 2120*).

For multivariable sets we define in a straightforward way important set operations. So the crossproduct of multivariable sets is a multivariable set where all the coordinates are ordered in sequence. Given $A = \{(a_1, \ldots, a_n) \mid a_1 \in A_1, \ldots, a_n \in A_n\}$ and $B = \{(b_1, \ldots, b_m) \mid b_1 \in B_1, \ldots, b_m \in B_m\}$ being multivariable, then the crossproduct of A and B is defined by

$$A \times B = \{(a_1, \ldots, a_n, b_1, \ldots, b_m) \mid a_1 \in A_1, \ldots, a_n \in A_n, b_1 \in B_1, \ldots, b_m \in B_m\}.$$

To access particular coordinates of elements of multivariable sets we define a *projection operation* $\cdot$ in the following way: Let $S = \{(v_1, v_2, \ldots, v_n) \mid v_1 \in S_1, v_2 \in S_2, \ldots, v_n \in S_n\}$ be a multivariable set, $V = (v_1, v_2, \ldots, v_n)$ be the ordered set of variables, and $s = (s_1, s_2, \ldots, s_n)$ an element of S, then we define to be a binary operation

$$\cdot : S \times V \to \bigcup_{j=1}^{n} S_j \text{ with } s \cdot v_i = s_i.$$

For ordered subsets $(v_i, v_j, \ldots) \in V$ we extend the projection operation by

$$\cdot : S \times 2^V \to \bigcup_{v \in 2^V} \underset{j \in v}{\times} S_j \quad \text{with } s\cdot(v_i, v_j, \ldots) = s\cdot v_i, s\cdot v_j.$$

Example: Let s = *(IBM, PC, 2120)* be an element of set *Computer*, then *s·make* = *IBM*, *s·type* = *PC* and *s·* (type, *cost*) = *(PC, 2120)*.

A function $f: A \to B$ whose domain $A = \{(a_1, \ldots, a_n) \mid a_1 \in A_1, \ldots, a_n \in A_n\}$ and range $B = \{(b_1, \ldots, b_m) \mid b_1 \in B_1, \ldots, b_m \in B_m\}$ are multivariable sets is called a *multivariable function* or *structured function*. In the same way as we defined the *projection operation* for multivariable sets, we define a projection operation for multivariable functions by

$$f\cdot b_i : A \to ((b_i), B_i) \quad \text{with } f\cdot b_i(a) = f(a)\cdot b_i$$

or

$$f\cdot(b_i, b_j, \ldots) : \mathrm{A} \to ((b_i, b_j, \ldots), B_i \times B_j \times \ldots)$$
$$\text{with } f\cdot(b_i, b_j, \ldots)(a) = f(a)\cdot(b_i, b_j, \ldots).$$

This is also a multi-variable function, and we often also write f_{b_i} or $f_{(b_i, b_j, \ldots)}$.

An I/O system whose input, output, and state sets are multivariable sets and state transition function and output function are multivariable functions is called a *multivariable* or *structured I/O system.* Obviously, from a structured I/O system an I/O system is derived by omitting the coordination of the sets and functions.

Besides the I/O system level, it is reasonable to use multivariable sets and functions also at the other levels of system specifications. Analogously to I/O system, we speak of *structured* IORO, *structured* IOFO, and *structured* multi-component and *structured* coupled systems as introduced in the next sections.

5.9 Multicomponent System Specification

Complex systems are often best modeled by collections of interacting components. It is usually much easier to identify simple components, model them independently, and then model the way in which they interact than to try to describe the overall behavior directly. To describe a multicomponent system in this manner, one has to define the component systems and specify how these systems work together.

To provide formal means to specify a system as a set of interacting components, we introduce *multicomponent systems* in this section and *networks of systems* (also called *coupled systems)* in the next. Whereas in networks of system specification individual component system are coupled by connecting their input and output interfaces in a modular way, components of multicomponent systems influence each other directly through their state transition functions.

In a multicomponent system specification, the system is structured into a set of interacting components, each with its own set of states and state transition function. Each component may be influenced by some other components—its *influencers*—and may influence other components—its *influencees*—by its state transition function. Furthermore, each component's state also might be influenced by the input of the system and it may contribute the output of the system. However, in contrast to coupled systems, components at this level are not stand-alone system specifications and do not employ their own input and output interface.

A *multicomponent system* is a structure

$$MC = \langle T, X, \Omega, Y, D, \{M_d\} \rangle,$$

where T, X, Y, Ω are the same as for the I/O system and

D is a set, the *set of component references.*

For all $d \in D$

$$M_d = \langle Q_d, E_d, I_d, \Delta_d, \Lambda_d \rangle$$

is a component with

Q_d is the set of states of the component d

$I_d \subseteq D$ is the set components influencing d — its influencers

$E_d \subseteq D$ is the set components influenced by d, its influencees

$\Delta_d \colon \times_{i \in I_d} Q_i \times \Omega \to \times_{j \in E_d} Q_j$ is the state transition function of d

$\Lambda_d \colon \times_{i \in I_d} Q_i \times \Omega \to Y$ is the output function of d.

A multicomponent system is composed of a set of components D. Each component d has its own set of states Q_d and contributes to the overall state transition and output of the system by its individual state transition function, Δ_d, and output function, Λ_d. Each component additionally defines a set of influencers, I_d, the components influencing it, and a set of influencees, E_d, which are the components influenced by it. The local state transition function takes the state set of the influencers and maps them into new states for the influencees. The local output functions takes the state sets of the influencers and defines its contribution to the overall output of the system.

A multicomponent system embodies a higher level of system knowledge than a structured I/O system in the sense that not only state coordinates are known but also the state set and transition and output functions are decomposed and identified with individual components. Each component contributes to the overall system behavior with its individual transition and output functions. A system specification at the I/O system or structured I/O system level is easily derived by forming the crossproduct of the state sets and state transition and output functions of the individual components. However, to be meaningful, as we will see in the subsequent chapters, special constraints must be obeyed by the set of influencees of the components when we consider a particular multicomponent formalism. For example, in the discrete time and differential equation cases, a component is allowed to change its own state only so that the set of influencees, E_d, is restricted to contain d as its single element and the output set of the multicomponent DTSS is a crossproduct of outputs sets Y_d belonging to components d. With this restrictions, the state set, state transition and output function of the I/O system can easily be defined as

$$Q = \times_{d \in D} q_d,$$

$$\Delta(q,\omega) \cdot d = \Delta_d\left(\times_{i \in I_d} q_i, \omega\right), \text{ and}$$

$$\Lambda(q,\omega) \cdot d = \Lambda_d\left(\times_{i \in I_d} q_i, \omega\right),$$

with d defining the part Y_d of the overall output Y that belongs to d (see Chapter 7 for more details).

These restrictions do not apply in the case in the discrete event case, where a component may change the state of others. In Chapter 7 on coupled system formalisms, we will learn the requirements for multicomponent system specifications in detail and show that a multicomponent system in a particular formalism defines a basic system in that formalism.

5.10 Network of System Specifications (Coupled Systems)

In the last section we introduced multicomponent systems where the components of a system interact directly through their state and state transition functions. In this section we introduce a higher level of specification where component systems are coupled through their output and input interfaces. We call this type of coupling *modular* and the system specification so derived a *coupled system specification* or *network of system specifications.*

In this form of system specification, *the components are themselves systems with their own input and output interfaces.* They are coupled together by instantaneous functions that take the output values of the components' influencers, as well as the external inputs to the overall system, and compute the input values for the components.

Immediately the question arises: What conditions on the individual component systems and on their coupling are needed to ensure that the resulting assemblage is well defined. In terms of systems theory, we want a network of system specifications again to *specify a system.* However, in this general a form, conditions that would guarantee well-defined resultants are not known. Fortunately, for basic system formalisms, introduced in subsequent chapters, such sufficient conditions are well known. We say that a system formalism has the property that it is *closed under coupling* if the resultant of any network of systems specified in the formalism is itself a system specified in the formalism. Furthermore, we develop constructive methods for deriving a resultant system from a network of system specifications.

Through the closure under coupling property, hierarchical model construction becomes feasible. Since a network of system specifications of particular system type is again a system specification of that type, it can be used as a component in a (bigger) coupled system specification.

In the following we will first introduce a general structure for coupled system specification. Then, we will get familiar with a special form of coupling of structured systems that is most important in simulation practice.

5.10.1 Coupled System Specification

A coupled system specification is a structure

$$N = \langle T, X_N, Y_N, D, \{M_d \mid d \in D\}, \{I_d \mid d \in D \cup \{N\}\}, \{Z_d \mid d \in D \cup \{N\}\} \rangle$$

where

X_N is the set of inputs of the network—the *external inputs*
Y_N is the set of outputs of the network—the *external outputs*
D is the set of *component references*.

For all $d \in D$,

$$M_d = \langle T, X_d, Y_d, \Omega, Q, \Delta, \Lambda \rangle \text{ is an I/O system.}$$

For all $d \in D \cup \{N\}$,

$$I_d \subseteq D \cup \{N\} \text{ is the } \textit{set influencers of d}$$
$$Z_d : \underset{i \in I_d}{\times} YX_i \to XY_d \text{ is the interface map for } d$$

with

$$\begin{aligned} YX_i &= X_i && \text{if } i = N \\ &= Y_i && \text{if } i \neq N \\ XY_d &= Y_d && \text{if } d = N \\ &= X_d && \text{if } d \neq N. \end{aligned}$$

The most general multicomponent system specification just described consists of the specification of the input/output interface of the network (X_N and Y_N), the specification of the components $d \in D$, which must be dynamic systems, and the coupling scheme ($\{I_d\}$ and $\{Z_d\}$). The set of influencers I_d of a component d may also contain the network N. The interface map Z_d specifies how the input values of component d are derived from the outputs or external inputs of its influencers $i \in I_d$. Through the general form of the coupling specification scheme employing interface maps, arbitrary couplings can be realized.

Exercise: Instead of using the XY notation used above, write out the interface map domains for the four special cases that arise (where the {source, destination} may be a component or the network).◆

Figure 16 shows an example of a two-component coupled system. The inputs of A are derived through interface map Z_A, which has X_N and Y_A as its domain. The interface map Z_B takes the elements of Y_A. Finally, the overall network output is defined by Z_N, which takes the output sets Y_A cross Y_B as its domain.

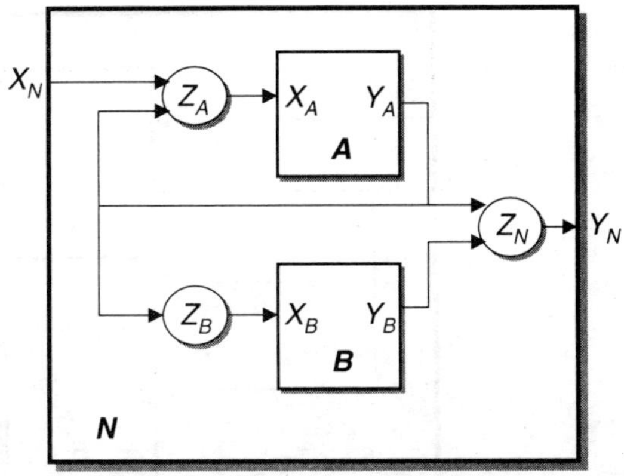

$I_A = \{N, A\}$, $I_B = \{A\}$, $I_N = \{A, B\}$

Figure 16 Example of a coupled system specification.

5.10.2 Coupled System Specification at the Structured System Level

Employing multivariable sets for the input and output sets in a coupled system specification allows us to derive a special coupled system formalism where coupling is done by directly connecting output and input ports. This way of coupling is the form, almost exclusively used in modeling practice. We will show how it maps to the general form just discussed.

Input/output and components specification is the same as in the general coupled system specification formalism. However, the coupling now is specified by three parts:

- The *external input coupling (EIC)*, couplings of network input ports to input ports of some components
- The *external output coupling (EOC)*, couplings of component output ports to output ports of the network
- The *internal coupling (IC)*, couplings of component output ports to input ports of components

Each coupling is a pair of pairs specifying the component and the port the coupling is beginning and a pair specifying the component and the port the coupling is ending. Figure 17 gives an example of a coupled system in so-called *block diagram* representation.

A *coupled system specification at the structured system level* is a structure

$$N = \langle T, X_N, Y_N, D, \{M_d \mid d \in D\}, EIC, EOC, IC \rangle,$$

where

$X_N = (IPorts_N, X_{N1} \times X_{N2} \times \ldots)$ is the multivariable set of inputs of the network with variables $Iports_N$

$Y_N = (OPorts_N, Y_{N1} \times Y_{N2} \times \ldots)$ is the multivariable set of outputs of the network with variables $Oports_N$

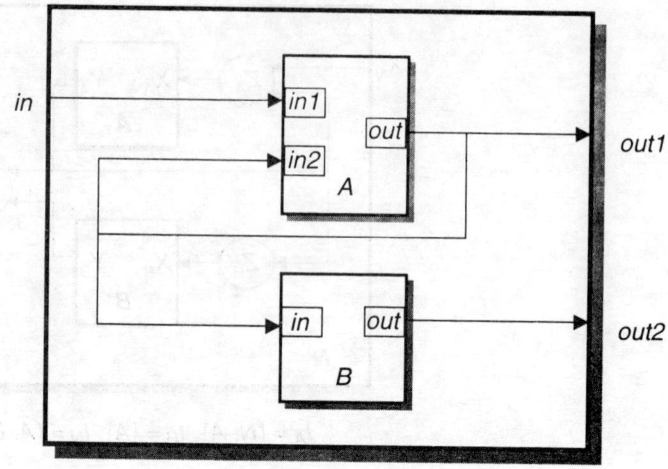

Figure 17 Block diagram representation of coupled system example.

D is the set of components, where $d \in D$ is a system,

$M_d = (T, X_d, Y_d, \Omega, Q, \Delta, \Lambda)$ specified at the structed system level

with $X_d = (IPorts_d, X_{d1} \times X_{d2} \times \ldots)$ and $Y_d = (OPorts_d, Y_{d1} \times Y_{d2} \times \ldots)$

$EIC \subseteq \{((N, ip_N), (d, ip_d)) \mid ip_N \in IPorts_N, d \in D, ip_d \in IPorts_d\}$

is the *external input coupling*

$EOC \subseteq \{((d, op_d), (N, op_N)) \mid d \in D, op_d \in OPorts_d, op_N \in OPorts_N\}$

is the *external output coupling*

$IC \subseteq \{((a, op_a), (b, ip_b)) \mid a, b \in D, op_a \in OPorts_a, ip_b \in IPorts_b\}$

is the *internal coupling*,

with the constraints that the range of the to-port must be a subset of the range of the from-port, i.e.,

$$\forall((N, ip_N), (d, ip_d)) \in EIC\colon\ range_{ip_N}(X_N) \subseteq range_{ip_d}(X_d)$$
$$\forall((d, op_a), (N, op_N)) \in EOC\colon\ range_{op_d}(Y_d) \subseteq range_{op_N}(Y_N);$$
$$\forall((a, op_a), (b, ip_b)) \in IC\colon\ range_{op_a}(Y_a) \subseteq range_{ip_b}(X_b).$$

From this form of coupling specification we are able to derive the set of influencers $\{I_d\}$ and interface maps $\{Z_d\}$. We state this formally as follows:

Theorem 3 Port-to-port coupling is a special case of general coupling.

Proof. The set of influencers I_d of all components $d \in D$ and network N is easily derived by gathering all components from which a coupling to d or N exists, i.e.,

$$\forall d \in D \cup \{N\}\colon I_d = \{i \mid ((i, fromport), (d, toport)) \in EIC \cup EOC \cup IC\}.$$

To define the interface maps Z_d and Z_N we first introduce a *resolution* operator ⊕. This is needed since we allow multiple couplings to a single input port or network output port. (Such couplings will be meaningful only for discrete event systems, a very important special case.) To simplify matters, we assume that at most one nonevent appears on converging wires at the same time. Then the operator takes the value that is unequal to the nonevent ∅. Formally, we define ⊕ as an operator taking an arbitrary number of arguments by

$$\begin{aligned} \oplus x &= x \\ \oplus x_1, x_2, \ldots, x_n &= x_i \quad \text{if } x_i \neq \varnothing \wedge \forall j \neq i \Rightarrow x_j = \varnothing \\ &= \varnothing \quad \text{otherwise.} \end{aligned}$$

This means that we take the value of x if x is the single argument of ⊕, we take the value of argument x_i if x_i is unequal to the nonevent ∅ and all the other arguments are equal to the nonevent, and we take the nonevent in all other cases.

So equipped, we define the map Z_d as a function that always takes the value of the *from port* of that coupling which is equal to the nonevent, if such a port exists. For simplicity, we'll assume that only one destination port of a component or the network receives input at any time. Then

$$\forall d \in D \cup \{N\}: Z_d : \underset{i \in I_d}{\times} YX_i \rightarrow XY_d,$$

with $Z_d(\ldots, yx_{i,fromport}, \ldots) = xy_{(d, toport)}$, where

$$xy_{(d,toport)} = \underset{\{(i,fromport) | ((i,fromport),(d,toport)) \in EIC \cup EOC \cup IC\}}{\oplus} yx_{(i,fromport)}.$$

In Chapter 7 we will adopt this type of system specification and introduce special coupled system formalisms that all have their unique restrictions. For these we will also show how a system at the I/O system level is derived from a coupled system specification.

5.11 Summary

The hierarchy of levels at which a system may be known or specified is summarized in Table 1. As the level in the table increases, we move in the direction of increasing structural specificity (i.e., from behavior to structure). Let us briefly restate what new knowledge is introduced at each level in the hierarchy.

At level 0 we deal with the input and output interface of a system.

At level 1 we deal with purely observational recordings of the behavior of a system. This is the set of I/O segment pairs called the I/O relation.

At level 2 we study the set of I/O functions that partitions a system's I/O relation. Each function is associated with an initial state of the system as it is described at level 3.

At level 3 the system is described by abstract sets and functions. The state space and transition and output functions are introduced at this level. The transition function describes the state-to-state transitions caused by the input

Table 1 Hierarchy of System Specifications

Level	Specification	Formal object
0	I/O frame	$\langle T, X, Y\rangle$
1	I/O relation observation	$\langle T, X, \Omega, Y, R\rangle$
2	I/O function observation	$\langle T, X, \Omega, Y, F\rangle$
3	I/O system	$\langle T, X, \Omega, Y, Q, \Delta, \Lambda\rangle$
4	Iterative specification	$\langle T, X, \Omega_G, Y, Q, \delta, \lambda\rangle$
5	Structured system specification	$\langle T, X, \Omega, Y, Q, \Delta, \Lambda\rangle$ with X, Y, Q, Δ, and Λ are structured
6	Nonmodular coupled multicomponent system	$\langle T, X, \Omega, Y, D, \{Md = (Q_d, E_d, I_d, \Delta_d, \Lambda_d)\}\rangle$
7	Modular coupled network of systems	$N = \langle T, XN, YN, D, \{M_d \mid d \in D\}, \{I_d \mid d \in D \cup \{N\}\}, \{Z_d \mid d \in D \cup \{N\}\}\rangle$

segments; the output function describes the state-to-observable-output mapping.

At level 4 we introduced a shorthand form of specifying a system at level 3 by presenting only its input generator segments and the state-to-state transitions caused by these segments. This level will serve us as a basis for introducing special basic modeling formalism in the subsequent chapters.

At level 5 the abstract sets and functions of lower levels are presented as arising as crossproducts of more primitive sets and functions. This corresponds to the form in which models are often informally described.

At level 6 a system is specified by a set of components, each with its own state set and state transition function. The components are coupled nonmodularly in that they influence each other directly through their state sets and state transition functions.

In contrast to the nonmodular couplings of level 6, at level 7 a system is specified as a modular coupling of components. The components are system specifications on their own and coupling is done by connecting their output and input interfaces.

We have shown how to convert a system specification at each level to one at the next lower level (except level 7, which is postponed until we introduce special network formalisms). Thus, by a multistep process we can express the observable behavior associated with system specified at any of the levels.

The process of going from a system specification at the highest level to the behavioral level is the formal equivalent of simulation of a model by a computer. The machine computes, step-by-step, successive states and outputs; each step involves the component-by-component calculation of state variable values. Sequences of states and outputs constitute trajectories, and collections of such trajectories constitute the behavior of the model.

We now have a full set of levels at which models can be constructed. For simulation purposes the more structured levels—the network, multicomponent, and structured system specifications—are most practical. However, the other levels play their role as well. This formal basis now will serve us for introducing well-known modeling formalisms for simulation modeling in subsequent chapters. In particular, we will introduce basic differential equation, discrete time, and discrete event formalisms as specializations of iterative specifications. Likewise, nonmodular and modular coupled differential equation, discrete time, and discrete event networks will be treated as specializations of multicomponent and network specifications.

5.12 Sources

The following are some of the pioneering works in mathematical systems theory.

1. Arnold, A., *Finite Transition Systems : Semantics of Communicating Systems.* Prentice Hall, Englewood Cliffs, NJ, 1994.
2. Harrison, M., *Lectures on Linear Sequential Machines.* Academic Press, New York, 1969.
3. Klir, G., *Introduction to the Methodology of Switching Circuits.* Van Nostrand, New York, 1972.
4. Mesarovic, M. D., and Y. Takahara, *Abstract Systems Theory.* Springer-Verlag, New York, 1989.
5. Mesarovic, M. D., D. Macko, and Y. Takahara, *Theory of Hierarchical Multilevel Systems.* Academic Press, New York, 1975.
6. Moore, E. F. (Ed.), *Sequential Machines: Selected Papers.* Addison-Wesley, Reading, Mass., 1964.
7. Padulo, L., and M. A. Arbib, *System Theory* Saunders, Philadelphia, 1974.
8. Wymore, W., *A Mathematical Theory of Systems Engineering: The Elements.* Wiley, New York, 1967.
9. Zadeh, L. A., and C. A. Desoer, *Linear Systems Theory, The State Space Approach.* McGraw Hill, New York, 1963.

   Unfortunately, these are mostly out-of-print—but many are available in libraries. More recent expositions are as follows.

10. Balakrishnan, A. V., *Elements of State Space Theory of Systems.* Springer-Verlag, New York, 1983.
11. Ho, Y.-C., (Ed.), *Discrete Event Dynamic Systems: Analyzing Complexity and Performance in the Modern World.* IEEE Press, 1994.
12. Klir, G. J., *Architecture of Systems Problem Solving.* Plenum Press, New York, 1985.
13. Pichler, F., and H. Schwaertzel (Eds.), *CAST(Computer Aided System Theory) Methods in Modelling.* Springer-Verlag, New York, 1992.
14. Takahashi, S., and Y. Takahara, *Logical Approach to Systems Theory.* Springer-Verlag, London, 1995.
15. Wymore, A. W. *Model-Based Systems Engineering: An Introduction to the Mathematical Theory of Discrete Systems and to the Tricotyledon Theory of System Design.* CRC Press, Boca Raton, FL, 1993.

II

Modeling Formalisms and Simulation Algorithms

6

Basic Formalisms: DEVS, DTSS, DESS

6.1 Basic System Specification Formalisms

Simulation modeling is not done by writing out a dynamic system structure itself, but indirectly, by using a *system specification formalism.* A system specification formalism is a shorthand means of specifying a system. It implicitly implies constraints on the elements of the dynamic system, and hence one only has to give the information necessary to distinguish this model from the others in the class. Such formalisms build subclasses of systems. We have already worked with these subclasses in Chapter 3 and we have seen the *DEVS* (*discrete event system specification*) formalism in Chapter 4. However, we have not seen how DEVS specifies a system, nor when such a specification is valid. This is the purpose of this chapter. We also introduce the *differential equation specified system* (*DESS*) and the *discrete time specified system* (*DTSS*) as the other basic formalisms for model specification.

Basic system specification formalisms allow a *local description of the dynamic* behavior of the system, i.e., we have to specify how the state changes at any particular point in time. From this local description it is possible to derive the global dynamic behavior of the corresponding dynamic system, and we call it the *dynamic interpretation* of the system formalism. Another way to look at the same process is that each of the formalisms can be interpreted as an iterative system specification (Chapter 5). Recall that an iterative system specification provides a set of input generators such that if we specify the system dynamics for these generators, then the rest of the system specification can be easily generated. Thus, if the DEVS, DTSS and DESS formalisms are cast as iterative system specifications, then the systems they specify are well characterized. In this chapter, however, we follow the spirit, but not the letter, of this approach. Rather, we will provide direct interpretations of the system behavior. The reason is that this provides a more understandable approach to the nature of the formalisms themselves. Nevertheless, the reader is encouraged to formulate the iterative system specifications through exercises.

At this point it will also help to examine the layout of the chapters in Part II as shown in Fig. 1. Here we see that this chapter introduces the DEVS, DTSS, and DESS formalisms, which are called "basic" in the following two senses. In the first sense, they are *fundamental* because all the systems we shall deal with are derived from these formalisms. In the second sense, we distinguish "basic" from "coupled" system formalisms, which are introduced in Chapter 7. Coupled system formalisms enable us to create networks of

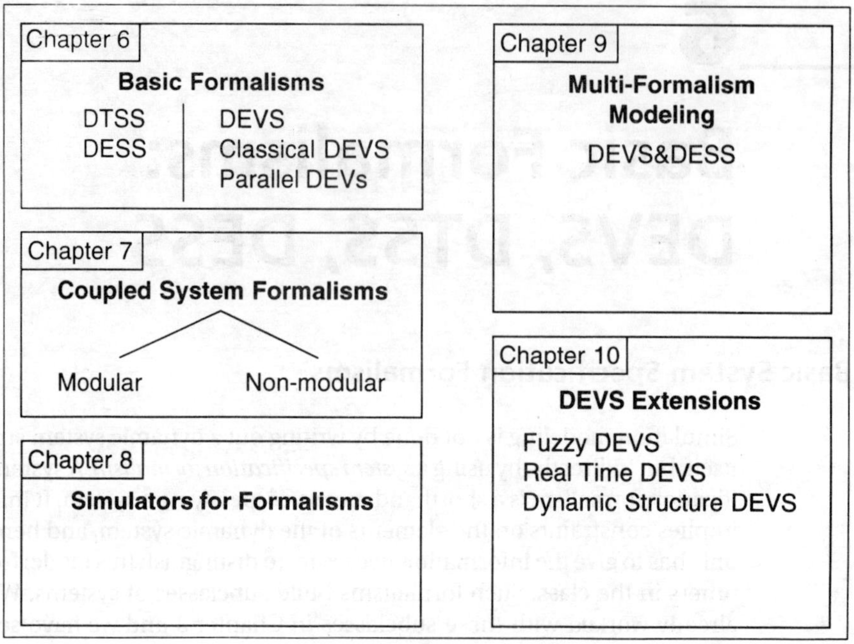

Figure 1 Layout of chapters.

systems as discussed in Chapter 5. (However, since the formalisms are closed under coupling, the resultant of the coupled system is a member of the same class of the systems and therefore has a basic specification for that class.)

Simulators for the formalisms are discussed in Chapter 8. When we implement a system specification by providing such a simulator, the basic formalism will be implemented as an *atomic* model class. To create an instance of such a class, the modeler uses the notation of the basic formalism. The coupled system formalism is then implemented by a *coupled* model class in which the modeler provides component and coupling information.

Chapter 9 introduces a formalism to enable using all three basic formalisms together. Chapter 10 discusses a number of extensions to the DEVS formalism that provide more capabilities to model complex real systems.

6.2 Discrete Event System Specification (DEVS)

Having already introduced DEVS in informal fashion in earlier chapters, we are now in a position to provide a more rigorous exposition in the context of system specification. We will review the basic formalism of Classic DEVS and also that of the more recent development of Parallel DEVS.

6.2.1 Classic DEVS

A basic *discrete event system specification* is a structure

$$DEVS = (X, Y, S, \delta_{ext}, \delta_{int}, \lambda, ta),$$

where

X is the set of inputs
Y is the set of outputs
S is the set of *sequential* states
δ_{ext}: $Q \times X \rightarrow S$ is the *external state transition function*
δ_{int}: $S \rightarrow S$ is the *internal state transition function*
λ: $S \rightarrow Y$ is the output function
ta: $S \rightarrow \Re_0^+ \cup \infty$ is the *time advance function*
$Q = \{(s,e) | s \in S, 0 = e = ta(s)\}$ is the set of *total states.*

6.2.2 Structure Specified by DEVS

The true meaning of a DEVS is expressed by the system that it specifies. So it is time to provide the mapping that will associate a system with a DEVS structure. Recall from Chapter 5 that a system is a structure $S = (T, X, \Omega, Y, Q, \Delta, \Lambda)$ where T is the time base, X is the input set, Y is the output set, Ω is the admissible set of segments over X and T, Q is a set, the *set of states* Δ: $Q \times \Omega \rightarrow Q$ is the state transition function, and Λ: $Q \times X \rightarrow Y$ is the output function.

The structure S specified by a DEVS is time invariant and has the following characteristics:

- Its time base T is the real numbers R (subsets such as the integers are also allowed).
- Its input set is $X^{\varnothing} = X \cup \{\varnothing\}$, i.e., the input set of the dynamic system is the input set of the DEVS together with a symbol $\varnothing \notin X$ specifying the nonevent.
- Its output set is $Y^{\varnothing} = Y \cup \{\varnothing\}$, i.e., the output set of the dynamic system is the output set of the DEVS together with a symbol $\varnothing \notin Y_M$ specifying the nonevent.
- Its state set is the total state set Q of the DEVS.
- The set Ω of admissible input segments is the set of all DEVS segments over X and T.
- The state trajectories are piecewise constant segments over S and T.
- The output trajectories are DEVS segments over Y and T.
- The state trajectory is defined as follows:
  Let ω: $<t_i, t_f] \rightarrow X^{\varnothing}$ be a DEVS segment and the state $q = (s, e)$ be the state at time t_i. Then we define

$\Delta(q, \omega <t_i, t_f]) =$

(1) $(s, e + t_f - t_i)))$ if $e + t_f - t_i < ta(s) \wedge \neg\exists t \in <t_i, t_f] : \omega(t) \neq \varnothing$
(no internal and external events)

(2) $\Delta((\delta_{int}(s), 0), \omega[t_i + ta(s) - e, t_f])$
if $e + t_f - t_i = ta(s) \wedge \neg\exists t \in <t_i, t_i + ta(s) - e) : \omega(t) \neq \varnothing$
(an internal event)

(3) $\Delta((\delta_{ext}((s, e+t-t_i), \omega(t)), 0), \varnothing[t,t] \cdot \omega[t,t_f])$

if $\exists t \in <t_i, \min\{t_f, t_i + ta(s) - e\}] : \omega(t) \neq \varnothing \wedge \neg\exists t' \in <t_i, t) : \omega(t') \neq \varnothing$

(an external event)

- The output function Λ of the dynamic system is given by

(4) $\Lambda(q,x) = \lambda(s)$ if $e = ta(s)$ and $\omega(t) = \varnothing$

$= \lambda(s)$ or $\varnothing$ if $e = ta(s)$ and $\omega(t) \neq \varnothing$

(only at internal events there is an output)

$\varnothing$ otherwise.

From the above definition we see that the dynamic behavior is not uniquely defined when both an internal events and an external event $\omega(t)$ occur at the same time, t. For good definition, we impose an order of processing where by the internal transition is executed first followed by the external transition. As mentioned earlier (Chapter 4), there are two approaches to deal with such collisions in DEVS-based simulation environments. In classical DEVS, the resolution is handled by the *Select* function, which will allow only one component to be activated at any time, thus assuring that the collision can't happen. In Parallel DEVS there is an additional transition specification that deals with the collision directly.

The recursive definition of dynamic behavior just given has to be interpreted in the following way: Beginning at time t_i the system has been in state s for e time units. The variable e defines the *elapsed time* the system has been in a particular state. The input values, the values of the input segment unequal to the nonevent, determine the *external events* causing the execution of the external transitions. The time advance function determines the time of the execution of the internal transitions. Whenever the elapsed time becomes equal to the value of time advance function, an *internal event* is scheduled. After each event the elapsed time is set to zero.

If there is no input in the whole interval $<t_i, t_f]$ and the total elapsed time $e + t_f - t_i$ at time t_f is smaller than the value of the time advance function $ta(s)$, then there is no event at all and only the elapsed time e has to be updated by the time elapsed during the interval (1). If there is no input until the execution of the first internal transition at time $t_i + ta(s) - e$, an internal event occurs and the internal transition function is executed (2). Note that the condition that no input occurs until the internal event does not include the time of the internal event ($\neg\exists\, t \in = t_i, t_i + ta(s) - e)$: $\omega(t) \neq \varnothing$) and so an external event may also occur at the same time. Only at internal events does an output unequal the nonevent also occur (4). If there is an input in the interval before the first internal event, then an external transition has to be executed (3). After the internal as well as external events, the recursive application of Δ to the new state and the remaining segment defines what happens in the sequel.

Exercise: Show how to formulate DEVS as an iterative system specification and characterize the system it specifies in this manner. (Hint: Represent a single cycle of DEVS operation by formulating the basis step in the recursion in the preceding definition and remove the rest of the recursion. The interested reader can refer to TMS 76 for the details.)◆

Informally, we can describe the dynamic behavior as follows:

Internal events: If at time t_i the DEVS has been in state s for $e = ta(s)$ time units, then the DEVS is scheduled to undertake its internal transition at time $tn = t_i + (ta(s) - e)$. When no external event input will arrive until time tn, then the DEVS will stay in state s until that time so that it has been in s exactly $ta(s)$ time units and then will transit from s to $s' := \delta_{int}(s)$ at time tn and set the elapsed time e to 0. Right before undertaking the internal transition, the DEVS will put out the value $\lambda(s)$. After the internal transition, the DEVS is scheduled for the next internal transition at time $tn + ta(s')$.

External events: Input values can arrive at arbitrary time instances at the input ports. If at time t_i the DEVS has been in state s for time $e = ta(s)$ and an external input arrives, then the DEVS has to execute its external transition function and the DEVS will transit from s to $s'' := \delta_{ext}(s, e, x)$ where it will remain either to the next external event or $ta(s'')$ time units. Again the elapsed time e is set to 0.

6.2.3 Legitimacy: When is the Structure Specified by a DEVS Really a System?

We have associated a structure with a DEVS, but how do we know that this structure is indeed a system? Since we employed recursion in the specification of the transition function of the system, we have to guarantee that this recursion always yields a unique result. For example, the DEVS could go into an infinite loop of internal events where time would not be advanced beyond a certain point. A property of a DEVS called legitimacy provides a necessary and sufficient condition for the system specified by a DEVS to be well defined.

To define legitimacy, we extend the internal transition function to its iterative form,

$$\delta_{int}^{+} : S \times \mathbf{I}_0^{+} \to S,$$

defined recursively by

$$\begin{aligned}
&\delta_{int}^{+}(s,0) = s \\
&\delta_{int}^{+}(s,n+1) = \delta_{int}(\delta_{int}^{+}(s,n)).
\end{aligned}$$

$\delta_{int}^{+}(s,n)$ is the state reached after n iterations starting at state $s \in S$ if no external events intervene. The function $\sum(s,n)$ accumulates the time the system takes to make these n transitions.

$$\sum : S \times \mathbf{I}_0^{+} \to \mathbf{R}_0^{+}$$

is defined recursively by

$$\begin{aligned}
&\sum(s,0) = 0 \\
&\sum(s,n) = \sum_{i=0}^{n-1} ta(\delta_{int}^{+}(s,i)).
\end{aligned}$$

Definition. A DEVS is legitimate if for each $s \in S$,

$$\lim_{n\to\infty} \sum(s,n) \to \infty.$$

Theorem 1 *Legitimacy Conditions for Well-Defined System Specification*

The structure specified by a DEVS is a system if, and only if, the DEVS is legitimate.

Proof: Let us define $\#(q,\omega)$ to be the number of internal events, i.e., the events of execution of the internal transition function, in interval $<t_i, t_f]$ given the input segment ω: $<t_i, t_f] \to X$ and the initial state q at time t_i. Then the system defined by the DEVS is well defined if, and only if,

$$\forall \omega:[t_i, t_f) \to X \in \Omega, q \in Q: \#(q,\omega) < \infty,$$

i.e., the number of internal events in any state trajectory is finite.

The proof proceeds by decomposing the input segment into its generator segments. In each such segment the number of events is given by $\#(s,m)$, where s is the initial state at the beginning of the segment and m exists if $\lim_{n\to\infty} \sum(s,n) \to \infty$.

Conversely, if for some s, there is a time t for which $\#(s,n) < t$ for $n = 0,1,2,\ldots$, then the state $\delta(s, 0, \varnothing_{t]})$ does not have an assigned value.

A *transitory state* is a state s for which $ta(s) = 0$.

Exercise: Show that a DEVS is not legitimate if there is a cycle in the state diagram of δ_{int} that contains only transitory states. (Hint: Once this cycle is entered, time will not advance.)◆

The deleterious effect of inadvertent zero-time-advance cycles is quite ubiquitous, especially in coupled, interactive models. They correspond to algebraic cycles in DTSS networks (see Chapter 15) and can arise in interactions of zero lookahead federates in distributed simulation (Chapter 11). Thus, legitimacy as the guarantor of a well-defined discrete event specification is more than a theoretical necessity.

The sufficient conditions for illegitimacy can be turned into necessary conditions as well in the special case of finite DEVS.

Theorem 2 *Conditions for Legitimate DEVS*

A DEVS M is legitimate under the following conditions:

(a) M is finite (S is a finite set): Every cycle in the state diagram of δ_{int} contains a nontransitory state (necessary and sufficient condition).

(b) M is infinite: There is a positive lower bound on the time advances, i.e., $\exists b \forall s \in S, ta(s) > b$ *(sufficient condition).*

Proof: Left as an exercise.

6.3 Parallel DEVS

The basic formalism of a *Parallel DEVS* model is

$$DEVS = (X, Y, S, \delta_{ext}, \delta_{int}, \delta_{con}, \lambda, ta)$$

with

X is the set of input events

S is the set of sequential states

Y is the set of output events

$\delta_{int}: S \rightarrow S$ is the internal transition function

$\delta_{ext}: Q \times X^b \rightarrow S$ is the external transition function, where X^b is a set of bags over elements in X

$\delta_{con}: S \times X^b \rightarrow S$ is the confluent transition function, subject to $\delta_{con}(s, \phi) = \delta_{int}(s)$

$\lambda: S \rightarrow Y^b$ is the output function

$ta: S \rightarrow \Re_0^+ \cup \infty$ is the time advance function

where $Q = \{(s,e) \mid s \in S, 0 < e < ta(s)\}$

e is the elapsed time since last state transition

The basic formalism of Parallel DEVS extends Classic DEVS by allowing bags of inputs to the external transition function. A bag of elements in X is similar to a set except that multiple occurrences of elements are allowed, e.g., $\{a,b,a,c\}$ is a bag. As with sets, bags are unordered. By using bags as the message structures for collecting inputs sent to a component, we recognize that inputs can arrive in any order and that more than one input with the same identity may arrive from one or more sources.

Parallel DEVS also introduces the confluent transition function, δ_{con}. This gives the modeler complete control over the *collision* behavior when a component receives external events at the time of its internal transition, $e = ta(s)$, as in Fig. 2. Rather than serializing model behavior at collision times, through the Select function at the coupled model level, Parallel DEVS leaves this decision of what serialization to use, if any, to the individual component. Collision tie-breaking therefore becomes a more controllable local

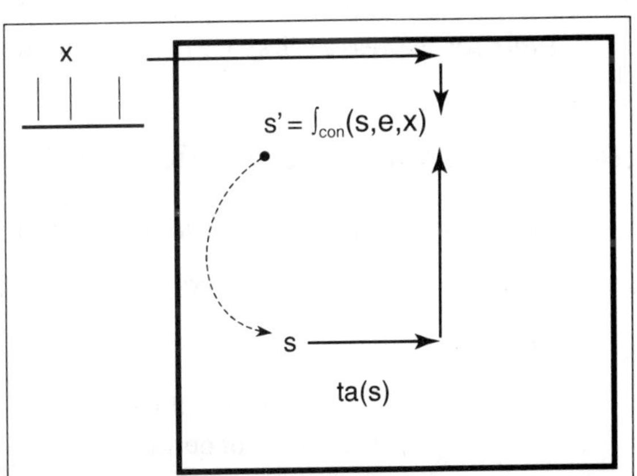

Figure 2 The confluent transition function in Parallel DEVS.

decision, as opposed to the global decision that it was in Classic DEVS. The default definition of the confluent function is

$$\delta_{con}(s,x) = \delta_{ext}(\delta_{int}(s),0,x)). \tag{1}$$

This is the same approach used in the defining the system specified by Classic DEVS. Here the internal transition is allowed to occur and this is followed by the effect of the external transition function on the resulting state (so the elapsed time clock is reset to zero). For example, if a job is just about to finish processing when a second one arrives, we let the first one finish and then start on the new one. Another possibility is

$$\delta_{con}(s,x) = \delta_{int}(\delta_{ext}(s,ta(s),x)),$$

which expresses the opposite order of effects. Of course, in general, the modeler can define δ_{con} without reference to the other functions so as to express special circumstances that occur when a confluence of external and internal events arises.

Exercise: Since bags are input to δ_{ext} and δ_{con}, we must consider the case where the input bags are empty. Show that for consistency we must have

$$ta(\delta_{ext}(s,e,\phi)) = ta(s) - e$$

and

$$\delta_{con}(s,\phi) = \delta_{int}(s). \blacklozenge$$

6.3.1 System Specified by Parallel DEVS

Defining the system specified by a Parallel DEVS follows along the lines of the same process for classic DEVS. Indeed, we can proceed by treating the input set underlying the system to be specified as X^b rather than X. Then the construction follows word for word except for the treatment of the case of confluent events, which of course, is now explicitly handled by δ_{con}.

Exercise: Express a cell space model (Chapter 3) as a Parallel DEVS.◆

6.4 Discrete Time System Specification (DTSS)

A *Discrete time system specification* is a structure

$$DTSS = (X,Y,Q,\delta,\lambda,c),$$

where

X is the set of inputs

Y is the set of outputs

Q is the set of states

$\delta: Q \times X \to Q$ is the *state transition function.*

Also,

$$\lambda : Q \to Y \quad \text{(Moore-type)}$$

or

$$\lambda : Q \times X \to Y \quad \text{(Mealy-type) is the output function}$$

and

c is a constant employed for the specification of the time base $c \bullet \mathfrak{I}$.

In the case that the output function is only a function of time and state, we again speak of a *Moore*-type system, and in the case it also depends on the input, we say likewise the system is of type *Mealy* (these names are taken from finite state machine theory context).

The structure specified by the DTSS is a structure

$$S = (T, X, \Omega, Y, Q, \Delta, \Lambda),$$

where

- The time base T has to be the set $c \bullet \mathfrak{I}$ isomorphic to the integers
- X, Y, and Q can be arbitrary sets
- The set Ω of admissible input segments is the set of all sequences over X and T
- The state and output trajectories are sequences over Q and T and Y and T, respectively

A DTSS defines the following dynamic behavior:

- Given an input segment $\omega: [t_1, t_2) \to X$ and an initial state q at time t_1, then we define the global transition function Δ of the dynamic system by

$$\begin{aligned} \Delta(q,\omega) &= q && \text{if } t_1 = t_2 \\ &= \delta(q, \omega(t_1)) && \text{if } t_1 = t_2 - c \\ &= \delta(\Delta(q, \omega_{t_1}^{-c)}), \omega(t_2 - c)) && \text{otherwise,} \end{aligned}$$

  where c is the constant in the definition of the time base $c \bullet \mathfrak{I}$.
- The output function Λ of the dynamic system is given by

$$\Lambda(q, x) = \lambda(q)$$

  in the case of Moore-type systems and

$$\Lambda(q, x) = \lambda(q, x)$$

  in the case of Mealy-type systems.

Exercise: Show that the structure is a system. (Hint: Essentially this requires showing that Δ is well-defined.)◆

Exercise: Show that the DTSS is itself an iterative specification of the system it specifies.◆

Exercise: Express a finite state machine as a DTSS. Do the same for cellular automata.◆

6.5 Differential Equation System Specification (DESS)

A *differential equation system specification* is a structure

$$DESS = (X, Y, Q, f, \lambda),$$

where

X is the set of inputs

Y is the set of outputs

Q is the set of states

$f: Q \times X \rightarrow Q$ is the *rate of change function*,

and

$\lambda: Q \rightarrow Y$ (Moore-type)

or

$\lambda: Q + X \rightarrow Y$ (Mealy-type) is the output function.

The structure associated with a *DESS* is $S = (T, X, \Omega, Y, Q, \Delta, \Lambda)$, where

- The time base T has to be the real numbers $\Re$
- X, Y, and Q are real-valued vector spaces $\Re^m$, $\Re^p$, $\Re^n$, respectively
- The set Ω of admissible input segments is the set of all bounded piecewise continuous input segments
- The state and output trajectories are bounded piecewise continuous trajectories

To define the state trajectory and state transition function we employ the iterative specification concept with the input generators taken to be the bounded continuous segments.

- Given a bounded continuous input segment ω: $<t_1, t_2> \rightarrow X$ and an initial state q at time t_1, the DESS requires that the state trajectory $STRAJ_{q,\omega}$ of the dynamic system at any point in time $t \in <t_1, t_2>$ satisfy the differential equation

$$STRAJ_{q,\omega}(t_1) = q$$
$$d\, STRAJ_{q,\omega}(t)/dt = f(STRAJ_{q,\omega}(t), \omega(t)).$$

Assuming the state trajectory is well defined, the transition function can be defined for every state, q and bounded countinuous input segment ω: $<t_1, t_2> \rightarrow X$, by

$$\Delta(q, \omega) = STRAJ_{q,\omega}(t_2).$$

- The output function of Λ the dynamic system is given by

$$\Lambda(q, x) = \lambda(q)$$

in the case of Moore-type systems and

$$\Lambda(q, x) = \lambda(q, x)$$

in the case of Mealy-type systems.

When is the System Specified by a DESS Well Defined?

We have to go back and justify the assumption that there is a unique, well-defined state trajectory determined for every state and input generator segment. It is known that the following condition guaranties that such unique solutions exist. The *Lipschitz condition* is stated as

$$\| f(q,x) - f(q',x) \| < k \| q - q' \|$$

for all pairs $q, q' \in Q$, and input values $x \in X$, where k is a constant and $\| \ \|$ is the Euclidean norm [2].

As you can see, we did not provide an explicit formula for the global transition function of the dynamic system. Instead, it was defined in terms of its state trajectories. However, when it is possible to find an analytical solution for the integral $F(t) = \int f(q, \omega)dt$, then we can explicitly specify the global transition function. In this case, Δ is defined by

$$\Delta(q, \omega) = q + F(t_2) - F(t_1),$$

where ω has domain $<t_1, t_2>$. Practical models often do not have tractable analytical solutions. Indeed, in many cases the complexity of the input signal forbids analytical integration. As discussed in Chapter 3, using digital computers to simulate DESS requires discrete approximation of the state trajectory and the state transition function.

Exercise: Express a linear time invariant system in the form of a set of matrices as a DESS. (Hint: Show that the Lipschitz condition is satisfied and write the integral solution F as before.)◆

Exercise: Show how to formulate the DESS as an iterative system specification and characterize the system it specifies in this manner. (Hint: Use the bounded continuous input segments as generators and the generator transition function as defined earlier. Show that the conditions required for the extension to piecewise continuous segments in Chapter 5 are satisfied.)◆

6.6 Summary

This chapter is key to the development of the theory that follows. The three basic system specification formalisms, DEVS, DTSS, and DESS, were defined. The system classes that they specify were characterized based on the ideas underlying the iterative system specification. Indeed, iteration is the manner in which the system's global transition function is defined and also the way in which the system's state trajectories are generated. Except for the DTSS, specific conditions are required for the iteration to be well defined—legitimacy in the case of DEVS, and the Lipschitz condition for DESS. Return to Fig. 1 for a map of the road ahead.

7

Basic Formalisms: Coupled Multicomponent Systems

In Sections 5.9 and 5.10 we introduced the concept of system specification at the multicomponent and network of systems (also called coupled systems) level. Both levels allow us to model systems by composing smaller systems together. In the multicomponent system specification, composition is done nonmodularly in that one component's state transitions can directly change another component's state. In contrast, the network of systems specification provides a means to couple stand-alone systems by connecting their output and input interfaces.

In Chapter 6 we introduced system specification formalisms as shorthand means to specify systems. A formalism defines a set of background conventions as features that are common to all systems of the class it specifies. We identified DESS, DTSS, and DEVS as the three fundamental system formalisms for simulation modeling.

The formalisms of Chapter 6 were at the I/O systems level or structured systems levels. In this chapter, we formulate the basic system formalisms at the *multicomponent* and the *network of systems* (coupled system) level. Further, for each formalism, we will provide conditions that guarantee that a coupling of systems in this formalism defines a basic system in the same formalism—we say that the formalism is *closed under coupling*. Closure under coupling allows us to use networks of systems as components in a larger coupled system, leading to hierarchical, modular construction.

Nonmodular system specification is important because many traditional forms of modeling (e.g., the classical world views of discrete event simulation) are nonmodular. However, the advantages of modular paradigms are decisive in the age of distributed simulation and model repositories. Thus, translation from nonmodular to modular specifications is an important topic of this chapter.

7.1 Discrete Event Specified Network Formalism

The discrete event specified network formalism (DEVN), also called the DEVS coupled model specification, provides a basis for modular construction of discrete event models. Such modular construction, although not, at the time of this writing, as common an approach as the nonmodular alternative, is destined to be more and more dominant. The reason is that modularity is more natural for distributed simulation and supports reuse through model repositories. Interoperability through distributed simulation with repository reuse is the goal of the High Level Architecture (HLA) standard being promulgated by the U.S. Department of Defense.

In discrete event coupled networks, components are DEVS systems coupled exclusively through their input and output interfaces. Components do not have the possibility to access and influence the states or the timing of other components directly. All interactions have to be done by exchanging messages. More specifically, the events generated by one component at its output ports are transmitted along the couplings to input ports where they cause external events and state transitions at the influenced components.

Besides treating Classic DEVS in the following discussion, we also will consider the revision called Parallel DEVS. We will discuss the closure under coupling of both, Classic and Parallel DEVS.

7.1.1 Classic DEVS Coupled Models

Recall the definition of coupled DEVS models in Chapter 4. Instead of repeating this definition here, we provide the more abstract version, which does not explicitly work with input/output ports but corresponds to the abstract definition of network of systems of Chapter 5. The translation from structured to abstract version follows the lines discussed in Chapter 5. The definition for DEVS coupled models adopted here differs only slightly from the general definition in Chapter 5 as the interface map Z_d for a component d is broken up into several interface mappings $Z_{i,d}$, one for each influencing component i. In addition to the general definition of coupled models, Classic DEVS coupled models employ a *Select* function that is used for tie-breaking in case of equal next-event times in more than one component.

The structure of the *DEVN* or *coupled DEVS model* is

$$N = \langle X, Y, D, \{M_d\}, \{I_d\}, \{Z_{i,d}\}\ Select \rangle,$$

with

X a set of input events

Y a set of output events

D a set of component references.

For each $d \in D$,

M_d is a *Classic DEVS* model.

For each $d \in D \cup \{N\}$,

I_d is the *influencer* set of d: $I_d \subseteq D \cup \{N\}, d \notin I_d$,

and for each $i \in I_d$,

$Z_{i,d}$ is a function, the i - to - d output translation with

$Z_{i,d}: X \to X_d$, if $i = N$

$Z_{i,d}: Y_i \to Y$, if $d = N$

$Z_{i,d}: Y_i \to X_d$, if $d \neq N$ and $i \neq N$.

Note that we use the influencer sets to specify the influence propagation in order to be consistent with the approach of Chapter 5. Earlier definitions, in the first edition of TMS and elsewhere, employed the influencee sets, since as we see later, this is more natural for Classic DEVS where only one imminent component is activated. However, either family of sets gives the same information and its more convenient to use the influencer sets for Parallel DEVS.

Exercise: Show that given the family of influencee sets we can derive the family of influencer sets, and conversely.

Finally, *Select* is a function

$$Select: 2^D \rightarrow D$$

with *Select* $(E) \in E$. *Select* is the tie-breaking function to arbitrate the occurrence of simultaneous events (see below).

Recall (Chapter 5) that the presence of N as a potential source or destination component is a device that makes it easy to represent external input and external output couplings.

Closure under Coupling of Classic DEVS

Given a coupled model, N, with components that are Classic DEVS, we associate with it a basic DEVS, called the *resultant*,

$$DEVS_N = \langle X, Y, S, \delta_{ext}, \delta_{int}, \lambda, ta \rangle,$$

where

$$S = \underset{d \in D}{\times} Q_d$$

and ta: $S \rightarrow \Re_0^+ \cup \{\infty\}$ is defined by

$$ta(s) = minimum\ \{\sigma_d \mid d \in D\},$$

where for each component d, $\sigma_d = ta_d(s_d) - e_d$, i.e., σ_d is the time remaining to the next event in component d.

Let the set of *imminents*, $IMM\ (s) = \{d \mid d \in D \wedge \sigma_d = ta(s)\}$. *Imminents* is the set of components that have minimum remaining time σ_d, i.e., they are candidates for the next internal transition to occur.

Let $d^* = Select\ (IMM\ (s))$. This is the component whose output and internal transition functions will be executed because it was selected using the tie-breaking function *Select*.

Now, we define δ_{int}: $S \rightarrow S$. Let $s = (\ldots, (s_d, e_d), \ldots)$. Then $\delta_{int}(s) = s' = (\ldots, (s_d', e_d'), \ldots)$,

where

$$\begin{aligned}
(s_d', e_d') &= (\delta_{int,d}(s_d), 0) && \text{if } d = d^* \\
&= (\delta_{ext,d}((s_d, e_d + ta(s)), x_d), 0) && \text{if } d^* \in I_d \text{ and } x_d = \varnothing \\
&= (s_d, e_d + ta(s)) && \text{otherwise,}
\end{aligned}$$

where $x_d = Z_{d^*,d}(\lambda_{d^*}(s_{d^*}))$. That means, the resultant's internal transition function changes the state of the selected imminent component d^* according to its (d^*'s) internal transition function and updates all influenced components according to the inputs produced by the output of d^*. In all other components, d, only the elapsed times, e_d, are updated.

We define δ_{ext}: $Q \times X \rightarrow S$, where $\delta_{ext}((s, e), x) = s' = (\ldots, (s_d', e_d'), \ldots)$ by

$$(s_{d'}, e_{d'}) = (\delta_{ext,d}((s_d, e_d + e), x_d), 0) \quad \text{if } N \in I_d \;\&\; x_d \neq \varnothing$$
$$= (s_d, e_d + e) \quad \text{otherwise,}$$

where $x_d = Z_{N,d}(x)$. That is, all components influenced by the external input x change state according to the input x_d transmitted to them as converted by their respective interface mappings. All other components increment their elapsed times by e.

Finally, we define the resultant's output function, λ: $S \rightarrow Y$:

$$\lambda(s) = Z_{d^*,N}(\lambda_{d^*}(s_{d^*})) \quad \text{if } d^* \in I_N$$
$$= \varnothing \quad \text{otherwise.}$$

This says that we translate the output of the selected imminent component, d^*, to an output of the coupled model through interface map $Z_{d^*,N}$. This, of course, is only for the case in which d^* actually sends external outputs.

7.1.2 Parallel DEVS Coupled Models

The structure of a *coupled DEVS model* for Parallel DEVS is almost identical to that for Classic DEVS except for the absence of the *Select* function:

$$N = \langle X, Y, D, \{M_d\}, \{I_d\}, \{Z_{i,d}\}\rangle$$

with X, Y, D, I_d, and $Z_{i,d}$ having the same interpretation as for Classic DEVS coupled models

and for each d in D,

$$M_d \text{ is a } \textit{Parallel DEVS} \text{ model.}$$

Closure under Coupling of Parallel DEVS

We consider a Parallel DEVS coupled model

$$N = \langle X, Y, D, \{M_d\}, \{I_d\}, (Z_{i,d}\}\rangle.$$

We demonstrate closure under coupling by constructing the resultant of the coupled model and showing it to be a well-defined Parallel DEVS. The resultant is (potentially) a Parallel DEVS:

$$DEVS_N = \langle X, S, Y, \delta_{int}, \delta_{ext}, \delta_{con}, \lambda, ta\rangle.$$

As with Classic DEVS, the state set is a crossproduct, $S = \times_{d \in D} Q_d$. Likewise, the time advance function is defined by

$$ta(s) = minimum\,\{\sigma_d | d \in D\}, \text{ where } s \in S \text{ and } \sigma_d = ta(s_d) - e_d.$$

The major difference with Classic DEVS comes in the definitions of the remaining functions. To make these definitions, we partition the components into four sets at any transition. Let $s = (\ldots, (s_d, e_d), \ldots)$. Then *IMM(s)* are the imminent components whose outputs will be generated just before the next transition. Since there is no *Select* function, all of the imminents will be activated. *INT(s)* is the subset of the imminents that have no input messages. *EXT(s)* contains the components receiving input events but not scheduled for an internal transition. *CONF(s)* contains the components receiving input events and also scheduled for internal transitions at the same time. *UN(s)* contains the remaining components. Formally,

$IMM = \{d \mid \sigma_d = ta(s)\}$ (the imminent components)

$INF(s) = \{d \mid i \in I_d, i \in IMM(s) \wedge x_d^b \neq \Phi\}$,

where $x_d^b = \{Z_{i,d}(\lambda_i(s_i)) \mid i \in IMM(s) \cap I_d\}$ (components about to receive inputs)

$CONF(s) = IMM(s) \cap INF(s)$ (confluent components)

$INT(s) = IMM(s) - INF(s)$ (imminent components receiving no input)

$EXT(s) = INF(s) - IMM(s)$ (components receiving input but not imminent)

$UN(s) = D - IMM(s) - INF(s)$.

Output Function

The output is obtained by collecting all the external outputs of the imminents in a bag:

$$\lambda(s) = \{Z_{d,N}(\lambda_d(s_d)) \mid d \in IMM(s) \wedge d \in I_N\}.$$

Internal Transition Function

The resultant internal transition comprises four kinds of component transitions: internal transitions of *INT(s)* components, external transitions of *EXT(s)* components, confluent transitions of *CONF(s)* components, and the remainder, *UN(s)*, whose elapsed times are merely incremented by *ta(s)*. (The participation of *UN(s)* can be removed in simulation by using an absolute time base rather than the relative elapsed time.) Note that, by assumption, this is an internal transition of the resultant model, and there is no external event being received by the coupled model at this time.

We define

$$\delta_{int}(s) = (\ldots, (s'_d, e'_d), \ldots),$$

where

$(s'_d, e'_d) = (\delta_{int,d}(s_d), 0)$ for $d \in INT(s)$,

$(s'_d, e'_d) = (\delta_{ext,d}(s_d, e_d + ta(s), x_d^b), 0)$ for $d \in EXT(s)$,

$(s'_d, e'_d) = (\delta_{con,d}(s_d, x_d^b), 0)$ for $d \in CONF(s)$,

$(s'_d, e'_d) = (s_d, e_d + ta(s))$ otherwise

where x_d^b is as defined earlier.

External Transition Function

To construct δ_{ext} of the resultant, let

$$\delta_{ext}(s,e,x^b) = (\ldots,(s'_d,e'_d),\ldots),$$

where $0 < e < ta(s)$ and

$$(s'_d,e'_d) = (\delta_{ext,d}(s_d,e_d+e,x_d^b),0) \quad \text{for } N \in I_d \wedge x_d^b \neq \Phi$$
$$(s'_d,e'_d) = (s_d,e_d+e) \quad \text{otherwise,}$$

where $x_d^b = \{Z_{N,d}(x) / x \in x^b \wedge N \in I_d\}$.

The incoming event bag x^b is translated and routed to the event bag, x_d^b, of each influenced component, *d*. The resultant's external transition comprises all the external transitions of the influenced children. Note that by assumption, there are no internally scheduled events at this time ($e < ta(s)$).

The Confluent Transition Function

Finally, we construct the δ_{con} of the resultant. This is what happens in the coupled model when some of the components are scheduled to make internal transitions and are also about to receive external events. Fortunately, it turns out that the difference between δ_{con} and the earlier defined δ_{int} is simply the extra confluent effect produced by the incoming event bag, x^b, at elapsed time $e = ta(s)$. By redefining the influencee set $INF(s)$ as $INF'(s)$, which includes the additional influencees from the incoming couplings, I_N, we develop three similar groups for δ_{con}.

Let $INF'(s) = \{d \,|\, (i \in I_d, i \in IMM(s) \vee N \in I_d) \wedge x_d^b \neq \Phi\}$, where $x_d^b = \{Z_{i,d}(\lambda_i(s_i)) \,|\, i \in IMM(s) \wedge i \in I_d\} \cup \{Z_{N,d}(x) \,|\, x \in x^b \wedge N \in I_d\}$. (This is a union of bags, so common elements are retained. The first bag collects outputs from imminent components that are coupled to the receiving component, *d*. The second bag collects external inputs that are sent to the receiver through the external input coupling.)

$$CONF'(s) = IMM(s) \cap INF'(s)$$
$$INT'(s) = IMM(S) - INF'(s)$$
$$EXT'(s) = INF'(s) - IMM(s).$$

We define

$$\delta_{con}(s,x^b) = (\ldots, (s'_d, e'_d), \ldots),$$

where

$$(s'_d,\ e'_d) = (\delta_{int,d}(s_d), 0) \quad \text{for } d \in INT'(s),$$
$$(s'_d,\ e'_d) = (\delta_{ext,d}(s_d,e_d+ta(s),x_d^b),0) \quad \text{for } d \in EXT'(s),$$
$$(s'_d,\ e'_d) = (\delta_{con,d}(s_d,x_d^b),0 \quad \text{for } d \in CONF'(s),$$
$$(s'_d,\ e'_d) = (s_d,e_d+ta(s)) \quad \text{otherwise,}$$

where x_d^b is as defined previously.

Hierarchical consistency is achieved here by the bag union operation that gathers all external events, whether internally or externally generated, at the same time into one single event group. By such consistency, we mean that a component would experience the same inputs independently of the manner in which we chose to decompose a model (see Ref. [3] for more details).

From the definition of the δ_{int}, δ_{con}, and δ_{ext}, we see that they are special cases of one encompassing transition function, $\delta(s, e, x^b)$ applied to each component. As shown in Fig. 1, δ_{int} is applied to imminent (non-confluent) components, i.e., when $(s, e, x^b) = (s, ta(s), \Phi)$; δ_{con} is applied to confluent components, i.e., $(s, e, x^b) = (s, ta(s), x^b)$ where $x^b_d \neq \Phi$; finally, δ_{ext} is applied to receiver (nonconfluent) components, i.e., (s, e, x^b) where $0 < e < ta(s)$ and $x^b_d \neq \Phi$.

The overall transition function is the basis for implementation of coupled Parallel DEVS (Chapter 11). In terms of the special case functions, it is defined by

$$\delta(s,e,x^b) = \delta_{ext}(s,e,x^b) \qquad \text{for } 0 < e < ta(s), \text{ and } x^b \neq \Phi$$
$$\delta(s,ta(s),x^b) = \delta_{con}(s,x^b) \qquad \text{for } x^b \neq \Phi$$
$$\delta(s,ta(s),\Phi)) = \delta_{int}(s).$$

Exercise: Write the generic transition function

$$\delta(s,e,x^b) = (\ldots,(s'_d,e'_d),\ldots)$$

for the resultant of a coupled model in terms of the generic functions of its components.◆

7.2 Multicomponent Discrete Event System Formalism

Recall (Chapter 5) that in nonmodular coupling, components directly influence each other through their state transitions. In DEVS multicomponent nonmodular coupled models, events occurring in one component may

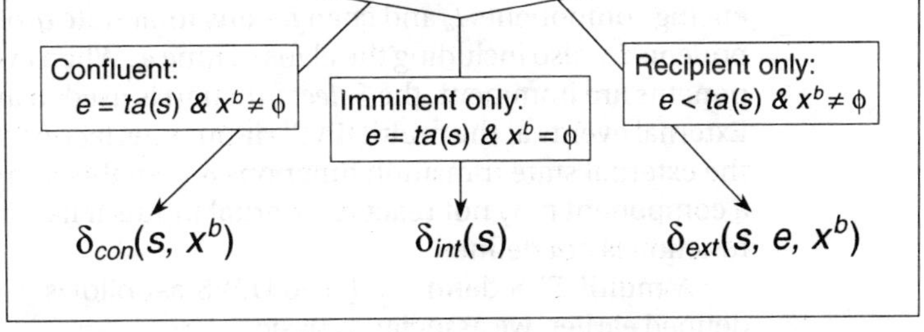

Figure 1 The overall transition function.

result in state changes and rescheduling of events in other components. The simulation strategies realized in many commercial simulation languages and systems, known as "world views," fall into the category of multicomponent DEVS. In this section, we will make the connection from the system theoretical DEVS approach to these discrete event simulation strategies. However, before we introduce the formalism for multicomponent DEVS, we formulate the GOL event model discussed in Chapter 3 as a multicomponent DEVS.

A multicomponent DEVS is a structure

$$\text{multiDEVS} = \langle X, Y, D, \{M_d\}, Select \rangle,$$

where

X, Y are the input and output event sets
D is the set of component references
$Select$: $2^D \rightarrow D$ with $Select(E) \in E$ is a tie-breaking function employed to arbitrate in case of simultaneous events

For each $d \in D$,

$$M_d = \langle S_d, I_d, E_d, \delta_{ext,d}, \delta_{int,d}, \lambda_d, ta_d \rangle,$$

where

S_d is the set of sequential states of d,

$Q_d = \{(s, e_d) | s \in S_d, e_d \in \Re\}$ is the set of total states of d,

$I_d \subseteq D$ is the set of influencing components,

$E_d \subseteq D$ is the set of influenced components,

$\delta_{ext,d}$: $\underset{i \in I_d}{\times} Q_i \times X \rightarrow \underset{j \in E_d}{\times} Q_j$ is the external state transition function

$\delta_{int,d}$: $\underset{i \in I_d}{\times} Q_i \rightarrow \underset{j \in E_d}{\times} Q_j$ is the internal state transition function

λ_d: $\underset{i \in I_d}{\times} Q_i \rightarrow Y$ is the output event function

ta_d: $\underset{i \in I_d}{\times} Q_i \rightarrow \Re_0^+ \cup \{\infty\}$ is the time advance function.

A multiDEVS works in the following way: Internal events are scheduled individually by each component $d \in D$ by the individual time advance functions ta_d. When an event occurs in one of the components, it is executed, and this results in state changes through the internal transition function $\delta_{int,d}$ and eventually output events for the multiDEVS defined in the output function λ_d. Note that the transition function depends on total states q_i of the influencing components I_d and changes any total state q_j of the influenced components E_d, also including the elapsed time e_j. When events in different components are imminent, the *Select* function is used to arbitrate among them. External events at the multiDEVS's input interface can be handled by any of the external state transition functions $\delta_{ext,d}$ of the components, d. However, a component may not react to external inputs if its external state transition function is not defined.

A multiDEVS defines a basic DEVS as follows. Given a multiDEVS as defined earlier, we associate a basic

$$\text{DEVS} = \langle X, Y, S, \delta_{ext}, \delta_{int}, \lambda, ta \rangle,$$

where $S = \times_{d \in D} Q_d$.

We define

$$ta(s) = \min\{\sigma_d \mid d \in D\}$$

with $\sigma_d = ta_d(\ldots, q_i, \ldots) - e_d$ as the remaining time until the next scheduled event in d.

We define the next scheduled component $d^* = Select(\{d \mid \sigma_d = ta(s)\}$ and

$$\delta_{int}((s_1,e_1),(s_2,e_2),\ldots,(s_n,e_n)) = ((s_1',e_1'),(s_2',e_2'),\ldots,(s_n',e_n'))$$

with

$$\begin{aligned}
(s_j',e_j') &= (s_j,e_j + ta(s)) && \text{if } j \notin E_{d^*} \\
(s_j',e_j') &= \delta_{int,d^*}((\ldots,(s_i,e_i + ta(s)),\ldots)) \cdot j && \text{if } j \in E_{d^*}
\end{aligned}$$

with $i \in I_{d^*}$, i.e., the internal state transition of the DEVS is defined by the state transition of the next scheduled component d^*.

The output of the system is defined by the output event of d^*,

$$\lambda(s) = \lambda_{d^*}(\ldots, q_i, \ldots), i \in I_{d^*}.$$

The external transition function δ_{ext} upon occurrence of an input event x is defined by the crossproduct of the external state transition functions

$$\delta_{ext,d}((\ldots, q_i, \ldots), e, x)$$

of all components $d \in D$. We define the overall external transition function by

$$\delta_{ext}(((s_1,e_1),(s_2,e_2),\ldots,(s_n,e_n)),e,x) = ((s_1',e_1'),(s_2',e_2'),\ldots,(s_n',e_n'))$$

with

$$\begin{aligned}
(s_j',e_j') &= (s_j,e_j + e) && \text{if } j \notin E_d \\
(s_j',e_j') &= \delta_{ext,d}((\ldots,(s_i,e_i + e),\ldots)).j && \text{if } j \in E_d.
\end{aligned}$$

Cellular Automata Multicomponent DEVS of GOL Event Model

We illustrate the general ideas of event coupling in multicomponent systems by recalling the discrete event cell space model introduced in Chapter 3. Clearly such a model is a multicomponent DEVS model with identical components, uniform arrangement, and uniform couplings. The set of influencing components $I_{i,j}$ as well as the set of influenced components $E_{i,j}$ for a cell i,j are the set of all neighboring cells plus the cell itself. The time advance function of a cell takes care of scheduling its birth and death based on its current fitness and the sum of its neighbors' states. (Note that the time advance is infinity in case that no event is scheduled to happen.) A state event in one cell can influence the time advance of its influencees, possibly causing them to be rescheduled. We will see in the next chapter how the simulation algorithm takes care to plan the events in time - in particular, how events in influenced components $E_{i,j}$ are rescheduled upon changes in a neighboring cell.

For the state set of each cell $M_{i,j}$ we consider the set of pairs,

$$S_{i,j} = \{(state_{i,j}, fitness_{i,j}) \mid state_{i,j} \in \{0,1\}, fitness_{i,j} \in$$

with variables $state_{i,j}$ to denote the actual dead or alive state of the cell and the $fitness_{i,j}$ parameter representing the current fitness of the cell. Additionally, we employ a help variable $sum_{i,j}$ representing the sum of the alive neighbors

$$sum_{i,j} = \left|\{(k,l) \mid (k,l) \in I_{i,j}, state_{k,j} =\right.$$

and an auxiliary variable $factor_{i,j}$ representing the increase or decrease of the fitness parameter

$$factor_{i,j} = \begin{cases} 1 & \text{if sum}_{i,j} = 3 \\ -2 & \text{if } state_{i,j} = 1 \ \& \ (sum_{i,j} < 2 \mid sum_{i,j} > 3) \\ 0 & \text{otherwise.} \end{cases}$$

Given the current $fitness_{i,j}$ and based on the value of $factor_{i,j}$ we easily can compute the time to the next zero crossing and hence the time advance. Note that only in the dead state with a positive $factor_{i,j}$ and in the alive state with negative $factor_{i,j}$ events are scheduled. Formally,

$$ta_{i,j}(q_{i,j}, q_{i,j+1}, q_{i+1,j}, q_{i,j-1}, q_{i-1,j}, q_{i+1,j+1}, q_{i+1,j-1}, q_{i-1,j+1}, q_{i-1,j-1})$$
$$= \begin{cases} -fitness_{i,j} / factory_{i,j} & \text{if } ((state_{i,j} = 1 \ \& \ factor_{i,j} < 0) \mid \\ & (state_{i,j} = 0 \ \& \ factor_{i,j} > 0)) \\ \infty & \text{otherwise.} \end{cases}$$

Finally, the state transition function has to realize time scheduled birth or death of a component. It actually carries out the birth and death in the cell itself and additionally updates the fitness parameter in all the influenced components.

$$\delta_{int,i,j}(q_{i,j}, q_{i,j+1}, q_{i+1,j}, q_{i,j-1}, q_{i-1,j}, q_{i+1,j+1}, q_{i+1,j-1}, q_{i-1,j+1}, q_{i-1,j-1}) =$$
$$(q'_{i,j}, q'_{i,j+1}, q'_{i+1,j}, q'_{i,j-1}, q'_{i-1,j}, q'_{i+1,j+1}, q'_{i+1,j-1}, q'_{i-1,j+1}, q'_{i-1,j-1})$$

where for all influcnced neighboring components $(k,l) \in E_{i,j} - \{ij\}$

$$q'_{k,l} = \langle state_{k,l}, \min\{6, fitness_{k,l} + factor_{k,l} * e_{k,l}\}, 0\rangle$$

i.e., the fitness is updated based on the elapsed time since the last state change, and for the cell i,j itself

$$q'_{i,j} = (state'_{i,j}, fitness'_{i,j}, 0)$$

with

$$state'_{i,j} = \begin{cases} 0 & \text{if } state_{i,j} = 1 \\ 1 & \text{if } state_{i,j} = 0 \end{cases}$$

$$fitness'_{i,j} = \begin{cases} -2 & \text{if } state_{i,j} = 1 \\ 0 & \text{if } state_{i,j} = 0 \end{cases}$$

i.e., the alive and dead state is flipped and the fitness parameter is either initialized with −2 in case of a death or initialized with 0 in case of a birth.

7.2.1 Event Scheduling Models

We come back now to discuss the world views of discrete event simulation, first considered in Chapter 3, in the context of multicomponent DEVS. There are three common types of discrete event simulation strategies employed in discrete event simulation languages and packages—the *event scheduling*, the *activity scanning*, and the *process interaction* world views, the last being a combination of the first two. A strategy makes certain forms of model description more naturally expressible than others. We will model the "pure" forms of these strategies, that is, the forms in which only the features inherent to the basic conception are employed.

Event-oriented models work with prescheduling of all events, and there is no provision for activating events by tests on the global state. Event scheduling strategy can be captured by the multicomponent DEVS as introduced earlier.

Implementing Event Scheduling Simulation Systems in Imperative Programming Languages

Because of its simplicity, event scheduling simulation is the preferred strategy when implementing customized simulation systems in procedural programming languages. One takes the approach that the components' states are realized by arbitrary data records and the state transition functions by several procedures that operate on these data. Most important, each active component defines a sort of "control state" similar to the DEVS's phase variable to denote different events types it has to process. For each such event type, one procedure is coded that implements the state transition for the event type. We can say that the set of event types $S_d^{control} = \{ev_1, ev_2, ev_3, \ldots ev_n\}$ divides the state transition function δ_d of component d into n functions $\delta_d^{ev_i}$, each describing the activity of the component d when started in one of its control states, ev_i. At an event the component branches to one of its event routines depending on the control state (Algorithm 1). On such a model implementation an event list simulation algorithm can be realized that sorts components into the event list depending on their event times and then takes them out in sequence to process.

```
Component d
    S_d^control = {ev_1, ev_2, . . ., ev_n}
    δ_ss ((S_d^control, . . . ))
      case S_d^control
        ev_1 : call event-routine_1
        ev_2 : call event-routine_2
        . . . .
        ev_n : call event-routine_n
```

Algorithm 1 Event scheduling model implementation.

7.2.2 Combined Event Scheduling, Activity Scanning Simulation Strategy

We now augment the event-oriented scheme to allow for activating components by means of co/ntingency tests. Referring to Fig. 2, we can understand the additional model description power attained by these means. Suppose

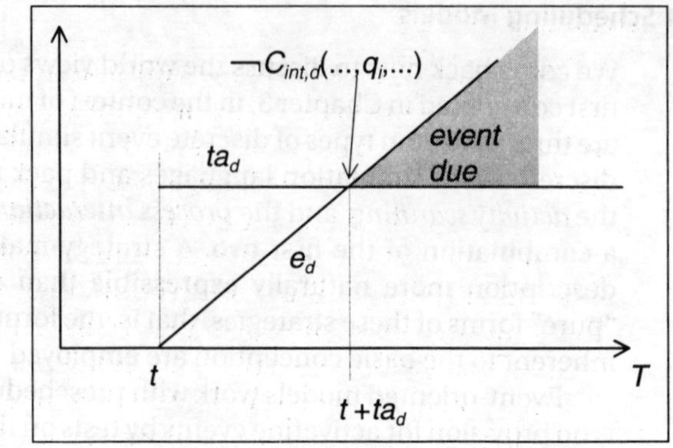

Figure 2 The meaning of due events.

that at time t component d is in state s_d with an elapsed time e_d of 0 (meaning that d just entered state s_d with an event at time t). Then a time of next event is scheduled at time $t + ta_d((\ldots, q_i, \ldots))$. Unless d is rescheduled by the action of another imminent component, it will be activated at this time to undertake an internal transition. In the pure event scheduling strategy this will in either case result in a change of state in d and in a redefinition of its next activation time.

In contrast, in the activity scanning approach, events can be conditioned on a contingency test. When its time has expired and if the contingency test evaluates to true, the event will occur and the state will change. Otherwise, the event is said to be *due*. This means that the elapsed time component e_d is allowed to become greater than the time advance, so the total state set of a component d is $Q_d = \{(s_d, e_d) \mid s_d \in S_d, e_d \geq 0\}$. Once it becomes due, an event must be checked at any global change of state to see if its activation condition has become true. Whenever this condition becomes true, the event can be activated.

To capture the activity scanning strategy, we introduce so-called *activity scanning multicomponent* DEVS as follows:

$$ASDEVS = \langle X, Y, D, Select \rangle,$$

with the same interpretation as for basic multicomponent DEVS. However, the components $d \in D$ are

$$M_d = \langle S_d, E_d, I_d, \delta_{ext,d}, C_{int,d}, \delta_{int,d}, \lambda_d, ta_d \rangle$$

with S_d, E_d, I_d, $\delta_{ext,d}$, $\delta_{int,d}$, λ_d, ta_d the same as in the basic multicomponent DEVS. Additionally, an activity scanning DEVS employs an *event condition function* $C_d: \times_{i \in I_d} Q_i \rightarrow Bool$.

An activity scanning DEVS works in the following way: Each component has its own state transitions whose occurrence is conditioned by the event condition function. Whenever the time elapses and the event condition becomes true, the component is ready to be activated. The *Select* function is used to arbitrate between components having true event conditions simultaneously. Formally, with an ASDEVS = $(X_N, Y_N, D, Select)$ we associate the following DEVS,

$$DEVS = \langle X, Y, S, \delta_{ext}, \delta_{int}, \lambda, ta \rangle,$$

with $S = \times_{d \in D} Q_d$. In the definition of the time advance function, let $\sigma_d = ta_d(\ldots, q_i, \ldots) - e_d$ be the time left to the next time in d. We distinguish two cases. For case (1), if $\exists\, d \in D: \sigma_d \le 0 \wedge C_{int,d}(\ldots, q_i, \ldots)$, i.e. if at current simulation time t there is a component that is ready to be activated, then we define $ta(s) = 0$. Otherwise we have case (2) and we have to advance the time to the time of the next activatable component, i.e., we define $ta(s) = min\,\{\sigma_d \mid d \in D \wedge \sigma_d > 0 \wedge C_{int,d^*}(\ldots, q_i, \ldots)\})$. In either case, we define $d^* = Select\,(\{d \mid \sigma_d \le ta(s) \wedge C_{int,d}(\ldots, q_i, \ldots)\})$ as the next activatable component. The internal transition function $\delta_{int}(s)$, the output function $\lambda(s)$, and the external transition function $\delta_{ext}(s, e, x)$ are defined in the same way as for event scheduling DEVS.

7.2.3 Process Interaction Models

Process interaction simulation strategy is basically a combined event scheduling–activity scanning procedure. The distinguishing feature is that a model component description can be implemented as a unit rather than being separated into a number of unconnected events and activity routines. The advantage is that the program structure maintains a closer relation to the model structure and by scanning the source code, the reader gets a better impression of the model's behavior.

Each component's dynamic behavior is specified by one (or more) routines that describe the state changes during the component's life cycle as a sequential program. This sequential program can be interrupted in two ways:

1. By the specification of time advance
2. By a contingency test

Whenever such an interrupt occurs, the component pauses until the activation condition is satisfied, i.e., either the specified time advance has elapsed or the contingency test has become true. Hence, an important state variable in a process is its *program counter,* which defines its activation point and, therefore, the next state transition to be executed. The program counter represents a control state in each component. It usually shows the particular phase of processing that a component is in. Thus, it is comparable to the phase variable employed in DEVS models.

The process interaction world view further breaks down into two views. Each view corresponds to a different assumption as to what are the active and passive components in building models of manufacturing or other processing systems. In the first view, the active components are taken to be the entities that do the processing, e.g., the machines, servers, and so on. In the second approach, the active components are the flowing elements, that is, the customers, workpieces, packets, etc. Whereas the first is regarded to be the prototypical process interaction world view, the second is regarded as a variation of the first and often referred to as the *transaction world view.*

7.2.4 Translating Nonmodular Multicomponent DEVS Models into Modular Form

Multicomponent systems with nonmodular couplings, directly access and write on each other's state variables. In the sense of modular couplings, this means a violation of modularity. In the sequel, we give a procedure for translating nonmodular coupled systems into modular form. Moreover, we will show that such a translation is always possible. The procedure works by identifying the dependencies between components and converting them into input and output interfaces and modular couplings. *Modularization* is the term used for such introduction of input/output interfaces.

We distinguish two forms of nonmodular couplings, which we have to treat differently. In case (1) component *A* has write access to a variable v of another component *B* (Fig. 3). In modular form, this has to be transformed into a communication from *A* to *B* through a modular coupling. The situation is modularized by giving *A* an output port, *vout*, and *B* an input port, *vin*, and by a coupling from *vout* to *vin*. Whenever, in the original transition function, *A* wants to write to v, in the modular form, *A* has to initiate an output event at *vout* with the same output value. Through the coupling, this results in an input event at *vin* of *B*. The external transition function of *B* has to react by writing the received value into its variable v.

In case (2), component *B* has read access to a variable u of component *A*. This situation is more complicated because *B* always has to have access to the actual value of the variable. The situation is solved in that *B* holds a copy of the state information of u in its own memory. Now, whenever *A* changes the value of u, *B* has to be informed of the change. This is accomplished by a coupling from *A* to *B* through ports *uout* and *uin* in a similar way as in case (1). In this way *B* always has an actual value of variable u in its own state variable *ucopy* (Fig. 4).

7.2.5 State Updating in Distributed Simulation

An important form of state updating occurs in distributed simulation, e.g., in the HLA run-time infrastructure, as illustrated in Fig. 5. The components of a coupled model are mapped onto different computers, or nodes, in a network. To maintain knowledge of the states of other components, replicas of these components are retained on the node dedicated to a component.

State updating is employed to keep the local replicas, or proxies, up to date. In a more advanced concept, the proxies are not full copies of their counterparts, but are smaller versions that are valid simplifications (homo-

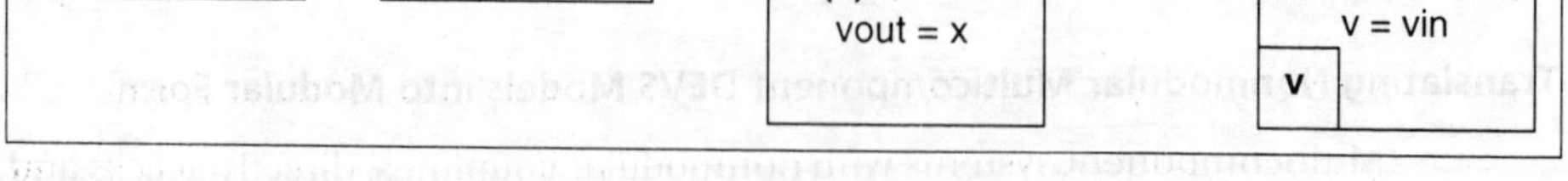

Figure 3 Component *A* has write access to variable v of component *B*.

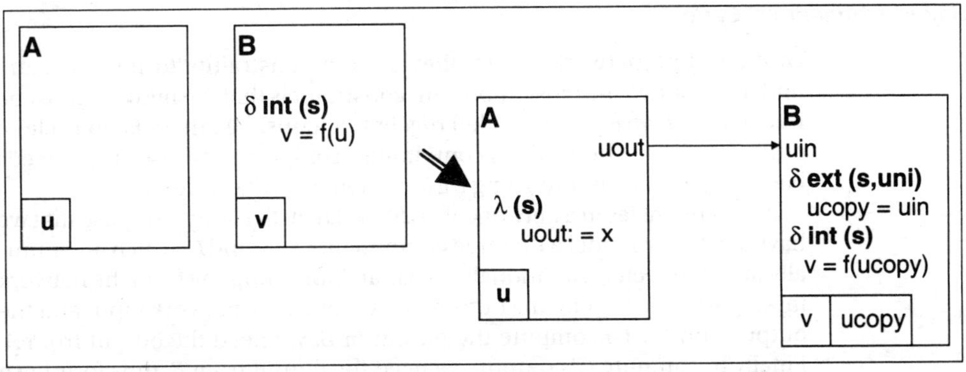

Figure 4 Component *B* has read access to variable *u* of component *A*.

morphisms or endomorphisms) in the experimental frame of the simulation study.

7.3 Discrete Time Specified Network Formalism

In Chapter 3, we learned to know how to model digital sequential networks as built from elementary flip-flops and Boolean gates. Digital networks are examples of networks of discrete time system components. In this section, we introduce the discrete time specified network formalism (DTSN) as a general discrete time formalism at the coupled system level. We specify discrete time networks as couplings of basic discrete time systems and of instantaneous functions, that is, memoryless models.

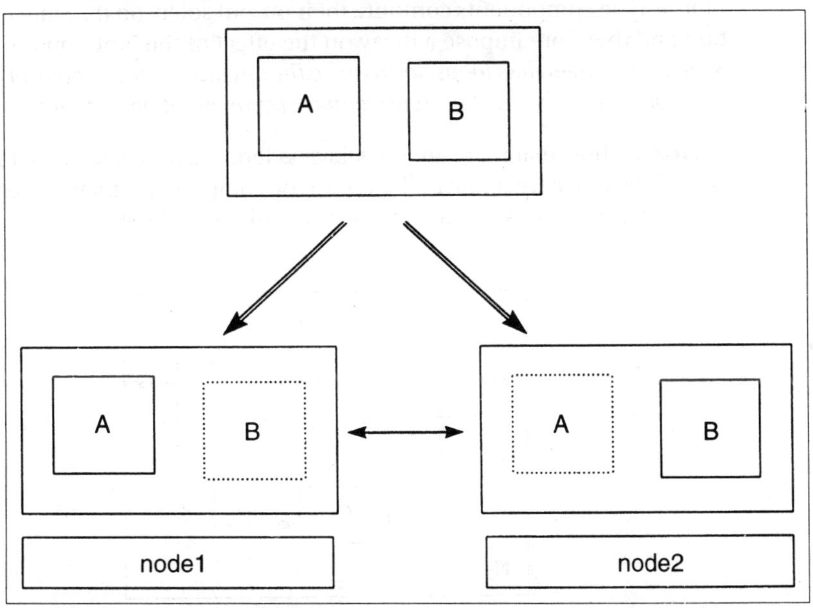

Figure 5 State updating in distributed simulation.

Delay-less (Algebraic) Cycles

Discrete time networks must obey certain constraints to fulfill closure under coupling. The most important constraint is that the network must be free of any *delayless* (also called *algebraic*) loops, i.e., there is no cycle of output-to-input connections containing a component whose output feeds back to its input without going through some non-zero delay.

Dependencies in a network of DTSS will help to clarify. Suppose that we have a network model with three components *A*, *B*, and *C*, which are mutually interconnected. Additionally, *A* has an input coupling from the network input port. To compute the output of *A* we need the network input and the output from *C*. To compute the output of *B*, we need the output from *A*. Finally to compute *C*'s output, we need the output from *B*, thus forming a cycle of dependencies. Now suppose that there are no delays between input and output in any of the components. This means that all the components impose their input-to-output constraints on the ports at the same time. Then, given an input on the input port, we can try to solve for consistent values on the other ports. If there is an unique solution for every input, then a consistent system can result. This approach is commonly adopted in differential algebraic equation models [9]. However, we can obviate the problem by requiring that no algebraic loops be present. For example, we require that in the cycle of Fig. 6, there is at least one component whose current output can be computed without knowledge of the current input.

Exercise: Give examples of choices for the components in Fig. 6 that create algebraic loops with consistent solutions. Do the same for inconsistent solutions.◆

Recall from Chapter 6 that in Mealy-type systems and in instantaneous functions, the output directly depends on the input as well as the state. Only Moore-type components compute their output solely on the state information and therefore impose a delay on the effect of the input on the output. *So to banish delayless loops, we require that in any feedback cycle of coupled components, there must be at least one component of type Moore.*

Exercise: Show that there are no delayless loops if, and only if, the following is the case: When we remove all Moore-type components, then the remaining components form a set of directed acyclic subnetworks.◆

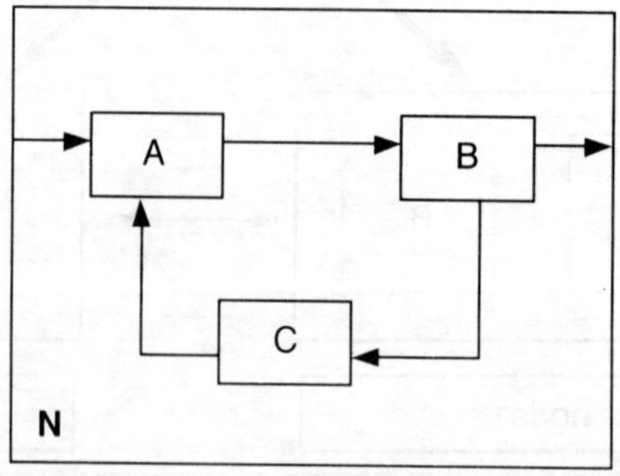

Figure 6 Dependencies in a network of DTSS.

Definition of Discrete Time Coupled Models

A discrete time specified network (DTSN) is a coupled system

$$N = \langle X,Y,D,\{M_d\},\{I_d\},\{Z_d\},h_N \rangle,$$

where X, Y, D, $\{M_d\}$, $\{I_d\}$, $\{Z_d\}$ defined as in the general multicomponent formalism in Section 5.9 and h_N is a constant time advance employed for the specification of the time base $h_N * \Im$. To be well defined, a discrete time network has to fulfill the following constraints:

- The components M_d are basic DTSS or FNSS
- No delayless cycles are allowed, i.e., in a feedback loop there has to be at least one component whose outputs can be computed without knowledge of its input or $\neg\exists\, d_1, d_2, \ldots, d_n \in D \cap \{d \mid d \in D \wedge d$ is a FNSS or d is of type *Mealy*$\} : d_1 \in I_{dn} \wedge d_i \in I_{d_{i-1}}, i = 2, \ldots, n$
- The time base h_N of the network and all its components must be identical.

Closure Under Coupling of DTSS

We now will show that the DTSS formalism is closed under coupling under the conditions just given. Recall that for the detection of algebraic loops it is crucial to decide if a component is of type Moore or Mealy. Therefore, in the process of characterizing the resultant of a DTSN we will develop a procedure to tell whether it is of type Moore or Mealy.

Given a discrete time specified network DTSN, we associate with it the following basic discrete time specified system:

$$DTSS_N = \langle X, Y, Q, \delta, \lambda, h \rangle,$$

where $Q = \underset{d\in D}{\times} Q_d$, $h = h_N$, and $\delta: Q \times X \to Q$ and $\lambda: Q \to Y$ or $\lambda: Q \times X \to Y$ are defined as follows.

Let $q = (q_1, q_2, \ldots, q_d, \ldots) \in Q$ with $d \in D$ and $x \in X$. Then $\delta((q_1, q_2, \ldots, q_d, \ldots), x) = q' = (q'_1, q'_2, \ldots, q'_d, \ldots)$ is defined indirectly through

$$q'_d = \delta_d(q_d, x_d)$$

with $x_d = Z_d(\ldots, y_j, \ldots)$, where for any $j \in I_d$

$$y_j = \begin{cases} \lambda_j(q_j) & \text{if } j \text{ is of type Moore} \\ \lambda_j(q_j, x_j) & \text{if } j \text{ is of type Mealy} \\ \lambda_j(x_j) & \text{if } j \text{ is of type function, respectively.} \end{cases}$$

Note that y_j has a well-defined value in the second and third cases because of the assumption that no algebraic loops are present.

Now the output function, $\lambda: Q \to Y$ or $\lambda: Q \times X \to Y$ is defined as $Z_N(\ldots, y_j, \ldots)$, $j \in I_N$ with y_j is defined as above.

At this stage, we do not yet have a way of deciding whether we have a function $\lambda : Q \to Y$ depending just on state q or it is a function $\lambda : Q \times X \to Y$ also depending on the input x, i.e., if the resulting system is of type Moore or type Mealy. However, having such a decision procedure is essential in hierarchical networks because of the requirement that no delayless cycles exist. Recall that this requires that at least one Moore-type component to be present in all feedback loops. Thus, in hierarchical construction, we need to know whether a network that we are encapsulating as a component is of type Mealy or Moore. The following procedure enables us to decide. We examine the subnetwork of all Mealy and memoryless components. If in this network we find an input from the network that is connected to an output to the network through Mealy-type components or instantaneous functions, then the network is of type Mealy; otherwise, it is of type Moore. (Since there are no algebraic cycles, the connection from the network to itself really represents a coupling from the external input to the external output.) Formally, we present this procedure in the theorem in the Appendix.

7.4 Multicomponent Discrete Time System Formalism

Recall from Section 5.9 that a multicomponent system employs a set I_d of influencing components and a set E_d of components that the component itself influences. We have seen an example of a multicomponent discrete time system—the Game of Life cellular automaton in Chapter 3. In this case, an individual component has a set of influencing components, called its *neighbors.* Its state transition function defines new state values only for its own state variables and does not set other components' states directly. It only influences them indirectly because the state transitions of the other components depend on its own state. Therefore, the next state function of the overall multicomponent system can be visualized as having all the components look at the state values of their individual influencers and simultaneously compute the next state values for their state variables. We have already seen how this inherently parallel computation can be done on a sequential computer. In Chapter 8 and 10 we will formulate appropriate simulators for each of the formalisms that are amenable to both sequential and parallel computation.

A *Multicomponent Discrete Time System Specification* is a structure

$$\text{multiDTSS} = \langle X_N, D, \{M_d\}, h_N \rangle$$

with

X_N is an arbitrary set of input values

h_N is the time interval to define the discrete time base

D is the index set.

For each $d \in D$, the component M_d is specified as

$$M_d = \langle Q_d, Y_d, I_d, \delta_d, \lambda_d \rangle,$$

where Q_d is an arbitrary set of states of d, Y_d is an arbitrary set of outputs of d, $I_d \subseteq D$ is the set of influencers of d, $\delta_d: \times_{i \in Id} Q_i \times X \to Q_d$ is the state transition function of d, and $\lambda_d: \times_{i \in Id} Q_i \times X \to Y_d$ is the local output function of d. (The set of influences E_d of d usually employed in multicomponent models—see Section 5.9—is defined implicitly to be the set $E_d = \{d\}$, having d as the unique element.)

In a multiDTSS, the set of components jointly generate the dynamics of the system. Each of the components owns its local state set, a local output set, and local state transition and output function. Based on the state of the influencing components $i \in I_d$ and on the current input value, the component determines its next state and its contribution to the overall output of the system. In this way, the resultant of a multiDTSS is a DTSS that is built from the crossproduct of the components.

Formally, a multiDTSS = $\langle X, D, \{M_d\}, h_N\rangle$ specifies a DTSS = $\langle X, Y, Q, \delta, \lambda, h\rangle$ at the I/O system level as follows: $Q = \underset{d\in D}{\times} Q_d$, $Y = \underset{d\in D}{\times} Y_d$, $\delta(q,x)$ is defined by

$$\delta(q,x)\cdot d = \delta_d((\ldots, q_i, \ldots), x),$$

$\lambda(q)$ is defined by

$$\lambda(q)\cdot d = \lambda_d((\ldots, q_i, \ldots))$$

with $i \in I_d$, and

$$h = h_N.$$

Spatial DTSS: Cellular Automata

Recall the cellular automata discussed in Chapter 3. Those can be formulated as special cases of the multicomponent DTSS formalism. For example, consider a two-dimensional automaton such as the Game of Life. The multcomponent DTSS model can be specified as follows:

$$\text{multiDTSS} = \langle X, D, \{M_{ij}\}, h_N\rangle$$

X is the empty set since there is no input to the model; $h_N = 1$, since the time base is the set of integers, $\{0,1,2,\ldots\}$; $D = \{(i,j) \mid i \in I, j \in I\}$ is the index set.

For each $(i,j) \in D$, the component M_{ij} is specified as

$$M_{i,j} = \langle Q_{i,j}, Y_{i,j}, I_{i,j}, \delta_{i,j}, \lambda_{i,j}\rangle,$$

where $Q_{i,j} = \{0, 1\}$, $Y_{i,j}$ is empty set since there are no outputs. The set of influencers $I_{i,j}$ is defined by its neighbors $(i, j+l)$, $(i+l, j)$, $(i, j-l)$, $(i-l, j)$, $(i+l, j+l)$, $(i+l, j-l)$, $(i-l, j+l)$, and $(i-l, j-l)\}$. Let

$$sum = q_{i,j+1} + q_{i+1,j} + q_{i,j-1} + q_{i-1,j} + q_{i+1,j+1} + q_{i+1,j-1} + q_{i-1,j+1} + q_{i-1,j-1}$$

be the sum of all neighbors of a cell at i,j. Then we define $\delta_{i,j}$: $x_{k,l} \in {}_{Ii,j}Q_{k,l} \rightarrow Q_{i,j}$ by

$$\begin{aligned}
&\delta_{i,j}(q_{i,j}, q_{i,j+1}, q_{i+1,j}, q_{i,j-1}, q_{i-1,j}, q_{i+1,j+1}, q_{i+1,j-1}, q_{i-1,j+1}, q_{i-1,j-1})\\
&= 1 \quad \text{if } q_{i,j} = 1 \ \& \ (sum = 2 \mid sum = 3)\\
&= 0 \quad \text{if } q_{i,j} = 1 \ \& \ (sum < 2 \mid sum > 3)\\
&= 1 \quad \text{if } q_{i,j} = 0 \ \& \ sum = 3\\
&= 0 \quad \text{if } q_{i,j} = 0 \ \& \ sum \neq 3.
\end{aligned}$$

$\lambda_{i,j}$ is not specified since there is no overall output.

In general, any cellular automaton has a multidimenional geometrical grid structure that is formalized as an Abelian group. A *neighborhood* template is specified as a subset of the group and defines the influencers of the cell at the origin, or zero element, of the group. By uniformity, the influencers of the cell at any other point can be obtained by translating the neighborhood template to that point, i. e., $I_{i,j} = N + (i,j)$, where N is the neighborhood template. The cells all have isomorphic component structures: basically, the same state sets and the same state transition functions. In other words, a cellular automaton can be specified by one neighborhood template and one component structure.

Exercise: Show that the Game of Life multicomponent formalization just given can be put into the space invariant form just described. (Hint: Relate the influencers of cell (i,j) to those of cell $(0,0)$, hence to a neighborhood template and show that the transition function $d_{i,j}$ can be expressed as a function of state values assigned to the appropriate elements in this template.)◆

Exercise: Formulate a space-invariant DEVS cell space formalism analogous to the DTSS formalism for cellular automata just discussed. Express the discrete event form of the Game of Life in this formalism.◆

7.5 Differential Equation Specified Network Formalism

Networks of differential equation specified systems (DEVN) are analogous to discrete time networks and the same ideas apply. Let us introduce networks of differential equation specified systems in the following by translating the considerations of discrete time networks to the continuous domain.

Recall from before that discrete time networks are specified as modular couplings of basic discrete time systems and memoryless instantaneous functions. In the continuous domain we have basic differential equation specified systems and again instantaneous functions. The whole network describes a basic differential equation as the crossproduct of the continuous components where the input rates are defined based on the influencers'outputs.

We introduce the *differential equation specified network* (DESN), analogous to discrete time networks, as a coupled system

$$N = \langle X, Y, D, \{M_d\}, \{I_d\}, \{Z_d\} \rangle$$

with the following constraints:

- X and Y have to be real vector spaces,
- The components $d \in D$ have to be DESS or FNSS,
- No algebraic cycles are allowed, i.e., in a feedback loop there has to be at least one component the output of which can be computed without knowledge of its input

Closure under Coupling of DESS

Given a differential equation specified network DESN, we are able to associate with it the basic differential equation specified system,

$$DESS_N = \langle X, Y, Q, f, \lambda \rangle,$$

where $Q = \times_{d \in D} Q_d$ and $f: Q \times X \rightarrow Q$ and $\lambda: Q \rightarrow Y$ or $\lambda: Q \times X \rightarrow Y$, defined similarly to δ and λ in DTSN,

However, not only must f be well defined, it must also satisfy the Lipschitz condition:

$$\|f(q,x) - f(q',x)\| \leq k\|q - q'\|$$

The proof that this is true will follow from the observation that f is composed of a sequence of coordinate functions, *fd*, taking the form of the nonmodular DESS specification to be discussed below. We will show that if each of the coordinate functions in the latter specification satisfies a Lipschitz condition, then so does the composite function. Since by assumption, in the present case, the f_d are the rate-of-change functions of well-defined DESS specifications, they do indeed satisfy the Lipschitz condition. Thus, on the basis of a proof yet to come, f satisfies the Lipschitz condition.

7.6 Multicomponent Differential Equations Specified System Formalism

In a similar way to the DTSS case, we formulate a multicomponent differential equation system specification, *multiDESS*, with nonmodular coupling. Recall that the basic DESS formalism does not define a next state function directly, but only through rate-of-change functions for the individual continuous state variables. In the multicomponent case, the individual components define the rate of change of their own state variables based on the state values of their influencers. Let us first define the general formalism and then discuss the modelling approach by considering partial differential equations—a special model type showing much resemblance to the cellular automata in the discrete time domain.

A multicomponent differential equation system specification is a structure

$$\text{multiDESS} = \langle X, D, \{M_d\} \rangle,$$

where X is the set of inputs, a real valued vector space $\Re m$, and D is the index set. For each $d \in D$, the component M_d is specified as

$$M_d = \langle Q_d, Y_d, I_d, f_d, \lambda_d \rangle,$$

where Q_d is the set of states of d, a real valued vector space $\Re n$, Y_d is the set of outputs of d, a real valued vector space $\Re n$, $I_d \subseteq D$ is the set of influencers of d, $f_d: \times_{i \in I_d} Q_i \times X \rightarrow Q_d$ is the rate of change function for state variables of d and $\lambda_d: \times_{i \in I_d} Q_i \times X \rightarrow Y_d$ is the local output function of d. The set of influences E_d of d is again defined to be the set $\{d\}$. We require that each f_d satisfies a Lipschitz condition:

$$\|f_d(q,x) - f_d(q',x)\| \leq k_d\|q - q'\|.$$

In a multiDESS, the derivative function of each component defines the rate of change of its local state variables. Formally a multiDESS = $\langle X_N, D, \{M_d\} \rangle$ specifies a DESS = $\langle X, Y, Q, f, \lambda \rangle$ at the I/O system level in the following way:

$$Q = \times_{d \in D} Q_d, \; Y = \times_{d \in D} Y_d,$$

$f(q,x)$ is defined by

$$f(q,x)\cdot d = f_d((\ldots,q_i\ldots),x),$$

and $\lambda(q)$ is defined by

$$\lambda(q)\cdot d = \lambda_d((\ldots,q_i,\ldots)),$$

with $i \in I_d$.

Now, we must show that the resultant derivative function satisfies the Lipschitz condition:

$$\left\|f(q,x)-f(q',x)\right\| \le k\left\|q-q'\right\|.$$

This will follow from the fact that each of its coordinate functions satisfies such a condition by the constraint placed on these functions given before. We demonstrate how this works using two coordinates only:

$$\begin{aligned}
&\left\|f(q_1,q_2,x)-f(q_1',q_2',x)\right\| \\
&= \left\|(f_1(q_1,q_2,x)-f_1(q_1',q_2',x), f_2(q_1,q_2,x)-f_2(q_1',q_2',x))\right\| \\
&\le \left\|(f_1(q_1,q_2,x)-f_1(q_1',q_2',x)\right\| + \left\|f_2(q_1,q_2,x)-f_2(q_1',q_2',x)\right\| \\
&\le k_1\left\|(q-q'\right\| + k_2\left\|(q-q'\right\| \\
&\le (k_1+k_2)\left\|q-q'\right\|.
\end{aligned}$$

Spatial DESS: Partial Differential Equation Models

Partial differential equation models emerge from an extension of differential equations where space coordinates, as well as time, are introduced as independent variables. A partial differential equation specified system therefore shows variations in time as well as in space.

Partial differential equation systems require a science of their own and a whole discipline deals with the solution of such differential equation systems. We will only give an short glimpse of them here to place them into our framework of simulation modeling formalisms.

For our exposition, let us consider a simple example of a general flux-conservative equation in one variable u. The equation

$$\frac{\partial u}{\partial t} = -v\frac{\partial u}{\partial x}$$

expresses that the change of the variable u in time is equal to the negative velocity, $-v$, multiplied by the change of the variable u in the spatial dimension x. The result of this equation is a wave that propagates with velocity v along the x dimension.

The approach to solve problems such as this one, which is a representative of the so-called *hyperbolic* partial differential equation, leads to the discretization of the space and time dimensions. Let us first introduce a discretization of space. The entire observation interval $[x_0, x_1]$ with length l is divided into k equal pieces, each $\Delta x = l/k$ wide. Then we get k *mesh points* for which we set up equations to express the changes over time. In the so-called *forward time centered space* (FTCS) approach, this is done for each mesh point j by replacing the spatial derivative $\frac{\partial u_j}{\partial x}$ of u at point j by the difference of the neighboring states divided by the length of the spatial interval

$$\frac{u_{j-1} - u_{j+1}}{2\Delta x}$$

(note the similarity to the Euler integration method) giving an equation for the time derivative of variable u at point j

$$\frac{\partial u_j}{\partial t} = -v\frac{u_{j-1} - u_{j+1}}{2\Delta x}$$

for each mesh point j. Obviously, we have a multiDESS with k components and influencers set $I_j = \{j-1, j+1\}$ for each component j, as well as derivative functions as just defined.

Usually, when solving partial differential equations the model is set up by also discretizing the time dimension. When we apply the same difference method for discretizing the time dimension, namely dividing the time interval into intervals of equal length Δt, we can replace the time derivative of u at spatial point j and time point n+1 by the difference of the value at time n+1 minus the value at time n divided by Δt (Euler integration)

$$\frac{u_j^{n+1} - u_j^n}{\Delta t}$$

Inserting this term into the equation above and solving it for u_j^{n+1} we finally obtain an equation for state at mesh point j for time n+1

$$u_j^{n+1} \doteq u_j^n - v\frac{u_{j-1}^n - u_{j+1}^n}{2\Delta x}\Delta t.$$

What have we accomplished finally? Starting with a partial differential equation with derivatives in time and space dimension, we have discretized space and time. With the discretization of space we obtained a continuous multi-component model in cellular form with equal derivative functions for the cells. With the discretization of time we finally have obtained a cellular automaton with neighborhood $\{j-1, j+1\}$, time step Δt, and equal next state function for cell j.

7.7 Summary

After defining modular and nonmodular coupled models and showing how a nonmodular system can be transformed into modular form for DEVS, let us conclude this chapter with a comparison of the two approaches.

From the procedure for translating nonmodular couplings into modular form, it is clear that nonmodular systems are easier to build in the conception phase, because the whole system can be built as one gestalt without breaking up the interrelations of components. Components do not have to maintain information about their neighbors since they are allowed to access other's state information directly.

However, this deceptive advantage soon becomes undermined when one considers such issues as testing components or their reusability. Components in modular coupled models are systems by themselves. From their interface description one has a clear understanding what the inputs to this systems can be and what one can expect as outputs. The input and output interfaces unambiguously show what each component needs to get from, and what it provides to other components. A component's dynamic behavior depends only on its inner state and its inputs. Such a module is much easier to comprehend and test for correctness. And modeling coupled systems in a bottom-up approach using well-tested components is much less error-prone than developing complex systems as one big unit.

Also, modular system components lend themselves to reusability. Again, the interface description gives a clear understanding where a component can be used. An interface-based classification of components [12] is useful for organizing families of compatible components. We will come back to this question of reusability of simulation models when we discuss the organization of model bases and the architecture of modeling and simulation environments in the third part of the book.

Finally, modular coupled models best fit the needs of distributed simulation since their components can be assigned to network nodes in a straightforward manner.

7.8 Sources

Kiviat [10] was the first to characterize the different world views of discrete event simulation, while Tocher [13] was the first to provide a formal representation of the activity scanning world view. Nance [11] characterized the time flow mechanisms for discrete event simulation. Renewed interest in activity scanning strategy is emerging in distributed simulation contexts (see Chapter 11). Process interaction world view discussions can be found in Refs. [4,7]. The hierarchical, modular approach to discrete event simulation was introduced by Zeigler [15], and its relation to testing, reusability, and distributed simulation is discussed in Ref. [16].

1. Bossel, H., *Modeling and Simulation.* Ak Peters, Ltd., 1994.
2. Burden, Richard L., and J. Douglas Faires, *Numerical Analysis,* 4th ed. PWS-KENT Publishing Company, 1989.
3. Chow, A., "Parallel DEVS: A Parallel, Hierarchical, Modular Modeling Formalism and its Distributed Simulator." *SCS Transactions on Simulation.* **13**(2), 55–102 (1996).
4. Cota, B. A., and R. G. Sargent, "A Modification of the Process Interaction World View." *ACM Transactions on Modeling and Computer Simulation* **2**(2), 109–129 (1992).
5. DiBenedetto, E., *Partial Differential Equations.* Birkhäuser, Boston, 1995.
6. Fishwick, P., *Simulation Model Design and Execution.* Prentice Hall, 1995.
7. *Process View of Simulation.* Elsevier, New York, 1977.

8. Gould, Harvey, and Gould, H. and Jan Tobochnik, J. *An Introduction to Computer Simulation Methods, Parts 1 and 2.* Addison-Wesley, 1988.
9. Hairer, E. and G. Wanner, *Solving Ordinary Differential Equations II. Stiff and Differential-Algebraic Problems.* Springer-Verlag, 1991.
10. Kiviat, P., "Simulation Languages." In *Computer Simulation Experiments with Models of Economic Systems* (T. H. Saylor, Ed.), Wiley, New York, 1971.
11. Nance, R. E., "On Time Flow Mechanisms for Discrete Event Simulators." *Manag. Sci* **18**(1), 59–73 (1971).
12. Thomas, C., "Interface-Based Classification of Simulation Models," WSC 94, Orlando, FL, 1994.
13. Tocher, K. D., "Simulation Languages." In *Progress in Operations Research* (J. Aronsky, Ed.). Wiley, New York, 1969.
14. Wolfram, Stephen, Ed., *Theory and Application of Cellular Automata.* World Scientific, Singapore, 1986.
15. Zeigler, B. P., *Multifaceted Modeling and Discrete Event Simulation.* Academic Press, London, 1984.
16. Zeigler, B. P., *Object-Oriented Simulation with Hierarchical Modular Models.* Academic Press, Boston, 1990.

Appendix

The following theorem gives the condition under which a network is of type Moore.

Theorem. *Characterization of Moore-type Networks*

Let $IMealy_d = \{e \mid e \in I_d$ and e is of type Mealy or Function or $e = N\}$ be those influencers in set I_d that are of type Mealy, Functions, or the network itself, and let

$$IMealy_d^+ = IMealy_d \cup \bigcup_{e \in IMealy_d} IMealy_e^+$$

be the transitive closure of $IMealy_d$. Then the network N is of type Moore if and only if $N \notin IMealy_N^+$.

Proof: Let $IMealy_N^0 = \{N\}$ and for $i = 1,2,\ldots$ let

$$IMealy_d^i = (\bigcup_{e \in IMealy_N^{i-1}} I_e) \cap \{d \mid d \text{ is of type Mealy or FNSS or } d = N\}$$

be the indirect influencers of type Mealy of network output y_N at level i. As no algebraic cycles are allowed and the set of components is finite, $\exists i \in \Im^+$ such that $IMealy_N^i = \{\}$ and let n be the maximum i with $IMealy_N^i \neq \{\}$. Obviously,

$$IMealy_N^+ = \bigcup_{i=1,\ldots,n} IMealy_N^i$$

For $i = 1,\ldots, n+1$, let

$$IMoore_N^i = \bigcup_{e \in IMealy_N^{i-1}} I_e \cap \{d \mid d \text{ is of type Moore}\}$$

be the influencers of type Moore of the Mealy influencers at level i–1. Then for $i = 1, \ldots, n$ and $\forall e \in IMealy_N^{i-1}$, it follows that $I_e \subseteq IMealy_N^i \cup IMoore_N^i$. Now, since $IMealy_N^{n+1} = \{\}$, $\forall e \in IMealy_N^n$ we have $I_e \subseteq IMoore_N^{n+1}$

(a) We first show if N is of type Moore, it is required that $N \notin IMealy_N^+$, and then from above follows $N \notin IMealy_N^i$ for $i = 1, \ldots, n$.

The output of network N is defined as a function Z_N dependent on the output of the Mealy and Moore influencers at level 1, $y_N = Z_N(\ldots, \lambda_{d_1}(q_{d_1}, x_{d_1}), \ldots, \lambda_{e_1}(q_{e_1}), \ldots)$, for all $d_1, e_1 \in I_N$, $d_1 \in IMealy_N^1$, $e_1 \in IMoore_N^1$. And for all $d_1 \in Imealy_N^1$ the output $\lambda_{d_1}(q_{d_1}, x_{d_1})$ is computed using their input x_{d_1}. However, inputs x_{d_1} are computed by functions Z_{d_1}, which are dependent on influencers of d_1, which are in the level 2 Mealy or Moore influencers of N, $x_{d_1} = Z_{d_1}(\ldots, \lambda_{d_2}(q_{d_2}, x_{d_2}), \ldots, \lambda_{e_2}(q_{e_2}), \ldots)$ for all $d_2, e_2 \in I_{d_1}$, $d_2 \in IMealy_N^2$, $e_2 \in IMoore_N^2$.

The inputs x_{d_2} of the Mealy influencers d_2 are again computed in the same way using the influencers of d_2, which are in the level 3 Mealy and Moore influencers of N. We continue this process until we come to level n components' inputs. For these, however, the set of influencers of type Mealy is empty and the inputs are definitely only dependent on the Moore type components, $X_{d_n} = Z_{d_n}(\ldots, \lambda_{en+1}(q_{en+1}), \ldots)$ for all $e_{n+1} \in I_{d_n}$, $e_{n+1} \in IMoore_N^{n+1}$.

This shows that if $N \notin IMealy_N^+$, following the lines of computations of outputs of Mealy type influencers of the network output above, the network output y_N is finally only a function of the state vector $(\ldots, q_d, \ldots)$, $d \in D$.

(b) The proof that, if $N \in IMealy_N^+$, the output of N is also dependent on the input x_N of N and the network therefore is of type Mealy follows the lines of proof (a).■

8

Simulators for Basic Formalisms

In the view of the hierarchy of system specifications (Chapter 5), simulation is actually a transformation from higher-level system structure knowledge to the I/O relation observation level (Fig. 1). Typically, we are given a system specification (e.g., a coupled model) together with the initial state values for all the state variables and time segments for all input ports at the model's interface. The task of a simulator is to generate the corresponding state and output trajectories. To do this, it has to realize the background conventions associated with the particular formalism in which the model is expressed. For example, a simulator that is given a differential equation must be written to accept piecewise continuous input trajectories and produce such trajectories for the state and output variables. In this chapter we construct corresponding simulation objects and algorithms for the DEVS, DTSS, and DESS modeling formalisms.

We erect a framework that exploits the hierarchical, modular construction underlying the high level of system specifications. Although each formalism requires its specific interpretation, the framework is generic and is based on the same concepts we have already seen in the context of system formalisms (Chapter 5 and 7):

- The basic specification structure of each formalism is supported by a class of atomic models. For example, we can write the elements of a basic DEVS in the atomic class.
- Each such atomic class has its own *simulator* class.
- The coupled model structure of each formalism is supported by a class of coupled models. For example, we can write the elements of a coupled DEVS in the *coupled* class.
- Each such coupled model class has its own simulator class, called *coordinator.*
- Simulator objects adhere to a generic message protocol that allows others to coordinate with them to execute the simulation.
- Assignment of coordinators and simulators follows the lines of the hierarchical model structure, with simulators handling the atomic-level components, and coordinators handling successive levels until the root of the tree is reached.

Figure 2 shows the mapping of a hierarchical model to an abstract simulator associated with it. Atomic simulators are associated with the leaves of the hierarchical model. Coordinators are assigned to the coupled models

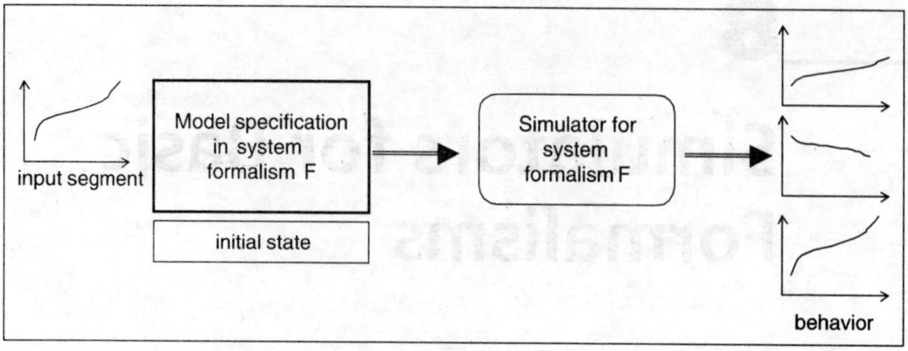

Figure 1 A simulator realizes the background conventions of its modeling formalism.

at the inner nodes of the hierarchy. At the top of the hierarchy a *root-coordinator* is in charge to initiate the simulation cycles.

Although the framework is defined in terms of message passing, it can be realized in different ways, and it can be optimized depending on the performance requirements. Indeed, we may refer to such simulators as *abstract simulators* in the sense that they characterize what has to be done to execute atomic or coupled models with hierarchical structure, not necessarily how it is to be done.

The ability to break down the simulation of hierarchical DEVS and other formalisms in terms of hierarchical simulators ultimately depends on the closure under coupling of such formalisms. Later (Chapter 11) we exploit closure under coupling to develop another approach to simulation of DEVS models, particularly Parallel DEVS models.

8.1 Simulators for DEVS

In Chapter 3 we have seen that discrete event simulation works by maintaining a list of events sorted by their scheduled event times. Events are executed by taking them from the event list in sequential order and doing the

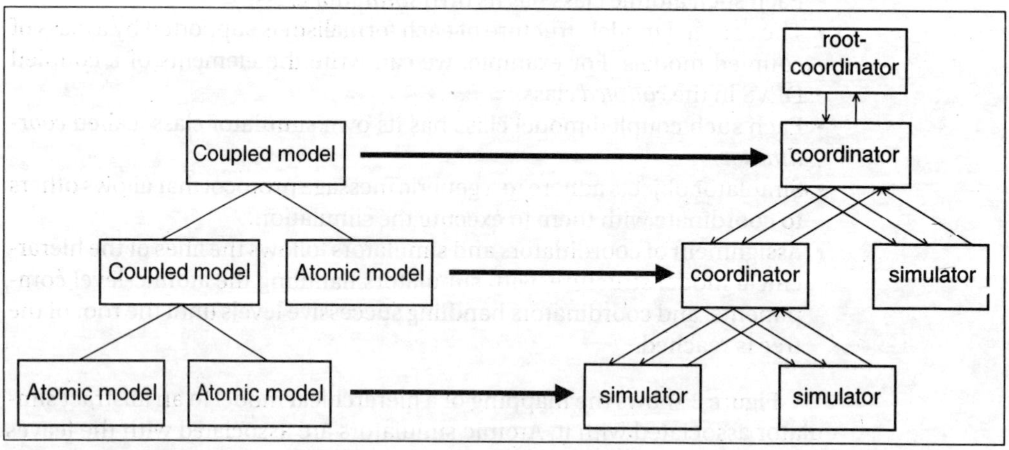

Figure 2 Mapping a hierarchical model onto a hierarchical simulator.

state transitions. Executing events results in new events being scheduled and inserted into the event list as well as events being canceled and removed from the event list.

Based on these general considerations, we formulate simulation schemes for modular hierarchical DEVS. We formulate simulators for atomic DEVS and coordinators for coupled DEVS. Then we show that a hierarchical structure of simulators and coordinators correctly simulates a DEVS coupled model. The event list in such architectures takes on a hierarchical structure that has an intrinsically efficient time management scheme. Moreover, this approach has the advantage that hierarchical DEVS can be readily transformed into executable simulation code. Finally, it has the advantage that it *supports formalism interoperability.* To explain: We will formulate simulators for multicomponent DEVS in nonmodular form that capture major world views (Chapter 7). Because of the polymorphic protocols, these simulators appear to coordinators as if they were basic DEVS. Generalizing this *DEVS-Bus* concept, we will show that it allows the integration of modular components formulated in different modeling approaches, not just those restricted to the ones considered so far.

A hierarchical simulator for hierarchical DEVS coupled model models consists of *devs-simulators* and *devs-coordinators* and uses four types of messages (Fig. 3). An initialization method (i, t) is sent at the initialization time from the parent simulator object to all its subordinates. The scheduling of events is done by the internal state transition message $(*, t)$ and are sent from the coordinator to its imminent child. An output message (y, t) is sent from the subordinates to their parents to notify them of output events. The input message (x, t) is sent from the coordinator to its subordinates to cause external events.

8.1.1 Simulator for Basic DEVS

An interpretation of the dynamics of a DEVS is given by considering the *devs-simulator* for DEVS. The simulator employs two time variables *tl* and *tn*. The first holds the simulation time when the last event occurred and the

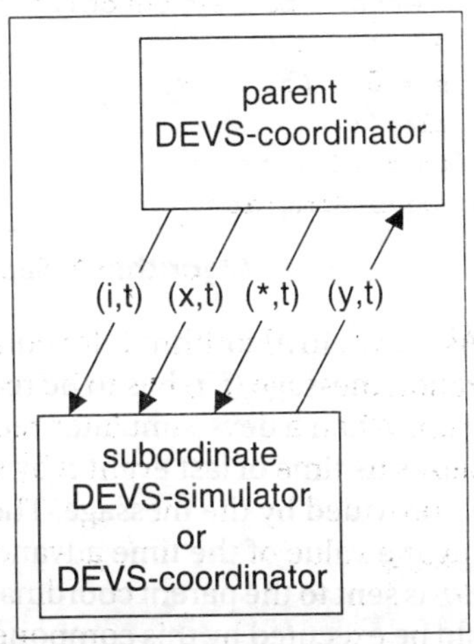

Figure 3 DEVS simulator protocol.

second holds the scheduled time for the next event. From the definition of the time advance function of DEVS it follows that

$$tn = tl + ta(s).$$

Additionally, if it is given the global current simulation time, *t*, the simulator can compute from these variables the elapsed time since the last event,

$$e = t - tl,$$

and the time left to the next event,

$$\sigma = tn - t = ta(s) - e.$$

The time of next event, *tn* is sent to its simulator's parent to allow for correct synchronization of events.

```
Devs-simulator
variables:
  parent    // parent coordinator
  tl        // time of last event
  tn        // time of next event
  DEVS        // associated model
          with total state (s, e)
  y          // current output value of the associated model
   when receive i-message (i, t) at time t
    tl = t - e
    tn = tl + ta(s)
   when receive *-message (*, t) at time t
    if    t != tn then
      error: bad synchronization
    y = λ (s)
    send y-message (y, t) to parent coordinator
    s = δint (s)
    tl = t
    tn = tl + ta(s)
   when receive x-message (x, t) at time t with input value x
    if not (tl ≤ t ≤ tn) then
      error: bad synchronization
    e = t - tl
    s = δext (s, e, x)
    tl = t
    tn = tl + ta(s)
 end Devs-Simulator
```

Algorithm 1 Simulator for Basic DEVS.

As shown in Algorithm 1, for correct initialization of the simulator a initialization message (*i, t*) has to be received at the beginning of each simulation run. When a devs-simulator receives such an initialization message, it initializes its time of last event *tl* by subtracting the elapsed time *e* from the time *t* provided by the message. The time of next event *tn* is computed by adding the value of the time advance *ta*(*s*) to the time of last event *tl*. This time *tn* is sent to the parent coordinator to tell it when the first internal event should be executed by this component's simulator.

An internal state transition message (*, t) causes the execution of an internal event. When a *-message is received by a devs-simulator, it computes the output and carries out the internal transition function of the associated DEVS. The output is sent back to the parent coordinator in an output message (y, t). Finally, the time of the last event tl is set to the current time and the time of the next event is set to the current time plus the value of the time advance function $ta(s)$.

An input message (x, t) informs the simulator of an arrival of an input event, x, at simulation time, t. This causes the simulator to execute the external transition function of the atomic DEVS given x and the computed value of elapsed time, e. As with internal events, the time of the last event tl is set to the current time and the time of the next event is set to the current time plus the value of the time advance function $ta(s)$.

In Chapter 6 we defined the dynamic interpretation of DEVS by defining the global state transition Δ in points (1), (2), (3), and output function Λ in point (4) of the I/O system associated with the DEVS. In the following we state and prove the theorem that the devs-simulator interprets the DEVS as defined by the I/O system.

Theorem 1

Under the assumption that at initial time t_i the system has been in state s for e time units and the parent coordinator provides an i-message at initial time t_i before any other message, x-messages for every event-input of the current input segment ω: $<t_i, t_f] \rightarrow X$, and *-messages when the simulation time t is equal the value tn of the simulator in a timely ordered sequence, then the state $(s, t - tl)$ at any event time t corresponds to the state trajectory of the I/O system associated with the DEVS. Likewise, the outputs sent out in y-messages correspond to the output trajectory.

Proof: The proof follows the dynamic definition of the global state transition and output function of the DEVS (compare Chapter 6). In particular, we show that, if at time $t = tl$, $(s, t - tl) = (s, 0)$ is correct, then the state after the execution of the next x- or *-message is correct. We also show that tn always represents the time of the next scheduled event.

Let (s, e) be the correct state at time $t = t_i$. After the i-message at time $t = t_i$, variable tl is set to $t_i - e$. Obviously, state $(s, tl - tl) = (s, 0)$ was the correct state at time. Also, variable tn is set to $tl + ta(s)$ as required.

Let $(s, 0)$ be the correct state at time tl and let $tn = tl + ta(s)$ be the time of the next scheduled event. Then, by the preceding assumption, either an x-message or a *-message has to be received, depending on whether an input event or internal event will occur next.

Let the next message be an x-message with input value $x = \omega(t)$ at time $t \leq ta(s)$. Then following the commands of the x-message (Algorithm 1), the state is set to $s' = \delta_{ext}(s, t - tl, x)$, tl is set to t, and finally, tn is set to $tl + ta(s)$. Obviously $(s', t - tl) = (s', 0)$ finally corresponds the global state transition function $\Delta(s, \omega_{(tl, t)})$ according to point (3) $(\Delta(\delta_{ext}(s, e - t - t_i, x), 0), \varnothing_{(t, t)}) = (\delta_{ext}(s, t - tl, x), 0)$, with $t_i = tl$ and $e = 0$.) Also, tn is set to $tl + ta(s)$, which by definition is the time of the next scheduled event.

In the case that there is no input event until time tn, then by assumption above the next message is a *-message at time tn. As $tn = tl + ta(s)$, $t - tl = ta(s)$

as required by point (2) in Chapter 6. Following the commands of the *-message, one sees that the state is set to $s' = \delta_{int}(s)$ and $tl = t$. This corresponds to the definition of $\Delta(s, \omega_{(tl,t)})$ according to point (2) of Chapter 6. Also, tn is set to $tl + ta(s)$.

The devs-simulator guarantees that it sends out an output $\lambda(s)$ in a y-message exactly when there is an internal transition at time tn. Hence, the trajectory constructed from the y-messages (y, t) sent out from the devs-simulator at internal event times tn and constant value $\varnothing$ between these events corresponds to the output function definition Λ in point (4) of the I/O system specification of DEVS in Chapter 6.■

8.1.2 Simulators for Modular DEVS Networks

In a simulator for a DEVS coupled model, each model component is handled by its own simulator, which is assumed to correctly simulate it. A coordinator assigned to the network is responsible for the correct synchronization of the component simulators and handling of external events arriving at the network inputs. To perform its task, the coordinator makes use of the protocols of its subordinates and provides the same protocol to its parent.

The coordinator implements an event list algorithm to take care for the correct synchronization of its components. It maintains an event list which is a list of pairs of component simulators with their times of next event. This list is sorted by the event times tn and, when the tn times of components are equal, by the *Select* function of the coupled model. The first component in the event list defines the next internal event within the scope of the coordinator. This minimum next event time,

$$tn = \min\{tn_d \mid d \in D\},$$

is provided to the parent of the coordinator as its next event time. In a similar way, the time of last event of the coordinator is computed by

$$tl = \max\{tn_d \mid d \in D\}$$

as the last time when an event occurred in one of the subordinate simulators. Additionally, a coordinator has to handle input events arriving at the network's input interface.

```
Devs-coordinator
  variables:
  DEVN = (X, Y, D, {M_d}, {I_d}, {Z_i,d}, Select)
    //the associated network
  parent        // parent coordinator
  tl            // time of last event
  tn            // time of next event
  event-list
    // list of elements (d, tn_d) sorted by tn_d and Select
  d*            // selected imminent child
when receive i-message (i, t) at time t
  for-each d in D do
    send i-message (i, t) to child d
```

```
  sort event-list according to tn_d and Select
  tl = max {tl_d | d ∈ D}
  tn = min {tn_d | d ∈ D}
when receive *-message (*, t) at time t
  if t != tn then
    error: bad synchronization
  d* = first (event-list)
  send *-message (*, t) to d*
  sort event-list according to tn_d and Select
  tl = t
  tn = min {tn_d | d ∈ D}
when receive x-message (x, t) at time t with external input x
  if not (tl ≤ t ≤ tn) then
    error: bad synchronization
  //consult external input coupling to get children influenced by
  //the input
  receivers = {r | r ∈ D, N ∈ I_r, Z_N,r (x) ≠ Φ}
  for-each r in receivers
    send x-messages (x_r ,t) with input value x_r = Z_N,r (x) to r
  sort event-list according to tn_d and Select
  tl = t
  tn = min {tn_d | d ∈ D}
when receive y-message (y_d*, t) with output y_d* from d*
  //check external coupling to see if there is an external out-
  //put event
  if d* ∈ I_N & Z_d*,N(y_d*) ≠ Φ then
    send y-message (y_N ,t) with value y_N = Z_d*,N(y_d*) to parent
  //check internal coupling to get children influenced by out-
  put y_d* of d*
  receivers = {r | r ∈ D, d* ∈ I_r, Z_d*,r(y_d*) ≠ Φ}
  for-each r in receivers
    send x-messages (x_r,t) with input value x_r = Z_d*,r (y_d*) to r
end Devs-coordinator
```

Algorithm 2 Coordinator for DEVS coupled model.

As mentioned above, the coordinator responds to, and sends, the same types of messages as do devs-simulators. As shown in Algorithm 2, it may receive a message (i, t) for initialization purposes, internal state transition messages $(*,t)$ to execute internal events, and input messages (x,t) for external events. It sends the events at the network output interface back to its parent in output messages (y,t). Additionally, the coordinator has to handle the *y*-messages received from its subordinates.

When a devs-coordinator receives an *i*-message, it forwards it to each of its children. When all the children have handled their *i*-messages, it sets its time of last event *tl* to the maximum of the times of last event of the children and its time of next event *tn* to the minimum of the times of next event of its children.

When a devs-coordinator receives a *-message, the message is transmitted to its imminent child, which is the first in the event list. The imminent child executes its state transition and may send output messages (y,t)

back. After the completion of the internal event and all the external events caused by the output of the imminent component, the time of the next event is computed as the minimum of the next event times of its children.

When a coordinator receives an output message (y_{d^*}, t) that carries the output information of its selected imminent child, it consults the external output coupling of the DEVS network to see if it should be transmitted to its parent coordinator, and the internal couplings to obtain the children, and their respective input ports, to which the message should be sent. In the first case, an output message (y_N, t) carrying the external network output y_N is sent to the parent coordinator. In the second case, the output message (y_{d^*}, t) is converted into input messages (x_r, t) with $x_r = Z_{d^*,r}(y_{d^*})$, indicating the arrival of external events at the influenced components, r.

When a coordinator itself receives an input message (x, t) from its parent coordinator, it consults the external input couplings of the DEVS network to generate the appropriate input message for the subordinates influenced by the external event. Input messages ($Z_{N,r}(x)$, t) are sent to all children, r, influenced by the external input x. After that, the event times are updated.

In Section 7.1 we defined how a discrete event network DEVN defines an atomic DEVS system. Now we will show that the devs-coordinator implements a devs-simulator for the $DEVS_N$ associated with DEVN. This allows us to treat a coordinator of a DEVS network in the same way as a simulator for an atomic DEVS. Also, we have to guarantee that the coordinator sends messages to the subordinates as required by the assumptions in the correctness theorem for the DEVS simulator.

Theorem 2

Under the assumption that at initial time t_i the components states are (s_d, e_d), meaning that component d has been in state s_d for e_d time units and the superior coordinator provides an i-message at initial time t_i before any other message, x-messages for every input event of the current input segment ω: $<t_i, t_f] \rightarrow X$ arriving at the network inputs, and *-messages when the simulation time t is equal the value tn of the coordinator in a timely ordered sequence, then the devs-coordinator

(i) implements the correct devs-simulator operations for the $DEVS_N$ with total state $((\ldots, (s_d, t - tl_d), \ldots), t - tl)$ associated with the coupled system N, and

(ii) provides the correct synchronization for the subordinate simulators associated with components d.

Proof: (i) *Correct implementation:* We show that (i) holds by showing that the commands in the i-, x-, and *-messages of the coordinator are equivalent to the messages of a simulator for the $DEVS_N$ associated with a coupled DEVS.

(i.1) To implement i-messages, a devs-coordinator has to implement commands $tl = t - e$, $tn = tl + ta(s)$ given the state $s = (\ldots, (s_d, e_d), \ldots)$ at initial time t_i. Since the last state change in component d was e_d time units prior to time t_i, the last state change within the scope of the network N was $e = min\{e_d \mid d \in D\}$ prior to t_i. After i-messages are sent to the children d, tl_d is equal to $t - e_d$. The variable tl is set to $max\ \{tl_d \mid d \in D\}$. Now, since $tl = max\ \{t - e_d \mid d \in D\}$, we have $tl = t - min\ \{e_d \mid d \in D\}$ or $tl = t - e$, as required by a devs-simulator.

In the coordinator, tn is set to $min\{tn_d \mid d \in D\}$. Let $e_d = tl_d - tl$ be the elapsed time at time tl. Then $\sigma_d = ta_d(s_d) - e_d$ is the time remaining for component d at time tl. $DEVS_N$ requires that $ta(s) = min\{\sigma_d \mid d \in D\} = min\,\{ta_d(s_d) - e_d \mid d \in D\}$, and according to the devs-simulator, $tn = tl + ta(s)$. Hence, we have to show that $min\,\{tn_d | d \in D\} = tl + min\,\{ta_d\,(s_d) - e_d | d \in D\}$. Now, $min\,\{tn_d \mid d \in D\} = min\,\{tl_d + ta_d\,(s_d) \mid d \in D\} = min\,\{tl - e_d + ta_d\,(s_d) \mid d \in D\} = min\,\{tl + ta_d(s_d) - e_d \mid d \in D\} = tl + min\,\{\sigma_d \mid d \in D\}$, as required.

(i.2) To implement *-messages, a devs-coordinator has to implement commands to compute the output $\lambda(s)$ and send it back to the parent, compute the next state using $\delta_{int}(s)$ and set tl to t and tn to $tl + ta(s)$ of the $DEVS_N$ (compare Section 7.1.1). Following the operations of the devs-coordinator, we see that d^* is computed by computing the imminents as $\{d \mid d \in D \wedge tn_d = min\,\{tn_c \mid c \in D\}\}$ and selecting one of them using function *Select*. This corresponds to the selection of the child d^* in $DEVS_N$ by *Select* $(IMM(s))$ with $IMM(s) = \{d \mid d \in D \wedge \sigma_d = ta(s)\}$. When a *-message is sent to the coordinator, this results in a y-message being sent back carrying the output $y_{d^*} = \lambda_{d^*}(s_{d^*})$. This output is converted to $Z_{d^*,N}(y_{d^*})$, providing the required output $\lambda(s)$ of the $DEVS_N$. If it is unequal to the nonevent, it is sent as an output of the DEVN to the parent coordinator which is in correspondence to the operation of the devs-simulator. After that, x-messages with inputs $x_r = Z_{d^*,r}(y_{d^*})$ are sent to the influencees r of d^*; this results in computation of $s_r' = \delta_{ext,r}\,(s_r,\, t - tl_r,\, x_r)$ and setting of tl_r to t, resulting in total state $(s_r', t - tl_r) = (s_r', 0)$ for component r, $r \in D$ with $d^* \in I_r$. This corresponds to the second point of δ_{int} of $DEVS_N$. In the *-message of d^*, the internal transition function computes $s_{d^*}' = \delta_{int,d^*}\,(s_{d^*})$ of d^* and tl_{d^*} is set to t, resulting in state $(\delta_{int,d^*}\,(s_{d^*}),\, t - tl_{d^*}) = (\delta_{int,d^*}\,(s_{d^*}),\, 0)$ as required in the first point of the definition of δ_{int}. All other components have not received messages and no change occurred. For those, by definition e_d should be increased by $ta(s)$ according to the third point of δ_{int}. Now, e_d was equal to $tl - tl_d$ before the *-message arrived and $t = tn$, $tn - tl = ta(s)$ at arrival of the *-message. As tl is set to t $(= tn)$, tl is increased by $ta(s)$, and hence $e_d = tl - tl_d$ is increased by $ta(s)$ as required. Also, tn is set to $tn = min\,\{tn_d \mid d \in D\}$, which is equivalent to $tn = t + ta(s)$ as shown in (i.1).

(i.3) To implement receiving of x-messages at time t with input x, a devs-coordinator has to implement commands to compute the next state by δ_{ext} and set tl to t and tn to $tl + ta(s)$ (compare Section 7.1.1). By following the operations of the devs-coordinator, we see that the x-messages with inputs $x_r = Z_{N,r}\,(x)$ are sent to the influencees of N to compute $s_r' = \delta_{ext,r}\,(s_r,\, t - tl_r,\, x_r)$. After computation of the new state s_r' and setting of tl_r to t, the state of r is equal to $(s_r', t - tl_r) = (s_r', 0)$ as required in the first point of the definition of δ_{ext} for $DEVS_N$. All other components have not received messages, so no changes occurred (point 2 of δ_{ext}). Again, since $e = t - tl$ and setting tl to t, $e_d = tl - tl_d$ is increased by e as required. Again tn is set *to* $tn = min\,\{tn_d \mid d \in D\}$, which is equivalent to $tn = t + ta(s)$ as shown in (i.1).

(ii) *Correct synchronization:* The devs-coordinator, by assumption, receives an i-message at time t_i prior to any other message and sends i-messages to its children; hence, the subordinate simulators receive correct i-messages at time t_i. Now, *-messages are sent at times $t = tn$ to component d^*, which is one of the imminents, $\{d \mid d \in D \wedge tn_d = min\,\{tn_e \mid e \in D\}\}$. As tn is defined by $min\ \{tn_d \mid d \in D\}$, it follows that $t = tn = tn_{d^*}$ as required. When receiving x-messages at times t, $tl \le t \le tn$, and when receiving y-messages at times $t = tn$, since tn is defined by $min\ \{tn_d \mid d \in D\}$, $t \le tn$ implies $t \le tn_d$. At the first i-message tl is defined by $max\ \{tl_d \mid d \in D\}$; hence, $tl_d \le tl$ is true after the i-message. At every message at time t, tl is set to t and only those tl_d's of children d that received message are changed to t. The others are left unchanged; hence, never is $tl_d > tl$. Hence, $tl_d \le tl \le t \le tn \le tn_d$, as required to guarantee correct timely order of messages.■

8.1.3 The Root-Coordinator

The root-coordinator implements the overall simulation loop (Algorithm 3). It accomplishes its task by sending messages to its direct subordinate, corresponding to the all-inclusive coupled model, to initiate their simulation cycles. In our terminology, we call the message to initiate a new simulation cycle for an event a *-message. The subordinate of the root-coordinator responds by reporting back its time of next state transition (*tn*). Thus, the root-coordinator first sends a message to initialize the simulator (*i*-message) and then in a loop sends *-messages with times *tn* to its subordinate to initiate the simulation cycles until some termination condition is met.

```
devs-root-coordinator
 variables:
   t        // current simulation time
   child    // direct subordinate devs-simulator or -coordinator
 t = t0
 send initialization message (i, t) to child
 t = tn of its child
 loop
      send (*, t) message to child
      t = tn of its child
  until end of simulation
end devs-root-coordinator
```

Algorithm 3 Root-coordinator for DEVS abstract simulator.

From the root-coordinator we require that it provides the correct synchronization for its subordinate.

Theorem 3
The devs-root-coordinator provides the correct synchronization for the subordinate devs-simulator.

Proof: Directly follows by the operations of the root-coordinator.■

8.2 DEVS Bus

After introducing abstract simulator concepts for Classic DEVS, we will show how other discrete event modeling approaches can be integrated into the framework. The DEVS bus concept for interoperating with diverse discrete event modeling formalisms is illustrated in Fig. 4. Any formalism to be integrated must be wrapped in a DEVS form through a suitably defined simulator. Its models can then be coupled to other such models and executed through a standard coordinator. Moreover, as we shall show in Chapter 9, DEVS is capable of expressing models formulated in the other major formalisms (DTSS and DESS), so these can also be integrated into an all-DEVS simulation environment supporting multiformalism modeling.

We begin by developing simulators for event scheduling and activity scanning/process interaction formalisms. These formalisms have already been characterized as nonmodular multicomponent DEVS (Chapter 7). However, we made them compatible with basic DEVS by adding the requisite input/output interface features (basically, external transition and output functions). The simulators exploit these extensions to adhere to the DEVS bus protocol.

8.2.1 Simulator for Event Scheduling Multicomponent DEVS

Earlier we defined *event scheduling multicomponent DEVS* as a formalism for models formulated in the event scheduling strategy. Recall that event scheduling models are built from several components that are coupled in a non-modular way. In distinction to the other formalisms, in event scheduling the only means to bring events to execution is by prescheduling them in the future.

In the following we present a simulator for multicomponent DEVS with event scheduling strategy that realizes the general simulation scheme for this modeling strategy. Moreover, the formulation as a simulator object and the provision of input/output interfaces allows use of such models as components in hierarchical simulators together with components formulated in other strategies. We present the simulator object first and then show that it realizes a simulator for basic DEVS associated with multi-component DEVS.

The simulator for event scheduling DEVS is similar to simulators of basic DEVS, but realizes its own event handling for the model components. For this purpose, it uses variables to hold its time of last event tl and time of next event tn, as well as variables tl_d and tn_d for all its components. Furthermore, an event list is used to sort the components based on their event times and *Select* order.

As shown in Algorithm 4, upon the receipt of an initialization message (i,t), first of all the event times tl_d and tn_d are set to

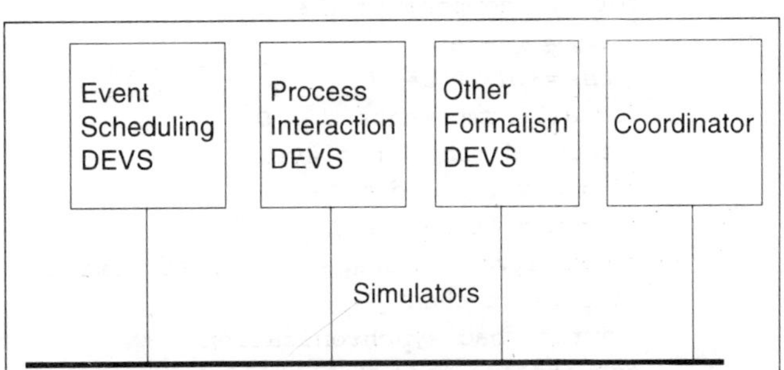

Figure 4 DEVS bus.

$$tl_d = t - e_d$$

and

$$tn_d = tl_d + ta_d((\ldots, q_i, \ldots)),$$

respectively, where $(\ldots, q_i, \ldots)$ denote the state vector formed by the states of the influencing components $i \in I_d$. Based on the next event times tn_d and the *Select* order, the components d are inserted into the event list. Finally, the global last event time tl of the multicomponent model is the maximum of the last event times of the components, and the global next event time tn is the minimum of the next event times of the components.

Upon receipt of a state transition message $(*, t)$, the next state transition within the components of the multicomponent model has to be executed. Therefore, we employ the event list and retrieve the first element d^* in the event list, which is the component with minimal tn_d, hence $t = tn_{d^*}$. We execute the state transition $\delta_{int,d^*}((\ldots, q_i, \ldots))$ of d^* that may change the states of all influenced components $j \in E_{d^*}$. As a result the time advance values of the components may change, which requires the reinsertion of the components with their new event times. Finally, the global event times tl and tn are updated appropriately.

We formulated event scheduling DEVS to also allow for external events. Upon receipt of an external input message (x, t), the external state transitions of all the components affected by the input are executed. As for internal state transitions, we have to reschedule all components changed by the external event.

```
Esdevs-simulator
  variables:
    parent      // parent coordinator
    tl          // time of last event
    tn          // time of next event
    ESDEVS = (X, Y, D, {Md}, Select)
    with components Md = (Sd, Id, Ed, δext,d, δint,d, λd, tad)
      with states qd = (sd, ed)
      time of last event tld and time of next event tnd
        and local outputs yd
    event-list = list of pairs (d, tnd) sorted by tnd and Select
when receive i-message (i, t) at time t
  for all components d ∈ D
    tld = t - ed
    tnd = tld + tad((. . ., qi, . . .))
  for all components d ∈ D
    sort (d, tnd) into event-list
  tl = max {tld | d ∈ D}
  tn = min {tnd | d ∈ D}
when receive *-message (*, t) at time t
  if t != tn then
    error: bad synchronization
  (d*, tnd*) = first (event-list)
  (. . ., qj, . . .) = δint,d*((. . ., qi, . . .))
```

```
    for all components j ∈ Ed*
      tlj = t - ej
      tnj = tlj + taj((. . ., qi, . . .))
      remove (j, tnj) and
      reinsert (j, tnj) into event-list
    tl = t
    tn = min {tnd | d ∈ D}
  when receive x-message (x, t) at time t with input value x
    if not (tl ≤ t ≤ tn) then
      error: bad synchronization
    for all components d ∈ D if defined δext,d
      (. . ., qj, . . .) = δext,d((. . ., qi, . . .), t-tld, x)
      for all components j ∈ Ed
        tlj = t - ej
        tnj = tlj + taj((. . ., qi, . . .))
        remove (j, tnj) and
        reinsert (j, t + tnj) into event-list
    tl = t
    tn = min {tnd | d ∈ D}
  end Esdevs-Simulator
```

Algorithm 4 Simulator for event scheduling multicomponent DEVS.

Theorem 4

Under the assumption that at initial time t_i the components of the system have been in state s_d for e_d time units and the superior coordinator provides an *i*-message at initial time t_i before any other message, *x*-messages for every event input of the current input *segment* ω:$<t_i, t_f] \to X$, and *-messages when the simulation time *t* is equal the value *tn* of the simulator in a timely ordered sequence, then the simulator for an event scheduling multicomponent DEVS realizes a simulator for the basic DEVS associated with the event scheduling DEVS as defined in Chapter 7.

Proof: The proof follows the lines of the definition of the basic DEVS associated with the event scheduling DEVS in Section 7.2.1 and is similar to the proof for the devs-coordinator.■

8.2.2 Simulator for Activity Scanning and Process Interaction Multicomponent DEVS

In addition to prescheduling of events, activity scanning and process interaction models also allow for conditional events, that is, events whose execution is dependent on a test of the global state. Recall that events can become due when the event time has come but the event condition does not evaluate to true. The event has to wait until some influencing states change so that the event condition allows the event to be executed. A simulator for activity scanning DEVS, therefore, has to check the conditions of due events at any state change to see if they are ready to be executed.

A simulator object for activity scanning DEVS employs two lists (1) the *future event list* (FEL), which serves to store the events scheduled for the future (essentially, similar to the events-list in the event scheduling simulator), and (2) the *current-events-list* (CEL), which is used to store the components whose event times have come. Events are sorted in one of those lists depending on their event times—if the time is greater than the current time *t*, the event is inserted into the FEL; if it is equal or smaller the current simulation time, the event goes into the CEL. Hence, the CEL also contains all the due events. At any state change all events in the CEL have to be checked to see if they are ready to be executed. While the FEL is sorted by the event time, the CEL is sorted by the *Select* order. This guarantees that the events are always executed according to the priority specified by *Select*.

In its remaining features, the simulator is similar to that of the event scheduling DEVS. Let us look at the main differences. In the initialization message, the components are inserted into the FEL or the CEL depending on their event times. Upon receiving a state transition message (*, *t*) with a new event time *t*, all events with that event time are removed from the FEL and inserted into the CEL. Then the CEL is scanned from the beginning, that is, in *Select* order, to find the first component with true event condition. This event is executed. The influenced components are rescheduled, either in the FEL or the CEL. Then, the CEL is again scanned from the beginning for the next executable event. Finally, when no executable events are left, the next event time *tn* is computed as the smallest scheduled time in the FEL. (See Algorithm 5.)

```
Asdevs-simulator
  variables:
    parent      // parent coordinator
    tl          // time of last event
    tn          // time of next event
    ASDEVS = (X, Y, D, {M_d}, Select)
    with components M_d = (S_d, I_d, E_d, δ_ext,d, C_int,d, δ_int,d, λ_d, ta_d)
      with states q_d = (s_d, e_d)
      time of last event tl_d and time of next event tn_d
      and local outputs y_d
    FEL = List of pairs (d, tn_d) sorted by tn_d and Select
    CEL = List of pairs (d, tn_d) sorted by Select
when receive i-message (i, t) at time t
  for all components d ∈ D
    tl_d = t - e_d
    tn_d = tl_d + ta_d((. . ., q_i, . . .))
  for all components d ∈ D
    if (tn_d ≥ t)
      insert (d, tn_d) into FEL
    else
      insert (d, tn_d) into CEL
  tl = max {tl_d | d ∈ D}
  tn = min {tn_d | d ∈ FEL}
when receive *-message (*, t) at time t
  if t != tn then
    error: bad synchronization
  take out all elements (d, tn_d) with tn_d = t from FEL and
      reinsert (d, tn_d) into CEL
```

```
SCAN:          // try to execute the due events
    for (d*, tn_d*) in CEL do
        if C_int,d*((..., q_i, ...)) then
            (..., q_j, ...) = δ_int,d*((..., q_i, ...))
          for j ∈ E_d* do
              remove (j, tn_j) from FEL or CEL
              tl_j = t - e_j
              tn_j = tl_j + ta_j((..., q_i, ...))
              if tn_j > t   then insert (j, tn_j) into FEL
                            else insert (j, tn_j) into CEL
          endfor
          exit to SCAN
        endif
    endfor
  tl = t
  tn = min {tn_d | d ∈ FEL}
when receive x-message (x, t) at time t with input value x
  // similar as for event scheduling DEVS but with current event
  // scanning
  end Asdevs-Simulator
```

Algorithm 5 Simulator for activity scanning multicomponent DEVS.

In the same way as for event scheduling multicomponent DEVS, we can formulate a theorem that proves the simulator correctness, i.e., it interprets the model in conformity with the DEVS associated with the activity scanning DEVS formalism. Finally, having constructed DEVS protocol compliant simulators for event scheduling, activity scanning, and process interaction strategies, we can state:

Corollary
Simulators exist for nonmodular multicomponent DEVS that enable models in such formalisms to interoperate in hierarchical, modular DEVS models as if they were basic atomic DEVS models.

8.3 Simulators for DTSS

The simulator for a hierarchical discrete time system has to implement the fixed step algorithm to compute the state and output values given an input value at each instant of the discrete time base. Recall (Chapter 6) that for a DTSS one has to specify a constant h that gives a constant time advance at each simulation step. Also, recall that a DTSS employs a next state function that computes the state value at the next time step given the state value at the current time and the input at the current time. An output function computes the output at any time instant based on the current state.

Hence, a DTSS simulator is a simple algorithm that jumps from one simulation step to the next and computes the next state and output values. However, through the dependencies between the different components in a coupled system, namely, that the output of one component defines the input for others, the right sequence for executing the state transitions and output functions in the individual components is crucial. Recall that components of DTSS networks can be of three different types: DTSS models of Moore-type, DTSS models of Mealy-type and memoryless FNSS, the main difference being that for Moore-type systems the output is computed solely based on the current state, whereas for the output of Mealy-type and FNSS models, we need the current input to compute the current output. The Moore-type components are those that break algebraic loops. A scheduling sequence for a network of DTSS, therefore, has to compute the outputs of the Moore-type components solely based on the current state and then, subsequently, go to the others to compute the current output when the current input is available. At the end of the sequence we come back to the Moore-type components to compute the next states.

In the following we present a hierarchical simulator for discrete time systems which assumes networks consisting only of Moore-type components and memoryless functions. This leads to a simpler scheme compared to networks also containing Mealy-type components. (In Ref. [5] a more general scheduling algorithm for hierarchical models is presented that also works with Mealy type systems and Mealy type networks. It is also optimized in requiring only a single traversal of components in each simulation step.)

A hierarchical simulator for hierarchical, coupled DTSS models consists of *dtss-simulators* and *dtss-coordinators* and uses three types of messages (Fig. 5). An initialization method (i, t) is sent at the initialization time from the parent simulator object to all its subordinates. The parent sends a *-message to tell its subordinates to compute their outputs. A state transition message (x, t) is sent to the subordinates to trigger the execution of the state transition. The subordinates send an output message (y, t) to their parent.

8.3.1 Simulator for Atomic DTSS

The *dtss-simulator* implements the simulation algorithm for an atomic DTSS (of the Moore-type). To take care of the feedback loops, a dtss-simulator provides two messages at each time step. The *-message is used

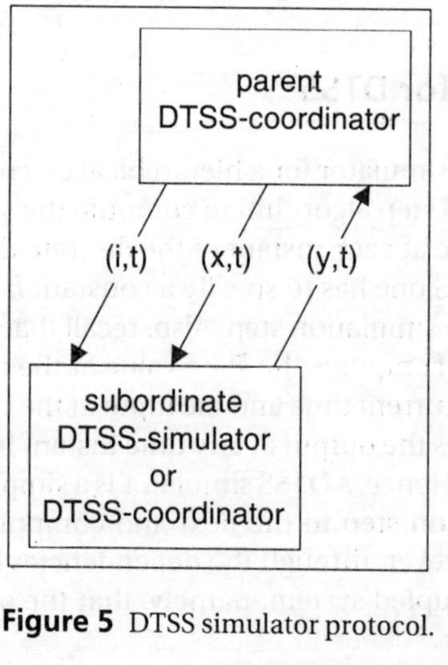

Figure 5 DTSS simulator protocol.

to generate the output and the x-message is used to execute the state transition. Note that viewed as a DEVS, the *-message causes an output but no internal transition, while the x-message causes an external transition. So, as we shall see later, a DTSS can be represented as an externally stimulated DEVS with no internal autonomy.

A dtss-simulator (Algorithm 6) has to have access to the model description and employs variables to store the sequential state q of the DTSS, the current output y, and the simulation time tn of its next state transition. It implements the protocol messages as follows. The initialization message (i, t) is intended to be called at the beginning of the simulation experiment that sets the time of the first state transition. In every simulation cycle at a state transition time t, we suppose that first a *-message is received to compute the output using $\lambda(q)$ based on the current state q. This value is sent back in a y-message. Afterwards, an x-message delivers the input value x for time t. Based on the input value, the state transition can be applied and the new state $\delta(q, x)$ determined. The time is set to the time of the next state transition, $t+h$.

```
Dtss-moore-simulator
  variables:
    DTSS = (X, Y, Q, δ, λ, h)     // associated model
      with state q
    y     // the current output value of the associated model
    tn    // time of next state transition
when receive message (i, t) at time t
    tn = t
when receive message (*, t) at time t
    if (t != tn) then
      synchronization error
    y = λ (q)
    send y in message (y, tn) to parent
when receive message (x, t) with input value x
    if (t != tn) then
      synchronization error
    q = δ (q, x)
    tn = tn + h
end Dtss-moore-simulator
```

Algorithm 6 Simulator for Moore-type DTSS.

Theorem 5

For input segments ω: $[t_1, t_m) \rightarrow X$, for initial state q_0 at time t_1 and under the assumption that the superior coordinator provides an i-message at initial time t_1 prior to any other message, exactly one *-and one x-message for times $t_i \in [t_1, t_m)$, with $t_i = t_{i-1} + h$, with input $\omega(t_i)$ in a timely ordered sequence, then the state q at any time t_i corresponds to the state, and the outputs y sent out in y-messages correspond to the output trajectory of the I/O system associated with the DTSS.

Proof: The proof follows the line of the definition of the I/O system associated with the DTSS in Chapter 6.

We prove by induction that if state q before the execution of an x-message at time $tn = t_i$ is the correct state, $\Delta(q_0, \omega_{[t_1, t_n)})$, then the state after the execution of an x-message is the correct state, $\Delta(q_0, \omega_{[t_1, t_n]})$ where now $tn = t_i + h$. After the i-message at time t_1, the state q_0 by definition represents the correct state and hence $q = \Delta(q_0, \omega_{[t_1, t_1)}) = \Delta(q_0, \omega_{[t_1, t_n)})$. Following the commands of the x-message at time $t_i = t_n$ with input $\omega(t_i)$, q is set to $\delta(q, \omega(t_i)) = \delta(\Delta(q_0, \omega_{[t_1, t_i]}), \omega(t_i)) = \delta(\Delta(q_0, \omega_{[t_1, t_i]}), \omega(t_i)) = \Delta(q_0, \omega_{[t_1, t_{i-h}]})$ by the definition of Δ. After setting of $tn = t_i + h$, we have $q = \Delta(q_0, \omega_{[t_1, t_n]})$.

As state $q = \Delta(q_0, \omega_{[t_1, t_{i+n}]})$ is correct state at time t_i and by assumption a *-message is received before an x-message at time t_i, the output $\lambda(q) = \Lambda(q, x)$, as required by the I/O system for DTSS.■

8.3.2 Simulator for Instantaneous Functions

Recall from Chapter 6 that function specified systems (FNSS) are elementary systems that do not own a state but compute the output values based on the current input values. Also recall from Chapter 7 that FNSS can occur as components in networks of DTSS. We therefore define a simulator for FNSS that appear as components in DTSS networks. The *fnss-simulator* (Algorithm 7) simply has to react to x-messages at any time step t by the computation of the output $\lambda(x)$.

```
Fnss-simulator     // for memoryless models
  variables:
    Fnss = (X, Y, λ)     // associated memoryless model
    y    // the current output value of the associated model
  when receive message (x, t) with input value x
    y = λ(x)
    send y in y-message (y, t) to parent coordinator
end Fnss-simulator
```

Algorithm 7 Simulator for memoryless FNSS.

Theorem 6

For input segments $\omega:[t_1, t_m) \rightarrow X$ and under the assumption that the superior coordinator sends an x-message for time $t_i \in [t_1, t_m)$ with input $\omega(t_i)$ in a timely ordered sequence, then the outputs $\lambda(\omega(t_i))$ correspond to the I/O system associated with the FNSS.

Proof: Directly follows from the definition of the I/O system for FNSS in Chapter 6.■

8.3.3 Simulator for Nonmodular Multicomponent DTSS

Multi-component DTSS are DTSS with several components, each with its own set of states and state transition function. A simulation algorithm for a multicomponent DTSS has to traverse the components to update their states by executing their state transition functions. Also, it has to apply the components' *individual* output functions, which together define the output of the multicomponent system.

A simulator for multicomponent DTSS (Algorithm 8) looks similar to a simulator for Moore-type DTSS. In the *-message, the output values of all components are computed and the overall output is sent back to the parent in a y-message. In the x-message, the new states are computed and stored in temporary variables, q'_d. Then, the time is advanced and the state variables are set to the values stored in the temporary variables.

```
Mcdtss-simulator
  variables:
    MCDTSS = (X, D, {M_d}, h)
      with d ∈ D, M_d = (Q_d, Y_d, I_d, δ_d, λ_d) // associated model
    {q_d | d ∈ D}      // states of components d
    {q_d' | d ∈ D}     // temporary variables to hold new states of
                       // components d
    {y_d | d ∈ D}      // the outputs of the components d
     tn                // time of next state transition
when receive message (i, t) at time t
  tn = t
when receive message (*, t) at time t
  if (t != tn) then
    synchronization error
  for all components d ∈ D do
    y_d = λ_d(. . ., q_i, . . .), i ∈ I_d
  send message (y, tn) with y = (X_{d∈D}, y_d) to parent
when receive message (x, t) with input value x
  if (t != tn) then
    synchronization error
  for all components d ∈ D do
    q_d' = δ_d((. . ., q_i, . . .), x), i ∈ I_d
    tn = tn + h
    for all components d ∈ D do
    q_d = q_d'
    end Mcdtss-simulator
```

Algorithm 8 Simulator for multicomponent DTSS.

Exercise: Show as an exercise that a simulator for multicomponent DTSS realizes a dtss-simulator for the basic DTSS associated with the multicomponent DTSS.◆

Exercise: Investigate conditions under which saving of states in temporary variables is not needed. In general, develop an algorithm for finding a sequence of component traversal that minimizes the number of temporary variables needed. (Hint: see TMS76, Section 16.6, Min Cycle Break Set).◆

8.3.4 Simulators for Coupled DTSS

After having defined simulators for basic and multicomponent DTSS, we now define a *coordinator* for networks of DTSS. A coordinator for a DTSS network uses the protocol of its subordinates, that is, it sends i–, *–, and x-messages messages, and receives y-messages from them, and it provides the same protocol to its parent. Therefore, a coordinator can serve as a subordinate simulator for a coordinator of a larger encompassing network. Seen through the identical protocol, coordinators and simulators are indistinguishable to superior coordinators.

The main task of the dtss-coordinator (Algorithm 9) is to schedule the components in the right sequence. The scheme is data-driven—only when all component's inputs are available is the component ready to go.

A *-message of a dtss-coordinator has to compute the output of the network (to provide the same protocol as a dtss-simulator). It does this by forwarding the *-message to all the Moore-type components to cause them to compute their outputs. The outputs are received in the y-messages and are stored (in variables xy_d) to be used for the computations of the inputs for components and the network outputs. After all Moore-type components have sent their outputs, a recursion takes place in which all instantaneous functions that have their inputs ready are sent x-messages to compute their outputs. We require in this scheme that the network is of type Moore, and this guarantees that the output of the network can be determined and sent back (see Theorem in Chapter 7, Appendix).

The ensuing x-message, which delivers the network input x_N for the time step, causes all other functions to be scheduled. Finally, all the Moore-type components can be sent x-messages with their respective input values to undertake their state transitions.

```
Dtss-coordinator
  variables:
    N = (X_N, Y_N, D, {M_d}, {I_d}, {Z_d}, h)
        // the network associated with the coordinator
    MOORE = {d ∈ D | d is of type Moore}
    FNSS  = {d ∈ D | d is of type FNSS}
    {xy_d | d ∈ D ∪ {N}}
      // variables to store the output values for components d
      // and the network input
    tn    // time of next state transition
  when receive message (i, t) at time t
    for d ∈ D do
      send i-message (i, t) with time t to d
    tn = t
  when receive message (*, t) with time t
    if t != tn
      synchronization error
    for d ∈ MOORE do
      send message (*, t) with time t to d
    while (∃ d ∈ FNSS : ∀i ∈ I_d : xy_i at time t is available
        & d not scheduled for time t) do
      send x-message (x_d, t) with x_d = (Z_d(. . ., xy_i, . . .),
      i ∈ I_d, to d
      mark d scheduled for time t
    endwhile
  when receive x-message (x_N, t) with input value x_N
    if t != tn
      synchronization error
```

```
    set xy_N to x_N
    while (∃ d ∈ D : ∀i ∈ I_d : xy_i at time t is available
        & d not scheduled for time t) do
      send x-message (x_d, t) with x_d = (Z_d (. . ., xy_i, . . .),
      i ∈ I_d, to d
      mark d scheduled for time t
  endwhile
  when receive y-message (y_d, t) with output value y_d from com-
  ponent d
    set xy_d to y_d
    if (∀i ∈ I_N : xy_i at time t is available
        & network output not sent for time t) then
      send y-message (y_N, t) with y_N = (Z_N (. . ., xy_i, . . .),
      i ∈ I_N, to parent
      mark network output sent for time t
end Dtss-coordinator
```

Algorithm 9 Coordinator for coupled DTSS.

We now state and show that a dtss-coordinator realizes a dtss-simulator for the $DTSS_N$ associated with the coupled DTSS. Again the proof directly follows from the definition of the DTSS associated with the coupled system and from the comparison of the message code of the dtss-coordinator and dtss-simulator. Also, the coordinator propagates the correct synchronization to its subordinate simulators.

Theorem 7

For input segments $\omega[t_1, t_m) \rightarrow X$, for initial state $q_0 = (\ldots, q_{d_0}, \ldots)$, $d \in D$, at time t_1 and under the assumption that the superior coordinator provides an *i*-message at initial time t_1 prior to any other message, exactly one *- and one *x*-message for times $t_i \in [t_1, t_m)$, with $t_i = t_{i-1} + h$, with input $x = \omega(t_i)$ in a timely ordered sequence, then (i) the dtss-coordinator implements the correct dtss-simulator operations for the atomic DTSS with total state $(\ldots, q_d, \ldots)$ associated with the DTSS network *N* and (ii) provides the correct synchronization for the subordinate simulators associated with components *d*.

Proof: (i) To prove (i) we show the correspondence of the messages of the coordinator and the simulator for the $DTSS_N$ associated with network *N*.

The *i*-message of the coordinator clearly corresponds because both set *tn* to *t*.

The *-message of a dtss-simulator computes the output $\lambda(q)$ and sends it back. The output λ of the $DTSS_N$ is defined as $Z_N(\ldots, y_i, \ldots)$, $i \in I_N$. Hence the task of the *-message of the coordinator is to compute $Z_N(\ldots, y_i, \ldots)$ and send it back in a *y*-message. The *-message causes *-messages to be forwarded to all Moore type components, which compute their outputs and send them back in *y*-messages. After that, all FNSS for which all inputs are available are sent *x*-messages with input $Z_d(\ldots, y_i, \ldots)$, $i \in I_d$ to compute their outputs. As the network is of type Moore, it is guaranteed that finally all the influencers' outputs of the network are available and the output $Z_N(\ldots, y_i, \ldots)$ can be sent back.

Upon receipt of an x-message with a network input x, the simulator computes the next state $\delta(q, x)$. The $DTSS_N$ requires that the state transitions $\delta_d(q_d, x_d)$ of all the individual components be done. This is accomplished by sending x-messages with the respective inputs $Z_d(\ldots, y_i, \ldots)$ to all the simulators in a sequence as outputs of influencers become available. As algebraic loops are not allowed, it is guaranteed that such a sequence always exists.

(ii) Since by assumption, a coordinator receives a *-message followed by an x-message at every time step and forwards these messages to its subordinates, it is guaranteed that the subordinates also receive the messages in correct order.■

Exercise: The main problem in simulating hierarchical DTSS networks that also contain Mealy-type components arises from the fact that the output of the network might be defined by Mealy-type components, but it might still be able to compute it without the knowledge of the network input. The input for a Mealy-type component might come from a Moore-type component (or from another Mealy-type component whose input, however, comes from a Moore-type). With computing the outputs of the Moore-types and scheduling the Mealy-type components with available inputs one time step ahead, it is possible to compute the output of a network without the knowledge of the input. This, however, requires that the network coordinator handles components operating at different time steps. Extend the coordinator for DTSS networks to allow also handling of Mealy-type components.◆

8.3.5 The Root-Coordinator

The root-coordinator for a DTSS abstract simulator has to initiate the stepwise execution of the overall DTSS simulation cycles. It accomplishes its task by sending *-messages followed by x-messages (with possibly empty input value x) to its subordinate every state transition time, tn (Algorithm 10).

```
dtss-root-coordinator
  t        // current simulation time
  child    // direct subordinate simulator or coordinator

  t = t0
  send initialization message (i, t) to child
  t = tn of its child
  loop
      send (*, t) message to child
      send (x, t) message to child
      t = tn of its child
  until end of simulation

end dtss-root-coordinator
```

Algorithm 10 Root-coordinator for DTSS abstract simulator.

From the root-coordinator we require that it provides the correct synchronization for its subordinate.

Theorem 8
The dtss-root-coordinator provides the correct synchronization for the subordinate simulator.

Proof: Directly follows by the operations of the dtss-root-coordinator.■

8.4 Simulators for DESS

After defining simulation schemes for discrete time systems, let us now make a step toward simulation of continuous systems. Simulation of discrete time systems on digital computers is relatively simple as they employ a discretized time base. This allows a next-state function to determine how the state at a particular time instant is computed given the state and the input at the previous time instant. In Chapter 3, we have stated the fundamental problem of simulating continuous models on digital computers—how to compute continuous time behavior in discrete steps. We have identified numerical integration methods as the principal means to accomplish this task. We also have identified two main categories of integration methods—*causal* and *noncausal* methods. Recall that causal methods use state values at past and present time instants to compute the state value at the next time instant. Noncausal methods can also use estimates of state values at time instants later than the current time.

In this section we formulate simulation concepts for DESS systems to correspond with the abstract simulators already introduced for DEVS and DTSS. In fact, an abstract simulator for DESS—for causal as well as for noncausal methods—shows much resemblance to the abstract simulator for DTSS. In particular, coordinators for DESS networks can employ the same scheduling scheme. The main difference is that in coordinators for DTSS, the *- and x-messages are used for the computation of outputs and state transitions in one simulation step, while in the coordinators of DESS each phase in an integration step requires its own *- and x-messages. Therefore, we will present the simulators for basic DESS—for the causal and noncausal integration methods—in the following, and the reader is referred to the DTSS coordinator as well as the simulator for FNSS to formulate the simulation architecture for coupled systems.

8.4.1 Causal Simulator for DESS

Recall from Chapter 3 that a causal method uses m past state and derivative values to estimate the state at the next time instant. With these considerations in mind, we formulate a general scheme for a causal simulator for atomic DESS (Algorithm 11). To implement a causal method of order m, a simulator must save the m past values of the model state values, q, derivatives, r, and inputs, x. With them, and the simulation step size h, the causal integration method determines an estimate for the state at the time instant $t_{i+1} = t_i + h$ by

$$q\left(t_{i+1}\right) = CasualMethod\left(\left[q\left(t_{i-m}\right),\ldots,q\left(t_i\right)\right],\left[r\left(t_{i-m}\right),\ldots,r\left(t_i\right)\right],\right.$$
$$\left.\left[x\left(t_{i-m}\right),\ldots,x\left(t_i\right)\right],h\right),$$

with *CausalMethod* being a function (usually linear) dependent on the particular method in hand. The state value in turn directly gives an estimate for the output value by applying the output function

$$y(t_i) = \lambda(q(t_i)).$$

As already indicated in Chapter 3, and clearly from the simulator definition, at start of the simulation, past state values may not be available. This requires special provision to be taken for startup. We do not specify any particular scheme here, but assume that this is covered by the integration method.

Aside from these issues, the simulator appears similar to the simulator of atomic DTSS.

```
Dess-causal-simulator
  variables:
    DESS = (X, Y, Q, f, λ)    // associated model
    [q(t_{i-m}), . . ., q(t_i)]    // is a vector of state values
    [r(t_{i-m}), . . ., r(t_i)]    // is a vector of derivatives
    values
    [x(t_{i-m}), . . ., x(t_i)]    // is a vector of inputs
    h                              // integration stepsize
  when receive message (i, t_i) at time t_i
    initialize [q(t_{i-m}), . . ., q(t_i)],
               [r(t_{i-m}), . . ., r(t_i)],
               [x(t_{i-m}), . . ., x(t_i)]
               using initialization specified by CausalMethod.
  when receive message (*, t_i) at time t_i
    y = λ (q(t_i))
    send y in message (y, t_i) to parent
  when receive message (x, t_i) with input value x
    x(t_i) = x
    q(t_{i+1}) = q(t_i+h) = Causal Method ( [q(t_{i-m}), . . ., q(t_i)],
                                            [r(t_{i-m}), . . ., r(t_i)],
                                            [x(t_{i-m}), . . ., x(t_i)], h)
end Dess-causal-simulator
```

Algorithm 11 Causal simulator for basic DESS.

Exercise: Formulate a causal simulator for multicomponent DESS.◆

8.4.2 Noncausal Simulator for DESS

Recall from Chapter 3 that noncausal integration methods work in phases. In predictor phases, estimates of future values are computed. In the corrector phase, the state values for the time instant are finally determined. A DESS simulator with a noncausal method (Algorithm 12), therefore, has to provide for these different phases.

As for a causal method, a simulator using a noncausal method may employ vectors to store the *m* past state, derivative, and input values. In addition, it also needs vectors to store n predicted values. In one simulation cycle, in n predictor phases the vectors $q'(i)$ for $i = 1, .., n$ are filled by

$$\begin{aligned} q'(k+1) = kth - Predictor\Big(\ & [q(t_{i-m}),\ldots,q(t_i),q'(1),\ldots,q'(k)],\\ & [r(t_{i-m}),\ldots,r(t_i),r'(1),\ldots,r'(k)],\\ & [x(t_{i-m}),\ldots,x(t_i),x'(1),\ldots,x'(k)],\\ & h\Big), \end{aligned}$$

and then in the final corrector phase these values are used to compute the corrected state and output value for time t_{i+1},

$$\begin{aligned} q(t_{i+1}) = Corrector\Big(\ & [q(t_{i-m}),\ldots,q(t_i),q'(1),\ldots,q'(n)],\\ & [r(t_{i-m}),\ldots,r(t_i),r'(1),\ldots,r'(n)],\\ & [x(t_{i-m}),\ldots,x(t_i),x'(1),\ldots,x'(n)],\\ & h\Big). \end{aligned}$$

In the simulator of Algorithm 12, we use a oounter k to distinguish between the different predictor and corrector phases. Based on the counter, we decide if an output has to be computed based on the current state or a state estimate, if an input received represents the k-th estimate or corrected value, and if we should make the next prediction or the final correction.

A simulator is supposed to start an integration loop by first receiving a *-message to compute the output. At the first *-message, k is 0 and the output is computed based on the state $q(t_i)$. In a later message with a k value unequal 0, we have to compute the output for the k-th state estimate $q'(k)$.

If an input is received in an x-message with $k = 0$, it represents an input stemming from some corrected (and not estimated) output y at time t_i and, therefore, the value is stored as normal input $x(t_i)$. Otherwise, the input represents an estimate and the value is stored as an input estimate $x'(k)$. Then k is increased by 1 and taken modulo n+1. This allows us to undertake exactly n predictions before getting 0 again and making the correction. With a k between 1 and n, the k predicator values are computed. With a value of $k = 0$, we have already computed the n predictor values and can compute the corrected value for the next time step t_{i+1}.

```
Dess-non-causal-simulator
  variables:
    DESS = (X, Y, Q, f, λ)          // associated model
    [q(t_i-m), . . ., q(t_i)]       // is a vector of past states
                                    // values
    [r(t_i-m), . . ., r(t_i)]       // is a vector of past derivatives
                                    // values
    [x(t_i-m), . . ., x(t_i)]       // is a vector of past inputs
                                    // values
    [q'(1), . . ., q'(n)]           // is a vector of predicted states
                                    // values
    [r'(1), . . ., r'(n)]           // is a vector of predicted
                                    // derivatives values
```

```
    [x'(1), . . ., x'(n)]      // is a vector of predicted inputs
    h                          // integration stepsize
    k                          // indicator for the phase of the
                               // integration

when receive message (i, t_i) at time t_i
  initialize [q(t_{i-m}), . . ., q(t_i)],
             [r(t_{i-m}), . . ., r(t_i)],
             [x(t_{i-m}), . . ., x(t_i)]
             using initialization specified by integration
             method.
  k = 0

when receive message (*, t_i)
  if k = 0 then y = λ (q(t_i))
           else y = λ (q' (k))
  send y in message (y, t_i) to parent

when receive message (x, t_i)
  if k = 0 then x(t_i) = x
           else x' (k) = x
  k = (k + 1) mod (n+1)
  if k > 0 then
    q'(k) = kth-Predictor
    ( [q(t_{i-m}), . . ., q(t_i), q'(1), . . ., q'(k-1)],
    [r(t_{i-m}), . . ., r(t_i), r'(1), . . ., r'(k-1)],
    [x(t_{i-m}), . . ., x(t_i), x'(1), . . ., x'(k-1)],
    h )
  else
  q(t_{i+1}) = Corrector
                    ( [q(t_{i-m}), . . ., q(t_i), q'(1), . . ., q'(n)],
                      [r(t_{i-m}), . . ., r(t_i), r'(1), . . ., r'(n)],
                      [x(t_{i-m}), . . ., x(t_i), x'(1), . . ., x'(n)],
                      h ).

  t_i = t_i + h

end Dess-non-causal-simulator
```

Algorithm 12 Noncausal simulator for basic DESS.

Exercise: Formulate noncausal simulator for multicomponent DESS.◆

As we have indicated already, for DESS coupled models, the same scheduling scheme used in DTSS coordinators can be employed to schedule the components in the correct computational sequence. In a simulator with a noncausal integration method, the main difference is that the coordinator is supposed to receive n+1 *- and x- messages and forward those to its subordinates before the integration cycle is completed and the time can be advanced.

Exercise: Formulate causal and noncausal coordinators for coupled DESS models.◆

8.5 Summary

In this chapter we have erected a framework of abstract simulators that parallels the framework of system formalisms introduced in the previous chapters. We have shown that the simulators for atomic models correctly generate their behavior. And we have shown the correctness of the coordinators by showing that each coordinator realizes a simulator for the basic model associated with the coupled model (the resultant under closure of coupling).

The coordinators and simulators obey the same polymorphic protocol, which allows them to work together in an transparent way. A coordinator need not know of the type of its subordinate, whether coordinator or simulator. The polymorphic simulator protocols, however, will also serve a further purpose. They will allow us to define simulation schemes for a multiformalism modeling and simulation methodology. Multiformalism models are built by coupling together models in different formalisms. They may also be simulated by coordinating the different abstract simulators in the DEVS bus concept to be described. This will be the topic of the next chapter.

Simulation is a computationally hard task and has to be implemented efficiently. The simulation protocols defined in this chapter have to be seen as abstract schemes without considering implementation details and performance requirements. In particular this is true for the distribution of outputs and translation to inputs according to the coupling schemes in coupled models. Especially in continuous simulation, where values have to be exchanged multiple times within one simulation cycle, communication must be implemented most efficiently. We will return to communication issues when discussing distributed simulation in later chapters.

8.6 Sources

The abstract simulator concept for DEVS first appeared in Zeigler [9] and was extended to the other basic formalisms by Praehofer [6]. The DEVS bus was defined and prototyped by Kim [4] in relation to distributed simulation and the High Level Architecture (HLA).

1. Burden, R. L., and J. D. Faires, *Numerical Analysis.* PWS-Kent Publishing, Boston, 1989.
2. Chu, Y., *Digital Simulation of Digital Systems.* McGraw-Hill, New York, 1969.
3. Horowitz, E., and S. Sahni, *Fundamentals of Data Structures in Pascal, 4th ed.* Computer Science Press, 1990.
4. Kim, J. Y., and Tag G. Kim, "A Heterogeneous Simulation Framework Based on DEVS BUS and High Level Architecture," WCSC-98, 1998, Washington, DC.
5. Korn, G., and J. Wait, *Digital Continuous System Simulation.* Prentice Hall, Englewood Cliffs, NJ, 1978.

6. Praehofer, H., "System Theoretic Formalisms for Combined Discrete–Continuous System Simulation." *Int. J. Gen. Sys.* **19**(3), 219–240 (1991).
7. Press, W. H., *Numerical Recipes in C,* 2nd ed. Cambridge University Press, 1992.
8. Sedgewick, R., *Algorithms, 2nd ed.* Addison Wesley, 1991.
9. Zeigler, B. P., *Multifaceted Modeling and Discrete Event Simulation.* Academic Press, London, 1984.

9 Multiformalism Modeling and Simulation

We have introduced three basic formalisms (DEVS, DTSS, and DESS), all based on the unifying framework afforded by the general dynamic systems formalism. Although these formalisms describe subclasses of systems, they are, nevertheless, generic formalisms in the sense that they encompass a wide variety of systems. In contrast, a multitude of more *specialized* formalisms have been developed. Such formalisms are proposed, and sometimes accepted, because they provide convenient means to express models for particular classes of systems and problems. Formalisms such as Petri nets and Statecharts, on the discrete event side, and Systems Dynamics and Bond Graphs, on the continuous side, are widely employed. However, many real-world phenomena cannot be fit into the Procrustean bed of one formalism at a time. More generally, the ambitious systems now being designed, such as an automated highway traffic control system, cannot be modeled by a pure discrete or continuous paradigm. Instead, they require a combined discrete/continuous modeling and simulation methodology that supports a *multiformalism* modeling approach and the simulation environments to support it. Before continuing to discuss multiformalism modeling—the use of many formalisms in the same model—we provide brief introductions to some of the more influential ones. We will focus on the strengths, and also the limitations, of each formalism, for it is these attributes that motivate the integrative approach that systems theory provide.

9.1 Brief Introduction to Specialized Formalisms

We will briefly consider some popular continuous formalisms and discrete event formalisms.

9.1.1 DESS Subformalisms: Systems Dynamics and Bond Graphs

Systems Dynamics, developed by Forrester [10], is widely used in natural systems and business and social systems modeling. It conceptualizes differential equations in stylized terms such as auxiliary, rate, and level variables and patterned couplings with an associated graphical representation.

In terms of a DESS network, level variables are the outputs of integrators, whereas auxiliary and rate variables are the outputs of memoryless functions (see Chapters 3 and 7).

Bond graphs, originated by Paynter [18], provide another graphically based approach to continuous system modeling, yet with an entirely different targeted class of systems and user group. Bond graphs generalize the current/voltage relationships of electrical circuits to other physical phenomena such as fluid flow and mechanical interactions. Bond graph models actually do not describe differential equations directly, but represent the dependencies between the system variables in a nondirected manner. For example, current can be considered to cause voltage across a resistor or the other way around, depending on whether the energy is coming from a current or voltage source. By fixing which variables are given (input) and which variables of the system should be computed (state and output), one particular DESS can be derived from a set of possibilities. Bond graphs are thus capable of representing dynamic systems at a higher level of abstraction than DESS.

The current/voltage metaphor is very useful in analyzing and designing system of components built from different energetic media since it affords a common basis for interfacing such components. However, the metaphor may need to be strained to fit the accepted ways of understanding phenomena in a field, thereby making it hard to adopt. Table 1 summarizes the main features of these formalisms, emphasizing the objectives, advantages, and limitations of each.

Although traditionally continuous systems have been the targets of modeling and simulation, in recent years there has emerged a multiplicity of formalisms for discrete event dynamic systems [13].

9.1.2 DEVS Subformalisms: Petri Nets and Statecharts

The classical *Petri net model* is a 5-tuple (*P, T, I, O, M*). *P* is a finite set of places (often drawn as circles) representing conditions. *T* is a finite set of transitions (often drawn as bars) representing events. *I* and *O* are sets of input and output functions mapping transitions to bags of places. *M* is the set of initial markings. Places may contain zero or more tokens at a moment in time. Tokens in Petri nets model dynamic behavior of systems. The execution of Petri nets is controlled by the number and distribution of the tokens. A transition is enabled if each of its input places contains at least as many tokens as there exists arcs from that place to the transition. When a transition is enabled, it may fire. When a transition fires, all enabling tokens are removed from its input places, and a token is deposited in each of its output places. Petri nets have been employed in a wide variety of modeling applications. Peterson [19] provides a good introduction. Fishwick [8] discusses Petri nets in the context of modeling and simulation. Because of their limited expressive power, there have been myriad extensions to overcome particular limitations. Berthomieu [2] provides an example of the extension to timed nets. Sanders [22] developed a stochastic extension for simulation-based performance evaluation.

Table 1 Basic Features of System Dynamics and Bond Graphs

Formalism	Systems dynamics	Bond graphs
Target systems	Social/industrial/ecological systems	Engineering systems with a variety of electrical, mechanical, thermal elements
Structure	Network of auxiliary, rate, and level elements	Vertices and arcs labeled in various ways
Main feature	Methodology for continuous system model construction	Generalized current/voltage variables; nondeterministic
Analysis method	Simulation	Solution based on causal direction assignments
Analysis objective	Growth of populations, use of resources, feedback effects	Equilibrium solutions, derivation of dynamic state equations
Advantages	Simplifies differential equation model building with graphical elements	Supports multidisciplinary modeling
Limitations of the basic formalisms	Graphical elements can capture limited subset of all dynamic behaviors	Nonintuitive representations, electrical metaphor may be strained in many cases

Statecharts describe a system's behavior over time, control, timing, and conditions and events that cause changes in a system's operation. Statecharts evolved from state-transition diagrams originally developed to depict the behavior of relatively simple digital systems. Such diagrams use a combination of arrows and boxes to indicate transitions among a system's states. Statecharts contain features that permit depiction of hierarchical states, concurrent or parallel processes, and timing. These features are essential to depicting the behavior of complex systems, allowing a designer to express even subtle semantics of system logic concisely and unambiguously. See Harel [12] for an introduction to Statecharts.

Summaries of the Petri net and Statechart formalisms are provided in Table 2.

Table 2 Basic Features of Petri Nets and Statecharts

Formalism	Petri nets	Statecharts
Target systems	Systems with interacting concurrent components	Real-time software systems
Structure	Place, transition, input function, output function, initial markings	State transition diagrams
Main feature	Event-conditional transitions	State generalization, orthogonality, broadcasting
Analysis method	Reachability analysis	Simulation, reachability analysis
Analysis objective	Logical analysis; performance evaluation (with stochastic, timed extensions)	Logical analysis
Advantages	Large research community; simple and common graphical notations	Expressive power greater than Petri nets; widely used in industry
Limitations of the basic formalisms	Not modular; time is not considered; not suitable for implementation	Partially modular, complex semantics

9.2 Multiformalism Modeling

Two approaches to multiformalism modeling are depicted in Fig. 1. To *combine* formalisms we have to come up with a new formalism that subsumes the original ones. This is the case with DEV&DESS, which combines DEVS and DESS, the *discrete event* and *differential equation* system specification formalisms and which will be subject of the next section. Another approach to multiformalism modeling is to *embed* one formalism into another. For example, it is not hard to see that the systems dynamics and bond graph formalisms can be embedded in the DESS formalism—indeed, each is a way of writing a set of ordinary differential equations. Similarly, it can be shown that the Petri net and Statechart formalisms can be embedded into the DEVS

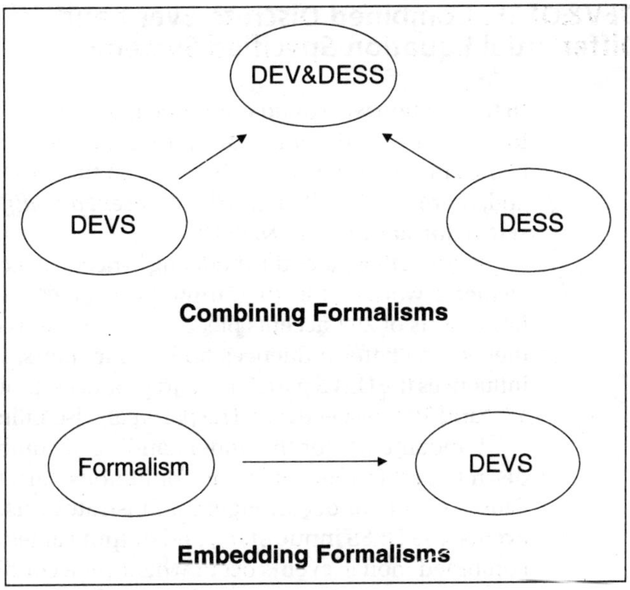

Figure 1 Multiformalism approaches.

formalism. Indeed, any discrete event behavior can be expressed as a DEVS model—we leave the demonstration of this fact for later (Chapter 15).

Now let's consider embeddings of one major formalism in another one. Traditionally, differential equations have been solved with numerical integration in discrete time. In formal terms, this means that DESS has been embedded into DTSS. However, we will show later (Chapter 16) that, especially for parallel and distributed execution, event-based simulation of continuous systems has greater potential for efficient processing at comparable accuracy. For example, recall the event-based Game of Life model from Chapter 3. In this example the continuous behavior of the fitness parameter was abstracted to an event model by only considering the relevant events. What justified this error-free abstraction was the fact that each cell had piecewise constant input and output trajectories (the birth/death state). As we will see later (Chapter 16), piecewise constancy of input and output is a sufficient condition for any system to have an exact DEVS representation. Further, since the continuous dynamics of the fitness function were quite simple (piecewise linear), we were able to easily predict the times to the next life cycle events.

Embedding the other formalisms (DESS and DTSS) into DEVS is attractive, since then both discrete and continuous components are naturally included in the same environment. But, with continuous and discrete components interacting, we still need the DEV&DESS formalism to provide the basics of how such interaction should occur and to provide a formalism in which embedding DESS into DEVS can be rigorously analyzed. Moreover, for combined models that cannot be feasibly embedded into DEVS, we must employ the DEV&DESS formalism.

9.3 DEV&DESS: Combined Discrete Event and Differential Equation Specified Systems

In this section we extend our modeling framework by introducing a system formalism for combined discrete/continuous modeling. The formalism comes into being by a combination of the DEVS and the DESS formalism and, therefore, is called the *discrete event and differential equation specified system* formalism (DEV&DESS).

Figure 2 illustrates the modeling concept, which has both DEVS and DESS elements working together. Input ports of X^{discr} accept event segments and input ports of X^{cont} accepts piecewise continuous or piecewise constant segments. The latter influences both model parts, while the event input only influences the DEVS part. Each part produces its own corresponding outputs, Y^{discr} and Y^{cont}, respectively. The parts can also influence each other's state.

Fundamental for the understanding of combined modeling is how the discrete part is affected by the continuous part, that is, how the DESS part causes events to occur. Figure 3 illustrates this. In the intervals between events, the DESS input, state, and output values change continuously. In a combined model, events occur whenever a condition specified on the continuous elements becomes true. Typically, the condition can be viewed as a continuous variable reaching and crossing a certain threshold or whenever two continuous variables meet (in which case, their difference crosses zero). In such situations, an event is triggered and the state is changed discontinuously. An event that is caused by the changes of continuous variables is called a *state event* (in distinction to internal events of pure DEVS, which are scheduled in time and are called *time events*).

We will now define the *combined discrete event and differential equation system specification (DEV&DESS)*. For simplicity and clarity we define the formalism *without allowing for time events.* However, such an extension can easily be achieved by adding time scheduling of events from the basic DEVS formalism. Moreover, we will show that a fully functional DEVS behavior can

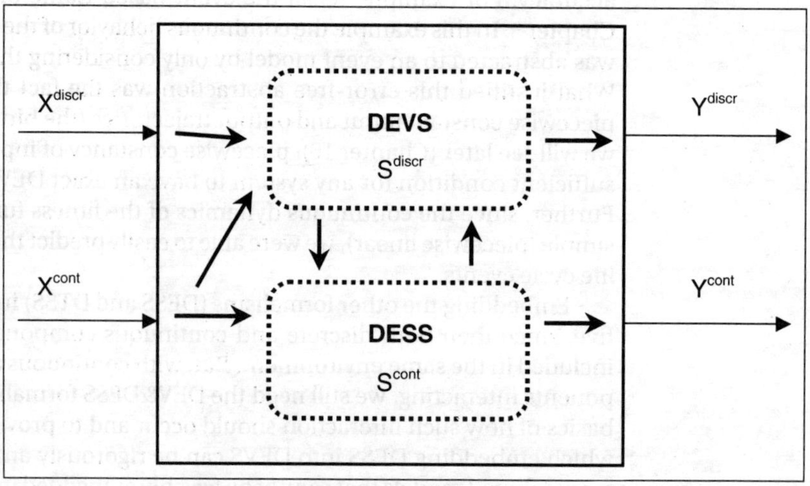

Figure 2 DEVS and DESS combined model.

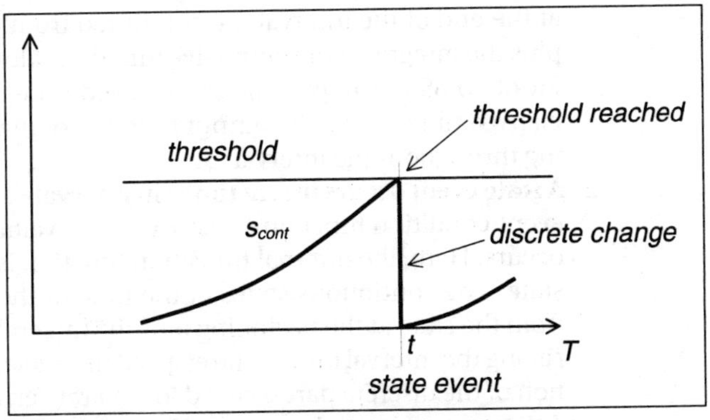

Figure 3 State event.

be embedded into the DEV&DESS formalism as it stands, so nothing is lost from the behavior point of view (although simulation efficiency will suffer).

$$\text{DEV\&DESS} = \left\langle X^{discr}, X^{cont}, Y^{discr}, Y^{cont}, S, \delta_{ext}, C_{int}, \delta_{int}, \lambda^{discr}, f, \lambda^{cont} \right\rangle$$

where

X^{discr}, Y^{discr} are the set of event input and output from DEVS

$X^{cont} = \left\{ \left(x_1^{cont}, x_2^{cont}, \ldots \right) \middle| \; x_1^{cont} \in X_1^{cont}, x_2^{cont} \in X_2^{cont}, \ldots \right\}$ is the structured set of continuous value inputs with input variables x_i^{cont}

$Y^{cont} = \left\{ \left(y_1^{cont}, y_2^{cont}, \ldots \right) \middle| \; y_1^{cont} \in Y_1^{cont}, y_2^{cont} \in Y_2^{cont}, \ldots \right\}$ is the structured set of continuous value outputs with output variables y_i^{cont}

$S = S^{discr} \times S^{cont}$ is the set of states as a Cartesian product of discrete states and continuous states

$\delta_{ext}: Q \times X^{cont} \times X^{discr} \rightarrow S$ is the external state transition function, where $Q = \left\{ \left(s^{discr}, s^{cont}, e \right) \middle| \; s^{discr} \in S^{discr}, s^{cont} \in S^{cont}, e \in \Re_0^+ \right\}$ is the set of total states

$\delta_{int}: Q \times X^{cont} \rightarrow S$ is the internal state transition function

$\lambda^{discr}: Q \times X^{cont} \rightarrow Y^{discr}$ is the event output function

$\lambda^{cont}: Q \times X^{cont} \rightarrow Y^{cont}$ is the continuous output function to define the continuous output variable values

$f: Q \times X^{cont} \rightarrow S^{cont}$ is the rate of change function

$C_{int}: Q \times X^{cont} \rightarrow$ Bool is the *state event condition function* for conditioning the execution of the state events

The semantics of a DEV&DESS are informally described as follows:

1. **Intervals $<t_1, t_2>$ with no events:** Only the continuous states and the elapsed time *e* change. The derivative function together with the value output function specify the continuous behavior. The continuous states

at the end of the interval are computed from the state at the beginning plus the integral of the derivative function *f* along the interval (see behavior of DESS in Chapter 6). The elapsed time *e* is increased by the total elapsed time $t_2 - t_1$. The output function of the continous part is operating throughout the interval.

2. **A state event occurs first at time *t* in interval $<t_1, t_2>$:** At time *t* the internal event condition function $C_{int}(s(t),x^{cont}(t))$ evaluates to true—a state event occurs. Here, the internal transition function is executed to define a new state. The continuous states at the time of the transition are computed from the state at the beginning plus the integral of the derivative function *f* along the interval until *t*. The elapsed time is set to 0, and the output function of the discrete part is called to generate an output event at time *t*.
3. **A discrete event at the external input port occurs first at time *t* in interval $< t_1, t_2>$:** Here, the external transition function is executed to define a new state at time instant *t*. The continuous states at the time of the transition are computed from the state at the beginning plus the integral of the derivative function *f* along the interval until *t*. Likewise, the continous output is generated until *t*. The elapsed time is set to 0 at time *t*.

9.3.1 A Simple Example: DEV&DESS Model of a Barrel Filler

Manufacturing typically involves processes that combine both continuous and discrete event phenomena, and Fig. 4 illustrates *DEV&DESS* modeling using a filling process. Filling a barrel is a continuous process; however, control input and output is discrete. Control comprises loading the barrel in place, turning on the liquid flow, and stopping the flow when the barrel fills up. The model has one continuous input port *inflow* and one discrete input port *on/off*. It has one discrete output port, *barrel*, and one continuous output port, *cout*, for observing the contents. There is also a continuous state variable *contents* and a discrete state variable *valve*. The derivative of the continuous state variable *contents* is given by the input value of *inflow* when the system *valve* is *open*, and it is zero when the *valve* is *closed*. The system switches between these two phases according to the discrete input at the discrete input port *on/off*. Barrels are sent out at the discrete output port *barrel* whenever the variable *contents* reaches the value 10, a state event. At that point, *contents* is reinitialized to 0.

BarrelFiller = $\langle X^{cont}, X^{discr}, Y^{cont}, Y^{discr}, S^{cont}, S^{discr}, \delta_{ext}, C_{int}, \delta_{int}, \lambda^{discr}, f, \lambda^{cont}\rangle$

X^{cont} = {inflow | inflow $\in \Re$}

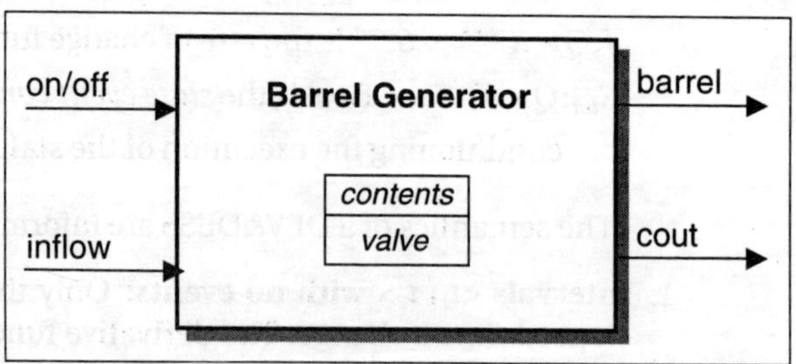

Figure 4 Barrel generator model.

```
Xdiscr = {on/off | on/off ∈ {on, off}}
Ycont  = {cout | cout ∈ ℜ}
Ydiscr = {barrel | barrel ∈ {10-liter-barrel}}
Sdiscr = {valve | valve ∈ {open, closed}}
Scont  = {contents | contents ∈ ℜ}}
δext ((contents, valve), e, inflow, on/off)
  if on/off = on then
       valve := open
  elseif on/off = off then
       valve := closed
Cint ((contents, valve), e, inflow)
     contents == 10
δint ((contents, valve), e, inflow)
     contents = 0
λdiscr ((contents, valve), e, inflow)
  barrel = 10-liter-barrel—send out 10-liter-barrel at port
  barrel
f ((contents, valve), e, inflow)
   case valve
      open: d contents / dt = 0
      closed: d contents / dt = inflow
λcont ((contents, valve), e, inflow)
   cout = contents
```

Algorothm 1 Example of a DEV&DESS model: Barrel Filler

Figure 5 depicts how elements in the barrel model influence each other. The phase is set by the external transition function, which is triggered by discrete input *on/off*. The derivative for the continuous state *contents* (derivative function *f*) is defined based on the value of the *valve* variable. If the the valve is open, the derivative is equal to the *inflow*. If the valve is closed, the rate of

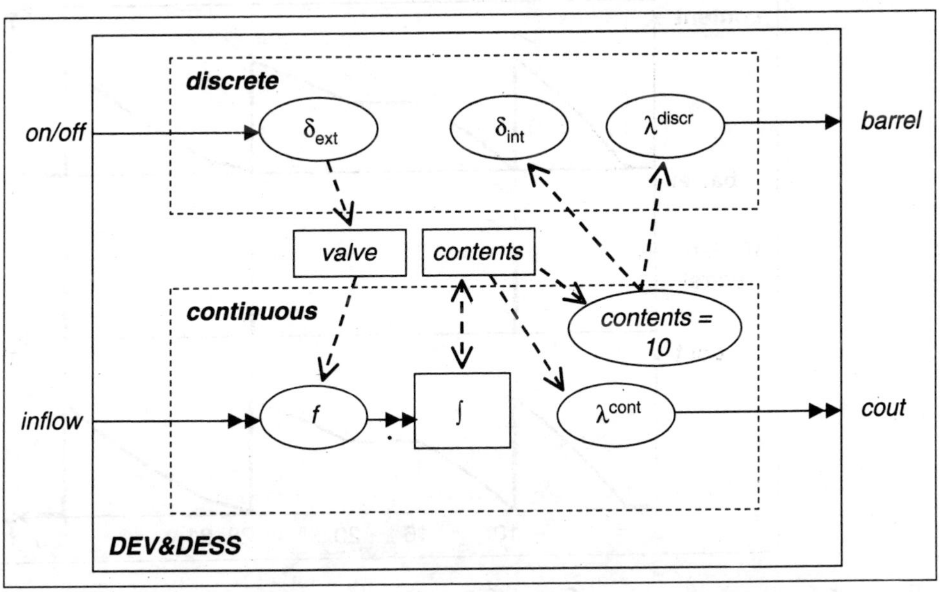

Figure 5 Functions dependencies of barrel model.

change is 0. The internal events are triggered by the internal condition function (*contents* = 10) and change the *contents* variable as well as produce the *barrel* output. The continuous output contents is solely determined by the state variable *contents.*

Figure 6 shows the trajectories of a sample experiment of the barrel filler system. Initially the *valve* is *closed* and the value of *contents* is 0. After some time, filling is turned on by an input signal *on.* The continuous input *inflow* is considered to be dependent on the level of an inflow tank and will decrease as the tank empties. The contents increases dependent on the inflow until it reaches 10 and a state event occurs. Filling is stopped (input *off*), the first barrel is released, *contents* is set back to 0, and filling is resumed

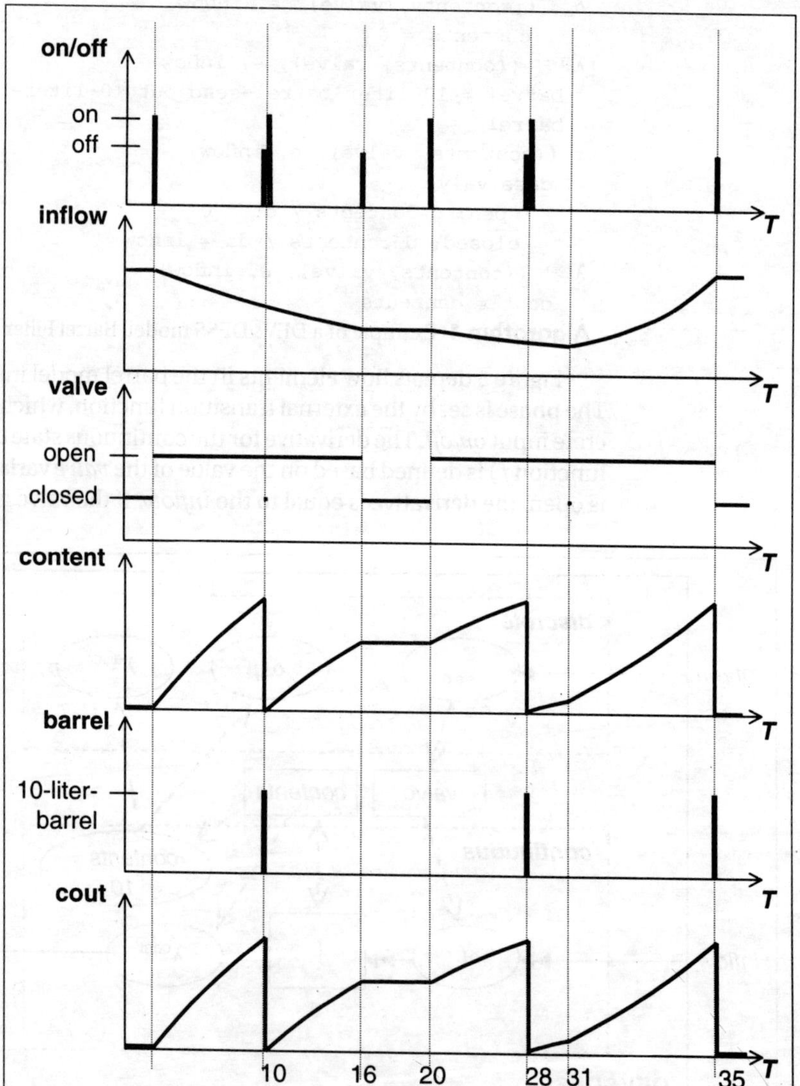

Figure 6 Barrel generator trajectories.

immediately by an input signal *on*. The filling of the second barrel is interrupted by an external event at the discrete input port *on/off* and filling is stopped. After some time there is a second external event, which activates the model again, and the filling resumes. The barrel is released at time 28. During the filling of the third barrel, there is a discontinuity of the inflow resulting from the tank being filled up again.

Exercise: Consider that the inflow in the example above is constant. Then the system can be modeled by a classic DEVS. (Hint: See the GOL event model in Section 3.3 and Section 7.2.) Build the DEVS model for the barrel filler problem.◆

Exercise: Extend the barrel filler model so that it detects when the inflow is too low and at that point stops the filling process and also issues an output notice that warns of this condition.

For a complete example of DEV&DESS modeling and simulation, see Praehofer *et al.* [21].◆

9.3.2 System Specified by a DEV&DESS

As always, the true meaning of a specification is the I/O system it specifies. Determining this meaning requires three steps:

1. Constructing the putative I/O system, $S = (T, X, \Omega, Y, Q, \Delta, \Lambda)$, from the specification
2. Working out the conditions that guarantee that the system is well defined
3. Proving that the conditions are indeed sufficient for the system to exist

Appendix A contains details of steps 1 and 3. Let's consider step 2. Clearly, for the combination to exist, the DESS portion must specify a well-defined system on its own. Recall that to determine unique continuous state trajectories, the derivative function has to satisfy the Lipschitz condition (Chapter 6). However, the property of legitimacy defined for time events for DEVS must be adapted for DEV&DESS. We define the property of *state-event-legitimacy* in the same way legitimacy is defined for pure DEVS.

Definition. State-Event-Legitimacy

Let us define $\Sigma'(q, \omega)$ to be the number of state events, i.e., the events of execution of the internal transition function, in interval $<t_1, t_2]$ given the input segment $\omega: <t_1, t_2] \rightarrow X$ and the initial state q at time t_1. Then we say that a DEV&DESS is *state-event-legitimate*, if and only if

$$\forall \omega:<t_1, t_2] \rightarrow X \in \Omega,\ q \in Q: \Sigma'(q,\omega) < \infty,$$

i.e., the number of state events is finite for all admissible input segments.

Steps 1 and 2 enable us to state and prove the following theorem.

Theorem 1

A DEV&DESS specifies an I/O system if and only if the derivative function f has unique solutions and if the system is state-event-legitimate.

The proof is in the Appendix.

9.4 Multimodeling with DEV&DESS

Many real-world phenomena cannot be modeled by one single model but require a set of complementary models that together are able to describe the whole process. A model that subsumes several different models is termed a *multimodel.* The DEV&DESS formalism is an appropriate means to implement multimodels.

In a multimodel, depending on a current state the process is in, one out of the set of models will be applicable and will describe the process appropriately. The transitions from a state to a next state with a different applicable model signifies a qualitative change in the dynamic behavior. We call such qualitative states *phases* and qualitative changes in behavior *phase transitions.*

Phase transitions can either be caused from outside or arise inside the system when particular situations occur. Let us clarify the ideas by considering two rather simplified versions of transmission systems, viz., a vehicle with a stick-operated transmission system and a vehicle with a rudimentary automatic transmission system that changes gears at particular speeds only. The phases of the system obviously are given by the different gears that determine different system behaviors, that is, different reactions of the vehicle. In the model of the hand-operated system, the gears are determined from outside. Thus, the phase transitions are determined by the external transition function. In the model of the automatic system, however, the gear changes occur when the speed reaches certain thresholds. The phase transitions can be modeled by state events. The different gears are directly associated to certain subsets of the continuous speed variable as depicted in Fig. 7. The different phases and phase transitions define a partition of the continuous state space into mutual exclusive blocks that show qualitatively different behaviors.

Exercise: Elaborate a model of a real transmission system where the gear changes are dependent not only on the current speed, but also on the current acceleration. Also consider that changes to higher gears and lower gears occur at different thresholds.◆

In a DEV&DESS representation of a multimodel, the phase transition are modeled either by external events, if determined from outside, or by internal state events, if caused internally. Let us concentrate on modeling phase transitions by internal events in the following. In such a multimodel, the underlying n-dimensional continuous state space is partitioned into different blocks where the state events for the phase transitions define the block boundaries. Each block in a partition corresponds to particular phase and each phase may have associated with it a unique continuous dynamic behavior. The current phase value implies the currently applicable continuous

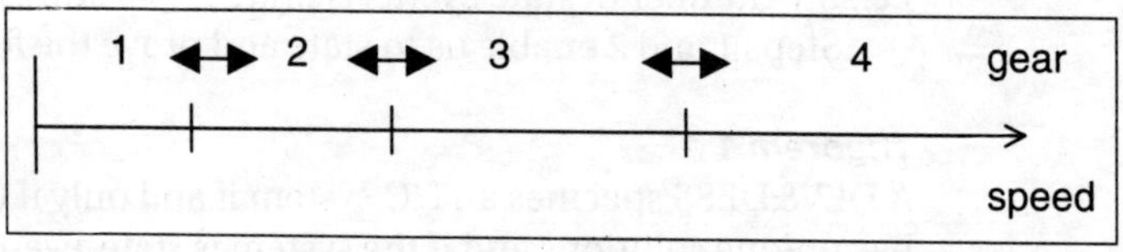

Figure 7 State partitioning of automated transmission system.

model and the phase transitions define the qualitative changes in system behavior. (See Fig. 8.)

The continuous state space of the DEV&DESS multimodel then is an n-dimensional real vector space

$$S^{cont} = \left\{ (s_1, s_2, \ldots, s_i, \ldots, s_n) \mid s_i \in \Re \right\}.$$

The discrete state space has phase variables $phase_i$ for each dimension i of the continuous state space. Each phase variables has a discrete range (e.g., the integers $\Im$) used to denote the blocks of the partition:

$$S^{discr} = \left\{ (phase_1, phase_2, \ldots, phase_i, \ldots, phase_n) \mid phase_i \in \Im \right\}.$$

Also, for each dimension i, a set of threshold values

$$TH_i = \left\{ th_{i,1}, th_{i,2}, \ldots, th_{i,p}, \ldots, th_{i,ni} \mid th_{ij} \in \Re \right\}$$

define continuous state values where phase transitions have to occur. Let's agree that if $s_i \in [th_{i,p}, th_{i,p+1})$, then $phase_i = p$. The internal event condition evaluates to true whenever $phase_i$ is equal to p and the continuous variable s_i cross a threshold and leaves block $[th_{i,p}, th_{i,p+1})$, i.e.,

$$C_{int}(s, x^{cont}) = true \text{ if } \exists i\text{: } phase_i = p \wedge s_i \notin [th_{i,p}, th_{i,p+1})$$
$$= false \text{ otherwise.}$$

The internal state transition function defines the new phase in case of a threshold crossing, i.e., $\delta_{int}(s, x^{cont}).phase_i = phase_i'$ with

$$\begin{aligned} phase_i' &= phase_i + 1 && \text{if } phase_i = p \wedge s_i \geq th_{i,p+1} \\ &= phase_i - 1 && \text{if } phase_i = p \wedge s_i < th_{i,p} \\ &= phase_i \text{ otherwise.} \end{aligned}$$

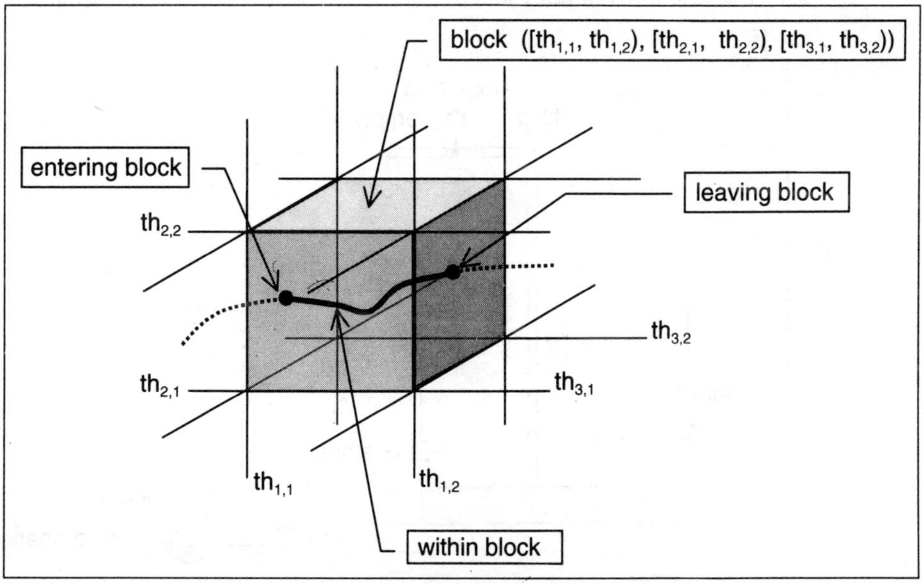

Figure 8 Three-dimensional state space with thresholds.

The discrete state vector ($phase_1$, $phase_2$, . . ., $phase_i$, . . ., $phase_n$) of phase variables is employed to define individual continuous behaviors for the blocks in the state partition. In each block denoted by phase variables values (p_1, p_2, . . ., p_i, . . .), a different derivative may be defined for dimension *i* by a unique function $f_{i(p_1, p_2, \ldots, p_i, \ldots)}$, i.e.,

$$ds_i/dt = f_{i(p_1,p_2,\ldots,p_i,\ldots)}(s, x^{cont}) \text{ if } (phase_1, phase_2, \ldots phase_i, \ldots) = (p_1, p_2, \ldots p_i, \ldots).$$

9.4.1 Example: Pot System with Command Inputs and Threshold Value Outputs

Let us now look at an example from hybrid systems domain. Actually, the following model shows elements of output partitioning as well as multimodeling. Figure 9 shows a two-dimensional system of a pot that can be heated and cooled, filled and emptied. The two dimensions are the *temp* and the *level* dimension representing the liquid level and the liquid temperature, respectively. The system has two discrete command inputs—the *heat-com* and the *fill-com* input—with three different commands for each: *heat-it, cool-it, stop-heating* and *fill-it, empty-it, stop-filling,* respectively. The system's discrete outputs are given by four simple threshold sensors, viz., *is-cold, is-hot, is-empty,* and *is-full.* The values for output sensors are *on* and *off* and they react at particular threshold values of the two continuous state variables *level* and *temp.* Each state dimension is partitioned into three mutual exclusive blocks according to the threshold-sensor output values. Figure 10 shows the state partitioning together with a sample state trajectory. There are 3 times 3 mutual exclusive blocks, which have different sensor output values and which are denoted by the phases *cold, t-betw, hot* and *emtpy, l-betw, full,* respectively. With different blocks we have different derivatives. For example, in the whole block *hot* the *temp* and *level* derivatives change because the

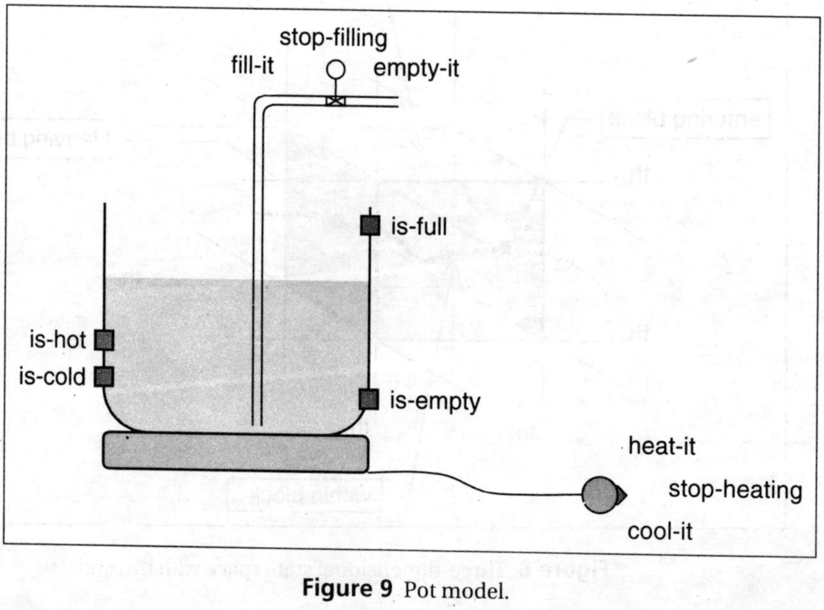

Figure 9 Pot model.

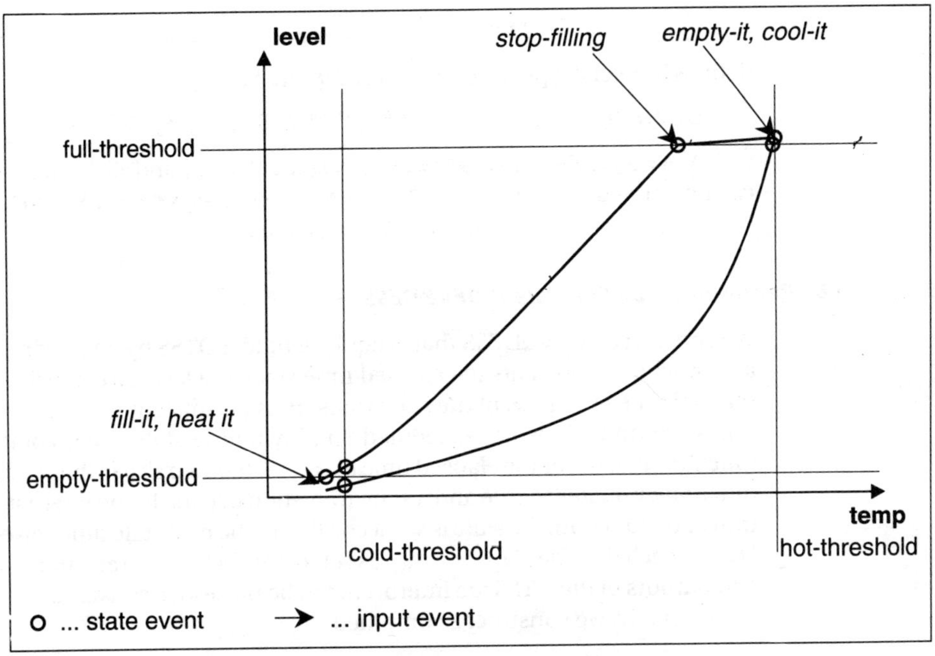

Figure 10 Pot state space partitioning.

liquid begins to boil. The temperature does not increase any more, but the level decreases through evaporation.

We come back to thresholds and phase partitioning of continuous processes in Chapters 16 and 13 when discussing DEVS representation of continuous systems and event-based control, respectively.

9.5 Coupled DEV&DESS: Network of Multiformalism Models

Having the basis of the DEV&DESS formalism puts us in a position to use DEVS&DESS as basic components in suitably defined networks as we did for the basic formalisms in Chapter 7. So now we will introduce a coupled system formalism for combined DEV&DESS that supports modular, hierarchical construction of DEV&DESS models. Then we will show how the basic formalisms, DESS, DTSS, and DEVS are interpreted as special types of DEV&DESS. Such "wrappings" give us interpretations of the basic formalisms in the context of multiformalism coupled systems. Moreover, we also are justified in using these wrappings as components in such networks. So we turn to interpreting the basic formalisms as special cases of DEV&DESS.

9.5.1 Basic Formalisms are Subsumed by DEV&DESS

DESS Are Special DEV&DESS

Basic DESS can obviously be interpreted as DEV&DESS by omitting all the event parts of the combined formalism. Therefore, a basic differential equation specified system,

$$\text{DESS} = (X_{dess}, Y_{dess}, Q_{dess}, f_{dess}, \lambda_{dess}),$$

defines a special type of combined DEV&DESS,

$$\text{DEV\&DESS} = (X^{discr}, X^{cont}, Y^{discr}, Y^{cont}, S, \delta_{ext}, C_{int}, \delta_{int}, \lambda^{discr}, f, \lambda^{cont}),$$

with $X^{cont} = X_{dess}$, $Y^{cont} = Y_{dess}$, $S^{cont} = Q_{dess}$, $f = f_{dess}$, $\lambda^{cont} = \lambda_{dess}$, and all the event parts can be omitted, i.e., $X^{discr} = \{\}$, $Y^{discr} = \{\}$, $S^{discr} = \{\}$, $\delta_{in}((s, e), x^{cont}) = s$, $\delta_{ext}((s, e), x^{cont}) = s$, $\lambda^{discr}((s, e), x^{cont}) = \varnothing$; and $C_{int}((s, e), x_c) = false$.

DTSS Can Be Represented by Equivalent DEV&DESS

We construct a DEV&DESS that is equivalent to a DTSS by employing variable e, which represents the elapsed time since the last state transition, to schedule the execution of the state transitions at constant time intervals h. The state transitions are scheduled employing the state event condition function. Whenever the elapsed time e reaches the step size h, the condition function evaluates to true and a state transition occurs. In the internal state transition function, the state is set according to the next state function of the DTSS (recall that the elapsed time e is set to 0 at each state transition). Input and outputs of the DTSS are interpreted to be piecewise constant.

Formally, we construct a combined

$$\text{DEV\&DESS} = \langle X^{discr}, X^{cont}, Y^{discr}, Y^{cont}, S, \delta_{ext}, C_{int}, \delta_{int}, \lambda^{discr}, f, \lambda^{cont} \rangle$$

from a

$$\text{DTSS} = \langle X_{dtss}, Y_{dtss}, Q_{dtss}, \delta_{dtss}, \lambda_{dtss}, h_{dtss} \rangle$$

in the following way: $X^{cont} = X_{dtss}$, $X^{discr} = \{\}$, $S^{cont} = \{\}$, $S^{discr} = Q_{dtss} \times \{h\}$ with $h = h_{dtss}$, $y^{cont} = \{\}$, $y^{discr} = Y_{dtss}$. The state event condition function $C \times X_c \to Bool$ is defined by

$$C_{int}((q_{dtss}, h), e, x^{cont}) = true \quad \text{if } e \geq h$$
$$= false \quad \text{otherwise.}$$

The internal transition function $\delta_{int}: Q \times X^{cont} \to S$ is built by

$$\delta_{int}((q_{dtss}, h), e, x^{cont})$$
$$= (\delta_{dtss}(q_{dtss}, x_{dtss}), h).$$

The discrete output function $\lambda^{discr}: Q \times X^{cont} \to Y^{cont}$ is given by

$$\lambda^{discr}((q_{dtss}, h) e, x^{cont}) = \lambda_{dtss}(q_{dtss}, x_{dtss})$$

for Mealy-type systems and

$$\lambda^{discr}((q_{dtss}, h), e, x^{cont}) = \lambda_{dtss}(q_{dtss})$$

for Moore-type systems.

The derivative function $f: Q \times X^{cont} \to \{\}$ and the continuous output function $\lambda^{cont}: Q \times X^{cont} \to \{\}$ are omitted.

Theorem 2

A DEV&DESS so constructed is behaviorally equivalent to the original DTSS

The theorem can easily be proven by showing that there exists a system isomorphism from the state component q_{dtss} of the DEV&DESS and the state of the original DTSS. We come back to system isomorphism in the third part of the book.

DEVS Can Be Represented by Equivalent DEV&DESS

In a similar way as for DTSS, we describe a procedure for constructing a DEV&DESS from a basic DEVS. In particular, we again employ the elapsed time variable e and the state event condition function to realize the scheduling of internal events. The internal condition function evaluates to true whenever the elapsed time reaches the value of the time advance given by the DEVS.

We construct a combined

$$\text{DEV\&DESS} = \left\langle X^{discr}, X^{cont}, Y^{discr}, Y^{cont}, S, \delta_{ext}, C_{int}, \delta_{int}, \lambda^{discr}, f, \lambda^{cont} \right\rangle$$

from a

$$\text{DEVS} = \left\langle X_{devs}, Y_{devs}, S_{devs}, \delta_{ext,devs}, \delta_{int,devs}, \lambda_{devs}, ta_{devs} \right\rangle$$

in the following way: $X^{cont} = \{\}$, $X^{discr} = X_{devs}$, $S^{cont} = \{\}$, $S^{discr} = S_{devs}$, $Y^{cont} = \{\}$, $Y^{discr} = Y_{devs}$.

The state event condition function C_{int}: $Q \times X^{cont} \rightarrow Bool$ is defined by

$$\begin{aligned} C_{int}((s_{devs}, e)) &= true \quad \text{if } e \geq ta_{devs}(s_{devs}) \\ &= false \quad \text{otherwise.} \end{aligned}$$

The internal transition function δ_{int}: $Q \times X^{cont} \rightarrow S$ is built by

$$\delta_{int}((s_{devs}, e)) = \delta_{int,devs}(s_{devs}).$$

The derivative function f: $Q \rightarrow \{\}$ and the continuous output function λ^{cont}: $Q \rightarrow \{\}$ can be omitted.

Theorem 3

A DEV&DESS so constructed is behaviorally equivalent to the original DEVS.

Once again the proof requires constructing a system isomorphism between the DEV&DESS and the DEVS. In particular, it has to be shown that the internal state transitions are scheduled at the same times.

Exercise: Show that a clock working in continuous time with a reset port can be realized as a DEV&DESS without using the elapsed time component, e. (Hint: Use a constant derivative.) This shows that the role of the elapsed time component can be played by such a clock.◆

9.5.2 Coupled DEV&DESS Formalism

We have shown that basic DESS are special DEV&DESS and also how to embed DEVS or DTSS into DEV&DESS. So now we can use a basic formalism wherever we can use a DEV&DESS. With that capability we introduce networks of DEV&DESS in order to get a method supporting the construction of networks of components specified in any one of the formalisms—this is a *multi-formalism modeling methodology.*

Let us first examine how we would intuitively like to interpret the couplings of multiformalism components. Then we will show how this is naturally achieved in the coupled DEV&DESS formalism. Fundamental to this enterprise is the interpretation of couplings of discrete outputs to continuous inputs and vice versa. Recall (Chapter 5) that event segments can be translated to piecewise constant segments and vice versa. Hence, we have a means for interpretation of couplings of event outputs to continuous inputs and piecewise constant outputs to event inputs. However, *arbitrary couplings of continuous outputs* to discrete inputs cannot be allowed. The reason is that a continuously changing segment would mean an infinite number of events—and this is not allowed for event segments. Therefore, we allow only couplings of *piecewise constant* continuous outputs to discrete inputs.

Multiformalism system couplings interpretations shows the couplings of the different basic formalisms. Each box shown should be interpreted as its wrapped DEV&DESS version. The interpretation is as follows:

- *Coupling of DTSS to DEVS:* In a coupling of an output of a DTSS to a DEVS, each output at regular intervals from the DTSS means an external event at the DEVS. As the outputs of the DTSS are interpreted as discrete in the context of multiformalism systems, the output segment of a DTSS is an event segment with events at regular intervals that result in external events at the state transition times of the DTSS (Fig. 11a).
- *Coupling of DEVS to DTSS:* In a coupling of an output of a DEVS to an input of a DTSS, the value of the last output event that occurred prior to the state transition of the DTSS should define the input value at its next state transition time. In the context of multiformalism models, the input of DTSS is continuous. Hence, the event output of the DEVS is translated into a piecewise constant input segment for the DTSS that results in the required behavior (Fig. 11b).
- *Coupling of DEVS to DESS:* In a coupling from an event output of a DEVS to a continuous input of a DESS, we would like the events to define discrete changes of the continuous input values. The translation of event segments to piecewise constant segments accomplishes this. The input of a DESS coming from a DEVS is piecewise constant, a subclass of the class of piecewise continuous segments allowed (Fig. 11c).
- *Coupling of DESS to DEVS:* The output of a DESS is a continuous segment, i.e., for every point in time a value is defined. Such a segment cannot be interpreted as an event segment because it would mean an infinite number of events. Thus, arbitrary couplings of continuous outputs of DESS to inputs of DEVS are not allowed. However, we allow couplings when the output is guaranteed to be piecewise constant. Piecewise constant segments are translated into event segments (Fig. 11d).
- *Coupling of DTSS to DESS:* In couplings of DTSS to DESS, the discrete outputs of the DTSS at regular intervals should mean a new constant output value until the next output occurs. The translation of the event segment of the DTSS into piecewise constant segments at the continuous interface of the DESS accomplishes just this (Fig. 11e).

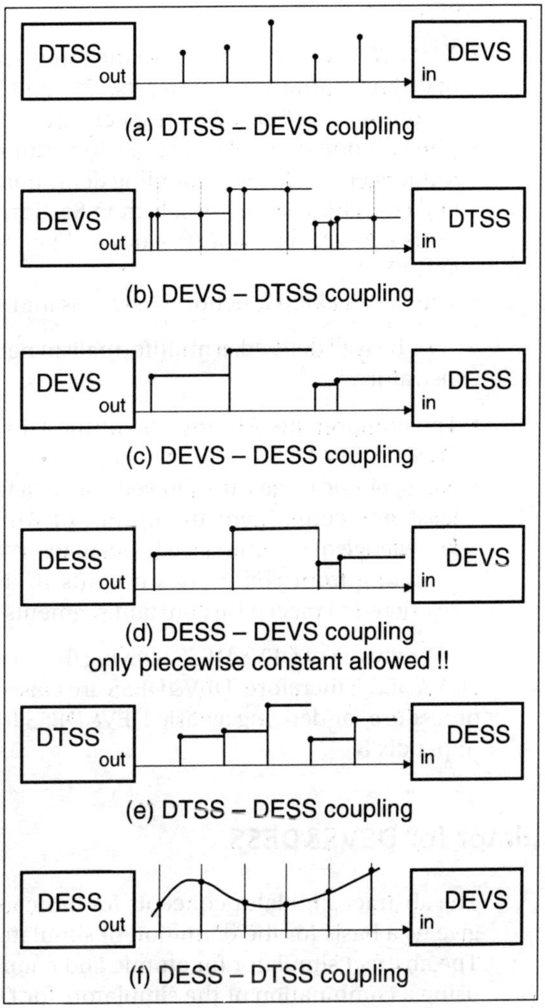

Figure 11 Multiformalism system coupling interpretations.

- *Coupling of DESS to DTSS*: In a coupling of a DESS to a DTSS, the current continuous output value of the DESS is supposed to define the input value for the state transition of the DTSS. As the input of the DTSS is interpreted to be continuous in multiformalism networks, the DTSS just takes the current continuous value at any particular state transition time (Fig. 11f).

Exercise: Consider the coupling interface between two DTSSs with different time step sizes. In particular consider using an averaging function in the mapping of fast output to slow input. (Hint: See Laffitte [14].)◆

Formally, we define a multiformalism network as a coupled system

$$\text{MFN} = \langle X^{discr} \times X^{cont}, Y^{discr} \times Y^{cont}, D, \{M_d\}, \{I_d\} \{Z_d\}, Select \rangle,$$

where

- $X^{discr} \times X^{cont}$ and $Y^{discr} \times Y^{cont}$ are the input and output sets, which consist of of discrete input and ouput sets, X^{discr} and Y^{discr}, and continuous input and output sets, X^{cont} and Y^{cont}, respectively.
- The components' references D and components systems $\{M_d\}$ as well as influencers set $\{I_d\}$ and coupling definitions $\{Z_d\}$ are defined as in the general coupled system formalism in Section 5.10 with Z_d divided into functions $Z_d^{discr}: \times_{i \in I_d} XY_i \rightarrow XY_d^{discr}$ and $Z_d^{cont}: \times_{i \in I_d} XY_i \rightarrow XY_d^{cont}$ according to YX_d^{discr} and YX_d^{cont}.
- The tie-breaking function *Select* is as for DEVS coupled models.

To be well defined, a multiformalism network has to fulfill the following constraints:

- The components M_d must be of the DEVS, DEVN, DTSS, DTSN, DESS, DTSN, DEV&DESS, or MFN type
- No algebraic cycles are allowed, i.e., in a feedback loop there has to be at least one component the output of which can be computed without knowledge of its input (see DTSS networks in Chapter 7)
- Coupling from continuous outputs to inputs of DEVS components is restricted to piecewise constant segments

A network of DEV&DESS obeying these constraints itself specifies a basic DEV&DESS; therefore, DEV&DESS are closed under coupling. We provide a procedure for deriving a basic DEV&DESS from a network of DEV&DESS in Appendix B.

9.6 Simulator for DEVS&DESS

The abstract simulator concepts for basic models formulated in Chapter 8 give us a basis for the definition of simulators for mutliformalism models. The abstract simulator for atomic and coupled DEV&DESS can be defined using a combination of the simulators for DEVS and DESS with additional handling of state events. This means that we have to detect state events, report state events, and execute them, which will require several additions in the continuous as well as the discrete parts of the abstract simulators.

The structure of an abstract simulator contains as discrete part an extended DEVS simulation protocol and as continuous part an extended DESS simulation protocol. These two parts are synchronized by a special root coordinator. In simulation, the two parts alternate in model execution. While the discrete part executes the state transition at the event times, the continuous part computes the state trajectories in between.

The abstract simulator for DEV&DESS has to allow the simulation of multiformalism models consisting of DEVS, DESS, and DTSS components. A simulator for multiformalism models is built up by simulators for basic formalisms as introduced in Chapter 8 and with a combined devs&dess-coordinator as their overall integrator. Additionally, the conversion of input and output segments between the different type of models is accomplished by special *interface objects*. We will present the dev&dess-simulators and dev&dess-coordinators first, and then introduce interfaces for basic model types in the sequel.

9.6.1 The DEV&DESS-Simulator and -Coordinator

Handling of state events is the main extension necessary for the simulation of combined models. This includes the following:

- The detection of state events
- The determination of their exact times
- Scheduling such events for execution.

Such state event handling has to occur during integration and therefore has to be undertaken by the continuous part. The execution of the state events, once determined, is identical to the exection of internal scheduled events in pure DEVS.

Recall that state events occur when continuous variables reach certain values, e.g., a threshold, or when continuous variables meet, e.g., when two objects hit. The state event then is specified by an equality or inequality expression such as

$$expr_1 = expr_2, expr_1 < expr_2, \text{ or } expr_1 > expr_2.$$

Inequality expressions are usually transformed by subtracting one side from the other so that there is zero on one side, i.e.,

$$expr_1 - expr_2, >|<| = 0.$$

State event detection then can be accomplished by checking for zero-crossing, i.e., whenever the $expr_1 - expr_2$ changes sign in an integration step, a state event must have occurred in between. An approximation method is then used to determine the exact time of the event.

Several different methods are used for the approximation of zero-crossings. The best-known method is the bisection method. Basically, it employs a binary search mechanism at the integration interval in which the state event occurred (Fig. 12). When a state event occurred during an inte-

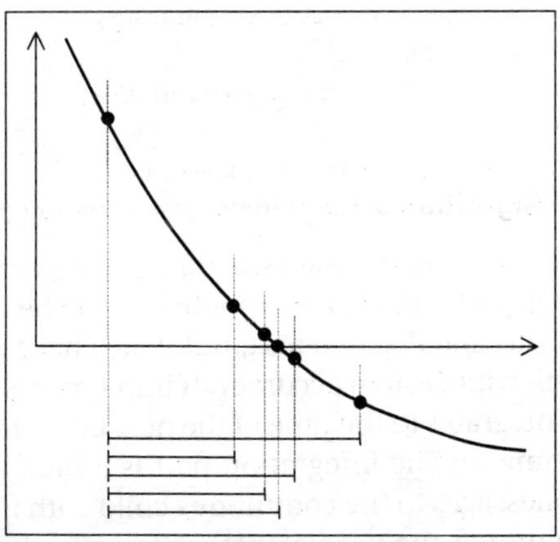

Figure 12 Bisection method to search for state event times.

gration step, the interval is halved and a new integration step is undertaken with the half step size. If the state event still occurs, one knows that it is in the first half and this half is considered further. Otherwise, one knows that the state event is in the second half and the second half is investigated further. This process is continued until the time of the state event is approximated to a predefined accuracy.

Let us now discuss the extensions that are necessary for a continuous simulator to handle state events. Recall from Chapter 8 that a dess-simulator (we discuss the causal version here; extension to noncausal integration methods is straightforward) upon the receipt of an x-message computes the state for next time step $t+h$. In the combined simulator, we have to check for the occurrence of a state event in each integration step. Whenever a zero-crossing for the new state at $t+h$ has occurred (which is recognized by the state event condition function C_{int}), a state event has been detected and is reported in a *state event message* (*se-message*) to the discrete part.

```
dev&dess-simulator extends devs-simulator, dess-causal-
  simulator
  when receive message (x, t_i) with input value x
    q(t_{i+1}) = q(t_{i+h}) = Causal Method ( [q(t_{i-m}), . . ., q(t_i)],
                                              [r(t_{i-m}), . . ., r(t_i)],
                                              [x(t_{i-m}), . . ., x(t_i)], h)
    if (C_int(q(t + h), x(t + h))) then
      tn : = t + h
    else
      tn = ∞
    if tn has changed then
       send se-message (se, tn) with time tn to discrete parent
end dev-dess-simulator
```

Algorithm 2 Causal simulator for basic DEV&DESS

The discrete part then schedules the execution of a state event and reports this state event upward to the parent coordinator. Finally, the message arrives at the root-coordinator.

```
dev-dess-coordinator extends devs-coordinator
  when receive se-message (se, t) with time t from child c
     tn = t
     if tn has changed then
         send se-message (se, tn) with time tn to parent
end dev-dess-coordinator
```

Algorithm 3 Coordinator extensionfor coupled DEV&DESS

In the combined simulation scheme the root-coordinator has important duties. Not only is it responsible for the alternating execution of the continuous and discrete part, but it also has to take care that the state events are hit with desired accuracy. It implements the overall event loop where it first integrates to the time of the next event *tn* and executes the internal event at time *tn*. The integration part is done in a loop where it sends integration messages to the continuous child with integration stepsize *dh*, which computes as the normal integration stepsize *h* or the time interval to the next internal event (*tn* – *t*), whichever is smallest.

After each integration step, the root coordinator checks if an *se*-message has been received from the discrete part and a state event has occurred. Then, in a further loop the root-coordinator iterates to the state event by successive integration steps with different time intervals *dh* until the time of the state event has been hit with the desired accuracy. The different time intervals *dh* are computed based on the approximation methods in hand. Then the discrete part takes over and triggers the execution of the internal event by a *-message to its discrete child.

```
root-coordinator
   variables:
     child - direct subordinate simulator or coordinator
     tn - time of next event of overall child
     h - desired time step
     t - current simulation time

   t = t0
   send initialization message (i, t) to discrete and
     continuous child
   tn = tn of its child

   loop
     // integration loop
     while (t < tn) do
       dh = if (t + h < tn) then dh = h else dh = tn - t
       //make-intgration step
       state-event-detected = false
       send (*, t, dh) to continuous child
       send (x, t, dh) to continuous child
       if state-event-detected then
         // iterate to state event
         loop
           dh = compute new dh based on approximation method
           // make integration step with new time step dh
           state-event-detected = false
           send (*, t, dh) to continuous child
           send (x, t, dh) to continuous child
         until state-event-detected && accuracy reached
       t = t + dh
     end while
     //execute event
     send (*, tn) message to discrete child
     t = tn
   until end of simulation

   when receive se-message (se, tn_c) with time tn_c from
     discrete child
     state-event-detected = true
     if tn_c < tn do
       tn = tn_c
 end root-coordinator
```

Algorithm 4 Root-coordinator in DEV&DESS abstract simulator

9.6.2 Integrating Different Modeling Formalisms

The dev&dess-coordinator can serve as an integrator for multiformalism model simulation. However, interfaces are needed to transform the messages of the simulators and coordinators for the different model types (Fig. 13). In particular, they have the task to transform the input messages as required by the interpretation of the modeling formalisms in a multi-formalism network as defined in Section 9.5. In the following we define the interfaces for the messages for the different model formalisms. All other messages not specified in the interfaces should be regarded as being forwarded directly to the simulator or coordinator object.

DEVS-Interface

The interface for DEVS receives the continuous input values. It checks if they are different from the last received. If so, it sends an *x*-message to its simulator or coordinator reporting the change event in the input value (recall that the inputs have to be piecewise constant so that only a finite number of changes occur).

```
devs-interface
   xs^cont–variable to save last continuous inputs
   when receive input message (x^cont, t)
      when x^cont ≠ xs^cont then
         send (x^cont, t) to devs-simulator or devs-coordinator
         xs^cont = x^cont
end devs-interface
```

Algorithm 5 devs-interface

DTSS-Interface

The interface for DTSS may receive inputs from DEVS, from DESS, and also from different DTSS components, possibly operating with different step sizes *h*. All these inputs are stored for the next state transitions. When a dtss-

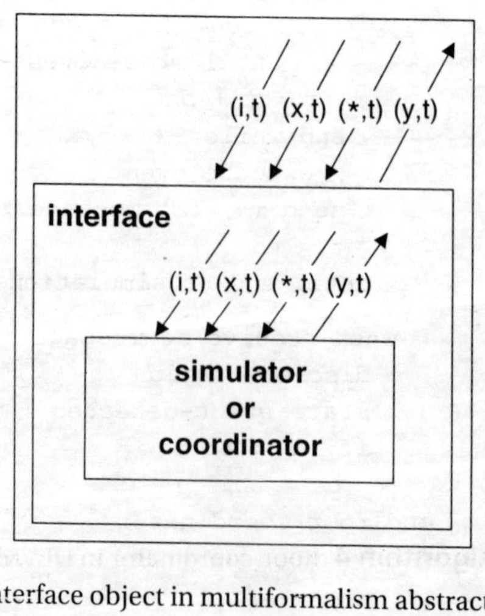

Figure 13 Interface object in multiformalism abstract simulator.

interface receives a *-message at the time of its next state transition, *tn*, it sends a *-message to its dtss-simulator or -coordinator to compute the output and then an *x*-message with stored input values to undertake the state transition.

```
dtss-interface
   xs—variable to save last input
   when receive input message (x, t)
      xs = x
   when receive (*,t)     // execute state transitions
      send (*, t) to dtss-simulator or dtss-coordinator
        // compute output
      send (xs, t) to dtss-simulator or dtss-coordinator
        // state transition
      tn = tn + h
end dtss-interface
```

Algorithm 6 dtss-interface

DESS-Interface

When a dess-interface receives a discrete input event, it stores the values to interpret its inputs as piecewise constant trajectories.

```
dess-interface
   xs^discr—variable to save last discrete inputs
   when receive input message (x^discr, t) with discrete
     input x^discr
      when x^discr ≠ xs^discr then
         xs^discr = x^discr
end dess-interface
```

Algorithm 7 dess-interface

Exercise: Show that the interface objects together with their simulators or coordinators realize the simulation protocol as required for the basic formalisms in multiformalism networks (Section 9.5.1).◆

9.7 Sources

State events are an integral part in many continuous simulation languages. A thorough investigation of the problems associated with state events was done by Cellier [3,4]. The system framework for combined modeling was first introduced by Praehofer [20,21]. The term multimodeling stems from Ören [17] and has been elaborated by [8] and [9]. A multimodeling approach also has been developed to study automated highways control architectures [5,7]. Hybrid systems modeling and analysis is part of an effort to establish a methodology for event-based intelligent control of continuous systems [1,11,15]. Some references to widely adopted formalisms are Forrester [10], Harel [12], Paynter [18], and Peterson [19]. Cellier [4] provides an in-depth discussion of systems dynamics and bond graphs. An example of employing Statecharts within a DEVS simulation environment for co-design of hardware and software is given in Schulz [23].

1. Anstaklis, P., M. D. Passino, and S. J. Wang, "Towards Intelligent Autonomous Control Systems." *Journal of Intelligent and Robotic Systems* **1**(4), 315–342 (1989).
2. Berthomieu, B., and Michael Diaz, "Modeling and Verification of Time Dependent Systems Using Time Petri Nets." *IEEE Transactions on Software Engineering* **17**(3), 259–273 (1991).
3. Cellier, F. E., *Combined Discrete/Continuous System Simulation by Use of Digital Computers:* Techniques and Tools. Ph.D. Thesis, Swiss Federal Institute of Technology, 1979.
4. Cellier, F. E., "Combined Discrete/Continuous System Simulation—Application, Techniques, and Tools." *Proceedings of the 1986 Winter Simulation Conference,* SCS, 1986.
5. Deshpande, A., A. Göllüu, and P. Varaiya, "A Formalism and a Programming Language for Dynamic Networks of Hybrid Automata." In *Hybrid Systems IV.* LNCS, Springer-Verlag, 1997.
6. Elmqvist, H., F. E. Cellier, and M. Otter, "Object-Oriented Modeling of Hybrid Systems." *Proc. ESS'93,* SCS European Simulation Symposium, Delft, The Netherlands, 1993.
7. Eskafi, F. H., *Modeling and Simulation of the Automated Highway System.* Ph.D. Thesis, University of California at Berkeley, 1996.
8. Fishwick, P. A., *Simulation Model Design and Execution: Building Digital Worlds.* Prentice Hall, Englewood Cliffs, NJ, 1995.
9. Fishwick, P., and B. P. Zeigler, "A Multi-model Methodology for Qualitative Model Engineering." *ACM Transactions on Modeling and Simulation* **2**(1), 52–81 (1992).
10. Forrester, J. W., *World Dynamics.* Wright-Allen Press, Cambridge, MA. 1972.
11. Grossmann, R. L., A. Nerode, A. P. Raun, and H. Ritschel, *Hybrid Systems,* Vol. 736, *Lecture Notes in Computer Science.* Springer-Verlag, Berlin, 1993.
12. Harel, David, and Amir Pnueli, "STATEMATE: A Working Environment for the Development of Complex Reactive Systems," *IEEE Transactions on Software Engineering* **16**(4), 403–414 (1990).
13. Ho, Y. C. *Discrete Event Dynamic Systems: Analyzing Complexity and Performance in the Modern World.* IEEE Press, 1994.
14. Laffitte, J., and R. M. Howe, "Interfacing Fast and Slow Subsystems in the Real-Time simulation of Dynamic Systems." *Trans. of SCS* **14**(3), 115–126 (1997).
15. Meystel, A., "Intelligent Control: A Sketch of the Theory." *Journal of Intelligent and Robotic Systems* **2**(4), 97–107 (1989).
16. Olson, J. T., "Combined Discrete/Continuous Simulation of Process Plans and Applications in Discrete Part Manufacturing," Master Thesis in ECE Dept. Tucson, University of Arizona, 1997,
17. Ören, T. I. "Dynamic Templates and Semantic Rules for Simulation Advisers and Certifiers." In *Knowledge-Based Simulation: Methodology and*

Application (P. A. Fishwick and R. B Modjeski, Eds.). Springer-Verlag, Berlin, 1989.

18. Paynter, H. M., *Analysis and Design of Engineering Systems.* MIT Press. Cambridge, MA, 1961.
19. Peterson, James L., *Petri Net Theory and the Modeling of Systems.* Prentice-Hall, Englewood Cliffs, NJ, 1981.
20. Praehofer, H., "System Theoretic Formalisms for Combined Discrete-Continuous System Simulation." *Int. J. Gen. Sys.* **19**(3), 219–240 (1991).
21. Praehofer, H., F. Auernig, and G. Reisinger, "An Environment for DEVS-Based Multi-formalism Modeling and Simulation." *Discrete Event Dynamic Systems: Theory and Applications* **3,** 119–149 (1993).
22. Sanders, W. H., and L. M. Malhis, "Dependability Evaluation Using Composed SAN-Based Reward Models." *J. Parallel and Distributed Computing, Special Issue on Petri Net Models of Parallel and Distributed Computers,* **15**(3), 238–254 (1992).
23. Schulz, S., J. W. Rozenblit, M. Mrva, and K. Buchenrieder, "*Model-Based Codesign*", *IEEE Computer,* **31**(8), 60–74. August 1998.
24. Thoma, J. U., *Simulation by BondGraphs.* Springer-Verlag, New York, 1989.

Appendix A: The System Specified By a DEV&DESS

The DEV&DESS system specification = $\langle X^{discr}, X^{cont}, Y^{discr}, Y^{cont}, S, \delta_{ext}, C_{int}, \delta_{int}, \lambda^{discr}, f, \lambda^{cont}\rangle$ relies on the following background conventions, and these become the corresponding elements in the I/O system $S = \langle T, X, \Omega, Y, Q, \Delta, \Lambda\rangle$ that it specifies:

- The time base T is the real numbers $\Re$
- $X = X^{cont} \times (X^{discr} \cup \{\emptyset\})$ is the set of inputs of the system being specified, with the symbol $\emptyset \notin X^{discr}$ specifying the nonevent
- X^{discr} can be an arbitrary set
- X^{cont} is a structured set $X^{cont} = \{(x_1^{cont}, x_2^{cont}, \ldots, x_i^{cont}, \ldots, x_n^{cont}) \mid x_i^{cont} \in X_i^{cont}\}$ with X_i^{cont} are the reals
- $Y = Y^{cont} \times (Y^{discr} \cup \{\emptyset\})$ is the set of outputs of the dynamic system
- Y^{discr} can be an arbitrary set
- Y^{cont} is structured set $Y^{cont} = \{(y_1^{cont}, y_2^{cont}, \ldots, y_i^{cont}, \ldots, y_n^{cont}) \mid y_i^{cont} \in Y_i^{cont}\}$ with Y_i^{cont} are the reals
- $Q = S^{cont} \times Q^{discr}$ is the set of states of the specified system. This system state set has a typical element $q = (s, e) = (s^{cont}, s^{discr}, e)$, i.e., a tuple containing the DESS state, s^{cont}, the DEVS state, s^{discr}, and the elapsed time, e
- S^{discr} can be an arbitrary set
- S^{cont} is structured set $S^{cont} = \{(s_1^{cont}, s_2^{cont}, \ldots, s_i^{cont}, \ldots, s_n^{cont}) \mid s_i^{cont} \in S_i^{cont}\}$ with S_i^{cont} are the reals
- The set Ω^{discr} of admissible input segments of the discrete inputs is the set of all event segments over X^{discr} and T

- The allowable input segment Ω_i^{cont} for input variable x_i^{cont} are bounded piecewise continuous segments over X_i^{cont} and T
- The state trajectories of the discrete states S^{discr} are piecewise constant segments over S^{discr} and T
- The state trajectories of the continuous states S^{cont} are piecewise continuous segments over S^{cont} and T
- The output trajectories of the discrete outputs Y^{discr} are event segments over Y^{discr} and T
- The allowable output segment for output variable y_i are piecewise continuous segments over Y_i^{cont} and T

The global transition function, Δ, of the I/O system is defined as follows: Let ω: $<t_1, t_2] \rightarrow X$ be the input segment and the state $q = (s, e) = (s^{cont}, s^{discr}, e)$ be the state at time t_1. Then we define Δ by

1. Intervals $<t_1, t_2>$ with no events:

$$\Delta(q,\omega) = \left(s^{cont}(t_2), s^{discr}(t_2), e(t_2)\right) = \left(\left(s^{cont}(t_1) + \int_{t_1}^{t_2} f(s(\tau),\omega(\tau))\, d\tau, s^{discr}(t_1), e(t_1) + t_2 - t_1\right)\right.$$

$$\text{if } \neg\exists t \in <t_1, t_2]: C_{\text{int}}\left(s(t), x^{cont}(t)\right) \wedge \neg\exists t \in <t_1, t_2]: \omega^{discr}(t) \neq \varnothing.$$

2. An state event occurs first at time t in interval $<t_1, t_2>$:

$$\Delta(q,\omega_{t]}) = \left(s^{cont}(t_2), s^{discr}(t_2), e(t)\right) =$$

$$\left(\delta_{\text{int}}\left(\left(s^{cont}(t_1) + \int_{t_1}^{t_2} f(s(\tau),\omega(\tau))\, d\tau, s^{discr}(t_1)\right),\right.\right.$$

$$\left.\left. x^{cont}(t)\right), 0\right)$$

$$\text{if } \exists t \in <t_1, t_2]: C_{\text{int}}\left(s(t), \omega^{cont}(t)\right) \wedge \neg\exists t' \in <t_1, t]: \omega^{discr}(t') \neq \varnothing.$$

3. An event input at a discrete input occurs first at time t in interval $<t_1, t_2>$:

$$\Delta(q,\omega_{t]}) = \left(s(t), e(t)\right) =$$

$$\left(\delta_{ext}\left(\left(s^{cont}(t_1) + \int_{t_1}^{t_2} f(s(\tau),\omega(\tau))\, d\tau, s^{discr}(t_1)\right),\right.\right.$$

$$\left.\left. x^{cont}(t), e(t_1) + t - t_1, \omega(t)\right), 0\right)$$

$$\text{if } \exists t \in <t_1, t_2]: \omega^{discr}(t) \neq \Phi \wedge \neg\exists t' \in <t_1, t]: C_{\text{int}}\left(s(t'), \omega^{cont}(t')\right).$$

The output function Λ is defined by

$$\Lambda^{cont}(q,x) = \lambda(q, x^{cont})$$

$$\Lambda^{discr}(q,x) = \lambda^{discr}(q, x^{cont}) \qquad \textit{if } e = 0$$

$$\Lambda^{discr}(q,x) = \varnothing \qquad \textit{otherwise.}$$

After executing the external or state events, the same considerations apply to the new state and the remaining segment.

Appendix B: The System Specified By a Multiformalism System—Closure Under Coupling of Networks of DEV&DESS

DEV&DESS systems are closed under coupling, i.e., networks of DEV& DESS are themselves DEV&DESS systems. The resulting system can be regarded as a crossproduct of the component systems. The sequential state, inputs, and outputs are defined by the crossproduct of the states, inputs, and outputs of the system description of the components. The state event condition function is the disjunction (logical *or*) of the state event condition functions of all components. This means that a state event occurs whenever one of the components' state event condition evaluates to true. The internal and external state transition functions are defined analogously to a network of DEVS (Chapter 7).

Theorem 4. *Closure under Coupling of DEV&DESS*
The resultant of coupled DEV&DESS is well defined and is itself a DEV& DESS.

Proof. Given a DEV&DESS coupled model,

$$MFN = \left\langle X^{discr} \times X^{cont}, Y^{discr} \times Y^{cont}, D, \{M_d\}, \{I_d\}\{Z_d\}, Select \right\rangle,$$

we associate with it the following basic DEV&DESS:

$$\text{DEV\& DESS} = \left\langle X^{discr}, X^{cont}, Y^{discr}, Y^{cont}, S, \delta_{ext}, C_{int}, \delta_{int}, \lambda^{discr}, f, \lambda^{cont} \right\rangle$$

where $X^{discr} = X_N^{discr}$, $X^{cont} = X_N^{cont}$, $Y^{discr} = Y_N^{discr}$, $Y^{cont} = Y_N^{cont}$, $S = \times_{d \in D} Q_d$.

A continuous input of a component d in the network is defined by the couplings of the continuous outputs of its influencers, i.e., $x_d^{cont} = Z_d^{cont}(\ldots, \lambda_i^{cont}(q_i^{cont}, x_i^{cont}), \ldots)$ with $i \in I_d$. Then the derivative function f: $Q \times X^{cont} \to S$ is the crossproduct over the derivative functions f_d of the components $d \in D$, i.e., $f(q, x_N^{cont}) \cdot d = f_d(q_d, x_d^{cont})$. The continuous output function λ^{cont}: $Q \times X^{cont} \to Y^{cont}$ is derived from the external output couplings of the continuous output variables, i.e., $Z_N^{cont}(\ldots, \lambda_i^{cont}(q_i, x_i^{cont}), \ldots)$ with $i \in I_N$.

The state event condition function C_{int}: $Q \times X_c \to Bool$ is defined by the disjunction of the condition functions of the components, i.e., $C_{int}(q, x^{cont}) = \bigvee_{d \in D} C_{\text{int},d}(q_d, x_d^{cont})$, and the state transition and output functions are as follows:

Let $IMM(s) = \{d \mid d \in D \wedge C_{int,d}(q_d, x_d^{cont})\}$ be the set of components that have a condition evaluating to true and $d^* = Select(Imminent(s))$ select one of them using the tie-breaking function *Select*. Then we define δ_{int}: $Q \times X_N^{cont} \to S$, $\delta_{int}((s, e), x_N^{cont}) = s' = (\ldots, (s_d', e_d') \ldots)$ by

$$\begin{aligned}
\left(s_d', e_d'\right) &= \left(\delta_{int,d}\left(q_d, x_d^{cont}\right), 0\right) && \text{if } d = d^* \\
&= \left(\delta_{int,d}\left(s_d, e_d + e, x_d^{cont}, x_d^{discr}\right), 0\right) && \text{if } d^* \in I_d \ \& \ x_d^{discr} \neq \\
&= \left(s_d, e_d + e\right) && \text{otherwise,}
\end{aligned}$$

where $x_d^{discr} = Z_d^{discr}(\varnothing, \varnothing, \ldots \lambda_{d^*}^{discr}(s_{d^*}) \ldots, \varnothing, \varnothing)$.

We define δ_{ext}: $Q \times X^{cont} \times X^{discr} \to S$,

$$\delta_{ext}\left((s,e),x^{cont},x^{discr}\right)=s'\left(\ldots,\left(s_{d'},e_{d'}\right)\ldots\right)\text{ by}$$

$$\left(s_{d'},e_{d'}\right)=\left(\left(\delta_{ext,d}\left(s_d,e_d+e,x_d^{cont},x_d^{discr}\right),0\right)\right)\quad\text{if } N\in I_d \text{ and } x_d^{discr}\neq\varnothing$$

$$=\left(s_d,e_d+e\right)\quad\text{otherwise,}$$

where $x_d^{discr}=Z_d^{discr}\ (\varnothing,\varnothing,\ldots,x^{discr},\ldots,\varnothing,\varnothing)$.

And we define $\lambda^{discr}:S\to Y$ by

$$\lambda^{discr}(s)=Z_N^{discr}\left(\varnothing,\varnothing,\ldots,\lambda_{d^*}^{discr}\left(s_{d^*}\right),\ldots,\varnothing,\varnothing\right)\quad\text{if } d^*\in I_N$$

$$=\varnothing\quad\text{otherwise.}$$

The rest of the proof shows that the resultant is well defined.■

10

DEVS-Based Extended Formalisms

This chapter introduces several extensions of DEVS. As already indicated, such extensions expand the classes of system models that can be represented in DEVS and hence within both the DEVS bus and the parent systems theory formalism. As depicted in Fig. 1, we summarize the extensions as follows:

- *Dynamic Structure DEVS*: Allows a model to change structure during a simulation run.
- *Symbolic DEVS*: Represents the time base in symbolic form allowing time relations ships symbolic times such as inter-arrival-time and service time.
- *Real Time DEVS*: Allows a DEVS model to be developed in a simulation environment and executed in real time rather than model time.
- *Fuzzy DEVS*: Provides fuzzy versions of the DEVS concepts to enable easier incorporation of uncertainty into the model.

A theme of the last three extensions is that they all involve extending the time advance function. In Symbolic DEVS this is a consequence of the symbolic time base. Real Time DEVS allows the time advance function to produce a time interval rather than a single value. The interval, called a time window, allows uncertainly in the time advance function to be stated as a lower and upper bound within which a transition must take place. The bigger this window, the more uncertain we are of the transition time, or the less control we wish to exert over the transition. The use of a time window also appears in the control-oriented Boundary-Based DEVS to be discussed in Chapter 13. It is also used in the simulation of Parallel DEVS, where it takes the form of a time granule that enables scattered events to be clustered together for concurrent execution. Fuzzy DEVS provides a linguistic interpretation of time advance values such as small, medium, and large.

10.1 Stochastic Systems: Conventional Approach to Uncertainty

DEVS extensions such as Fuzzy DEVS can be placed in a larger framework as alternatives to the conventional stochastic approach to including uncertainty in dynamic systems [13]. Thus, we start with some background on stochastic modeling. Stochastic behavior in simulation programs is usually obtained by including pseudo-random-number generators into component models. The first edition, TMS76, formulated a concept of an ideal random number generator as a deterministic algorithm whose output sequences pass suitable

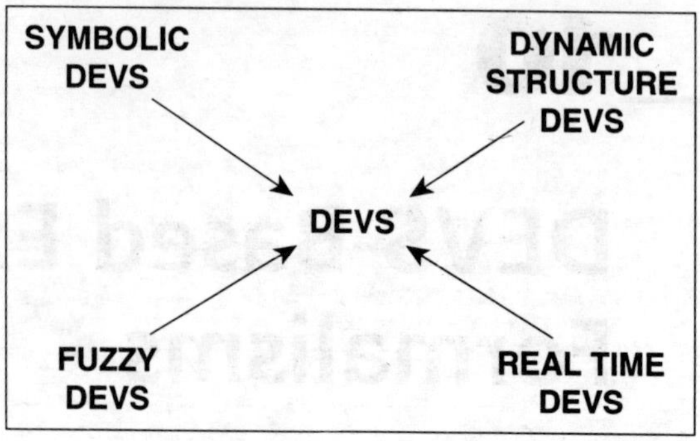

Figure 1 DEVS extensions.

tests such as for uniform distribution and zero-correlation properties [1]. A call to an ideal random number generator yields a number in the range [0,1], which is fed to a function, called a random variable. Outputs of a random variable have frequency distributions such as uniform, exponential, or normal.

As an example of stochastic simulation, let's compare a multiserver architecture with two such architectures, each having half the number of processors. This is an answer to the question: Should a bank continue to form one line for all tellers, or should it require customers to line up at tellers as in the typical supermarket?

Let customers be generated with an interarrival time that is exponentially distributed with mean $1/\lambda$. This makes the arrival rate λ. Similarly, each processor has a processing time with an exponential distribution with mean $1/\mu$ and service rate μ. A four-processor architecture is depicted in queuing theory terms in Fig. 2a.

The same notation for two architectures in parallel is shown in Fig. 2b. Note that the arrivals are split into two separate groups, each with half the arrival rate of the four-processor architecture.

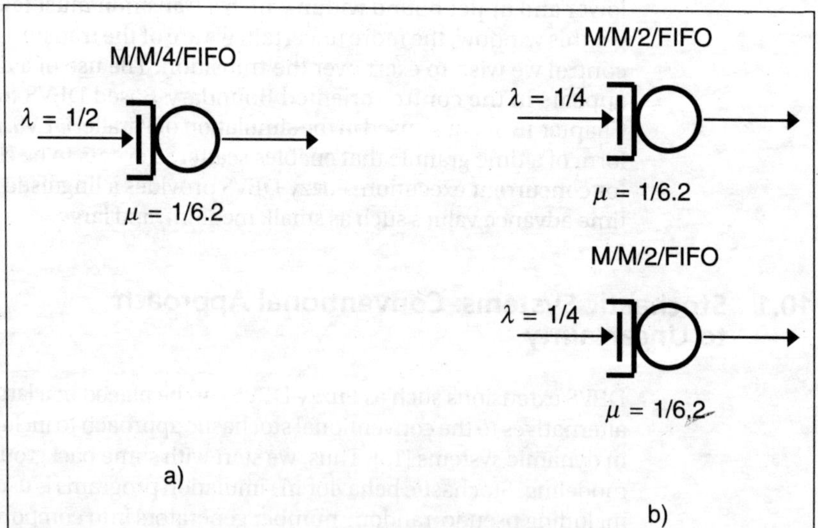

Figure 2 Queuing theory depiction of a four-processor architecture. M stands for exponential; FIFO is first in, first out.

The turnaround time, or system residence time, of a job is the time it spends in a queue plus the time it spends being processed. The mean turnaround time for M/M/2/∞/FIFO and M/M/4/∞/FIFO can be computed analytically and are equal to 15.52 and 10.00, respectively. Thus, the all-in-one-line is better for the customer.

In fact, these alternatives are two extremes in an adaptive architecture in which servers can be moved between stations as needed. Although the extremes have analytic solutions for some statistics, dynamic structure models such as adaptive architectures require simulation for analysis and comprehension. We discuss an extension to DEVS that supports dynamic structure next.

10.2 DSDEVS (Dynamic Structure DEVS)

Allowing changes in model structure during execution is a challenging area of development in modeling and simulation research. Such structural change can better reflect real-world dynamics in which drastic changes in behavior regimes occur in an event-like fashion—so that between such structure-transforming events the dynamics can be portrayed as ordinary system behavior. For example, a parachute that opens on the way down can be represented in two regimes, before and after it opens, with the structure change event switching from the first regime to the second. Other examples are societies that change their organizational structure over time, the evolution of neural connectivity, biological evolution, and so on [18,19]. The multimodeling approach of Chapter 9 is one way to express such variable structure at the I/O system level. Another approach discussed here focuses on structure change at the coupled model level.[1]

In DSDEVS (Dynamic Structure DEVS), introduced by Barros [2,3,5], basic models are the same as classic DEVS basic models, but the structure of coupled models can change over time. For example, processors can be moved from one site to another depending on the workloads at the sites.

A DSDEVS coupled model (*dynamic structure network*) is defined by Barros [5] as

$$DSDEVN_{\Delta} = \langle X_{\Delta}, Y_{\Delta}, \chi, M_{\chi} \rangle,$$

where

Δ is the DSDEVS network name

X_{Δ} is the input event set of the DSDEVS network

Y_{Δ} is the output event set of the DSDEVS network

χ is the DSDEVS *network executive* name

M_{χ} is the model of χ.

The DSDEVS network is defined with a special component, the *network executive* χ. M_{χ}, the model of the executive, is a DEVS basic model and is defined by the structure

$$M_{\chi} = \langle X_{\chi}, S_{\chi}, Y_{\chi}, \delta_{int_{\chi}}, \delta_{ext_{\chi}}, \lambda_{\chi}, ta_{\chi} \rangle.$$

[1] This section is based on the material in Barros [5].

This model keeps information about network composition and coupling. The DSDEVS formalism relies on the underlying simulation environment to map changes in network-related state variables of χ into changes in network structure. A state $s_\chi \in S_\chi$ has information about the structure of the DSDEVS network and is defined by the 6-tuple

$$s_\chi = \left(D^\chi, \{M_i^\chi\}, \{I_i^\chi\}, \{Z_{i,j}^\chi\}, SELECT^\chi, V^\chi\right),$$

where

D^χ is the set of components

M_i^χ is the model of component i, for all $i \in D^\chi$

I_i^χ is the influence of i, for all $i \in D^\chi \cup \{\chi, \Delta\}$

$Z_{i,j}^\chi$ is the i-to-j output to input function, for all $j \in I_i^\chi$

$SELECT^\chi$ is the *Select* function

V^χ represents other state variables that the executive may employ for its decision making.

The state variables are subject to the following constraints:

$\chi \notin D^\chi$ (the executive cannot be removed)

$M_i^\chi = \langle X_i, S_i, Y_i, \delta_{int_i}, \delta_{ext_i}, \lambda_i, \tau_i \rangle$ is a DSDEVS basic model, for all $i \in D^\chi$

$i \notin I_i^\chi$ for all $i \in D^\chi \cup \{\chi, \Delta\}$ (self loops are not allowed)

$SELECT^\chi : \Pi \to D^\chi \cup \{\chi\}$, where

$\Pi = 2^{D^\chi \cup \{\chi\}} - \{\}$

$SELECT^\chi(A) \in A$

$Z_{\Delta,j}^\chi : X_\Delta \to X_j$

$Z_{i,\Delta}^\chi : Y_i \to X_\Delta$

$Z_{i,j}^\chi : Y_i \to X_j$

$Z_{k,\chi}^\chi(y) \neq \phi \Rightarrow Z_{k,j}^\chi(y) = \phi$

for $k \in D^\chi \cup \{\Delta\}$ and for all $j \in I_k^\chi - \{\chi\}$, where ϕ represents the non-event.

The last constraint states that if a model sends an external event to the executive, then the executive is the only component receiving an external event. Since the underlying formalism is Classic DEVS, this constraint is added to prevent any ambiguity that may arise when several components, including the executive, receive an input. In this case, the behavior of the system would depend on the external event handling order because of changes in structure that might be done by the executive.

Since the coupling information of the network is located in the executive state, transition functions can change this state and thereby change the structure of the network. Usually the state variables represented by V^χ are used to keep information about when and how changes take place.

The 5-tuple $(D^{\chi},\{M_i^{\chi}\},\{I_i^{\chi}\},\{Z_{i,j}^{\chi}\},SELECT^{\chi})$, defined in the executive state, is referred to as the *network structure.* Any change in one of these variables is called a *change in structure.* We define changes in structure in a broad sense, ranging from the simple change of the *Select* function to more com plex changes, such as the addition and deletion of components and links.

10.2.1 DSDEVS Closure Under Coupling

To use a formalism for representing large simulation models, one must guarantee that it allows model building in a hierarchical and modular manner. Model musts obey the rules stated in Chapter 7 for hierarchical and modular construction:

- A basic model is a hierarchical model
- A coupled model whose components are hierarchical models is a hierarchical model (closure under coupling)
- Nothing else is a hierarchical model

Since DSDEVS basic formalism is DEVS, closure under coupling can be accomplished by demonstrating that the resultant of a DSDEVS coupled model is equivalent to a DEVS.

Theorem 1
Every DSDEVS coupled model is equivalent to a DEVS basic model.

The proof is given in Barros [5].

As described by the definition of the resultant transition functions δ_{ext} and δ_{int}, the network structure can change when the executive performs an internal or external transition. Since all structure information is kept in the executive state, any change in structure can be accomplished by the executive transition functions. The DSDEVS thus provides a formalism to represent and simulate a subclass of systems with a time-varying structure.

The theorem suggests that in principle, a dynamic structure model can be transformed into a Classic DEVS model and executed without any support for dynamic structure. However, in real applications, this transformation will be prohibited by model complexity. In such applications, it would be very difficult, or even impossible, to represent the range of complex dynamic structure systems without the help of a formalism with complete structural semantics.

Exercise: Show how to embed a DEVS coupled model into a DSDEVS coupled model. (Hint: Use a "degenerate" executive with a single decision state.)◆

10.2.2 Example: Adaptive Processing Architectures

We illustrate the use of the DSDEVS formalism to represent a system that can move servers (modeled as simple processors with queues (Chapter 4) from one service station to another [7].

Figure 3 shows the DEVS coupled model at the top level. Nodes serve jobs arriving at the input ports. A Control component observes the workloads of the nodes and makes decisions about changes in structure. The Control

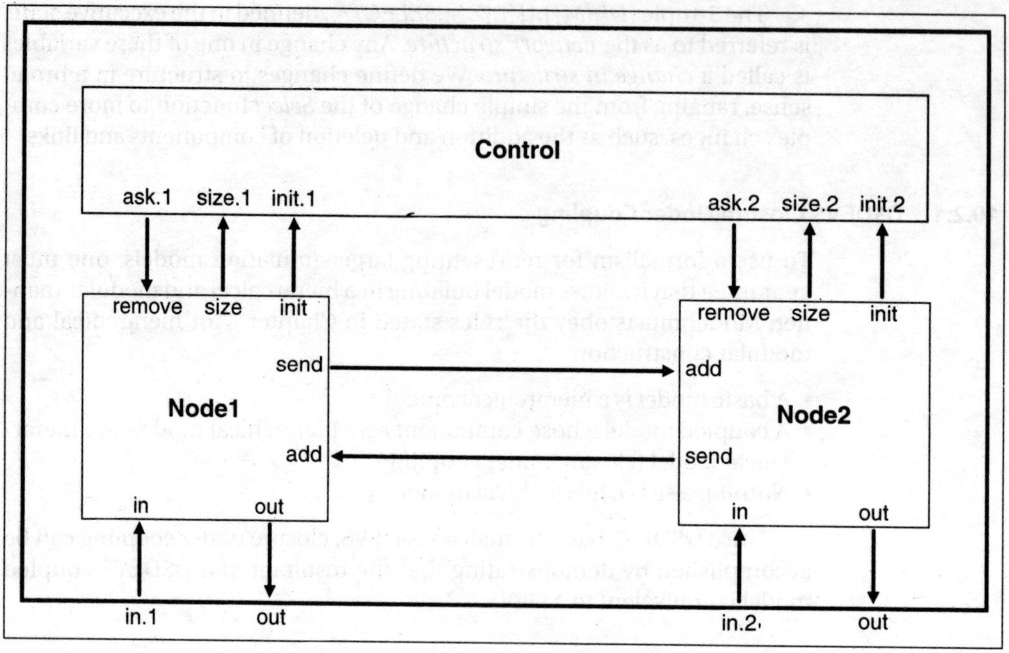

Figure 3 Network block diagram.

model observes the state of each queue (via ports **size**) and when necessary, idle servers are moved from one node to another (via ports **ask**).

When the simulation starts, each node sends its initial state to the Control model using the port **init.** When customers arrive or leave, each node updates Control information using the port **size.**

The Node Model

The node represented in Fig. 4 is a dynamic structure network model and thus has the ability to change its structure by adding or removing servers. The *queue* component implements the DSDEVS network executive. Changes in structure are initiated by the queue transition functions. Aside from the ability to add and remove servers, the queue component is similar to a processor with a queue (Chapter 4; see also Section 10.3).

When a client arrives to port **in@0,** it is sent to an existing idle server or is placed in a FIFO queue if all servers are busy. When a client arrives from a server, it is sent through port **out@0.** If there are clients waiting, the first is chosen and sent to the idle server. If the queue is empty, the server becomes idle.

An idle server is removed from a node in response to a message on the **remove** port. After the server is removed, it goes to the port **send** and will be received on the **add** port of the other node. When a new server arrives, a client is removed from the queue and placed in service. The port **size** is used to communicate node information such as the number of idle servers and customers in queue.

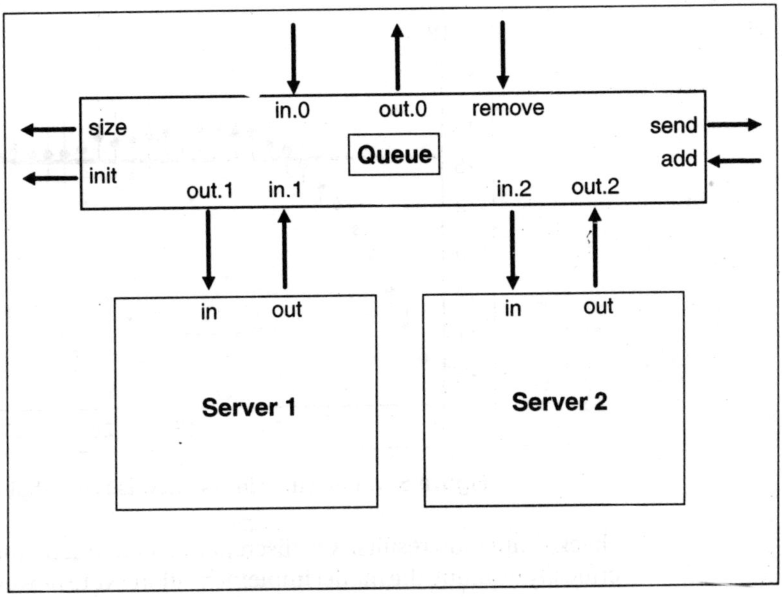

Figure 4 Block diagram of a node.

The queue discipline used in this example is FIFO, but because of the modularity of the model, we can replace it by another discipline without changing the network architecture.

For the sake of simplicity we limit our discussion to a network of two queues and four servers. However, the same principles could also be used to control more complex networks. The decision rule to change a server is:

> if there is an idle server in node$_i$ and (size of the queue in node$_j$ – number of servers in transit to node$_j$) > T then move an idle server from node$_i$ to node$_j$, where T is the threshold level.

For simplicity, assume that moving a server requires zero time. Then the performance of the queuing network will range between two extremes: (1) an equivalent system with one node having all the servers when $T=0$; and (2) a system with two nodes and no movable servers when $T=\infty$. These were the alternatives mentioned earlier (Fig. 2).

One-hundred one simulation runs were made to plot each point with associated confidence interval, $\alpha = 0.05$.

Figure 5 plots mean turnaround time, W = *service time* + *time spent in the queue,* for several values of T. The black line represents the value of W for $T=\infty$. As threshold increases, the network behaves more and more as two independent nodes, and as a consequence turnaround time increases. As there is no delay associated with server change, the smallest turnaround time occurs when threshold level $T=0$, i.e., a server can be moved to a site as quickly as needed.

A useful methodology for verifying simulation models is illustrated here. Extremes such as $T=0$ and $T=\infty$ that have analytic solutions can be used to

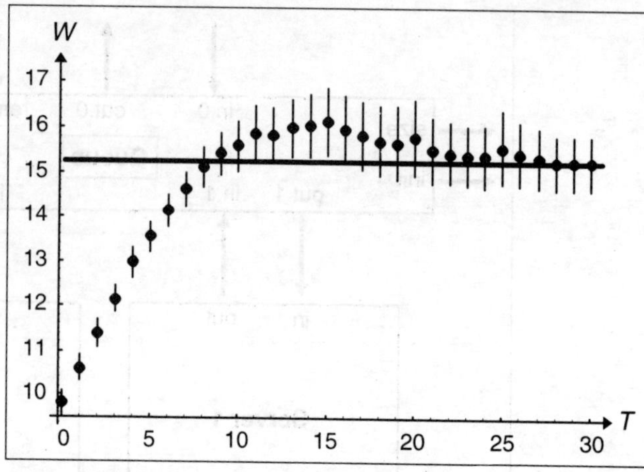

Figure 5 Waiting time in system versus threshold level.

check simulation results. Any discrepancy should send the modeler back to critically examine the model implementation. Note however, between such extremes analytic models may not exist and simulation becomes the only way to gain quantitative predictions from complex models. See [Barros 4] for more information on the DELTA/DSDEVS simulation environment and more sophisticated dynamic structure models and Ref. [6] for a generalization to the other basic system formalisms.

10.3 Symbolic DEVS

Symbolic DEVS represents events occurring in symbolic time.[2] Rather than focusing on statistical summaries obtained through stochastic simulation, the objective is to explore multiple model behaviors simultaneously and in orderly fashion. By allowing times to be expressed symbolically, Symbolic DEVS generates a family of trajectories that represent all possible state trajectories resulting in a particular state. Such a family can be employed to trace a detected fault back to its root cause, or to find timing constraints on a systems transitions that satisfy a target performance requirement, and so on. Symbolic DEVS is thus an example of automated reasoning [20].

The basic Symbolic DEVS is a structure

$$M = \langle X, S, Y, \delta_{int}, \delta_{ext}, \lambda, ta \rangle,$$

where X is the set of external (input) event types, S is the sequential state set; Y is the output set; δ_{int}: $S \times LP^{+}_{0}, \infty \rightarrow S$ is the internal transition function where the LP^{+}_{0}, ∞ is the vector space of linear polynomials over nonnegative reals with ∞ adjoined; δ_{ext}: $Q \times S \rightarrow S$ is the external transition function where $Q = \{(s,e) \mid s \in S, 0 \leq e \leq ta(s)\}$; $\lambda: S \rightarrow Y$ is the output function; and $ta: S \rightarrow 2^{LP+0}, _{\infty}$ is the time advance function where *ta(s)* is a finite, nonempty set of linear polynomials.

[2] This section is based on the material in Chi [8].

In conventional DEVS, the time base and its operations and relations are performed over the field of real numbers. In Symbolic DEVS, this field is extended to the linear polynomials over the reals. For example, the expression "*5 + 2 × travel-time + delay-time*" is a legal time value and might represent the time taken to make a round-trip journey. When *travel-time* and *delay-time* are assigned numerical values, this expression evaluates to a real number. Thus, precise knowledge of any event time can be readily incorporated by setting its symbol to a real value. Therefore, Symbolic DEVS is truly an extension of conventional DEVS and reduces to the latter when all times are real-valued. In contrast to stochastic discrete event simulation, Symbolic DEVS can generate a symbolic representation of a family of trajectories as opposed to a sampled subset based on probability distributions.

10.3.1 Symbolic DEVS Coupled Models

A coupled model of Symbolic DEVS components is nondeterministic since the minimum of a set of next event times is not unique. Thus, trajectories split into treelike structures. Each minimal element in a set of next event times represents a possible state transition; in making the choice of such an element, we generate a set of constraints asserting that it is less than all other minimal elements. This constraint applies to the trajectory branch just initiated. Likewise, constraints are accumulated and inferenced to constrain minimal next event times in subsequent branchings. For example, asserting "$t_1 < t_2$" at one branch and "$t_2 < t_3$" at a subordinate one requires also that "$t_1 < t_3$" in the latter's subtree. Since symbolic times are linear expressions, we can adopt techniques from linear programming to efficiently manage and inference the constraint sets [21].

10.3.2 Example: Performance Evaluation of Basic Architectures

With Classic DEVS (or Parallel DEVS) we can investigate the performance of architectures such as that shown in Fig. 2 under various conditions and parameter settings. However, there are some simple considerations that determine such statistics as the smallest turnaround time and maximum throughput that these architectures can achieve. Unless we have some insight into the governing constraints, it unlikely that we would come up with them through sampling their behaviors with stochastic simulation. We can gain such insight by employing Symbolic DEVS with the same models.

In Symbolic DEVS, we set the processing time of each processor and interarrival time of the generator (*G*) to the symbols *processing-time* and *inter-arrival-time*, or *P* and *T* for short, respectively. In order to mark the trajectory that can allow the optimal performance, the goal condition is set as "every processor maintains the busy state for as long as possible and no jobs are lost." Every multiprocessor architecture consists of a coordinator (*CO*) with three attached identical processors (*P1, P2,* and *P3*) as shown in Fig. 6. The multiserver farms out jobs to processors, keeping track of those that are busy.

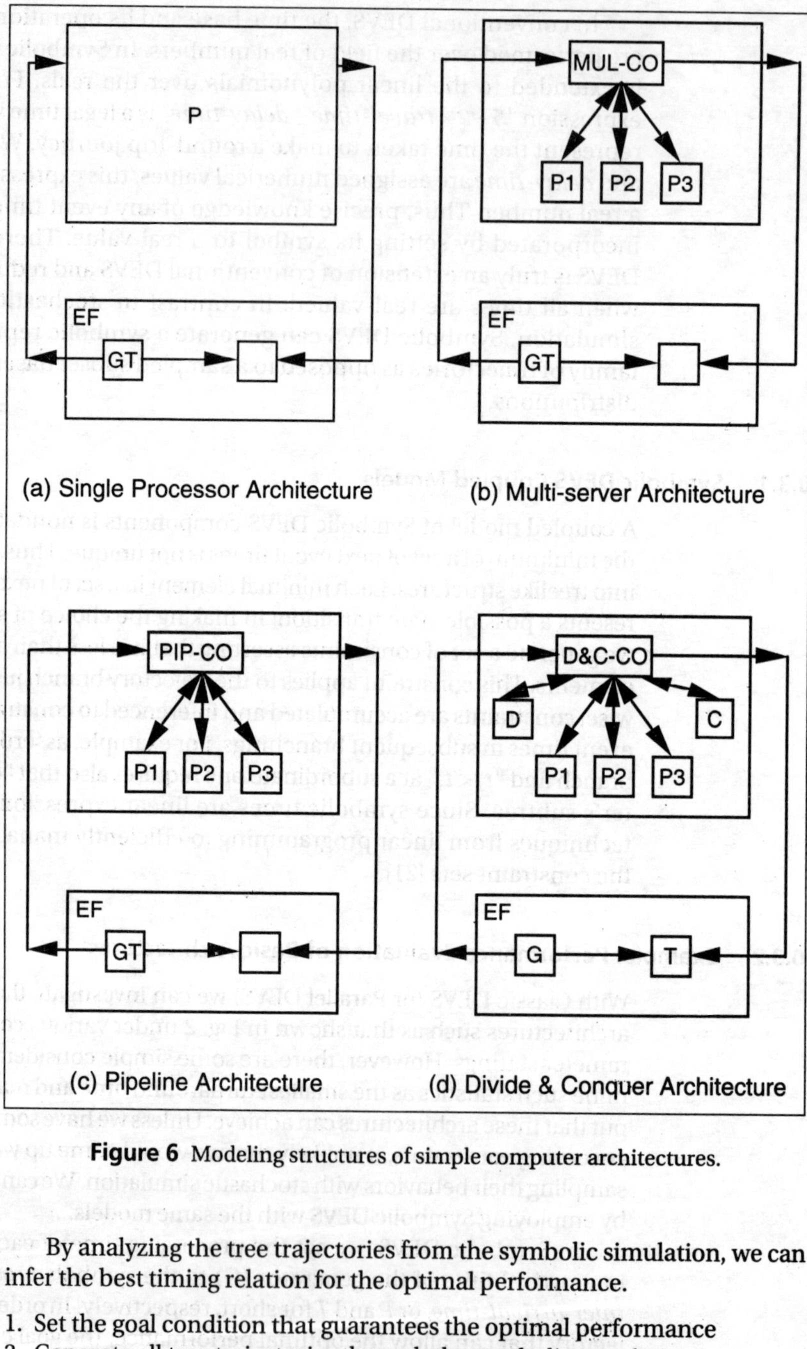

Figure 6 Modeling structures of simple computer architectures.

By analyzing the tree trajectories from the symbolic simulation, we can infer the best timing relation for the optimal performance.

1. Set the goal condition that guarantees the optimal performance
2. Generate all tree trajectories through the symbolic simulation
3. Analyze the timing constraints that satisfy the goal condition

Figure 7 shows the generated tree trajectories and the timing relation of each trajectory where the generator outputs three jobs to the single-processor architecture. To see how the tree is generated, consider the root node where the symbolic simulation starts. We start with a job just having

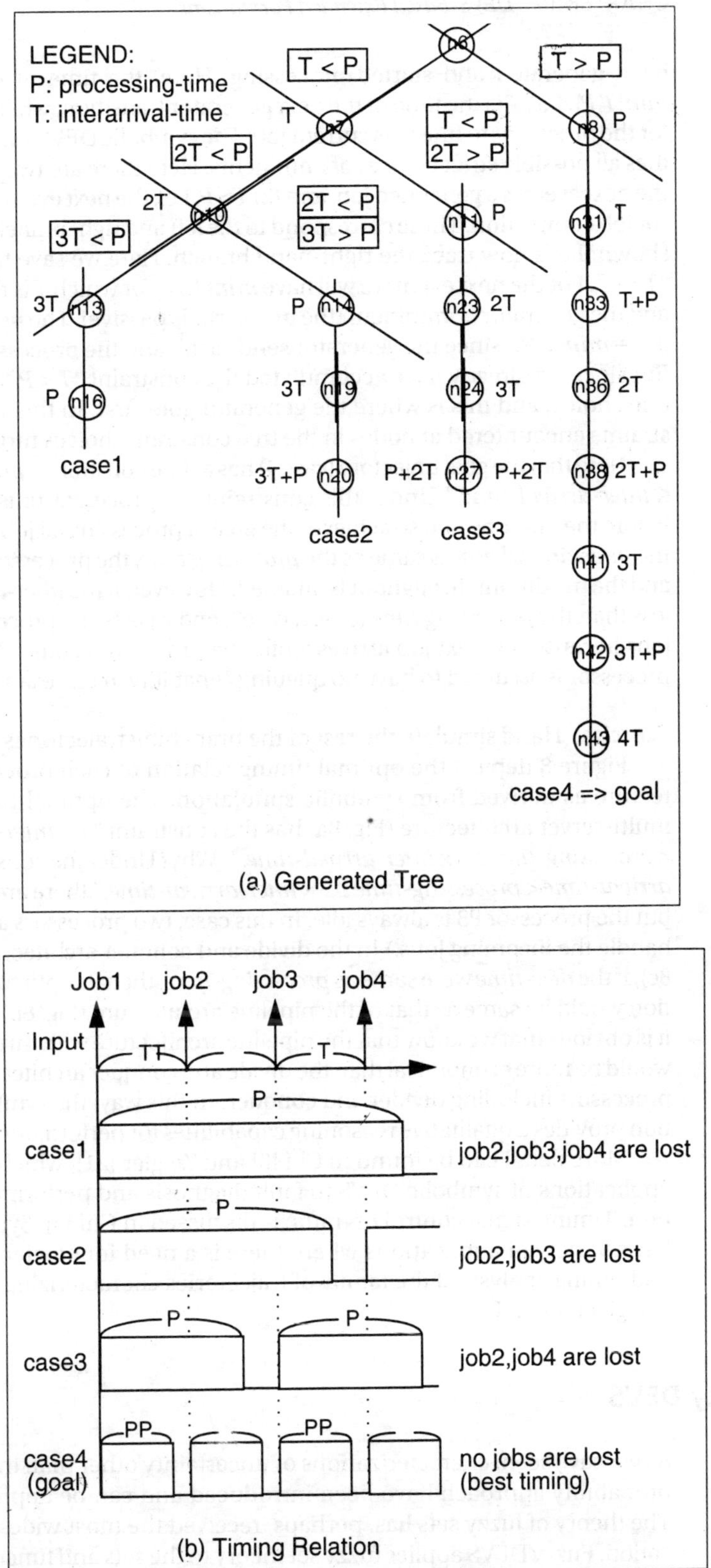

Figure 7 Generated tree and timing relation of single-processor architecture.

been generated and started processing. Here, the time of next event is $min\{T,P\}$, i.e., T is the time of the next generator transition, while P is the time for the processor to finish its current job. The symbolic DEVS simulator examines all possible strict choices of imminents. Here there are two: (1) $T < P$, i.e., the next event is a generated job, and (2) $T > P$, i.e., the next event is the processor job completion. These correspond to the left and right branches of the tree shown. Let's now track the right-hand branch. Here we save the constraint "$T < P$". For the next event we will have $min\{T, \infty\}$ for which T is the minimum and the generator is imminent (the processor is passive). The next event time is $T + min\{T,P\}$, since the generator sends a job and the processor accepts it. But since we already have accumulated the constraint "$T < P$", there is only one choice, and this is where the generator goes first. In this way, the constraints encountered at nodes in the tree constrain choices further on.

Note that the goal trajectory (case 4) has a time constraint "*processing-time* ≤ *inter-arrival-time.*" Under this constraint the processor finishes each job before the next one and so achieves the goal of processing all jobs. Similarly, if the *inter-arrival time* is same as the *processing time,* the processor is kept busy and the maximum throughput is attained. However, if the *inter-arrival time* is less than the *processing time* (case1, case2, and case3), the processor will lose jobs because the next job arrives while the processor is busy. Note that the processor is assumed to have no queuing capability in this example.

Exercise: Hand simulate the rest of the branching trajectories in Fig. 7.◆

Figure 8 depicts the optimal timing relation of each processing architecture as derived from symbolic simulation. The optimal timing for the multi-server architecture (Fig. 8a) has the constraint "2 × *inter-arrival-time* < *processing-time* ≤ 3 × *inter-arrival-time.*" (Why? Under the constraint "*inter-arrival-time* < *processing-time* ≤ 2 × *inter-arrival-time,*" there are no lost jobs, but the processor P3 is always idle. In this case, two processors are enough to handle the incoming jobs.) In the divide and conquer architecture case (Fig. 8c), if the *d&c-time* were same as *processing-time,* then its optimal timing relation would be same as that of the pipeline architecture (Fig. 8b). In this case, it is obvious that we know that the pipeline architecture with three processors would be more economical than the divide and conquer architecture with five processors including divider and conquer. In this way, the symbolic simulation provides a qualitative reasoning capabilities for performance evaluation.

More detail can be found in Chi [8] and Zeigler [21], which also discuss applications of symbolic DEVS to fault diagnosis and performance evaluation. Timing signal control of traffic is discussed in Chi [9]. Symbolic DEVS has a variety of applications where there is a need for efficient generation and timing analysis of the family of trajectories characterizing all scenarios of a given model.

10.4 Fuzzy DEVS

As we have seen, characterizations of uncertainty other than the traditional probability approach have been introduced and can be applied to DEVS. The theory of fuzzy sets has, perhaps, received the most widespread application. Fuzzy DEVS applies fuzzy set theory to the sets and functions defined

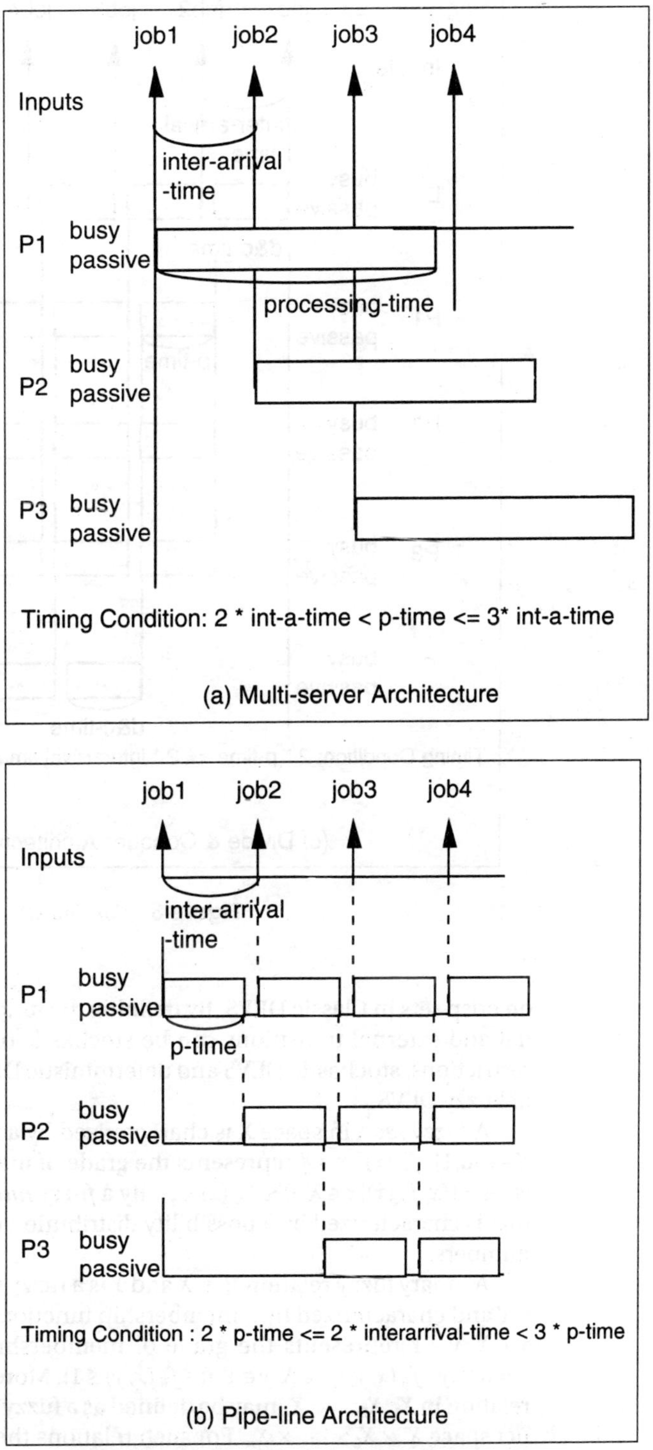

Figure 8 Timing relations for optimal performance.

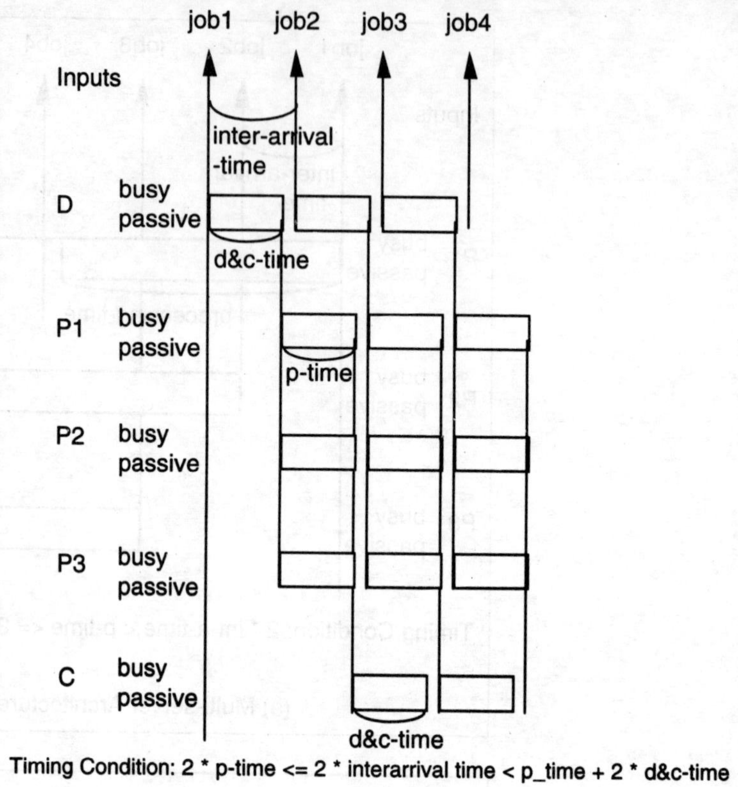

(c) Divide & Conquer Architecture

Figure 8 (*Continued*)

on crisp sets in Classic DEVS. By defining the functions on fuzzy sets, internal and external transitions can be stochastic or possibilistic. By further restrictions, stochastic DEVS and deterministic DEVS become special cases of Fuzzy DEVS.

A *fuzzy set* $\tilde{A}$ in space X is characterized by a membership function $f_{\tilde{A}}$: $X \rightarrow [0,1]$. $f_{\tilde{A}}(x)$, $x \in X$ represents the grade of membership of x in $\tilde{A}$. That is, $\tilde{A} = ((x, f_{\tilde{A}}(x) | x \in X, 0 \leq f_{\tilde{A}}(x) \leq 1)$. By a *fuzzy number,* we mean a number that is characterized by a possibility distribution or is a fuzzy subset of real numbers.

A binary fuzzy relation $\tilde{R}$ in X and Y is a fuzzy set in the product space $X \times Y$ and characterized by a membership function $f_{\tilde{R}} : X \times Y \rightarrow [0,1]$. $f_{\tilde{R}}(x,y)$, $x \in X$, $y \in Y$ represents the grade of membership of (x, y) in $\tilde{R}$. That is, $\tilde{R} = \{((x,y), f_{\tilde{R}}(x, y)) | x \in X, y \in Y, 0 \leq f_{\tilde{R}}(x, y) \leq 1\}$. More generally, an n-ary fuzzy relation in $X_1, X_2, \ldots, X_n$ may be defined as a fuzzy set in the Cartesian product space $X_1 \times X_2 \times \cdots \times X_n$. For such relations the membership function is of the form $f_{\tilde{R}}(x_1, x_2, \ldots, x_n)$, where $x_i \in X_i$, $i = 1,2, \ldots, n$.

10.4.1 Basic Fuzzy DEVS Formalism

A *Fuzzy DEVS* is defined by

$$\tilde{M} = \langle X, S, Y, \tilde{\delta}_{int}, \tilde{\delta}_{ext}, \tilde{\lambda}, \tilde{ta} \rangle$$

where

X: input events set

S: sequential states set

Y: output events set

$\tilde{\delta}_{int}: S \times S \to [0,1]$: fuzzy internal transition function

$\tilde{\delta}_{ext}: Q \times X \times S \to [0,1]$: fuzzy external transition function

$Q = \{(s,e) \mid s \in S, 0 \le e \le ta(s)\}$: total state of $\tilde{M}$

where $ta(s)$ is the defuzzified value of $\tilde{ta}(s)$

$\tilde{\lambda}: S \times Y \to [0,1]$: fuzzy output function

$\tilde{ta}: S \times \tilde{N} \to [0,1]$: fuzzy time advance function

$\tilde{N} =$ set of fuzzy numbers in $R_{0,\infty}$.

Internal (external) transitions between states constitute a fuzzy relation characterized by a fuzzy internal (external) transition function that represents the possibility of each state transition. That is, $\tilde{\delta}_{int}$ and $\tilde{\delta}_{ext}$ in the preceding definition are membership functions of the internal transition relation on $S \times S$ and of the external transition relation on $Q \times X \times S$, respectively. $\tilde{\delta}_{int}(s_t, s_{t+1})$ is the grade of transition from the present state s_t to the next state s_{t+1} when the elapsed time reaches at the time advance of the state s_t. $\tilde{\delta}_{ext}(s_t, x_t, s_{t+1})$ is the grade of transition from the state s_t to the next state s_{t+1} when the input event x_t is applied before the time advance of the state s_t.

Outputs from states also constitute a fuzzy relation characterized by a fuzzy output function that represents the possibility of each output event from state. That is, $\tilde{\lambda}$ is the membership function of the output relation on $S \times Y$. $\tilde{\lambda}(s_t, y_t)$ is the grade that the output becomes y_t, given that the present state is s_t and the elapsed time is reached at the time advance of the state s_t.

We can also extend the underlying time base to a set of fuzzy numbers, as $\tilde{N}$ in the formalism, defined in real numbers. These fuzzy numbers may be linguistic such as "small" and "large." $\tilde{ta}(s, \tilde{n})$ where s is a state and $\tilde{n}$ is a fuzzy number in $\tilde{N}$, is the grade (possibility) of the time advance value of the state s to be $\tilde{n}$. Note that a state may have more than one time advance value with an appropriate possibility.

Although we formalized the Fuzzy DEVS as a whole, only a part of the characteristic functions may be fuzzified depending on the characteristics of the system to be modeled.

Fuzzy Matrix Representation

For finite sets, a useful representation of fuzzy relations is the fuzzy matrix. Figure 9 shows an example of the fuzzy matrices of the transition and output functions. For example, assume that $X = \{x_1, x_2, \ldots, x_m\}$ and $S = (s_1, s_2, \ldots, s_n)$.

$X = \{x1, x2, x3\}$

$Y = \{y1, y2\}$

$S = \{s1, s2, s3\}$

$$R_{int} = \begin{array}{c|ccc} & s1 & s2 & s3 \\ \hline s1 & 0.8 & 0.2 & 0.2 \\ s2 & 0.6 & 0.1 & 0.3 \\ s3 & 0.9 & 0.3 & 0.2 \end{array} \qquad R_{out} = \begin{array}{c|cc} & y1 & y2 \\ \hline s1 & 0.7 & 0.5 \\ s2 & 0.6 & 0.9 \\ s3 & 0.7 & 0.2 \end{array}$$

$$R_{ext}(x^1) = \begin{array}{c|ccc} & s1 & s2 & s3 \\ \hline s1 & 0.5 & 0.8 & 0.2 \\ s2 & 0.7 & 0.4 & 0.2 \\ s3 & 0.2 & 0.7 & 0.6 \end{array} \qquad R_{ext}(x^2) = \begin{array}{c|ccc} & s1 & s2 & s3 \\ \hline s1 & 0.4 & 0.6 & 0.7 \\ s2 & 0.5 & 0.7 & 0.3 \\ s3 & 0.1 & 0.4 & 0.8 \end{array} \qquad R_{ext}(x^3) = \begin{array}{c|ccc} & s1 & s2 & s3 \\ \hline s1 & 0.8 & 0.3 & 0.3 \\ s2 & 0.9 & 0.4 & 0.3 \\ s3 & 0.5 & 0.3 & 0.2 \end{array}$$

Figure 9 Fuzzy matrix representation.

Then, the internal transition relation is defined by a fuzzy matrix of order n such that, $R_{\text{int}} = [r_{ij}]$, $1 \le i \le n$, $1 \le j \le n$, where r_{ij} denote the *(i,j)*th entry of the matrix and $r_{ij} = \tilde{\delta}_{\text{int}}(s_i, s_j)$. This means that the possibility of the transition from a state s_i to a state s_j is the r_{ij}. For the external transition relation, a fuzzy matrix is associated with each input event. For each $x \in X$, $R_{ext}(x)$ is a fuzzy matrix such that $R_{ext}(x) = [s_{ij}]$, $1 \le i \le n$, $1 \le j \le n$, where $s_{ij} = \tilde{\delta}_{ext}(s_i, x, s_j)$. This means that the possibility of the transition from a state s_i to a state s_j given an input event x is the s_{ij}. The output relation is defined by a fuzzy matrix such that $R_{out} = [t_{ij}]$, $1 \le i \le n$, $1 \le j \le p$, where $t_{ij} = \tilde{\lambda}(s_i, y_j)$.

Fuzzy State Transition

Let x_t, y_t, s_t denote respectively the input, output, and state of a DEVS model M. Consider state transitions of the form $s_{t+1} = \delta_{int}(s_t)$ when $e = ta(s_t)$ or $s_{t+1} = \delta_{ext}(s_t, x_t)$ when $e < ta(s_t)$ (ignoring the effect of e), and (ii) the output function of the form $y_t = \lambda(s_t)$ when $e = ta(s_t)$, where e means the elapsed time of the state s_t. Classic DEVS is said to be deterministic because s_{t+1} and y_t are uniquely determined by s_t and x_t. In contrast, a Fuzzy DEVS model $\tilde{M}$ is nondeterministic because s_{t+1} and/or y_t are not uniquely determined by s_t and x.

The grade of the membership of a state s_{t+1} in the fuzzy state set $\tilde{s}_{t+1}$, denoted $\mu_{\tilde{s}_{t+1}}(s_{t+1})$, is obtained by the max-min rule:

1. By internal transition when $e = ta(s_t)$,

$$\mu_{\tilde{s}_{t+1}}(s_{t+1}) = \max_{s_t \in S} \min\left(\mu_{\tilde{s}_t}(s_t), \tilde{\delta}_{\text{int}}(s_t, s_{t+1})\right).$$

2. By external transition when $e < ta(s_t)$,

$$\mu_{\tilde{s}_{t+1}}(s_{t+1}) = \max_{s_t \in S} \min\left(\mu_{\tilde{s}_t}(s_t), \tilde{\delta}_{ext}(s_t, x_t, s_{t+1})\right)$$

The grade of the membership of an output y_t in the fuzzy output set $\tilde{Y}_t$, denoted, $\mu_{\tilde{Y}_t}(s_t)$, is obtained when $e = ta\,(s_t)$ as

$$\mu_{\tilde{y}_t}(Y_t) = \max_{s_t \in S} \min\left(\mu_{\tilde{s}_t}(s_t), \tilde{\lambda}(s_t, y_t)\right),$$

where $\tilde{s}_t$ is a fuzzy state and x_t is a nonfuzzy input.

Figure 10 shows the dynamics of the Fuzzy DEVS model Fuzzy Matrix Representation. The initial state, denoted $\tilde{S}_0$, is a fuzzy set $\tilde{S}_0 = \{(s_1, 0.9), (s_2, 0.7), (s_3, 0.7)\}$. Assume that crisp input events x_1 and x_3 activate two external transitions before an internal transition. Each external transition creates a new fuzzy state in which the grade of the membership of each state is calculated using the max-min rule. The new states caused by the input events x_1 and x_3 are $\tilde{S}_1 = \{(s_1, 0.5), (s_2, 0.8), s_3, 0.6)\}$ and $\tilde{S}_2 = \{(s_1, 0.8), (s_2, 0.4), (s_3, 0.3)\}$, respectively. Next, the internal transitions all occur simultaneously from all states if we assume $ta(s)$ is a constant. The internal transitions generate fuzzy state $\tilde{S}_3 = \{(s_1, 0.8), (s_2, 0.3), (s_2, 0.3)\}$. Outputs are generated from state $\tilde{S}_2$ just before the internal transitions. These output events also constitute a fuzzy set, $\tilde{Y} = \{(y_1, 0.7), (y_2, 0.5)\}$ by the max-min rule. These outputs may be applied to another Fuzzy DEVS model as input events.

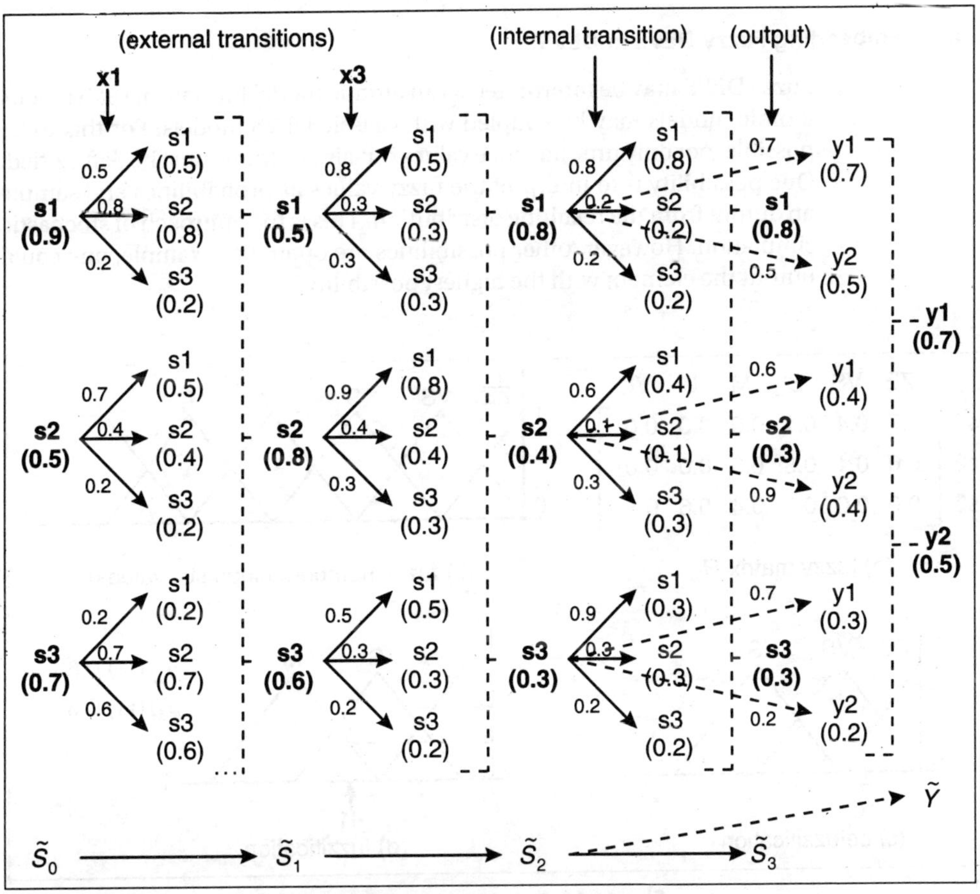

Figure 10 State trajectory of Fuzzy DEVS model.

Fuzzy Time Advance

The Fuzzy-DEVS formalism extends the underlying time base to a set of fuzzy numbers defined over the reals. The fuzzy numbers used as time advance of a state may be defuzzified to be a crisp value when the actual time advance value is needed.

Figure 11 shows an example of the concept of the fuzzy time advance. The matrix representation of fuzzy time advance values of the states, s_1, s_2 and s_3 is shown in Fig. 11a. The fuzzy numbers used in the figure are defined in terms of triangular fuzzy number as depicted in Fig. 11b. The fuzzy numbers ZE, VS, S, M, L, and VL represent the linguistic terms "near zero," "very small," "small," "medium," "large," and "very large," respectively. The time advance value, for example, of the state s_1 may be "near zero" with possibility 0.7, "very small" with possibility 0.4, and "small" with possibility 0.1. We can obtain a crisp time value t_0, as in Fig. 11c, from this fuzzy time advance by using some defuzzification method such as the center of gravity. The fuzzification of a crisp time value t_1 may result in a fuzzy time value of "small" with possibility 0.6 and "medium" with possibility 0.3, as in Fig. 11d.

10.4.2 Embedding Fuzzy DEVS in DEVS

Fuzzy DEVS may be interpreted as an atomic model formalism such that its atomic models may be coupled with Classic DEVS models. For this to be possible, not only time advance values but also outputs must be defuzzified. One possibility is to interpret the fuzzy values as probabilities and sample an output from the resulting distribution. This is the approach of stochastic simulation. However, other possibilities are open. For example, one could output the element with the highest possibility.

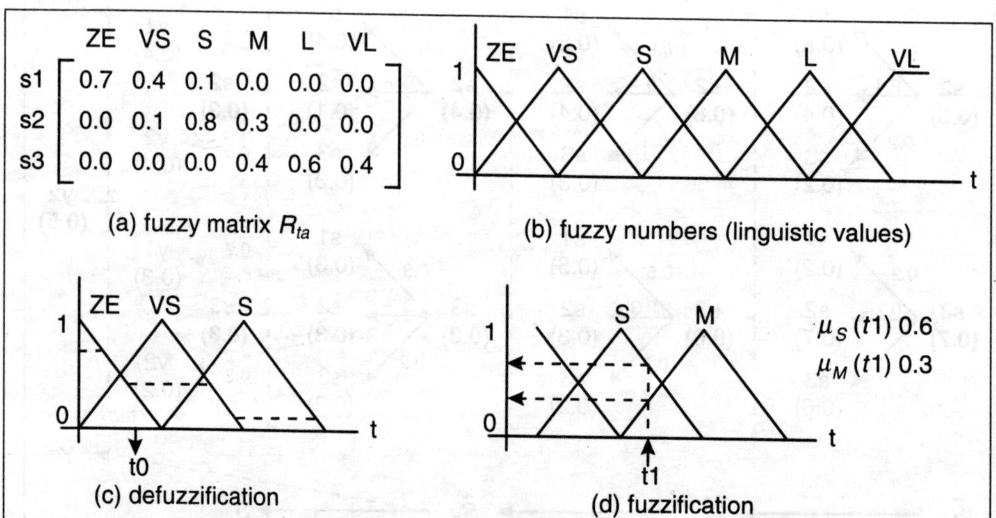

Figure 11 Fuzzy time advance.

10.4.3 Example: Fuzzy DEVS Model for Boiler System

Figure 12 depicts a Fuzzy DEVS model of boiler system. The system consists of two subsystems, a burner and a boiler tank, each of which is modeled as an atomic model. We modeled the burner subsystem as a fuzzy model and the boiler tank as a deterministic one.

We concentrate only on the burner model in the following discussion. Input events are "on" and "off" to turn on and off the burner, respectively. We assume that the burner system has some possibility for some unusual or faulty operations. The burner, for example, may be actually fired or not if the switch is on when its initial state is "OFF." More specifically, when the input event "on" is applied to the model whose initial state is "OFF," the possibility of state transition to the state "IGN" is 0.8 and the possibility to remain "OFF" is 0.3. This situation models a faulty behavior of the burner, which may be difficult to represent under the deterministic DEVS formalism.

In state "IGN" there are two possible internal transitions, one of which is to the state "ON" with possibility 0.8 and the other to the state "OFF" with possibility 0.4. The model generates an output event "B_on" (burner-on) or "B_off" (burner-off) according to the transition. For simplicity, the possibility of output events is the same as that of internal transitions. However, in general, the possibility of an output event is independent of that of internal transition in Fuzzy DEVS. Other transitions and output events are modeled similarly.

Figure 13 shows some trajectories from the initial state "OFF" and input events "on," "off," and "on" are applied to the burner model in order. From these trajectories, we can get the most possible state trajectory (OFF,IGN,

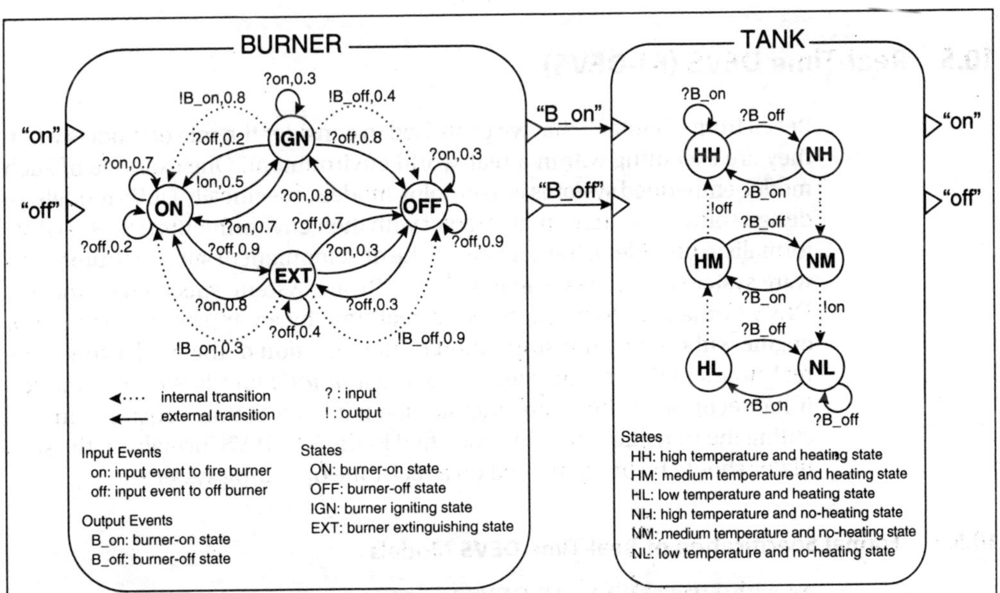

Figure 12 Fuzzy DEVS model of boiler system.

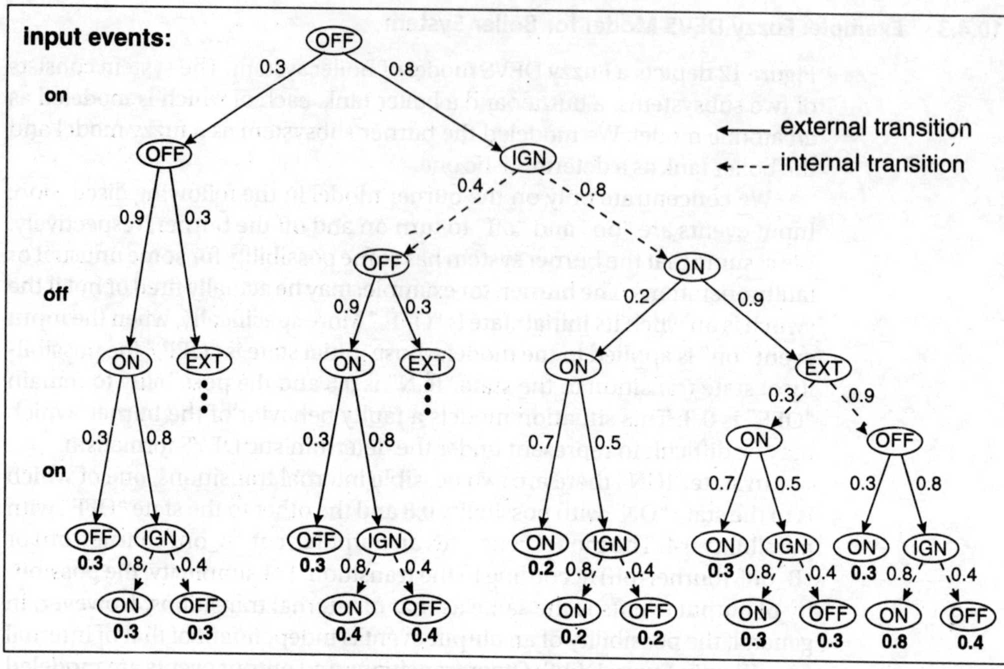

Figure 13 State trajectories of burner subsystem.

ON,EXT,OFF,IGN,ON), and its possibility is 0.8. Analysis of all the trajectories can give us more information. For example, the possibility that the burner subsystem will stay in the state "OFF" in spite of the applied input events is 0.3.

10.5 Real-Time DEVS (RT-DEVS)

Recall from Chapter 2 that we promised to consider the role of models when they are executing within a real-world environment. One example of such model-embedded systems is to employ models, specifically DEVS models, to design software systems that interact with their environments. The RT-DEVS formalism provides a framework for the development of such real-time software systems. The idea is to enable a software system, specified by the RT-DEVS formalism, to be executed in real time by an appropriate simulator engine without any transformation or modification of the model code. The real-time simulator is an extension of the *simulator* for Classic DEVS models (Chapter 8). Since the RT abstract simulator has a real-time constraint in executing the transition function specified in the RT-DEVS formalism, the simulator should be implemented on a real-time operating system.

10.5.1 Formal Specification of Real-Time DEVS Models

As with Fuzzy DEVS, RT-DEVS formalism extends the DEVS formalism only in atomic DEVS models. Coupled DEVS RT-DEVS formalism remains the same as the original except that a coupled RT-DEVS model has no specification of selection function. This is because a simulation clock in RT-DEVS is no longer a virtual clock but a real-time clock, which is not controllable by simulation algorithms. An atomic RT-DEVS model, RTAM, is defined as follows:

$$RTAM = \langle X, S, Y, \delta_{ext}, \delta_{int}, \lambda, ti, \psi, A \rangle,$$

where

$X, S, Y, \delta_{int}, \lambda$: same as classic DEVS
ti: an interval time advance function
ψ: an activity mapping function
A: a set of activities with the constraints
$\psi: s \rightarrow A$
$ti: s \rightarrow R^{+}_{0,\infty} \times R^{+}_{0,\infty}$
$\delta_{ext}: Q \times X \rightarrow S$, an external transition function

where Q is the total state set of $RTAM = \{(s,e) | s \in S, 0 \le e \le ti(s)|_{\max}\}$.

Note that an atomic RT-DEVS has activities, a mapping function, and an interval time advance function that are not defined in the Classic DEVS formalism. Associated with each state *s* is an *activity*, $\psi(s)$. This is an executable function whose completion is required for an atomic RT-DEVS model to transit from one state to another. Thus, an activity function requires actual execution time to be spent during simulation. Three actions, receiving and sending events and modifying states, are excluded from activities.

The execution time for an activity is nondeterministic in nature. In contrast to Symbolic DEVS and Fuzzy DEVS, the RT-DEVS formalism modifies the time advance function, now called *ti(s)*, to specify the time interval in which an activity is expected to complete operation. Thus, the nondeterministic execution time for an activity is specified in terms of minimum and maximum time defined for each state. For example, if an estimated execution time for an activity *computing* associated with a state *BUSY* is *comp_time*, then *ti*(*BUSY*) would be [*comp_time* – ε, *comp_time* + ε]. Proper choice of the value of ε is critical for validity of the model, it should reflect the actual variation of normal execution times for the computing activity.

10.5.2 Execution of RT-DEVS Models

RT-DEVS models are not simulated on a logical time base as are other DEVS models. Instead, they are executed in real time. As with abstract simulators for Classic DEVS, execution of RT-DEVS models requires a one-to-one correspondence between a model and an associated simulator. An *RT-simulator* and a *RT-coordinator* are associated with atomic RT-DEVS and a coupled RT-DEVS, respectively.

As with Classic DEVS, the *RT-simulator* algorithm handles two primary types of messages, (*,*t*) and (*x*,*t*). The following are pseudo codes for its processing of these messages.

RT-Simulator :: when receive (*,t)
    if $ti_N|_{min} \le t \le ti_N|_{max}$ then
        $y := \lambda(s)$;
        $s := \delta_{int}(s)$;
        $t_L := t$;
        $ti_N := [t_L + ti(s)|_{min}, t_L + ti(s)|_{max}]$;
        $a := \psi(s)$;
    else
        error;
    end if

As with the simulator algorithm in the original DEVS, "when receive (*,*t*)" specifies how the RT-simulator reacts to a (*,*t*) message transmitted from a higher level RT-coordinator. The RT-coordinate issues the (*,*t*) only when an activity associated with the current state of an atomic RT-DEVS model is completed and no (*x*,*t*) has been received. Except for checking that the actual execution time, *t* falls within the allowed bounds, the simulator is similar to the one defined for Classic DEVS (Chapter 8). The response to an (*x*,*t*) message is also similar to the classic DEVS simulator behavior, except that the current activity is aborted and replaced by the activity prescribed by the new state, $\delta(s,e,x)$.

An RT-coordinator for RT-DEVS differs from a coordinator defined for Classic DEVS in that it needs to concurrently execute two types of control threads for monitoring: (1) the occurrence of external events and (2) internally executing activities. The RT-coordinator needs only one monitoring thread for all atomic RT-DEVS models within a coupled model and one activity thread for each atomic RT-DEVS model. Concurrent execution of such threads requires supports provided from an underlying real-time operating system. Such supports may include suspending of executing activities at an occurrence of an external event and resuming it after handling the event.

Timing Discrepancy in Execution of RT-DEVS Models

Simulation of RT-DEVS models requires executing internal and external transition functions, output functions and activities, all in real time. Thus, timing discrepancies can arise during simulation. In fact, RT-DEVS models usually run slower than the minimum time advance specified within the model. Two sources of timing errors need to be considered.

The first source is from execution times of transition and output functions for an atomic RT-DEVS model—recall that these are not included in the execution times of activities. The second source stems from the fact that execution time for an activity varies with each execution depending on the state of the simulation environment. In the worst case, the timing errors are accumulated as the simulation proceeds. In some cases, such errors can be corrected by compensations made during scheduling within *RT-simulators* [11,12,17,22].

10.5.3 Example of RT-DEVS: Elevator Control

An elevator control system controls one or more elevators. The system has to schedule elevators to respond to the requests from passengers at various floors, and control the motion of the elevators between floors. For each elevator, there are several elevator buttons, elevator lights for indicating the floors to be visited, and an elevator motor, which is controlled by commands such as move-up, move-down, and stop, and an elevator door, which is controlled by commands to open and close the door. For each floor, there are up and down floor buttons, which are pressed by passengers needing to use an elevator, and a corresponding pair of floor lights to indicate the directions that have been requested. At each floor for each elevator, there are a pair of direction lights to indicate whether an arriving elevator is heading in the up or down direction. For the top and bottom floors, there is only one floor button, one floor light, and one direction light per floor. There is also a floor arrival sensor at each floor in each elevator shaft to detect the arrival of an elevator. The elevator buttons, floor buttons, and floor arrival sensors are asynchronous. The other I/O devices are all passive. The elevator and floor lights are switched on by the hardware, but must be switched off by software. The direction lights are switched on and off by the software.

Figure 14 shows a hierarchical modular composition of components and couplings for an elevator control system. The system is composed of an experimental frame (EF) and an elevator control system (ECS) which controls the system. The experimental frame is a DEVS simulation concept that provides a modular capability to stimulate and observe a system. Here, EF is decomposed into two atomic models, Gen(erator) and Trans(ducer). The Gen model generates requests and the Trans model measures the service time of each request. Although it was originally developed for DEVS performance simulation, the experimental frame concept is advantageous in the real-time context as well. For example, the complete frame may be employed during testing of the control system while the transducer portion may remain for recording while in actual operation.

The ECS model has three atomic models: FloorControl, which manages a floor and accepts passengers' requests at each floor; ElevatorControl,

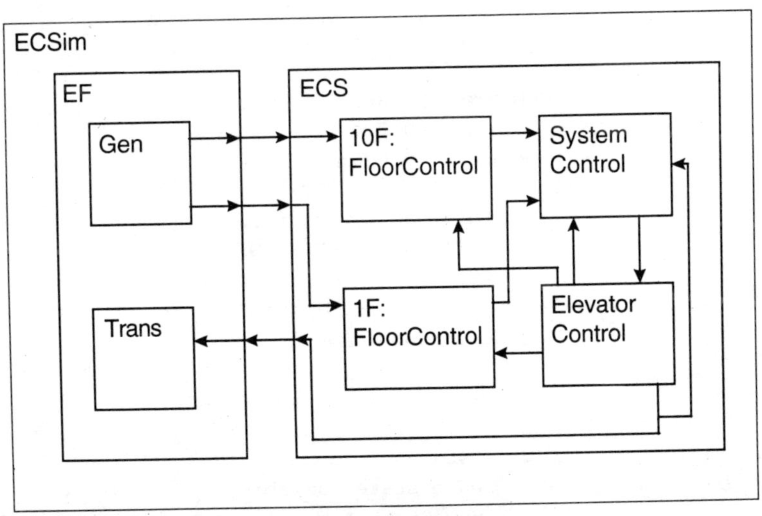

Figure 14 Elevator control example.

which manages an elevator and accepts passengers' requests in the elevator as well as the requests from an atomic model SystemControl; and SystemControl, which manages the whole system and schedules the requests of FloorControls.

The following code shows the implementation of ElevatorControl model in C++. (This code would be the output of a translator, as will be discussed.) The ElevatorControl model has two state variables, curFloor and curReq, and eight phases. The curFloor state variable represents the current floor of the elevator, and curReq contains the request being processed. The starting phase is IDLE. When receiving a request from the SystemControl model, the ElevatorControl model checks the destination first and makes its associated elevator move upward or downward as necessary. It takes approximately 2 seconds to open the elevator door ([1.9,2.1]). Then, the controller waits for about 5 seconds ([4.9,5.1]) in a WAIT phase. The door may be closed while waiting if a passenger presses the close button. Since requests can be queued in the SystemControl model, the controller does not accept more than one request at once before finishing the current request.

Phases can have associated activities. For example, an OPEN phase has an activity, doorOpen, which opens the elevator door, and a STOP phase does motorStop. A MOVE phase is a superphase that has two subphases, MOVE_UP and MOVE_DOWN. While the current floor is same as the request being processed, internal transitions occur from the MOVE phase to itself. Because the phase is a superphase, however, the current phase is either the MOVE_UP or MOVE_DOWN phase. Furthermore, because the phase keeps its history, the next phase is same as the current one (elevator continues to move in the same direction). When the requested floor is reached, the next phase is the STOP phase regardless of the current phase.

An extract of C++ code for the ElevatorControl Model is as follows:

```
class ElevatorControl : public AtomicModel
{
   // State variables
   int umid;
   Integer phase;
   Integer curFloor;
   Request curReq;
public:
   // Phase enumeration
   enum { IDLE, OPEN, STOP, WAIT, CLOSE, MOVE_UP, MOVE_DOWN,
   NPHASES };
ElevatorControl::ElevatorControl(const char* name)
   : AtomicModel(name)
{
   // Define input/output events
   X = "request";
   Y = "status", "done";
   // Define state variables
   S = new State("phase", phase, NPHASES, "IDLE", "OPEN",
"STOP", "WAIT", "CLOSE", "MOVE_UP", "MOVE_DOWN"),
```

```
new State("destFloor", destFloor),
new State("curFloor", curFloor),
new State("curReq", curReq);
  // Initialize state variables
  umid = int(this);
  curFloor = -2;
  // Set starting phase
  phase = IDLE;
}
```

Note the one-to-one correspondence between the ElevatorControl methods and the elements in the RT-DEVS formalism (Fig. 15). The external transition function (extTransfn) handles external requests and sensor inputs. The internal transition function (intTransfn) handles continued movement in the absence of input. The time advance function (TimeInterval) provides time windows in which inputs are expected. As part of the output function, the activity function (activityfn) generates actuator commands.

10.5.4 Real-Time Simulation and RT-DEVS

Real-time simulation requires timely completion in physical time for the execution of a simulated model. Such simulation deals with an information-open, or *reactive*, real-time system. A real-time system, by nature, consists of

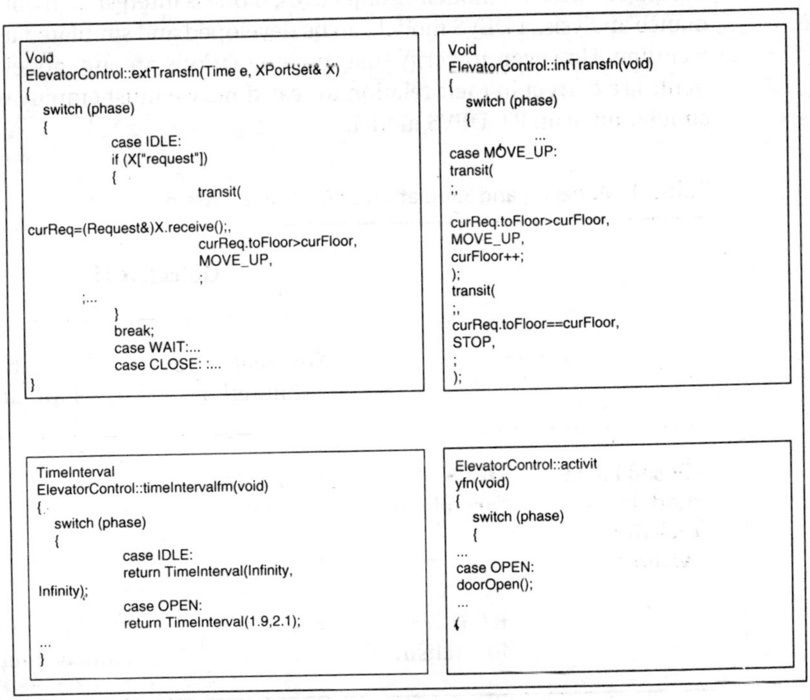

Figure 15 Elevator control.

a computing system and an external environment. The environment consists of live components, possibly including humans, which have temporal interactions with the computing system. To simulate the real-time system, one can model only the computing system while leaving the real component and any human participants as they are. An example of such real-time simulation is a simulator for training pilots to fly airplanes. We call such simulation *interactive real-time* simulation. However, to analyze certain aspects of their operation, such a reactive system can be modeled as an information-closed form. In this case, simulation models represent any live components, humans, and the computing system itself. Such simulation is called *transformational real-time* simulation.

Recall from Chapter 2 that in reactive real-time simulation, the execution time of a model must be synchronized with physical time, at which stimuli are generated from a live component and/or a human participant. Thus, hard deadlines on model execution time are required for timely interactions between the model and its external environment. On the other hand, in transformational real-time simulation, logical time advances in the model are synchronized with predefined physical times. To meet such physical time constraints, the logical time advances can be uniformly enlarged or contracted, if necessary, so long as they do not violate the required event orderings. Table 1 summarizes modeling and simulation of real-time systems in information-closed form using the DEVS or RT-DEVS formalism. Basically, closed-form modeling of real-time systems can employ either the DEVS formalism or the RT-DEVS formalism. The choice should be based on modeling objectives. If one is interested in only performance analysis, a DEVS model can be developed and simulated using logical time. However, to verify that the interactions among model components are correct in their relation to real-time, we must employ real-time simulation of an RT-DEVS model.

Table 1 Modeling and Simulation of Real-time System

		Objectives for	
		Non-real-time simulation	**Real-time simulation**
Closed Form modeling of real-time systems	**DEVS formalism**	Performance analysis	N/A
	RT-DEVS formalism	N/A	Verification of timely interaction

10.6 Summary

Each of the extensions just discussed suggests an important direction in which simulation modeling in general, and the DEVS formalism in particular, can be enhanced. Incorporating dynamic structure capabilities in DEVS environments will greatly expand the range of phenomena that can be studied. Fuzzy DEVS enables a "softer" approach to discrete event modeling and is an alternative to classical stochastic representation of uncertainty. Symbolic DEVS enables searching through a space of possible models, each one described in the standard manner. RT-DEVS leaves the domain of models executing in logical time and enters the domain of real-time software systems. As of this writing, these extensions are isolated penetrations into the future of simulation environments. Integrating them in a comprehensive environmental framework, as discussed in Part IV, would enable modelers to employ them in plug-and-play fashion.

10.7 Sources

1. Aggarwal, S., "Deterministic Representation of Probabilistic Systems by Ergodic Machines." *Math. Sys. Theory* **10,** 345–361 (1977).
2. Barros, F. J., "Dynamic Structure Discrete Event System Specification: A New Formalism for Dynamic Structure Modeling and Simulation." *Proceedings of the 1995 Winter Simulation Conference,* Arlington, VA, 1995, pp. 781–785.
3. Barros, F. J., "Dynamic Structure Discrete Event System Specification: Formalism, Abstract Simulators and Applications." *Transactions of the Society for Computer Simulation* **13**(1), 35–46 (1996).
4. Barros, F. J., "Structural Inheritance in the Delta Environment." *Proceedings of the Sixth Annual Conference on AI, Simulation and Planning in High Autonomy Systems,* La Jolla, CA, 1996, pp. 141–147.
5. Barros, F. J., *Modeling and Simulation of Dynamic Structure Discrete Event Systems: A General Systems Theory Approach.* Ph.D. Dissertation, Department of Informatics Engineering, University of Coimbra, 1996.
6. Barros, F. J., 1997. Modeling Formalisms for Dynamic Structure Systems. *ACM Transactions on Modeling and Computer Simulation.* Vol. 7, No. 4, pp. 501–515.
7. Barros, F. J., and B. P. Zeigler, 1996. Adaptive Queueing: A Study Using Dynamic Structure DEVS. *International Transactions in Operational Research,* Vol. 4, No. 2, pp. 87–98.
8. Chi, S. D., "Model-based Reasoning Methodology Using the Symbolic DEVS Simulation." *Trans. of SCS* **14**(3), 141–152 (1997).
9. Chi, S. D., J. Lee, and Y. Kim, "Using the SES/MB Framework to Analyze Traffic Flow." *Trans. of SCS* **14**(4), 211–221 (1991).
10. Dubois, D., and H. Prade, *Fuzzy Sets and Systems.* Academic Press, New York, 1980.

11. Hong, J. S., H. S. Song, "A Formal Method for Object-Oriented Real-time Software Development," Ph.D. Thesis, EE Dept., KAIST, Dec. 1997.

12. Hong, J. S., H. S. Song, T. G. Kim, and K. H. Park, "ReDEVS Executive: A Seamless Realtime Software Development Framework," *Discrete Event Dynamic Systems* **7,** 355–375 (1997).

13. Joslyn, C., "The Process Theoretical Approach to Qualitative DEVS." In *AI, Simulation and Planning in High Autonomy Systems.* EPD, University of Arizona; San Diego, 1996.

14. Kandel, A., and S. C. Lee, *Fuzzy Switching and Automata.* Crane Russak, 1979.

15. Klir, G., and T. Folger, *Fuzzy Sets, Uncertainty, and Information.* Prentice-Hall, Englewood Cliffs; NJ, 1988.

16. Kwon, Y., H. Park, S. Jung, and T. Kim, "Fuzzy-DEVS Formalism: Concepts, Realization and Applications." In *AI, Simulation and Planning in High Autonomy Systems.* EPD, University of Arizona, San Diego, 1996.

17. Seong, M. Cho, and T. G. Kim, "Real-time DEVS Simulation: Concurrent, Time-Selective Execution of Combined RT-DEVS Model and Interactive Environment," Proc. of SCSC-98, July 19–22, 1998, Reno, NV, pp. 410–415.

18. Uhrmacher, A. M., and B. P. Zeigler, "Variable Structure Models in Object-Oriented Simulation." *Int. J. Gen. Systems* **24**(4), 359–375 (1996).

19. Vahie, S., and B. P. Zeigler. "Dynamic Neuronal Ensembles: Issues in Representing Structure Change in Object-Oriented, Biologically-based Brain Models." Presented at Intl. Conf. on Semiotics and Intelligent Systems, Washington, DC, 1996.

20. Wos, L., "Automated Reasoning." In *Artificial Intelligence, A Knowledge-based Approach* M. W. Firebaugh, Ed.). PWS-KENT, 1988.

21. Zeigler, B. P., and S. D. Chi, "Symbolic Discrete Event System Specification," *IEEE Trans. on Systems, Man, Cybernetics,* Dec., pp. 1428–1443 (1992).

22. Zeigler, B. P., and J. Kim, "Extending the DEVS-Scheme Knowledge-based Simulation Environment for Real-Time Event-based Control." *IEEE Trans. on Robotics and Automation* **9**(3), 351–356 (1993).

11

Parallel and Distributed Discrete Event Simulation

In Chapter 8 we presented simulators for DEVS models. These simulation algorithms can be called *abstract simulators* since they represent the processing that has to be done to execute DEVS models. As such they can be executed on sequential single processor systems using, for example, event list algorithms to keep track of the times-of-next-event. However, for a number of compelling reasons, discrete event simulation execution on multiple machines can be an attractive alternative in various applications:

- Models and their simulators are usually dispersed among many physical locations and there is great potential benefit to sharing such resources. *Distributed Simulation* is the name given to the networking of geographically dispersed simulators of model components to execute a single overall model. The simulators are called federates and the coupled model is called a federation in HLA (Chapter 1).
- The computational demands imposed by large-scope, high-resolution simulations (Chapter 13) are moving the preferred platforms from single-processor systems to multiprocessor architectures. Multiprocessor architectures consist of a number of serial processors interconnected through a communications network to enable coordination of their execution and sharing of data. *Parallel simulation* refers to the design of such systems to enable processors to execute the model *concurrently* (or as is often said, in *parallel*).

Whether one uses the term "parallel" or "distributed" (or both) to describe a simulator is largely a matter of objectives in its design. Such objectives include:

- Increased speed: if done right, the time required for a simulation run can be reduced in proportion to the number of processors it is allocated
- Increased size of models: the combined memory capacity of all processors may be employed
- Exploiting the greater data handling or graphics capability provided by specialized nodes
- Interoperability and sharing of resources

A simulation architecture might be called parallel if its main goal is reducing execution time. In contrast, as already indicated, distributed simulation often connotes the goal of interoperating geographically dispersed simulators. While parallel simulation depends on properly distributing model execution among processors, the farmed-out work need not be in the form of recognizable model components, or federates, that would characterize distributed simulation.

In this chapter we discuss the basics of *parallel/distributed discrete event simulation* (PDES) algorithms for discrete event models, especially DEVS models, on multiprocessor systems. In our discussion, we'll assume that a model is divided into distinct components and each one is executed on a distinct processor. Although real-world systems naturally operate in parallel, the sharing of information they do in exploiting this intrinsic parallelism turns out to be rather difficult. The reasons for this are the strong causal dependencies that exist between the model components. When components are simulated on distinct processors, such dependencies require careful synchronization to ensure execution correctness.

Several approaches to parallel/distributed simulation have been developed in two decades of research. They are categorized as *conservative* or *optimistic* depending on whether *causality violations* are strictly avoided or allowed to occur but detected and repaired. In this chapter we discuss the basics of these approaches to simulation of coupled DEVS models on multiprocessor machines.

11.1 Problem Characterization of Parallel Discrete Event Simulation

To get some insight into the problems occurring in parallel execution of discrete event models, let us recall the essentials of discrete event simulation. Recall from the introduction to simulation algorithms in Chapter 8 that computer simulation means to generate the behavior of a model as specified by its dynamic definition starting from a given initial state. In the sequential simulation algorithms we assumed that the behavior is generated in strict temporal order. However, this is not really required. Let us consider a model with two components that actually are not coupled and strictly separated (Fig. 1). For such a model, it does not matter if the behaviors of the two components are generated in strict sequential order. We could, for example, first generate the complete behavior of the first component from the starting

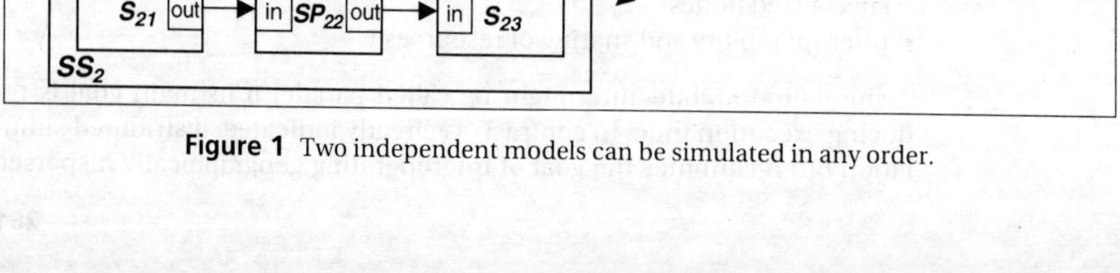

Figure 1 Two independent models can be simulated in any order.

time to the final time and then start again from the beginning and generate the behavior for the second component. Or, we could assign the parts to two different processors and simulate them (independently) in parallel—the result is the same.

However, completely independent model components are not the general rule. Model components may run independently for a limited time interval, but then show dependencies, eventually to run independently again afterwards. Dependencies in discrete event models occur through events. When an event in one component directly or indirectly influences events in another component, then we say that there is a *causal dependency* of events. To guarantee execution correctness, the generation must preserve what is called *causality*, i.e., that the causes have to precede the effects [12]. For an arbitrary event E_j all the events E_i on which it depends must be processed prior to processing the event E_j. An event E_j depends on an event E_i if E_i schedules event E_j, if E_i alters states used by E_j, or if E_i schedules events E_k and E_j depends on E_k. Additionally, the dependency relation is transitive, i.e., if E_k depends on E_j and E_j depends on E_k, then E_k depends on E_i. It is intuitively clear that all the events E_i on which E_j depends must be processed prior to E_j. Dependencies among events form an irreflexive partial ordering of events. Furthermore, we have to require that the dependency relation not be cyclic and the time associated with an event E_j must not be less than any event E_i it depends on [23].

To discuss dependencies between model components, let us restrict the discussion to modular coupled models as presented in Chapter 7. Actually, most parallel discrete event simulation systems adopt a modular modeling approach (model components are usually called *logical processes* in the PDES simulation literature).

In a modular coupled model, dependencies between components are exclusively through input/output couplings. Thus, dependencies show as dependencies between output and input events. In the model of Fig. 2, the two serial server models are now linked to a model F (fork) at the input side and a component J (join) at the output side. Figure 3 shows the partial ordering of an exemplary sequence of input–output events. The ordering shows us that no direct dependencies exist between the two serial servers and, hence, they still can be simulated independently, but events have to be synchronized at the outputs of F and inputs of J.

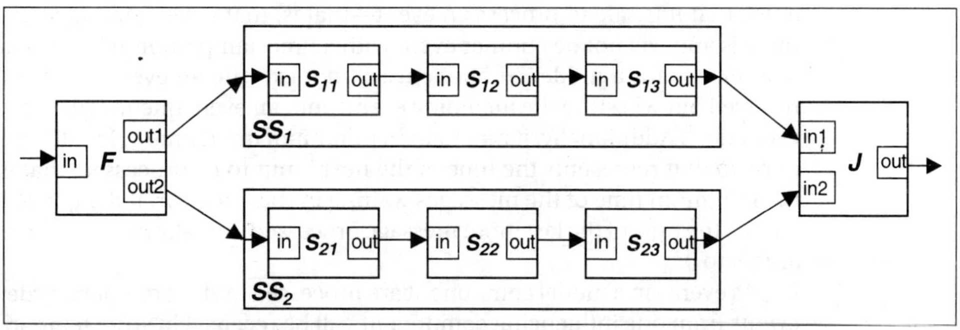

Figure 2 Two independent model components SS_1 and SS_2 with synchronization points F and J.

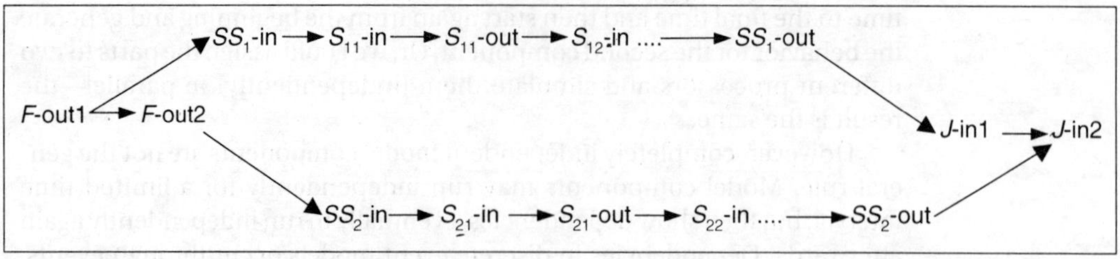

Figure 3 Dependency relation of input–output events.

Sequential simulation algorithms guarantee causality between events by generating, from this partial ordering, a total ordering of events according to the event times [12,23]. Parallel discrete event simulation, however, has to exploit the partial ordering to find events that can be processed in parallel. Fujimoto [12] defines conditions for correct simulation (without causality violations) as follows:

Causality constraint: A simulation of a model consisting of modular components which exclusively communicate through their modular input/output couplings obeys the causality constraint, if and only if each modular component simulator processes the events in nondecreasing timestamp order.

Parallel discrete event simulation schemes are based on this constraint. While conservative PDES strictly avoids violating the causality constraint, optimistic approaches temporarily violate it but then will detect and repair the violations.

11.2 Conservative Parallel Discrete Event Simulation

Conservative PDES approaches were introduced in the late 1970s by K. M. Chandy and J. Misra [3,4]. Since then several variations, improvements, and optimizations have been developed. However, all of them are based on the principal idea that *causality violations are strictly avoided.* Let us discuss the fundamental ideas by reviewing the original approach in more detail.

Considering the causality constraint presented earlier, we see that the fundamental problem a simulator of a component is faced with is to guarantee that it is safe to process an event—that is, that it can guarantee that there is and will not be another event with a timestamp prior to that event. A simulator for a model component will not execute an event when it is received but will store the incoming events into an event queue ordered by event time. Additionally, it maintains a minimum input time t_{ip} for all input ports *ip* that represents the time of the next input to be processed, that is, the minimum time of the messages waiting in the queue or, if the queue is empty, the time of the last input message processed. Initially the input times are set to 0.

As events in a model component are processed in strict temporal order, events from one influencing component will be received in strict temporal order. Hence, when a model component is influenced only by one other component, it is guaranteed that the events are received in temporal order and actually can be processed as soon as they are received. The difficulties, however, arise when a component is influenced by more than one other component. In Fig. 4 we take a closer look at component *J* which, receives input events from two influencing components. When it has received an event from SS_2 at some time t_{in2}, but the last event from SS_1 was at time t_{in1} with $t_{in1} < t_{in2}$, it cannot guarantee that it will not receive an event for SS_1 at a time between t_{in1} and t_{in2}. The event at t_{in2} cannot be guaranteed to be next and cannot be processed. The simulator is blocked until it eventually receives an event from SS_1. Generally, a simulator blocks when it has not received events from all its influencing components.

This problem in conservative parallel simulation schemes becomes crucial when event communication is not distributed uniformly. Consider once again our model from Fig. 2. It might happen that accidentally all the outputs from *F* are sent to only one of the servers, for example to SS_1. Then at component *J*, the input queue coming from the first server fills up while the second stays empty. The component is blocked and cannot advance.

By blocking components' simulators when inputs from some influencers are absent, the causality constraint can be fulfilled; however, it is not guaranteed that the simulator advances. Misra [23] expresses this as follows: *The approach guarantees that whatever event happens in the simulator also happens in the model. However, the opposite is not true, it cannot be guaranteed that what happens in the model also happens in the simulator.*

The scheme to avoid deadlock is by *null-messages* and *lookahead* properties of models [3,23,25]. Lookahead is the ability of a model to predict that it will not have outputs for a certain period in the future. Null messages are used to announce the absence of outputs and are used by influenced components for synchronization. Fig. 5 shows how blocking is broken by null messages. When the component *F* has an event at one of the output ports, let's say at time 10, it also puts out a null-message at the other output port announcing that it has advanced to time 10 and will not have an output prior to 10. This information is forwarded through the serial server to *J*, and any input received prior to 10, already waiting in the input queue, can be processed.

With this scheme we are able to prevent blocking, but we cannot break deadlock arising from feedback loops. Consider the model in Fig. 6, where a feedback loop has been introduced from *J* back to *F*. The null message with

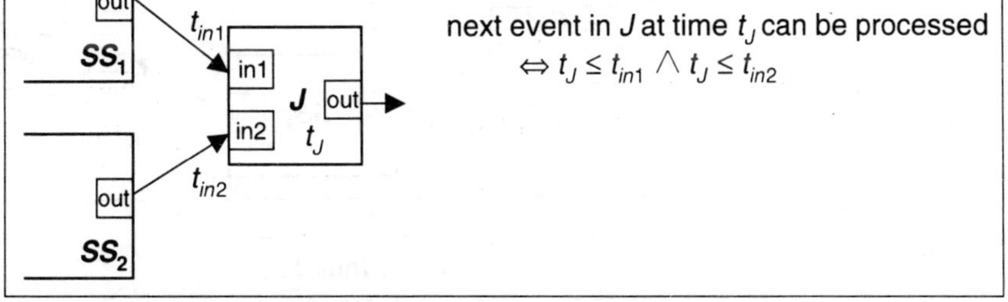

Figure 4 Example situation in simulating component *J*.

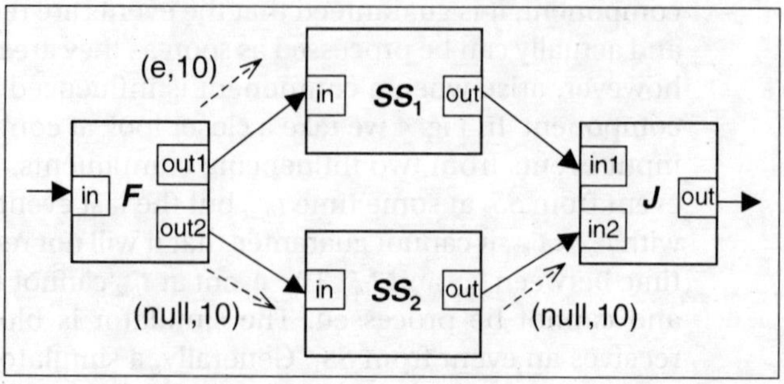

Figure 5 Breaking blocking situation in component *Join* by null messages.

time 10 from *F* traveling through SS_2 propagates back to *F* but does not allow *F* to advance—it cannot process the next event waiting at its other input port because time has only advanced to 10. Similarly, for *J* to process the event scheduled for time 13 it must know that no message on its other port will arrive earlier than 13. As observers we know that the earliest next scheduled event is at time 13 and that it should be processed, but this information is not available in the conservative scheme. In general, if there are feedback loops in the model and message population is relatively small, i.e., only a few messages are transmitted in comparison to the number of couplings, or if the unprocessed messages become clustered in one portion of the model, deadlock may occur very frequently [12].

To break deadlock, the *lookahead* property of a model is used. In looking ahead, a processor makes a promise not to produce an output event before a given time. For example, when a processor knows the earliest time it will receive the next event at its input and it knows its internal state of processing (*s* and *tn*), it can predict that the next output will at least be in some time in the future. This is called lookahead and is computed by either of the following:

- A minimum time estimate when the next output will be produced assuming that no input is received (cannot be smaller then the next internal event scheduled within the component)

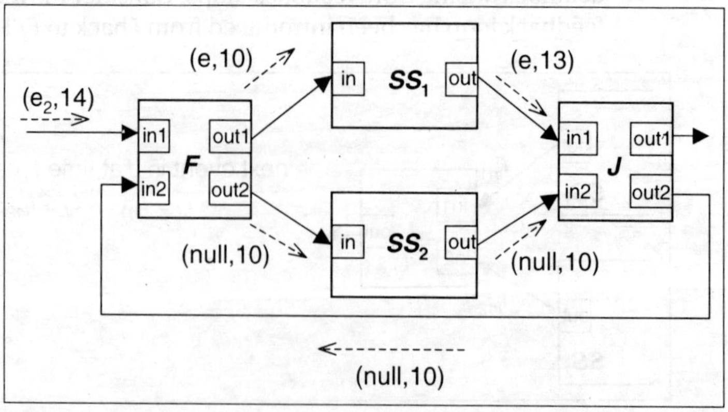

Figure 6 Deadlock situation cannot be broken by null messages alone.

- A minimum time estimate when the next output will be produced, assuming there is an input

In its simplest form, lookahead is given in form of *minimum propagation delay,* which represents a minimum time span an input needs to propagate through the system to the output. For example, let's assume that components' output events are equal to internally scheduled next event times and the model has a minimum propagation delay. Then the earliest time of an next output is the minimum of the time of next event and the minimum input time plus the minimum propagation delay.

The performance of a conservative scheme is heavily dependent on lookahead. Models that lack good lookahead properties are difficult to simulate with such schemes. Examples of such models are servers that can have zero service times or that can be preempted. A preemptive server can be interrupted and have its job completion scheduled at an earlier time than was predicted—thus, it can't be relied upon to produce reliable lookahead promises.

In Fig. 7, the deadlock can be broken assuming that the servers have a minimum propagation delay of 1 time unit. Component *F* will send a null message with time 10 to component S_{21}. This will be forwarded to the next in line with an improved output time of 11. Going through all the servers, the null-message arrives at *J* with an improved lower bound of 13, and the deadlock is broken, since *J* can now proceed to execute the event scheduled for 13.

Exercise. In general, several iterations through the feedback loops might be necessary to advance the time so that deadlock can be broken. Consider that the next message waiting at input port *in*1 of *J* is at time 15. Show how deadlock is broken by two iterations of null messages.◆

An alternative to strictly avoiding deadlock is to let deadlock happen, detect it, and recover from it. Several deadlock detection and recovery methods have been proposed [2,4,23,30]. We will not further discuss deadlock detection. Instead, we continue by formulating a parallel conservative, hierarchical simulator for DEVS models working with deadlock avoidance.

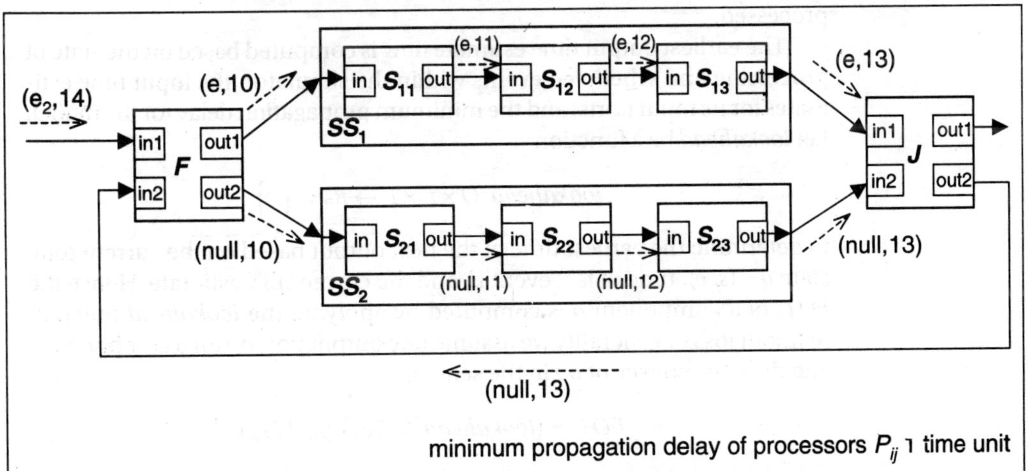

Figure 7 Breaking deadlock in the feedback loop.

11.2.1 Conservative Parallel DEVS Simulator

In this section we introduce an approach to conservative parallel simulation of modular DEVS models. It is a scheme that relates to several conservative approaches, most notably the original Chandy–Misra approach with deadlock avoidance [3,23] and the Yaddes algorithm [8].

In the definition of the simulator we will make some simplifying assumptions. In particular, we will not consider simultaneous events and we will formulate the simulator for nonhierarchical models only.

Principal Idea

The principal idea behind the conservative DEVS simulator presented here is to maintain a network of correlated *earliest output time* (EOT) and *earliest input time* (EIT) estimates, which matches the output-to-input coupling structure of the coupled model. The EOT/EIT estimates represent the times that are distributed with the null-messages. They have to be maintained in parallel to the event communication and event processing.

The earliest input time estimate $EIT_{i,ip}$ for an input port *ip* of a component *i* gives the information that no input will be received at that port at a lower time. It can be computed by considering all earliest output time estimates of all influencing output ports. So for an input port *ip* of a component *i* the earliest input time computes as

$$EIT_{i,ip} = \min\{EOT_{o,op} \| ((o,op),(i,ip)) \in IC\}.$$

The minimum of the EITs of all input ports *ip* for a component *i* determines a lower bound on the time of next input received by *i:*

$$EIT_i = \min_{ip}\{EIT_{i,ip}\}.$$

This EIT now provides the required information to determine that an event is safe. Obviously, any event with a time lower than EIT can be processed.

The earliest output time estimate now is computed based on the state of processing and scheduled events within the simulator, the input time estimates for its input ports, and the minimum propagation delay for the model. Let *lookahead* be a function

$$lookahead: Q \times T \times T \rightarrow R_0^+ \cup \{\infty\}$$

to determine the earliest time of the next output based on the current total state $q = (s, e)$, time of last event *tl*, and the current EIT estimate. Hence the EOT_o of a component *o* is computed by applying the *lookahead* function (without loss of generality we assume one output port *op* for a component *o* and drop the subscript *op* in the sequel)

$$EOT_o = (lookahead_o(s_o, e_o), tl_o, EIT_o).$$

For example, when the model *o* has a minimum propagation delay, D_o, and the next output events are equal to the time of next event, tn_o, the lookahead function is

$$lookahead_o\left(\left(s_o, e_o\right), tl_o, EIT_o\right) = \min\left\{tn_o, EIT_o + D_o\right\}$$

with $tn_o = tl_o + ta_o(s_o)$ as usual.

To be meaningful, we require that

$$lookahead_o\left(q_o, tl_o, EIT_o\right) \geq \min\left\{EIT_o, tn_o\right\}, \tag{1}$$

i.e., the earliest output time estimate computed should not be smaller than the next possible event. We speak of a *positive lookahead* if

$$lookahead_o\left(q_o, tl_o, EIT_o\right) > EIT_o \tag{2}$$

i.e., the lookahead function can predict a nonzero period that an input needs to propagate to the output.

The following theorem states absence of causality violations.

***Theorem 1** No Causality Violations*

A simulator i of an atomic DEVS that processes events only when they have time smaller or equal to the minimum input time estimate EIT_i computed as defined earlier does process the events in time stamp order.

Proof: Directly follows from the definition of EIT_i being the minimum of the $EOT_{o,op}$ of all influencing components o. ■

Additionally, we can state and prove the following theorem guaranteeing the absence of deadlock.

***Theorem 2** No Deadlock*

Under the condition that in every feedback loop there is at least one component i with a positive lookahead ($lookahead_i(q_i, tl_i, EIT_i) > EIT_i$), the simulator does not deadlock and always can proceed forward in time.

Proof: The proof works by showing that at least the component i^* with minimum time of next event tn_{i^*} is not blocked.

Let us first consider the computation of EOT_i for components i with $EIT_i \geq tn_i$. For such a component it follows from (1) that

$$EOT_i \geq tn_i. \tag{3}$$

For all components with no input ports we have $EIT_i = \infty$. Hence, all input-free components fulfill condition (3).

Let i^* be a component simulator with minimum next event time tn_{i^*}:

$$tn_{i^*} = \min_i\left\{tn_i\right\}. \tag{4}$$

We show that this component is never blocked, i.e., $EIT_{i^*} > tn_{i^*}$.

Let us consider all paths ($i^* = i_0, i_1, i_2, \ldots$) of direct and indirect influencers of component i^* according the coupling structure of the model. For all pairs of components i_k, i_{k+1} in those paths based on the computation of EIT by the minimum of the EOT of the influencers, it is guaranteed that $EIT_{i_k} \leq EOT_{i_{k+1}}$ and there is at least one path with $EIT_{i_k} = EOT_{i_{k+1}}$. From those paths we select the one with $EIT_{i_k} = EOT_{i_{k+1}}$ for all k. Without loss of generality, let us consider that there is exactly one such path. In this path we have

$$EIT_{i_k} = EOT_{i_{k+1}} = lookahead_{i_{k+1}}\left(q_{i_{k+1}}, tl_{i_{k+1}}, EIT_{i_{k+1}}\right). \tag{5}$$

We distinguish two cases:

(a) The path $(i^* = i_0, i_1, i_2, \ldots, i_{n-1}, i_n)$ ends at an input-free component i_n
(b) The path forms a cycle $(i^* = i_0, i_1, i_2, \ldots i_n = i_0 = i^*)$

(a) The path ends at an input-free component i_n: For i_n we have $EIT_{i_n} = \infty$; hence, $EIT_{i_n} > tn_{i_n}$. From (4) it follows that $tn_{i_n} > tn_{i^*}$, and using (1) we conclude $EOT_{i_n} > tn_{i^*}$. With (5) we have $EIT_{i_{n-1}} > tn_{i^*}$. With the same considerations we conclude that $EOT_{i_{n-1}} > tn_{i^*}$, and hence $EIT_{i_{n-2}} > tn_{i^*}$. Continuing until i^* we can conclude $EIT_{i^*} > tn_{i^*}$.

(b) The path forms a cycle: In a path forming a cycle $(i^* = i_0, i_1, i_2, \ldots i_n = i^*)$ it follows by (1) that $EOT_{i^*} \geq \min\{tn_{i^*}, EIT_{i^*}\}$. From that, from $EIT_{i_{n-1}} = EOT_{i^*}$, and from (4) it follows that $EOT_{i_{n-1}} \geq \min\{tn_{i^*}, EIT_{i^*}\}$. Continuing, we can conclude that for all components i_k in the network

$$EOT_{i_{k+1}} = EIT_{i_k} \geq \min\{tn_{i^*}, EIT_{i^*}\}. \tag{6}$$

Hence, also for $i_n = i^*$ we have $EIT_{i_n} = EIT_{i^*} \geq \min\{tn_{i^*}, EIT_{i^*}\}$; thus,

$$EIT_{i^*} \geq tn_{i^*}. \tag{7}$$

From this result we conclude that either $EIT_{i^*} > tn_{i^*}$ and the component i^* is not blocked or $EIT_{i^*} = tn_{i^*}$. $EIT_{i^*} = tn_{i^*}$, however, requires that

$$EOT_{i_{k+1}} = EIT_{i_k} = tn_{i^*} \tag{8}$$

for all component i_k in the cycle. Hence, also $EOT_{i_k} = EIT_{i_k}$ and then $lookahead_{i_k}(q_{i_k}, t, EIT_{i_k}) = EIT_{i_k}$. Hence, there is no component i_k in the cycle with a real lookahead as required in (2). This is in contradiction of the theorem requiring at least one component with a real lookahead in every feedback loop. ■

The practical result of this theorem and proof is that at least the EIT estimate of the imminent component (with minimum next event time) can be advanced until the next internal event can be executed. Hence, the simulator never can deadlock.

Conservative DEVS Simulator

In a parallel simulator for a modular coupled DEVS model, the coordinators no longer control the individual simulators, which now do their event processing autonomously. The coordinators serve only to distribute the output values, as well as to forward next-event time estimates as will be described in the following.

Figure 8 shows the structure of a conservative parallel abstract simulator. There are conservative parallel simulators for handling the parallel event processing. Each such parallel simulator has attached a conventional sequential DEVS simulator (as defined in Chapter 8), which is employed to do the event processing under the control of the parallel simulator. The parent coordinator is responsible for distribution of outputs and output time estimates only according to the coupling structure. The coordinator has to be realized in a distributed form on a distributed computer architecture.

The parallel DEVS simulator maintains a queue, *Iq*, to store the received, yet unprocessed, input messages. As shown in Algorithm 1, it also maintains

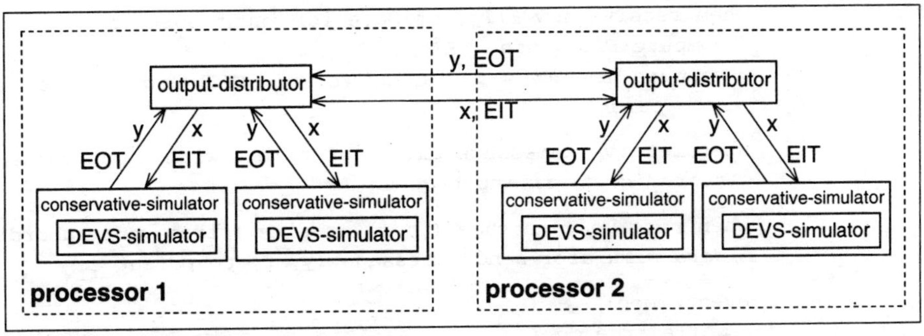

Figure 8 Structure of the parallel abstract simulator.

variables for the EOT and EIT estimates. When the parallel simulator receives an initialization message, it first forwards it to its devs-simulator, which initializes the *tl* and *tn* times. Then the parallel simulator initializes its input queue to empty and its input time estimates to 0. Also, it already computes its first output time estimate considering the lookahead. This is sent out and eventually will make events in other simulators safe.

When it receives an *x*-message, the input is not processed immediately but stored in the event list. When it receives new input time estimates, it updates its EOT and sends new estimates back for distribution. Outputs from its devs-simulator are forwarded directly to the parent output distributor.

The kernel of the parallel simulator is the infinite event loop, which processes external and internal events as long as it is safe to do so. It sends *- or *x*-messages to its associated sequential simulator, whichever is next. After each event the EOT estimate is updated and new estimates are sent out.

```
Conservative-devs-simulator
 variables:
  parent          // parent output distributor
  devs-simulator  // associated DEVS simulator or coordinator
  tn              // time of internal event (maintained by
                     the devs-simulator)
  tl              // time of last event (maintained by the
                     devs-simulator)
  Iq              // queue to store the external input
                     messages
  EIT             // earliest input time estimate
  {EIT_ip}        // earliest input time estimate for all
                     input ports ip
  EOT             // earliest output time estimate
  lookahead       // function to compute the lookahead of the
                     model

 when receive i-message (i, t) at time t
  send i-message (i, t) to devs-simulator
  EIT = 0, EIT_ip = 0
  compute new EOT = lookahead (q, tl, EIT) and send it back
    to parent
```

```
when receive new EIT_ip estimate for input port ip
  compute EIT = min_ip {EIT_ip}
  compute new EOT = lookahead (q, tl, EIT) and send it back
   to parent

when receive x-message (x, t) at time t with input value x
  store (x, t) in input-queue Iq

when receive y-message (y, t) at time t from your subordinate
  devs-simulator send y-message (y, t) to parent

event-loop:
  while true do
    (x, tx) is first in Iq // (x, tx) = (null, ∞) if Iq is empty
    if (tn ≤ EIT && tn ≤ tx) then // process internal event
      send (*, tn) message to your devs-simulator
    else if (tx ≤ EIT && tx < tn) // process external event
      remove first of input queue Iq
      send (x, tx) message to your devs-simulator
    compute new EOT = lookahead(q, tl, EIT) and send it back to
      parent
    endwhile
  end event-loop
end Devs-Simulator
```

Algorithm 1 Conservative parallel DEVS simulator.

Some Comments on the Conservative Simulator

After defining the general scheme for conservative parallel DEVS simulation, let us now discuss some issues that have been neglected so far.

Simultaneous events: Simultaneous events are difficult to deal within conservative PDES. Recall that in the Classic DEVS abstract simulator of Chapter 8, the coordinator for the coupled system was in a position to decide on the component to be activated next based on the *Select* function of the coupled model. However, in the parallel scheme there is no overall coordinator and the choice of which component should go first has to be distributed to the individual simulators.

One way to solve simultaneous events in distributed way is to extend the content of a message so that it also contains the name of the source component [18]. Then it is possible to resolve two simultaneous times by comparing the sources based on the *Select* order. For example, if an external input event and an internal event have the same time, the internal event will be first when the component itself has priority over the component sending the input, and conversely. However, this does not take account of the possibility that the selected event will have canceled or rescheduled the event that was not activated. Parallel DEVS does away with the *Select* function altogether, and its simulator is not subject to this problem.

Runtime efficiency and optimizations: Overhead through the EOT-EIT computations (null messages) can be a large compared to event execution. Various approaches are known to reduce this overhead. They deal with the questions of when to compute and distribute new estimates. Approaches range from sending the information from time to time, sending only when all processors are blocked, to sending them only on demand. Each approach has its advantages and disadvantages [21,23,25,27].

Another important issue is the load balancing between different processors. A processor having a heavy load compared to the others will slow down the others by lagging behind and blocking them. Unfortunately, good load balancing often depends on the simulation runs and cannot be fixed in advance [40]. Dynamic load balancing where the assignment of components to processors is changed dynamically is a way to tackle this problem.

Models with lookahead properties: Conservative parallel discrete event simulation protocols depend on good lookahead capabilities of the models. Also they only work for uniform and heavy message populations [12]. Also, lookahead values need to be large for a distributed simulator to outperform its sequential counterpart [29]. It has been shown that when message traffic is low, null-message overhead is overwhelming. Conservative schemes, therefore, are unlikely to be useful as protocols for general-purpose simulation systems.

11.3 Optimistic Parallel Discrete Event Simulation

Optimistic parallel discrete event simulation stands in contrast to the conservative approaches, as it takes risks that might violate causality. The simulator continues to execute the events even when it cannot guarantee that they are safe to execute. As a consequence, a simulator may get ahead in simulated time of its influencers and, therefore, may receive a message with time smaller than its local simulation time, a so-called *straggler* event. That means a causality violation has occurred—it has to be detected and repaired by "rolling back" in simulated time to take into account the new message. At a rollback a simulator has to

- Set back the state before the straggler event
- Annihilate any outputs already sent with simulated time greater than the time of the straggler event

Obviously to accomplish this, an optimistic simulator must store

- The state information to set back the state
- The input messages to redo the inputs after rollback
- The outputs to be able to annihilate the output events later than the rollback time

In the following we try to illustrate rollback by an example. Figure 9 shows a sample simulation run by means of the input, state, and output trajectories. In the simulation shown in Fig. 9a, three inputs i_1, i_2, and i_3 are received and processed and outputs o_1 and o_2 are sent until time 9. In Fig. 9b, a straggler input event i_4 is received at time 4. This necessitates setting the simulation time back to time 4, resetting the state at that time, undoing the outputs at time 6 and 9, and then stepping forward again in time, which means processing the straggler input i_4 and redoing processing of the inputs i_2 and i_3.

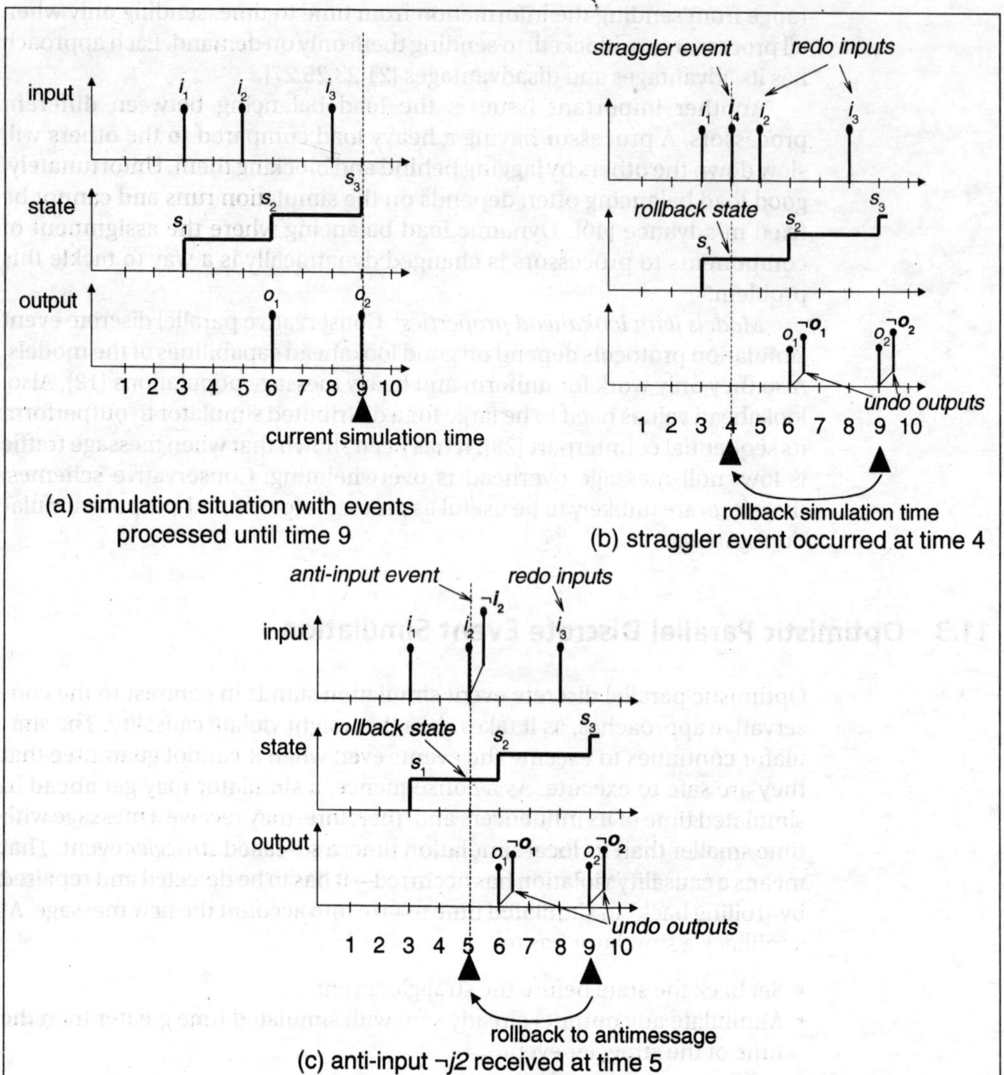

Figure 9 Straggler event and rollback.

While setting back the state in case of a rollback is straightforward and only requires storing past state values, to undo outputs will affect the influenced components and therefore can be cumbersome. It requires special messages—so-called *anti-messages*—to be sent out to annihilate the effects of the outputs. These have to be handled by the receiving components in similar way as straggler inputs. Figure 9c illustrates the handling of anti-messages at the receiving component. An anti-input is received to undo the input i_2. The anti-message is handled similarly to a straggler event, that is, the state is set back to time 5, the input i_2 is deleted from the input queue, and the outputs after that time have to be undone. Then, with the cleared input queue and cleared outputs, the component again proceeds to process the events left after time 5.

State saving represents a main overhead in optimistic parallel simulation schemes, especially for memory requirements. Obviously, with the progress in simulation run, the memory required to save the state history would increase indefinitely and the simulator would soon run out of memory. Therefore, in optimistic schemes saved information that is not needed any longer, i.e., that lies in the past so that no rollback to it will occur, can be deleted. This is called *fossil collection*. What we need to implement fossil collection is a time horizon for which we can guarantee that no rollback will occur prior to the time horizon.

Such a time can easily be found. Imagine that the individual processors i have executed events at different times tl_i. One of them will have minimum time tl_{i^*}. Obviously, no processor can generate an output event prior to this minimum time. Also, let's assume that there are some events sent and not yet received. Let's assume that tx is the minimum of these times. Obviously no processor can receive an event with time prior to tl_{i^*} or tx. The minimum of these times is the time horizon we need for fossil collection and is generally known as the *global virtual time* (*GVT*).

This approach for optimistic parallel discrete event simulation outlined above is generally referred to as the *Time-Warp* algorithm [14,15]. Other approaches exist. In the next section, we will formalize a DEVS simulator based on Time-Warp and then discuss and present another approach to optimistic simulation, a *riskfree optimistic* algorithm, in the last section.

11.3.1 Time-Warp DEVS Simulator

Parallelization of hierarchically coupled DEVS is possible using the optimistic synchronization technique of conventional Time-Warp and sequential hierarchical scheduling of the conventional DEVS abstract simulator. The whole model is partitioned into distinct components where one component is assigned to one processor. We assume that the model component assigned to one processor is one single coupled model, and we have one overall coordinator at one processor.

Now, hierarchical scheduling is used with some modifications locally within a processor; Time-Warp is employed for synchronization of global simulation between processors. Figure 10 shows the hierarchical structure of the optimistic parallel abstract simulator. The simulators and coordinators are extended to meet the needs of optimistic simulation, i.e., to do state saving and rollback. An overall root-coordinator for each processor realizes the Time-Warp mechanism.

The optimistic simulators and coordinators are formalized to extend the abstract DEVS simulators and coordinators. Algorithm 2 shows the optimistic simulator extension for basic DEVS. It employs a queue, *Sq*, to store the state information, *s*, together with time of last event, *tl*, and time of next event, *tn*. At each conventional message, initialization, internal event, and external event, the message is forwarded to the conventional devs-simulator and then state and times are saved. Additionally, the optimistic simulator realizes the rollback message, which looks up the state queue *Sq* to restore state *s* and times *tl* and *tn* for the time of the rollback.

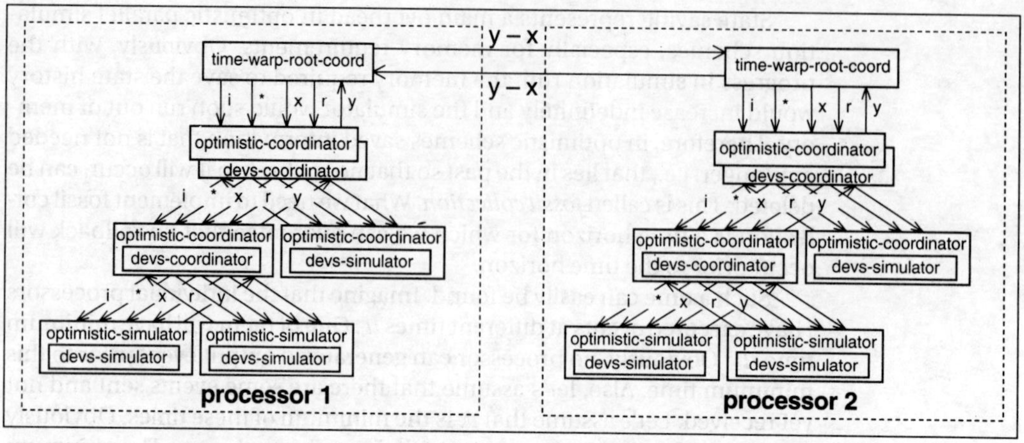

Figure 10 Structure of the parallel optimistic abstract simulator.

```
Optimistic-devs-simulator
variables:
  parent          // parent coordinator
  devs-simulator  // associated sequential DEVS simulator
  Sq              // queue to store the state s plus times tl
                     and tn

  when receive i-message (i, t) at time t
    send i-message (i, t) to devs-simulator
    initialize Sq by inserting initial state and times (s, tl, tn)
  when receive x-message (x, t) at time t with input value x
    send x-message (x, t) to devs-simulator
    save state and times (s, tl, tn) in Sq
  when receive *-message (*, t) at time t
    send *-message (*, t) to devs-simulator
    save state and times (s, tl, tn) in Sq
  when receive rollback-message (¬, t) at time t
    roll back to state (s, tl, tn) at time t
  when receive y-message (y, t) with output y from devs-simulator
    send y-message (y, t) to parent
end Optimistic-devs-simulator
```

Algorithm 2 Optimistic simulator for basic DEVS.

The coordinator extension for optimistic simulation (Algorithm 3) forwards the conventional messages unchanged to the subordinates or parent. Additionally, it takes care of rollbacks. When receiving a rollback message for time *t*, it forwards it to all children *d* with time of last event tl_d greater than the time *t* of the rollback. In that way the global state of the associated coupled model is set back to the state at time *t*. Afterwards the times *tl* and *tn* are reinitialized based on the times of the children.

```
Optimistic-devs-coordinator
variables:
    parent              // parent coordinator
    devs-coordinator    // associated sequential DEVS simulator
when receive rollback-message (¬, t) at time t
  for-each d in D with tl_d > t do
    send rollback-message (¬, t) to d
  tl = max (tl_d | d ∈ D)
  tn = min (tn_d | d ∈ D)
// all other messages directly forwarded to devs-coordinator
  and parent
end Optimistic-devs-coordinator
```

Algorithm 3 Optimistic coordinator for coupled DEVS.

An overall root-coordinator in each processor realizes the Time-Warp mechanism (Algorithm 4). In particular, it stores input and output events from, and to other processors, takes care of anti-messages, and is involved in global synchronization (*GVT* and *global-IOq*). In an event loop the root-coordinator sends *-messages for next internal events or *x*-messages for queued input events to its child to process them optimistically. Inbetween, it takes care for global synchronization and fossil collection. Also, whenever it asynchronously receives messages from other processors, it handles them. When an output message is received from the child, the output is stored in the output queue *Oq* and then sent to the influenced processors immediately. Also, it is stored in the global event queue, *pending-IOq,* to mark it as a sent, but not yet received, message. When the output is transmitted to the receiving processor as an input in an *x*-message, it takes the output event out from the pending global event queue, *pending-IOq,* and stores the input event in the input queue. Then it sees if it is a straggler event. If so, a rollback message is sent to the child to restore the state at time of the rollback and anti-messages are sent out for all outputs in the output queue with later time. When an anti-message requests cancellation of an input event, the corresponding input message is deleted from the input queue and a rollback is carried out in analogous manner.

Global event synchronization is through the global virtual time, *GVT.* It is computed as the minimum of the last event times tl_i in all processors *i* and the minimum of the pending events in *pending-IOq.* Fossil collection can be carried out based on the *GVT,* i.e., all events prior to *GVT* can be freed (usually this is carried out periodically by traversing all simulators and examining their state queues *Sq*).

```
Time-Warp-root-coordinator for processor i
 variables
   t              // current simulation time
   child          // subordinate optimistic simulator or
                     coordinator
   Iq             // queue to store the input events
   Oq             // queue to store the output events
   pending-IOq    // global queue to store the sent, not yet
                     received output events
```

```
  tl              // time of last event within the scope of the
                     root-coordinator

event-loop:
  t = t0
  initialize Iq and Oq empty
  send initialization message (i, t) to child
  tl = tl_child
  while true do
    let (x, tx) be next input event in Iq with smallest time tx
    if tx ≤ tn_child then
      t = tx
      send (x, t) to child
    else
      t = tn_child
      send (*, t) message to child
    tl = tl_child
    GVT = min {min {tl_i | for all processors i}, min{ ty | (y, ty)
    ∈ pending-IOq}
      do fossil collection for states, inputs,
      and outputs with time t < GVT
  end while
when receive y-message (y, t) from child
  save output event (y, t) in Oq
  send request to put (y, t) into global pending-IOq
  send (y, t) to influenced processor

when receive x-message (x, t) from influencing processor
  send request to remove output (y, t) correlating to input
  event (x, t) from pending-IOq
  save input event (x, t) in Iq
  if (t < tn_child) then    // rollback
    send rollback message (¬, t) to child
  for all output events (y, ty) in Oq with ty > t do
    send anti-messages (¬y, ty) to influenced processors
    delete (y, ty) from output queue Oq

when receive anti-message (¬x, t) from influencing processor
  if (t < tn_child) then    //rollback
    send rollback message (¬, t) to child
  for all output events (y, ty) in Oq with ty > t do
    send anti-messages (¬y, ty) to influenced processors
    delete (y, ty) from output queue Oq
  delete input event (x, t) corresponding to (¬x, t) from Iq
end Time-Warp-root-coordinator
```

Algorithm 4 Time-Warp root-coordinator.

Some Comments on the Time-Warp Simulator

Hierarchical models and process granularity: As in the conservative scheme, the question arises at what level of the coupled model parallelization should occur. Actually, in the preceding simulator we assumed that one process handles one coupled model assigned to one processor. However, the scheme also works with more processes and smaller coupled components. Actually, it is possible to parallelize the coupled model simulator at any granularity down to the atomic model level. What we have to do is to use a Time-Warp root-coordinator for each process to handle the interprocess synchronization.

However, let's examine the consequences of using multiple processes or only one process at one processor. To clarify this issue, let's consider the example in Fig. 11. In Fig. 11a one process *i* is responsible to handle the whole coupled model *N* with four components, *A*, *B*, *C*, and *D*. The compo-

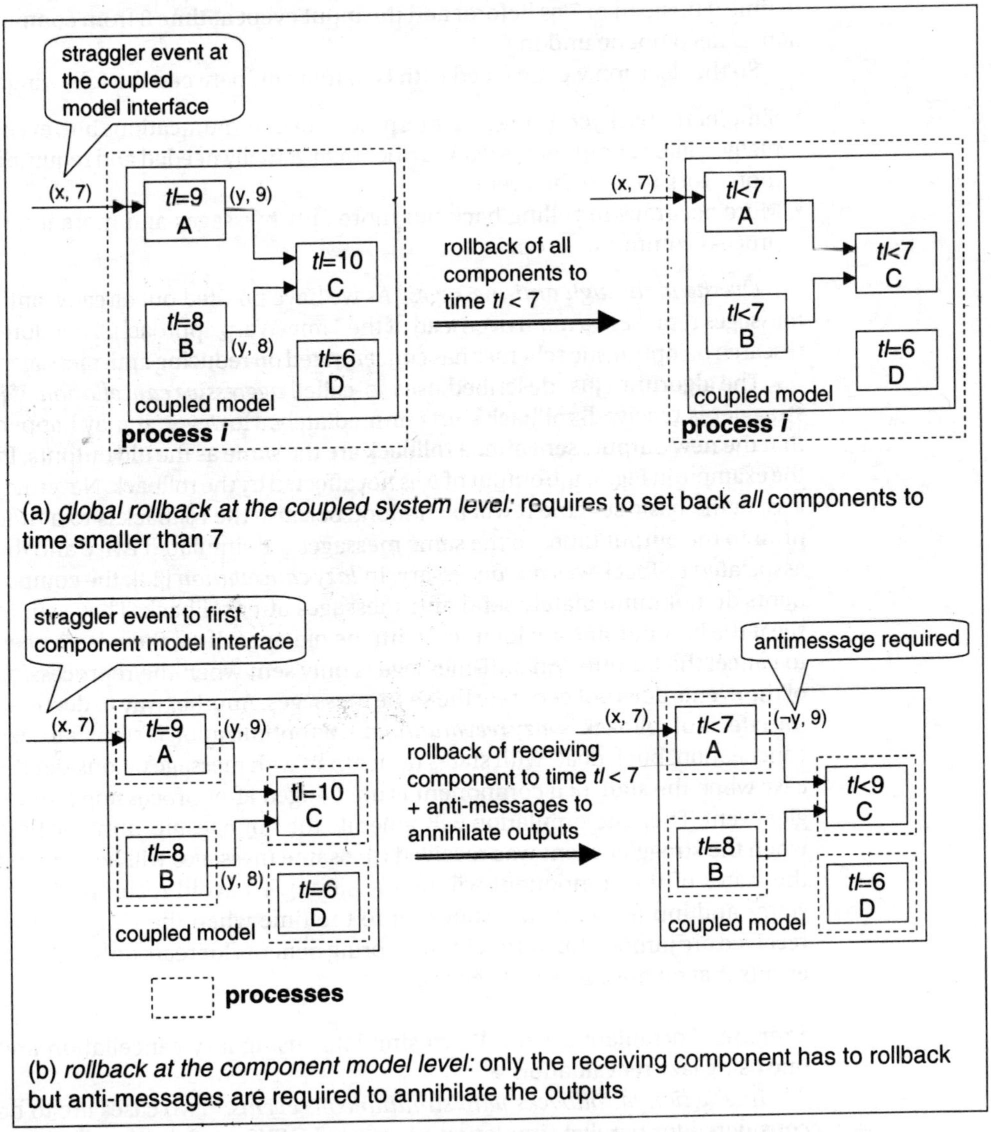

Figure 11 Comparison of rollback at the coupled model and component model level.

nents have just processed events at times 9, 8, 10, and 6, respectively, with output events from *A* to *C* at time 9 and from *B* to *C* at time 8. When a straggler event arrives at time 7 at the coupled system interface, all the components with time of last event *tl* greater than 7 have to be rolled back. However, output events need not be undone (since the receiving processors have been rolled back, anyway), and therefore no anti-messages are required.

In Fig. 11b each component is handled by a process and components are synchronized using Time-Warp. In this configuration the straggler event is handled directly by simulator of component *A*. Only component *A* will roll back to a smaller rollback time but has to send out anti-messages to annihilate its later outputs. In our example, this will cause component *C* to roll back to time 9 (instead of 7 as before) and the input event at time 8 from component *B* need not be undone.

So the decision we are faced with is to trade off between the following:

- Simpler rollback requiring less interprocessor communications but, eventually, rolling components back further than actually needed and requiring more work to redo the events
- More accuracy in rolling back but more anti-messages and more interprocess communications

Overhead through anti-messages: As we have pointed out already, anti-messages represent a main overhead of the Time-Warp approach. Therefore, research on optimistic schemes has concentrated on reducing anti-messages.

The algorithm just described uses so-called *aggressive cancellation.* If a straggler is received, rollback starts immediately. However, it may happen that the new outputs sent after a rollback are the same as the old outputs. In the example in Fig. 9, the output of o_1 is not affected by the rollback. Nevertheless, in the basic scheme it will be undone because the rollback is to a time prior to the output time. So the same messages are simulated twice and the associated rollback was not necessary. In *lazy cancellation* [23], the components do not immediately send anti-messages after rollback. They wait to see if the new outputs are identical with the old ones. If so, there is no need to cancel the outputs. An anti-message is only sent when the reprocessing of the events does not generate the same messages. Another way to decrease the effects of rollback is *lazy reevaluation.* This optimization is similar to lazy cancellation, but it deals with states rather than with messages. Consider the case when the state of a component is unchanged after processing a straggler event. Then the simulation will generate the same results until the time when the straggler event was received (the same messages will be sent and the states of the component will be the same). To avoid recomputing of states and input events, the states up to the time when the straggler was received are jumped forward. This may bring benefits for read-only or query events that do not cause state changes.

Exercise: Formulate a Time-Warp simulator using lazy cancellation and one using lazy reevaluation.◆

Interaction of rollbacks with simultaneous events: Two cases are to be considered for parallel simulation of coupled DEVS models: simultaneous events and nonsimultaneous events. The former has two subcases: simultaneous external input events and simultaneous internal events. These cases are illustrated in Fig. 12. In (a), an output from A is sent as simultaneous input events (X_B, X_C) to components B and C, mapped into different processors; (b) shows simultaneous execution of internal events ($*_A$, $*_B$) when A and B are mapped into different processors and each sends simultaneous outputs to C. Finally (c) illustrates execution of ($*_A$, $*_B$) when A and B are mapped into different processors and have the same timestamps but are executed at different times.

Exercise: Fill in Table 1 with indications of whether or not rollback is needed and whether or not it must be propagated for each of the cases in Fig. 12. For example, in case (a), rollback is not needed.◆

11.3.2 Riskfree Optimistic DEVS Simulator

Several alternatives to classical Time-Warp have been developed, which try to further reduce the overhead through anti-messages and basically deal with the question of whether an output should be sent once scheduled or should be held back to reduce the risk of having to undo it [9]. *Riskfree optimistic parallel simulation* is the extreme version of this approach and has shown to be an attractive alternative [37]. It refrains from sending nonsafe events between different processors altogether. Only within the processor events are processed optimistically. Hence, when a straggler event is received by a processor, rollback occurs but is local to the processor and therefore less costly. In the following section we formulate a riskfree optimistic variation of our optimistic DEVS simulator. The scheme we present here is supposed to work well on low-grained parallel machines, typically multiprocessor machines with shared memory.

To illustrate the objectives behind this riskfree optimistic simulation protocol, let's recall the discussion of parallel simulation at the beginning of the chapter. When model components may run independently for a limited time interval and only show dependencies at distinct points in time, they are good candidates for parallelization (Fig. 2). Let's assume that we have such model components and we have assigned them to distinct processors.

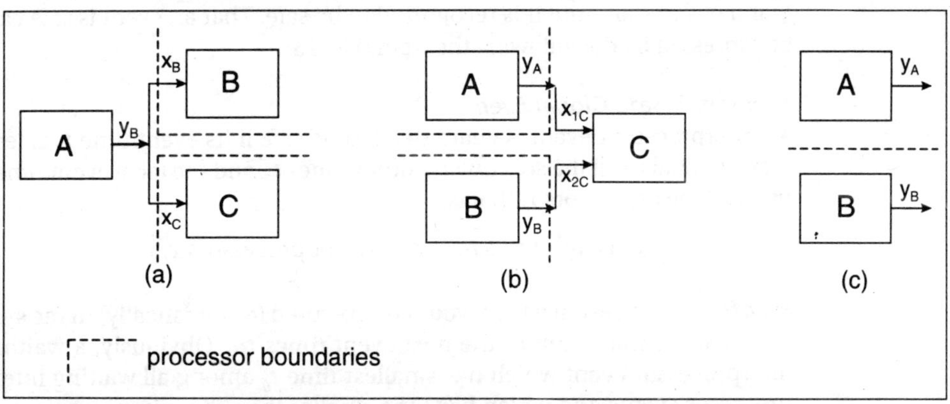

Figure 12 Parallel simulation of DEVS models.

Table 1 Parallelization in Hierarchical Simulation of DEVS Models

	Parallelization		
	Simultaneous events		**Nonsimultaneous events**
	External (*x, t*)events, case (a)	**Internal (*, *t*) events, case (b)**	**Internal (*, *t*) events, case (c)**
Time-warp/rollback	No	?	?
Propagation of rollback	?	?	?

Therefore, communication between these model components occurs infrequently. Also, let's assume that we have succeeded in balancing the load uniformly at the different processors and they progress with similar speed. Then, when we run the simulation, each processor will get quite a lot done until it has to communicate with another processor. If we succeed in keeping interprocessor communication frequency low and keeping overhead small, progress will be great compared to overhead.

The riskfree scheme presented here is based on this idea. We let the processors run independently and try to make the overhead at communication points small. Events local to each processor are processed sequentially but optimistically. However, any outputs that have to be forwarded to components running on another processor are held back until it can be guaranteed that it is safe to process them. That means interprocessor events are processed conservatively.

To guarantee that interprocessor events are safe, a global synchronization mechanism is employed. Each processor i has its local next event time tn_i. A model output to a different processor j is scheduled with output time t_{ij} and has to wait until it is recognized to be safe. That an event is safe can be expressed by the following theorem (Fig. 13).

***Theorem 3** Safe Global Event*

An interprocessor event is guaranteed to be safe if its event time t_{ij} is less than or equal to all the scheduled output times t_{xy} and the local event times tn_x of all the processors x, that is,

$$t_{ij} \text{ is } \textit{safe} \text{ if } t_{ij} \le tn_x \wedge t_{ij} \le t_{xy} \text{ for processors } x, y.$$

***Proof*:** The next event which would be executed (optimistically) in the system is at the minimum of the next event times tn_x. Obviously, a waiting interprocessor event which has smallest time t_{ij} among all waiting interprocessor events and which has time smaller than the minimum time of

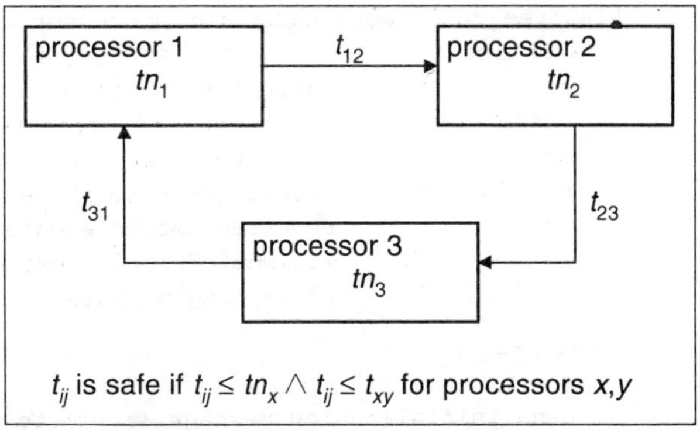

Figure 13 Risk-free optimistic event synchronization: An output event is safe to process if it is less than or equal to all the other output events scheduled and less than or equal to the local next event times of all processors.

next *tn* is the event with smallest event time in the system. Such an event cannot be influenced by any other event in the system and therefore is safe to process. ■

Therefore, the global synchronization of a riskfree optimistic DEVS simulator has to compute the minimum of the *tn*-times and channel times t_{ij} for all processors. We call this, in correspondence to the Time-Warp mechanism, global virtual time (*GVT*). In this protocol, the *GVT* is used to control interprocessor communication as well its original role of controlling fossil collection.

A riskfree version of an optimistic DEVS abstract simulator can be formalized based on the Time-Warp abstract simulator presented in the last section. Actually, the optimistic simulators and coordinators are used without modification and only the synchronization mechanism in the root-coordinator is changed. Algorithm 5 shows the root-coordinator for the riskfree optimistic approach. Let us concentrate on the main differences from the Time-Warp version. The riskfree version does not need an input queue, since incoming events are guaranteed to be safe and can be processed immediately. In the event loop only the internal events are scheduled optimistically. When the root-coordinator receives an output from its child, it sees if this output is safe, i.e., its time is equal to the *GVT*. If so, it is sent out immediately. Otherwise, the output event is held back in the output queue, *Oq*. With the advance of the GVT, queued output events eventually become safe and are released for distribution to other processors.

Whenever an input message (x, t) is received, a *local* rollback may result. Rollback is handled by sending a rollback message to the child for setting back all states to a time prior to *t*. Afterwards, the input event is processed immediately. Note that we can dispense with anti-messages.

Global synchronization is carried out in a similar way to Time-Warp, i.e., by updating the (redefined) *GVT*. In addition to the local event times and the pending events, output events waiting in the output queues *Oq* also have to be considered.

```
Riskfree-root-coordinator for processor i
 variables
   t              // current simulation time
   child          // subordinate riskfree simulator or coordinator
   Oq             // queue to store the output events
   pending-IOq    // global queue to store the sent, yet not
                     received output events
   tn             // minimum of local next event time and times
                     of waiting outputs

 event-loop:
   t = t0
   send initialization message (i, t) to child
   loop
     t = tn_child
     send (*, t) message to child
     tn_i = min (tn_child, min{ty | (y, ty) ∈ Oq})
     GVT = min (min {tn_j | for all processors j}, min{ty | (y, ty)
       ∈ pending-IOq})
     for all output events (y, ty) in Oq with ty = GVT do
       put (y, ty) into pending-IOq
       send (y, ty) to influenced processor
       delete (y, ty) from Oq
     endfor
     do fossil collection for states with time t < GVT
   until end of simulation

 when receive y-message (y, t) from child
   if (t ≤ GVT) then
     put (y, t) into pending-IOq
     send (y, t) to influenced processor
   else save output event (y, t) in Oq
 when receive x-message (x, t) from influencing processor
   remove (y, t) corresponding to input event (x, t) from
     pending-IOq
   if (t < tn_child) then // rollback
     send rollback message (¬, t) to child
   send x-message (x, t) to child
 end riskfree-root-coordinator
```

Algorithm 5 Riskfree optimistic root-coordinator.

11.4 Parallel DEVS Simulator

Recall that Parallel DEVS was designed so that the parallelism intrinsic to DEVS coupled models could be exploited to allow as much parallel processing as possible without engaging in optimistic processing. In each processing cycle, all imminent components can be executed in parallel in an output generation step. In a subsequent input processing step, all imminents and the components they influence can be executed in parallel.

Thus, the abstract simulator for Parallel DEVS affords a scheme for PDES that is relatively straightforward to implement, exploits parallelism in moderately to highly active models, and involves no rollback, deadlock, or other overhead associated with conservative and optimistic PDES schemes (Algorithm 6).

In contrast to Classic DEVS, a basic Parallel DEVS model receives a bag of inputs rather than a single input. If the input bag is not empty, processing depends on whether or not the component is imminent. If not, its simulator employs the model's external transition function to process the input. If the model is imminent, the confluent transition function is used instead. An imminent component that does not receive input executes its internal transition function.

```
Parallel-Devs-simulator
  variables:
    parent  // parent coordinator
    tl      // time of last event
    tn      // time of next event
    DEVS    // associated model
               with total state (s, e)
    y       // output message bag

  when receive i-message (i, t) at time t
    tl = t - e
    tn = tl + ta(s)

  when receive *-message (*, t) at time t
    if t = tn then
      y = λ(s)
      send y-message (y, t) to parent coordinator
  when receive x-message (x, t) {
    if (x = Φ and t = tn) then
      s = δint (s)
    else if (x != Φ and t = tn) then
      s = δcon (s, x)
    else if (x != Φ and (tl ≤ t ≤ tn))
      e = t - tl
      s = δext (s, e, x)
      tl = t
      tn = tl + ta(s)
  end Parallel-Devs-Simulator
```

Algorithm 6 Simulator for basic Parallel DEVS.

In contrast to Classic DEVS, where imminents were sequentially activated, in Parallel DEVS all imminents are allowed to execute concurrently. The outputs of these imminents are collected into a bag called the mail. The mail is analyzed for the part going out because of the external output coupling and the parts to be distributed internally to the components due to the internal coupling. The internal transition functions of the imminents are not executed immediately, since they may also receive input at the same model time.

```
Parallel-devs-coordinator
  variables:
    DEVN = (X, Y, D, {M_d}, {I_d}, {Z_i,d})
                              // the associated coupled model
    parent                    // parent coordinator
    tl                        // time of last event
    tn                        // time of next event
    event-list                // list of elements (d, tn_d) sorted
                                 by tn_d
    IMM                       // imminent children
    mail                      // output mail bag
    y_parent                  // output message bag to parent
    {y_d}                     // set of output message bags for
                                 each child d

  when receive i-message (i, t) at time t
    for-each d ∈ D do
      send i-message to child d
    sort event-list according to tn_d
    tl = max {tl_d | d ∈ D}
    tn = min {tn_d | d ∈ D}

  when receive *-message (*, t)
    if t != tn then
      error: bad synchronization
    IMM = {d | (d, tn_d) ∈ (event-list & tn_d = tn}
    for-each r ∈ IMM
      send *-messages (*, t) to r

  when receive x-message (x, t)
    if not (tl ≤ t ≤ tn) then
      error: bad synchronization
    //consult external input coupling to get children influenced
      by the input
    receivers = {r | r ∈ children, N ∈ I_r, Z_N,r(x) ≠ Φ}
    for-each r in receivers
      send x-messages (Z_N,r(x), t) with input value Z_N,r(x) to r
    for-each r ∈ IMM and not in receivers
      send x-message (Φ, t) to r
    sort event-list according to tn_d
    tl = t
    tn = min {tn_d | d ∈ D}

  when receive y-message (y_d, t) with output y_d from d
    if this is not the last d in IMM
      add (y_d, d) to mail
      mark d as reporting
    else if this the last d in IMM
    //check external coupling to form sub-bag of parent output
    y_parent = Φ
    for each d ∈ I_N & d is reporting
      if Z_d,N(y_d) ≠ Φ then
        add y_d to y_parent
```

```
    send y-message (y_parent, t) to parent
    //check internal coupling to get children r who receive
      sub-bag of y
      for each child r with some d ∈ I_r & d is reporting & Z_d,r
        (y_d) ≠ Φ
      for each d ∈ I_r & d is reporting & Z_d,r(y_d) ≠ Φ
        add Z_d,r(y_d) to y_r
      send x-messages (y_r, t) to r
    for-each r ∈ IMM & y_r = Φ
      send x-messages (Φ, t) to r
    tl = t
    tn = min {tn_d | d ∈ D}
    sort event-list according to tn_d

  end Parallel-devs-coordinator
```

Algorithm 7 Coordinator for Parallel DEVS coupled model.

For executing models with thousands or millions of components, it was found that concurrency could be markedly improved if a less strict test for being imminent than equality were to be employed [41]. Let t_N be the minimum of all the times-of-next-event and let g be a positive number called the granule size. Then instead of requiring strict equality, we allow a component to be imminent if its time-of-next-event is within g of the global minimum, i.e. we use the relation ≡ defined by

$$t_n \equiv t_N \text{ if } \left(t_N \leq t \leq t_N + g\right).$$

This can greatly increase the number of imminents by including all those that scheduled no later than g after the true global minimum. Of course there is a trade-off here—the larger the granule, the greater the concurrency, but also the greater the potential for introducing timing error. (Note: ≡ is a "tolerance," not an equivalence relation, since transitivity does not hold.) The concept of a granule is consistent with the DEVS extensions that allow the time advance function to return a time window as opposed to a single value, as discussed in Chapter 10 (RT-DEVS). The advantage in the latter approach is that, unlike the single global time granule, each component can have a time window that is appropriate to the level of error tolerance needed in the simulation.

11.5 Summary

Table 2 compares the different protocols for distributed parallel simulation of discrete event models. As you can see, all have their pros and cons. The selection of a right protocol is heavily dependent on the model in hand and must be considered carefully.

11.6 Sources

The simulation protocols just introduced came into being by gathering many ideas that emerged in the past 20 years of parallel and distributed simulation (PDS) research. In their seminal work, Chandy and Misra introduced basic

Table 2 Comparison of PDES Approaches

Scheme	Approach	Overhead	Pros	Cons
Chandy-Misra conservative	Process events in strict time stamped order (causality preservation) w/ deadlock avoidance	Null messages, lookahead computation	Relatively simple to implement	Does not exploit all parallelism and not intrinsically load balancing Relies on lookahead capabilities of the models Only works for heavy message load and uniform message distribution Simultaneous events are problematic
DEVS version	Exploits knowledge of internal events in lookahead			
Time warp optimistic	Permits causality violation Detects violations and remedies using rollback	State, message saving, fossil collection Anti-messages Global virtual time computation	Can exploit feedback-free couplings	Complex logic is difficult to implement and verify Simultaneous events are problematic
Riskfree DEVS version	Refrain from output until safe	Similar to Time Warp, except no anti-messages and rollback is local	Relatively easy to implement	
Parallel DEVS	Riskfree and strict causality adherence	Global minimum time synchronization Simultaneous output collection and distribution	Easy to implement Expoits simul-taneous events Works well for active models with feedback couplings	Does not exploit parallelism in feedback-free couplings

concepts for conservative distributed simulation [3–4]. They defined causality requirements for correct distributed execution of events and schemes to fulfill them. Several variations and improvements have been developed. Notable impact to our presentation came from the Bounded Lag Algorithm of Lubachevsky [21], the global window synchronization scheme of Nicol [25], the Yaddes algorithm [8] and the shared memory implementation of Wagner, Lazowska, and Bershad [38]. Lubachevsky's algorithm is synchronous: With every synchronization cycle, it computes input time estimates for each simulator process based on minimum propagation delays and so-called *opaque periods*—lookahead computed dynamically based on the current state. To limit the overhead needed to compute the input time estimates, the bounded lag restriction bounds the difference in the local simulation times of all simulator processes from above by a known finite constant *B*. The global window synchronization algorithm [25,27] is another synchronous algorithm that tries to exploit static and dynamic lookahead capabilities to define *global time windows* during which event processing is safe. The Yaddes algorithm [8] uses a data flow network to compute input time estimates to guarantee safe event processing. The algorithm is tailored for network models that have a lot of feedback loops, such as digital logic models, and therefore are difficult to parallelize using Chandy-Misra or Time Warp.

Optimistic distributed simulation has been introduced by Jefferson [13,14] and implemented in the Time-Warp operating system [15]. Ferscha [9] defines an adaptive optimistic scheme where sending of optimistic interprocessor events is assessed for risk before sending. Riskfree optimistic schemes were first introduced by Dickens and Reynolds and have been used in the implementations of the Breathing Time Buckets algorithm by Steinman [37]. Excellent reviews of the different approaches can be found in Fujimoto [12] and Righter and Walrand [34].

Page [28] pointed out that research on PDS has often not related itself to the broader context of modeling and simulation methodology in general. Constraints imposed by other parts of the model development life cycle may have greater impact than local considerations characterizing PDS research. Also, considerations of modeling formalisms can provide useful guidance. For example, classical world views, discussed in Chapter 7, can provide useful guidance for PDS methods [29].

The PDS research relating to the DEVS formalism has from the start worked within the modeling and simulation methodology described in this book. Parallel simulators for DEVS modular hierarchical models have been implemented by various researchers [2,40]. Reisinger [33] implemented a combined conservative/riskfree optimistic simulator based on the EOT-EIT network presented in section 11.2.1. Christensen implemented a Time-Warp DEVS-simulator in Ada using the Time-Warp operating system [6]. Parallel simulation of DEVS models by parallelizing simultaneous external and simultaneous internal events and a mapping of hierarchical DEVS models in a hypercube computer was presented by Seong *et al.* [35,36]. Discussion of ordering of simultaneous events in parallel simulation of DEVS models can be found in Kim *et al.* [18]. Time Warp parallel simulation of hierarchical DEVS with local hierarchical scheduling was presented in Kim *et al.* [17] with experimental results for a benchmark with various workloads.

A riskfree version using the approach presented in Section 11.3.2 has been implemented by Reisinger.

Parallel DEVS and its distributed abstract simulator were formulated by Chow [5]. The DEVS-C++ environment [41] implements Parallel DEVS using an approach based on closure under coupling [39] and is the basis for HLA compliant implementation [42].

1. Bagrodia, R., K. Chandy, and J. Misra, "A Message-Based Approach to Discrete-Event Simulation." *IEEE Trans. on Software Eng.* **SE-13**(6), 654–665 (1987).
2. Bain, W. L., and D. S. Scott, "An Algorithm for Time Synchronization in Distributed Discrete Event Simulation." *Proceedings of the SCS Multiconference on Distributed Simulation* **19**(3), 30–33 (1988).
3. Chandy, K. M., and J. Misra, "Distributed Simulation: A Case Study in Design and Verification of Distributed Systems." *IEEE Trans on Software Eng.* **SE-5**(5), 440–452 (1979).
4. Chandy, K. M., and J. Misra, "Asynchronous Distributed Simulation via a Sequence of Parallel Computations." *Comm. ACM* **24**(11), 198–205 (1981).
5. Chow, A., "Parallel DEVS: a Parallel, Hierarchical, Modular Modeling Formalism and Its Distributed Simulator." *SCS Transactions on Sim* **13**(2), 55–102 (1996).
6. Christensen, E. R., *Hierarchical Optimistic Distributed Simulation: Combining DEVS and Time Warp*. Doctoral Dissertation, University of Arizona, Tucson, AZ, 1990.
7. Concepcion, A. I., and B. P. Zeigler, "DEVS Formalism: A Framework for Hierarchical Model Development." *IEEE Trans. on Software Engineering* **14**(2), 228–241 (1988).
8. DeBenedictus, E., S. Ghosh, and M.-L.-Yu, "A Novel Algorithm for Discrete Event Simulation." *IEEE Computer*, June, pp. 21–33 (1991).
9. Ferscha, A., "Probabilistic Adaptive Direct Optimism Control in Time Warp." In *Proc. 9th Workshop on Parallel and Distributed Simulation*, pp. 120–129, 1995.
10. Fujimoto, R. M., "Performance Measurement of Distributed Simulation Strategies." In *Proc. of the 1988 SCS Conference on Distributed Simulation*, San Diego, CA, 1988, pp. 14–20.
11. Fujimoto, R. M., "Lookahead in Parallel Discrete Event Simulation." In *Proc. of the International Conference on Parallel Processing*, Silver Spring, MD, IEEE 1988, pp. 34–41.
12. Fujimoto, R. M., "Parallel Discrete Event Simulation." *Comm. ACM* **33**(10), 30–53 (1990).
13. Jefferson, D., "Virtual Time." *ACM Trans. on Programming Languages and Systems* **7**(3), 404–425 (1985).
14. Jefferson, D., and H. Sowizral. "Fast Concurrent Simulation Using the Time Warp Mechanism." In *Proc. SCS Distr. Sim. Conf.*, 1985, pp. 63–69.
15. Jefferson, D., Beckmann, B., Wieland, F., L. Blume, and M. Diloreto, "Distributed Simulation and the Time Warp Operating System." In *Proc.*

of the 11th ACM Symposium on Operating System Principles, ACM, 1987, pp. 77–93.

16. Jha, V., and R. L. Bagrodia, "A Unified Framework for Conservative and Optimistic Distributed Simulation." In *Proc. of the 8th Workshop on Parallel and Distributed Simulation,* pp. 12–19, 1994.
17. Kim, K. H., Y. R. Seong, T. G. Kim, and K. H. Park, "Distributed Simulation of Hierarchical DEVS Models: Hierarchical Scheduling Locally and Time Warp Globally." *Transactions of SCS* **13**(3), 135–154 (1996).
18. Kim, K. H., Y. R. Seong, T. G. Kim, and K. H. Park, "Ordering of Simultaneous Events in Distributed DEVS Simulation." *Simulation: Practice and Theory* **5,** 253–268 (1997).
19. Kim, K. H., T. G. Kim, and K. H. Park, "Hierarchical Partitioning Algorithm for Optimistic Distributed Simulation of DEVS Models," *Journal of Systems Architecture* **44**, 433–455 (1998).
20. Lin, Y.-B., and E. D. Lazowska, "A Study of Time Warp Rollback Mechanisms." *ACM Trans. on Modeling and Computer Simulation* **1**(1), 52–83 (1991).
21. Lubachevsky, B. D., "Efficient Distributed Event-Driven Simulations of Multiple-Loop Networks." *Comm. ACM* **32**(1), 111–131 (1989).
22. Lubachevsky, B., A. Weiss, and A. Shwartz. "An Analysis of Rollback-based Simulation." *ACM Trans. on Modeling and Computer Simulation* **1**(2), 154–193 (1991).
23. Misra, J. "Distributed Discrete Event Simulation." *ACM Computing Surveys* **18**(1), 39–65 (1986).
24. Nicol, D., "Parallel Discrete-Event Simulation of FCFS Stochastic Queuing Networks." *SIGPLAN Notices* **23**(9), 124–137 (1988).
25. Nicol, D., "Performance Bounds on Parallel Self-Initiating Discrete-Event Simulations." *ACM Trans. on Modeling and Computer Simulation* **1**(1), 24–50 (1991).
26. Nicol, D. M., and P. F. Reynolds, "Problem Oriented Protocol Design." In *Proc. 1984 Winter Simulation Conference,* December 1984, pp. 471–474.
27. Nicol, D., and S. Roy, "Parallel Simulation of Timed Petri-Nets." In *Proc. of the Winter Simulation Conf.,* 1991, pp. 574–583.
28. Page, E. H., "In Defense of Discrete-Event Simulation." *ACM TOMACS* **3**(4), 281–283 (1993).
29. Page, E. H., *"Zero Lookahead in a Distributed Time-Stepped Simulation.* McLean, VA, MITRE, 1998.
30. Peacock, J. K., J. W. Wong, and E. G. Manning, "Distributed Simulation Using a Network of Processors." *Computing Networks* **3**(1), 44–56 (1979).
31. Preiss, B., "The Yaddes Distributed Discrete Event Simulation Specification Language and Execution Environment." *In Distributed Simulation 89.* SCS Press, 1989, pp. 139–144.
32. Reed, D. A., A. D. Malony, and B. D. McCredie, "Parallel Discrete Event Simulation Using Shared Memory." *IEEE Trans. on Software Eng.* **14**(4), 541–553 (1988).

33. Reisinger, G, and H. Praehofer, "Object-Oriented Realization of a Parallel Discrete Event Simulator." *Eurosim. Congress 95*, Vienna, Austria, Sept. 1995, pp. 327–332.

34. Righter, R., and J. C. Walrand, "Distributed Simulation of Discrete Event Systems." *Proceedings of the IEEE* **77**(1), 99–113 (1989).

35. Seong, Y. R., S. H. Jung, T. G. Kim, and K. H. Park, "Parallel Simulation of Hierarchical Modular DEVS Models: A Modified Time Warp Approach." *Int. J. in Computer Simulation* **5**, 263–285 (1995).

36. Seong, Y. R., T. G. Kim, and K. H. Park, "Mapping Hierarchical, Modular Discrete Event Models in a Hypercube Computer." *Simulation: Practice and Theory* **2**, 257–275 (1995).

37. Steinman, J., "SPEEDES: A Unified Framework to Parallel Simulation." In *Proc. 6th Workshop on Parallel and Distributed Simulation*, pp. 75–83, 1992.

38. Wagner, D., E. Lazowska, and B. Bershad, "Techniques for Efficient Shared-Memory Parallel Simulation." *In Distributed Simulation 1989*. SCS Press, 1989, pp. 29–37.

39. Zeigler, B. P., and D. Kim, "Design of High Level Modeling/High Performance Simulation Environments." In *10th Workshop on Parallel and Distributed Simulation*, Philadelphia, 1996, pp. 214–217.

40. Zeigler, B. P., and G. Zhang. "Mapping Hierarchical Discrete Event Models to Multiprocessor Systems: Concepts, Algorithm, and Simulation." *Journal of Parallel and Distributed Computing* **9** (1990).

41. Zeigler, B. P., V. Moon and G. J. Ball, "The DEVS Environment for High-Performance Modeling and Simulation." *IEEE C S & E* **4**(3), 61–71 (1997).

42. Zeigler, B. P., G. Ball, and H. J. Cho, "Implementation of the DEVS Formalism over the HLA/RTI: Problems and Solutions." *Simulator Interoperability Workshop*, Orlando, FL., 1999. http://www.sisostds.org

III

System Morphisms: Abstraction, Representation, Approximation

12

Hierarchy of System Morphisms

The essence of modeling lies in establishing relations between pairs of system descriptions. As discussed in Chapters 1 and 2, these relations pertain to a variety of situations:

- The validity of a model representation of a real system
- The validity of a lumped model relative to a base model
- The validity of a system description at one level of specification relative to a system description at a higher or lower level
- The correctness of a simulator with respect to a model

Based on the arrangement of system levels shown in Fig. 1, we distinguish between vertical and horizontal relations. A vertical relation is called an *association mapping.* It takes a system at one level of specification and generates its counterpart at another level of specification. The downward motion in the structure-to-behavior direction formally represents the process by which a simulator generates the behavior of a model. It was presented in Chapter 5. The opposite upward mapping relates a system description at a lower level to one at a higher level. While the downward association of specifications is straightforward, the upward association is much less so. Recall from Chapter 1 that this is because to travel in the upward direction requires us to acquire or specify additional system knowledge. Many structures exhibit the same behavior. Thus recovering a unique structure from a given behavior is not possible except in special circumstances, called *justifying conditions.* Please refer to Chapters 14 and 15 of the first edition of *Theory of Modeling and Simulation* [15] for a detailed discussion of these conditions.

In this chapter we will treat the horizontal relations that relate systems at the same level of specification. Corresponding to each of the various levels at which a system may be known, described, or specified is a relation appropriate to a pair of systems residing at that level. We call such a relation a *preservation relation* or *system morphism* because it establishes a correspondence between a pair of systems whereby features of the one system are preserved in the other.

For system morphisms, we take the point of view illustrated in Fig. 2, where S represents a "big" system and S' a "small" system. For example, S could be a base model and S' a lumped model. Accordingly, the basic orientation is that a part of the behavior of the big system S is mapped on the small system S' and the morphism is taken to be *surjective.* System S' therefore represents part of the system S with a certain degree of accuracy (Fig. 2a). On the other hand, we also may employ mappings that go in the other direction,

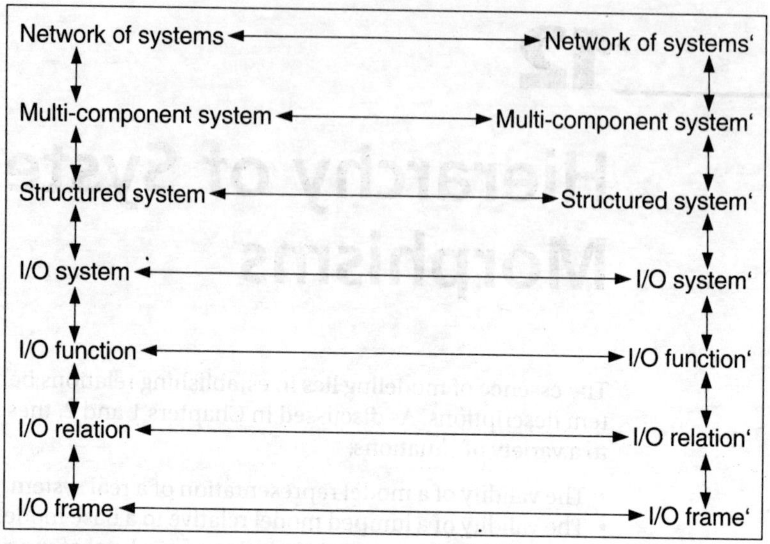

Figure 1 Hierarchy of system specifications, association mappings (vertical), and morphisms (horizontal).

i.e., from the small system to the big one, and we have an *injective* mapping. This ensures that all the behavior of small S' is covered by big S (Fig. 2b).

We shall develop morphisms appropriate to each level of system specification. These morphisms are such that higher level morphisms imply lower level morphisms. This means that a morphism that preserves the structural features of one system in another system at one level also preserves its features at all lower levels. We will show this by employing the association mappings introduced in Chapter 5. For example, consider a morphism between systems at the I/O System Level in Fig. 1. This morphism must be defined so that it induces a morphism at the I/O Function Level between the associated systems at that level and indeed, between the associated systems at the I/O Relation and I/O Frame levels.

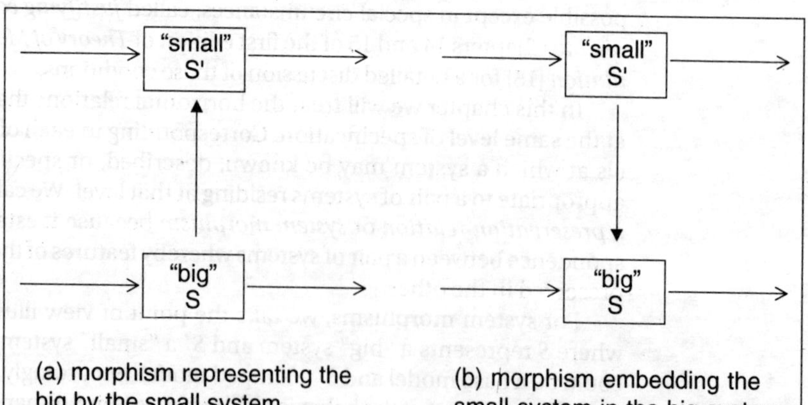

Figure 2 Morphisms between a big system and a small system.

12.1 The I/O Frame Morphism

Recall from Chapter 5 that an I/O frame defines the input and output interface of a system in the form of an input and an output set. We relate two systems $IO = \langle T, X, Y\rangle$ and $IO' = \langle T', X', Y'\rangle$ at the I/O frame level by defining functions to relate the input and outputs interfaces. Let $g: (X', T') \rightarrow (X, T)$ be a function to derive a segment over X given a segment over X'. Let $k: (Y,T) \rightarrow^{onto} (Y', T')$ map in the opposite direction (as in Fig. 4).

If input sets X and X' are identical, output sets Y and Y' are identical, and functions g and k are identity mappings, then IO and IO' are isomorphic at the I/O frame level. Systems isomorphic at the I/O frame level are said to be *compatible*.

12.2 The I/O Relation Observation Morphism

Let S and S' be represented by I/O relation observation (T, X, Ω, Y, R) and $(T', X', \Omega', Y', R')$, respectively. As indicated just now, we want to represent the condition wherein the I/O behavior R' of small S' can be "found in" the I/O behavior R of big S. We take this to mean that if we apply an input segment ω' to S' and observe an output segment ρ', there ought to be an I/O pair $(\omega, \rho) \in R$ corresponding to $(\omega', \rho') \in R'$ (note that this is an example of an mapping from a small system to a big system). This correspondence is to be established by mappings between the segment spaces as follows.

Let $g: \Omega' \rightarrow \Omega$. We call g an *encoding* map or *encoder*. If we apply $\omega' \in \Omega'$, it tells us which $\omega \in \Omega$, namely $g(\omega')$, to apply to S.

Let $k:(Y, T) \rightarrow^{onto} (Y', T')$. We call k a *decoding map,* or *decoder*. If we observe an output segment $\rho \in (Y, T)$ in the big system, it tells which $\rho' \in (Y', T')$ this represents, namely $k(\rho)$.

The condition that every pair $(\omega', \rho') \in R'$ has a corresponding pair $(\omega, \rho) \in R$ can now be stated as follows: An I/O relation morphism from $\langle T', X', \Omega', Y', R'\rangle$ to $\langle T, X, \Omega, Y, R\rangle$ is a pair (g, k) such that

1. $g: \Omega' \rightarrow \Omega$
2. $k: (Y, T) \rightarrow^{onto} (Y', T')$
3. For every pair $(\omega', \rho') \in R'$, there exists $(\omega,\rho) \in R$ such that $\omega = g(\omega')$ and $k(\rho) = \rho'$.

Let us now consider the other case, where a big system S is mapped to a small one S'. Here we are confronted with a situation where the little system has to represent the I/O behavior of the big system up to a certain accuracy.

Let $g: \Omega \rightarrow^{onto} \Omega'$ now be an encoding of the input trajectories from the big system S to the small system S'. If we apply $\omega \in \Omega$, it again tells us to apply $g(\omega)$ to S'. However, some information in Ω might get lost through this mapping. Therefore, it is not possible to find a decoder k that uniquely determines an output segment of the big system. Instead we employ a mapping $k: (Y, T) \rightarrow^{onto} (Y', T')$ from the big system to the small one, which allows us to set the I/O behavior of the system, in to correspondence. We formulate this as follows:

1. $g: \Omega \rightarrow^{\text{onto}} \Omega'$
2. $k:(Y, T) \rightarrow^{\text{onto}} (Y', T')$
3. For every pair $(\omega, \rho) \in R$, there exists $(\omega', \rho') \in R'$ such that $\omega' = g(\omega)$ and $\rho' = k(\rho)$.

This means that for every I/O pair in the big system *S*, there is a I/O pair in *S'* such that these pairs correspond through mappings *g* and *k*. Or in other words, whatever we can observe in the big system we also can observe in the little system—usually at coarser level of granularity.

Example. *Sampled Data Representation of Continuous I/O Signals*
As an example of a I/O behavior morphism, let us consider discrete time encoding of continuous input and output segments. The system *S* in Fig. 3 has a continuous I/O behavior. We encode the input and output segments of *S* by discrete time segments of system *S'*, employing coding functions *g* and *k* as follows.

IORO = $\langle T, X, \Omega, Y, R\rangle$ with $T = X = Y = \Re$ and Ω is the set of bpc segments.
IORO' = $\langle T', X', \Omega', Y', R'\rangle$ with $T' = X' = Y' = \Re$ and Ω is the set of piecewise constant segments with constant length *s* (sample rate). The encoding function $g: \Omega \rightarrow \Omega'$ is defined by $g(\omega)(t) = \omega(t')$; where t' is a multiple of sample rate *s* and just smaller or equal to *t*. In the same way we define $k(\rho)(t) = \rho(t')$.

Obviously, in sampled representation some information has been lost and the original segments cannot be reconstructed to their full extent (however, for bandwidth-constrained signals, there is a sufficiently high sampling rate to permit the original signal to be reconstructed to the desired accuracy).

12.3 The I/O Function Morphism

Corresponding to the level of system knowledge characterized by the I/O function observation (where the starting state of an experiment is given) is the following preservation concept.

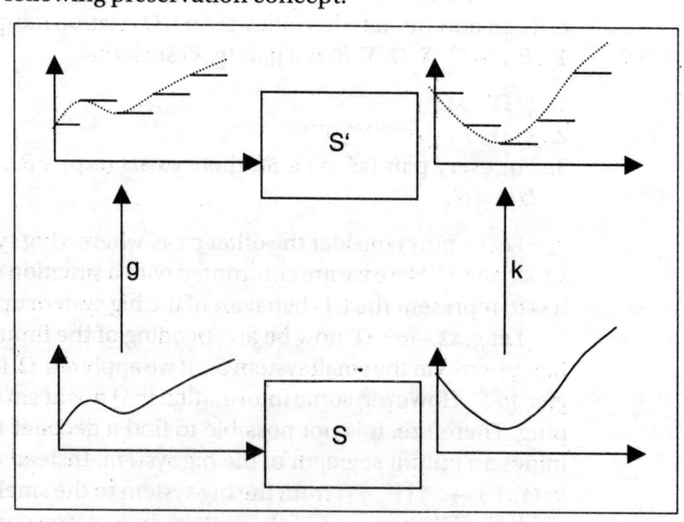

Figure 3 Digital representation of continuous I/O signals.

An I/O function morphism from an IOFO = (T, X, Ω, Y, F) to an IOFO′ = $(T', X', \Omega', Y', F')$ is a pair (g, k) where

1. g: $\Omega' \to \Omega$.
2. k: $(Y, T) \to^{\text{onto}} (Y', T')$.
3. For each $f' \in F'$ there is an $f \in F$ such that $f' = k \circ f \circ g$, i.e., for all $\omega' \in \Omega'$, $f'(\omega') = k(f(g(\omega')))$.

We say that f, f', g, and k form a commutative diagram as shown in Fig. 4. This is interpreted as follows: Suppose the little system S' is in a state whose I/O function is f'. Now an input segment ω' is injected into S' and an output segment $\rho' = f'(\omega')$ is observed—this is the top arrow. On the other hand, suppose the big system S is in a state whose I/O function is f. Then we encode ω' to obtain $\omega = g(\omega')$, inject ω into S, observe the result $\rho = f(\omega)$, and decode ρ to $k(\rho)$— this is the arrow path labeled with g, f, and k. The result is the same for both processes, namely $f'(\omega') = k(f(g(\omega')))$.

Thus, an I/O function morphism runs from S' to S if and only if each of the I/O functions of S' can be realized by an I/O function of S using the same pair (g, k)—every "capability" of small S' can be found in big S with uniform encoding and decoding rules.

Example: Scaling a System to Different Rates

To relate two systems that are essentially the same except that they operate at different rates, let IOFO be derived from the differential equation

$$\frac{dy}{dt} = x$$

and the IOFO′ be derived from the differential equation

$$\frac{dy}{dt} = \tau x.$$

Then both systems IOFO and IOFO′ are integrators, but IOFO′ runs at a rate τ times that of IOFO (consider their responses to a constant input, for example).

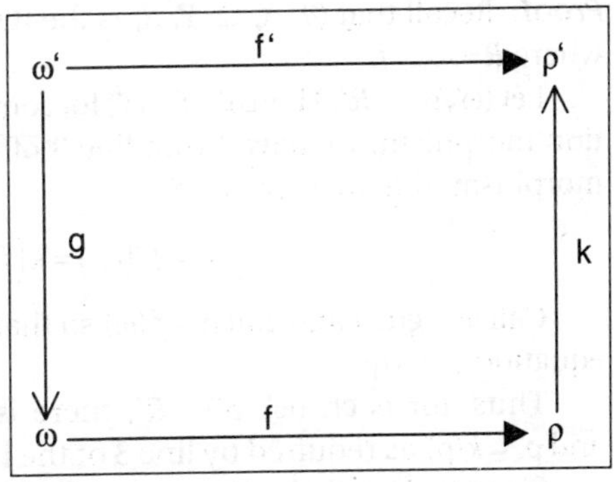

Figure 4 Commutative diagram of I/O function observation.

Let $g: \Omega' \to \Omega$ be given by

$$g(\omega')(t) = \omega'\left(\frac{t}{\tau}\right),$$

with $l(g(\omega')) = l(\omega') \times \tau$, with $l(\omega)$ and $l(\omega')$ being the length of ω and ω', respectively.

Let $k:(Y, T) \to^{\text{onto}} (Y', T')$ be given by

$$k(\rho)(t') = \rho(\tau t'),$$

with $l(k(\rho)) = l(\rho) \times (1/\tau)$, with $l(\rho)$ and $l(\rho')$ again being the length of ρ and ρ'.

Note that g dilates (stretches) a segment to τ times its original width, whereas k does the inverse dilation. (All segments are assumed to begin at zero.)

Exercise: Show that (g, k) is an I/O function morphism for IOFO and IOFO′.◆

Exercise: Show that if $T = T'$, $X = X'$, $\Omega = \Omega'$, and $Y = Y'$, the case $F' \subseteq F$ is given by the I/O function morphism (id, id), with id being the identity mapping.◆

Exercise: The preceding morphism at the IOFO observation level is an example of a morphism from a small system to a big system. Develop, analogous to Fig. 4, a corresponding IOFO morphism concept from a big system to a small system.◆

12.3.1 IOFO System Morphism Implies IORO System Morphism

We now show that an I/O function observation morphism also implies the existence of a weaker morphism at the I/O relation observation level.

Theorem 1

If (g, k) is an I/O function morphism from IOFO $= \langle T, X, \Omega, Y, F\rangle$ to IOFO′ $= \langle T', X', \Omega', Y', F'\rangle$, then (g, k) is also an I/O relation morphism from the IORO associated with IOFO to the IORO′ associated with IOFO′.

Proof: Recall that $\langle T, X, \Omega, Y, R\rangle$ is the IORO associated with (T, X, Ω, Y, F) where $R = \cup_{f \in F} f$.

Let $(\omega', \rho') \in R'$. Then $\rho' = f'(\omega')$ for some $f' \in F'$. Since (g, k) is an I/O function morphism, we have (from line 3 of the definition of the I/O function morphism) that for some $f \in F$,

$$\rho' = f'(\omega') = k(f(g(\omega'))).$$

Call $\omega = g(\omega')$ and call $\rho = f(\omega)$ so that $(\omega, \rho) \in R$. Now by the foregoing equation $\rho' = k(\rho)$.

Thus, for each $(\omega', \rho') \in R'$, there is a pair $(\omega, \rho) \in R$ with $\omega = g(\omega')$ and $\rho' = k(\rho)$ as required by line 3 of the I/O relation morphism definition.

Since (g, k) satisfies lines 1 and 2 of the I/O function and relation morphism directly, we have proved that (g, k) is an I/O relation morphism.■

Exercise: Show directly that $F' \subseteq F$ implies $R' \subseteq R$ (as would be inferred by applying Theorem 1 with $(g,k) = (id, id)$).◆

12.4 The I/O System Morphism

Moving to the next level, we know more about the insides of S and S'. Therefore we have a morphism that preserves the specified structural features. As a specialization, this morphism includes the classical notion of homomorphism (Chapter 1). Since the major element introduced at this level is the state space, we must include an additional mapping that establishes a correspondence between the big and small state sets. We refer to the new morphism as a *system morphism* or a *generalized homomorphism.*

A system morphism from big system $S = \langle T, X, \Omega, Y, Q, \Delta, \Lambda, \rangle$ to small system $S' = \langle T', X', \Omega', Y', Q', \Delta', \Lambda' \rangle$ is a triple (g, h, k) such that

1. $g: \Omega' \to \Omega$
2. $h: \bar{Q} \to^{\text{onto}} Q'$, where $\bar{Q} \subseteq Q$
3. $k: Y \to^{\text{onto}} Y'$

and for all $q \in \bar{Q}$, $\omega' \in \Omega'$,

4. $h(\Delta(q, g(\omega'))) = \Delta'(h(q), \omega')$ *(transition function preservation)*
5. $k(\Lambda(q)) = \Lambda'(h(q))$ *(output function preservation)*[1]

In interpreting line 4, which pertains to the preservation of the state transitions, we start the big system in one of the states q in the restricted set $\bar{Q}$. The map h yields a corresponding state in the small system $q' = h(q)$. We then inject a segment ω' into S' and its encoded version $g(\omega')$ into S—sending them to states $\Delta'(q', \omega')$ in S' and $\Delta(q, g(\omega'))$, respectively. These states also correspond under h, i.e., $h(\Delta(q,g(\omega'))) = \Delta'(q', \omega')$.

Line 5, pertaining to the output function preservation, is interpreted as follows. When big system S is in state q and small system S' is in corresponding state $q' = h(q)$, the output values observed in these states are $y = \Lambda(q)$ and $y' = \Lambda'(q')$, respectively. The value y' is also obtained by decoding y with k, i.e., $y' = k(y)$ or $\Lambda'(q') = k(\Lambda(q))$ (Fig. 5).

Exercise: Show that for the equation in line 4 to be well defined (both sides defined and equal), $\bar{Q}$ must be closed under $g(\Omega')$, i.e., for all $q \in \bar{Q}$, $\omega' \in \Omega'$, $\Delta(q, g(\omega')) \in \bar{Q}$.◆

Consider systems S and S' described over the same observational base, i.e., $T = T'$, $X = X'$, $Y = Y'$, and $\Omega = \Omega'$. S' is a homomorphic image of S if (g, h, k) is a system morphism, where g and k are identity maps and $\bar{Q} = Q$. The map h is said to be a *homomorphism* in this case. Obviously, for compatible systems, S and S', the homomorphism conditions 4 and 5 manifest themselves as

4. $h(\Delta(q,\omega)) = \Delta'(h(q),\omega)$
5. $\Lambda(q)) = \Lambda'(h(q))$

If, in addition, h is a one-to-one, it is an isomorphism, and S and S' are said to be *isomorphic.*

[1] We assume output function $\Lambda: Q \to Y$ only dependent on state in the sequel.

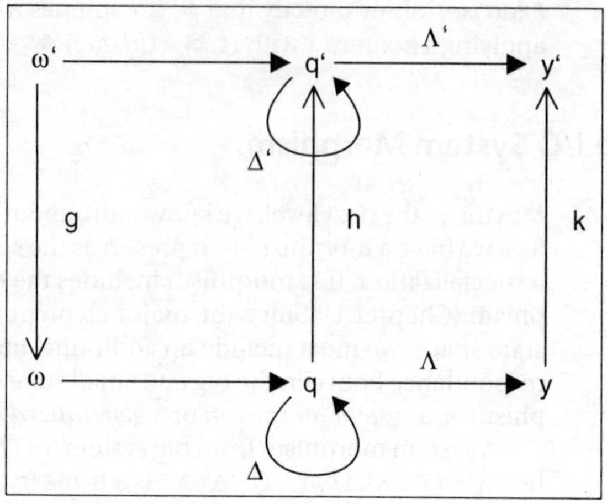

Figure 5 Commutative diagram showing the I/O system morphism.

When S' is a homomorphic image of S, both systems turn out to have the same I/O function behavior, but the difference is that the state space of S' may be much "smaller" than that of S—all the state space Q of S is lumped by h onto that Q' of S'.

When S and S' are isomorphic, there is no essential difference in their structural descriptions at the I/O system level, although they may differ very significantly at higher levels of specification involving more structural detail.

Example:* *Linear System Homomorphism
Let S and S' be compatible linear systems specified by $\{A, B, C\}$ and $\{A', B', C'\}$, respectively (in discrete time, let a common field F be assumed).

The existence of a homomorphism from S to S' can be reduced to relatively simple relation involving the specifications $\{A, B, C\}$ and $\{A', B', C'\}$ as shown by the following theorem.

Theorem 2
Let $H: Q \to^{\text{onto}} Q'$ be a linear mapping. Then H is a homomorphism from S to S' if and only if the following conditions hold:

1. $A'H = HA$
2. $HB = B'$
3. $C'H = C$

Exercise: Prove the theorem for the discrete case using the linear machine formalism in Section 3.2.6.◆

12.4.1 I/O System Morphism Implies IOFO and IORO Morphism

We now show that if S' is a homomorphic image of S, then S and S' have the same I/O function behavior. This result will be generalized to demonstrate that the holding of a general preservation relation between systems at the I/O system level implies the existence of preservation relations at the lower (behavioral) levels. However, some additional considerations will have to be brought in to achieve this generalization. So we start with the most straightforward case first.

We say that two states (of the same or different systems) are behaviorally equivalent if they have the same I/O function, i.e.,

$$q \equiv q' \quad \text{if} \quad \tilde{\beta}_q = \tilde{\beta}'_{q'}.$$

We say that two systems S and S' are behaviorally equivalent if $\tilde{B}_S = \tilde{B}_{S'}$, i.e., if for each state $q \in Q$, there is a state $q' \in Q'$ such that $\tilde{\beta}_q = \tilde{\beta}_{q'}$ (q and q' are equivalent), and conversely.

Exercise: Show that $\tilde{B}_S = \tilde{B}'_{S'} \Rightarrow R_S = R'_{S'}$ (S, S' are relationally equivalent).◆

We can now consider the fundamental theorem on behaviorally equivalence of compatible systems.

Theorem 3

Let $h\colon Q \rightarrow^{\text{onto}} Q'$ be a homomorphism from S to S'. Then $\tilde{B}_S = \tilde{B}'_{S'}$ (S and S' are behaviorally equivalent).

Proof: We show first that for each $q \in Q$, $h(q)$ is equivalent to q. Consider the last output function $\beta'_{h(q)}$. For $\omega \in \Omega$,

$$\begin{aligned}
\beta'_{h(q)}(\omega) &= \Lambda'\big(\Lambda'(h(q), \omega)\big) \\
&= \Lambda'\big(h(\Delta(q,\omega))\big) && \text{(from 4 of homomorphism of compatible systems)} \\
&= \Lambda\big(\Delta(q,\omega)\big) && \text{(from 5 of homomorphism of compatible systems)} \\
&= \beta_q(\omega).
\end{aligned}$$

Since h is onto Q', every state q' of S' has a representative state $q \in h^{-1}(q')$ such that $h(q) = q'$. Thus, $\tilde{B}_{S'} = \{\tilde{\beta}'_{q'} | q' \in Q'\} = \{\tilde{\beta}'_{h(q)} \mid q \in Q\} \subseteq \tilde{B}_S$. But also, since h is defined on all of Q, for each $q \in Q$ there is a state $h(q) \in Q'$; thus, $B_S \subseteq B_{S'}$. Thus, $\tilde{B}_S = \tilde{B}_{S'}$. ■

The essence of the preceding theorem generalizes to a broader class of system morphisms. First we have the following theorem.

Theorem 4

If (i, h, i) is a system morphism from S to S', then (i, i) is an I/O function morphism from IOFO_S to $\text{IOFO}_{S'}$ (hence, an I/O relation morphism from IORO_S to $\text{IORO}_{S'}$). In other words, if S' is a homomorphic image of a subsystem of S, then $\tilde{B}'_{S'} \subseteq \tilde{B}_S$ and $R'_{S'} \subseteq R_S$.

Proof: An easy corollary of the preceding theorem.

We now would like to show, more generally that, if (g, h, k) is a system morphism from S to S', there is also an I/O function morphism from S to S'. Unfortunately, this is not necessarily true for an arbitrary encoding g. To see why, consider the following lemma.

Lemma 1

Let (g, h, k) be a system morphism from S to S'. Then for each $q \in Q$, we have

$$\beta'_{h(q)} = k \circ \beta_q \circ g.$$

Exercise: Prove the lemma.◆

This tells us that the *last output* functions of corresponding states match up, but it does not allow us to conclude that the same is true for the I/O functions, which are obtained by applying the last output functions to successive left segments to obtain segment-to-segment mappings. The correspondence between last outputs must be maintained as this extension is being performed. More specifically, the g mapping must preserve left segmentation. Also, since the k map of the I/O function morphism cannot look at the input segment, the g map must allow such a map to be definable on the basis of k alone.

Thus, let us say that $g: \Omega' \to \Omega$ is *invertible* if

1. *g preserves left segmentation:* $\omega'_{t>}$ is a left segment of $\omega' \Rightarrow g(\omega'_{t>})$ is a left segment of $g(\omega')$
2. *g is one-to-one on length:* $l(\omega'_1) = l(\omega'_2) \Leftrightarrow l(g(\omega'_1)) = l(g(\omega'_2))$

These properties of g are precisely the ones enabling us to match up instants in an observation interval of the small system with uniquely corresponding instants in the corresponding observation interval of the big system. This is shown by the following lemma.

Lemma 2

g is an invertible coding if and only if there is a one-to-one (partial) function $MATCH: T'^{+}_0 \to T^{+}_0$ such that

$$MATCH(l(\omega')) = l(g(\omega'))$$

$$g(\omega'_{t>}) = g(\omega')_{MATCH(t)>}.$$

With this matching of computation instants $l(\omega')$ and $l(g(\omega'))$, we can define a decoding map $\bar{k}: (Y, T) \to (Y', T')$ as follows.

For any $\rho \in (Y, T)$, $\bar{k}(\rho)$ has length $l(\bar{k}(\rho)) = MATCH^{-1}(l(\rho))$ and

$$\bar{k}(\rho)(t') = k(\rho(MATCH(t'))) \quad \text{for } t' \in \text{dom}\,(\bar{k}(\rho)).$$

Exercise: Check that $\bar{k}$ is well defined in carrying any segment ρ of the big system to a unique segment $\bar{k}(\rho)$ of the small system.◆

Now, using the two previous lemmas, we can obtain a strengthened lemma.

Lemma 3

Let (g, h, k) where g is invertible, be a system morphism from S to S'. Then for each $q \in Q$,

$$\beta'_{h(q)} = \bar{k} \circ \beta_q \circ g,$$

where $\bar{k}$ is defined as before.

Exercise: Prove the lemma.◆
Finally we have the desired theorem.

Theorem 5
If (g, h, k), where g is invertible, is a system morphism from S to S', there is an I/O function morphism $(g, \bar{k})$ from $IOFO_S$ to $IOFO_{S'}$, and hence an I/O relation morphism from $IORO_S$ to $IORO_{S'}$.

The proof follows the lines of the above theorem and is left as an exercise for the reader.

Exercise: If h is a homomorphism from S to S', show that for each $q' \in Q'$, the set $h^{-1}(q')$ is a set of equivalent states.◆

We learn in the next section that the converse of the last statement is also true. That is, if we are given a partition of the sates of S whose blocks consist of equivalent states, we can construct a homomorphic image of S.

12.4.2 The Lattice of Partitions and the Reduced Version of a System

Any system has a "reduced version" that represents the most that can be inferred about the structure of S from external observation, i.e., its behavior. Seen from the opposite direction—going from structure to behavior—it turns out that the reduced version is also the system having the "minimal" state set needed to generate the behavior. Thus, the reduced version S_R of a system S has a number of interesting and useful properties that are important in structural inference [15] and system representation (Chapter 15).

From here on we restrict our attention to systems whose input segment set Ω contains the null segment Φ. This segment has the useful property that $\Delta(q, \Phi) = q$ for any system state q, and $\Phi \bullet \omega = \omega$ for any segment ω. This restriction is a matter of convenience, since essentially the same results can be obtained without it.

State partitioning is the means to define a reduced version of a system. Let us therefore first review basic concepts and operations of partitions of sets.

Let P_A denote the set of all partitions of a set A. It is well known that P_A is a lattice with underlying partial order $\leq$ given by

$$\pi_1 \leq \pi_2 \Leftrightarrow \left(\forall a, a' \in A\right)\left(a\ \pi_1\ a' \Rightarrow a\ \pi_2\ a'\right).$$

We say that π_1 is a *refinement* or π_2 or π_1 *refines* π_2.

Two operations are defined for partitions. The *least upper bound* (lub) and *greatest lower bound* (glb) operators are denoted by $\cap$ and $\cup$, respectively. The glb operator is defined so that $\pi_1 \cap \pi_2$ is the greatest partition with

$$a\left(\pi_1 \cap \pi_2\right)a' \Leftrightarrow a\left(\pi_1\right)a' \,\&\, a\left(\pi_2\right)a'.$$

The lub operator is defined so that $\pi_1 \cup \pi_2$ is the smallest partition with

$$a\left(\pi_1 \cup \pi_2\right)a' \Leftrightarrow \exists a = a_1, a_2, \ldots, a_n = a'$$

such that $a_i(\pi_1)a_{i+1}$ for all odd i & $a_i(\pi_2)a_{i+1}$ for all even i.

These definitions satisfy the required conditions, namely, that $\pi \leq \pi_1$ & $\pi \leq \pi_2$ implies $\pi \leq \pi_1 \cap \pi_2$ and $\pi_1 \leq \pi$ & $\pi_2 \leq \pi$ implies $\pi_1 \cup \pi_2 \leq \pi$. The finest partition 0 (the partition with all blocks containing a single element) is defined by

$$a0a' \Leftrightarrow a = a'$$

and the coarsest partition I (the partition with one block only containing all elements) is defined by

$$aIa' \Leftrightarrow a, a' \in A.$$

A partition of a state set of a dynamical system is said to be a *congruence* relation ≡ if and only if

$$q \equiv q' \Rightarrow (\forall \omega \in \Omega)(\Delta(q,\omega) \equiv \Delta(q',\omega)),$$

i.e., if two states are congruent, all next states for all input segments are congruent.

Theorem 6

The set of all congruence relations ≡ of a state set Q of a system with state transition Δ forms a sublattice of all partitions P_Q of state set Q.

Exercise: Prove this.◆

The equivalence relation induces a partition on the set Q consisting of the equivalence classes that we denote by

$$Q/\equiv_R = \{[q]_{\equiv_R} \mid q \in Q\}.$$

where $[q]_{\equiv R}$ denotes the block containing q. Furthermore, we call a congruence relation *output consistent* if and only if congruent states are behavioral equivalent:

$$q \equiv q' \Rightarrow \Lambda(q) = \Lambda(q').$$

We are able to apply the behavioral equivalence relation introduced in Section 12.4.1 to states of the same system. Doing so we obtain an output consistent congruence relations.

Theorem 7

A equivalence relation ≡ induced by a homomorphism $h: Q \rightarrow^{\text{onto}} Q$ on a state set Q is

(a) congruent
(b) output consistent

Proof:

Exercise: Show that $\beta_q(\omega \bullet \omega') = \beta_q(\omega) \bullet \beta_{\Delta(q,\omega)}(\omega')$.◆

$$\text{(a)}\quad q \equiv q' \Rightarrow \tilde{\beta}_q = \tilde{\beta}_{q'} \Rightarrow (\forall \omega \in \Omega)(\tilde{\beta}_q(\omega) = \tilde{\beta}_{q'}(\omega))$$

$$\Rightarrow (\forall \omega \in \Omega)(\forall \omega' \in \Omega)(\tilde{\beta}_q(\omega\omega') = \tilde{\beta}_{q'}(\omega\omega'))$$

$$\Rightarrow (\forall \omega \in \Omega)(\forall \omega' \in \Omega)(\tilde{\beta}_q(\omega)\,\tilde{\beta}_{\Delta(q,\omega)}(\omega') = \tilde{\beta}_{q'}(\omega)\,\tilde{\beta}_{\Delta(q',\omega)}(\omega'))$$

$$\Rightarrow (\forall \omega \in \Omega)(\forall \omega' \in \Omega)(\tilde{\beta}_{\Delta(q,\omega)}(\omega') = \tilde{\beta}_{\Delta(q',\omega)}(\omega'))$$

$$\Rightarrow (\forall \omega \in \Omega)(\Delta(q,\omega) \equiv \Delta(q',\omega))$$

(b) $q \equiv q' \Rightarrow \tilde{\beta}_q(\Phi) = \tilde{\beta}_{q'}(\Phi) \Rightarrow \Lambda(\Delta(q,\Phi)) = \Lambda(\Delta(q',\Phi))$
$\Rightarrow \Lambda(q) = \Lambda(q')$■

The reduced version S_R of a system $S = \langle T, X, \Omega, Y, Q, \Delta, \Lambda\rangle$ is defined as follows. Let $\equiv_R$ be the *maximal* output consistent congruence relation. Then we define S_R as

$$S_R = \langle T, X, \Omega, Y, Q/\equiv_R, \Delta/\equiv_R, \Lambda/\equiv_R\rangle,$$

where $\Delta/\equiv_R: Q/\equiv_R \times \Omega \rightarrow Q/\equiv_R$ is defined by

$$\Delta/\equiv_R\left([q]_{\equiv_R}, \omega\right) = \left[\Delta(q,\omega)\right]_{\equiv_R}$$

and $\Lambda/\equiv_R: Q/\equiv_R \rightarrow Y$ is defined by

$$\Lambda/\equiv_R\left([q]_{\equiv_R}\right) = \Lambda(q).$$

Theorem 8
If S is a system, so is S_R.

Proof: Use the preceding lemma to show that $\Delta/\equiv_R$ and $\Lambda/\equiv_R$ are well defined. Then check that $\Delta/\equiv_R$ has the composition property.■

We say that S is **reduced** if for all pairs $q, q' \in Q$, $\tilde{\beta}_q = \tilde{\beta}_{q'} \Rightarrow q = q'$. In other words, each state q has a distinct I/O function $\tilde{\beta}_q$ associated with it.

Exercise: Show that S is reduced if and only if for each distinct pair $q, q' \in Q$, there is an input segment ω that will cause S to respond with different output segments when started in states q and q'.◆

The following theorem presents the important properties of reduced version S_R of the system S.

Theorem 9

(a) S_R is reduced.
(b) S_R is a homomorphic image of S.
(c) S_R is behaviorally equivalent to S.
(d) For any system S', if S' is behaviorally equivalent to S and S' is reduced, S' is isomorphic to S_R.

Proof: We show first by a straightforward expansion

$$\tilde{\beta}_{[q]_{\equiv_R}} = \tilde{\beta}_q \quad \text{for all } q \in Q.$$

Then (a) and (c) follow immediately for this result. For (b), we consider the mapping $h: Q \rightarrow Q/\equiv_R$ given by $h(q) = [q]_{\equiv_R}$. Then by direct verification h is a homomorphism.

For (d) we establish a mapping h': $Q' \rightarrow Q/\equiv_R$ of states to their corresponding equivalence classes just as h does. Using the same approach we can show h' is a homomorphism and since S' is reduced, it is also one-one. Thus, isomorphism is established.■

The theorem establishes that the reduced version of a system is rather special—it is a homomorphic image of any other behaviorally equivalent system and is thus called *minimal* (in finite state systems it has the smallest number of states). It is also *unique* in the sense that any way of arriving at the reduced version will result in a system that is isomorphic to it.

12.5 System Morphism for Iteratively Specified Systems

We have seen in Chapter 5 that it is possible to implicitly specify a system structure by providing an iterative specification, G. For iterative specifications we will define an appropriate system morphism with the following natural requirement: If the morphism runs from G to G', then when G is expanded to S_G and G' is expanded to $S_{G'}$, this will imply the existence of a system morphism running from S_G to $S_{G'}$.

To develop the concept, we must first construct an input segment encoding map in such a way that a segment can be encoded by composing the encoded versions of the generators in its mls decomposition.

Thus, let Ω_G and Ω'_G be an admissible set of generators. Let $\bar{g} : \Omega'_G \to \Omega^+_G$ be a *generator encoding* map, so that with each generator $\omega' \in \Omega'_G$ (the little input generator set) there is associated a segment $\bar{g}\,(\omega')$, its coded version (which is not necessarily a generator of the big input set generator set). We extend $\bar{g}$ to an encoder $g: \Omega'^+_G \to \Omega^+_G$ by the definition

$$g(\omega') = \bar{g}(\omega'_1)\,\bar{g}(\omega'_2)\ldots\,\bar{g}(\omega'_n) \qquad \text{for } \omega' \in \Omega'^+_G,$$

where $\omega'_1, \omega'_2, \ldots \omega'_n$ is the mls decomposition for ω'. Now g is well defined because of the uniqueness of the mls decomposition.

For iterative specifications $G = \langle T, X, \Omega_G, Y, Q, \delta, \lambda\rangle$ and $G' = \langle T', X', \Omega'_G, Y', Q', \delta', \lambda'\rangle$, a *specification morphism from* G′ to G is a triple $(\bar{g}, h, k)$ such that

1. $\bar{g} : \Omega'_G \to \Omega^+_G$
2. h: $\bar{Q} \to^{\text{onto}} Q'$, where $\bar{Q} \subseteq Q$.
3. k: $Y \to^{\text{onto}} Y'$

and for all $q \in \bar{Q}$, $\omega' \in \Omega'_G$

4. $h(\delta^+(q, \bar{g}\,(\omega'))) = \delta'(h(q), \omega')$ (*transition function preservation*)
5. $k(\lambda(q)) = \lambda'(h(q))$ (*output function preservation*)

Note that lines 4 and 5 are very similar to lines 4 and 5 of the I/O system morphism definition. The major difference is that, in the present specification morphism, the transition function preservation need only be checked for the generators of the little system Ω'_G.

We say that $\bar{g}$ is *generator preserving* if $\bar{g}\,(\Omega'_G) \subseteq \Omega_G$. Since in this case, for each generator $\omega' \in \Omega'_G$, $\bar{g}\,(\omega')$ is also a generator, the function δ need not be extended, and line 4 can read

$$4'.\ h(\delta\,(q, \bar{g}\,(\omega'))) = \delta'(h(q), \omega').$$

This means that the specification morphism can be checked directly by examining the generator transition functions δ and δ'.

12.5.1 Iterative Specification Morphism Implies I/O System Morphism

The next theorem establishes the procedure for expanding a specification morphism into a system morphism. The importance of this, as we have indicated, comes in checking whether a system morphism runs from a big to a little system. To establish such a morphism we need to verify only that a specification morphism runs from the *iterative specification* of the one to that of the other. The expansion procedure is then guaranteed by the theorem and need not be carried out.

Theorem 10
If $(\bar{g}, h, k)$ is a specification morphism from G to G', then (g, h, k) is a system morphism from S_G to $S_{G'}$, where g is the extension of $\bar{g}$.

Proof: We need show only that line 4 holds in the system morphism definition. This is done using induction on the proposition

$$P(n) \equiv \Big[\text{if } \omega' \in \Omega_G'^{+} \text{ has the mls decomposition } \omega_1', \omega_2', \ldots \omega_n' \\ \text{then for all } q \in \bar{Q}: h\big(\delta^+(q, g(\omega'))\big) = \delta'^+\big(h(q), \omega'\big)\Big].$$

$P(1)$ is just line 4 of the specification morphism definition. Assuming that $P(n-1)$ holds, we can show that $P(n)$ holds. Let ω' have mls decomposition $\omega_1', \omega_2', \ldots, \omega_n'$ and let $q \in \bar{Q}$. Then write

$$\begin{aligned}
h\big(\delta^+(q, g(\omega_1'\omega_2'\ldots\omega_n'))\big) &= h\big(\delta^+(q, \bar{g}(\omega_1')g(\omega_2'\ldots\omega_n'))\big) && \text{(definition of } g) \\
&= h\big(\delta^+(\delta(q, \bar{g}(\omega_1')), g(\omega_2'\ldots\omega_n'))\big) && \text{(composition property of } \delta^+) \\
&= \delta'^+\big(h(\delta(q, \bar{g}(\omega_1'))), \omega_2'\ldots\omega_n'\big) && (P(n-1) \text{ using } \omega_2', \ldots, \omega_n' \text{ as the mls decomposition of } \omega_2'\ldots\omega_n') \\
&= \delta'^+\big(\delta'(h(q), \omega_1'), \omega_2'\ldots\omega_n'\big) && (P(1)) \\
&= \delta'^+\big(h(q), \omega_1'\omega_2'\ldots\omega_n'\big) && \text{(composition property of } \delta^{+\prime})
\end{aligned}$$

Thus, $P(n)$ holds, and by the principle of induction, the theorem, which asserts $P(n)$ for all n, is established.■

Exercise: Show that if (g, h, k) is a system morphism from S_G to $S_{G'}$, then $(\bar{g}, h, k)$ is a specification morphism from G to G' where $\bar{g} = g \mid \Omega_G'$. Thus there is a system morphism from S_G to $S_{G'}$ if and only if there is a specification morphism from G to G'.◆

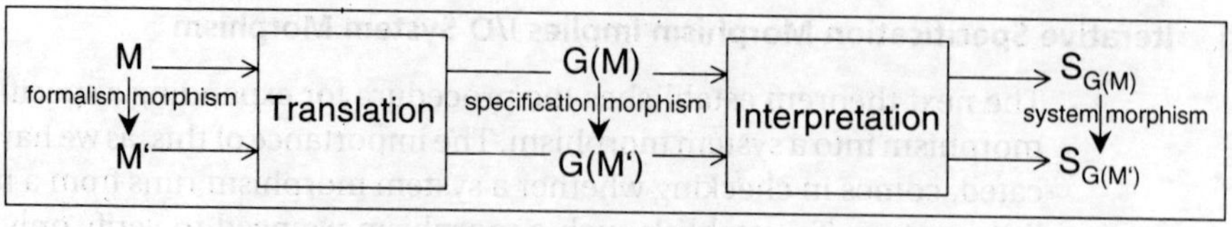

Figure 6 Specialization of specification morphisms.

12.5.2 Specialization of Morphisms for Iteratively Specified Systems

Just as we can further specialize the iterative specification schemes to the discrete time, differential equation, and discrete event cases, we can provide appropriate specializations of the specification morphism. The procedure is depicted in Fig. 6.

We shall describe the expansion for the discrete time and discrete event cases.

DTSS Specification Morphisms

Let $M = \langle X_M, Y_M, Q_M, \delta_M, \lambda_M, h\rangle$ and $M' = \langle X'_M, Y'_M, Q'_M, \delta'_M, \lambda'_M, h'\rangle$ be DTSS. The appropriate morphism is as follows: $(\overline{\overline{g}}, h, k)$ is a *discrete time morphism* from M to M' if

1. $\overline{\overline{g}} : X'_M \to X^+_M$
2. $h: \overline{Q}_M \to^{\text{onto}} Q'_M$, where $\overline{Q}_M \subseteq Q_M$
3. $k: Y_M \to^{\text{onto}} Y'_M$

and for all $q \in \overline{Q}$, $x' \in X'_M$,

4. $h(\delta^+_M(q, \overline{\overline{g}}(x'))) = \delta'_M(h(q), x')$
5. $k(\lambda_M(q)) = \lambda'_M(h(q))$

The translation to a specification morphism is very straightforward in this case. The generator segments for DTSS are as follows: $\Omega_{G(M')} = \{\omega_x \mid x \in X, \omega_x : <0, 1> \to \{x\}\}$. The translated morphism is $(\overline{g}, h, k)$ running from $S_{G(M)}$ to $S_{G(M')}$, where $\overline{g} : \Omega_{G(M')} \to \Omega_{G(M)}$ is defined by $\overline{g}(\omega_x) = \omega_{\overline{\overline{g}}(x)}$.

Discrete Event Case

We give as an example the construction of a homomorphism for discrete event specifications. Let $M = \langle X_M, Y_M, S_M, \delta_{ext,M}, \delta_{int,M}, \lambda_M, ta_M\rangle$ and $M' = \langle X'_M, Y'_M, S'_M, \delta'_{ext,M}, \delta'_{int,M}, \lambda'_M, ta'_M\rangle$ be legitimate DEVSs, where $X_M = X'_M$, $Y_M = Y'_M$. A DEVS homomorphism from M to M' is a map $\overline{h}$ such that

$$\overline{h} : S_M \to^{\text{onto}} S'_M,$$

and for all $(s, e) \in Q_M$, $x \in X_M$,

1. $\overline{h}(\delta_{ext,M}(s, e, x)) = \delta'_{ext,M}(\overline{h}(s), e, x))$
2. $\lambda'_M(\overline{h}(s)) = \lambda_M(s)$
3. $\overline{h}(\delta_{int,M}(s)) = \delta'_{int,M}(\overline{h}(s))$
4. $ta'_M(\overline{h}(s)) = ta_M(s)$

The translation of the homomorphism $\bar{h}$ to a specification morphism is given by

Theorem 11
Let $\bar{h}$ be a DEVS homomorphism from M to M'. Let $h: Q_M \rightarrow^{\text{onto}} Q'_M$ be a map such that $h(s, e) = (\bar{h}(s), e)$ for all $(s, e) \in Q_M$. Then $\bar{h}$ is a (specification) homomorphism from $G(M)$ to $G(M')$.

Proof: The proof employs the following sequence of assertions, which are left to the reader as an exercise.

(a) h is an onto map.
(b) $\#((s, e), \varnothing_\tau) = \#((\bar{h}\,(s), e), \varnothing_\tau$ where $\#(q, \omega)$ is the number of transitions for initial state q and input segment ω (see Chapter 6, Section 6.2.3).
(c) $\bar{h}\,(\delta_{int,M}(s) = \delta'_{int,M}(\bar{h}(s))$
(d) $h(\delta_G(s, e, \varnothing_\tau)) = \delta'_G(h\,(s, e), \varnothing_\tau)$
(e) $h(\delta_G(s, e, x_\tau)) = \delta'_G(h\,(s, e), x_\tau)$
(f) $\lambda'(h(s)) = \lambda(s)$.

Assertions (d), (e), and (f) show that (i, h, i) is a specification morphism from $G(M)$ to $G(M')$, and since h has domain Q_M, h is a homomorphism from $G(M)$ to $G(M')$.■

12.6 The Structured System Morphism

A system at the structured system level differs from an I/O system by its structuring of sets and functions. The sets of a structured system takes the form of a multivariable set $S = (V, S_1, S_2, S_3, \ldots)$ identifying an ordered set of variables $V = (v_1, v_2, \ldots, v_n)$. The functions are multivariable, which means that they take a multivariable set as its domain and a multivariable set as its range. Recall that a multivariable function $f: A \rightarrow B$ can be represented as a crossproduct of coordinate functions $f \cdot v_i : A \rightarrow ((v_i), B_i)$ with one function for each variable v_i of the range set B_i. We want a morphism at this level not only to preserve the relations between input, states, and output sets of the big and little system as defined at the I/O system level, but also to preserve the structural properties as defined by the structuring of sets and transition and output functions.

To introduce a morphism at the structured system level, we construct a system homomorphism from the big to the little system. Let S be the big system and S' the little system, both at the structured system level. There is a structured system homomorphism $h: Q \rightarrow^{\text{onto}} Q'$ from S to S' if h is a I/O system homomorphism for the two I/O systems associated with S and S', respectively, and we require that the homomorphism takes a special form as follows:

Let *coord:* $V \rightarrow^{\text{onto}} V'$ be a mapping from the variable set V of Q onto the variable set V' of Q'. Let $V_{v'_i} = coord^{-1}\,(v'_i)$ be the subset of variables of V mapped to v'_i. Then we require that the homomorphism h from Q onto Q' be composed of functions

$$h_{v_i'}:Q\cdot V_{v_i'}\rightarrow Q'\cdot v_i'$$

for each $v_i' \in V'$. Thus, a structured systems homomorphism is constructed as a composite of local coordinate maps. Because of its construction the structure morphism can be rephrased to emphasize that the global homomorphism condition reduces to a series of local function preserving conditions

$$h_{v_i'}\left(\Delta(q,\omega)\cdot V_{v_i'}\right) = \Delta'\left(h(q),\omega\right)\cdot v_i'.$$

Example:* *Structure Morphism for Linear Systems

For simplicity consider a linear system having no inputs and outputs. Such a system is specified by a single matrix A and *we* have either a discrete time specification $M = \langle Q, \delta\rangle$ in which Q is a vector space over a field and $\delta(q) = Aq$ or a continuous time system $S_A^{cont} = \langle T, Q, \delta\rangle$ in which $T = R$, Q is a vector space over the reals and $\delta(q, 0_t) = e_q^{At}$, where we use 0_t (zero-valued input of length t) to represent the running of the system for an observation interval of length t.

For two systems specified by A and A' we know from Example 3 that a linear map $H: Q \rightarrow^{\text{onto}} Q'$ is a homomorphism just in case

$$A'H = HA$$

But now let us restrict H so that it carries out an aggregation. This permits us to derive conditions on A which allow S_A to be lumped to a system S'_A.

Let $\{e_1, e_2, \ldots, e_n\}$ be a basis for Q so that every element q of Q is represented by a list $(q_1, q_2, \ldots, q_n)$ such that $q = \Sigma_{i=1}^{n} q_i e_i$. Thus the basis vectors $\{e_i\}$ become the coordinates of a coordinatization of Q, and their range sets are the same underlying field. Note that another choice of basis set $\{f_1, f_2, \ldots, f_n\}$ would induce another coordinatization of Q, where each element q would be represented by a list $(q_1', q_2', \ldots, q_n')$. The primed q's are related to the unprimed q's because $q = \Sigma_{i=1}^{n} q_i' f_i = \Sigma_{i=1}^{n} q_i e_i$. (Linear algebra, of course, tells us that all such bases have the same number of elements.)

With respect to basis $\{e_i\}$, the linear mapping $A: Q \rightarrow Q$ is represented by a matrix $[a_{ij}]$ so that the operation $\bar{q} = Aq$ is represented by

$$\begin{bmatrix}\bar{q}_1\\ \vdots \\ \bar{q}_n\end{bmatrix} = \begin{bmatrix} a_{11} & \cdots & a_{1n} \\ \vdots & & \vdots \\ a_{n1} & \cdots & a_{nn}\end{bmatrix}\begin{bmatrix} q_1 \\ \vdots \\ q_n\end{bmatrix}$$

or in other words,

$$\bar{q}_i = \sum_{j=1}^{n} a_{ij} q_j \qquad \text{for} \quad i = 1, 2, \ldots, n$$

Exercise: In the discrete time case show how the foregoing operation provides a structure for the transition function δ.◆

Not let us consider a partition of the coordinates $D = \{e_1, \ldots, e_n\}$. Call the partition $D' = \{e_1', \ldots, e_m'\}$ so that each e_i is a subset of D, disjoint from the rest, and the union of all such blocks is exactly D. For example, if $D = \{e_1, e_2, \ldots, e_n\}$, then D' might be $\{e_1', e_2', e_3'\}$, where $e_1' = \{e_1, e_2, e_3\}$, $e_2' = \{e_4, e_5, e_6\}$, and $e_3' = \{e_7, e_8\}$.

Now D' will serve as the coordinate set for our little system, and each coordinate will have the same range set. This will be the same field given previously. Thus the state set Q' of the little system will be a vector space of dimension m where each element q' is represented by a list $(q'_1, \ldots, q'_m)$ such that $q' = \Sigma_{i=1}^{m} q'_i e'_i$.

Our coordinate mapping $d : D \overset{\text{onto}}{\to} D'$ is the natural one given by $d(e_i) = e'_j$, where $e_i \in e'_j$. In our example, $d(e_1) = e'_1$, $d(e_4) = e'_2$, and so on.

Exercise: Show that because D' is a partition of D, d is well defined and onto.◆

Now we will require that $H: Q \to Q'$ operate by summing up the coordinate values in a block, separately for each block. In other words, for each coordinate e'_i, the local mapping $h_{e'_i}$ is given by

$$h_{e'_i}(q_j, q_k, \ldots, q_s) = q_j + q_k + \cdots + q_s$$

where $e'_i = \{e_j, e_k, \ldots, e_s\}$. Then H is the aggregation of the $\{h_{e'_i}\}$.

Actually it is easy to show that H has a very simple specification, namely, that for each $e_j \in D$,

$$He_j = d(e_j)$$

Exercise: Show that the preceding statement is true. Also show that H is onto.◆

This leads to a very simple matrix representation for H, consisting entirely of columns containing exactly one 1 and the rest zeros. Also at least one 1 is found in any row. In our example, H is represented by

$$\begin{bmatrix} 1 & 1 & 1 & 0 & 0 & 0 & 0 & 0 \\ 0 & 0 & 0 & 1 & 1 & 1 & 0 & 0 \\ 0 & 0 & 0 & 0 & 0 & 0 & 1 & 1 \end{bmatrix}$$

Now we ask under what circumstances is there a linear map $A' : Q' \to Q'$ for which $A'H = HA$? This is answered in

Theorem 12 Conditions for Lumpability

Given A and linear aggregation H, there is a matrix A' such that $A'H = HA$ if and only if for each $e'_r \in D'$, and $e_j, e_k \in e'_p$, we have

$$\sum_{e_i \in e'_r} a_{ij} = \sum_{e_i \in e'_r} a_{ik}$$

The conditions in Theorem 12 place special requirements on matrix A, namely, that if it is blocked off according to the partition D' in both vertical and horizontal directions, *sums of elements down columns within blocks must be equal.*

Exercise: Convince yourself that Theorem 8 is true by one or more of the following methods.◆

(*a*) Argue directly from the basic meaning of homomorphism in the sequential machine case.

(*b*) Examine the matrix equation $A'H = HA$ when H takes the special matrix form indicated.

(*c*) Give a formal abstract algebra proof, examining the equation $A'He_j = HAe_j$ for an arbitrary basis vector e_j.

The lumpability condition expresses a principle of "uniformity of influence" that we meet with again in Chapter 13. It requires that for every pair of blocks e'_r and e'_p, the total influence of block e'_r on elements of e'_p be the same for all the elements of e'_p.

12.7 Multicomponent System Morphism

A morphism at the multicomponent system level should preserve not only the structural properties of the state set, but also the coupling structure between pairs of component systems. Therefore, a morphism at this level will consist, first, of local mappings of blocks of components in the big system to their representatives in the small system and, second, of *coupling preservation conditions* guaranteeing that the components in the big and the little system are coupled in like manner. We show that under the coupling preservation conditions, the composite of the local preservation conditions define a global morphism at the I/O system level. For simplicity of exposition, we assume that the two multicomponent systems to be related are compatible and a homomorphism is established between them.

Let $MC = \langle T, X, \Omega, Y, D, \{M_d\}\rangle$ be a big multicomponent system with components $M_d = \langle Q_d, E_d, I_d, \Delta_d, \Lambda_d\rangle$, and let $MC' = \langle T', X', \Omega', Y', D', \{M'_{d'}\}\rangle$ be a little multicomponent system with components $M'_{d'} = \langle Q'_{d'}, E'_{d'}, I'_{d'}, \Delta'_{d'}, \Lambda'_{d'}\rangle$. Since MC and MC' are compatible, it follows that $X = X'$, $Y = Y'$, $T = T'$, and $\Omega = \Omega'$.

Let $coord: D \rightarrow^{onto} D'$ be a mapping from the set of components D of MC onto the set of components D' of MC'. Let $D_{d'} = coord^{-1}(d')$ be the subset of components of D mapped to d'. We'll call $D_{d'}$ the *representing block* of d'. Note that since *coord* is a function, the representing blocks, $D_{d'}$ form a partition of D. Then we require that the global map

$$h: \times_{d \in D} Q_d \rightarrow \times_{d' \in D'} Q'_{d'}$$

from the state set of MC onto that of MC' be composed of *local* functions

$$h_{d'}: \times_{d \in D_{d'}} Q_d \rightarrow Q'_{d'}$$

for each $d' \in D'$ defined on the states of representing blocks.

To guarantee the preservation of the structural properties, we require that the influences between components in the little systems also be present, at a finer level, in the big system (*coupling preservation condition*). Note that this allows some of the influences in the big system to be lost in the small system. However, no new ones can appear in the small system that are not present in the big one.

Formally, for all the influencing components $I'_{d'}$ of a component d' in the small system, there also must be an influence in the big system, i.e.,

$$\forall d' \in D' \forall i' \in I'_{d'} \exists d \in D_{d'} \exists i \in D_{i'} : i \in I_d,$$

and in the same form for the set of influenced components $E'_{d'}$ of components d',

$$\forall d' \in D' \forall e' \in E'_{d'} \exists d \in D_{d'} \exists e \in D_{e'} : e \in E_d.$$

The two conditions guarantee that the set of influencers and influencees are preserved under the coordinate mapping, i.e.,

$$\bigcup_{i' \in I'_{d'}} D_{i'} \subseteq \bigcup_{d \in D_{d'}} I_d$$

and

$$\bigcup_{e' \in E'_{d'}} D_{e'} \subseteq \bigcup_{d \in D_{d'}} E_d.$$

Exercise: Prove this.◆

Figure 7 shows an example multicomponent system homomorphism from a big multicomponent system *MC* to a little multicomponent system *MC'*. Subsets of components of *MC* are mapped to components of *MC'*. The dependencies between components in *MC'* also can be observed in *MC*.

Assuming these coupling preservation conditions, we present the structure morphism as a series of local preservation conditions for the local mapping of each small system component, d', as follows. Let

$$h_{I'_{d'}} : \underset{i \in \underset{i' \in I'_{d'}}{\times} Q_i}{\times} Q_i \rightarrow \underset{i' \in I'_{d'}}{\times} Q'_{i'}$$

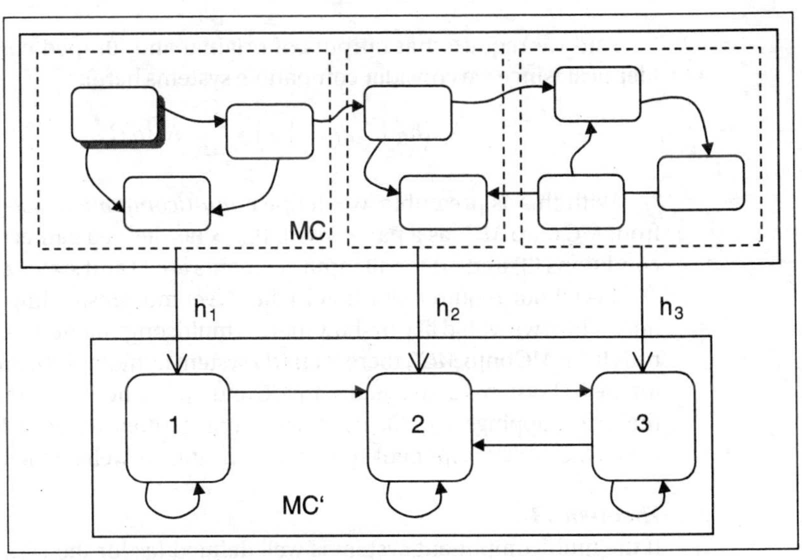

Figure 7 Multicomponent system homomorphism from the "big" system *MC* onto the "little" system *MC'*.

be the mapping from the state sets of the big system's influencers of the representatives of d' to the state sets of the small system's influencers of d'. This mapping is defined by

$$h_{I'_{d'}}(\ldots,q_i,\ldots).\ i' = h_{i'}(\ldots,q_i,\ldots).$$

Similarly, let

$$h_{E'_{d'}}: \underset{\substack{e \in \cup D_{e'} \\ e' \in E'_{d'}}}{\times} Q_e \rightarrow \underset{e' \in E'_{d'}}{\times} Q'_{e'}$$

be the mapping from the state sets of the big system influencees of the representatives of d' to the state sets of the small system influencees of d'. This mapping is defined by

$$h_{E'_{d'}}(\ldots,q_j,\ldots)\cdot j' = h_{j'}(\ldots,q_j,\ldots).$$

Let $q = (\ldots, q_d, \ldots)$ denote a state of the big system and $q' = (\ldots, q'_{d'}, \ldots)$ denote a state of the little system. When we apply the transition function of component d' in the little system to the mapped states of all the big system influencers of the representatives of d' we get

$$\Delta'_{d'}\left(h_{I'_{d'}}(\ldots,q_i,\ldots),\omega\right). \tag{1}$$

On the other hand, when we apply the transition functions Δ_d of all the representatives $d \in D_{d'}$ and then apply the mapping $h_{E'_{d'}}$ to get the states of the influences of d', we get

$$h_{E'_{d'}}\left(\underset{d \in D_{d'}}{\times} \Delta_d(q \cdot I_d, \omega)\right). \tag{2}$$

We require that computations (1) and (2) yield the same result:

$$\Delta'_{d'}\left(h_{I'_{d'}}(\ldots,q_i,\ldots),\omega\right) = h_{E'_{d'}}\left(\underset{d \in D_{d'}}{\times} \Delta_d(q \cdot I_d, \omega)\right). \tag{3}$$

And we require that outputs of original and lumped components be identical (since we consider compatible systems here):

$$\Lambda'_{d'}\left(h_{I'_{d'}}(\ldots,q_i,\ldots),\omega\right) = \underset{d \in D_{d'}}{\times} \Lambda_d(q \cdot I_d, \omega). \tag{4}$$

With this as preamble, we define a *multicomponent system morphism* from *MC* onto *MC'* as a pair <*coord*, $\{h_{d'}\}$> (as defined earlier) that satisfies conditions (3) and (4) for all input segments $\omega \in \Omega$ and states $q \in Q$.

Recall our requirement that higher level morphisms imply lower level ones. Thus, we would like to show that if a multicomponent system morphism runs from *MC* onto *MC'*, there is an I/O system homomorphism $h: Q \rightarrow^{onto} Q'$ for the I/O systems associated with *MC* and *MC'*, where h is the composite of the local mappings $\{h_d\}$. Clearly, this can only be done for those formalisms in which the multicomponent system specification is well defined.

Theorem 13

If the multicomponent system is well defined (as for the DTSS, DESS, and DEVS), the existence of a morphism at the multicomponent system level implies the existence of an associated morphism at the I/O system level.

Proof: The proof follows from the definition of the I/O system associated with a multicomponent system as discussed in Chapters 5 and 7. For reasons of simplicity in the following we show this for the DTSS case, where $E_d = \{d\}$ for all components d, and for identical input and output interfaces. For such systems the global state transition function is defined by the crossproduct of the global state transitions functions of the individual components (see Chapters 5 and 7):

$$\Delta(q,\omega)\cdot d = \Delta_d\left(\underset{i\in I_d}{\times} q_i,\omega\right).$$

To show the preservation of state transitions, we have to show that

$$h(\Delta(q,\omega)) = \Delta'(h(q),\omega)$$

(see definition of homomorphism in Section 12.4). With h defined by the crossproduct of local mappings $h_{d'}$, i.e., $h \cdot d'(q, \omega) = h_{d'}(q \cdot D_{d'}, \omega)$ and with $E_d = \{d\}$, the homomorphism requirement (3) simplifies to

$$\Delta'_{d'}\left(h_{I'_{d'}}(\ldots,q_i,\ldots),\omega\right) = h_{d'}\left(\underset{d\in D_{d'}}{\times} \Delta_d(q\cdot I_d,\omega)\right).$$

From the definition of h and $h_{I'_{d'}}$ it follows that $h_{I'_{d'}}(\ldots, q_i, \ldots) = h(q) \cdot I'_{d'}$. With that observation in hand we conclude that

$$\Delta'_{d'}\left(h_{I'_{d'}}(\ldots,q_i,\ldots),\omega\right) = \Delta'(h(q),\omega)\cdot d'$$

and

$$h_{d'}\left(\underset{d\in D_{d'}}{\times} \Delta_d(q\cdot I_d,\omega)\right) = h_{d'}\left(\Delta(q,\omega)\cdot D_{d'}\right) = h(\Delta(q,\omega))\cdot d',$$

and finally,

$$\Delta'\cdot d'(h(q),\omega) = h(\Delta(q,\omega))\cdot d'$$

for all $d' \in D'$, as required.

The output preservation condition can be shown in a similar way.

12.8 The Network of Systems Morphism

In a manner similar to that for multicomponent systems, we'll define a morphism at the coupled systems level. Besides preserving the dependencies among components, we also require that the interface mappings be preserved under the morphism. Recall that an interface mapping specifies how outputs of influencing components define the inputs of their influencees. Again for simplicity of exposition we assume compatible network systems and restrict our attention to homomorphisms.

Let $N = \langle T, X_N, Y_N, D, \{M_d\}, \{I_d\}, \{Z_d\}\rangle$ be a big network and $N' = \langle T', X'_{N'}, Y'_{N'}, D', \{M'_{d'}\}, \{I'_{d'}\}, \{Z'_{d'}\}\rangle$ be a little network where N and N' are compatible. Let *coord:* $D \rightarrow^{\text{onto}} D'$ be a mapping from the set of components D of N onto the set of components D' of N' and $D'_{d'} = \text{coord}^{-1}(d')$ as defined for multicomponent systems. Then we desire that the composite of local maps $h_{d'}\colon \underset{d\in D_{d'}}{\times} Q_d \rightarrow Q'_{d'}$ become a homomorphism

$$h: \times_{d\in D} Q_d \to \times_{d'\in D'} Q'_{d'}$$

for the I/O systems associated with N and N'.

To guarantee the preservation of the structural coupling properties between components, we additionally require that for each component d' in the small system there exist a mapping

$$g_{d'}: \times_{d\in D_{d'}} (X_d, T) \to (X'_{d'}, T)$$

from the composite set of input segments of the block representing d' of the big system to the input segments of d'. In the same way, we require a mapping

$$k_{d'}: \times_{d\in D_{d'}} (Y_d, T) \to (Y'_{d'}, T)$$

from the composite set of output segments of the block $D_{d'}$ to the output segments of the component d'.

First we require local structure preservation relations for mappings $h_{d'}$ and $g_{d'}$ for state transitions (*state transition preservation conditions*). The preservation conditions for state transitions say that state transitions in components $d \in D_{d'}$ and component d' must correspond under mappings $h_{d'}$ and $g_{d'}$:

$$h_{d'}\left(\times_{d\in D_{d'}} \Delta_d(q_d, \omega_d)\right) = \Delta_{d'}\left(h_{d'}\left(\times_{d\in D_{d'}} q_d\right), g_{d'}\left(\times_{d\in D_{d'}} \omega_d\right)\right). \tag{1}$$

Second, we require that the input/output behavior be preserved under mappings $h_{d'}$, $g_{d'}$, and $k_{d'}$ (*input output behavior preservation condition*). Let ω_d be the inputs in $d \in D_{d'}$ and $\rho_d = \tilde{\beta}_d(q_d, \omega_d)$ be the corresponding output segment for initial state q_d. Let $\omega'_{d'}$ and $\rho'_{d'} = \tilde{\beta}'_{d'}(q'_{d'}, \omega'_{d'})$ denote input/output pairs in the little system. Then we require that input and output pairs in $d \in D_{d'}$ and d' correspond under mappings $h_{d'}, g_{d'}$ and $k_{d'}$

$$k_{d'}\left(\times_{d\in D_{d'}} \tilde{\beta}_d(q_d, \omega_d)\right) = \tilde{\beta}'_{d'}\left(h_{d'}\left(\times_{d\in D_{d'}} q_d\right), g_{d'}\left(\times_{d\in D_{d'}} \omega_d\right)\right) \tag{2}$$

with $d \in D_{d'}$ (Fig. 8).

Finally, we require that the coupling relations of the big system be preserved in the little system (*coupling preservation relations*). This manifests itself as a commutative diagram as depicted in Fig. 9. When we take the outputs of the influencers $i \in I_d$ of components $d \in D_{d'}$ in the big system and apply the interface mappings Z_d to get the inputs ω_d of $d \in D_{d'}$ and then apply the coding mapping $g_{d'}$ to all ω_d, we obtain the input $\omega'_{d'}$. This value must be the same as if we first applied the coding function $k_{i'}$ to obtain all the outputs $\rho_{i'}$ of components i' influencing d' in the little system and then applied the interface mapping $Z'_{d'}$ to the outputs $\rho'_{i'}$ of $i' \in I'_{d'}$, i.e.,

$$g_{d'}\left(\times_{d\in D_{d'}} Z_d\left(\times_{i\in I_d} \rho_i\right)\right) = Z'_{d'}\left(\times_{i'\in I'_{d'}} k_{i'}\left(\times_{i\in D_{i'}} \rho_i\right)\right). \tag{3}$$

We define a *network of systems morphism* from N onto N' as a structure $\langle coord, \{k_{d'}\}, \{g_{d'}\}, \{h_{d'}\}\rangle$ (as defined earlier) such that $\{k_{d'}\}, \{g_{d'}\}$ and $\{h_{d'}\}$ satisfy the coupling preservations, state transition preservation, and input/output preservation conditions.

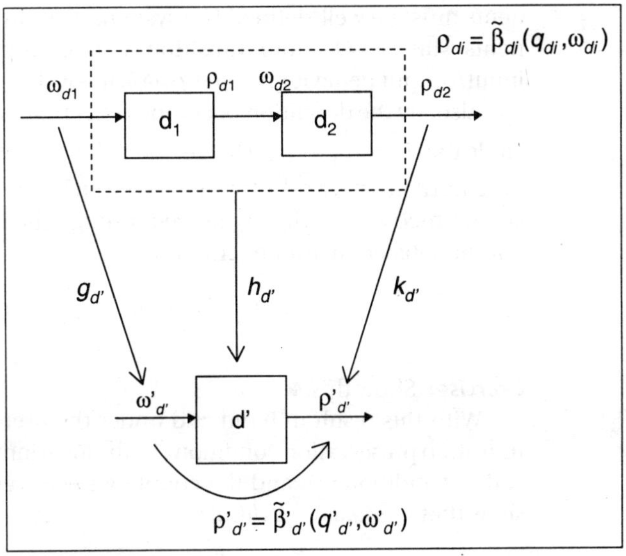

Figure 8 Input/output pairs preservation relation.

Theorem 14

If the network of systems is well defined, the existence of a network of systems morphism $\langle coord, \{k_{d'}\},\{g_{d'}\},\{h_{d'}\}\rangle$ which fulfills the coupling preservations, state transition preservation, and input/output preservation conditions implies the existence of an associated morphism at the I/O system level.

Proof: The proof works by considering the definition of the I/O system associated with a network of systems and showing that the homomorphism at the I/O system level is equivalent to the local homomorphism relations $h_{d'}$ under the local structure and coupling preservation conditions as defined earlier.

Recall from Chapter 7 that a network of systems in a particular formalism defines a basic system in that formalism by taking the crossproduct of the components' state $\underset{d\in D}{\times} Q_d$ and local state transitions and output functions and by mapping outputs to inputs by the interface mappings Z_d. As compo-

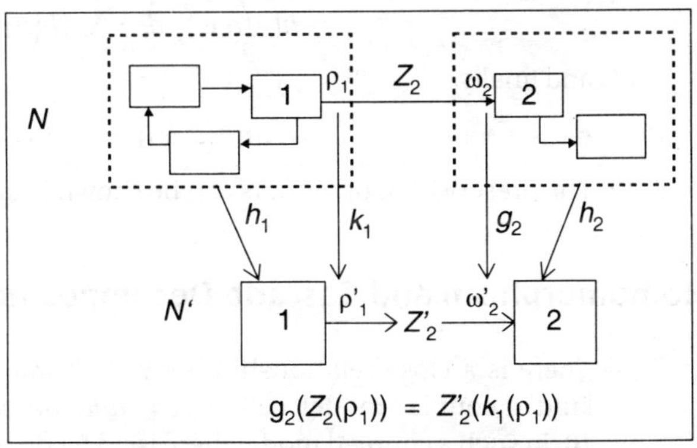

Figure 9 Network of systems morphisms.

nents must be well-defined I/O systems, we can conclude that the components' state set Q_d, state transition Δ_d, and output functions Λ_d, as well as input/output behavior $\rho_d = \tilde{\beta}_d(q_d, \omega_d)$, are well defined.

Also, by the definition of components inputs $x_d = Z_d(\times_{i\in I_d} y_i)$, we can conclude that $\omega_d = Z_d(\times_{i\in I_d} \rho_i)$. Hence, the definition of the global state transition function Δ of a network of systems is given by the crossproduct of local transition functions Δ_d with ω_d derived through the interface maps Z_d from the output behavior of influencing systems:

$$\Delta(q,\omega)\cdot d = \Delta_d\left(q_d, Z_d\left(\times_{i\in I_d} \tilde{\beta}_i(q_i,\omega_i)\right)\right). \tag{4}$$

Exercise: Show this.◆

With this result in hand and under the prerequisites of the local state transition preservation condition (1), the local input/output behavior preservation condition (2), and the coupling preservation condition (3), we can show that $h(\Delta(q,\omega)) = \Delta'(h(q), \omega)$, with $h: \times_{d\in D} Q_d \rightarrow \times_{d'\in D'} Q'_{d'}$ defined by

$$h(q)\cdot d' = h_{d'}(q\cdot D_{d'}),$$

is a system homomorphism as follows. By using (3) we can transform (1) into

$$h_{d'}\left(\times_{d\in D_{d'}} \Delta_d\left(q_d, Z_d\left(\times_{i\in I_{d'}} \rho_i\right)\right)\right) = \Delta'_{d'}\left(h_{d'}\left(\times_{d\in D_{d'}} q_d\right), Z_{d'}\left(\times_{i'\in I'_{d'}} k_{i'}\left(\times_{i\in D_{i'}} \rho_i\right)\right)\right)$$

and by using (2) we obtain

$$h_{d'}\left(\times_{d\in D_{d'}} \Delta_d\left(q_d, Z_d\left(\times_{i\in I_d} \tilde{\beta}(q_i,\omega_i)\right)\right)\right) = \Delta'_{d'}\left(h_{d'}\left(\times_{d\in D_{d'}} q_d\right), Z'_{d'}\left(\times_{i'\in I'_{d'}} \tilde{\beta}_{i'}\left(h_{i'}\left(\times_{i\in D_{i'}} q_i\right), g_{i'}\left(\times_{i\in D_{i'}} \omega_i\right)\right)\right)\right).$$

The forms of Δ_d and $\Delta'_{d'}$ just shown, however, correspond to definition of Δ and Δ' for the network system in (4), and we can conclude

$$h_{d'}\left(\Delta(q,\omega)\cdot D_{d'}\right) = \Delta'_{d'}\left(h_{d'}\left(q\cdot D_{d'}\right), \omega'_{d'}\right).$$

From the definition of h as the crossproduct of $h_{d'}$, we directly conclude

$$h\left(\Delta(q,\omega)\right)\cdot d' = \Delta'_{d'}\left(h(q), \omega'_{d'}\right).$$

and finally,

$$h\left(\Delta(q,\omega)\right) = \Delta'\left(h(q), \omega\right).$$

The preservation of outputs can be shown in similar way.■

12.9 Homomorphism and Cascade Decompositions

There is a close relationship between homomorphism and a particular kind of coupled model, called a *cascade composition.* As illustrated in Fig. 10, in such a coupled model there is no feedback from the second, or *Back,* component to the first, or *Front,* component. When we are able to construct a homomorphic realization of a system using a cascade composi-

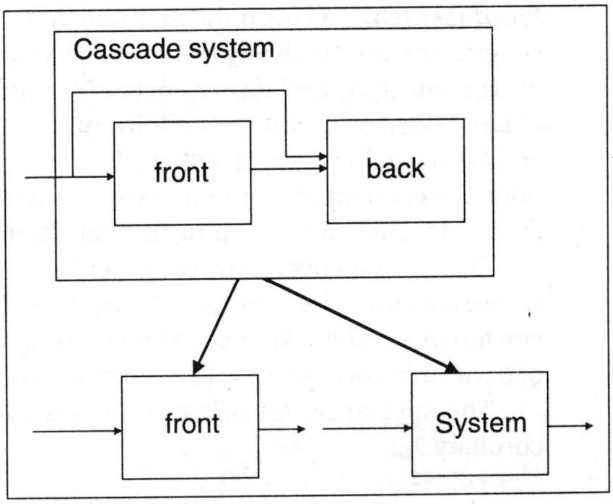

Figure 10 Cascade composition with homomorphic mappings.

tion, we say that the system has a *cascade decomposition*. There is a complete theory of cascade decomposition for finite automata due to Krohn and Rhodes [7] that used algebraic semigroup theory to break down machines into two kinds of primitives called reset and simple group machines—these are memory-losing and memory-retaining automata, respectively, which are not further decomposable. Our approach follows that of Paul Zeiger [13] in avoiding semigroup theory and rephrases a theorem of Westerdale [11] that shows directly how any strongly connected finite state system can be decomposed into a memory-losing front component and a memory-retaining back component.

To discuss cascade decomposition into the two kinds of elements, we need to generalize the congruence partition of Section 12.4 to allow blocks to overlap. Given a system $S = \langle T, X, \Omega\ Y, Q, \Delta, \Lambda\rangle$, we define a *cover* to be a family (set) of subsets of Q whose union includes Q. A cover is *maximal* if no subset is included in any other. A partition is a (maximal) cover for which all the sets are disjoint. Just as with congruence partitions, a cover has the *congruence property* if all transitions carry subsets into subsets.

A *cascade composition* is a coupled model containing two component systems, called Front and Back, in which there is no coupling from Back to Front (Fig. 10). A cascade composition *homomorphically realizes* a system $S=\langle T, X, \Omega, Y, Q, \Delta, \Lambda\rangle$ if there is a mapping $h: F\times B \rightarrow Q$ such that h is a homomorphism, where F and B are the state sets of Front and Back, respectively, and h must be an onto mapping (covering all of Q) but may be partial (not necessarily defined on all of $F \times B$). When h is one-to-one we call the realization *isomorphic*.

The basic connection between intrinsic properties of a system (having a congruent cover) and its amenability to cascade decomposition is stated as follows:

***Theorem 15** Cascade Decomposition*

If a cascade composition homomorphically realizes a system S, then there is a maximal cover of Q with the congruence property. Conversely, given a cover of the latter kind, we can construct a cascade realization of S.

Proof (sketch): (i) Given the mapping $h: F \times B \rightarrow Q$, we then identify set of states associated with any front state f as $Q_f = h(f,B) = \{q \mid h(f,b) = q$, for some $b\}$. The sets $\{Q_f \mid f \in F\}$ form a cover of Q (since h is onto) and is maximal (no Q_f is included in another by definition). This cover has the congruence property because there is no feedback from the Back to the Front—the destinations under an input segment of any two states (f,b) and (f,b') with the same f are states that have the same front element (which depends only on f).

(ii) Given a cover with congruence, we construct a front component whose states are the subsets of the cover in the same manner as the reduced version of a system. We use the back component to disambiguate the state of S within a cover subset. The transitions are defined as needed.■

The specialization of covers to partitions is stated as the following corollary.

Corollary

The projection of a cascade composition on the front component is a homomorphism and induces a congruence partition. Given a system having a congruence partition, we can construct a cascade composition to *isomorphically* realize the system.

Exercise: Prove the corollary.◆

Note that we can define an isomorphic realization because a state is found in exactly one partition block. Thus, the front component is guaranteed to have fewer states than the original system. In contrast, since a cover may have overlapping subsets, a system state may have multiple representations, and the front component can be larger than the original system. However, we need the state expansion provided by a cover to identify the memory-losing and memory retaining components in a system.

Given $S = \langle T, X, \Omega, Y, Q, \Delta, \Lambda \rangle$, we can extend Δ to subsets of Q, i.e., $\Delta : 2^Q \times \Omega \rightarrow 2^Q$, by defining $\Delta(Q',\omega) = \{\Delta(q,\omega) \mid q \in Q'\}$ for any subset Q'.

Exercise: Show that the extended transition function also satisfies the composition property: $\Delta(Q',\omega\upsilon) = \Delta(\Delta(Q',\omega)\ \upsilon)$.◆

A system S is *strongly connected* if $\Delta(Q,\Omega) = Q$, i.e., every pair of states has an input segment that takes the first to the second. An input segment σ is a *synchronizer* if $|\Delta(Q,\sigma)| = 1$, i.e., if it maps every state to a particular state—this resets or clears all past memory. S is *synchronizable* if it has a synchronizer.

An input segment ω is a *permutation operator* if the state mapping induced by ω is a permutation mapping (one-to-one and onto). For a finite state system, this is equivalent to $|\Delta(Q,\omega| = |Q|$, i.e., states are at most shuffled around but never contracted into a smaller set. S is a *permutation system* if all its input segments are permutation operators.

Clearly, synchronizable systems and permutation systems at the extremes of a continuum of memory-losing systems. Interestingly, if a finite state, strongly connected system is not one of the extremes, it is a combination of them in a well-defined manner:

Theorem 16
Every strongly connected finite state system (a) is a synchronizable system, (b) is a permutation system, or (c) has a cascade decomposition into a synchronizable front system and a permutation back system.

Proof (sketch): Let $S = \langle T, X, \Omega, Y, Q, \Delta, \Lambda\rangle$ be a strongly connected finite state system that is not synchronizable or a permutation system. Let the *contraction size* of $\omega \in \Omega$ be the size of its range i.e., $|\Delta(Q,\omega)|$. By definition, the contraction size of a synchronizer is 1. Since S is not synchronizable, call σ a *quasi-synchronizer* if it has the smallest contraction size (>1) of all $\omega \in \Omega$. Let the range of σ be R, i.e., $\Delta(Q,\sigma) = R$. Since S is not a permutation system, R is a proper subset of Q. Since S is strongly connected, we can show that the family of sets $\{\Delta(R,\omega) \mid \omega \in \Omega.\}$ is a maximal cover of Q with congruence property (illustrated in Fig. 11). Moreover, each of the subsets has the same cardinality.■

Exercise: Use the composition property of the extended transition function to establish the congruence property and to show that each of the subsets of the cover has cardinality $= |R|$, i.e., for all $\omega \in \Omega \; |\Delta(R,\omega)| = |R|$.◆

Using the Cascade Decomposition Theorem, we construct a cascade composition whose front component is based on the cover. In this front component, the underlying quasi-synchronizer becomes a true synchronizer. Since all subsets have the same cardinality, the back component has a state set of this cardinality and the induced operations on the back component state set are all permutations.

Exercise: Relate the state expansion of the cascade decomposition to the contraction size of the quasi-synchronizer.◆

The contraction size of a quasi-synchronizer determines the memory loss properties of a finite state, strongly connected system. If the contraction size is unity, there is an input segment that erases all memory. If this segment is a generator, this is like having a button that resets the machine to a ground state. Otherwise, we can synchronize down only to a subset of states whose cardinality is the contraction size. A non–strongly connected finite state system can be decomposed into strongly connected components [2] to which the theorem applies.

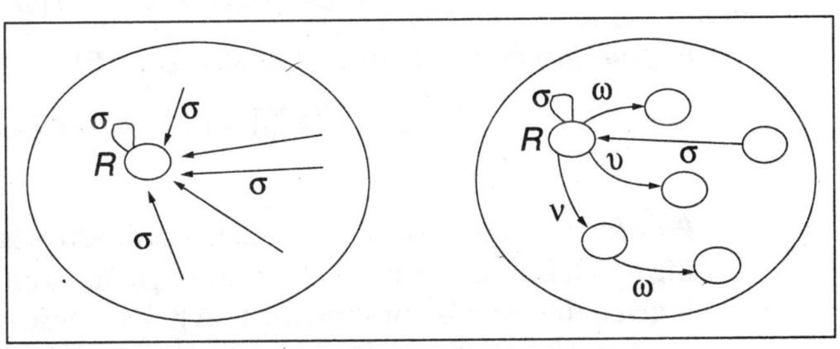

Figure 11 Illustrating the cover with congruence property induced by a quasi-synchronizer.

12.10 Characterization of Realizable I/O Relations and Functions

Consider the IORO, IOFO, and I/O system level of system description. Given an I/O system S, we have seen how to associate the lower level objects $IOFO_S$ and $IORO_S$ with it. Our definition of IORO and IOFO, however, allowed considerable freedom, and we would like to know whether every such object can be associated with some system. The problem can be phrased as follows: An IORO is said to be realizable if there exists an I/O system S such that IORO = $IORO_S$. In other words, an IORO is realizable if we can find a system that has exactly the same IORO associated with it.

Our problem, then, is to characterize the classes of realizable IOROs and IOFOs by looking for necessary and sufficient conditions that will distinguish a realizable IORO or IOFO from a nonrealizable IORO or IOFO. The simpler these conditions are to check, the more useful characterization we will have achieved. After all, one characterization of a realizable IORO is given by the definition of "realizable" itself. But given an IORO, this would require us to search through all possible systems to determine whether there is, or is not, a system S for which IORO = $IORO_S$.

Our characterization are based on the characterization of realizable I/O functions.

A function f is said to be *realizable* if there is an I/O system $S = \langle T, X, \Omega, Y, Q, \Delta, \Lambda\rangle$ and a state $q \in Q$ such that $f = \tilde{\beta}_q$.

Theorem 17

A function $f: \Omega \to \mathrm{P}$ is realizable if and only if the following conditions hold.

1. *Ω and P are of the right form:* There are sets X, Y, and a time base T such that
$$\Omega \subseteq (X,T) \text{ and } \mathrm{P} \subseteq (Y,T).$$
2. *Ω is closed under translation and composition.*
3. *f is length preserving and in step:* For all $\omega \in \Omega$, $\mathrm{dom}(f(\omega)) = \mathrm{dom}(\omega)$.
4. *f is time invariant:* For all $\omega \in \Omega$, $\tau \in T$,
$$f(TRANS_\tau(\omega)) = TRANS_\tau(f(\omega)).$$
5. *f is causal:* For all $\omega, \omega' \in \Omega_0$ $(= STR(\Omega))$, and $t \in \mathrm{dom}(\omega) \cap \mathrm{dom}(\omega')$,
$$\omega_{t>} = \omega'_{t>} \Rightarrow f(\omega)_{t>} = f(\omega')_{t>}.$$
6. *f has last values defined:* For all $\omega \in (X, T)_0$,
$$f(\omega)(l(\omega)) \in Y \Leftrightarrow \omega \in \Omega_0.$$

Proof: The necessity of the six listed properties is established by considering the definition of an I/O function $\tilde{\beta}_q$ of an arbitrary system S. The reader is given the exercise of showing that $\tilde{\beta}_q$ has these properties.

For establishing sufficiency, we suppose that a function f has the given properties. Based on these properties, we construct a system S_f^* which realizes f, using the following lemmas.

***Lemma 4** f Preserves Left Segmentation*

For all $\omega \in \Omega_0$, $t \in \text{dom}(\omega)$,

$$f(\omega)_{t>} = f(\omega_{t>}).$$

Proof: It follows easily from the definition of left segmentation that $\omega_{t>} = (\omega_{t>})_{t>}$. Setting $\omega = \omega$ and $\omega' = \omega_{t>}$ in the causality property 5, we have $f(\omega)_{t>} = f(\omega_{t>})_{t>}$. But by the length-preserving property 3, $\text{dom}(f(\omega_{t>})) = \text{dom}(\omega_{t>}) = \langle 0, t\rangle$, so $f(\omega_{t>})_{t>} = f(\omega_{t>})$. Thus, $f(\omega)_{t>} = f(\omega_{t>})$, as desired.■

***Lemma 5** f Is Specifiable by a Last Value Function $\tilde{f}$*

There exists a function $\tilde{f}: \Omega_0 \to Y$ such that for all $\omega \in \Omega_0$, $t \in \text{dom}(\omega)$, $f(\omega)(t) = \tilde{f}(\omega_{t>})$.

Proof: Define $\tilde{f}: \Omega_0 \to Y$ by $\tilde{f}(\omega) = f(\omega)(l(\omega))$ for $\omega \in \Omega_0$. By property 6, $\tilde{f}$ is defined for every $\omega \in \Omega_0$. Moreover,

$$\begin{aligned} f(\omega)(t) &= f(\omega)_{t>}(t) && \text{(property of left segmentation)} \\ &= f(\omega_{t>})(t) && (f \text{ preserves left segmentation.}) \\ &= \tilde{f}(\omega_{t>}) && \left(\text{definition of } \tilde{f}, \text{ noting that } l(\omega_{t>}) = t\right).\blacksquare \end{aligned}$$

With the help of Lemma 5, we construct an object $S_f^* = \langle T, X, \Omega, Y, Q^*, \Delta^*, \Lambda^*\rangle$, where Ω is the given domain of f and T, X, Y are the sets guaranteed to exist by property 1. In addition, $Q^* = \Omega_0$, $\Delta^*: \Omega_0 \times \Omega \to \Omega_0$ is defined by

$$\Delta^*(\omega, \omega') = \omega \bullet STR(\omega')$$

and $\Lambda^*: \Omega_0 \to Y$ is defined by $\Lambda^* = \tilde{f}$.

We are assuming for simplicity that the null segment $\Phi \in \Omega_0$ so that in particular $\Delta^*(\Phi, \omega) = STR(\omega)$. (If $\Phi \notin \Omega_0$, we set $Q^* = \Omega_0 \cup \{\Phi\}$, slightly complicating the definition of Λ^*.)

By Lemma 5, Λ^* is well defined, and it is easy to check that S_f^* is a system, which moreover is time invariant.

Finally, note that for $\omega \in \Omega_0$,

$$\beta_\Phi(\omega) = \Lambda^*(\Delta^*(\Phi, \omega)) = \tilde{f}(\omega),$$

so that $\beta_\Phi | \Omega_0 = \tilde{f}$, and it is then easy to check that $\tilde{\beta}_\Phi = f$. Thus, S_f^* realizes f as required.

Having this characterization of realizable functions, we cán develop a characterization for realizable IOFOs.

***Theorem 18** Characterization of Realizable IOFOs*

An IOFO = (T, X, Ω, Y, F) is realizable if and only if the following conditions hold.

1. Each function $f \in F$ is realizable.
2. The set F is closed under derivatives:

$$f \in F \Rightarrow \forall \omega \in \Omega, \quad \overline{fL_\omega} \in F.$$

Here, $\tilde{f}$ is the last output function guaranteed to exist by the realizability of f, $\tilde{f}L_\omega$ is called the ωth derivative of $\tilde{f}$ and is defined by $\tilde{f}L_\omega(\omega') = \tilde{f}(\omega\omega')$ for all $\omega' \in \Omega$, and $\bar{\bar{\tilde{f}}}L_\omega$ is the segment-to-segment mapping specified by $\tilde{f}L_\omega$.

Proof: The necessity of the condition follows by considering an arbitrary system and examining its associated IOFO. Let $S = \langle T, X, \Omega, Y, Q, \Delta, \Lambda\rangle$ and $\text{IOFO}_s = \langle T, X, \Omega, Y, \tilde{\text{B}}_s\rangle$, where, as we recall, $\text{B}_S = \{\tilde{\beta}_q | q \in Q\}$. Clearly, each $\tilde{\beta}_q$ is realizable. Moreover, the reader should verify that $\tilde{\beta}_q L_\omega = \tilde{\beta}_{\Delta(q,\omega)}$, i.e., the derivatives of the I/O function of state q are the I/O functions of all the states accessible from q. Thus, $\tilde{\text{B}}_S$ is closed under derivatives.

To show that the conditions are sufficient, we construct a system S for which IOFO_S is the given IOFO. Since each function f is realizable, we can construct a system S_f^* that realizes it. Now each of these systems has the same state space Ω_0, but it is an easy matter to relabel each of these sets so that they are disjoint.

Naturally, the transition and output functions are likewise altered. For example, let $S_f^* = \langle T, X, \Omega, Y, \Omega_0 \times \{f\}, \Delta_f^*, \Lambda_f^*\rangle$, where $\Delta_f^*((\omega, f), \omega') = (\omega\omega', f)$, and $\Lambda_f^*(\omega, f) = \tilde{f}(\omega)$. We can then "lay all the separate systems next to each other" in an operation called the disjoint union. Formally this results in an object $S_F^* = \langle T, X, \Omega, Y, Q_F^*, \Delta_F^*, \Lambda_F\rangle$, where $Q_F^* = \cup_{f\in F}(\Omega_0 \times \{f\})$, $\Delta_F^*|(\Omega_0 \times \{f\}) = \Delta_f^*$ and $\Lambda_F^*|(\Omega_0 \times \{f\}) = \Lambda_F^*$. It is easy to check that S_F^* is a time-invariant system. Moreover, we claim that $\text{IOFO}_{S_F^*} = \text{IOFO}$. Certainly $F \subseteq \tilde{\text{B}}_{S_F^*}$, since f is realizable by S_f^*, a part of S_F^*. On the other hand, given $q \in \dot{Q}_F^*$, it belongs uniquely to some component $\Omega_0 \times \{f\}$, i.e., $q = (\omega, f)$ for some $\omega \in \Omega_0$ and $f \in F$. But since (ω, f) is accessible from $(\varnothing, f)$, we have that $\tilde{\beta}_{(\omega,f)}$ is a derivative of $\tilde{\beta}_{(\Phi,f)}$. Noting that $\tilde{\beta}_{(\Phi,f)} = f$ and that F is closed under derivatives, we have that $\tilde{\beta}_{(\omega,f)} \in F$. This allows us to conclude that $\tilde{\text{B}}_{S_F^*} \subseteq F$, hence $\tilde{\text{B}}_{S_F^*} = F$, as required.

Finally, we have the following corollary.

Corollary: ***Characterization of Realizable IOROs***

An IORO $\langle T, X, \Omega, Y, R\rangle$ is realizable if and only if there is a realizable IOFO $\langle T, X, \Omega, Y, F\rangle$ such that $R = \cup_{f\in F} f$.

12.10.1 Canonical Realization

Given a realizable I/O function, there is at least one I/O system that realizes it. More than this, from Section 12.4.2, there is a reduced version of this system that has minimality and uniqueness properties. In fact, from the preceding discussion, we can see that every system that realizes the function has to have states representing the function and its derivatives. Indeed, if the system uses only these states, then we call it the *canonical realization* of the function. It is easy to see that the canonical realization is both of the following:

- *Minimal,* defined as being a homomorphic image of a subsystem of any realization of the function
- *Unique,* in being isomorphic to any other minimal realization

Given a realizable IOFO, there is similarly a canonical realization for it. However, given an IORO, there may be several distinct IOFOs that can be associated with it. But, under a condition called system identifiability, a unique IOFO, and canonical realization, exist [14].

12.11 Summary

The hierarchy of preservation relations runs parallel to the hierarchy of system specification levels. For each level of system specification, there is a corresponding relation that preserves features introduced at this level. Recall that as the level increases, more and more structure is introduced by the system specification. Accordingly, higher level morphisms preserve more structure than do lower level ones. Thus, higher level morphisms are stronger in the sense of preserving more structure and it is natural that the existence of a stronger morphism relating a pair of systems should imply the existence of a weaker morphism relating the same pair. In fact, we showed that for each level, a morphism between two system specifications at that level implies a morphism between their associated specifications at lower levels.

The utility of a high-level morphism, however, lies in the guarantee that a lower level morphism exists, not necessarily in the actual construction of the latter. Indeed, the higher level morphisms allow us to check—by comparison of structures—whether two systems are behaviorally equivalent without having to compare their behavior directly. For example, a homomorphism at the multicomponent and network of systems level allows us to check several smaller local preservation conditions together with coupling preservation conditions and automatically conclude that a global homomorphism exists. For this reason, higher level morphisms are important in model simplification and in simulator verification.

Although stronger preservation relations imply weaker ones, the reverse is not generally true. This means that as a rule we cannot infer structure uniquely from behavior [15]. Inductive modeling based on the DEVS formalism and applying nonmonotonic logic is discussed in Sarjoughian [9, 10].

12.12 Sources

Homomorphisms of general algebras and systems are discussed by Cohn [3] and Foo [4]. The relationship between I/O function morphism and the system morphism is derived from Krohn [7] and by Hartmanis [5]. Realization of I/O functions is discussed in a number of books, e.g., Kalman [6] and Zemanian [16]. Category theory provides a foundation for abstract properties of morphisms and has been used to characterize canonical realizations [8]. Aggregations in control theory are treated in Aoki [1]. Yamada [12] discusses behavioral and structural equivalences in cellular spaces.

1. Aoki, M., "Control of Large Scale Dynamic Systems by Aggregation." *IEEE Transactions on Automatic Control* **13**(3), 246–253 (1968).
2. Bavel, Z. and D. E. Muller, "Connectivity and Reversibility in Automata." *Journal of the ACM* **17**(2), 231–240 (1970).
3. Cohn, P., *Algebra*, Vol. 1. Wiley, New York, 1974.

4. Foo, N. Y., *Homomorphic Simplification of Systems.* Doctoral Dissertation, University of Michigan, Ann Arbor, 1974.
5. Hartmanis, J., and R. E. Stearns, *Algebraic Structure Theory of Sequential Machines.* Prentice Hall, Englewood Cliffs, NJ, 1969.
6. Kalman, R. E., P. L. Falb, and M. A. Arbib, *Topics on Mathematical Systems Theory.* McGraw-Hill, New York, 1962.
7. Krohn, K. B., and J. L. Rhodes, "Algebraic Theory of Machines." In *Mathematical Theory of Automata.* Polytechnic Press, Brooklyn, New York, 1963, pp. 371–391.
8. Rattray, C., "Abstract Modelling of Complex Systems." In *Systems: Theory and Practice* (R. Albrecht, Ed.). Vienna, 1998.
9. Sarjoughian, H. S., *Inductive Modeling of Discrete-Event Systems: A TMS-based Non-monotonic Reasoning Approach.* Doctoral Dissertation, ECE Dept., University of Arizona, Tucson, 1995, p. 256.
10. Sarjoughian, H. S., and B. P. Zeigler, "Inductive Modeling: A Framework Marrying Systems Theory and Non-monotonic Reasoning." In *Hybrid II, Lecture Notes in CS* (P. Antsaklis and A. Nerode, Ed.), Springer Verlag, 1996, p. 417–435.
11. Westerdale, T. H., "An Automaton Decompostion For Learning System Environments." *Inform. & Comp.* **77**(3), 179–181 (1988).
12. Yamada, H., and S. Amoroso, "Structural and Behavioral Equivalences of Tessellation Automata," *Information and Control* **18**(1), 1–31 1971.
13. Zeiger, H. P., "Cascade Synthesis of Finite-State Machines." *Information and Control* **10**(4), 419–433 (1967).
14. Zeigler, B. P., "Canonical Realization of General Time Systems," *Information Science* **12,** 179–186 (1971).
15. Zeigler, B. P., *Theory of Modelling and Simulation.* Wiley Interscience, New York, 1976.
16. Zemanian, A. H., *Realizability Theory for Continuous Linear Systems.* Academic Press, New York, 1962.

13

Abstraction: Constructing Model Families

Abstraction is key to constructing models for simulation. Traditionally, it has been considered to be a black art, a craft without a scientific basis. However, the importance of methodological support for abstraction is becoming increasing evident. Complex distributed simulation systems are being developed that are intended to support interoperation of models at different levels of resolution. Such designs presuppose effective ways to develop and correlate the underlying abstractions. However, discussions of abstraction still often proceed through individual anecdotal experiences with little cumulative impact. This chapter presents concepts and approaches, based on the morphism concepts of Chapter 12, for effectively working with abstraction in model construction.

Abstraction is the process underlying modeling whereby a relatively sparse set of entities and relationships is extracted from a complex reality. We can also define abstraction as *valid simplification.* Thus, to understand and support the abstraction process, we must have concepts for *model validity* and for *model simplification.* A model's complexity is measured in terms of the time and space required to simulate it. Validity is preserved through appropriate morphisms at desired levels of specification. Thus, abstraction methods, such as aggregation, will be framed in terms of their ability to reduce the complexity of a model while retaining its validity relative to the modeling objectives and experimental frame (Chapter 2).

In this chapter, we first develop three different measures of complexity. Then we use the M&S framework (Chapter 2) and the morphism specification hierarchy (Chapter 12) to develop a quite general theory of aggregation as well as an approach to developing DEVS abstractions for control. We discuss the importance of maintaining not just one model, but an integrated family of models, to allow flexibility in both calibration and application. The concept of parameter morphism is then introduced to support the organization of models in an integrated family.

13.1 Scope/Resolution/Interaction Product

As we have said, *abstraction* refers to a method or algorithm applied to a model to reduce its complexity while preserving its *validity* in an experimental frame. The inevitable resource (time and money) constraints placed on project budgets require working with models at various levels of abstraction. The more detail included in a model, the greater the resources required of a simulator to execute it and of the development team to build it. We refer to the time and memory required to execute a model as its *computational complexity.* The time and cost of development is its *developmental complexity.*

We usually can relate the computational and developmental complexity to the *scope* and *resolution* of a model. *Scope* refers to how much of the real world is represented; *resolution* refers to the number of variables in the model and their precision or granularity. Scope is a relation between the model and the portion of the real world it is intended to represent. Typically, the larger the scope, the greater the number of components in the model. However, this need not be the case since, for example, the model may represent the real-world portion of interest as a single component. Consequently, we will use *size,* the number of components in a coupled model, as correlating better with complexity, but most of the time we won't be too wrong if we think of scope as strongly determining size. We will also identify resolution as the number of states in a component, and if we are referring to the model as a whole, then we assume that all components have the same state set (Fig. 1). We say that the complexity of a model depends on the amount of detail in it, which in turn, depends on the *size/resolution* product. "Product" is used symbolically here, i.e., we don't necessarily multiply size and resolution—what we do instead is discuss several measures in which increasing the size (number of components) and resolution (number of states per component) lead to increasing complexity. Some times we get a better handle on the complexity of a model by including the interactions among components in the product—in this case, we will refer to it as the *size/resolution/interaction* product.

13.1.1 Complexity

Three kinds of complexity can be understood in terms of the size/resolution/interaction product.

- *Analytic complexity:* This is the number of states that have to be considered to analyze, i.e., fully explore, the global state space of the coupled model. The number of states in the coupled model is the cardinality of the crossproduct of the local state sets,

$$|Q| = |Q_1| \times |Q_2| \times \cdots \times |Q_n|.$$

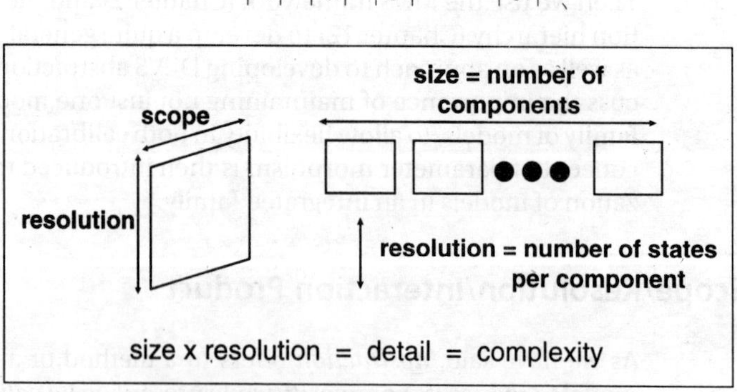

Figure 1 Size/Resolution Product.

Recall that the coupled model states are called *global* states in contrast to the *local* state sets of the components. Sometimes the increase in states is called "state space explosion" since it involves all the combinations of states and is exponential in the number of components. For example, if each component has m states, then the global space of n components has m^n states. Here we see the size/resolution "product" in that increases in both component numbers (size) and component state size (resolution) increase the crossproduct.

- *Simulation complexity:* This measures the computational resources required to execute the model. There may be many measures that are relevant depending on the resource under focus, time (e.g., execution time) or space (e.g., memory size), and the simulator class considered. Space required is proportional to number of components and the space required for the current state of each—e.g., m states can be coded in $log\ m$ bits, yielding a size/resolution "product" of $n \log m$ bits. A basic discrete time scanning algorithm may take time proportional to nm^d (where d is the number of influencees, a measure of the interactions in a model) to do a global state transition. A discrete event algorithm can reduce this by a factor related to the model activity. In Chapter 16 we will discuss complexity related to the message traffic required in distributed simulations. In general, size/resolution "products" for simulation complexity are much smaller than for analytic complexity, since simulation samples, but does not explore all, the global states.

Exercise: Let a discrete time model such as in Chapter 3 have n components, each with m states and d influencees. Compute the time required to do a global state transition for the basic simulation algorithm that examines each component and looks up a table of next states at each time step.◆

Exercise: For the same model assume that the fraction of "active" components is a and that a discrete event algorithm (Chapter 3) can limit its scan to only the active components with negligible overhead. What is its time complexity? How does this change when the overhead to manage the list of active components is taken into account?◆

- *Exploratory (search) complexity:* This relates to the resources required to explore a space of models. For example, to evaluate M models requires a time complexity of $M \times$ *size/resolution product*, where the latter depends on the particular analytic or simulation approach used. The size of the model space, M, also depends on the structure of the coupled model and its parameterization. In the worst case, this can grow superexponentially—the number of transition functions that are possible for an input free discrete time model having n components with m states each is enormous:

For example, a model with 10 components having 2 states each has 2^{10} or approximately 1000 states, and there are approximately 1000^{1000}, i.e., ~ 10^{3000} such models.

Exercise: Imagine a table with two columns and S rows. The left-hand column for current states is filled in, while the right-hand column is blank. Each way of filling in the right-hand column constitutes a different transition function. Show that the number of ways of filling in the right-hand column is S^S.◆

Clearly, real-world processes can never explore all the structures in such *Vast* design spaces[1] whether such processes be natural (evolution, human intelligent) or man-made (artificially intelligent). We can limit our explorations by imposing parameterized structures on such spaces and then considering only the parameter combinations. For example, there are only approximately 1000 cellular automata having 9 neighbors (including the center cell) with 2 states each, which is independent of the number of cells and is *Vastly* smaller than the unconstrained search space.

Exercise: Show that there are m^d cellular automata having d neighbors (including the center cell) with m local states. How many linear cellular automata of this type are there? (In a linear transition function, the next state can be specified as weighted sum of the neighbor states.)◆

In general, the size/resolution product strongly impacts the size of the space of models to explore. Unconstrained, such spaces are *vast* with cardinalities as high as SR^{SR} (where SR is the size/resolution product). By imposing parameterized structures on them, we can reduce the spaces to more manageable levels—with the risk that something (actually, possibly a *vast* number of things) of interest maybe left out!

13.1.2 Size/Resolution Trade-Off: Simplification Methods

Since complexity depends on size/resolution product, we can reduce complexity by reducing the size of a model or its resolution (or both). Given a fixed amount of resources (time, space, personnel, etc.) and a model complexity that exceeds this limit, there is a trade-off relation between size and resolution. We may be able to represent some aspects of a system very accurately, but then only a few components will be representable. Or we may be able to provide a comprehensive view of the system, but only to a relatively low resolution. *Abstraction* is a general process and includes various simplification approaches, such as those outlined in Table 1. We will discuss these approaches in more detail in Section 13.2.

As indicated, various methods can be used to reduce the complexity of a model as measured by the size/resolution/interaction product. Note that some methods may primarily affect the size, and others the resolution, of a model. The reduction in interactions here might be measured by the number of influencees, or more in depth, by the computational complexity of the functions that implement these interactions. Computer science has characterized this kind of complexity. The challenge in any case is to reduce complexity while preserving the validity of a model with respect to its counterpart real system in desired experimental frames.

Most abstraction methods work on the structure of a *base* model in an attempt to achieve a valid *lumped* model (and hence work at levels 3 and 4

[1] Vastness is a technical concept discussed in [7].

Table 1 Some Common Abstractions

Simplification method	Brief description	Affects primarily
Aggregation	Combining groups of components into a single component that represents their combined behavior when interacting with other groups	Size and resolution
Omission	leaving out	
	• components	Size
	• variables	Resolution
	• interactions	Interactions
Linearization	Representing behavior around an operating point as a linear system	Interactions
Deterministic/stochastic replacement		
Deterministic => Stochastic	Replacing deterministic descriptions by stochastic ones can result in reduced complexity when algorithms taking many factors into account are replaced by samples from easy-to-compute distributions.	Interactions
Stochastic => Deterministic	Replacing stochastic descriptions by deterministic ones, e.g., replacing a distribution by its mean	Interactions
Formalism transformation	Mapping from one formalism to another, more efficient one, e.g., mapping differential equation models into discrete event models	

of the specification hierarchy, which support state and component descriptions). The homomorphism concept then provides a criterion for valid simplification. Error is introduced when exact homomorphism is not achieved. However, the abstraction may still be valid if the error does not grow so as to exceed the tolerance for goodness of fit (see Chapter 14).

Modelers must trade off the advantages of model abstraction against the costs. For example, benefits in reduced run-time and memory requirements may be accompanied by an inevitable loss of predictive accuracy. The objectives of the M&S effort should drive the choice of which trade-offs to make.

The benefits of abstraction include the ability to perform more rapid analysis and wider ranging exploration at lower cost. This may be crucial in initial attacks at a problem and in gaining an overall understanding of how all the components interact (seeing the forest rather than the trees). Also, abstractions can be more generic and widely applicable than models tuned to specific circumstances. Models based on abstractions can be based on a few general principles in pristine form and hence more reusable than detailed models. Nevertheless, models at various levels of size and resolution are indispensable. More detailed models help in understanding phenomena in the messy real world away from the control of the laboratory. They are necessary for achieving realism, for example, in virtual simulations, where new designs (say for a high-speed airplane) must be tested under conditions as near as possible to what they will experience in reality.

You might think that you should go about constructing detailed models first—and then derive abstractions from them using simplification methods only when you are compelled to do so by complexity considerations. Unfortunately, often the data to calibrate and validate high-resolution models are not available. On the other hand, data may be available in more aggregate form that enables calibrating lower resolution models. This calls for an approach, called "integrated families of variable resolution models" [5], where models are constructed in ways that support cross-calibration and validation. The parameter morphism concept to be discussed soon facilitates such an approach since it explicitly records how parameters of base and lumped models are related.

13.1.3 How Objectives and Experimental Frame Determine Abstraction Possibilities

We return to finite state homomorphisms to demonstrate the importance of objectives and experimental frames to attaining valid abstractions. Recall that homomorphisms can be equivalently rephrased in terms of partitions of the state set. A homomorphism corresponds to a partition that has the congruence property with respect to the transition function and that refines the output partition (Chapter 12). For finite state systems, there is a well-known procedure that generates the desired partition. As illustrated in Fig. 2, one starts an iterative process with the output partition. If this does not

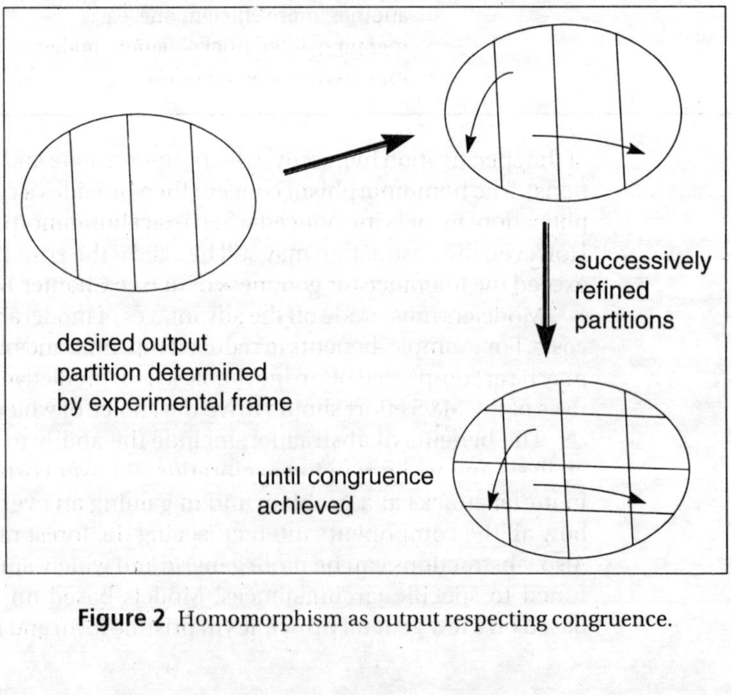

Figure 2 Homomorphism as output respecting congruence.

satisfy the congruence property, then the partition is refined by breaking up blocks that send transitions to different blocks. The resulting partition is tested for congruence and this process continues iteratively until the congruence property is satisfied. The process must terminate since the finest partition—in which each state is in its own block—is the limit. Given a finite state system, the set of congruent partitions is a constructive property of its state transition function. However, which of these partitions can match the output requirements is determined by the output partition. And the latter is determined by the experimental frame. The higher the resolution required to compute the desired output, the finer the output partition. The finer the output partition, the finer the congruence required to refine it.

Exercise: Why doesn't the iteration stop after one step? (Hint: At each step, the partition blocks get smaller, with all states coherently going to the same blocks of the *previous* partition, but not necessarily to the now *smaller* blocks.)◆

Exercise: Some finite state systems have no nontrivial homomorphisms. Show that a n-counter has congruence partitions that correspond to the factors of n. What can you conclude if n is prime?◆

13.2 Integrated Families of Models

To make our discussion concrete, we will introduce an example of an integrated model family.

13.2.1 Integrated Model Family Example: Space Travel

Space ships traveling from earth to other planets and moons will someday be common. We'll develop a base model as a dynamic structure DEVS& DESS. The base model will itself include many simplifications, and we'll indicate what simplifications, we're introducing from the outset and what general category they illustrate. From the base model, we'll construct two abstractions, one useful for short-term control and scheduling of the flights, the other for long-term logistical planning. Thus, our overall modeling objectives are to construct a space travel planning, scheduling, and control system and test it against a realistic base model (Fig. 3). The planning model predicts the efficiency of alternative routing policies for given cargo demands (input time trajectory) based on numbers of ships in the various routes. Basically, it is asking whether the right number of ships will be available at the right places at the right times. The control model will be a DEVS that abstracts the routes of ships and their times of travel, ***without*** retaining the details of such travel. It can be used to keep track of individual ships and schedule them for picking up and delivering cargo. This abstraction, an example of "transformation of formalism" simplification, supports the design of an event-based controller that can be implemented as a real-time DEVS (Chapter 10). Chapter 17 discusses the general methodology of which this is an example. The logistics model will help us to develop and illustrate the principles underlying simplification by aggregation.

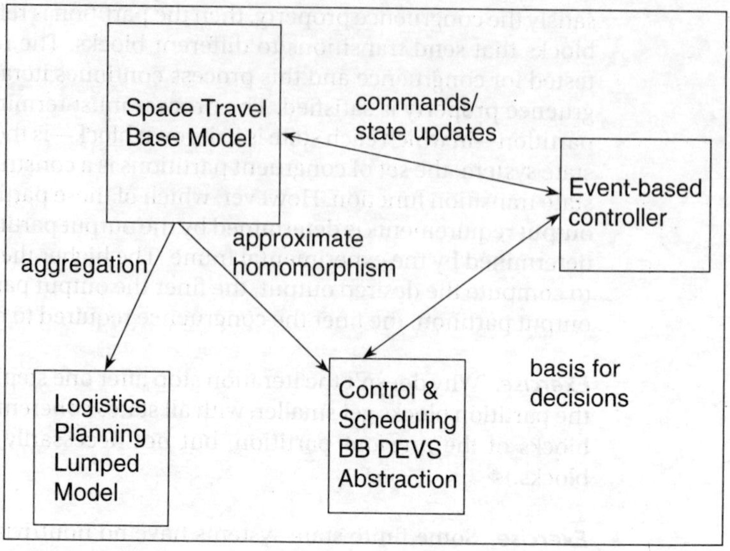

Figure 3 Space system integrated model family.

13.2.2 Space Travel Base Model

Imagine a single space ship starting at earth and destined for the moon and Mars. One of the strong influences on its travel is gravity. Recall that gravity is a force exerted on a body by all other bodies in relation to their mass and their distance. Theoretically, we might have to include the gravitational forces of the earth, moon, and Mars on the ship (if not all the other planets and objects), but practically these influences are only significant when the ship is near enough to one and then, since the planets are far apart, only this one has any influence. Thus, as an example of "omission" (Table 1), we leave out the gravitational influences of all but the most dominant body (if any—in between planets, there is no influence). But now have the problem of deciding when the ship is within the gravitational field of one of the bodies or in free flight.

Why DEV&DESS?

The motion of the ship is well described by the differential equations of Newtonian mechanics. But the crisp partitioning of space based on gravitational strength is best handled by conditions and state events. Thus, DEV&DESS is the natural formalism for the model. We can define a sphere around the earth, say, within which the ship's equations of motion include the influence of earth's gravity. When the ship crosses into, or out of, this sphere, its equations of motion must be changed accordingly.

Since the sphere cuts out gravitational force that might be there in reality (although small), there is potential for error in this "omission" approximation. Fortunately, it is a once-only situation and the error should not affect the overall behavior (more of this in Chapter 14).

Why Dynamic Structure?

When the ship enters or leaves one of the gravitational spheres, its motion equations change considerably. An elegant way to effect this change is to have the state event trigger a structural change as supported by DS-DEVS (Chapter 10). Figure 4a shows that we can have a component for free flight and for each gravitational region. When the ship crosses a boundary it is sent from the model for the current region to the model for the region it enters.

Why Distributed Simulation?

Another way to look at structure change is to assign the components to computers in a distributed simulation (Fig. 4b). This makes sense if we are tracking a large number of ships where at any time, there may be many ships orbiting any of the bodies or in free flight between them. We can think of each computer as a server specialized in its particular gravitational conditions and spatial properties. This exploits the parallelism in the model, especially if interaction between ships occurs only between those in close proximity. Then interprocessor message traffic is limited to migrations from one gravitational zone to another.

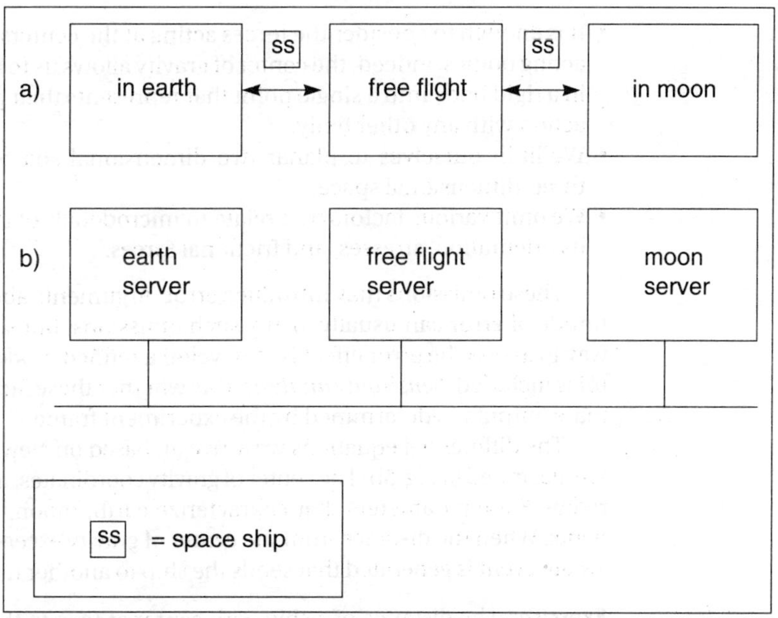

Figure 4 Dynamic structure architecture.

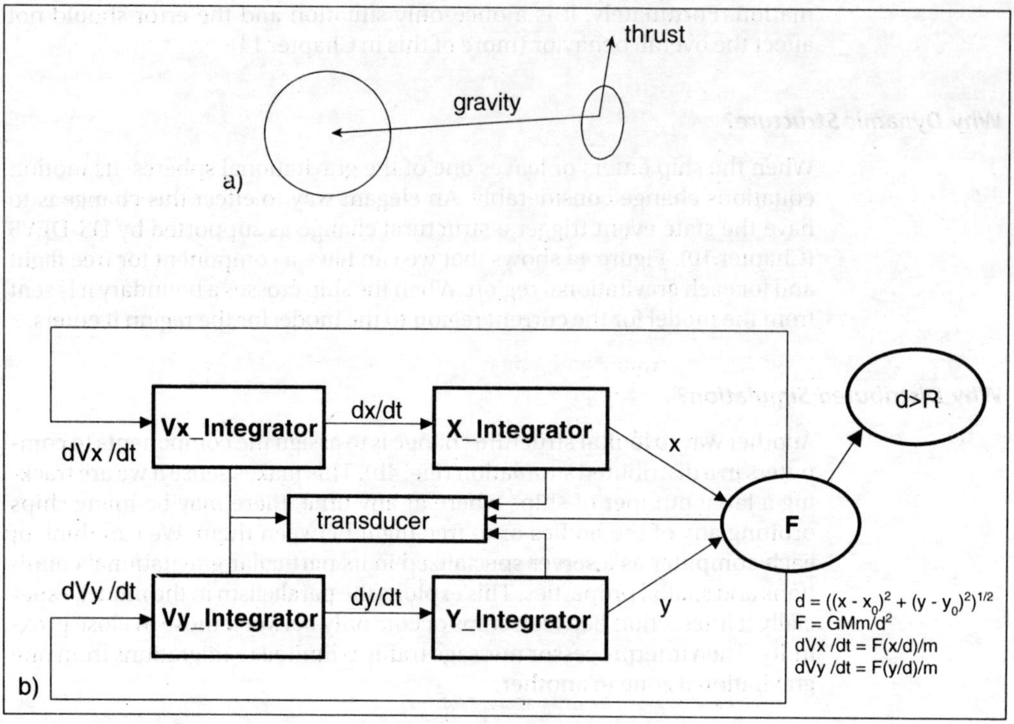

Figure 5 (a) Forces on a space ship. (b) DEV&DESS coupled model for kinetics.

Figure 5a illustrates how the forces on a space ship are analyzed. Some of the simplifications employed are as follows:

- It is enough to consider the forces acting at the centers of gravity of interacting bodies; indeed, the center of gravity allows us to aggregate particles in a rigid body into a single point that represents their gravitational interaction with any other body.
- We limit ourselves to planar two-dimensional space, thus simplifying three-dimensional space.
- We omit various factors that relate to microdetails of the vehicle, such as its orientation, stresses, and frictional forces.

These omissions may introduce error. Arguments about orders of magnitude of error can usually justify such omissions, but sometimes the only way to assess the error effect is to develop a refined model in which the factor is included. *Sensitivity analysis* tests whether these factors affect the ultimate outputs as determined by the experiment frame.

The differential equations we arrive at, based on Newtonian mechanics, are illustrated in Fig. 5b. The center of gravity coordinates, mass M, and escape radius R are parameters that characterize earth, moon, and Mars components. When the distance from the center of gravity exceeds the threshold R, a state event is generated that sends the ship to another model component.

Exercise: The distance of a ship with center at (x,y) to the center of gravity of a massive body (x_0,y_0) is $d = ((x - x_0)^2 + (y - y_0)^2)^{1/2}$. The force of gravity pulls along the line joining the two centers and has magnitude $F = GMm/d^2$, where G is the gravitational constant, and M and m are the masses. The force is projected in the x and y directions in proportions $p_x = x/d$ and $p_y = y/d$, respectively. Using this information, develop and simulate the model in Fig. 5.◆

Exercise: To maintain a circular orbit with radius D and speed v around a massive body requires a centripetal force, mv^2/D. Show that with $d = D$ (constant), the coordinate dynamics in Fig. 5 separate into independent second-order linear oscillators (Chapter 3) for such orbits with frequency $\omega = (GM/d^3)^{1/2}$. It is remarkable indeed that a nonlinear fourth-order system has such linear second-order subsystems. Let $(x_0,y_0) = (0,0)$. Starting at $x = 0$, $y = D$, what initial velocities v_x and v_y will start the system in a circular orbit with radius D?◆

The complete model of a space ship is a coupled model containing the kinetic component from Fig. 5 connected to its propulsion component, which supplies the thrust. Sending such a model on an input port to a server coupled model is illustrated in Fig. 6. When the server receives such a model, it supplies it the parameters (center coordinates, mass and its escape radius) that characterize its region of space. However, clearly it leaves unchanged the position and velocity coordinates and propulsion variables characterizing the space ship state at the moment it enters the server's region of operation.

13.3 Aggregation: Homogeneity/Coupling Indifference Principles

As illustrated in Fig. 7, *aggregation* is an abstraction method that maps a coupled model into another, less complex coupled model, with the intent of preserving behavior in some applicable experimental frame. The mapping

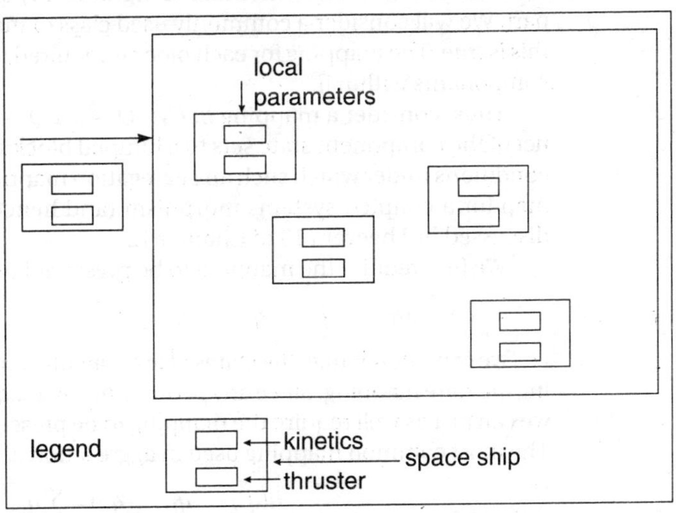

Figure 6 Server coupled model with space ship component clients.

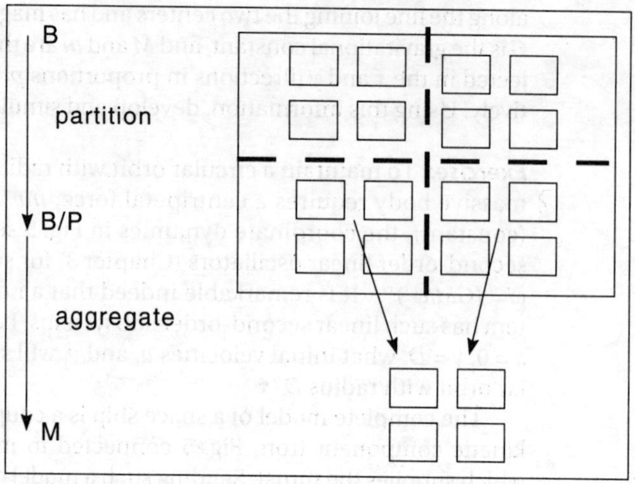

Figure 7 Aggregation: first partition, then lump.

process is a composition of two steps. In the first, the component set is partitioned into blocks. As in Chapter 12, each block can be described as a coupled model, and these block coupled models can be coupled to recapture the full behavior of the original coupled model. Thus, this step does not involve any abstraction *per se*, but results in a change in structure, called *deepening*, since we have added an extra hierarchical layer in the model. In the second, the block coupled models are abstracted to simpler versions and are formed into a final coupled model with suitably abstracted coupling.

Figure 8 illustrates how aggregation acts on the base block models and their couplings. The components in each base block model are aggregated into the corresponding lumped block. To enable nontrivial abstraction, the state set of a lumped block must be significantly smaller than its counterpart. We will consider a commonly used class of mappings that ensure that this is true. The mapping for each block is required to *erase the identity* of the components within it.

Thus, consider a mapping $h: Q_1 \times Q_2 \times \ldots Q_n \rightarrow Q$ from the crossproduct of the component state sets to a lumped block state set. We wish to find conditions under which such an aggregation mapping can serve as the local map for a coupled systems morphism (and hence a homomorphism) as discussed in Theorem 13 of Chapter 12.

We first require the mapping to be preserved under *transposition*;

$$h(q_1, \ldots, q_i, \ldots, q_j, \ldots, q_n) = h(q_1, \ldots, q_j, \ldots, q_i, \ldots, q_n);$$

i.e., we can interchange the states of any pair of components without changing the state mapping. Since any *permutation* is a sequence of transpositions, we can just as well require the mapping to be preserved under permutation. The most common mapping used in aggregation is the summation:

$$h(q_1, \ldots, q_i, \ldots, q_n) = \sum q_i,$$

which is clearly preserved under permutation (assuming real-valued states and the commutative and associative properties of addition!).

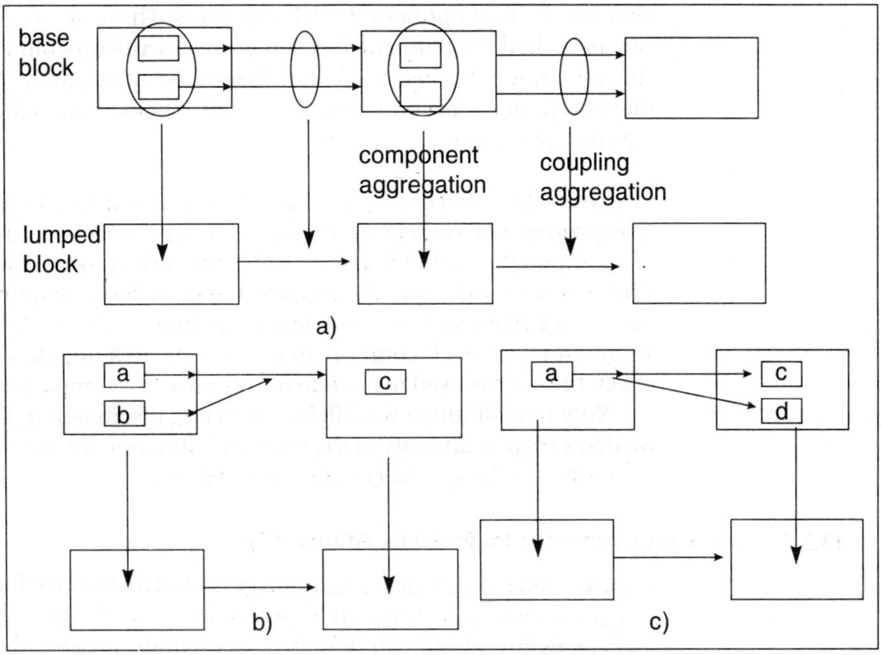

Figure 8 Coupling conditions imposed by identity erasing aggregation.

Exercise: Show that multiplication is also preserved under permutation. However, summation is often too coarse to achieve valid aggregations. We consider a more refined mapping called a *census,* in which we count the number of components in each state. Clearly, from a census of states we can compute the summation (if the states are summable) but not conversely. However, a census mapping is *also preserved under permutation* since by interchanging states of components we do not change the number in each state. So a census, while being a more refined aggregation than summation, is still nontrivial in the sense of erasing the identities of components.◆

Exercise: Imagine a census taker, C_S asking each component if it is in a particular state S. Show that C_S can be defined recursively by

$$\begin{aligned} C_S() &= 0 \\ C_S(q_1, \ldots, q_n) &= C_S(q_2, \ldots, q_n) + 1 \qquad \text{if } q_1 = S \\ &= C_S(q_2, \ldots, q_n) \qquad \text{otherwise.} \end{aligned}$$

Then if there are N states labeled with subscripts $0,1,\ldots,N-1$, a census-based aggregation mapping takes the form

$$h(q) = h(q_1, q_2, \ldots, q_n) = (C_0(q), C_1(q), \ldots, C_{N-1}(q)).\ \blacklozenge$$

The ability to perform a census of states implies that all components in a block have the same state set. We will go further and require block *homogeneity,* i.e., all components in a block have the same model structure: they are copies of each other. Of course, different blocks may have different characteristic component model structures. These aggregation mappings can be called *identity-erasing* since, for an unconstrained global state space, components lose their identities in the aggregation. We can also say that components become *anonymous* after being mapped by an identity-erasing aggregation.

Exercise: Show that for the unconstrained global state set of a block (the full crossproduct of its component states) it is impossible to recover the identity of a component in a block knowing only the state census. However, it is possible to recover the original state assignments (which component is in which state) if the block state set is suitably constrained. (Hint: Consider the constraint in which each component can only be in a unique set of states—in effect, the state is used to encode the identity of a component.)◆

Note that although we will be restricting discussion to finite state sets, we don't require linearity of the transition function. At the end of the chapter, we'll turn the special case of linear systems.

13.3.1 Coupling Conditions Imposed by Anonymity

As illustrated in Fig. 8, anonymity suggests that a restricted form of communication should hold between base blocks. In Fig. 8b, consider component *c* receiving input from component *a*. Anonymity suggests that any component, *b* in the same state as *a* could have been the one sending the same input. In other words, receiving component *c* can't distinguish between senders in the same state.

Similarly, in Fig. 8c, the sender *a* should not be able to direct output to a particular receiver; any output that can be responded to by a particular component *c* in state *s* can just as well be responded to by any other component *d* in the same block, if it is also in *s*. This suggests strong requirements on the coupling possibilities in the base model.[2]

To summarize, along with the identity-erasing aggregations we impose the following prerequisites on a base model partition:

- *Homogeneity:* Base model blocks must be homogeneous in structure (components in a block are isomorphic copies of each other).
- *Interblock coupling indifference:* No receiver can distinguish between senders residing in same block in the same state. Similarly, no sender can direct outputs that distinguish between receivers in same block in the same state.
- *Output desired by our experimental frame must be compatible with the partition*—as in Chapter 12, the partition on the states of the base model defined by the aggregation mapping must be finer than the partition imposed by the desired output mapping. More specifically, we must be able to compute the base model behavior of interest using only the census state counts available from the lumped model.

[2] We would like to claim that such requirements are necessary, i.e., imposed by the need to convert identity-erasing aggregations into homomorphisms. However, simple counterexamples can be given. Indeed, we 'll see soon that the uniform coupling requirement imposed by linear lumpability (Chapter 12) is actually weaker than the coupling indifference requirement.

We can show that these are sufficient conditions for the existence of a homomorphism enabling a base model to be abstracted to a lumped model based on identity-erasing blockwise aggregations.

Conjecture: *Existence of Identity-erasing Homomorphic Aggregations*

Let there be a partition on the components of a base model for which (1) blocks have homogeneous components (2) the coupling indifference conditions hold for all pairs of blocks, and (3) the base model output is computable from block model census counts. Then a lumped model exists for which there is a homomorphism based on an identity-erasing aggregation.

We will only be able to investigate such a conjecture within specific classes of systems. We will restrict our attention to DTSS (discrete time) coupled models as a special but representative case. To proceed will require us to formalize the coupling indifference conditions. Given any pair of blocks B, B' in a partition of components, let a receiving component, $c \in B'$ have all components in B as influencers and an interface map Z_c which is invariant under permutation, i.e.,

$$Z_c(q_1, \ldots, q_i, \ldots, q_j, \ldots, q_n) = Z_c(q_1, \ldots, q_j, \ldots, q_i, \ldots, q_n)$$

for all state assignments to B' and pairs of transpositions. This explicitly requires that receiving component c be indifferent to permutations of the sending block state, hence to the identities of sending components. We also require that each component in B' have the same interface map as c. This guarantees that receivers are indifferent to senders.

A general characterization of such an interface map is that it is a function, z of the state counts, i.e.,

$$Z(q_1, \ldots, q_i, \ldots, q_n) = z(C_0(q), C_1(q), \ldots, C_{N-1}(q)).$$

The underlying function may be nonlinear. For example,

$$Z(q_1, \ldots, q_i, \ldots, q_n) \quad \begin{aligned} &= 1 \quad \text{if } C_0(q) > C_1(q) \\ &= 0 \quad \text{otherwise} \end{aligned}$$

is a boolean function that compares the number of zeros and ones in the input. In general, although the aggregation mapping is linear, *the lumped models we construct may not be linear,* because for one thing, the coupling between components may be non-linear. Since we are not trying to linearize complex behavior, we are more likely to be able to find valid aggregations.

Exercise: Write out the underlying function z for the preceding case. Provide other examples of permutation invariant functions.◆

Fig. 9 illustrates a pair of blocks in a base model and the counterpart lumped model components. The coupling between base blocks is mediated by a permutation invariant map Z which sends the same output to each block subcomponent. In the lumped model, block states are represented by state count vectors. The coupling between blocks is given by z, the underlying block count function of Z.

In the following we investigate how to construct lumped models from a base model having a partition with the conditions stated in Theorem 13 of Chapter 12.

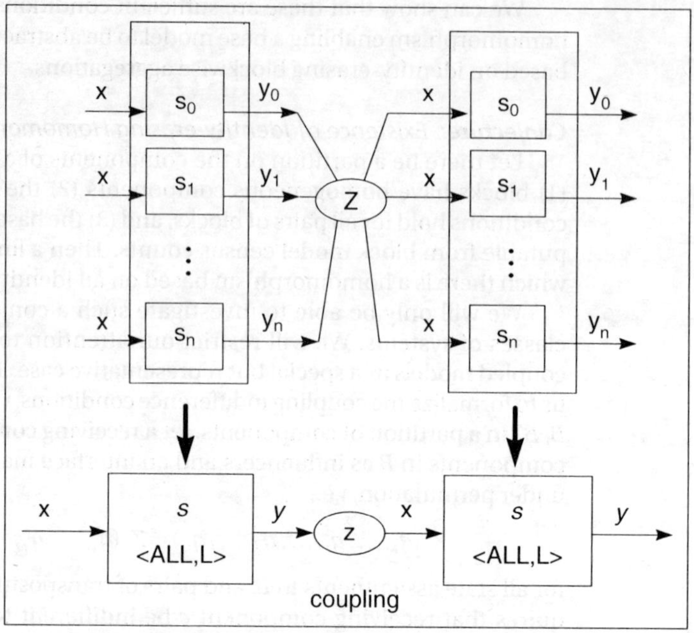

Figure 9 State census mapping.

13.3.2 Constructing Lumped Models Based on Identity-Erasing Aggregation

State Census Redistribution Under Equal Input

As in Fig. 9 let $\vec{n} = [n_0, n_1, \ldots, n_N]$ be the vector representing the census of states, i.e., n_i is the number of components in state i and there are N states labeled with subscripts $0,1,\ldots, N$. We call $\vec{n}$ a *census* vector for the block in question. How does the census change after all components in the block have received and input x? (Recall that all components in the block receive the same input due to the earlier construction.)

The redistribution of states is a linear operation and can easily be computed from the transition function of any component (all being identical). Let $ALL_{ij}[x]$ be the matrix that represents the *redistribution* under a state transition due to input x applied to all components. Then

$$\begin{aligned} ALL_{ij}[x] &= 1 \quad \text{if } \delta(s_j, x) = s_i \\ &= 0 \quad \text{otherwise,} \end{aligned}$$

i.e., there is a 1 in position (i,j) if, and only if, x sends s_j to s_i.

Let $\vec{n}$ be census at time t, then $\vec{n}' = [n'_0, n'_1, \ldots, n'_N]$, the distribution after each component has received input x, is given by $\vec{n}' = ALL[x] * \vec{n}$. This is true because

$$\begin{aligned} n'_i &= \sum ALL_{i,j}[x] * n_j \\ &= \sum \{n_j \,|\, \delta(s_j, x) = s_i\}. \end{aligned}$$

Exercise: Show that total number of components is preserved under a redistribution. State the criterion on the sums of the columns of the state census matrix that guarantees this preservation.◆

Output Census

Let $\vec{y} = [y_0, y_1, \ldots, y_n]$ be the census of outputs when the census of component states is $\vec{s}$. This is also a linear computation expressible by a matrix L, i.e., $\vec{y} = L * \vec{s}$, where

$$L_{i,j} = 1 \quad \text{if } \lambda(s_i) = y_j$$
$$= 0 \quad \text{otherwise,}$$

i.e., there is a 1 in position (i,j) of L if, and only if, s_i outputs y_j.

Exercise: Since each component produces one output, show that total number of components is preserved in the output census. State the criterion on the columns of the output census matrix that guarantees this to be true.◆

Theorem 1 *Existence of Identity-erasing Homomorphic Aggregations for DTSS Models*
Let there be partition on the components of a base model for which 1) blocks have homogeneous components, 2) the coupling between components in blocks is permutation invariant as in Figures 9 and 3) the base model output is computable from block model census counts. Then a lumped model exists for which there is a homomorphism based on an identity-erasing aggregation.

Proof: We will apply Theorem 13 of Chapter 12, which allows us to conclude that a homomorphism exists if we can show that a coupled system morphism exists.

Let $N = (T, X_N, Y_N, D, \{M_d\}, \{I_d\}, \{Z_d\})$ be network of DTSS components $\{M_d\}$ representing the base model. We construct a network $N' = (T, X'_{N'}, Y'_{N'}, D', \{M'_{d'}\}, \{I'_{d'}\}, \{Z'_{d'}\})$ for the lumped model. We define the mapping *coord:* $D \rightarrow^{onto} D'$ as the petition of base model components that places isomorphic components within the same block (which is possible by the homogeneity assumption). The block, $coord^{-1}(d')$, is called the block of d'.

The influencers $I'_{d'}$ are those lumped components whose blocks influence the block of d'. By assumption the coupling from such blocks to d' is governed by permutation invariant maps that feed the same input to each component in the block, as illustrated in Fig. 9. This allows us to define the lumped interface map $Z'_{d'}$ in terms of the count maps z_d underlying each base interface maps Z_d.

The lumped DTSS model $M'_{d'}$ that corresponds to the block of d' is constructed using the census mappings and matrix transformations discussed earlier.

Exercise: Given a component $M = (X, Y, S, \delta, \lambda)$ typical of the block $coord^{-1}(d')$ define $M'_{d'} = (X', Y', S' \delta', \lambda')$ appropriately. (Hint: X', Y', and S' are vector spaces of census vectors over sets X, Y, and S respectively, δ' is given by the *ALL* matrix defined by δ and, λ' is given the L matrix define by λ.).◆

To apply Theorem 13 of Chapter 12 we need to define the local maps, $h_{d'}$, $g_{d'}$ and $k_{d'}$ for each lumped component d. We easily identify the local state map $h_{d'}$ as the state census mapping for the block of d'. Recognizing the constraint that all inputs to components in a block are identical, the input map $g_{d'}$ becomes the identity mapping. Finally, the output map $k_{d'}$ is defined as the output census mapping. The theorem then states that a homomorphism will exist if the following conditions are met, where we rephrase the conditions in terms of DTSS networks and components.

1. *state transition preservation:* this is equivalent to requiring that the state census mapping preserve the state transitions of the components in a block under identical input. By construction using the *ALL* matrix, it does so.
2. *input output behavior preservation:* this is equivalent to output function preservation by the output census mapping. By construction, the *L* matrix output function enables the output census to do so.
3. *coupling preservations:* this requires the commutation of the interface maps in the base and lumped models. By construction, using the count maps ($z_{d'}$) underlying the interface maps (Z_d) gives the required preservation.

Exercise: In Fig. 9, show that outputs of the Z and z maps are equal if the block states are related by the census mapping (Hint: recall that z is the count map that underlies Z).◆

Having shown that the conditions required by Theorem 13 can be satisfied we can conclude that the state census maps are local homomorphisms that compose together to form a homomorphism at the I/O system level.■

To summarize, we have provided a general way to construct DTSS lumped models from DTSS base models based on identity-erasing aggregations. Base and lumped models constructed in this manner are related by a morphism at the coupled system level and therefore are homomorphic at the I/O system level.

In Section 13.3.3 we provide an example of such aggregated model construction.

Randomized Coupling

In the construction of Theorem 1, to guarantee that all components of a receiving block receive the same input from the sending block, we assumed *all-to-all coupling.* In such coupling all pairs of sending and receiving components are coupled. In real world examples this situation is unlikely to be found, but we can relax the requirement for for all-to-all coupling while still expecting that all receiving components received the same, or at least closely matching, inputs. We can think of each receiver as sampling the outputs of the sending block's population (its components). An error-free census emerges from sampling all of the population (which is all-to-all coupling). However, just as in random opinion polls, a large enough finite sample, under the appropriate stochastic conditions, would estimate the census as closely as desired. With this in mind, let the influencers (senders) of each receiver be selected at random and let the interface maps Z_d all have the same underlying count-based function z (Fig. 10). If the number of influencees (sample size) is the same for each receiver, their interface maps will receive approximately the same inputs and their outputs will also be approximately the same since all have the same underlying count-based function. We can even allow the interface maps to have different numbers of inputs provided that they all have the same underlying frequency-based maps, defined in the following exercise.

Exercise: Let $\vec{y}$ be census vector. By normalizing (dividing each count by the sum of all counts) we obtain a frequency (probability) distribution, $\vec{p}y$. Say that a count-based function z is *frequency based* if there is a function of z' with frequency distribution input such that for all $\vec{y}$, $Z(\vec{y}) = Z'(\vec{p}y)$ An interface map Z is *frequency-based* if its underlying count-based function is frequency-based. In other words, Z is sensitive only to the frequencies, not the actual counts, of the inputs. Two frequency-based maps are *frequency-equivalent* if they have the same underlying frequency-based function. Assuming that all interface maps are frequency-equivalent and sample a sending block's output without error (i.e., obtain the same frequency distribution of inputs), show that their outputs are all the same.◆

We say that the coupling between components in blocks is *randomized* if for each pair of blocks the receiving interface maps are all frequency-equivalent and sample without error.

Corollary 1. *Existence of Identity-erasing Aggregations for DTSS Models*

Let there be partition on the components of a base model for which (1) blocks have homogeneous components, (2) the coupling between components in blocks is randomized and (3) the base model output is computable from block model census counts. Then a lumped model exists for which there is a homomorphism based on an identity-erasing aggregation.

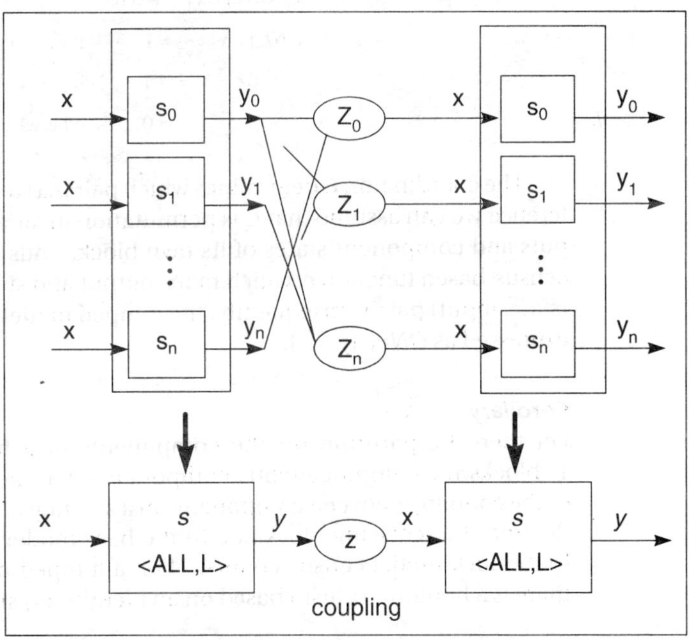

Figure 10 Randomized coupling.

Exercise: Prove the corollary using the definitions and exercise just discussed.◆

The result generalizes the discussion of the first edition of TMS that derived an approximate aggregation of a neural net base model based on firing frequencies. (See TMS76 Chapter 13 for details).

Exercise: Model a neuron with refractory period and threshold firing as a finite state DTSS. A base model containing billions of neurons is partitioned into blocks satisfying the homogeneity and inter-block indifference properties through randomized coupling. Construct a lumped model based on such a partition.◆

13.3.3 All-To-One Coupling

Fig. 11 illustrates another way in which the coupling indifference conditions may be satisfied. We assume that, in addition to the homogeneous set of components assumed earlier, the receiving block has a coordinator that receives all the inputs of the sending block. Based on state feedback from the other components, the coordinator sends an output that causes a non-trivial state change to at most one of these others. Receiver coupling indifference requires that the coordinator does not favor any particular component—it can only base its decision on the state of the component, not its identity.

Let *ONE*[*s*,*x*] be the vector that represents sending an input x to any one component in state s, with the restriction that $\delta(s,x) \neq s$ (i.e., x actually does cause a change in state). Then we can represent the change in census state count occasioned by input x to a component in state s by

$$\vec{s}' = \vec{s} + ONE[s, x] \quad \text{where}$$

$$ONE_i[s, x] \quad = 1 \qquad \text{if } \delta(s, x) = s_i$$

$$= -1 \qquad \text{if } s_i = s$$

$$= 0 \qquad \text{otherwise.}$$

The coordinator, C determines which pair (s,x) to use. By coupling indifference we can assume that C is permutation invariant in both sender outputs and component states of its own block. Thus there is an underlying census-based function c, which maps output and state censuses $(\vec{y}, \vec{s})$ to a (state, input) pair. Consequently, the lumped model state transition can be expressed as $ONE[c(\vec{y}, \vec{s})]$.

Corollary 2.

Let there be partition on the components of a base model for which 1) blocks have homogeneous components with additional coordinator, 2) the coupling between components in a sending block is only to the coordinator of a receiving block and 3) the base model output is computable from block model census counts. Then a lumped model exists for which there is a homomorphism based on an identity-erasing aggregation.

Exercise: Prove the corollary.◆

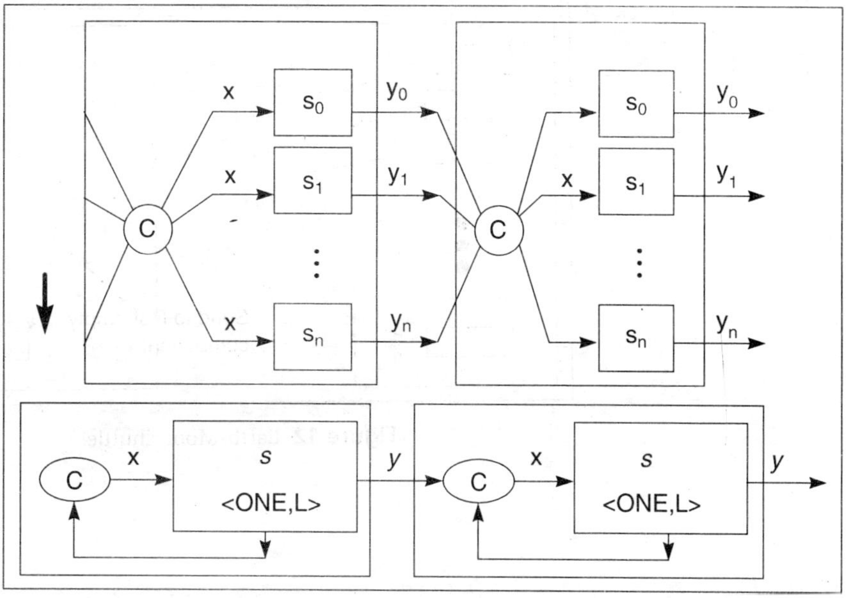

Figure 11 All-to-one coupling.

13.3.4 Example of Aggregation Model Construction: Space Travel

Consider the space travel system simplified to an earth-moon shuttle as in Fig. 12. Suppose there are 10 ships at any time shuttling between the two stations. Each base model block has 10 components where a component may be empty or be in a non-empty state representing a ship in transit. When a ship reaches its destination it is added to the opposite block for the return journey, being accepted by one, and only, one empty component. Supposing that an output of 1 is emitted when a ship reaches its destination, we send this output to a coordinator that routes it to the first empty component in some arbitrary order. Thus we have all-to-one coupling since any component in one block may send a ship to the coordinator in the other block. Moreover, the coupling satisfies the indifference requirement since neither identity of the sending or receiving component determine the coordinator's decision. Of course, only in a specific state can a transaction (ship hand-over) actually occur. To represent a ship's state of travel with a finite state set, we assume a fixed travel time in days and let the number days left represent the current state. For example, if it takes 3 days to travel from the earth to the moon, the state set of a component is {0, . . ,4} where 0 means "arrival", 4 means "empty", and the rest represent the days left to reach the moon. The transition and output functions are shown in Fig. 13. To represent a one day time step, when a component receives a 0, its state reflects the associated reduction in days left. The mapping into census matrices is also shown in Fig. 13.

The coordinator function is defined as follows:

$$Coord(y,s) = select(C_0(y), delta(s,0))$$

where *delta*(*s*,0) is the application of a 0 input to each of the components; *select*(1,*s*) is the state resulting from filling in the first empty component in

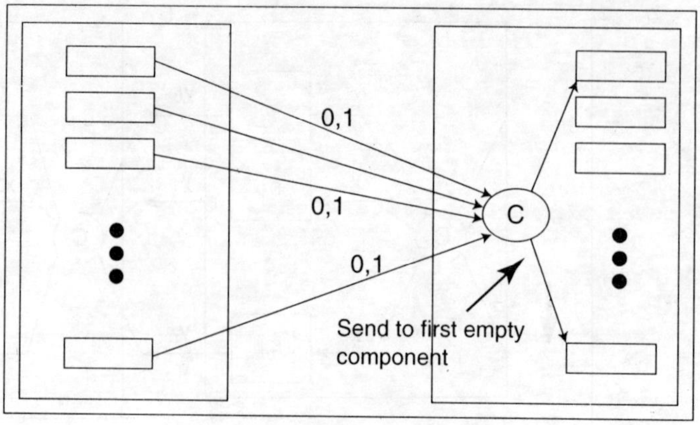

Figure 12 Earth-Moon shuttle.

some order and *select*(n,*s*) = *select*(n–1,*select*(1,*s*)). In other words, the reduction in days left is done first, then each ship arrival is assigned successively to a (different) empty component.

Exercise: Show that the expression for *Coord* implements the just given informal description.◆

As an example, let $\vec{s}$ = [3,2,1,0,4] be the current state of the earth-to-moon block (meaning 3 ships have just arrived at the moon, 2 are 1 day away, and so on, while there are 4 empty slots. Then the output census is $\vec{y} = L * \vec{s}$ = [7,3] i.e., 7 zero outputs and 3 one outputs (the just-arrived ships).

The coordinator first sends a zero input to all components in the moon-to-earth block. The effect on the state census is $\vec{s}' = ALL[0] * \vec{s}$ (If $\vec{s}$ = [0,1,1,2,6] is the state census of the block, then $\vec{s}'$ = [1,1,2,0,6] is the state census after the state shift to the left caused by the input 0, corresponding to the reduction in time left of all components except the six that are empty.).

The coordinator then iterates the *select* function 3 times on the moon-to-earth block. The effect on the state census is given by $\vec{s}' = \vec{s}$ + ONE[4,1]∗[3]. (If $\vec{s}$ = [1,1,2,0,6] is the state census of the block, then after receiving the 3 one inputs, we have

$$\vec{s}' = \begin{bmatrix}1\\1\\2\\0\\6\end{bmatrix} + \begin{bmatrix}0\\0\\0\\1\\-1\end{bmatrix}[3] = \begin{bmatrix}1\\1\\2\\3\\3\end{bmatrix}.$$

Exercise: Based on the example, express the state transition of a receiving lumped block caused by input from a sending block and confirm that

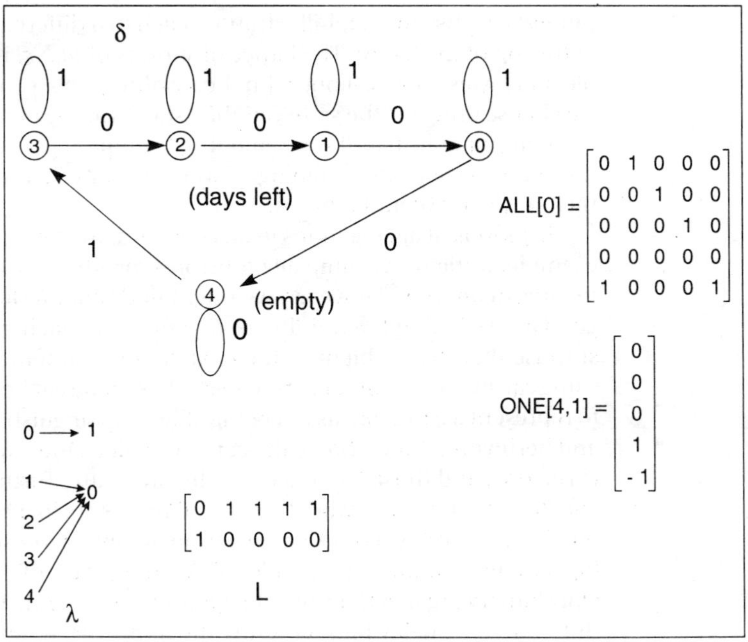

Figure 13 Census models for earth–moon block.

it can be expressed entirely in terms of the lumped model block census counts.◆

Exercise: Define, and implement, base and lumped models of the space travel example.◆

13.3.5 Constructing Aggregations Through State and Block Refinement

The homogeneity and coupling indifference requirements seem quite stringent. What if we can't achieve them on our first try at aggregation? As in the finite state reduction case, we can start an iterative process in which we attempt to refine block partitions and/or state sets to increase homogeneity and coupling indifference. Such a process may have to backtrack, since refinement of blocks and/or states to increase homogeneity may make it more difficult to achieve coupling indifference, and conversely. This can be understood from the example of the finite machine state reduction process, where successive refinements make it easier to control the source of transition arrows but more difficult to control their destinations. Unfortunately, since state sets are not necessarily finite, we cannot guarantee that an iterative process converges.

To understand how to refine the state set used as the basis for aggregation, we recall that components in the base model may have a number of state variables. This gives us a lattice of projective spaces, each one of which can serve as a state set basis for the aggregation mapping. For example, in Fig. 14, the underlying base model block is assumed to have components, each with three binary state variables, labeled *a,b,* and *c.* Five components are assumed for illustration, each in a different state as illustrated at the top of the figure. The lattice of subsets of *{a,b,c}* is shown in the middle and lowest layers, along with the resulting state census. For example, if we choose only *a* as the state variable (shown at the bottom), then there are two components in its 0 state, and three components in its 1 state. Refining the state space from *{a}* (going upward) we have either *{a,b}* or *{a,c}* with their respective counts shown.

Let's look at aggregations in an ecological food chain as a more realistic example. Initially, we lump all herbivores together in one block and all carnivores in another. However, we might find that our lumped model is not good at predicting the number of organisms in each group over time. We surmise that the problem is due to violation of interaction indifference—some carnivores eat other carnivores, while some eat herbivores. It is wrong to represent a carnivore as not being able to distinguish between carnivores and herbivores. So we break the carnivore block into two: those feeding on carnivores and those feeding on herbivores. After further experiments, we conclude that it won't work to allow all predators in a block to be active all the time. So we add a state variable to an organism's description, representing its state of hunger, in addition to keeping track of its dead/alive status. Only hungry organisms hunt, and upon success, they leave the hungry state. But now is the delay for reentering the hungry state uniform over the current blocks (homogeneity)?

So goes the iteration—at each stage, we try refining the blocks and the states to develop the lumped model specification. (We may also backtrack and combine blocks or states when a bad choice seems apparent.) The experimental frame—desired output—clearly plays a major role in where we stop. So do the properties of the real system (base model) itself—does it lend itself to component partitions with homogeneity and coupling indifference properties?

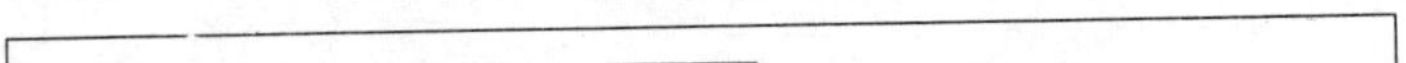

Figure 14 Illustrating state set choice and resulting state censuses.

Exercise: Refine the aggregation employed in the space travel logistics model so that it keeps track of the numbers of ships of the different types in addition to their position in space.◆

13.3.6 Time Scale Relations

Theorem 1 assumed that both base and lumped models were discrete time systems with the same time scale constants. Now, the time scale of the base model can be take as fixed since it represents the real system. However, the time scale of the lumped model offers another parameter for adjustment in seeking to satisfy the homogeneity and coupling indifference conditions. As discussed in Chapter 2, the more general form of morphism allows the base model to undergo several microtransitions for each lumped model transition. In the current context, this effect is achieved by choosing a bigger time scale for the lumped model than that of the base model. Why might it be easier to satisfy the homogeneity and coupling indifference conditions over a longer period? For an answer, we look to the internal dynamics of blocks which may act to reduce the differences among components. This dynamic behavior may also enable components to obtain random samples of each other's activities through interactions over time—in other words, by using time averaging to enhance space averaging. For example, the natural tendency of gases to diffuse irons out initial concentration differences. Stirring, or adding catalysts to, a container of chemical reagents will mix them together faster than diffusion. Wind in the atmosphere serves the same purpose with respect to the chemistry of air pollutants. The term "nearly-decomposable" systems refers to base models that support valid aggregations through such behaviors.

Exercise: Consider two chemicals that react to form a product. Each is injected into a container with a motorized stirrer to ensure a fast mixing process. Consider a partition of molecules in which the molecules of each chemical species occupies a block (called a compartment in this context). Derive a lumped model that considers only the concentrations (counts per unit volume) of the reactants and the product—a standard approach in chemistry and biochemistry. How are the homogeneity and coupling indifference requirements satisfied?◆

13.3.7 Universality/Applicability of Identity-Erasing Aggregations

Many modeling approaches have aggregation as their basis. The complexity of real-world systems, such as the foregoing ecosystem example, necessitates such lumping. And in many cases, such as for ideal gases and chemical reactions, such lumped models work quite well. In such cases, we can infer that the homogeneity and coupling indifference requirements are being met. In other cases, the truth of these assumptions may be in doubt. For example, rather than track individual customers (or items to be processed at the servers), queuing theory typically works with their numbers only (although classes of costumers are also considered). Such identity erasure greatly simplifies the analysis and leads to tractable results. However, identity erasure is questionable in relation to a real processing system where the coupling and homogeneity assumptions may not be warranted (see Chapter 8 of TMS76 for discussion of queuing model simplification). Actually, to consider such issues, we need to introduce a more rigorous way of measuring how well a model represents a real system or another model. In the next chapter, we'll discuss error and approximate morphisms. For example, an aggregation where the homogeneity and coupling indifference requirements are not met exactly is an approximate morphism. However, an approximate morphism may still incur errors that are acceptable in the desired experimental frame.

13.4 Abstractions for Event-Based Control

Returning to the space travel model family, the second model we consider is an abstraction that supports event-based control of space trips. In such an abstraction, called a *boundary-based DEVS,* we partition the state space of a base model in a manner that could support an exact DEVS representation as in Chapter 16. However, instead of constructing this representation, we construct a model that is truly an abstraction by focusing on the boundaries that define the partition. Since the base model is a DESS, and the lumped model is a DEVS, the method in Table 1 illustrated by this abstraction is that of "formalism transformation."

The space travel model in Fig. 15 furnishes the base model for such a transformation. Here the surfaces of the planetary and lunar bodies form the boundaries. All trips from one boundary to another are placed into the same equivalence class. For any such class, we retain only information about travel times in the form of a window bracketing the minimum and maximum times. A boundary-based DEVS is thus a variant of the real-time DEVS formalism in Chapter 10. Such a DEVS can be used to send control signals to a real system so as to drive it through a desired sequence of boundaries. In our example, this would be to move a ship around the solar system. The time window associated with a boundary-to-boundary trip can be used as information for control. If no word is heard from the space ship after the maximum allowed time has elapsed, a breakdown must have occurred and the controller should initiate corrective action such as a diagnostic procedure. If an arrival signal returns to the controller earlier than the minimum time, then a problem with the sensor communication system can be suspected. The formal definition is given next, followed by the example application to the space system.

13.4.1 Boundary-Based DEVS

A boundary-based DEVS is a structure

$$DEVS = (X, Y, S, \delta_{ext}, \delta_{int}, \lambda, ta),$$

where

- X = arbitrary set of symbols representing equivalence classes of input trajectories.
- $Y = B$, where B is set of symbols called *boundaries.*
- $S \subseteq B \times X$ is a set of symbols called *phases.*
- $\delta_{ext}(b, \phi, 0, x) = (b,x)$—inputs are accepted only immediately after an internal transition, i.e., when the base model state is on a boundary, then the

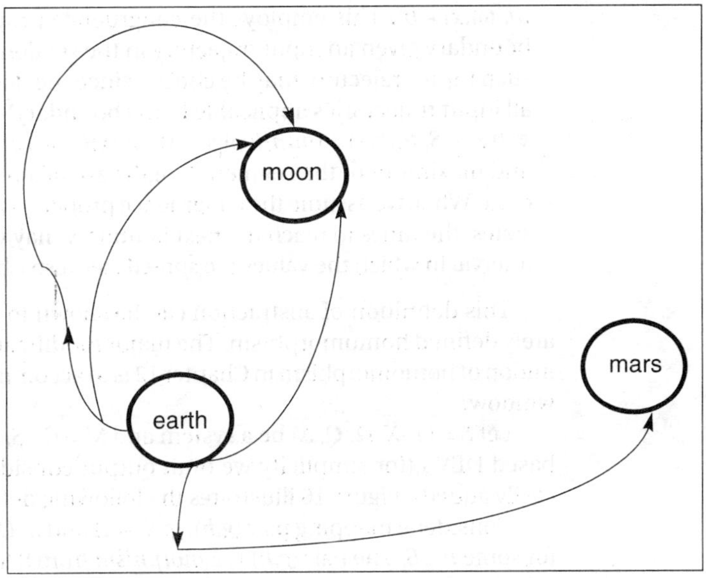

Figure 15 Space travel system illustrating congruence property.

change is only to store the input. The input is then applied in the subsequent internal transition, as follows:

- $\delta_{int}(b, x) = (b', \phi)$ where $b' \in B$ represents the boundary that the base model state reaches after the input trajectory represented by the input. After internal transition input, the store is nullified.
- $\lambda(x,b) = b \in Y$—the output is the current boundary.
- $ta(b, x) = [t_{min}, t_{max}]$, a time window representing the minimum and maximum times for the internal transition from (b, x) to (b', ϕ) i.e., from one boundary to the next. Also, $ta\ (b, \phi) = \infty$.

While we informally described the interpretation of a boundary-based DEVS, its relation as an abstraction of a base model can be formalized. A system S *abstracts* to a boundary-based DEVS if:

- There is a map of B into the subsets of Q, where the subsets associated with distinct boundaries are disjoint. For simplicity, let b stand both for the boundary symbol and the subset it represents.
- There is a map from X to subsets of Ω, where the subsets associated with distinct inputs are disjoint. For simplicity, let x stand both for the input symbol and the subset it represents.
- Congruence property of boundaries:

$$\forall (b, x) \in S, \forall q, q' \in b, \forall \omega \in x, \exists b' \in B \text{ such that}$$

$$\Delta(q, \omega) \in b' \text{ and } \Delta(q', w) \in b'.$$

This requires that all states starting on the same boundary are placed on the same destination boundary by all of the input segments belonging to same subset.

- $\forall (b,x) \in S,\ x \neq \phi,\ \exists\ b' \in B$ *such that* $\delta_{int}\ (b, x) = b'$ and $\exists \omega \in x$ *such that* Δ

$(q, \omega),x) \in b'$. This employs the congruence property to define the next boundary given an input trajectory in the set denoted by the input x (any such input trajectory may be chosen since the destination is the same for all input trajectories applicable to the boundary).

- $\forall(b,x) \in S$, $ta(b,x) = [min\{l(\omega)|\omega \in x\}, max\{l(\omega)|\omega \in x\}]$, where the minimum and maximum of the segment lengths are taken over all input segments $\omega \in x$. While we assume the congruence property with respect to inputs and states, the times to reach the next boundary may vary, thus resulting in an interval in which the values are spread (see also Chapter 10 on RT-DEVS).

This definition of abstraction can be shown to constitute an appropriately defined homomorphism. The major modification required in the definition of homomorphism in Chapter 12 is to accommodate the time advance window.

Let $S = (T, X, \Omega, Q, \Delta)$ be a system and $M = (X, S, \delta_{ext}, \delta_{int}, ta)$ a boundary-based DEVS (for simplicity we omit output considerations—these can be easily added). Figure 16 illustrates the following definition:

Consider a mapping pair (g,h), $g: X \rightarrow \Omega$ and $h: Q' \rightarrow S$ where $h(q) = (b, \phi)$ for some $b \in B$. The pair (g,h) is a *morphism from* S to M if $\forall q \in Q'$, $\forall x \in X$

$$\delta_{int}(\delta_{ext}(h(q), 0, x) = h(\Delta(q, g(x)) \quad (1)$$

and

$$l(g(x)) \in ta(b, x). \quad (2)$$

Because of the definition of h, the right-hand side of line (1) requires that starting on a boundary, the system winds up on another boundary under the input trajectory associated with x. The equation therefore requires that the destination boundary be the same as that produced in the DEVS. Line (2) requires that the time taken to make the boundary-to-boundary transition falls within the interval allowed by the time advance function.

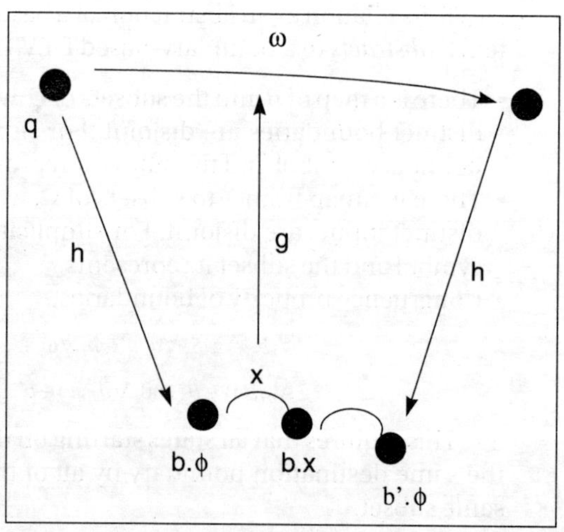

Figure 16 Illustrating a homomorphism from a model to a boundary-based DEVS.

Theorem 2
If a system *S* is abstracted to a boundary-based DEVS, *M*, then there is a morphism (as defined above) from *S* to *M*.

Exercise: Provide the proof.

13.4.2 DEVS Abstraction: Space Travel Example

Let's construct a boundary-based DEVS and show that it is abstracted from the space system described before. The DEVS will focus on the interplanetary journeys and will abstract away details of the trajectories of these journeys. Effectively it will place all those ships with the same source and destination in the same equivalence class and develop brackets on their travel times. (See Fig. 17.)

$$\textit{Boundary-Based DEVS, } M = (X, Y, S, \delta_{ext}, \delta_{int}, \lambda, ta)$$

$$x = \{\text{zero}, \text{earth-to-moon}, \text{earth-to-mars}, \text{ mars-to-earth},$$
$$\text{moon-to-earth}, \text{land-on-earth}, \text{ land-on-moon}, \text{ land on mars}\}$$

$$B = \{\text{earth\_surface}, \text{ moon\_surface}, \text{ mars\_surface}\}.$$

The interpretation of the boundary-based DEVS is formalized in the mappings that show it is an abstraction of the space travel system. Table 2 shows the mapping of *B* to subsets of *Q;* Table 3 shows the mapping of *A* to subsets of Ω.

The congruence requirement holds by construction. For example, for input earth-to-moon, all states on the earth's surface are taken by the selected input trajectories to states on the moon's surface. The same is true for the other inputs.

Exercise: Write an event-based controller that uses the boundary-based DEVS to monitor a multileg flight (one that touches on several moons and planets). Assume that the itinerary is given the controller as input.◆

Exercise: Write a DEV&DESS model of the space travel example in which the thrust of the space ship can vary within certain bounds. With this as a base model, formulate a procedure to determine the time windows for a boundary-based DEVS. (Hint: Using simulation of DEV&DESS base model, search for parameter settings that minimize and maximize the travel times from one planet to another.)◆

Exercise: The boundary-based DEVS, as defined earlier, is restricted so that there is always exactly one transition to a next boundary. We can relax this restriction and allow different next boundaries for a initial block and input. This would result in a nondeterministic abstraction, where a set of next boundary transitions are possible for states in a block and input. Formalize a nondeterministic boundary-based DEVS to represent such cases. (Hint: Consider the two-dimensional pot model in Chapter 9, Section 9.2.1, as an example. In the model, the output thresholds are the boundary crossings. For different states in a block, a threshold of either the *temp* or the *level* dimension might be reached next. See Ref. [13] for details.◆

Phase Definition Table

boundary	input	phase
earth_surface	ϕ	on_earth
earth_surface	earth-to-moon	travelling_earth-to-moon
moon_surface	ϕ	on_moon
earth_surface	earth-to-mars	travelling_earth-to-mars
...	...	...

current phase	next phase
on_earth	on_earth
travelling_earth-to-moon	entering_moon
travelling_earth-to-mars	entering_mars
	...

Internal Transition Table

phase	input	phase
on_earth	earth-to-moon	travelling_earth-to-moon
on_earth	earth-to-mars	travelling_earth-to-mars
on_mars	zero	mars_surface
	...	...

External Transition Table

phase	time window
on_earth	∞
travelling_earth-to-moon	[min travel time, max travel time]
on_moon	∞
travelling_earth-to-mars	[min travel time, max travel time]
...	...

Time Advance Windows

Figure 17 Table definition of space travel example.

13.5 Parameter Morphisms

Often we deal with parameterized models and our attempts to build abstractions of them are based on so-called parameter morphisms. As illustrated in Fig. 18, a *parameter morphism* maps both the state and parameter spaces of the base model to corresponding lumped model state and parameter spaces. The advantage of a parameter morphism is that it does not just work for a single isolated base model, but for a whole class of such models. Given the parameters of the base model, the parameter mapping uniquely determines the settings of the parameters of the lumped model, for which the state mapping becomes an (approximate) homomorphism. Such unique parameterization allows a "set and forget" approach to lumped model simulation. In contrast, without a parameter mapping we have to find the best setting of the parameters, typically by seeking to minimize the error in the homomorphism. Mapping of parameters is also important for cross model validation (see Chapter 15). Typically, a parameter morphism works only when restricted to a sub-

Table 2 Mapping of Boundaries to Subsets of *Q*

Boundary	Subset of Q
earth_surface	All states whose *x,y* coordinates lie on the surface of the sphere representing the earth
mars_surface	All states whose *x,y* coordinates lie on the surface of the sphere representing Mars
moon_surface	All states whose *x,y* coordinates lie on the surface of the sphere representing the moon
...	

space of state and parameter values. Another way of saying this is that there are assumptions underlying the abstraction—often, in practice, such assumptions are not all made as explicit as they should be.

13.5.1 Linear Systems Parameter Morphisms

Linear systems offer the quintessential parameter morphisms. The state mapping discussed in Chapter 12 is a blockwise summation and thus sat-

Table 3 Mapping of *x* to Subsets of Ω

Input	Subset of Ω
φ	$\{0_t>\mid t \in T\}$
earth-to-moon	$\{\omega \mid q$ is on earth's surface and $\delta(q, \omega\}$ is on moon's surface}
earth-to-mars	$\{\omega \mid q$ is on earth's surface and $\delta(q, \omega\}$ is on Mars' surface}
...	...

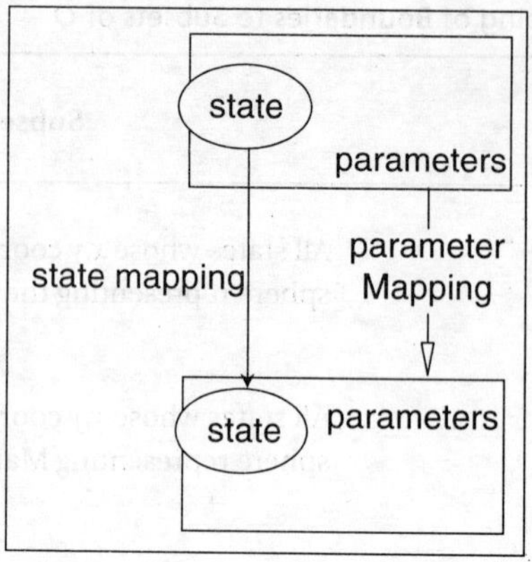

Figure 18 Parameter morphism. Parameters space mapping yields a lumped a model that is valid abstraction of the base model in some experimental frame.

isfies the identity-erasing requirements. However, since it does not preserve state counts, it imposes a less demanding form of interblock coupling indifference requirement then does the state-count-based aggregation. For example, if we create blocks {1,2} and {3,4} in a fourth-order linear transition matrix and focus on the influences of 3 and 4 on 1 and 2, we get the submatrix

$$\begin{bmatrix} - & - & g & g_1 \\ - & - & h & h_1 \\ - & - & - & - \\ - & - & - & - \end{bmatrix}$$

Lumpability requires that the sums of the sending block columns restricted to the receiving block rows be equal, namely, that $g + h = g_1 + h_1$. This states that the combined influence of 3 on {1,2} is equal to that of 4 on {1,2}. In general, components in a sending block equally influence, in an aggregate manner, any receiving block.

Exercise: Show that the equal influence requirement of lumpability for linear systems is less restrictive than the general coupling indifference requirement. (Hint: Show for the preceeding matrix that the coupling indifference requirement is that the sets $\{g, h\}$ and $\{g_1, h_1\}$ be equal (so $g = g_1$ and $h = h_1$ or $g = h_1$ and $h = g_1$), which implies (but is not implied by) the lumpability requirement.)◆

13.5.2 Example Lumpable: Linear DTSS and Parameter Morphisms

Figure 19 illustrates an example of a linear DTSS that is lumpable. Note that the influence of the top two delay components on the bottom two is through the same summation of their states. As we have seen, this strong requirement for coupling indifference is one way in which the linear lumpability conditions can be satisfied, but not the only way.

The matrix of the fourth-order (four delay) system and that of its lumped version are:

$$\begin{bmatrix} 0 & 0 & g & g \\ 0 & 0 & h & h \\ k & k & 0 & 0 \\ l & l & 0 & 0 \end{bmatrix} \rightarrow \begin{bmatrix} 0 & g+h \\ k+l & 0 \end{bmatrix}.$$

The aggregation, illustrated in Fig. 20, maps coordinates {1,2} to 1 and {3,4} to 2. Interpreted as a parameter morphism, the aggregation mapping does the following:

- Maps the state space of the base model to that of the lumped model:

$$h(q_1, q_2, q_3, q_4) = (q_1 + q_2, q_3 + q_4).$$

- Maps the parameter space of the base model to that of the lumped model:

$$p(g,h,k,l) = (g+h, k+l)$$

If we take the model in Fig. 19 as the parameterized base model, there is no restriction on the state space or parameter space for which the morphism works. However, consider the space of all fourth-order models that have the structure

$$\begin{bmatrix} 0 & 0 & g & g1 \\ 0 & 0 & h & h1 \\ k & k & 0 & 0 \\ l & l & 0 & 0 \end{bmatrix}$$

In this space, the restrictions justifying the morphism are that $g = g1$ and $h = h1$. In other words, the lumpability conditions are the assumptions underlying the parameter morphism.

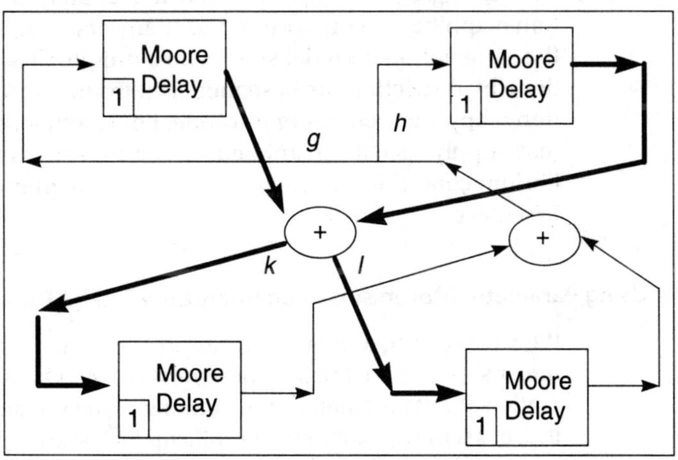

Figure 19 Linear lumpable system.

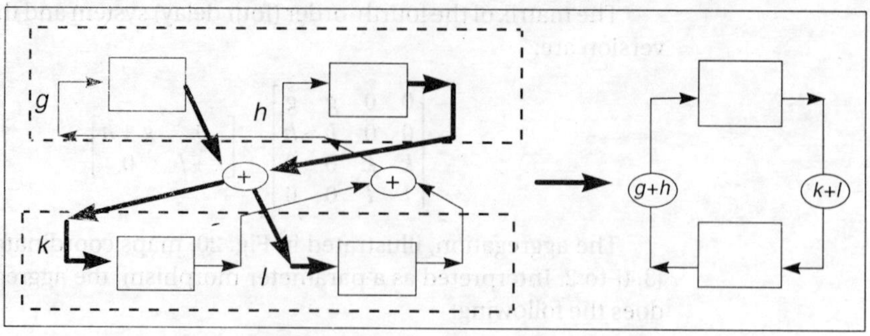

Figure 20 Aggregation mapping.

13.5.3 Constraints on Parameter and State Spaces: Disaggregation

We conclude from the foregoing discussion that parameter morphisms typically only work when parameters are restricted to a subset of the parameter space. Such constraints on validity should be included with the statement of the morphism. The same can be said for state space constraints. In many cases, lumped models can be constructed under assumptions that constrain the states for which the aggregation mapping is a valid morphism. Equilibrium conditions are often used for this purpose. Typically, when a model is in equilibrium, constraints exist on its parameters that make it easier to construct valid parameter morphisms. Of course, it is then important to include such constraints in the statement of the morphism. For example, it might be stated that the morphism is exact if the base model is operating in equilibrium and that it becomes approximate for other states. As indicated before, we will consider such approximations in the next chapter.

Disaggregation is a process where we wish to associate a base model state with a given lumped model state. Multiresolution modeling, where we may alternate between models at different levels of resolution, requires such disaggregation capabilities. Unfortunately, by its nature, an aggregation mapping is many-to-one, i.e., many base model states are mapped to the same lumped model state. Thus, unique dissagregation can only be done by restricting the base model states to a subset where the aggregation mapping becomes one-to-one. For example, equilibrium conditions may supply such a constrained subset. Indeed, as indicated earlier, equilibrium conditions may have justified the mapping as a morphism in the first place.

13.5.4 Using Parameter Morphisms in an Integrated Model Family

We have seen that parameter morphisms contain relations between parameter sets of model pairs. These relations can be used to propagate information about parameter values among models in an integrated model family. Let's see how parameter morphisms look and help propagate information in the space travel example. The base model in Fig. 21 contains detailed representations about the ports of call, routes, times, and individual ships in the

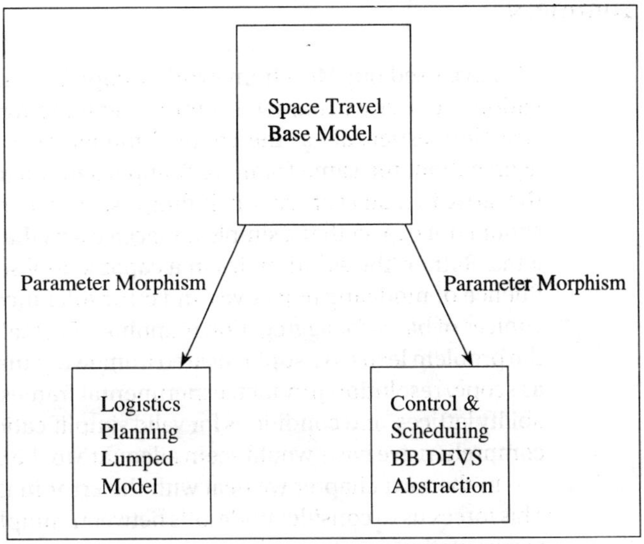

Figure 21 Parameter morphisms in space travel example.

system. Recall the morphisms we constructed in earlier sections to build the logistics and control models. These should now be extended to parameter morphisms so that they also transmit parameter information from the base model to the abstractions. This means that parameter values employed in the abstractions should be determined by formulas (rules, procedures; tables, etc.) from parameter values in the base model.[3] For example, the time windows in the boundary-based DEVS are derived from the minimum and maximum travel times of equivalent trajectories in the base model. Having a parameter morphism for such a window would not allow it to be frozen forever. For example, a new flight path might be made possible by new technology that significantly reduced the minimum time to travel from earth to the moon. Then the parameter morphism would cause the corresponding time window to be automatically updated. This might be done by placing demons in the model base that look for changes in the inputs of parameter formulas and invoke a recomputation of the formula when a change occurs. Other base model information that might change such as new ports of call (planets or moons), new routes, and new routing policies would also be propagated automatically by parameter morphisms.

Exercise: Express the relationship of parameters in the logistics model to those of the space travel base model. Consider how changes in base model parameters might be propagated to the logistics model.◆

For a detailed discussion of parameter propagation please see [18].

[3]It might be ideal if all such parameters could be set from the base model, but this might not be possible, since in practice the scope of the base model is itself limited and not all information in an abstraction can be derived from it.

13.6 Summary

We have used our M&S framework (Chapter 2) and the morphism specification hierarchy (Chapter 12) for understanding the issues in model abstraction, especially at the coupled model level. While our focus was on aggregation, the same framework applies to the multiresolution problems that arise in many contexts including distributed interactive simulation. We should not expect that a simple panacea exists that conquers all such problems. Rather, the solution lies in a capable tool set that recognizes the influence of modeling objectives and error tolerances, the multidimensional choices of bases for aggregation mappings. Formalizing such dimensions of the problem leads to a sophisticated framework that involves concepts such as scope/resolution product, experimental frames, applicability and derivability lattices, and conditions for valid simplification. Nothing less than this comprehensive basis would seem adequate to the demands of the problem.

In the next chapter we deal with the error in the abstraction explicitly. This forces us to consider trade-offs between complexity reduction and error accumulation.

13.7 Sources

Aggregation has been of interest in economic modeling [13,17], and ecological modeling [2,10] for some time. Axtell [1] reviews much of this literature and the issues raised. A more general summary, focusing on engineering and military application, is given by Caughlin [4]. A special issue of *Transactions of the Society for Computer Simulation* on model abstraction contains papers by Caughlin [3], Lee [14], Takahashi [18], and Zeigler [21].

Aggregation in queueing is discussed in [16] and [5]. Integrated families of models were introduced by Davis [6,7].

1. Axtell, R., *Theory of Model Aggregation for Dynamical Systems with Application to Problems of Global Change.* Pittsburgh, Carnegie Mellon University, 1992.
2. Cale, W. G., "Model Aggregation: Ecological Perspectives." In *Complex Ecology: The Part–Whole Relation in Ecosystems* (B. C. Patten and S. E. Jorgensen, Eds.). Prentice Hall PTR, Englewood Cliffs, NJ, 1995, pp. 230–241.
3. Caughlin, D., "Model Abstraction via solution of a General Inverse Problem to Define a Metamodel." *Trans. of SCS* **13**(5), 191–216 (1996).
4. Caughlin, D., and Alex F. Sisti, "A Summary of Model Abstraction Techniques," presented at the International Society for Optical Engineering (SPIE), 22–24 April, Orlando, FL, 1997.
5. Courtois, P. J., Decomposability: Queueing and Computer System Applications. Academic Press, New York, 1977, 201 pages.
6. "An Introduction to Variable-Resolution Modeling and Cross Resolution Model Connection." *Naval Logistics Jnl.* **42**(2), 151–182 (1995).

7. Davis, P. K., and R. Hillestad. "Families of Models That Cross Levels of Resolution: Issues for Design, Calibration and Management." In *Winter Simulation Conference.* IEEE Press, 1993.
8. Dennet, D. C., *Darwin's Dangerous Idea.* Simon and Schuster, New York, 1995.
9. Fishwick, P. A., "Abstraction Level Traversal in Hierarchical Modeling." In *Modelling and Simulation Methodology: Knowledge Systems Paradigms* (B. P. Zeigler *et al.*, Eds.). Elsevier North Holland, New York, 1989, pp. 393–429.
10. Fishwick, P. A., J. Sanderson, et al. (1998). "A Multimodelling Basis for Across-Trophic-Level Ecosystem Modeling: The Florida Everglades Example." *Trans. of SCS* **15**(2): 76–88.
11. Hartmanis, J., and R. E. Stearns, *Algebraic Structure Theory of Sequential Machines.* Prentice Hall, Englewood Cliffs, N J, 1969.
12. Hopcroft, J. E., *Introduction to Automata Theory, Languages, and Computation.* Addison-Wesley, 1979.
13. Ijiri, Y., "Fundamental Queries in an Aggregation Theory." *J. Am. Stat. Assoc.* **66**(5), 766–782 (1971).
14. Lee, K., and P. A. Fishwick, "A Methodology for Dynamic Model Abstraction." *Trans. of SCS* **13**(5), 191–217 (1996).
15. Praehofer, H., P. Bichler, and B. P. Zeigler, "Synthesis of Endomorphic Models for Event Based Intelligent Control." *Proc. AI, Simulation and Planning in High-Autonomy Systems,* Tucson, AZ, Sept. 1993. IEEE/CS Press, pp. 120–126.
16. Savory, P. A., and G. T. Mackulak, "Cycle Time Estimation for Simulating a Tandem Queuing System Using Aggregation Techniques." *Trans. of SCS* **13**(3), 125–134 (1997).
17. Simon, H. A., and A. Ando, "Aggregation of Variables in Dynamic Systems." *Econometrica* **29**(16), 111–138 (1961).
18. Takahashi, S., "General Morphism for Modeling Relations in Multimodeling." *Trans. of SCS* **13**(5), 169–178 (1996).
19. Zeigler, B. P., "Towards a Formal Theory of Modeling and Simulation: Structure Preserving Morphisms." *J. of the ACM,* 742–746 (1972).
20. Zeigler, B. P., *Multifacetted Modelling and Discrete Event Simulation.* Academic Press, London, 1984.
21. Zeigler, B. P., and Y. Moon, "Abstraction Methodology Based on Parameter Morphisms." In *Enabling Technology for Simulation Science, SPIE AeoroSense 97,* Orlando, FL, 1997.

14

Verification, Validation, Approximate Morphisms: Living with Error

This chapter deals with error—*verification* (how to check if a simulator is in error), and *validation* (how to check if a model is in error). The standard for error-free relations between entities in the framework for M&S is the morphism. But in the real world, error is inevitable and we must usually be satisfied with something less than the perfect agreement required by such morphisms. So we have to deal with *approximate* morphisms—relations that are close to, but not 100%, perfect morphisms.[1]

14.1 Verification

Verification is the attempt to establish that the simulation relation (Chapter 2) holds between a simulator and a model. Actually, as we have seen, the simulator may be capable of executing a whole class of models. In this case, we wish to guarantee that it can execute any of these models correctly. There are two general approaches to verification:

- Formal proofs of correctness
- Extensive testing

The basic concept in establishing correctness is that of **morphism,** and we have seen that morphisms can exist at different levels of the system specification hierarchy (Chapter 12). Since both model and simulator are known at the higher levels of structure, it is possible to apply system morphisms at such levels to prove correctness. In such a morphism, when a model should go through a state sequence, the simulator should go through a corresponding state sequence. Typically, a simulator is designed to take a number of *microstate* transitions to simulate a *macrostate* transition of the model. These

Material in this chapter adapted from D. Cloud and L. Rainey, Eds. *Applied Modeling & Simulation: An Integrated Approach to Development & Operation.* McGraw-Hill, New York, 1998, with permission.

[1]While we emphasize morphisms, alternative formulations emphasize statistical techniques [2].

are computation steps necessary to achieve the desired end result. Moreover, a simulator has a lot of apparatus, represented in its states, necessary to accommodate the whole class of models rather than a single one. The fact that morphisms propagate down the specification hierarchy (Chapter 12) has a practical application—if a designer can show that such a morphism holds between the simulator and any model in a class, then the simulator correctness will have been established for that class. In other words, any state trajectory of a model in the class will be properly reproduced by the simulator.

Formal proofs employ mathematical and logical formalisms underpinning the concepts in the systems specification hierarchy to rigorously establish the requisite morphism. Unfortunately, such proofs are difficult or impossible to carry out for large, complex systems. Moreover, they may also be prone to error since ultimately humans have to understand the symbols and carry out their manipulations. On the positive side, more automated tools are becoming available to relieve some of the burden.

In the absence of once-and-for-all proofs, extensive testing must be done to ensure that all conditions that could arise in simulator operation have been covered by test cases. Time and other resources limit the amount of testing that can be done. However, even though formal proofs are not employed, the morphism concept comes in handy since it offers a framework for laying out the combinations of inputs and states that have to be tested for thorough, yet efficient, testing [3].

14.2 Validation at the Behavioral Level

Validation is the process of testing a model for validity. Figure 1 illustrates how the experimental frame is critical in this process. The frame generates

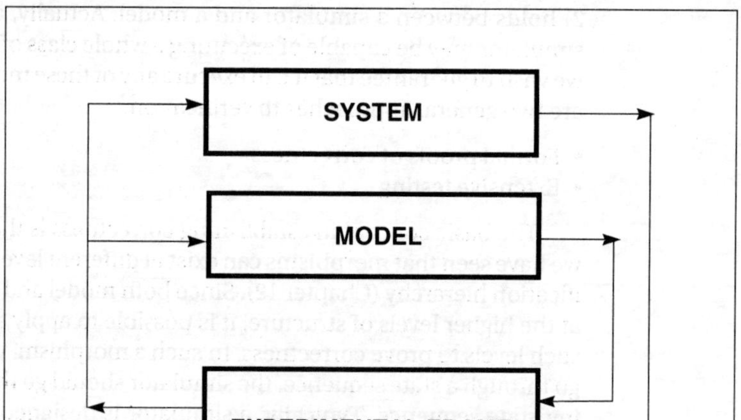

Figure 1 Validation within experimental frame.

input trajectories to both the source system and the model under test. The corresponding output trajectories of the model and system are fed back into the frame. Validity, whether replicative, predictive, or structural (Chapter 2), requires that these trajectories be equal. We will first discuss replicative validation as the basic level of the validation process in which trajectories are compared. Later we will consider predictive and structural validation.

The experimental frame is critical in assessing model validity since it provides the conditions under which both model and system are to be experimented with. Therefore, we'll examine the experimental frame concept in more depth before proceeding further. Recall that a frame is decomposed into generator, acceptor, and transducer components (Chapter 2). Table 1 presents some generator, acceptor, and transducer behaviors typically associated with continuous, discrete time, and discrete event system specifications.

Recall that a *generator* stimulates the system with input trajectories. In continuous systems such trajectories take the form of various kinds of *aperiodic* functions such as steps and ramps, or various *periodic* functions such as sine waves or square waves. In discrete event systems, arrival of events (such as jobs for processing) may be periodic or *stochastic* (random). In the latter case, we need to specify the probability distribution of the interarrival times, such as *uniform* or *exponential.* The type of processing required

Table 1 Typical Experimental Frame Components

System formalism	Typical generator	Typical acceptor	Typical transducer
DESS (continuous systems)			Final value
DTSS (discrete time)	Periodic: sine wave, square wave	Steady state	
	Aperiodic: step, ramp	Transient	Rise time
DEVS (discrete event)			
	Periodic arrivals	Small queues	Throughput
	Stochastic arrivals	Large queues	Turnaround time Utilization
	Workload characteristics		Failure rate Blocking rate

(*workload*) is also part of the generator specification.

We often make a distinction between the *transient* and *steady-state* characteristics of system behavior. The *acceptor* is the slot in the experimental frame where conditions limiting the observation of behavior, such as steady-state versus transient, can be specified. For example, if interest in transient behavior is specified, then the frame would extract only the parts of the trajectories shown within the corresponding box in Fig. 2.

The *transducer* processes the output trajectories, where such postprocessing may range from none at all (in which case the trajectories are directly observed) to very coarse summaries where only certain features of interest are extracted. For example, for transient conditions, we may be interested in the *rise time* (time to adjust to change). On the other hand, in steady-state conditions, the *final value* reached may be of interest. In discrete event systems, we might be interested in the *turnaround times* required to process jobs or in the *throughput* (rate of job completion). *Utilization* of various resources and occurrence of special events such as *failure* or *blocking* may be of interest.

Usually the many numbers produced are summarized into statistical quantities such as the *average, maximum,* or *minimum.* Data may also be grouped into classes called *quantiles* with associated breakpoints. For example, the *median* separates the data into two classes of equal sizes.

Please note that we have only mentioned some of the wide variety of features that can be formulated in experimental frames. Many features, while frequently associated with continuous systems, may also apply to discrete event systems, and conversely.

14.2.1 Quantitative Comparison

Recall that validation requires comparison of model and source system behavior. Please note that the comparison is only performed under the conditions of experimentation specified in the frame: that is, only under the

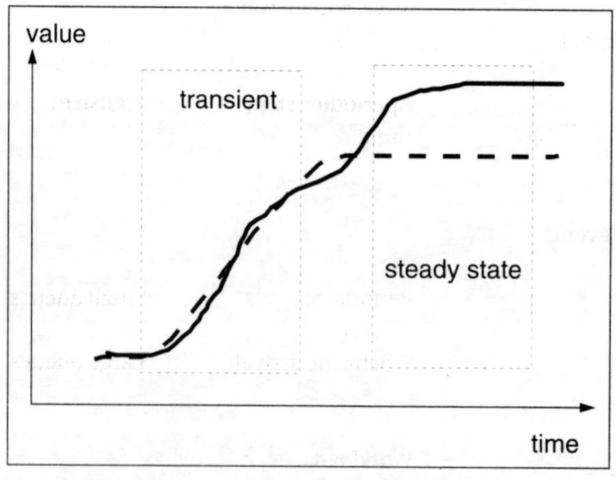

Figure 2 Experimental frame operating regions: transient versus steady-state conditions.

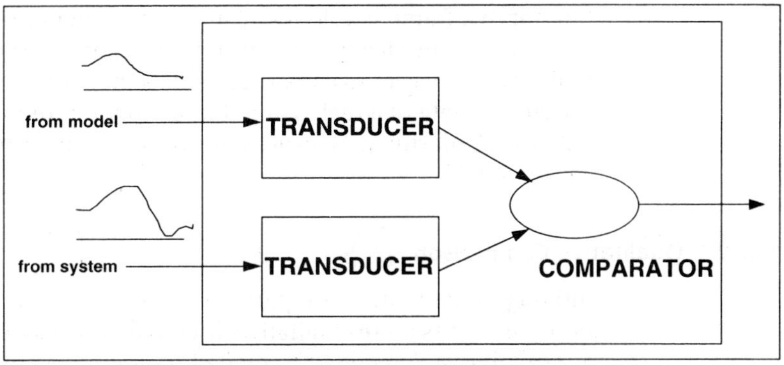

Figure 3 Comparing trajectories in an experimental frame.

input trajectories generated by the generator, the control conditions checked by the acceptor, and the output summaries performed by the transducer. Such a comparison is illustrated in Fig. 3, where the input trajectories are the respective output trajectories of the system and model. Each is summarized by a copy of the same transducer and the summaries are compared. In the conventional approach, comparison requires a *metric* and a *tolerance.* The metric provides a numerical basis for measuring *goodness-of-fit.* The *tolerance* is a positive number that determines when the fit is good enough.[2] When the fit is outside of tolerance, the model trajectory is judged not to be close enough to that of the system for the model to qualify as valid in the particular frame. On the other hand, if the fit is within tolerance, then the model validity is *confirmed*—but *not established,* since a possible infinitude of trajectories still need to be compared. Typical metrics are the familiar *distance measure in Euclidean space* (square root of sum of squared differences), *largest absolute difference,* and *city block distance* (sum of absolute differences).

When stochastic processes are employed, comparison involves a further consideration: how representative are the observed samples of the underlying spaces? Statistical techniques are then employed to judge significance in terms of the number of samples observed and the variance in their values. However, a word of caution: Statistical techniques often make assumptions characterizing the stochastic nature of the data sources, such as normal distributions. These are models themselves and may not be valid!

In doing such comparisons it is easy to forget that the choice of what to observe may have as great, or greater, bearing on validity judgments as the metrics and statistical procedures employed. For example, returning to Fig. 2, the two curves shown are very close (under most reasonable metrics) in the transient behavior but far apart in the steady-state region. Thus a model might be judged valid in a frame that focuses on transient behavior,

[2] Tolerance can be more abstractly defined as a relation on states independently of a metric. Insights into error propagation discussed later in the chapter can be obtained with such a formalization [5].

but not in a frame that looks at steady-state behavior. Or, a model might agree well in the steady-state region but not in the transition to it. Indeed, typically, it is easier to construct models that are accurate with respect to the steady state of a real system but are poor at representing its transient behavior. Unfortunately, especially nowadays, many processes are never in steady state!

14.2.2 Qualitative Comparison

Although quantitative comparison provides an objective basis for validation, it can miss more qualitative discrepancies or agreements that humans are capable of detecting if provided the right perspectives. Two methods attempting to provide such perspectives are *visualization* and *animation. Visualization* attempts to map complex numerical data into graphic structures that humans can more readily understand. Actually, simple graphical displays can suffice for illustrating this idea. Table 2 contains some behaviors that were first encountered in linear systems as displayed in figures of Chapter 3. However, the general trends—increasing, decreasing, oscillating—can be present in general. For example, models of the universe can be steady-state (fixed), expanding, or contracting. Graphical display makes it easy for us to immediately distinguish among such behaviors. The importance for validation is that if a model is supposed to manifest one of these behaviors but actually exhibits another, it is clearly invalid. Quantitative comparison is needed to make finer distinctions between behaviors that agree in their basic form, but qualitative comparison can quickly eliminate

Table 2 Some Behaviors That are Easily Distinguishable by Visual Means

Behavior	Description	Linear system example
Fixed	Variable is constant over time	Same
Indefinite increase	Variable is increasing over time	Exponential explosion
Indefinite decrease	Variable is decreasing over time	Exponential decay
Oscillation	Variable is oscillates between fixed values	Sine wave

models that are not even in the right ballpark. By subjecting models to such qualitative tests early in model development, it may be possible to eliminate wrong formulations and focus in promising directions long before serious quantitative comparison can be attempted. For example, recall the space travel example of Chapter 13, where a nonlinear fourth-order system orbiting system decomposes into two independent second-order linear oscillators when initialized to states that establish circular orbits. By initializing in such states, complex models of orbiting mechanics, which are supposed to be consistent with this easily identifiable oscillatory behavior, can easily be invalidated if they do not exhibit it.

Animation presents the simulated state behavior of a model in a movie-like form that corresponds to the underlying physical reality—as a simulation of manufacturing might show parts moving from one workstation to the next on conveyor belts. *Virtual reality* goes further by providing a sensation of actual presence in the simulation. Validation methodology can profit from such presentations, since humans can recognize events or configurations that seem to be in conflict with everyday experience. It is also possible to train *neural nets* or other artificial pattern recognizers to do such detection.

14.3 Performance/Validity (e.g., Speed/Accuracy) Trade-off

Recall (Chapter 13) that scope/resolution product is an indicator of the complexity of a model. Complexity is a measure of the resources required to analyze, simulate, and develop the model. Typically, the performance of a simulator will increase as the complexity of a model decreases. For example, the speed of a simulator (measured, say, in the number of model transition executions it can do in a given time) will usually increase as either the number of components or the number of states per component diminishes. We can similarly talk of the performance of model development or the model exploration process in terms of how long it takes to develop the model or how many alternatives can be examined in a given time, respectively.

So on one hand, performance can be expected to improve with reduced complexity. On the other hand, reducing the scope/resolution product often entails a loss of validity of the model—which, of course, has to be measured within an experimental frame of interest. Thus, often we are in a situation where we must sacrifice potential validity for improved performance of a development or simulation process. This performance/validity trade-off is illustrated in Fig. 4, where we see, conceptually depicted, performance increasing while validity decreases as the scope/resolution product is decreased. In such a situation, we can set a level of error tolerance that determines the level of error we can live with—any model with more error (less validity) cannot be accepted. The complexity reduction or performance improvement at that tolerance level is the best we can achieve. Of course, the purposes for which the model is being constructed or deployed should determine such threshold limits. We can include acceptance criteria within our experimental frame as well, so that the acceptance judgments could be automated.

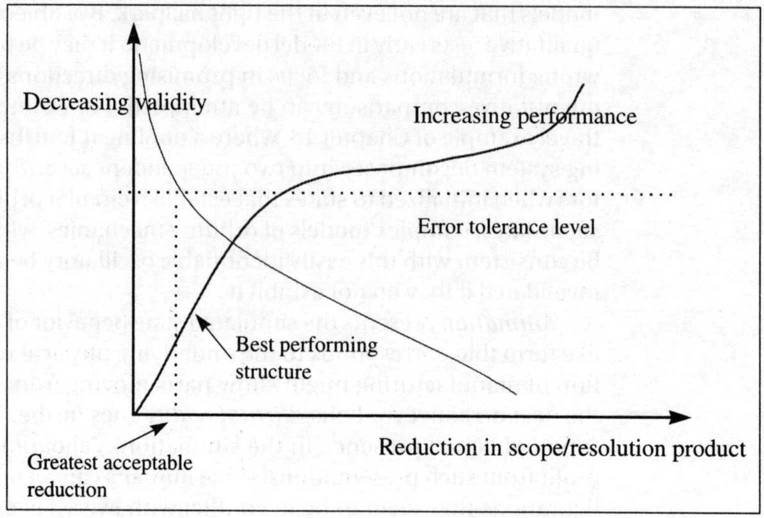

Figure 4 Performance/validity trade-off.

Before we look at an example, Fig. 5 reminds us that the trade-off space we are in is determined by our experimental frame. Thus, if we are demanding high resolution in model output, then error may increase beyond a tolerable level as the detail included in the model structure decreases. However, it may well be that if we require a lower level of resolution in the model output, then the error may be below tolerance, or even vanish, for the same level of detail included in the model. Indeed, the complexity in the model

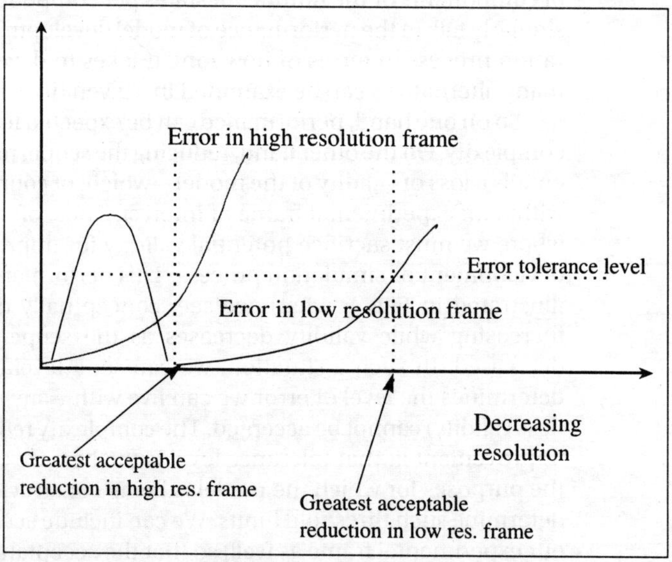

Figure 5 Breaking the speed/accuracy trade-off with choice of experimental frames.

may be much lower at the threshold of acceptability for the low-resolution frame than for its high-resolution counterpart. Correspondingly, the fastest simulation might be much faster in the low-resolution frame than in the high-resolution one. This graphically illustrates the importance of choosing experimental frames that are no more demanding than needed for the particular task at hand.

Exercise: Let the number of blocks in a state partition be the measure of model resolution. Let zero be the error tolerance level so that only true homomorphic lumped models are allowed. For an 8-counter (Chapter 13), with a desired output of size 4, draw the "curve" of error versus resolution as the latter decreases from 8 to 1. Do the same for an output of size 2. (Hint: The lattice of congruent partitions for an 8-counter is shown in Fig. 6.)♦

Example of speed/accuracy trade-off: Watershed Modeling

One example of such a trade-off is a speed/accuracy trade-off, where, for example, we investigate how the speed of a simulation program increases as we successively aggregate model components in coarser and coarser partitions.

Consider an experimental frame in which we are interested in surface water accumulation the bottom of a hill as in Fig. 7. As rainfall starts, the water starts rising and then reaches a maximum level some time after the rain stops. The experimental frame is interested in this runoff over time. The goodness-of-fit criterion is the maximum of the absolute difference between predicted and actual runoff. The error tolerance is 10% of rainfall input, assumed constant.

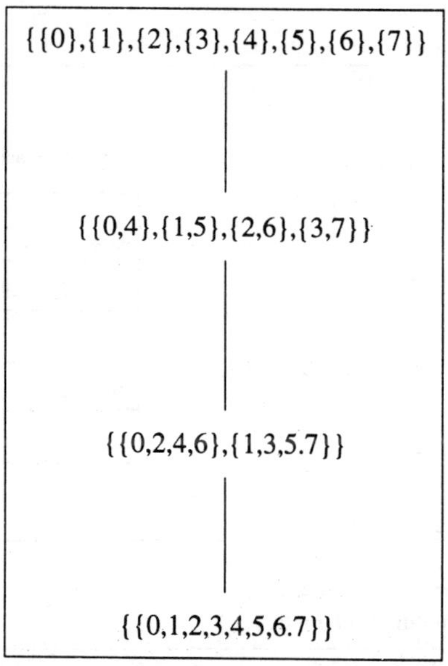

Figure 6 Lattice of partitions for 8-counter.

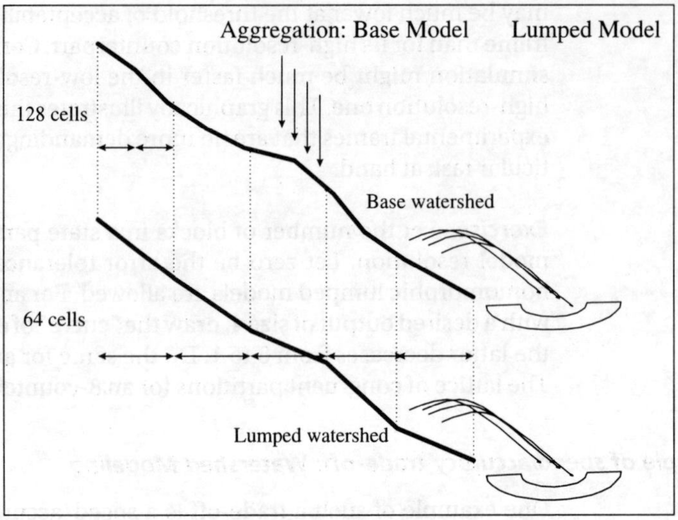

Figure 7 Aggregation mapping of high-resolution watershed models.

DEVS cell space models of surface watershed runoff and their implementation in high-performance environments are detailed in [9]. Starting with a base model of 128 cells, a lumped model of 64 cells was created by an aggregation mapping in which adjacent pairs of cells were combined into single cells. A second lumped model was created by using the same process to arrive at a model with 32 cells, and so on. The aggregation map is a parameter morphism (Chapter 13).

The effect of successive aggregation of cells on the accuracy and speed of simulation is shown in Fig. 8. As the resolution is reduced, simulation time

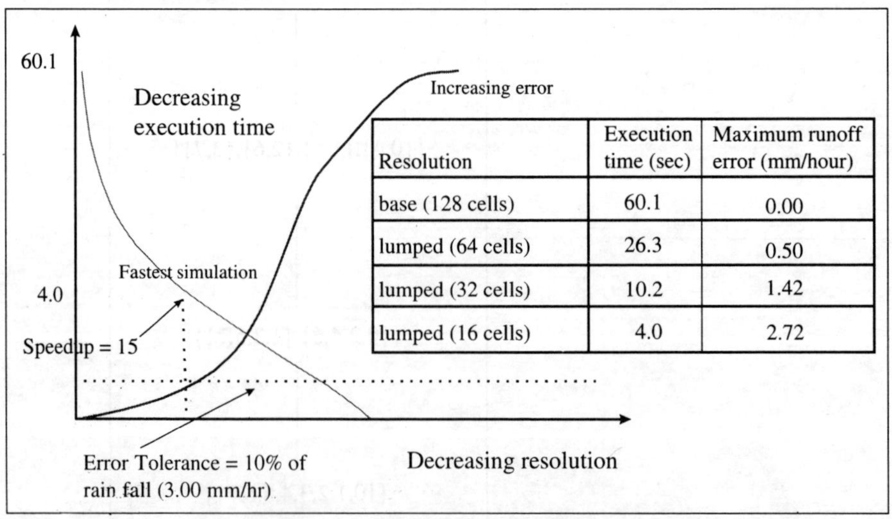

Resolution	Execution time (sec)	Maximum runoff error (mm/hour)
base (128 cells)	60.1	0.00
lumped (64 cells)	26.3	0.50
lumped (32 cells)	10.2	1.42
lumped (16 cells)	4.0	2.72

Figure 8 Speed/accuracy trade-off in aggregation.

decreases while error increases. We found that we could obtain a 15-fold speedup with an error tolerance of 10% of input rainfall by decreasing resolution by a factor of 8.

14.4 Approximate Morphisms and Error Behavior

14.4.1 Approximate Morphisms and the Specification Hierarchy

So far we have seen how loss of accuracy often arises from reducing the score/resolution product. But we have not discussed why this happens or what can be done about it. Since each level of the specification hierarchy (Chapter 5) offers a means to create a model of a real system, it also presents an opportunity to do so incorrectly. Recall that morphisms afford the means to compare systems at each level of the specification hierarchy (Chapter 12). This suggests a general concept of *approximate morphism*—if all the requirements for a morphism between systems specified at a particular level are not met, then we can call the morphism approximate, as opposed to exact. Thus, as illustrated in Fig. 9, there is an approximate morphism concept at each level of the specialization hierarchy. If there is an approximate morphism between a model and a real system at some level, then we can say that the model is in *error* as an account of the system at that level. As we have seen, just how big this error is depends on our choice of measure of agreement.

Figure 9 also suggests another important consideration—how do approximate morphisms behave as we descend the levels of the hierarchy? Recall

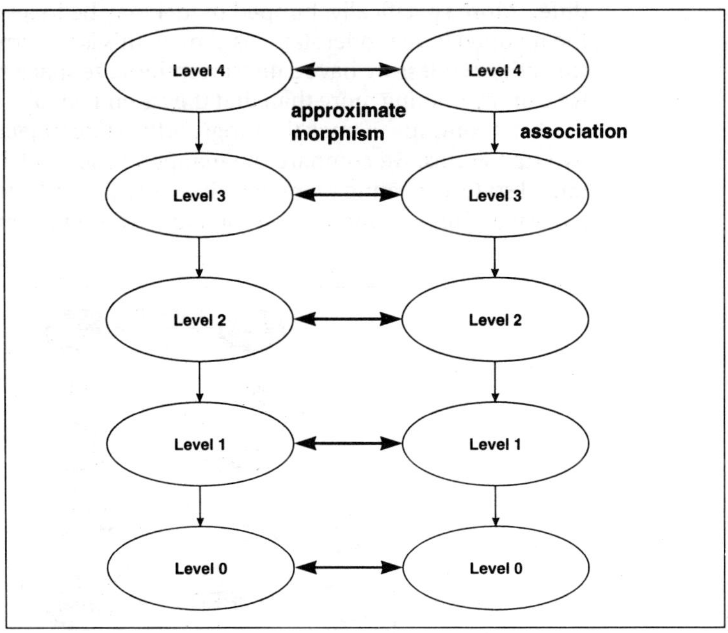

Figure 9 Approximate morphisms at system specification levels.

that given a system specification, there is a way to associate with it a system specification at the next lower level and this carries over to morphisms as well (Chapter 12). Thus, for example, given an exact morphism between a pair of systems at level 4, there is an exact morphism between the associated system specifications at level 3. When the morphism in question is only approximate, we might still expect that there will be an approximate morphism at the next lower level. So, for example, given an approximate morphism between a pair of systems at level 4, there is an approximate morphism between the associated system specifications at level 3. Recall that going down the levels corresponds to a simulation process, i.e., generating the behavior of the model given its structure. Thus, a disagreement in structure between a base model and a lumped model, as encoded in an approximate morphism at level 4, would show up ultimately in the mismatch in their behaviors as encoded in an approximate morphism at level 1. Errors in structure may not only be manifested immediately, but also at later times as they propagate through the simulation process.

14.4.2 Approximate Homomorphisms and Error Propagation

To understand how errors can propagate in the simulation process, we'll focus on approximate morphisms at the state transition level of specification. As illustrated in Fig. 10, let there be a mapping from the states of a base model to those of a lumped model. Let the base and lumped models be in states that correspond under this mapping and consider corresponding transitions in these states for both models. Were the state mapping to be an exact homomorphism, then the states after the transition would correspond under the mapping. However, in an approximate morphism, the states may differ. More specifically, lumped model may be in a state that differs from the mapped base model state. As shown, this is the error introduced in one transition. Unless we have a metric for the state space of the lumped model, we can say nothing more than that they aren't equal.

Let's continue to track the progress the state trajectories in Fig. 11. After two transitions, we compare the mapped base model state to the lumped model state, expecting them to be in error. Similarly, the mapped state trajectory of the base model and the lumped model state trajectory may be

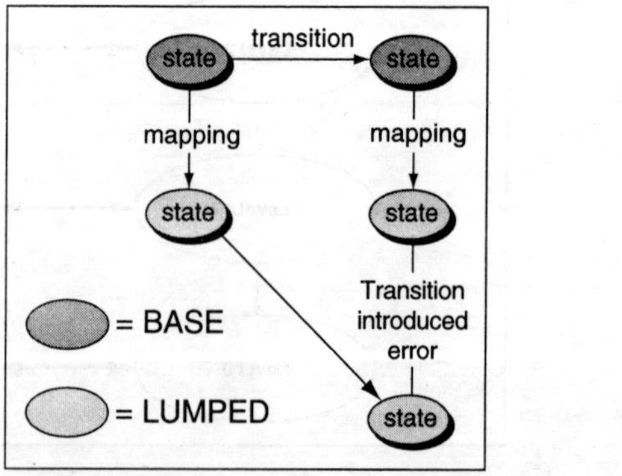

Figure 10 Error introduced in approximate homomorphism.

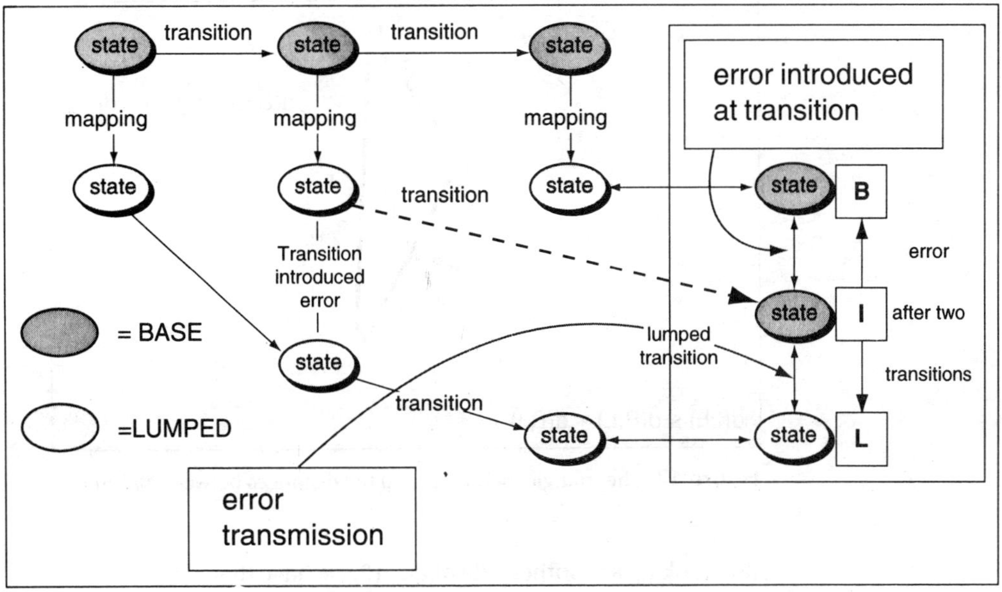

Figure 11 Error accumulation over time.

compared at every transition. Again, if we have a metric for judging the distance between trajectories, we can say how far apart these trajectories are. More than that, we may sometimes be able to discern how the error introduced at each transition (as in Fig. 10) propagates to affect the total error in subsequent transitions.

To see this, look at the box in Fig. 11. There look at a third state in the lumped state space, illustrated at the end of the dashed arrow. This state is obtained by applying the lumped model transition function to the lumped state that was the image of the base model state in the previous transition. In a metric space, it may be "intermediary" between the two states we are interested in—the mapped based model state and the lumped model state. Our goal is to link the error (which is distance between the latter two states) to their distances to the intermediary state. Why? Because these last two distances can be related to information available in a single transition.

As in Fig. 11, let's call the mapped base state *B;* the intermediary state *I;* and the lumped state *L.* Then notice that the distance between B and I is the error introduced in a single transition. And the distance between *I* and *L* is how the lumped model transition function treats two states: Does their separation increase, decrease, or stay the same after one transition?

Figure 12 depicts how the distances are interrelated using the triangle inequality for distance measures (called metrics), *d.* Basically, each side is less than the sum of the other two. Looking at the side *BL,* this tells us directly that

$$d(B,L) \le d(B,I) + d(I,L). \tag{1}$$

This means that if we have *upper bounds* on $d(B,I)$ (the error introduced in a single transition) and $d(I,L)$ (the error propagated from the last transition), then we have an *upper bound* on the error at this transition.

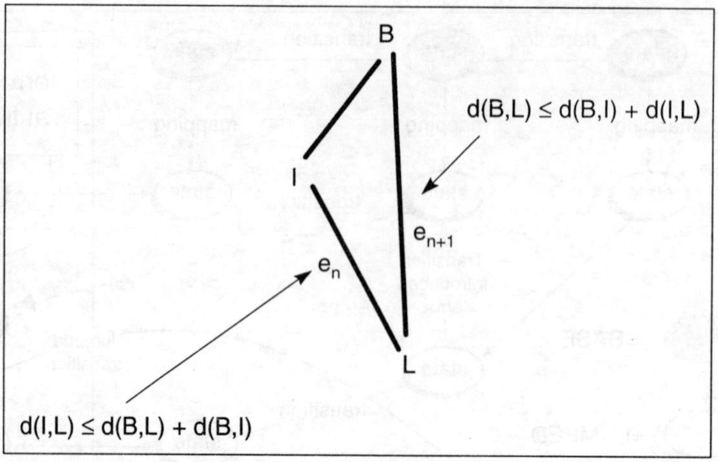

Figure 12 The triangle inequality and the distances between *B*, *I*, and *L*.

Also, looking at another side of Fig. 12, we have that

$$d(B,L) \geq d(I,L) - d(B,I). \tag{2}$$

So if we have a *lower bound* on the propagated error and an *upper bound* on the error introduced at this transition, then we have a *lower bound* on the error at this transition.

Error Propagation and Accumulation: Bounded and Unbounded Growth

Using the relationships just given, we can characterize the way error propagates over many transitions in terms of lumped model properties. Let ε_n be the error introduced at transition n and let e_n the total error at transition n where $e_0 = 0$ (since we start in corresponding states). Let Fig. 12 represent the situation at transition $n + 1$. This means we can interpret $d(B,I) = \varepsilon_n$, $d(B,L) = e_{n+1}$, and $d(I,L)$ as the error propagated by lumped model from the last transition.

Suppose we know that $d(I,L) \leq a_n \times e_n$, i.e., that the error at a transition grows no bigger than a factor a_n times what it was at the previous transition. Then equation (1) gives us

$$e_{n+1} \leq a_n \times e_n + \varepsilon_n.$$

If, at every transition $a_n < 1$, we let a be the largest of the a_n and we call a the attenuation factor. In this case, we have bounded growth of the error:

$$e_n \leq \frac{\varepsilon}{1-a},$$

where ε is the largest of the ε_n.

Exercise: Using the formula for sums of geometric terms, prove the bounded growth relation.◆

A more subtle bound on growth occurs when the magnification is greater than unity but is counteracted by the introduced error. We will encounter this situation in Chapter 16 (DEVS Representation).

Exercise: Show that if a is an upper bound for the error growth parameters a_n and ε is an upper bound for error introduced in each step ε_n, then the accumulated error is bounded by:

$$e_n \leq \frac{\varepsilon\left(a^n - 1\right)}{a-1}. \blacklozenge$$

Now consider the accumulated error e_N after N iterations and suppose that $a = 1 + b/N$. The term a^N becomes $(1 + b/N)^N$ which is bounded by exp(b) as N goes to infinity. Substituting in the bound for e_N and manipulating terms, we have that e_N is bounded by $N\varepsilon(\exp(b) - 1)/b$. For small b, we have $e_N \leq N\varepsilon$. This brings out the essential result to be used later—for $a = 1 + b/N$, the error grows at most linearly for large N. For convenience, we will not carry forward the proportionality factor as it will not change the essential results in Chapter 16.

If, on the other hand, we know that $d(I,L) \geq a_n \times e_n$, i.e., that the error grows no smaller than a factor a_n times what it was at the previous transition. Then equation (2) gives us

$$e_{n+1} \geq a_n \times e_n - \varepsilon_{n+1}.$$

If, at every transition, $a_n > 1$, we let A be the smallest of the a_n and we call A the amplification factor. Also let ε be the largest of the e_n. In this case, we have unbounded growth of the error:

$$e_{n+1} \geq A^n \times \varepsilon,$$

where ε is the smallest of the ε_n for sufficiently large A.

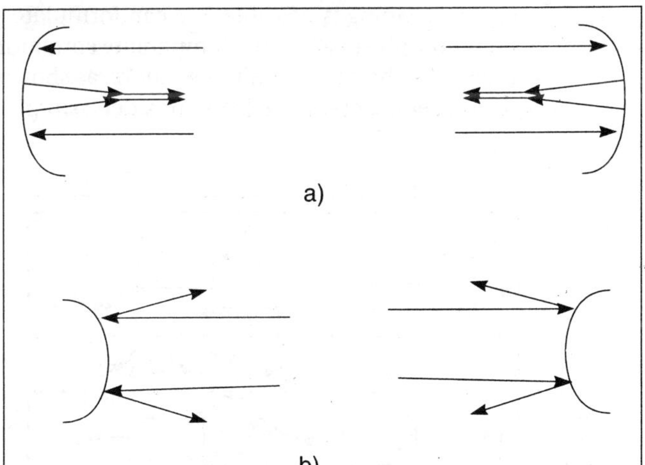

Figure 13 Illustrating (a) error attenuation and (b) error amplification.

Exercise: Using the formula for sums of geometric terms prove the unbounded growth relation.◆

Finally, if $a_n = 1$ and $\varepsilon_n = \varepsilon$ at every transition, then

$$\varepsilon \leq e_{n+1} \leq n\,\varepsilon,$$

where the growth may be linear at worst. We call this *neutral* growth of error.

Figure 13 shows how to visualize error propagation properties. Attenuation is illustrated in Fig. 13a, showing how the distance between trajectories may be reduced after a state transition. If errors are introduced in a trajectory bouncing between concave reflectors, the trajectory will remain close to where it would be if unperturbed. Contrast this with the error amplification that would arise if the reflectors are convex. In this case, an error introduced in the trajectory may cause it to be deflected in a direction far from the unperturbed case.

14.4.3 Example: Approximate Linear System Homomorphisms

Linear systems afford a direct means of illustrating the principles of error propagation. Recall that the requirement for exact homomorphism for linear DTSS systems is expressed by the lumpability condition. What happens if lumpability is not satisfied? We'll see that the concept of approximate homomorphism can be applied and that we can readily predict whether the error propagation will be bounded, unbounded or neutral. Look at the mapping

$$\begin{bmatrix} 0 & 0 & g & g1 \\ 0 & 0 & h & h1 \\ k & k & 0 & 0 \\ l & l & 0 & 0 \end{bmatrix} \rightarrow\rightarrow \begin{bmatrix} 0 & (g+g1+h+h1)/2 \\ k+l & 0 \end{bmatrix}.$$

If $g = g1$ and $h = h1$, then we have a lumpable system as discussed earlier. Intuitively, the closer g is to $g1$ and h and is to $h1$, the more likely that a usable lumping is possible. We can formulate a mapping that becomes a homomorphism when the lumpability conditions apply—this is to take the average of the sums within the blocks, as shown in the matrix on the left in the preceding mapping. Let's consider a simple special case:

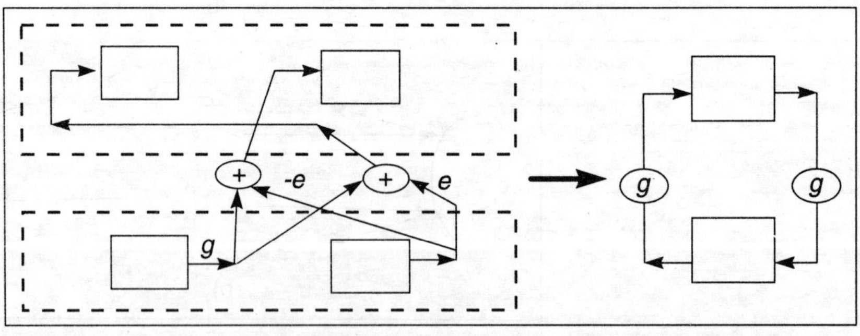

Figure 14 Approximate morphism.

$$\begin{bmatrix} 0 & 0 & g & e \\ 0 & 0 & -e & g \\ g/2 & g/2 & 0 & 0 \\ g/2 & g/2 & 0 & 0 \end{bmatrix} \to\to \begin{bmatrix} 0 & g \\ g & 0 \end{bmatrix}.$$

Here the average of the upper right-hand block is always g and the mapping is illustrated in Fig. 14. We expect that the lumped model is a better and better approximation to the base model as e goes to zero.

Table 3 shows simulation data that confirms our expectations—as e gets smaller so does the accumulated error at any particular time. More than this, other features of the table are in accordance with the error propagation concepts presented earlier.

To see this, consider the error propagation characteristics of the lumped model. Recall that we need to characterize how the lumped model treats the distances between pairs of states. Since the system is linear, we need only examine how the transition function treats distances relative to the origin. For an arbitrary state (x,y), the transformed state is

$$\begin{bmatrix} 0 & g \\ g & 0 \end{bmatrix} \begin{bmatrix} x \\ y \end{bmatrix} = \begin{bmatrix} gy \\ gx \end{bmatrix},$$

and the ratio of the distance of point (gx,gy) to the original point (x,y), is

$$\sqrt{\frac{g^2(x^2+y^2)}{x^2+y^2}} = g.$$

Thus, according to the error propagation theory, g plays the role of attenuation or amplification factor depending on its magnitude relative to 1. The transition function should cause unbounded error growth if $g > 1$ or neutral growth if $g = 1$. These predictions are borne out in Table 3. We see that for the same induced error, the error grows much faster in the unbounded growth condition. For $g < 1$, the theory predicts that error may grow but will reach a limiting value. The table indicates that the same induced error (0.1) grows

Table 3 Error in Approximate Morphism

g	*e*	Error at time 5	Error behavior
0.8	0.001	-0.002	Error decreases over time
0.8	0.01	-0.02	Decreases
0.8	0.1	-0.2	Decreases
0.8	0.0	0.0	Constant
1	0.1	0.4	Error increases over time
1.2	0.1	7.0	Increases exponentially

much more slowly than for the previous cases. In fact, the error actually starts to diminish with time. This is consistent with the theory that provides *an upper bound envelope* on error growth but says nothing as to whether it will be attained.

Although it involves more computation, the growth characteristics of any linear system are readily determined. Indeed, they correspond to the usual concepts of stability mentioned in Chapter 3.

14.5 Approximate Morphisms at the Coupled System Level

We have seen how error introduced in the transition function of a system can manifest itself in its behavior. This analysis applies to approximate morphisms at the I/O systems level. Now let's examine the level of coupled system specifications. Recall that this is the level at which we created aggregated models in Chapter 13. Any departure from the conditions guaranteeing exact morphisms (Theorem 1) is potentially a source of error. For example, a block of supposedly identical components may not really be homogeneous, but may have a diversity of subcomponents. Also, the interblock coupling indifference conditions may be violated. For example, in the all-to-all case, not all subcomponents may get the same inputs, as they should. Or in the randomized coupling case, not all subcomponents may get the same frequencies of inputs, as they should.

14.5.1 Error-Driven Aggregation Refinement

The iterative procedure for creating an aggregation discussed in Chapter 13, can be better formulated by explicitly linking it to error reduction. As illus-

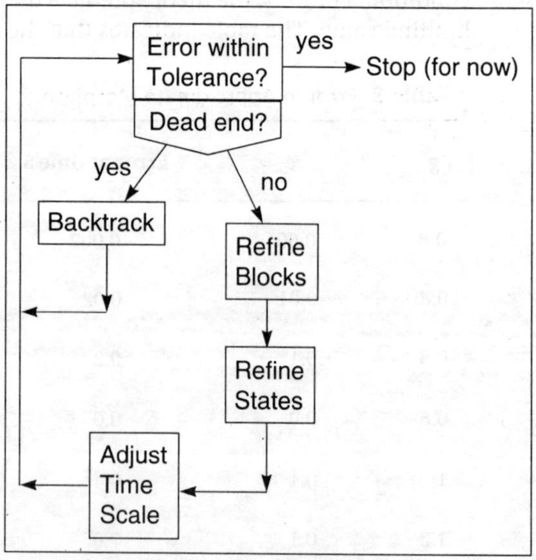

Figure 15 Aggregation search.

Table 4 Sources of Error and Corrective Actions in Fig. 15

Source of error	Corrective action
Inhomogeneity—base model blocks are not homogeneous in structure. The bigger the structural diversity of components in a block, the greater error is likely to be.	Further refine blocks so as to make them more homogeneous.
Interblock interaction skewing—preferential interactions between senders and receivers that violate the interblock indifference requirement.	Further refine blocks and/or further refine the state description of the components (add more state variables) so that interactions occur indifferently between blocks.
Output incompatibility—output desired by the experimental frame is too refined for the information preserved by the state count mappings of the base model blocks.	Further refine blocks and/or further refine the state description of the components so that the desired output can be computed from the block state censuses.

trated in Fig. 15, the procedure tries to reduce the error to below tolerance by reducing its possible sources. Table 4 identifies sources of error and possible corrective actions in executing the procedure in Fig. 15.

Also in line with the discussion in Chapter 13, we may adjust the time scale of the lumped model to look for near-decomposability.

So far the iterative procedure does not have any guidance as to which blocks or states to try to refine. In the next section we indicate how it might concentrate its efforts on components that are critical sources of error.

Identifying Critical Sources of Error

At the coupled model level, an approximate morphism is like an exact morphism, except that it allows local mismatches between blocks of components in the base model and their combined representations in the lumped model. Figure 16 illustrates how a global state transition in the base model may not map exactly to the corresponding global state transition in the lumped model. When we look at the divergence in the mapped base model successor state and the actual lumped model successor states, we will see one or more lumped model components where the mismatch occurs. We can distinguish between two kinds of components: critical and noncritical relative to error propagation. A component is *error-critical* if an error in its state propagates in successive transitions to other components and ultimately to the outputs we are interested in through our experimental frame. Accordingly, components whose errors do not ultimately affect the output of interest are noncritical. It is only the critical set of components that we should be concentrating on.

How can we determine if a component is error-critical or not? Two conditions are required for error-criticality:

- The component is a source of error growth—we have seen that a test for such growth is whether it has neutral or unbounded error growth characteristics.
- There is a path in the influence diagram from the component to the experimental frame specified output—the component can influence the output only if such a path exists.

These conditions give us some heuristic guidance in constructing lumped models through aggregation. If the error associated with the aggregation is over the tolerance limit, we should isolate the components in the lumped model that are error-critical. Then we should reexamine the base model block that mapped to an error-critical component. If it is not homogeneous, we try splitting it into two or more blocks that are (more) homogeneous. If its coupling indifference conditions are not fully satisfied, then we may try to refine it and/or its influencer blocks. In general, the conditions offer some guidance in isolating where to concentrate refinements of the current aggregation.

Effect of Error Accumulation

The situation with respect to error in aggregation can be viewed from the metaphor of the half empty/half full cup. All modeling can justifiably be

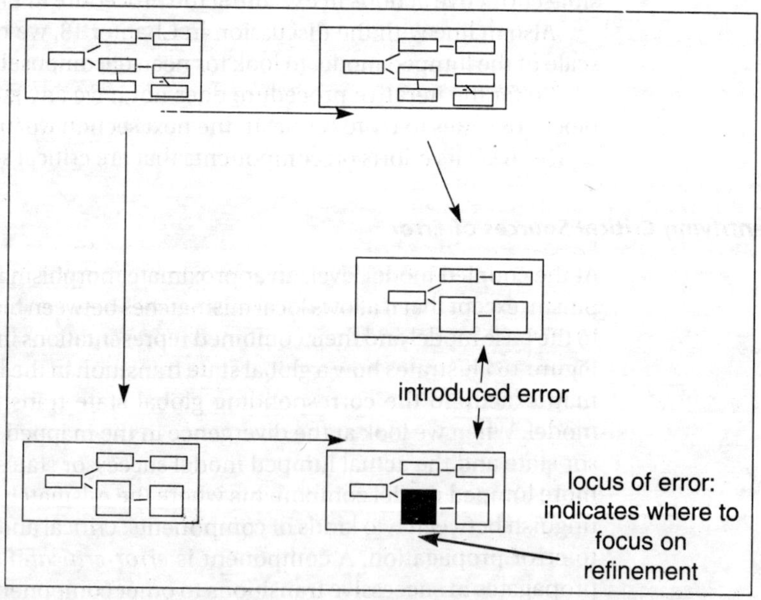

Figure 16 Localizing the source of error in a coupled model approximate morphism.

viewed as constructing lumped models. Therefore, all models are error prone. Although much research has been emphasizing the positive—that reasonable conditions justifying abstractions exist in reality (e.g., [4]), some work is more pessimistic [1]. Questions can be raised such as: What if most aggregations generate errors that grow with time? Can't such aggregated models still be useful? Can we use models in such a way as to compensate for their error accumulation? As indicated earlier, the approach to approximate morphism construction presented here provides some initial answers to such questions. The theory indicates that the dynamics of the lumped model determine how the error is transmitted from one transition to the next, whether it is magnified or attenuated. Thus, we may analyze the lumped model itself to assess its own credibility. One caveat—this is true only provided that the lumped model is close enough so that the bounds on error growth obtained from it are themselves applicable.

Also, the existence of certain lumped features may mitigate uncontrolled error accumulation. For example, error is controlled if the model periodically undergoes a memory erasing reset (all states synchronize to some particular state). Chapter 12 discussed a cascade decomposition of system into a synchronizable front component and a permutation back component. Since it is a permutation system, the back component represents the memory that cannot be erased. So the smaller it is, the more synchronizable the model is. Synchronizable models might be called self-correcting [7], but the degree to which this is true will depend on the length of the synchronizer input (relative to the duration of the simulation experiment) and the frequency with which a synchronizer input segment occurs.

14.6 Validation at Structural Levels

Recall that there are validity concepts that correspond to the levels of the specification hierarchy: *replicative, predictive,* and *structural validity,* respectively. The basic mode of validation is at the replicative level, since it involves comparison of observable data sets. The problem, then, is how to validate a model at the predictive and structure levels. Since we are trying to gain additional knowledge beyond that at the data system level, this is the problem of *climbing up the specification hierarchy.* In the case of predictive validation, the issue is whether the proper initial state of a model can be inferred from past system observations. In the case of structural validity, the additional issue is whether the structure of a model can be inferred to be the only one consistent with the observed data. Conditions known that justify such inferences are discussed in Chapter 15 of TMS 76. Unfortunately, this is an area where there is a dearth of appreciation for the problem and of computerized tools that might help determine whether the justifying conditions hold. So the issue is ignored at the cost of overconfidence in model prediction. Roughly put, the problem is that if our current model has not been shown to be structurally valid, the real system may in fact be represented by any one of the other model structures consistent with the observed data. Thus, further experimentation may well uncover a significant departure between our model and the real system.

14.6.1 Calibration, Parameter Identification, Sensitivity

Most models have free parameters whose proper values are unknown. *Calibration* is the process by which parameter values are adjusted so that the model best fits the system data. Unfortunately, as just seen, a model may be replicatively valid but not predictively valid. That is, just because it can be made to fit past data does not guarantee that it will fit future data (i.e., data that has not been employed in the calibration process). Indeed, parameters can be viewed as state variables and calibration as state identification. The problem then reduces to that of climbing up the specification hierarchy, as just mentioned. In other words, there is no guarantee that parameter assignments that result in best fits actually lead to credible predictions.

More confidence in the uniqueness of predictions can be obtained by assessing their sensitivity to various perturbations. One approach that is sometimes feasible is to try to locate all, or at least many, parameter assignments that result in good fit. One can then assess how much model predictions vary over the range of these parameter assignments.

Another possibility is to assess the sensitivity of model predictions to variations in the assumptions made in the model's construction. One particular form of this approach is to assess the impact of adding greater detail on the predictions. This can be viewed as investigating the variation of predictions over a family of higher resolution models that each map to the original lower resolution model.

A related approach is to systematically formulate known sources of error in such a way that the error actually obtained can be used to pinpoint the source [8].

14.6.2 Local/Global, Cross-Model Validation

Relations between high- and low-resolution models leads us to distinguish between local (applying to the model in focus) and *global* (applying to existing model base) validation. The latter refers to *cross-model* validation, e.g., between models at different levels of resolution. Global cross-validation places greater constraints on model calibration, since the parameter values must be consistent with related ones in other models. Parameter morphisms (Chapter 13) facilitate intermodel parameter correlations by providing mappings from base model parameters to lumped model counterparts. For example, suppose that a high-resolution model has been validated and there is a high degree of confidence in its parameter values. Then the parameter values in a low-resolution model that should be checked for consistency with these values. Indeed, if there is a parameter morphism running from the high-resolution to the low-resolution model, the parameters of the latter ("low-res") are computed directly from those of the former ("high-res").

Moreover, the direction of knowledge propagation does not necessarily always go from high to low. For example, if data exists to calibrate a low-resolution model, then its parameters should inform related high-resolution models. Indeed, in this case, the parameters of the "low-res" model constrain, but do not usually uniquely determine, those of the "high-res" model.

14.7 Sources

1. Axtell, R., *Theory of Model Aggregation for Dynamical Systems with Application to Problems of Global Change.* Pittsburgh, Carnegie Mellon University, 1992.
2. Balci, O., "Principles of Simulation Model Validation, Verification, and Testing." *Trans. of SCS* **14**(1), 3–12 (1997).
3. Barros, F. "Hierarchical Testing of Dynamic Structure Models: A Practical Approach." *Trans. of SCS* **15**(4); 181–189 (1998).
4. Cale, W. G., "Model Aggregation: Ecological Perspectives." In *Complex Ecology: The Part–Whole Relation in Ecosystems* (B. C. Patten and S. E. Jorgensen, Ed.) Prentice Hall, Englewood Cliffs, N.J., 1995, pp. 230–241.
5. Dal Cin, M., "Modeling Fault-Tolerant System Behavior." In *Systems: Theory and Practice* (R. Albrecht, Ed.), Springer, Vienna, 1998, pp. 213–234.
6. Raczynkski, S., "On A Metric Structure in the Space of Dynamic System Models." *Trans. of SCS* **15**(2), 1998.
7. Westerdale, T. H., "An Automaton Decompostion For Learning System Environments." *Inform. &. Comp.* **77**(3); 179–181 (1988).
8. Yuan, Z., H. Vangheluwe, and G. C. Vansteekiste, "An Observer-Based Approach to Modeling Error Identification." *Trans. of SCS* **15**(1); 20–33 (1998).
9. Zeigler, B. P. and Y. Moon, "DEVS Representation and Aggregation of Spatially Distributed Systems: Speed Versus Error Tradeoffs." *Trans. of SCS,* **13**(5); 179–190, (1996).

15

DEVS and DEVS-like Systems: Universality and Uniqueness

The DEVS Bus in Chapter 8 provides a means to interoperate models developed within traditional discrete event world views. But it would be even more reassuring to know that our DEVS Bus would be able to accommodate new modeling formalisms as they emerge. We would like to know how *universal* the DEVS representation is with respect to the class of all possible discrete event systems. We would also like to know how *unique* the DEVS formalism is—are there other discrete event formalisms that would support equivalent Bus-like interoperability? This chapter deals with these issues. Then as a start toward extending the DEVS Bus to a wider class of systems, we will show that the DEVS formalism includes the DTSS (discrete time system specification) formalism in a very strong sense. We continue extending the DEVS Bus concept to DESS (differential equation system specification) models in the next chapter.

Global vs Local (Component-wise) Representation

Before proceeding, we need to clarify our concept of representation of one formalism by another. Each of the formalisms DEVS, DTSS, and DESS define a subset of systems. Can the subset defined by DEVS "represent" the other two? The answer depends on the strength of the equivalence, or morphism, that we are interested in. Looking at Fig. 1, we say that formalism F *can represent a formalism F' with morphism type M*, if for every system specified by F' there is a system specified by F that simulates it in the sense that there is a morphism of type M that holds between them. For example, we say that the DEVS formalism can represent a formalism at the coupled system level if for every coupled model specifiable in the formalism, there is a DEVS coupled model which simulates it with a coupled system morphism. We'll call this *strong, local or component-wise* simulation, since we don't have to preprocess the model to get a DEVS simulation. Instead, we convert the components of the model individually to a DEVS representation and then run the resulting DEVS coupled model to generate the original behavior. Contrast this with *weak* or *global* representation in which we only know how to create a morphism given the model expressed in the basic formalism but not as a coupled system. In the latter case, any coupled model has to be first converted into its resultant form before being translated to a DEVS equivalent. This is not practical for complex coupled models.

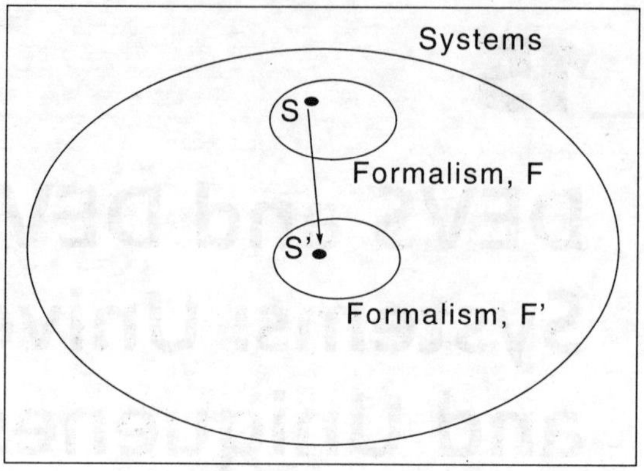

Figure 1 Formalism representation.

15.1 Relation Between Classical and Parallel DEVS: Is There One DEVS or Two?

Recall that we have introduced two apparently distinct DEVS formalisms—Classic DEVS and Parallel DEVS. Thus, the first question to ask is: Are there two DEVS or one? Or indeed, many? Is Parallel DEVS represented by Classic DEVS at the coupled systems level? The answer is not known at this writing. However, the answer to the global simulation counterpart can be shown to be "yes." Thus, in principle, Parallel DEVS does not extend the class of systems that can be specified by classic DEVS. This is expressed in the following theorem:

Theorem 1 *Classic DEVS and Parallel DEVS specify the same class of systems*

Given a Parallel DEVS MP = $(X, Y, S, \delta_{ext}, \delta_{int}, \delta_{con}, \lambda\ ta)$, there is a classic DEVS $MC = (X_{MC}, Y_{MC}, S_{MC}, \delta_{ext,MC}, \delta_{int,MC}, \lambda_{MC}, ta_{MC})$ that weakly represents it, and conversely.

Proof: **(Classic DEVS includes Parallel DEVS)** As suggested just now, we take the input set of the Classic DEVS to be a set of bags over X, i.e., $X_{MC} = X^b$. Similarly, $Y_{MC} = Y^b$. As a first approach the other components would be transferred over without change: $S_{MC} = S$, $\delta_{ext,MC} = \delta_{ext}$, etc. However, in the construction of the system, the classic DEVS employs the serialized composition in line (1) while δ_{con} controls tie-breaking in Parallel DEVS. We must show that classic DEVS can achieve the same effect using serialization. To do this, we arrange to let the Classic DEVS save the state of the parallel DEVS and apply δ_{con} to this saved state when needed. Thus, we set $S_{MC} = S \times S$, where the second component is employed to save the state after an internal transition, i.e., $\delta_{intMC}(s,s') = (\delta_{int}(s),s)$. We use the copy component only when a collision occurs, i.e., $\delta_{extMC}((s,s'),0,x) = (\delta_{con}(s',x),s)$. In mapping MC to the system it specifies, the serial interpretation of collision simulates the parallel interpretation, i.e.,

$$\begin{aligned}\delta_{S,MC}((s,s'),e,x) &= \delta_{extMC}(\delta_{intMC}(s,s'),0,x)\\ &= \delta_{extMC}((\delta_{int}(s),s),0,x)\\ &= (\delta_{con}(s,x),s).\end{aligned}$$

(Note that the Classic DEVS *MC* can tell when a collision has occurred because of the zero value for elapsed time.) Thus the state and output of the system specified by the Classic DEVS follow those of the Parallel DEVS.

(Parallel DEVS includes Classic DEVS) Given a Classic DEVS, we can easily embed it into a Parallel DEVS with the same structure by restricting the inputs of the latter to just bags of size one.

Exercise: Define a mapping from Classic DEVS to Parallel DEVS by projecting pairs of states (*s,s'*) to the state of the left element s. Show that this mapping is indeed a homomorphism.◆

The theorem shows that the basic formalisms are equivalent in the sense that any basic DEVS in one can be represented by a basic DEVS in the other. Also, by closure under coupling, any coupled model in one can also be represented in the basic formalism of the other. But it is an open question whether or not there is a constructive way to simulate a Parallel DEVS coupled model in a Classical DEVS coupled model, and conversely.

Exercise: Investigate the representation of classic DEVS by Parallel DEVS as the coupled system level, and the converse as well. This question has some interesting issues in it. For example, can Parallel DEVS (which is decentralized) realize the global (centralized). Select function of Classic DEVS? Conversely, can Classic DEVS realize the parallelism and confluence of Parallel DEVS (allowing it several steps to do this)? In each case, if the answer is yes, prove it? if not, provide a counterexample.◆

Since the Classic and Parallel DEVS are equivalent in terms of the class of systems they specify, which one we employ depends on other considerations. In the following, we will find that parallel DEVS affords convenient properties, since it easily handles the simultaneous component transitions inherent in discrete time simulation.

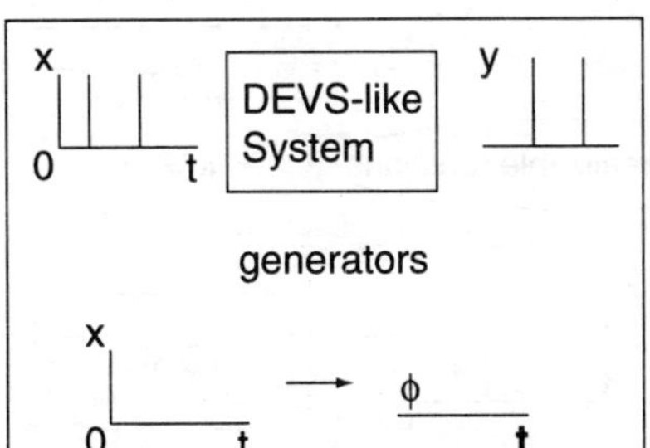

Figure 2 DEVS-like systems.

15.2 Universality and Uniqueness of DEVS

15.2.1 Systems with DEVS Interfaces

A system with DEVS input and output segments is illustrated in Fig. 2. It is not necessarily a DEVS, although it does receive and generate DEVS segments. Recall (Chapter 5) that a DEVS segment consists of an interval of null events punctuated by a finite number of nonnull events. The basic generators for such segments are of the form $x_{t>}$ as illustrated in the figure, where x is either an input in X or the null event, ϕ.

We call a system with DEVS interfaces *DEVS-like* for short. We will consider such systems to be a class of DEDS (discrete event dynamic systems) identified by Ho [2] as containing a variety of discrete event system formalisms, although no subsuming class was formally defined.

Since we want to be sure of taking all considerations into account in characterizing DEVS-like systems, we will start at the lowest level of the system specification hierarchy and work upwards (Fig. 3). At the lowest level we have pairs of input/output discrete event segments, the IORO of Chapter 5. Our basic problem is to characterize the I/O systems that realize such segments and see how closely they relate to the class of DEVS systems. We know that DEVS systems have such IOROs associated with them, but we don't know if there are other non-DEVS classes that also do so. In other words, what we would like to know is *whether the internal mechanisms of systems with DEVS interfaces are all essentially described by DEVS models.*

First we ask: Under what conditions do pairs of discrete event segments actually come from an I/O system? The answer is found in Chapter 12 which characterized realizable IOROs. Essentially the answer is that such pairs must be the union of functions (mapping the input segment sets to the output segment sets) that are realizable, meaning that they can be I/O functions associated with the states of an I/O system. Several properties were shown to be nec-

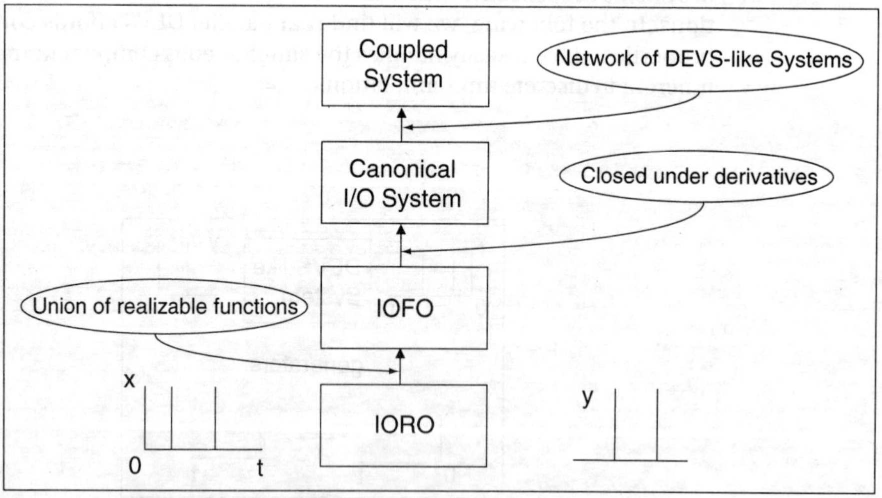

Figure 3 Hierarchy of DEVS-like system specifications.

essary and sufficient for an I/O function to be realizable, the most critical of which was causality—this allows the function to only use past input to determine past output (future input cannot influence past output). The collection of such functions constitutes the IOFO level of specification. For an IOFO to be realizable, it has to be closed under derivatives. One way to understand this is that if a function *f* is associated with a state, then each of the states it can access has a function that is derivative of *f*. Now if we take the functions of an IOFO as labels for states and follow their derivatives, we get a way of constructing an I/O system that realizes the IOFO. In fact, by Theorem 17 in Chapter 12, such a system is the canonical realization of the IORO—it is reduced, minimal, and unique up to isomorphism among all systems that realize the IOFO.

In the rest of this section, we'll assume that we are given a realizable I/O function with discrete event input and output segments. We know there is a canonical I/O system that realizes this behavior. What we don't know is whether this canonical realization is in any way related to a DEVS.

Continuing up the system hierarchy, we can formulate a way of coupling DEVS-like systems together. Indeed, the coupling rules for DEVS-like systems are identical to those for DEVS. We can also formulate both Classic and Parallel compositions of DEVS-like systems. We would then like to show that the class of DEVS-like systems is closed under such coupling. Once we have established that the internal structure of such DEVS-like systems is isomorphic to a DEVS, closure will naturally follow, as will the fact that all such coupled systems are strongly simulated by DEVS coupled models.

15.2.2 Behavior of DEVS-like Systems

We'll assume that the input segment sets, DEVS(X), have segments with zero length, which become generators, $\{x_0 \mid x_0 \in X\}$. The other generators are then the nonevent segments $\{\phi_{t>}\}$. The composition operation is illustrated in Fig. 4. Clearly, $x_{t>} = x_0\, \phi_{t>}$. For $x_0\, y_0$ we represent the result as the generic $(x+y)_0$. In Classic DEVS we would set $x+y=x$ to disallow more than one simultaneous external event. In Parallel DEVS, the input set, bags over X, allows the natural interpretation of + as the bag union operation. We obtain a well-defined concept of maximal length segmentation by selecting the nonnull events and the intervening nonevent segments as generator elements.

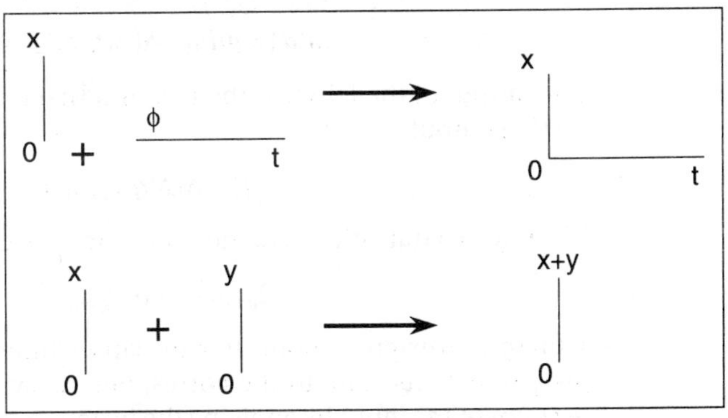

Figure 4 Composition of generators.

Exercise: Show that this definition of *mls* decomposition satisfies the requirements in Chapter 5.◆

A realizable DEVS-like system has a transition function Δ that satisfies the composition property (Chapter 5). Thus, we can write

$$\Delta(q, x_{t>}) = \Delta(q, x_0 \phi_{t>}) = \Delta(\Delta(q, x_0), \phi_{t>}).$$

Thus, there is an instantaneous mapping $\Delta_0: Q \times X \to Q$, such that $\Delta_0(q,x) = \Delta(q,x_0)$. Then

$$\Delta(q, x_{t>}) = \Delta(\Delta_0(q, x), \phi_{t>}).$$

This shows that an external event has an *instantaneous effect* on the state of the system. We call Δ_0 the *instantaneous input transition function.* In contrast, the effect of an input in a DESS cannot be exerted instantaneously in its state.

Exercise: Apply a constant input segment to a DESS. Show that as the length of the segment approaches zero, the state transition function approaches the identity. In this sense, an input does not have instantaneous effect.◆

Exercise: Identify the instantaneous input transition function in a system specified by a DEVS.◆

15.2.3 Universality of DEVS

We are now ready to show that the behaviors of DEVS-like systems are describable by DEVS.

Theorem 2 Universality Theorem for Systems with DEVS Interfaces
Every DEVS-like system is a homomorphic image of a DEVS I/O system.

Proof: Let $S = (T, X, \Omega, Y, Q, \Delta, \Lambda)$ be a DEVS-like system. We will construct a DEVS, $M = (X, Y, S, \delta_{ext}, \delta_{int}, \lambda, ta)$ to homomorphically simulate it. We set the DEVS sequential state set, $S = Q$, the state set of the DEVS-like system. The rest of the construction follows:

- The *time advance* from a state *q* is the time to the next nonnull output in *S*:

$$ta(q) = min\{t \mid \Lambda(\Delta(q, \phi_{t>})) \neq \phi\}.$$

- The output of the DEVS at the next internal event is the corresponding system output

$$\lambda(q) = \Lambda(\Delta(q, \phi_{ta(q)>})).$$

- The internal transition is to the state of the system at the next output:

$$\delta_{int}(q) = \Delta(q, \phi_{ta(q)>}).$$

- If there is an external input after an elapsed time *e*, the DEVS will immediately update its state to the corresponding system state and then take account of the input by applying the instantaneous effect function:

$$\delta_{ext}(q, e, x) = \Delta_0(\Delta(q, \phi_{e>}), x).$$

The total state set of the DEVS is $Q_{DEVS} = \{(q,e) | q \in Q, 0 \le e < ta(q)\}$. We define a mapping $h: Q_{DEVS} \to Q$, by $h(q,e) = \Delta(q, \phi_{e>})$. In other words, when the DEVS system is in total state (q,e), this means it has been resting in state q while the simulated system has been advancing under the null-event input for an elapsed time e. Thus, the state corresponding to (q,e) is indeed $\Delta(q, \phi_{e>})$.

Exercise: Show that h is a homomorphism from the system specified by the DEVS onto the DEVS-like system.◆

The problem now is that h is a homomorphism, not necessarily the isomorphism we will need for DEVS uniqueness. To be an isomorphism, h has to be onto and one-to-one. It is certainly onto, but to be one-to-one requires that for any pair of of distinct states (q,e) and (q',e') in Q_{DEVS}, the images $h(q,e)$ and $h(q',e')$ must also be distinct. This will not happen unless we define the DEVS appropriately. Let's look at an example to see why.

15.2.4 Example: DEVS Realization of DEVS-like System

Figure 5a depicts the accessibility diagram of a DEVS-like system. We'll define this diagram formally in a moment, but for now take it as the state transition diagram of the system with input restricted to null segments. Consider now how the homomorphism assigns DEVS states to map to the system states. Since state a is an initial state, we represent it in the DEVS by $(a,0)$. Since d is an output state, we need to represent it in the DEVS by a state $(d,0)$. Now all states with null output along the trajectory between a and d (such as c) are represented by (a,e), which maps to $\Delta(a, \phi_{e>})$, where e ranges between 0 and 2.

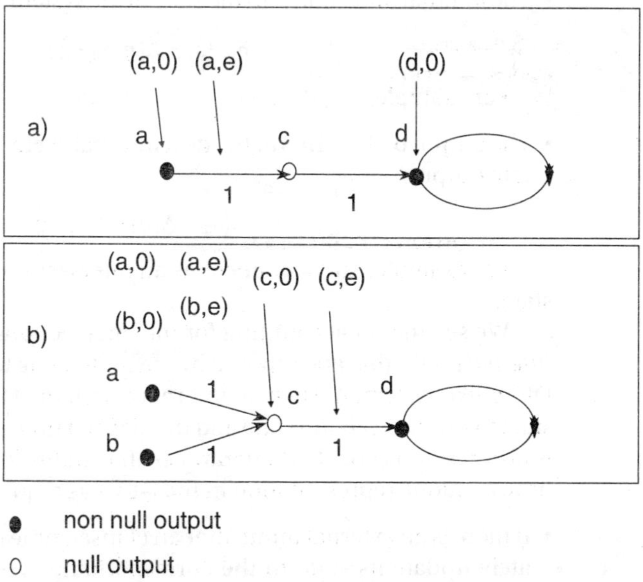

Figure 5 DEVS-like system example.

However, suppose there is a convergence of states as shown in Fig. 5b, where after 1 unit of time, the trajectories from distinct states a and b merge at c. Then state c is represented by both $(a, 1)$ and $(b, 1)$ in the DEVS, i.e., $\Delta(a, \phi_{1>}) = \Delta(b, \phi_{1>}) = c$. This violates the one-to-one requirement for isomorphism. To maintain bijectivity (one-to-oneness) we need to transition to $(c,0)$ in the DEVS. Thus, the time advance from $(a,0)$ is 1 (rather than 2, as before) and the internal transition to $(c,0)$ occurs at the end of this time (if no external events occur). Similarly, the time advance for $(b,0)$ is also 1. Thus, the states transiting out of c are represented only in one way, namely, by (c,e), and we have removed the redundant representation of these states in the DEVS.

15.2.5 Uniqueness of DEVS

The example illustrates the main issue in constructing an isomorphic DEVS realization of a DEVS-like system. To guarantee that the homomorphism mapping is one-to-one we have to use a sequential state set S that is a subset of Q, and such that every state q has a unique representation in the form of (s,e). In Fig. 5b, $S = \{a, b, c, d\}$. In constructing the simulating DEVS, we have to make sure that the DEVS has internal transitions to intersection states in addition to the output generating states already included. The revised definitions will look like the following:

- The *time advance* is the time to the next nonnull output or intersection state:

$$ta(s) = min\{t \mid \Lambda(\Delta(s, \phi_{t>})) \neq \phi \text{ or } \Delta(s, \phi_{t>}) \text{ is an intersection state}\}.$$

  For example, $ta(a) = 1$.

- The internal transition is to the state of the system at the next internal event:

$$\delta_{int}(s) = \Delta(q, \phi_{ta(s)>}).$$

  For example, $\delta_{int}(a) = c$.

- The output of the DEVS at the next internal event is the corresponding system output:

$$\lambda(s) = \Lambda(\Delta(s, \phi_{ta(s)>})).$$

  For example, $\lambda(a) = \phi$, since c is an intersection state, but not an output state.

We see that in accounting for the intersections we have added a set of *internal events* that are imposed by the underlying transition structure of the DEVS-like system. At such an internal event, the DEVS resets its sequential state to the intersection state and the elapsed time clock of the DEVS system is also reset to zero. This guarantees that states following the intersection have a unique representation in the DEVS as required for isomorphism.

- If there is an external input after an elapsed time e, the DEVS will immediately update its state to the corresponding system state and then take account of the input by applying the instantaneous effect function. However, the resulting state now has to be represented as one of the allowable pairs (*s,e*). Since the h mapping is now one-to-one, it has an inverse; we can map any system state into an (*s,e*) pair using this inverse:

$$\delta_{ext}(s,e,x') = h^{-1}\left(\Delta_0\left(\Delta\left(s,\phi_{e>}\right),x\right)\right).$$

Notice, however, that we have to modify the DEVS external transition to set the (*s,e*) pair, since the current function would require us always to set $e = 0$. The modification changes only the external transition function of a DEVS = (*X, Y, S,* δ_{ext}, δ_{int}, λ, *ta*). We extend the range of the function so that $\delta_{ext} : Q \times X \to Q$. In other words, $\delta_{ext}(s,e,x) = (s',e'$ for s' in S and e' *in* [*0, ta*(s')]. The system specified by a modified DEVS is the same as the before the modification, except that in response to an external input it resets the total state to the (*s,e*) pair.

This allows us to state the following lemma.

Lemma 1

Any reduced DEVS-like system has a DEVS realization that is isomorphic to it.

The actual proof of the lemma involves taking account of other possibilities where redundant state representation may exist. We rigorously analyze the transition structure of any DEVS-like system and show how to define a set of internal events (including the intersections) that enable us to construct the required isomorphic DEVS realization. The proof is given in the Appendix.

Putting together the lemma with the earlier discussion, we state that the *internal mechanism of any DEVS-like system is in fact exactly described by a modified DEVS:*

Theorem 3 *Uniqueness Theorem for Systems with DEVS Interfaces*

Every DEVS-like system has a canonical realization by a DEVS I/O system.

Proof: The reduced version of the given system always exists and is its canonical realization (Chapter 12). The lemma shows that this realization is isomorphic to a DEVS.

15.3 DEVS Representation of DTSS

Our first task in the implementing the DEVS Bus is to provide for DEVS representation of DTSS models. Since DESS models are traditionally simulated in discrete time, this offers an immediate path to representation of DESS models as well. However, we will subsequently look for direct and more efficient means of DEVS representation of DESS models.

It turns out that DEVS can strongly represent the DTSS formalism. In other words, we will show how coupled discrete time systems can be mapped component-wise and simulated in a DEVS environment. Our approach to this demonstration is to first develop DEVS representatives for each of the component types in DTSS coupled models. Then we show how the DEVS representatives are coupled in a manner preserving their DTSS counterparts to execute the DTSS simulation. Recall from Chapter 7 that there are four types of DTSS components to consider:

- *Input Free Moore DTSS:* These drive the simulation forward as the ultimate generators of the inputs in a closed coupled model.

- *Multiported memoryless FNSS:* These collect outputs from Moore components and transform them into inputs without using any state information.
- *Moore DTSS with input:* The outputs are generated for the next cycle based on the current input.
- *Mealy DTSS:* These include memoryless FNSS. In a well-defined network they form a *directed acyclic graph* (*DAG*) of computations, taking zero time and propagating from Moore outputs back to Moore inputs.

We examine each in turn.

15.3.1 Input-Free Moore

DEVS representation of an input-free Moore system is straightforward, since the input-free system acts as an uninterruptable generator with a fixed generation period (Chapter 5). Thus, given a *DTSS* $M = (Y_M, S_M, \delta_M, \lambda_M, h)$, define

$$DEVS_h = (Y, S, \delta_{int}, \lambda, ta),$$

where

$$Y = Y_M$$
$$S = S_M \times R_\infty^+$$
$$\delta_{int}(s,\sigma) = (\delta_M(s), h)$$
$$\lambda(s,\sigma) = \lambda_M(s)$$
$$ta(s,\sigma) = \sigma.$$

There is a reason we retain the sigma variable even though it is apparently always set to the predictable step time, h. This relates to the fact that initialization of coupled model DEVS simulations requires setting σ initially to zero (more on this in a moment).

15.3.2 Multiported FNSS

DEVS simulation of a memoryless function with a single input is straightforward. When receiving the input value, the model goes into a transitory state and outputs the computed output value. However, if there are multiple input ports, the system must wait for all inputs to be received before going into the output mode. Since inputs may be generated at different points in the processing, we cannot assume that all inputs come in the same message. Thus we formulate a FNSS (Chapter 7) with multiple input ports and define a DEVS to simulate it: Given *FNSS* $M = (X_M, Y_M, \lambda_M)$, where

$$IPorts = \{in_1, in_2, \ldots, in_n\}$$

$X_M = \{(p,v) \mid p \in Iports, v \in V\}$ is the set of input ports and values (for simplicity, we assume all ports accept the same value set)

$Y_M = \{(out,v) \mid v \in V_{out}\}$ is the single output port and its values,

define

$$DEVS = (X, Y, S, \delta_{ext}, \delta_{int}, \delta_{con}, \lambda, ta),$$

where

$$X = X_M$$
$$Y = Y_M$$
$$S = \{f \mid f\colon IPorts \to V^{\phi}\} \times R^{+}_{\infty}.$$

Since inputs need not all arrive together, we must keep track of their arrival status so that we can tell when all have been received. This is the purpose of the function *f* in the state of the DEVS. Each arriving input is cached (guarding against out-of-phase arrivals). The function *Ready* tells whether all have been received. *Value* extracts the tuple of values for output by λ. The internal transition function, δ_{int}, then resets the state to all empty input stores. Formally,

$$\delta_{ext}(f,\infty,e,(p_1,x_1),(p_2,x_2),\ldots,(p_n,x_n)) = (f',\sigma),$$

where

$$in_i = p_i \text{ and } f(in_i) = \phi \Rightarrow f'(in_i) = x_i$$
$$\text{otherwise } f'(in) = f(in)$$
$$\text{and } Ready(f') \Rightarrow \sigma = 0$$
$$\text{otherwise } \sigma = \infty$$
$$\delta_{int}(f,0) = (f^{\phi},\infty)$$
$$\lambda(f,0) = \lambda_M(value(f)) \quad \text{if } Ready(f)$$
$$= \phi \quad \text{otherwise}$$
$$ta(f,\sigma) = \sigma.$$

Exercise: Define *Ready* and f^{ϕ}.◆

15.3.3 Moore DTSS with Input

The DEVS representation of a Moore DTSS with input combines features of the memoryless and input free implementations. The DEVS waits for all input ports to be heard from before computing the next state of the DTSS and scheduling its next output by setting σ to *h*. This guarantees an output departure to trigger the next cycle. In the subsequent internal transition the DEVS continues holding in the new DTSS state waiting for the full complement of next inputs.

Exercise: Implement a Moore DTSS as a DEVS.◆

15.3.4 Mealy DTSS

A Mealy DTSS is represented as a DEVS is a manner similar to a memoryless function with the difference that the state is updated when all inputs are received. However, the output cannot be prescheduled for the next cycle. (Recall that a Moore system that also updates its state can preschedule its output because it depends only on the state (Chapter 7)). So the Mealy DEVS passivates after a state update just as if it were a memoryless element.

Exercise: Implement a Mealy DTSS as a DEVS.◆

15.3.5 DEVS Strong Simulation of DTSS Coupled Models

Now that we have all the component DEVS in place we can couple them together to strongly simulate a coupled model. First, we assume that the DTSS coupled model is well defined in that it has no algebraic (cycles of Mealy components that do not include a Moore component, Chapter 7). After this, we will see some interesting correlates between ill-defined DTSS networks and illegitimate DEVS counterparts.

Theorem 4

Given a well-defined DTSS coupled model, we can construct a DEVS that can simulate it in a componentwise manner (there is an exact morphism at the coupled model level from the DEVS coupled model to the DTSS coupled model).

Proof: For each DTSS component, define its DEVS representative in the manner discussed previously. Couple the DEVS representatives to each other in the same manner in which their counterparts are coupled in the DTSS network.

Start each of the DEVS components in the state of their DTSS counterpart. Let the σ's of all the Moore components be set to zero. This means that there will be an output generated from all such components. Now by construction, the DEVS coupled model preserves the topology of DTSS network. So the coupling of DEVS components that represent Mealy (including FNSS) systems forms a DAG that is isomorphic to the original. Thus, the outputs of the Moore components propagate through the DAG to the inputs of these components in the same manner that they do in the original. When they arrive, the Moore-representing DEVS components employ them to compute the next states and outputs of their counterparts and schedule these outputs to occur at the next time step. This is the basis for a proof by induction on the number of simulation cycles.

Exercise: Write the formal version of the proof and complete the proof by induction.◆

Is the DEVS just constructed legitimate? The next theorem makes a strong connection between DEVS illegitimacy and existence of algebraic cycles in DTSS networks.

Theorem 5

The previous DEVS simulation of a coupled DTSS is legitimate if, and only if, the coupled DTSS has no algebraic cycles.

Proof: Let the coupled DTSS be well defined. Then the subnetwork of Mealy components does not contain cycles. We show that the DEVS coupled model (actually its associated DEVS at the I/O system level) is legitimate. Since the DEVS coupled model preserves the topology of the original coupling, its representation of the Mealy DAG subnetwork propagates the computation through a series of transitory (zero time) states. Since there are no cycles, eventually activity reaches the inputs to the Moore-representing components. (In Parallel DEVS the computations at each level of the DAG all take place in parallel.) The computation of next states and outputs at the Moore-representing components has time advance $h > 0$. If there are no Moore components, then the coupled model has type Mealy. In this case, the DEVS response to input takes zero time before passivating. In either case, time advances by a fixed amount. Since there are no other sources of internal transitions in the DEVS (by the manner in which it constructed), it is legitimate.

In an ill-defined DTSS coupled model, a cycle exists within the subnetwork of Mealy components. This shows up as a cycle of transitory states in the representing DEVS. This cycle forms a zero time loop of DEVS internal transitions and make the DEVS illegitimate. ■

Example: DEVS Strong Simulation of DTSS Network
Figure 6 illustrates a DEVS component-wise simulation of the linear DTSS network discussed in Chapter 14. The DTSS Moore Delay (Chapter 3) is implemented as a DEVS with single input port and the summer as a two-input port memoryless system. The coupling shown preserves that of the simulated network.

Exercise: Define the DEVS representations of the Moore Delay, the summer, and the DTSS network.◆

15.4 Efficient DEVS Simulation of DTSS Networks

Recall the event-based simulation of cellular automata in Chapter 3 where the simulation algorithm is based on restricting state updates to only those components that can actually change state. Now that we have formalized

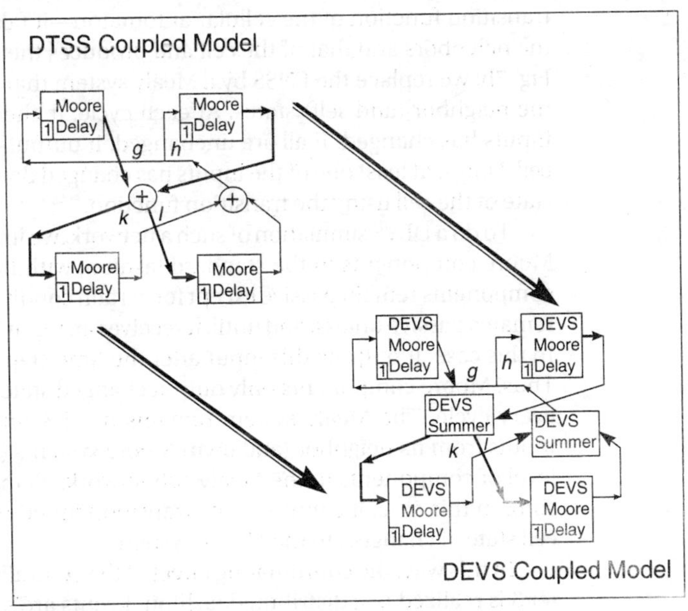

Figure 6 DEVS componentwise simulation DTSS linear network.

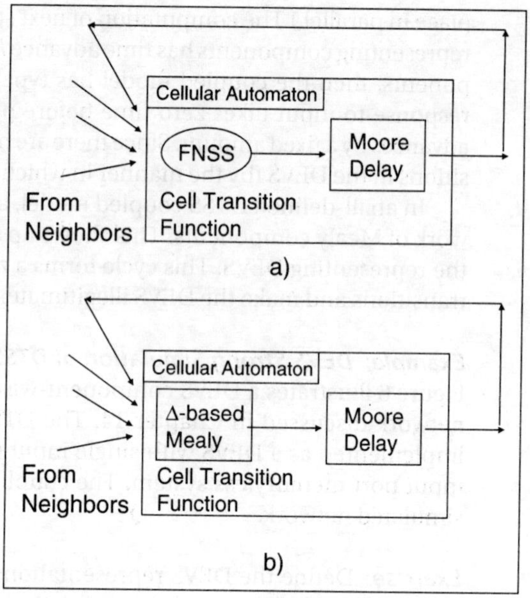

Figure 7 Cell automaton represented as FNSS-fronted delay component in DTSS network.

DEVS simulation of DTSS, we can investigate how to improve the efficiency of such simulation using the same idea. We can capture the essentials of cellular automata simulation by restricting attention to DTSS networks of Moore Delay components, each fronted by a FNSS. As shown in Fig. 7a, since the memory element is a unit delay, the memoryless element represents the transition function of the cellular automaton—it takes the current states of the neighbors and that of the cell and produces the next state of the cell. In Fig. 7b, we replace the FNSS by a Mealy system that stores the last values of the neighbor (and self) states. At each cycle, it checks whether any of the inputs has changed. If all are unchanged, it outputs the stored state of the cell. Only if at least one of the inputs has changed does it recompute the next state of the cell using the transition function.

To do a DEVS simulation of such a network, we implement the Mealy and Moore components in the standard fashion, with the exception that these components remain passive except for certain conditions. The Moore system remains passive unless, and until, it receives an input from the Mealy system. In this case, it outputs this input after the time step h and then passivates. Thus, Moore components only output changed states and do this in unison every cycle. The Mealy system remains passive until it receives changed inputs from its neighbor (and own) Moore systems (since there is only one level of components in the Mealy subnetwork, all inputs will arrive in unison). In this case, it computes the transition function and outputs the new cell state, if changed, to the Moore system.

In this way, the coordinating effect of the centralized event-list of Chapter 3 is realized in a distributed fashion. Events are scheduled at only those cells that can change because their neighbors have changed. Only if a cell state changes does it broadcast this news to its influencees.

Exercise: Write the DTSS change-based Mealy system just described and its DEVS-modified implementation as just discussed.◆

Exercise: Compare the straightforward and change-based DEVS simulations of some cellular automatan. Measure the activity in a cellular automato by the fraction of cells changing state. Show that the relative efficiency of change-based DEVS simulation over the baseline standard increases as the activity level decreases.◆

15.5 Summary

Are there discrete event systems that are not described by the DEVS formalism? To answer this question we put to work much of the systems theory built up in earlier chapters of the book. We first had to ask whether it matters which formalism, Classical or Parallel DEVS, we are talking about. It turned out that although the formalisms may differ at the coupled system level, they are equivalent at all lower levels. We could then formulate the main issue of DEVS expressibility in terms of discrete event behaviors and climbing up the system specification hierarchy to state space realizations of these behaviors. This approach enabled us to establish both the universality and uniqueness properties of the DEVS formalism. Indeed, not only can every discrete event behavior be realized by a DEVS I/O System but also a DEVS realization be constructed that is isomorphic to the reduced realization of the behavior. Thus, the DEVS formalism (in slightly extended form) can generate all discrete event behaviors (universality), and it can isomorphically represent their canonical internal structures (uniqueness). We went on to establish the ability of DEVS to represent an important subclass of systems—the DTSS, or discrete time models such as cellular automata and sampled data systems. This representation is stronger than that which follows from universality since it applies at the coupled system level, not just the I/O systems level. This component-wise mapping enables practical and efficient DEVS simulation of discrete time systems. We continue with exploration of the DEVS Bus concept in the next chapter where we examine its application to simulation of differential equation models.

15.6 Sources

Asahi [6] characterized DEVS-like systems and Sato [5] raised the issue of uniqueness of DEVS for discrete event systems. Sarjoughian [3,4] extended the iterative specification approach to provide a means of inferring DEVS structures from DEVS-like behaviors. Ho [2] defined DEDS (discrete event dynamic systems) and founded the *Journal of DEDS* to promote research in the area. Cassandras [1] provides applications of DEDS to control theory and performance analysis.

1. Cassandras, C. G., *Discrete Event Systems: Modeling and Performance Analysis.* Richard Irwin, New York, 1993.

2. Ho, Y. C. Special issue on discrete event dynamic systems. In *Proceedings of the IEEE,* 1989.
3. Sarjoughian, H. S., "Inductive Modeling of Discrete-event Systems: A TMS-based Non-monotonic Reasoning Approach." In *Electrical and Computer Engineering.* University of Arizona, Tucson, 1995, p. 256.
4. Sarjoughian, H. S. and B. P. Zeigler, "Abstraction Mechanisms in Discrete-event Inductive Modeling." In *Winter Simulation Conference.* San Diego, IEEE Press, 1996.
5. Sato, R. "Uniqueness of DEVS Formalism." In *AI, Simulation and Planning in High Autonomy Systems.* EPD, University of Arizona, San Diego, 1996.
6. Zeigler, B. P., and T. Asahi, "Behavioral Characterization of Discrete Event Systems, in *Simulation and Planning in High Autonomy Systems.* IEEE Press, Tucson, 1993.

Appendix: Isomorphically Representing DEVS-like Systems by DEVS

We prove the following lemma.

Lemma 2

Any reduced DEVS-like system has a DEVS realization that is isomorphic to it.

Proof: Let $S = (T, X, \Omega, Y, Q, \Delta, \Lambda)$ be a reduced DEVS-like system. As indicated in the main text, we need to extract a subset of states that will form the sequential state set S_{DEVS} of the simulating DEVS. Let's call these *milestone* states. Each state q must have a unique representation (s,e) where q is the state reached from a milestone, s, when no external events have been received for e units of time. We have to select a set of milestones that completely cover the state set Q in this sense.

Consider the autonomous subsystem with nonevent input segments, $\phi_{t>}$. The state diagram consists of all state trajectories responding to such inputs. Although for a multidimensional state space its detailed structure would be difficult to capture, the features needed for our purposes can be readily visualized. The composition property of Δ imposes a distinct structure on such state spaces that gives them a structure depicted in Fig. 8. The basic relation between states is *accessibility* or reachability:

$$q' \textit{ is accessible from } q \text{ if } (\exists t > 0)\Delta(q, \phi_{t>}) = q'.$$

The problem can now be stated as: Identify a set of milestones, S_{DEVS} such that

- Each milestone s has an associated *maximum time,* $T(s)$. Let the states accessed from s within time $T(s)$ be its *access* set, $Q(s) = \{\Delta(q, \phi_{e>}) \mid 0 \le e < T(s)\}$.
- The access sets are disjoint and cover Q, i.e., form a partition.

To solve this problem we first consider the following types of states:

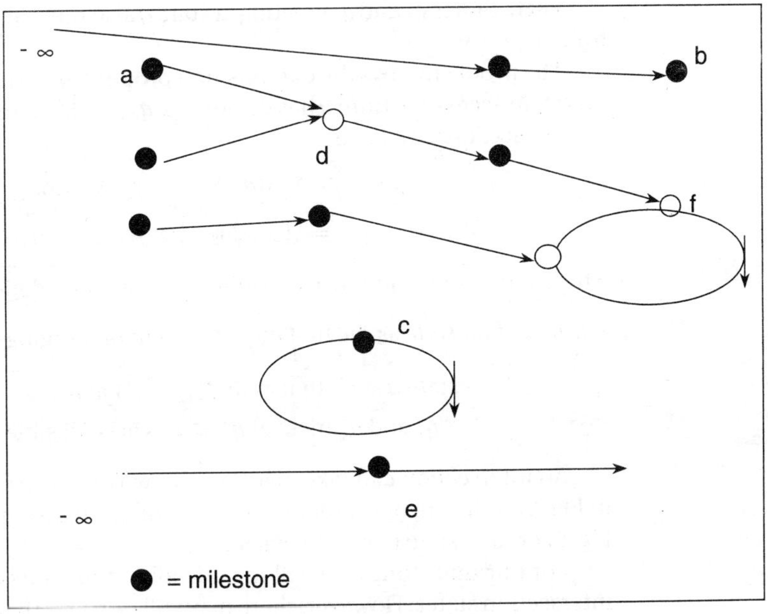

Figure 8 State transition structure.

- *Initial state* (e.g., *a* in Fig. 8): states that are not accessible from other states:

$$q \text{ such that} (\neg \exists q')\, q \text{ accessible from } q'$$

- *Final (equilibrium) state* (e.g., *b* in Fig. 8): states that can only access themselves:

$$q \text{ such that} (\forall t)\Delta(q, \phi_{t>}) = q$$

- *State on a finite cycle* (but not final) (e.g., *c* in Fig. 8):

$$q \text{ such that } (\exists t > 0)\Delta(q, \phi_{t>}) = q \text{ and } (\exists t' < t)\Delta(q, \phi_{t'>}) \neq q$$

- *State on an infinite cycle* (e.g., *e* in Fig. 8):

  q such that there is no initial state that accesses q and there is no final state or cycle of states that q accesses.

Fact: The states accessible from any state q include at most one final state or finite cycle of states.

Exercise: Prove the fact using the determinism (single-valued nature) of the transition function.

To identify intersection states, we'll need the following definition:

States q_1 *and* q_2 *meet at state* q if q is accessible from both q_1 and q_2, i.e.,

$$(\exists t > 0)\Delta(q_1, \phi_{t>}) = q \text{ and } (\exists t' > 0)\Delta(q_2, \phi_{t'>}) = q.$$

Fact: States q_1 and q_2 meeting at state q also meet at all states accessible from q.

The proof employs the composition property of the transition function. Any state accessible from q has the form $\Delta(q, \phi_{e>})$. Then replacing q by its two representations, we have

$$\begin{aligned}\Delta(q,\phi_{e>}) &= \Delta(\Delta(q_1,\phi_{t>}),\phi_{e>}) = \Delta(q_1,\phi_{t+e>})\\ &= \Delta(\Delta(q_2,\phi_{t'>}),\phi_{e>}) = \Delta(q_2,\phi_{t'+e>}),\end{aligned}$$

which shows the required accessibility. We can then define the following:

- *Intersection state* as the first meeting point of merging states:

$$\text{state } q \text{ such that } q_1 \text{ and } q_2 \text{ meet at } q$$
$$\wedge\, q_1 \text{ and } q_2 \text{ meet at } q' \Rightarrow q' \text{ is accessesible from } q$$

An intersection can take place where two distinct streams meet (e.g., *d* in Fig. 8) or where one stream curls back on itself forming a cycle (e.g., *f* in Fig. 8) or final state (e.g., *b* in Fig. 8).

For our milestones we will include all output states, initial, final, and intersection states. However, there may still be states that are not accessible from these states and do not access any of them. Since such states contain no intersections and no initial states, they must form self-contained cycles that are either finite (such as that containing *c* in Fig. 8) or infinite (such as that containing *e* in Fig. 8). Since the system is reduced we can't ignore such states—we have to assume they can access output states using external events. We choose an arbitrary state as a milestone for each such cycle.

There are five types of milestones. A *middle* milestone lies between two other milestones, to the left and right, in the sense that it is accessed by the first and accesses the second. A *right end* milestone only has a milestone on its left. A *left end* milestone only has a milestone on its right. An *isolated* milestone accesses no milestones. The last type is a milestone on an isolated finite cycle, which accesses itself.

We proceed to develop the access sets and maximum time for the milestones. We'll also need additional milestones.

As shown in Fig. 9, for a middle milestone *s* we assign to it all states that it accesses until the next milestone on the right. Its maximum time $T(s)$ is thus the time to access the next milestone.

Exercise: Show that the mapping from the interval $[0,T(s))$ to Q given by $f(t) = \Delta(s, \phi_{t>})$ is a one-to-one correspondence. (Hint: If the same state is accessed twice, then it forms a cycle contrary to assumption.)◆

For a milestone on an isolated cycle, we use the same approach, except that the next milestone is taken to be itself.

For a right end milestone, we define $T(s)$ = *infinity* and associate its full access set with it.

For a left end milestone *s*, we use the approach of a middle milestone. However, we have to take care of the infinite half stream on its left, namely, the set of states that access it. For each such state, *q*, there is a unique time *t*

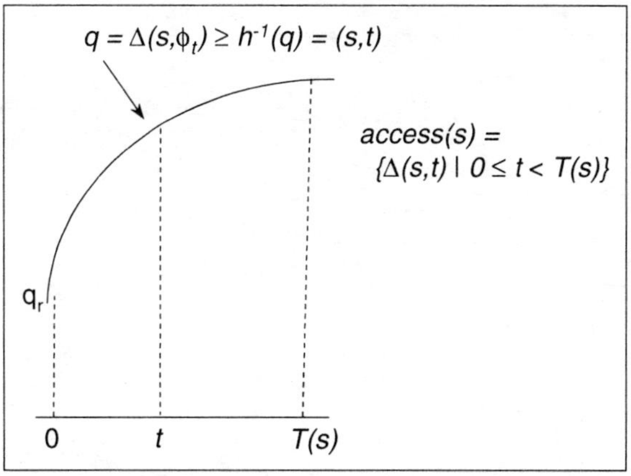

Figure 9 Access set structure.

for it to access to s (t such that $\Delta(q, \phi_{t>}) = s$). The case of an isolated milestone is handled in the same way.

Exercise: Show that the uniqueness of access time is true in view of the choice of milestones. We choose an arbitrary subset of the half stream as a set of middle milestones. This is done, for example, by adding the states $\{\ldots, \Delta^{-1}(s, \phi_{i>}), \ldots, \Delta^{-1}(s, \phi_{2>}), \Delta^{-1}(s, \phi_{1>})\}$ as milestones. Here $\Delta^{-1}(s, \phi_{i>})$ is the unique state that accesses s in time i.◆

Exercise: Use the composition property of the transition function to show that each additional milestone, $s_i = \Delta^{-1}(s, \phi_{i>})$ has a time $T(s) = 1$, and the mapping $[i,-1) \rightarrow Q$ given by $t \rightarrow \Delta(s_i, \phi_{t>})$ is one-to-one, as required.◆

The chosen set of milestones becomes the sequential state set of the simulating DEVS. The construction of the DEVS follows that in the text and is left as the next exercise.

Exercise: Define a DEVS with the milestones as its sequential states that is isomorphic to the given system, S. (**Hint:** Note that $ta(s) = T(s)$.)◆

16

DEVS Representation of Systems

Distributed simulation, the use of multiple computers for model execution (Chapter 11), is fast becoming the predominant form of simulation. One of the major advantages that it affords is to enable sharing of assets across large distances (potentially, connecting earth and space stations, for example). Another advantage is speed of computation when parallelism is exploited, particularly in high-performance "network in a box" computers. The major difference between distributed simulation and its nondistributed counterpart is that information and data are encoded in messages that travel from one computer to another over a network. This changes our perspective on simulation from one in which only computation matters to one in which communication matters just as much, and sometimes more. The brunt of simulation analyses in the past (e.g., in the design of numerical methods, (Chapters 3 and 8) had to do with trade-offs between accuracy and computation speed. And while these retain their importance (Chapter 13), our new perspective demands that we look at trade-offs between accuracy and communication resources as well. For example, we can ask what's the best architecture to simulate a model distributed among several sites, given limited bandwidth (bits/sec that can be transmitted) or given limited bandwidth and computer memory (the latter taking both computation and communication constraints into account). queries

Since messaging requires that continuous quantities be coded into discrete packets or cells and sent discontinuously, discrete event simulation is the most natural means to examine such problems. And since DEVS is the formalism representing system specification in discrete event terms, we turn to it as our vehicle for such study. However, the models to be simulated can't be restricted to discrete event form only, since many, especially those coming from the physical sciences, are cast in differential equation terms and may come packaged in discrete time simulators, the traditional way of simulating continuous systems.

16.1 DEVS Bus Revisited

The DEVS Bus (Chapter 15) provides the concepts we need. Recall (Chapter 7) that we could embed traditional discrete event world views into the DEVS formalism. In such a "wrapping," simulators for models expressed in various event-based formalisms can interoperate under the control of a standard DEVS coordinator. Figure 1 depicts an extended DEVS Bus in which this

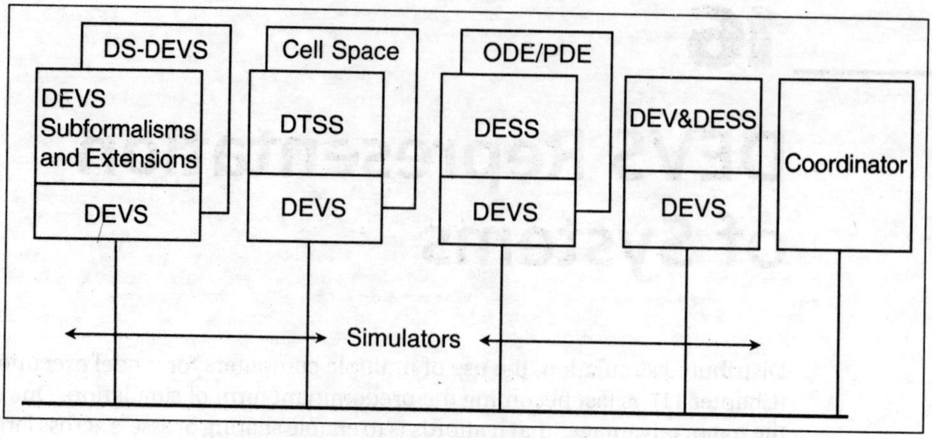

Figure 1 DEVS bus extended to nondiscrete event formalisms.

concept is extended to encompass the other major formalisms, DTSS and DESS. The idea is to provide means to represent DTSS and DESS models in DEVS form, thus providing an all-DEVS distributed simulation environment for any modeling domain. For example, we could have rule-based DEVS models representing intelligent agents communicating through a distributed network represented by cellular automata and interacting over terrain represented by spatially continuous (partial) differential equation models.

16.1.1 Approaches to DEVS Representation of Continuous Systems

To make the extended DEVS Bus a reality requires that we have workable representations of the DTSS and DESS formalisms in DEVS. We already have shown (in Chapter 15) how DEVS can simulate discrete time models at both the global and local levels. This provides a start toward practical means of wrapping the traditional kinds of differential equation models into DEVS. This chapter discusses approaches to strongly simulate DESS systems in DEVS. Since these are necessarily approximations, we need to establish the conditions under which the error can be made as small as desired. Backing off from such limiting case theorems, we need to study whether, and how the DEVS representation can provide more efficient simulation than the traditional discrete time simulation of differential equation systems.

Having established the means to simulate discrete time coupled models in componentwise DEVS manner, we are in a position to develop one approach to DEVS simulation of differential equation systems. This approach, the DEVS equivalent of traditional numerical integration, corresponds to the top pathway in Fig. 2. The major step in this approach is to discretize time to fixed time steps and employ standard numerical methods to obtain DTSS representations of the DESS components (Chapter 3). Since, as shown in Chapter 8 this can be done in a componentwise manner, we have a componentwise simulation by DTSS of DESS coupled models. Now applying the DEVS strong simulation of DTSS (Chapter 15), we can directly construct a DEVS coupled model to simulate the DTSS representation, and hence, the

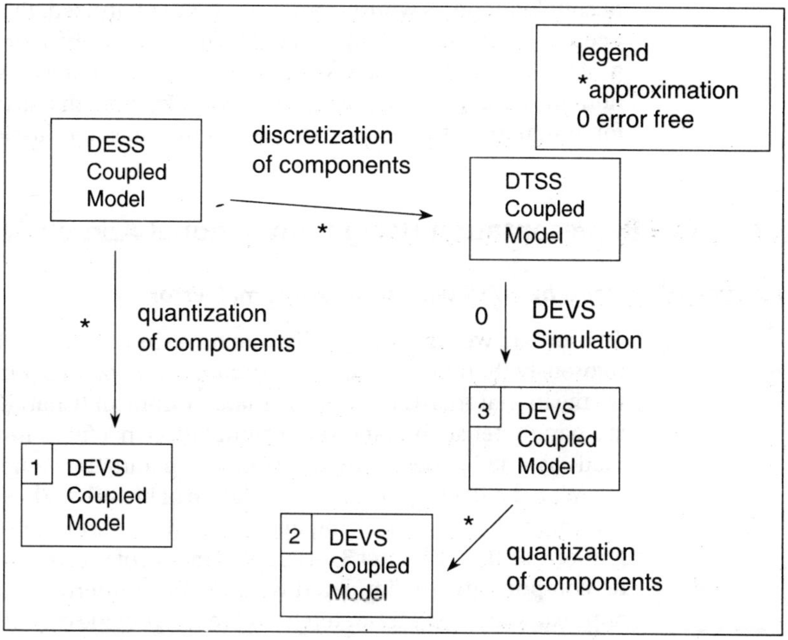

Figure 2 Approaches to DEVS simulation of DESS coupled models.

original DESS coupled in the required componentwise manner. Of course, as indicated in the figure, error may be introduced in the DTSS approximation of the DESS model, and this will carry over to the DEVS simulation. However, since the DEVS simulation of the DTSS stage is error free, the DEVS simulation will not suffer more error than the DTSS simulation.

However, in going second-hand through a DTSS simulation, we are not taking advantage of the reduced computation and message passing that a direct DEVS representation might provide. Thus, for our second approach to DEVS representation of DESS (the left-hand pathway in Fig. 2) we recall that DEVS offers an alternative way of handling continuous time. Instead of advancing time in discrete steps, we can advance time based on discrete events, where an event is a significant change in an input, state, or output variable. The key to handling the continuous variables of a DESS is to determine when a significant event occurs in a component. Such an event can then be reported to other components. We will introduce a significant event detector, called a quantizer, which monitors its input and uses a logical condition to decide when a significant change, such as crossing a threshold, has occurred. The concept of quantization will formalize the operation of significant event detectors. A quantum is a measure of how big a change must be to be considered significant.

To reduce local computation and message passing we would like to have the quantum size be large. However, the decision of what is a significant change can't just be made locally since it also involves other components. We are really asking how big a change must be before we need to tell others about it. The answer to this kind of question is through error analysis of coupled models whose components are quantized. Put another way, we need to look at closed loop behavior, i.e., how any error propagates through a network where feedback loops exist. Such analysis is well known for numerical integration of differential equation systems, so to prepare the way for our quantization approach, we first turn to such classical analysis.

16.2 DEVS Representation Using Conventional Approach

Simulation of Systems by DTSS with Arbitrarily Small Error

To proceed, we have to treat discrete time simulation of DESS models more rigorously than in Chapter 8. By *simulation with an arbitrarily small error* we mean that there is an approximate morphism (Chapter 14) where there is a parameter such that error accumulation in a finite time interval can be made as small as desired with a choice of parameter value.

We consider approximate simulation of DESS by DTSS first at the global, then at the local, level. Using numerical integration such as the Euler integration method (Chapter 3), a coupled model of integrator components can be componentwise simulated by a DTSS counterpart. The simulation is approximate for any time step $h > 0$. We will provide conditions under which the maximum error in a finite interval goes to zero as h goes to zero. We say that the DESS is *exactly discretizable* under these circumstances.

Our approach to DTSS representation will be first to formulate the required properties for systems specified at the I/O system level and then to specialize them to differential equation systems.

***Theorem 1** Sufficient Conditions for DTTS Simulation at the I/O System Level*

Let S by an I/O system have the following properties:

1. Lipschitz condition on state (upper bounding error growth): For small enough τ, there is $\alpha > 0$
$$\left\|\delta(q, x_{t>}) - \delta(q', x_{t>})\right\| \leq (1+\alpha\tau)\left\|q - q'\right\| \text{ for all } q, q' \text{ in } Q.$$
2. Lipschitz condition on input (upper bounding the error introduced at each transition):
$$\left\|\delta(q, \omega_{t>}) - \delta(q, \rho_{t>})\right\| \leq k\left\|\omega_{t>} - \rho_{t>}\right\|.$$
3. Bound on the input growth, for small enough τ:
$$max_{t\in<0,\tau>}\left\|\omega_{t>} - \omega(0)_{\tau>}\right\| \leq M_{max}\tau.$$
4. Norm-preserving output map:
$$\left\|\lambda(q) - \lambda(q')\right\| \leq \kappa\left\|q - q'\right\|.$$

(This is clearly true if the state appears as the output.)

Then there is a DTSS S_{DTSS} and an approximate morphism at the I/O system level from S_{DTSS} to S, where the error goes to zero as the time step h goes to zero.

Proof: Define S_{DTSS} so that it has the same input, state, and output sets as *S*. Since the state sets are both *Q*, we use the identity mapping as the approximate morphism. Consider the input segment ω and its discretized version, $\bar{\omega} = \omega(0)\omega(h)\ldots\omega((n-1)h)$. Define $\delta_{DTSS}(q, x) = \delta(q, x_{h>})$, where $x_{h>}$ is the constant input segment having value *x* for period *h*. The output functions of S_{DTSS} and *S* are the same.

The proof consists of two parts:

1. We must bound the state error introduced at each time step. Using this and the error growth bound in condition 3, we apply the error growth approach in Chapter 14 to bound the error in the state trajectory.
2. We must bound the error in the output trajectories generated from the same starting state by both systems. This we can do immediately given the norm-preserving condition 4 on the output map and the bound on the error in the state trajectory from 1.

The number of time steps in the interval <0,*T*> is

$$N = T/h.$$

The error introduced at the end of such a time step is

$$\begin{aligned}\varepsilon &= \left\|\delta(q,\omega_{h>}) - \delta_{DTSS}(q,\omega(0))\right\| \\ &= \left\|\delta(q,\omega_{h>}) - \delta(q,\omega(0)_{h>})\right\| \\ &\le k\left\|\omega_{h>} - \omega(0)_{h>}\right\| \text{ (using condition 2)} \\ &\le kh\, max_{t\varepsilon<0,h>}\left\|\omega_{h>}(t) - \omega(0)\right\| \text{ (definition of trajectory norm)} \\ &\le k\, M_{max} h^2 \text{ (using condition 3).}\end{aligned}$$

Since the magnification of the error in each time step is given by condition 1 as $(1 + \alpha h)$, and we can make *h* as small as desired, we use the error bound in Section 14.4.2 for $a = 1 + b/N$. Thus, the accumulated error is

$$e_T \le N\varepsilon = k\, M_{max}\, T\, h,$$

and the error goes to zero as *h* goes to zero.

16.2.1 DTSS Simulation of a DESS Integrator

Let S be a DESS integrator. The transition function of the integrator is

$$\delta\, S(q,\omega_{\tau>})) = q + \int_0^{\tau}\omega(t)dt,$$

where $\omega_{t>}$ is an admissible input segment. The output of the integrator is its state: $\lambda(q) = q$. The transition function of the discrete integrator employing Euler integration is an extension of the simple transition function,

$$\Delta(q,\omega_{t>}) = q + xt,$$

where $\omega_{t>}$ is represented by a piecewise constant segment $x_{t>}$.

Under suitable constraints on the derivative of its input segments, the integrator satisfies all the conditions of the exact discretizability in the theorem just given.

We say that an input segment ω is *BCS (bounded, continuous and smooth)* if

1. ω is a bounded, continuous function of its domain, and
2. ω is smooth (its derivative, $\frac{d}{dt}\omega(t)$ is finite at every point, t in its domain)

and the derivative function ω′ is bounded $\left(\omega'(t) = \frac{d}{dt}\omega(t)\right)$.

***Proposition 1** DTSS Simulation of DESS Integrator*
The DESS integrator with a BCS input segment set is an exactly discretizable system.

Proof: Using the integrator transition function it is easy to show that the integrator satisfies the two Lipschitz conditions. Indeed, condition 1 is satisfied because $\|\delta(q, x_{t>}) - \delta(q', x_{t>})\| = \|q - q'\|$, i.e., $\alpha = 0$. For condition 2 we have

$$\begin{aligned}
&\left\|\delta(q,\omega_{t>}) - \delta(q,\rho_{t>})\right\| \\
&= \left\| \int_0^{\tau} \omega(t) - \rho(t)dt \right\| \\
&\leq \int_0^{\tau} \left\| \omega(t) - \rho(t) \right\| dt \\
&= \|\omega - \rho\|,
\end{aligned}$$

i.e., $k = 1$.

Now for condition 3, which bounds the input growth for small enough τ. This follows from the bound on the derivative of the admissible input segments. We can identify $M_{max} = max\left\{\left\|\frac{d}{dt}\omega(t)\right\| t \in dom(\omega)\right\} = \|\omega'\|$, the largest derivative in the interval <0, τ>. This is because of the mean value theorem of calculus, which states that

$$\omega_{t>}(t) - \omega_{t>}(0) = t \times \frac{d}{dt}\omega(t') \text{ for some } t' \text{ in the interval } (0,\ t).$$

Thus,

$$max_{t \in <0,\tau>}\left\|\omega_{\tau>} - \omega(0)_{\tau>}\right\| \leq \tau\, max\left\{\left\|\frac{d}{dt}\omega(t)\right\| t \leq \tau\right\} \leq M_{max}\tau.$$

Since the output function is the identity, it preserves the state norm. Thus, the error bound for the integrator is given by $e_T \leq \|\omega'\|\, T\, h$. In other words, the larger the rate of change of input, the smaller the time step must be to reduce the error below a given tolerance. ■

16.2.2 Simulation of Coupled Systems by DTSS

***Theorem 2** Componentwise Simulation of Coupled Systems by DTSS with Arbitrarily Small Error*
A well-defined coupled model can be componentwise simulated with an arbitrarily small error by a DTSS coupled model.

Rather than work with an arbitrary coupled model, we will consider closing the loop around a single component (Fig. 3). This will demonstrate the essence of what is involved in a full-scale proof. By feeding back the output of the system *S* to its input, the resultant is an input-free system, *R*. Let *DS* be the DTSS representation of *S* and let *DR* be the representation of *R*, which, as shown, preserves the coupling from output to input. To show that we can make *DR* simulate *R* as closely as desired by reducing *h*, we would like to use Theorem 1 for the open loop case. It turns out that the most of the properties required in Theorem 1 still apply. The one exception is the input property, condition 3. This property has to be reconsidered since, because of feedback, we can't specify the input's properties independently of the system itself.

***Theorem 3** Feedback Simulation of a System by a DTSS with arbitrarily small error*

Let *S* be a system with the following properties:

1. (Replacing input property 3)
   Small excursion behavior: *S* stays close to its initial state for short duration inputs. For small τ, for all ω possible as feedback input (see below), there exists $m > 0$ such that

$$\left\|\delta_s(q,\omega_{\tau>})\right) - q\| \le m\,\tau.$$

2. Lipschitz condition on state (upper bounding error growth): For small enough τ,

$$\left\|\delta_s(q,x_{\tau>}) - \delta_s(q',x_{\tau>})\right\| \le (1+\alpha\tau)\left\|q-q'\right\| \text{ for all } q,q' \text{ in } Q.$$

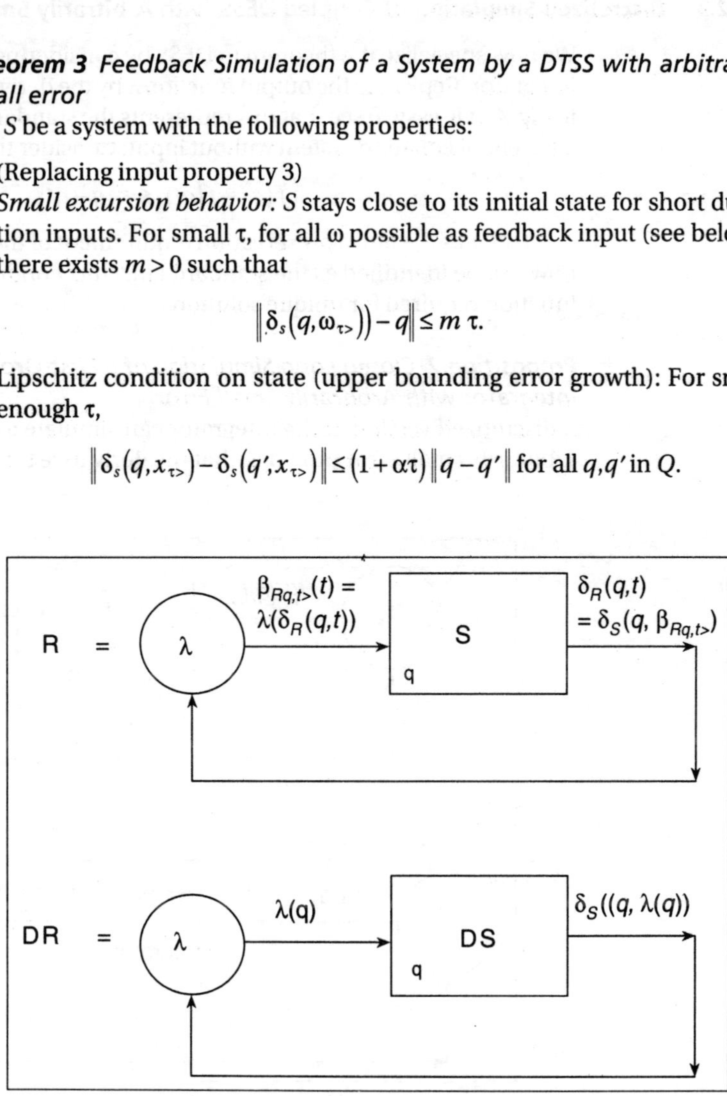

Figure 3 DTSS closed loop simulation of a system.

3. Lipschitz condition on input (upper bounding the error introduced by each segment):

$$\|\delta_s(q,\omega_{t>}) - \delta_s(q,\rho_{t>})\| \le k\|\omega_{t>} - \rho_{t>}\|.$$

4. Norm-preserving output map:

$$\|\lambda(q) - \lambda(q')\| \le \kappa\|q - q'\|.$$

Then a discretized version of S with feedback can simulate S with feedback with arbitrarily small error.

The proof is given in Appendix 1.

16.2.3 Discretized Simulation of Coupled DESS with Arbitrarily Small Error

We now specialize the theorem to DESS by considering the system S to be an integrator. Replacing the output function λ by the derivative function f results in Fig. 4. It is easy to see that this represents the standard form of a first-order differential equation system without input. Consider the condition

$$\|f(q) - f(q')\| \le \kappa\|q - q'\|.$$

This was the norm preservation requirement of the output function, but now can be identified as the standard Lipschitz condition on the derivative function required for unique solutions.

***Proposition 2** Closed Loop Simulation of a First-Order DESS by a Discrete Integrator with Arbitrarily Small Error*

A discretized version of the integrator can simulate a first-order DESS with arbitrarily small error provided that the derivative function is bounded.

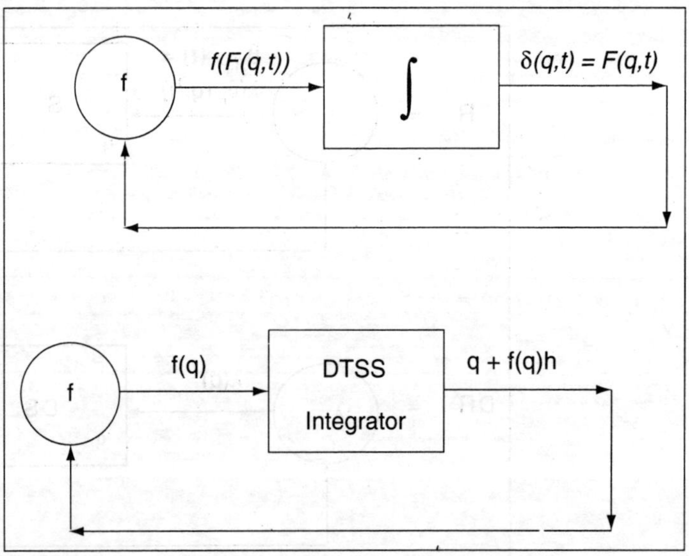

Figure 4 DTSS closed loop simulation of DESS integrator.

Proof: Recall that for the integrator we have $\delta_s(q,\omega_{\tau>}) = q + \int_0^\tau \omega(t)dt$. In Theorem 2, the Lipschitz conditions on state and input were already verified. We consider the following.

Small excursion behavior: For any $\omega = f(q)_{\tau>}$,

$$\left\| \delta_S(q,\omega_{\tau>})) - q \right\|$$
$$= \left\| \int_0^\tau \omega(t)dt \right\| \leq \tau \, max\{\| \omega(t) \| \,|t \leq \tau\}$$
$$\leq \tau \left\| f(q) \right\|.$$

Thus, $m = max\{\| f(q) \|\} = f_{max}$.

As already said, the norm preservation requirement is really the Lipschitz condition on the derivative in disguise and comes along with the fact that the system forms a DESS, thus $\kappa = L$. Recall that $k = 1$. Thus, from Appendix 1, $M = f_{max} L$ and the error is bounded by

$$e_T \leq hT\ Lf_{max}. \blacksquare$$

Exercise: Compare the error bound for the closed loop integrator with that of the open loop integrator (Theorem 1). Match up the parameters for the input segment as externally controlled with those where it is determined by feedback.◆

16.2.4 DEVS Representation of DESS via DTSS Simulation

Recall the two approaches to DEVS representation of DESS. The first is to employ standard numerical methods that result in a DTSS simulation of the DESS. Since a DEVS can componentwise simulate a DTSS coupled model with zero error, we have that a DEVS can componentwise simulate a DESS. The second is to map the DESS model directly into a DEVS. Taking the first approach, illustrated in Fig. 5, leads to the following theorem.

Theorem 4 *Componentwise Simulation of DESS by DEVS with Arbitrarily Small Error*

Let there be a well-defined DESS coupled model that can be componentwise simulated with an arbitrarily small error by a DTSS coupled model. Now a legitimate DEVS coupled model can simulate the DTSS coupled model with zero error. Thus, there is a legitimate DEVS coupled model that can similarly simulate the DESS with an arbitrarily small error.

16.3 Quantization: An Alternative Approach for DEVS Representation

The second approach to DEVS representation of DESS will be based on the concept of quantization. It requires a change in viewpoint. To simulate systems with a digital computer requires that we approximate a continuous trajectory with a finite number of values in a finite time interval. One way we

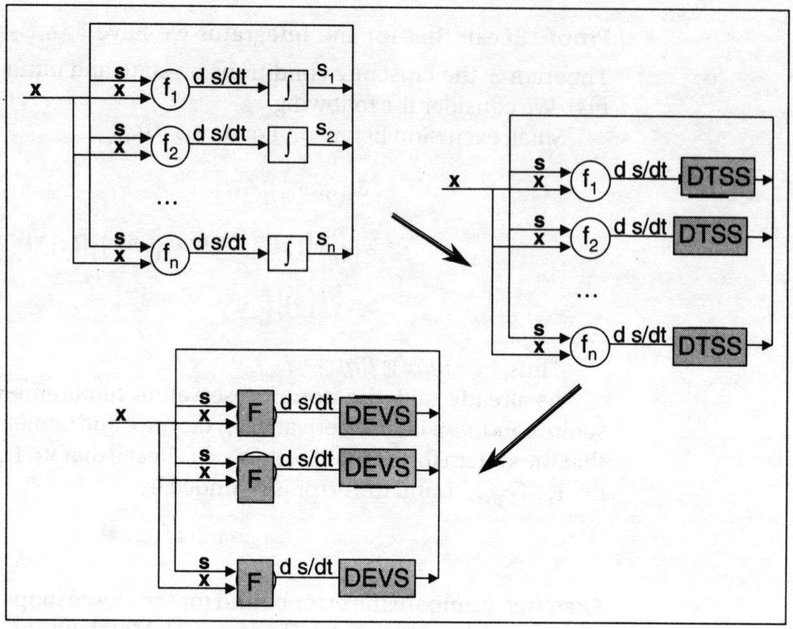

Figure 5 DEVS simulation of DESS coupled models via DTSS simulators.

have just seen is to discretize the time base to obtain a DTSS approximation. Rather than discretize the time base, we may partition the trajectory into a finite number of segments, each of which has a finite computation associated with it. One way to do this is to quantize the value space as illustrated in Fig. 6a. Quantization is a very general concept applicable to any value set, *X*. Figure 6b shows a partition π on *X* with a finite number of partition blocks (equivalence classes). Let $[x]$ denote the block containing point x, and let $\hat{x}$ be the representative of the block containing x. We'll return to consider the choice of representative.

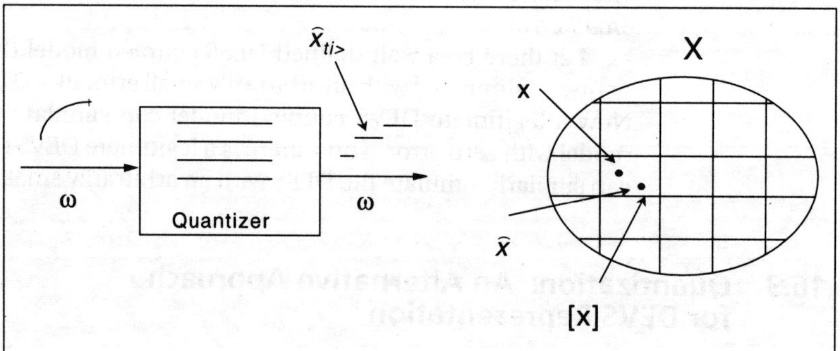

Figure 6 Quantization principles.

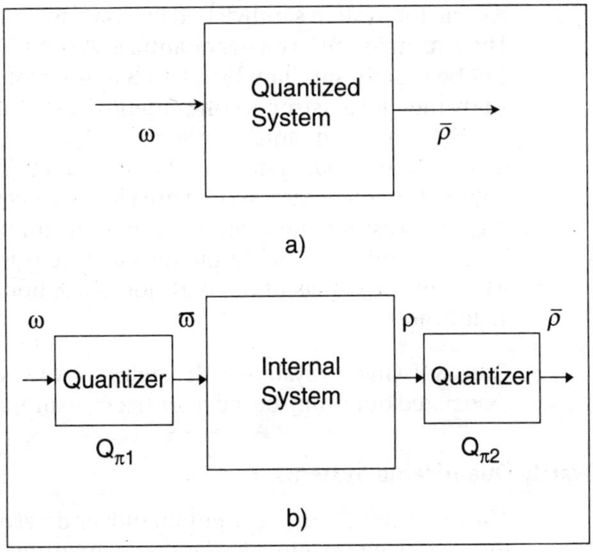

Figure 7 Quantized systems.

Let ω be a trajectory on interval <0,τ> mapping into *X*. Then a *quantization* of ω, based on π, is a piecewise constant segment over the same interval, ϖ defined by $\varpi = \hat{x}_{t_1>} \hat{x}_{t_2>} \ldots \hat{x}_{t_n>}$, where each constant segment $\hat{x}_{t_i>}$ pointwise represents a segment of ω whose range lies entirely in block $[\hat{x}_{t_i}]$, i.e., the representative of $\omega(t)$ is $\hat{x}_{ti}$ for all points *t* in the domain of $\hat{x}_{t_i>}$. To pick out the longest such segments, let *ti* be the largest time *t* such that $\omega(t)$ is in $[\hat{x}_{t_i}]$. Thus, a quantization is a maximum length segmentation[1] and the domain of each constant segment is well defined.

For a special quantization, we let the value set be a finite interval of the reals and let the partition π be given by an integer mesh, {. . . , –*D*,0,*D*,2*D*, . . . , *nD* . . .}, where a block is an interval $[nD, n+1D)$ and *D* is called the *quantum.* We call such a quantization *quantum-based.* Given a number *x*, the partition block [*x*] is computed as the integer floor of *x*/*D*. The latter value can also be designated as the representative of *x*, corresponding to rounding down. Other choices of representative are possible—for example, the half point, floor(*x*/*D*) + *D*/2. Quantization of an *n*-dimensional real-valued space can be done in many ways. One way is through the independent quantization of each dimension.

A *quantizer* is a system defined at the I/O function level, with its only function, Q_κ defined by $Q_\kappa(\omega) = \varpi$. Such systems have a number of properties to which we will return.

16.3.1 Quantized Systems

To study representation of DESS by DEVS we introduce quantized systems as in Fig. 7a. A *quantized system* can be decomposed into, and hence has the same behavior as, a system with input and output quantizers, as in Fig. 7b.

[1] This is a canonical means of breaking a segment into part (Chapter 5).

We call the system sandwiched between the quantizers the *internal system.* The reason for introducing quantized systems is that, as we shall show, they can be exactly simulate by a DEVS at the global level, opening the way to study their local (strong, componentwise) simulateability.

We denote a quantized system by $<Q_{x_1}, S, Q_{x_2}>$, the sequence of the input quantizer, internal system, and output quantizer, respectively. The output segments of quantized system are clearly piecewise constant. In the following, we'll restrict attention to continuous inputs segments with quantum-based quantizers. Such a quantized system is realizable as a DEV&DESS where the crossings of the partition block boundaries are implemented as state events.

Exercise: Given a system with single real-valued input and output ports and associated quantum-based quantizers, express it as a DEV&DESS.◆

16.3.2 Exactly Quantizable Systems

The quantum D_{in} of the input quantizer determines the *input sensitivity* of the quantized system. Similarly, the quantum D_{out} of the output quantizer determines the *output resolution.* Next we formulate conditions under which a quantized system approaches its internal system as both D_{in} and D_{out} go to zero. We call such systems *exactly quantizable.*

First, we note that no error propagation problem arises when we let D_{out} get smaller and smaller. The difference between the output trajectory of the internal system and its quantized counterpart emerging from the output quantizer is always at most D_{out}. Thus, we can safely make D_{out} as small as needed to make the quantized output match the output of the internal system as small as we like. So from here on, we won't worry about D_{out}.

However, to make the output of the internal system match that of the original system, we need to consider the size of the input quantum, D (we will drop the subscript from here on). Here, we must take into account the accumulation of the error introduced by the quantization. This occurs because the internal system has memory and can wind up in different states because of the different inputs. Moreover, as we have seen, once states have diverged, they may be forced into even greater divergence because of the amplification dynamics of the system. Thus, we must come up with conditions on the system that enable us to control this error propagation to as small as level as desired by reducing the input quantum.

First we formulate constraints on the system's input segment set that allow each of its segments to be given an mls (maximal length) segmentation in a uniform manner as a function of the quantum size D.

An input segment ω is *uniformly segmentable* if there is a small enough quantum size D_0 and positive numbers $Max > Min > 0$ such that for every $D_m = D_0/2^m$ $(m = 1,2,3\ldots)$,

1. There is a finite set of boundary crossings for a quantization based on D_m, i.e., the set $\{t\text{: } \omega(t) = nD_m$, for some integer $n\}$ is finite.
2. Let $\tau_1, \ldots, \tau_n$ be the set of intercrossing times $(\tau_i = \tau_i - \tau_{i-1})$. Then for $i = 1, \ldots, n$,

$$D_m/Max = \tau_{min} \leq \tau_i \leq \tau_{max} = D_m/Min.$$

This means that as we refine the quantization (by halving the quantum size at each stage), the upper and lower bounds on the lengths of the representing segments behave in a very well-defined manner: Both are proportional to the quantum size (D_m). In the following theorem, we will see that the smallest representing segment length, τ_{min}, upper bounds the number of segments, while the largest representing segment length, τ_{max}, upper bounds the error introduced by each segment.

An input segment set Ω is *uniformly segmentable* if every one of its segments is uniformly segmentable.

***Theorem 5** Sufficient Conditions for Exactly Quantizable Systems*
Let $<Q_{x1}, S, Q_{x2}>$ be a quantized system and let its internal system S have the same properties as in Theorem 1, except that the input property 3 is replaced by

3. The input segment set of S is uniformly segmentable.

Then there is an approximate morphism at the I/O system level from $<Q_{x1}, S, Q_{x2}>$ to S where the error goes to zero as the input quantum D goes to zero.

Proof: The state sets of the quantized system and its internal system are both Q, so we use the identity mapping as the approximate morphism. As illustrated in Fig. 7, consider the input segment ω and its quantized version, $\varpi = \hat{x}_{t1>}\ \hat{x}_{t2}\ldots\ \hat{x}_{tn>}$, both sent to S. The proof consists of two parts:

1. We must bound the state error at the end of the corresponding generator segments. Using this and the error growth bound in condition 3, we apply the error growth approach in Chapter 14 to bound the error in the state trajectory.
2. We must bound the error in the output trajectories generated from the same starting state by both systems. This we can do immediately given the norm-preserving condition 4 on the output map and the bound on the error in the state trajectory from 1.

By condition 1 (uniform segmentation), we have bounds *Min* and *Max* and a sequence of quantum sizes, $D_m = D_0/2^m$ ($m = 1,2,3\ldots$), such that for each D_m,

$$D_m/Max = \tau_{min} \le \tau_i \le \tau_{max} = D_m/Min.$$

Thus, if ω has length T, the number of segments in its domain is

$$N \le T/\tau_{min} = T\ Max/D_m.$$

The error introduced at the end of such a segment is

$$\varepsilon = \left\| \delta(q,\omega_{\tau>}) - \delta(q,x_{\tau>}) \right\| \le k \left\| \omega_{\tau>} - x_{\tau>} \right\|$$

using condition 2

$$\le k\tau\ max_\tau \left\| \omega_{\tau>}(\tau) - x_{\tau>}(\tau) \right\|$$

$$\le k\tau D_m.$$

The error is thus upper bounded by

$$\varepsilon_{max} = k\ D_m\ \tau_{max} = kD_m^2/Min.$$

Since the magnification of the error is given by condition 1 as $(1+\alpha\,\tau)$, we use error bound in Chapter 14 for $a = 1 + b/N$, and the accumulated error is

$$-e_T \le N\ \varepsilon_{max} = k\ D_m\ T\ Max/Min.$$

Thus, by choosing an m large enough that the quantum size D_m is as small as we need, we can make the error as small as we like. ■

Exercise: Express the required quantum size D_m as a function of the error tolerance, e_T. How do the bounds *Max* and *Min* influence the required quantum size?◆

Given an exactly quantizable system *S* and an error tolerance, there is a quantum value for the input quantizer that keeps the error within tolerance. Now there is also a *largest* quantum value that keeps the error within tolerance. We call this quantum value the input *sensitivity* of system *S* relative to the error tolerance and we say that *S* is *sensitizable* relative to the error tolerance. It may also happen that a system is *exactly* represented by its quantized version (i.e., with an error tolerance of zero). In this case, we omit the qualification and refer to the *sensitivity* of the system as the largest quantum size for which it is exactly represented.

16.3.3 Quantized Integrator: Approximation of DESS

Let *S* be a DESS integrator. Then $<Q_{x1}, S, Q_{x2}>$ will be called a *quantized integrator*. The transition function of the quantized integrator is an extension of the simple transition function,

$$\Delta(q, \omega_{t>}) = q + x \times t,$$

where $\omega_{t>}$ is represented by a piecewise constant segment $x_{t>}$ where x is the block representative of $\omega_{t>}(0)$. The output of the integrator is its state: $\lambda(q) = q$.

Under suitable constraints on the derivative of its input segments, the integrator satisfies all the conditions of the exact quantization theorem just given.

Theorem 6 *Quantized Simulation of DESS Integrator*
The DESS integrator with a uniformly segmentable input segment set is an exactly quantizable system.

Proof: By assumption, the input segment set is uniformly segmentable, and the remaining three conditions of Theorem 5 have already been shown to be satisfied. ■

Appendix 2 characterizes uniformly segmentable input sets for the continuous bounded set of inputs that are admissible for DESS.

16.3.4 Coupled Systems with Quantized Components

A coupling of quantized components is a coupled system specification (Chapter 5) in which the components are quantized systems and for which quantizers are present at the input and output interfaces (Fig. 8). As usual, our first concern is whether such specifications result in well-defined systems. Such networks operate very much like DEVS networks. Indeed, we shall see that they can be directly represented by DEVS equivalents.

Theorem 7

Quantized Moore Systems are closed under coupling.

Proof (sketch): We establish that coupling of quantized Moore systems has a well-defined resultant. For a global state of such a coupled model, there is a well-defined next-event time. This is the smallest of all times to next boundary crossing of the output quantizers of the components. Not considering external input, until the next event time, all outputs of the output quantizers remain constant, and therefore all inputs to input quantizers remain constant. (The interior systems of the components may, however, be undergoing state transitions in response to these constant inputs.) Consider an *internal event* that occurs when the time to next event has elapsed without an intervening *external event* (defined later). At such an internal event one or more outputs change, and the changed outputs are sent to the output quantizer as well as to the influenced components via the component interface maps. If boundaries of the input quantizers are crossed, these changes are transmitted as new input levels to the transition functions of the influenced interior systems. Since the latter are Moore systems, their individual next event times are greater than zero, and the global next event time is also greater than zero. Now consider the response of the network to an external event, i.e., an input causing a change in the output of the input quantizer. Here the external input causes a change in the output of the input quantizer before the next internal transition. When such an event occurs, the new level is transmitted through the input interface maps to the input quantizers of the receiver components. The same subsequent behavior can be observed as in the internal event case. Both internal and external events

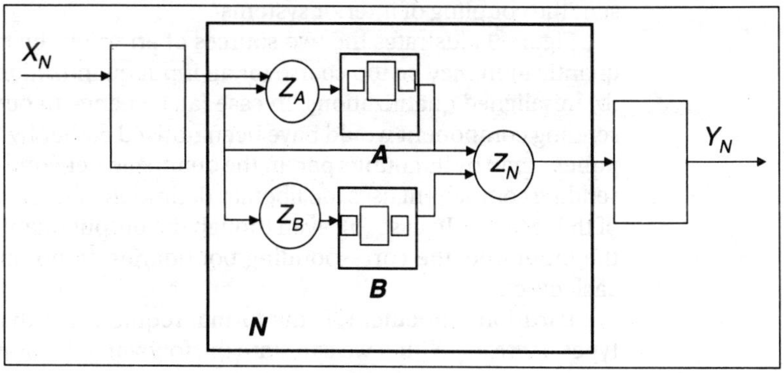

Figure 8 Coupled model of quantized systems.

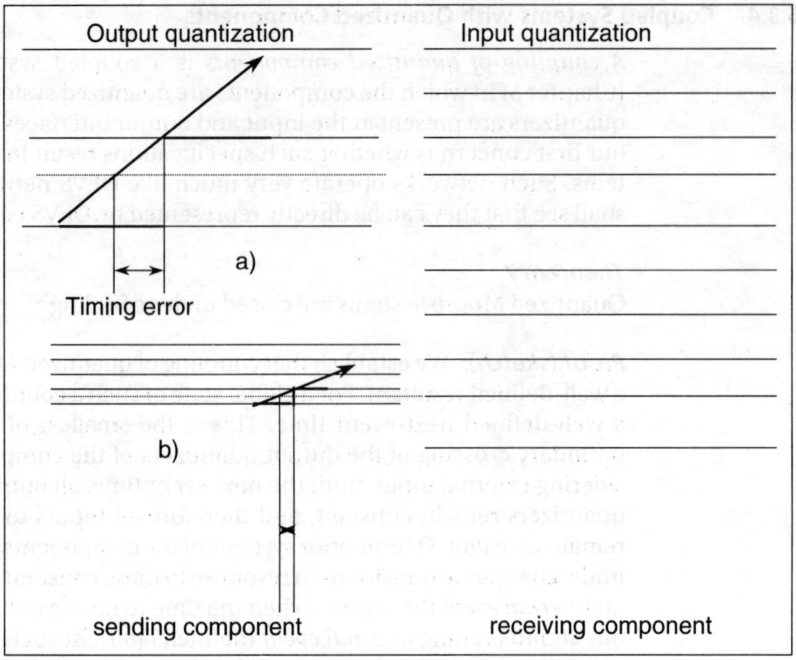

Figure 9 Conditions for error-free coupling.

can occur at the same time, i.e., a component output quantizer crosses a boundary at the same time that the input quantizer does. This *confluent behavior* is resolved by the component interface functions.

Closure under coupling follows, since now the resultant is a system that is sandwiched between the input and output quantizers. ■

Next consider the relationship of a coupling of quantized systems to a coupling of their interior systems. Suppose each of the interior systems is quantizable with zero error. We assume that in each case, the input quantization is that of the maximum quantum size given by the sensitivity. However, we can choose the output quantizations. Under what conditions on the latter quantum sizes will the coupling of quantized systems exactly represent the coupling of interior systems?

Figure 9 illustrates the two sources of error: (a) the fact that the output quantization may be too coarse for an input quantization it influences, and (b) misaligned quantizations. In case (a), a change in output of the original sending component would have been noticed earlier by the receiving component than by its counterpart in the quantized network. In other words, the sending component uses too liberal a definition of significance for the needs of the receiver. In case (b), even though the output quantum is smaller than the input one, the corresponding boundaries do not line up exactly with each other.

Partition refinement[2] is the formal requirement that obviates the two types of errors. With it we can state the following theorem.

[2] One partition refines another if every equivalence class in the first is contained in an equivalence class of the second (Chapter 12).

***Theorem 8** Component wise simulation of Systems with Finite Sensitivities* Given a coupled model of quantizable systems with given sensitivities. A coupled model of quantized systems can componentwise simulate the given coupled model under the conditions that the input quanta are the respective sensitivies and the output quantizations refine the input quantizations they influence.

Figure 10 illustrates an application of this theorem. The state of a sender (A) must be updated for two receivers (B and C) with different sensitivities. The theorem says that we must use output quantizations that refine the input quantizations that they influence. However, it does not require us to use the smallest quantum size 1 (that of C) for both receivers. We can use a quantum of 10 at the output of the sender for receiver B without loss of fidelity, while employing the finer quantization for output to receiver C. Anticipating DEVS simulation of the next section, in *this sensitivity-based updating,* the total number of messages sent by DEVS simulators of the quantized systems can be significantly reduced. As indicated by the reverse arrow, feedback (e.g., from B to A) allowed in such couplings and its benign effect has been accounted for in formulation of the theorem. Of course, as illustrated in the figure, information about others' quantum sizes must be retained in the component simulators.

16.3.5 Quantized Simulation of Coupled Systems with Arbitrarily Small Error

Let each component in a coupled model be an exactly quantizable system. Consider the coupled model with every component replaced by a quantized version. Under what conditions can the quantized coupled model simulate the coupled model with an arbitrarily small error?

As in the discrete time case, for simplicity we consider only a single system S shown in Fig. 11. By feeding back the output of the system S to its input, the resultant is an input-free system R.

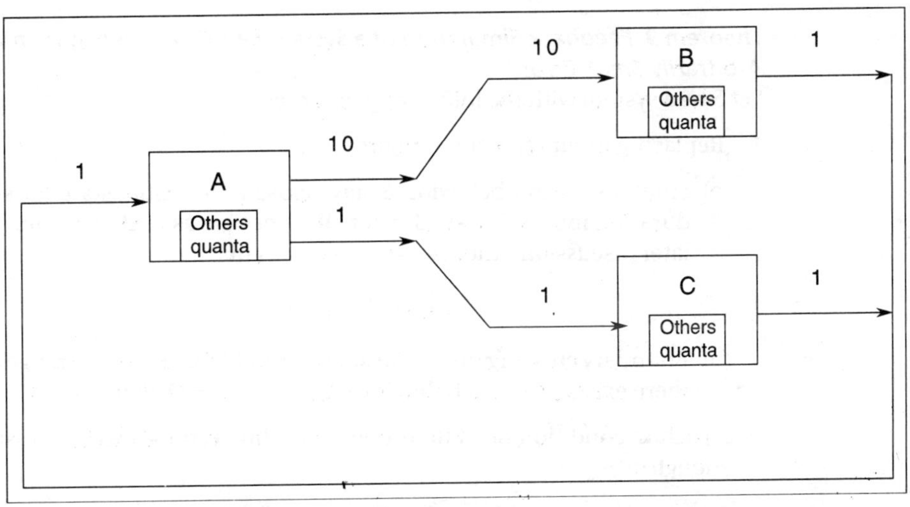

Figure 10 Selective updating based on sensitivity.

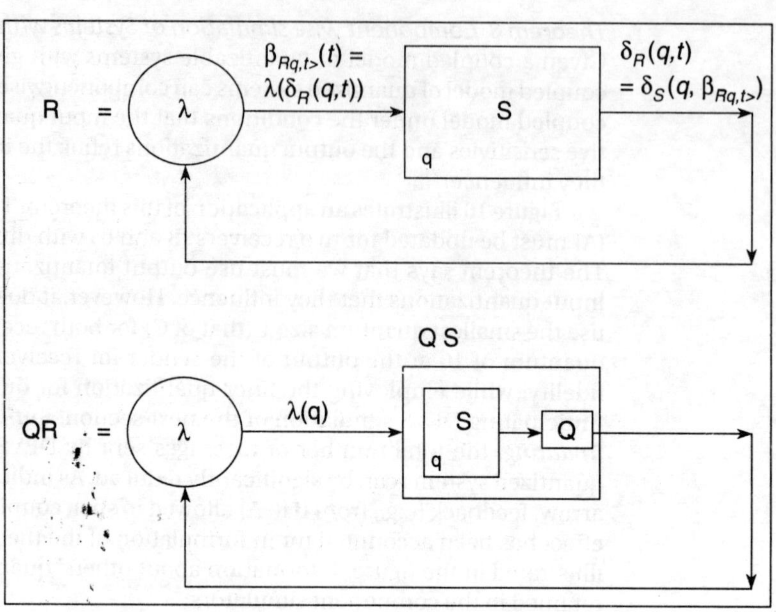

Figure 11 Quantized simulation of closed loop system.

Let *QS* be the quantized version of *S*. We consider only an output quantizer with quantum size *D*. We let *QR* be the coupled quantized version of *R*, which, as shown, preserves the coupling from output to input. To show that we can make *QR* simulate *R* as closely as desired by reducing *D*, we would like to use Theorem 5 for the open loop case. It turns out that the most of the properties required in Theorem 5 still apply. The one exception is the uniform segmentation property of the input. This property has to be reconsidered since, because of feedback, we can't specify the input's properties independently of the system itself.

***Theorem 9** Feedback Simulation of a System by a Quantized System with Arbitrarily Small Error*

Let *S* be a system with the following properties:

1. (Replacing input segmentation property)

   (a) Small excursion behavior: *S* stays close to its initial state for short duration inputs. For small τ, for all ω possible as feedback input (see later discussion), there exists $m > 0$ such that

   $$\left\|\delta_S\left(q,\omega_{\tau>}\right)\right) - q\right\| \leq m\,\tau.$$

   (b) Boundary crossing times: For small τ and *D*, for all *x* in the range of λ, there exists $M > 0$ such that if $\| \delta_S(q, x_{\tau>})) - q\| = D$, then $\tau \leq D/M$.

2. Lipschitz condition on state (upper bounding error growth): For small enough τ,

   $$\left\|\delta_s\left(q, x_{\tau>}\right) - \delta_s\left(q', x_{\tau>}\right)\right\| \leq \left(1 + a\tau\right)\left\|q - q'\right\| \text{ for all } q,q' \text{ in } Q.$$

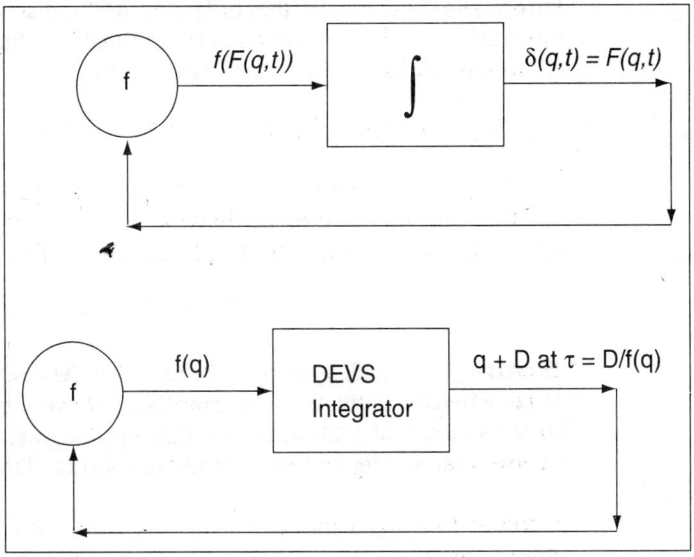

Figure 12 Closed loop quantized simulation of DESS.

3. Lipschitz condition on input (upper bounding the error introduced by each segment):

$$\left\| \delta_s(q, \omega_{t>}) - \delta_s(q, \rho_{t>}) \right\| \le k \left\| \omega_{t>} - \rho_{t>} \right\|.$$

4. Norm-preserving output map:

$$\left\| \lambda(q) - \lambda(q') \right\| \le \kappa \left\| q - q' \right\|.$$

Then a quantized version of S with feedback can simulate S with feedback with arbitrarily small error.

The proof is given in Appendix 3.

16.3.6 Quantized Simulation of Coupled DESS with Arbitrarily Small Error

We now specialize the theorem to DESS by considering the system S to be an integrator. As before, replacing the output function λ by the derivative function f in the feedback loop represents the standard form of a first order differential equation system. Figure 12 illustrates the quantized version of the coupled model.

Proposition 3 *Closed Loop Simulation of a First-Order DESS by a Quantized Integrator with Arbitrarily Small Error*

A quantized version of the integrator can simulate a first-order DESS with arbitrarily small error provided that the derivative is bounded above and below away from zero.[3]

[3] In future work, we will seek to strengthen this theorem so as not to required bounding away from zero.

Proof: The proof follows that of Theorem 9 for discretized simulation of the integrator. In addition, we have to establish the boundary crossing times condition. We have for a boundary event time τ

$$D = \left\| \delta_S\left(q, f(q)_{\tau>}\right) - q \right\| = \left\| \int_0^\tau f(q)dt \right\| = \tau \left\| f(q) \right\| \quad (f(q) \text{ is constant}).$$

So $\tau = D \| f(q) \|$ and $\tau < D/\min\{\|f(q)\|\} > 0$ (by assumption)).

Thus, in Theorem 9, we have $m = max\ \{\| f(q) \|\} = f_{max}$ and $M = min\ \{\|f(q)\|\} = f_{min}$. Thus, the error bound is (recall $k = 1$ and $\kappa = L$)

$$e_T \le D\, LT\, f_{max}^2 / f_{min}^2.$$

Exercise: The smallest value of the ratio *Max/Min* occurs when *Max* = *Min* = *M*, i.e., when the derivative is constant, so we have a straight line with slope *M*. Show by direct calculation that for this input segment a DEVS integrator has an error that is independent of *M* and proportional to *DT* as predicted.◆

Exercise: Investigate the error of the DEVS integrator by direct calculation for input segments: $\omega(t) = at^2$ and $w(t) = e^{at}$ in the interval $(1, T)$. Show that the dependence of the error is consistent with the ratio *Max/Min* in each case.◆

16.3.7 DEVS Representation of Quantized Systems

Recall that the reason for introducing the quantized system concept is that it bridges the gap between DESS models and their representation in DEVS. Since, as we now will show, DEVS can simulate quantized systems at both the I/O system and coupled system levels without error, the ability of quantized systems to represent DESS models directly carries over to DEVS.

***Theorem 10** Exact Simulation of Quantized Systems by DEVS at I/O System Level*

Every quantized system is simulateable (with zero error) by a DEVS at the I/O system (global) level.

Proof: Let $S = (T, X, \Omega, Y, Q, \Delta, \Lambda)$ be the internal system with input and output quantizers Q_{π_1} and Q_{π_2}, respectively.

Define a DEVS by $M = (X, Y, S, \delta_{ext}, \delta_{int}, \lambda, ta)$. Let $S = Q \times X$. The second component enables the DEVS to store its last input. Then,

- The *time advance* is the time to the next change in output produced by the output quantizer:

$$ta(q,x) = min\left(t \,\middle|\, Q_{\pi 2}\left\{\Lambda\left(\Delta(q, x_{t>})\right) \neq Q_{\pi 2}\left(\Lambda(q)\right)\right\}\right),$$

  i.e., the earliest elapsed time at which a change in output occurs.
- The output of the DEVS at the next internal event is the quantized output of *S* at that time:

$$\lambda(q,x) = Q_{\pi 2}\left(\Lambda\left(\Delta(q, x_{ta(q,x)>})\right)\right)$$

- Unless there is an external input, the DEVS will update its state to the state of the system at the next output:

$$\delta_{int}(q,x) = \Delta(q, x_{ta(q,x)} >.$$

- If there is an external event after an elapsed time, e, in <0,*ta*(*a*,*x*)>, the DEVS will immediately update its state to

$$\delta_{ext}(q,x,e,x') = (\Delta(q, x_{e>,}), x'),$$

i.e., it uses the current input to update the state of *S* and stores the new input from the input quantizer.

Appendix 3 shows how to construct the morphism to demonstrate exact simulation of the internal system by the DEVS system. ■

Combining DEVS exact simulation of quantized systems and the definitions of quantizable and sensitizable systems, we have the following theorem.

Theorem 11

Every exactly quantizable system is simulateable by a DEVS at the (global) I/O system level with arbitrarily small error. Every sensitizable system relative to a given error tolerance is approximately simulateable by a DEVS with error no larger than the error tolerance.

16.3.8 DEVS Repesentation of Quantized Integrator

The DEVS realization of the quantized integrator has the simple definition

$$M = (X, Y, S, \delta_{ext}, \delta_{int}, \lambda, ta),$$

where $X = Y = R$ and $S = R \times R \times \mathrm{I}$ and

- $\delta_{int}(q, x, n) = ((n + sign(x))\, D, x, n + sign(x))$
- $\delta_{ext}((q,x,n), e, x') = (q + xe, x', n)$
- $\delta_{con}((q,x,n), x') = ((n + sign(x))D), x', n + sign(x))$
- $\lambda(q,x) = (n + sign(x))D$
- $ta(q,x,n) = |\,((n+1)D - q)/x\,|$ $if\, x > 0\ and\ (n+1)D - q > 0$
  $= |\,(q - nD)/x\,|$ $if\, x < 0\ and\ |\,q - nD\,| > 0$
  $= |\,D/x\,|$ $if\, x \neq 0$ *and none of the above*
  $= \infty$ *otherwise* (*i.e.*, $x = 0$)

For an internal transition, we assume the model starts on a boundary and ends on a boundary, one quantum below or above it. As in Fig. 13a, starting on a boundary, the time advance computation merely divides *D* by the current input *x* (which is the derivative, or slope, after all). If we reach the upper boundary ($n + 1$) or lower boundary ($n - 1$), we output, and update, the state accordingly. Note that so long as the input remains the same, the time to cross successive boundaries will be the same. Figure 13b shows that when a new input is received, we update the state using the old input and the elapsed time. From this new state, *q*, the new time to reach either the upper or lower boundary is computed.

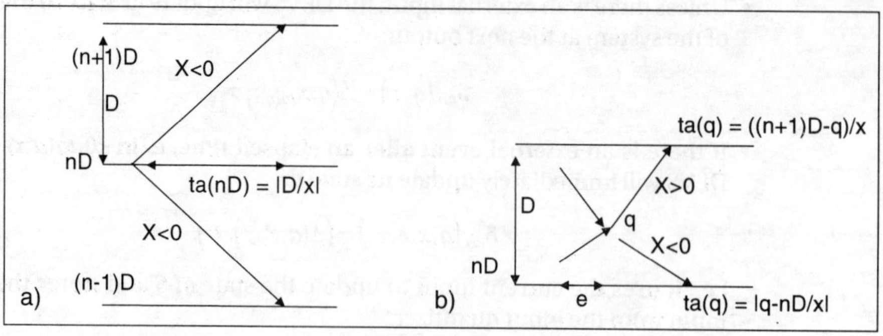

Figure 13 DEVS simulator of a quantized integrator.

The Quantized DEVS integrator greatly reduces the number of transitions and output messages needed to simulate an integrator. It can also greatly reduce the message size, to one bit. Since the only possible transitions are to the upper or lower boundaries, we need to send only the appropriate element of the two-valued set {+1, −1}. Of course, this requires that the receiver know the quantum size and the initial state of the sender.

Thus, there is a DEVS simulation of the quantized integrator with BCS inputs that can serve as an arbitrarily close representation of the integrator at the I/O system level. We still need to examine coupled networks of integrators to examine whether this error-free representation holds in the "closed loop" case.

Exercise: Show that the DEVS integrator model follows formally from the general form of DEVS representation of quantized systems.◆

Exercise: Write the quantized DEVS integrator that sends only +1 or −1 as appropriate at a boundary crossing.◆

16.3.9 DEVS Simulation of Coupled Quantized Systems

We will show that DEVS can strongly simulate coupled systems with quantized systems as components. Since, as we have just seen, quantized systems can approximate DESS models to an arbitrary degree of accuracy, we will conclude that DEVS can also strongly simulate DESS with arbitrarily small error.

***Theorem 12** Exact Simulation of Quantized Systems by DEVS at Coupled System Level*
Every coupling of quantized systems can be componentwise simulated (with zero error) by a DEVS coupled model.

Proof (sketch): Given a coupling of quantized systems, we have seen that each of the components can be simulated without error by a DEVS. Thus, we construct a coupled DEVS model in which each quantized component is mapped to its DEVS simulator. The coupling among DEVS simulators reflects that among the original components. The interface maps in the quantized network are retained without change for the DEVS coupled model. We employ the same morphism approach originally defined at the I/O system level, now refined to apply at the coupled system level.

Exercise: Complete the proof of the simulation showing that the global state transitions of the DEVS coupled model and those of the quantized system coupled model occur in synchronized fashion with corresponding results.◆

16.3.10 Quantization-Based DEVS Simulation of DESS

Combining the ability of DEVS to exactly simulate quantized systems and the ability of quantized systems to approximate DESS models yields the ability of DEVS to approximately coupled DESS models. This leads to the approach of Fig. 14. Given a network of integrators and memoryless functions, in the first step, we construct a quantized network for simulating it by replacing the integrators by their quantized equivalents. In the second step, we replace each of the quantized integrators by their DEVS equivalents and replace the interface maps by DEVS-equivalent memoryless function representations. The resulting network isomorphically simulates the quantized coupled model without error, and consequently, the original DESS coupled model with the error introduced by quantization. This gives the following theorem.

***Theorem 13** Quantization-based DEVS Simulation of DESS*
Any DESS can be simulated by a DEVS network at the coupled system level with an arbitrarily small error.

Exercise: Design a DEVS representation F of a memoryless function f to work in Fig. 14. Which is the correct approach: (a) waiting for all inputs to arrive before computing the output, or (b) computing the output as soon as any input changes? (See Chapter 15.)◆

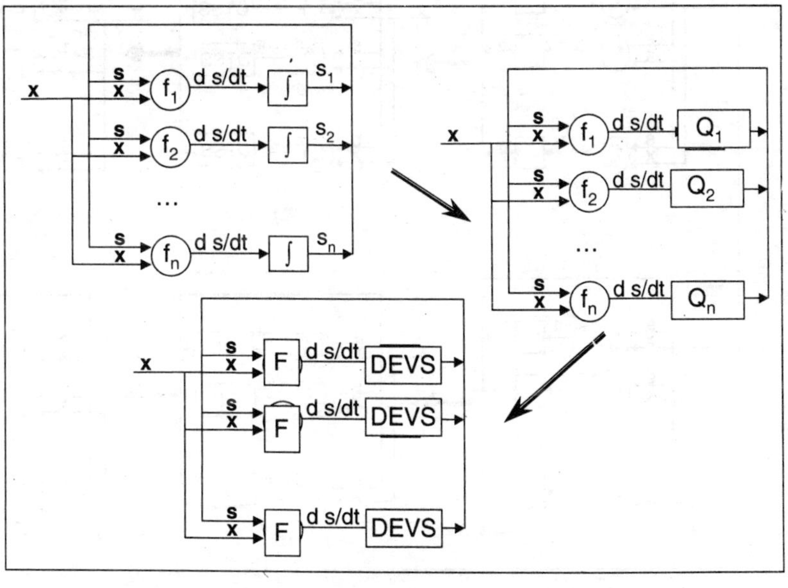

Figure 14 DEVS simulation of DESS coupled models via quantization.

16.4 Simulation Study of Quantization

Recall that the motivation for developing the quantization approach to system representation was to support the use of the DEVS Bus for both event-based and time-driven simulation. Using quantization, we are primarily looking for a way to reduce message traffic between components; however, reduction in computation and error trade-off are also important considerations. In this section we discuss an early simulation study that provides some promising results and helps us to focus on the issues more intensely.

Figure 15 reproduces the two approaches to quantization of DESS that we introduced. In the first (Fig. 15a), we employ conventional numerical methods to do the integration of the differential equations of each component in a coupled model (hence, a DTSS representation). We then attach a quantizer to the output, thus sending messages to other components only when large enough changes occur. We call this the *Quantized DTSS* approach. In the second approach (Fig. 15b), instead of using numerical analysis to do the integration, we directly quantize each integrator and represent it with a DEVS simulator. We call this the *Quantized DEVS* approach.

16.4.1 Some Indicative Simulation Results

To compare the Quantized DTSS and Quantized DEVS approaches, we chose an example with well-understood behavior that would enable us to compare both message reduction and error properties. Figure 16 shows the

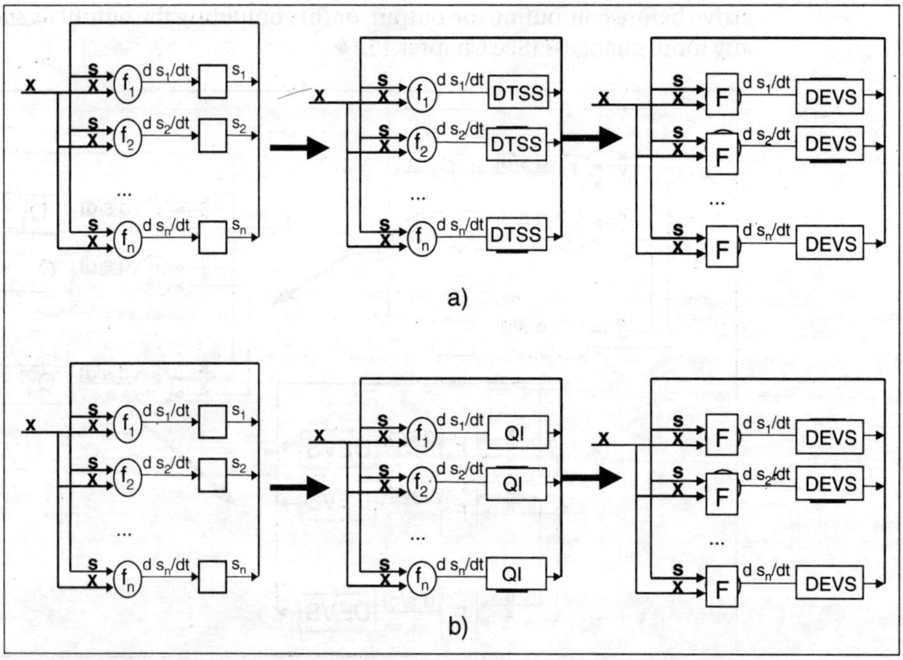

Figure 15 Quantized DTSS and Quantized DEVS simulation approaches.

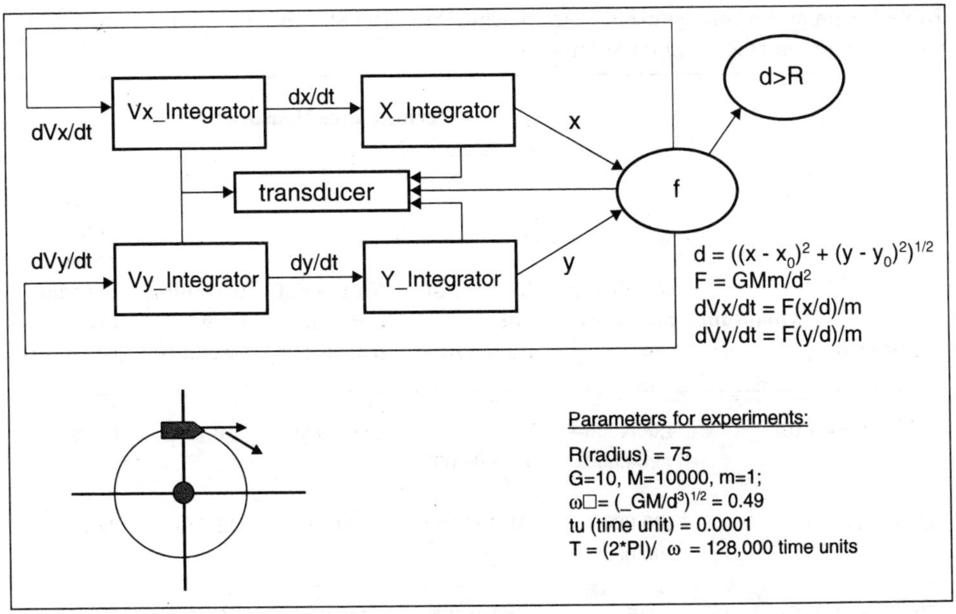

Figure 16 Test example.

example used. It is a DESS model of a Newtonian body orbiting around a fixed mass (e.g., earth around the sun).

Table 1 shows the results of experiments with the parameters shown in the figure. Since these tests were done on a sequential machine,[4] the execution time includes internal transitions, external transitions, output computations, and quantization checks. Although for the same quantum size, both approaches reduce the number of messages sent about equally, Quantized DEVS also significantly reduces the internal transitions and the computation time. (Internal transitions are required only at event times rather than at each time step as in DTSS.) Also, a major advantage of DEVS quantization is that since events are predicted at exact boundary crossings, only information about which boundary has been crossed need actually be sent—which can be many fewer bits than required for the state at the boundary. One approach is to send the integer multiple of the quantum requiring the receiver to multiply this integer by the quantum size to recover the original real state value. More dramatic savings can be obtained by sending only the *change* in boundary level. Because of the incremental nature of DEVS quantization, this change can be only +1 or −1, requiring only a *one-bit* transmission. Of course the receiver must keep track of the current boundary and know the proper quantization size to recover the actual state, as illustrated in Fig. 10. Also important is that the Quantized DEVS approach is much more accurate than the Quantized DTSS for the same quantum size. In other words, for the same accuracy, the DEVS method requires many fewer bits sent and smaller execution times. For example, compare the DTSS ($D = 0.01$)

[4] We used the DEVSJAVA environment using double precision for real number representation.

Table 1 Comparison of Quantization Approaches (Messages Shown as the Sum of Those Existing the Integrators and the Memoryless Function)

		Performance Measure				
Approach	**Quantum size**	**Number of messages sent**	**Number of bits transmitted**	**Number of internal transitions**	**Execution time (seconds)**	**Error (avg. deviation of radius from constant)**
DTSS ($h = 0.1$ tu)		4,000,000 + 200,000	384,000,000	4,000,000	118,774	0.0099
DTSS ($h = 1$ tu)		400,000 + 200,000	38,400,000	400,000	12,776	0.015
Quantized DTSS ($h = 1$ tu)	$D =$ 0.5	1,215 + 1,664	184,256	400,000	9,250	3.73
	$D =$ 0.1	6,256 + 8,330	933,504	400,000	9,243	1.47
	$D =$ 0.01	64,954 + 74,552	8,928,384	400,000	9,456	0.441
Quantized DEVS (with ±1)	$D =$ 0.5	1,272 + 1,710	2,982	1,272	219	0.441
	$D =$ 0.1	6,360 + 8,550	14,910	6,360	1,207	0.073
	$D =$ 0.01	63,602 + 85,510	149,112	63,602	13,130	0.007

with the DEVS ($D = 0.5$)—the DTSS requires sending approximately 3000 times the number of bits (each message contains 64 bits to represent a real number with double precision) and approximately 40 times the execution time to achieve the same (low) accuracy.

We also compared Quantized DEVS with "pure" DTSS, by which we mean using the DTSS without quantization. Effectively, this is Quantized DTSS with a quantum size matching the precision of the computer word size. The remarkable result is that the DEVS achieves a better accuracy than the pure DTSS ($h = 1$) with approximately the same execution time but with a reduction of approximately 250 times the number of bits transmitted. When we run the DTSS with $h = 0.1$, the results are even more dramatic. Now both have about the same accuracy, but the DEVS is 10 times faster and has a 2500-fold reduction in bits sent.

16.4.2 Comparing Quantized DEVS with Pure DTSS Simulation of DESS

How can we explain the remarkable gains in performance by Quantized DEVS displayed in this example? Is this example just a fluke, or is there something fundamentally different about the DEVS approach? The latter explanation is suggested by the fact that these results agree with earlier experiments showing a 1000-fold speedup in computation on massively parallel platforms using DEVS quantization [12]. This was a simulation study of surface water runoff using a high-resolution spatial cellular model of a large-scale watershed. The cells were modeled with ordinary differential equations and quantization was compared with a standard discrete time numerical method. To address this question we make the following conjecture.

Conjecture

For any exactly quantizable DESS coupled model, a DEVS componentwise simulation is never less, and often much more efficient, than a counterpart variable or fixed step simulation with the same final accuracy.

We now present a heuristic argument why this conjecture should be true:

Consider a DEVS simulation of a DESS network of integrators as in Fig. 15. By assumption for any given final error, there is a quantum size D that enables the simulation to stay within that error. Let us choose the largest D that satisfies the tolerance requirement, so that crossing a boundary later than required by this D will result in an error that is above the tolerance limit.

Let's look at a DEVS simulation cycle as illustrated in Fig. 17a. Each DEVS integrator i schedules itself for the next boundary crossing at $\tau_i = D/|x_i|$, where x_i is the current input derivative to integrator i. The time advance to the next event is then $\sigma = \min\{\tau_i\}$ and the imminent integrators are those for which $\tau_i = \sigma$. In Fig. 17a, the imminents are {1,4,6}. The coupling then determines which integrators receive outputs from these imminents. Imminents {1,6} send to {2,4, 7} in the figure (shown as heavy vertical arrows). The imminents and the influencees {1,2,4,6,7} then execute their transition functions—{1,6} the internal, {2,7}, the external function, and {4} the confluent function (which in the case of an integrator is the same as the external transition function). This results in new time advances for imminents and their influences (shown as dotted arrows for the latter Fig. 17a.) None of the remaining inte-

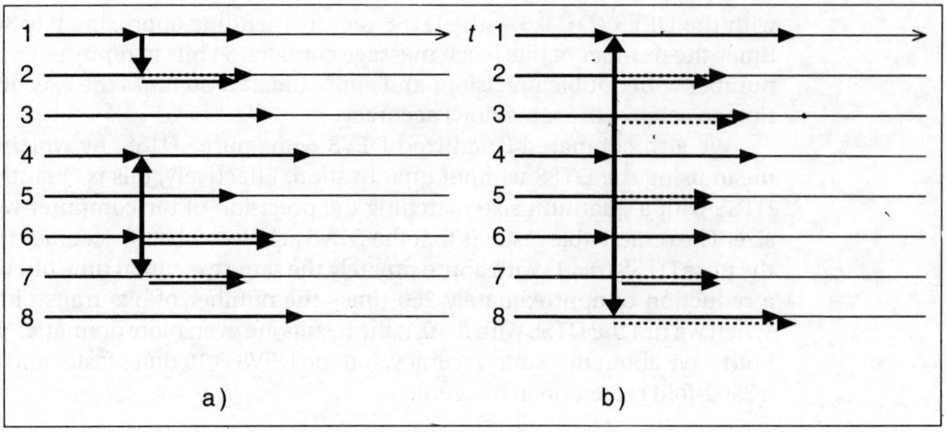

Figure 17 Comparing DEVS and DTSS simulation of DESS.

grators (e.g., {3,5,8}) executes computations and their next event times are unchanged. We are now ready for the next DEVS cycle.

To measure the complexity of such a cycle, we see that we need to obtain measurements from the imminents and their influencees. But we don't necessarily have to identify them at each cycle to do this. This is because the complexity of a run is determined by accumulating the measured elements in the individual cycles. We instrument each component to count its internal transitions, external transitions, and confluent transitions. This will catch all the executions without requiring us to identify the imminents and their influencees. We also have all outputs sent to a transducer, thus capturing all the messages sent from the imminents to influencees, again without necessarily identifying who did what when.

Now consider Fig. 17b, where we illustrate a synchronized variable step simulation strategy. The global time advance is again $\sigma = \min\{\tau_i\}$. Instead of activating only the imminents, however, we activate all the integrators at this time. They exchange messages as prescribed by the coupling and execute their integration step (external transition function). Thus, communication and computation occur at each event. We can call this a variable step integration method since at each cycle, σ may be different. Note that some integrators such as {3,5,8} are now updated that were not in the original DEVS simulation. Since we have chosen the quantum size for error tolerance, any increased accuracy that might result from such updating does not matter to us. (Had we wanted this improved accuracy, we should have said so in the beginning—we can always go back and do so!)

In our final case, at each cycle we set $h = D/Max$ where *Max* is the largest (magnitude of) derivative of all the inputs to the integrators. Here the time advance is fixed for the whole run, so we have a DTSS simulation with time step *h*. A bigger time step than *D/Max* runs the risk of increasing error, since we would be too late for the boundary crossing of the integrator(s) that receives this largest derivative input (and *D* was chosen as liberally as possible within the error tolerance). Thus, *D/Max* is the largest acceptable (constant) time step. Note that the updating in any cycle in which the maximum derivative is not present is superfluous, since the earliest required updating occurs later.

Corollary of Conjecture

To produce the same final error as a quantized DEVS simulation with quantum size D, a DTSS simulation must have step size

$$h \leq D/Max,$$

where *Max* is the largest (magnitude of) derivative.

In order of increasing complexity we have the quantized DEVS, the variable-step, and the fixed-step methods. All reduce the error below tolerance, but unless the maximum derivative is present at each cycle as input to each integrator, the DEVS will demonstrate many fewer transitions and much less message traffic. If we measure the *simultaneity* of the network by the fraction of *imminent* integrators at each cycle, we can see that DEVS simulation will be more efficient than both the variable and fixed step methods for small to moderately active states of coupled models. It is only for fully simultaneous states that persist for all of the run that a variable step method will equal the DEVS in performance. In addition, the maximum derivative has to be input to at least one integrator at each time cycle for the fixed time step method to match the DEVS performance.

Conjecture

Highly simultancous DESS networks are rare.

A number of arguments suggest that highly simultaneous networks are rare—in fact, the chances of finding one get vanishingly small as the number of components increase to infinity. To start, let's consider a stochastic characterization of the selection of derivatives. If we assume that each integrator chooses its derivative independently, then the chance that all integrators receive the same input derivative, let alone the same maximum value, decreases exponentially with the number of components. Of course, the derivative process may be highly correlated, since the underlying model is deterministic. Nevertheless, the exponential dependence on the number of integrators might well hold in any sequence of model transitions with any sort of interesting behavior.

For example, in a second-order linear oscillator, the integrators see sine wave inputs from each other that are 90 degrees out of phase. Indeed, when one integrator is getting the maximum value (amplitude times frequency) the other is getting the minimum, 0. Only every eighth of a cycle do the integrators see the same input magnitude, and as we shall see, the DEVS has approximately 30% fewer internal transitions. The fourth-order orbiting oscillator discussed earlier shows a much greater reduction for DEVS integration in internal transitions over the DTSS simulation with the same accuracy.

16.4.3 Insight from Second-Order Linear Oscillator

The linear oscillator shown in Fig. 18a provides a revealing example of the efficiency advantages of DEVS. It is well known that the exact behavior is characterized by sinusoidal oscillations with the integrators 90 degrees out of phase with each other.

Thus, while one is generating a sine wave, the other is generating a cosine wave. Indeed, from the input perspective of each one, we can replace the other with the corresponding sinusoidal generator in open loop fashion as in Fig. 18b & c. The derivative input trajectories are shown in Fig. 18d.

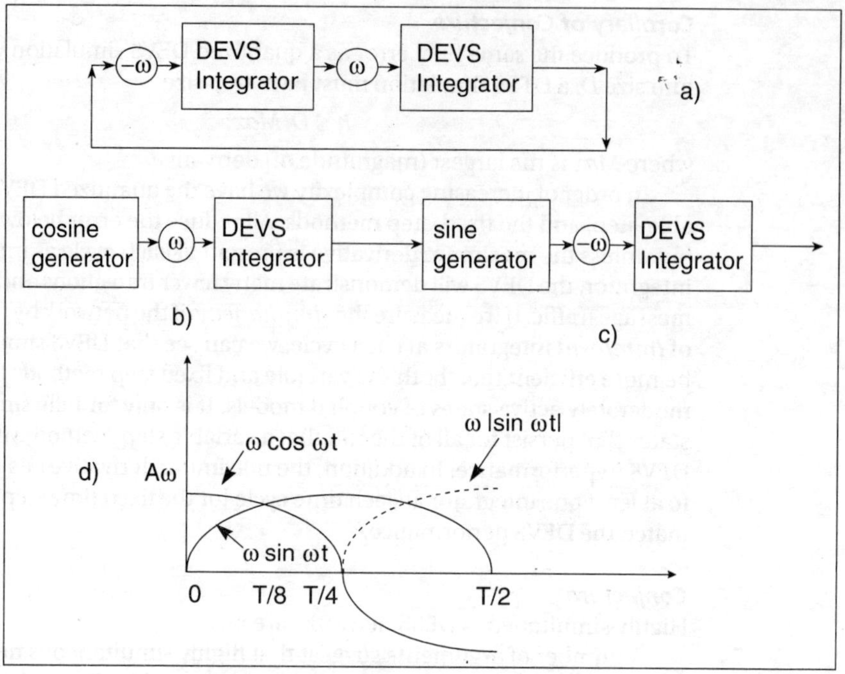

Figure 18 Second-order linear oscillator.

Taking into account that the step size is inversely related to the magnitude of the derivative, the same pattern of relative step sizes is repeated every eighth of a cycle. In every such period, one integrator always sees higher derivatives than the other, and they alternate among these fast and slow behaviors. Think of it this way: Whichever is currently the slow integrator needs the fast integrator to speed it up; conversely, the fast integrator needs the other to slow it down.

Now in the DEVS simulation, in every eighth of a cycle, the time advances of the fast integrator are smaller than those of the slow integrator. It is only at the end of this period that they are equal. As shown in Table 2, we can estimate the average time step by following the steps of one integrator through a quarter cycle containing its slow and fast phases. We predict that DEVS cuts down on the number of internal transitions and output messages by about 30% over the DTSS with the same error. In contrast, the variable step method is predicted to produce only a 10% reduction.

Exercise: Write the integral for the average time step of one integrator over a quarter cycle. Look up the integral in a table. In general, the average time step is not equal to the quantum divided by the average derivative. Compute the latter and compare.◆

Exercise: Write a short program to compute, given a quantum size, successive time step sizes in the DEVS and variable time step methods. As the quantum gets smaller, do your averages converge to those in the table?◆

Table 2 Predicted Comparison of DEVS and Variable Time Step Relative Baseline DTSS

Method	**Means to estimate**	**Internal transitions (output messages) relative to DTSS as gets small**
Fixed time step DTSS	*D* (set max. derivative =1)	1
Variable time step	Average of minimum time step of both integrators over one eighth cycle	0.9
Quantized DEVS	Average of time step of one integrator over one quarter cycle	$2/\pi \cong 0.64$

Exercise: Show that the requirement that $h \leq D/Max$ implies that $h/T \leq D/2\pi A$ for the oscillator, i.e., h/T and D/A are closely correlated. Explain why this should be so.◆

Simulation of a test case showed that the predictions of relative performance of quantized DEVS versus pure DTSS were remarkably close. We compared the Quantized DEVS with quantum sizes *D* shown in Table 3 against the DTSS with step sizes $h = D/max$ (where the maximum derivative is the amplitude multiplied by the frequency) with values shown in the table. Note that the ratio of messages sent (and internal transitions) is the same as predicted to two decimal places! The errors incurred in quantized DEVS are however, slightly higher than the corresponding DTSS values, although of the same order of magnitude. The data bits passed (using the DEVS binary output technique) are 100 times fewer for DEVS than for DTSS. The execution time for DEVS, although initially slightly larger, improves to about 40% that of DTSS as the quantum size decreases.

16.5 Conjectures for Further Research

Caveat: Effect of Integration Method

The results presented provide strong evidence for the claim that quantized DEVS can reduce the message traffic burden in distributed simulation as compared to quantized DTSS for the same accuracy. Moreover, they support the stronger conjecture that quantized DEVS does better than even pure DTSS in both message passing and total execution time, even for small

Table 3 Simulation Comparison of DEVS Quantization Approach with Pure DTSS: $\omega = 0.0001$, $A = 75$, Run Time = 62,800 (one cycle)

	Avg. error	Number of messages passed	Number of data bits passed	Number of internal transitions	Execution time (seconds)
DTSS	0.79	1,882 (0.64)	120,448	1,882	125
($h = 66.7$)					
($h = 13.3$)	0.16	9,418 (0.64)	602,752	9,418	550
($h = 1.33$)	0.016	94,198 (0.64)	6,028,672	94,198	10,140
Quantized DEVS	0.96	1,213	1,213	1,213	153
($D = 0.5$)					
($D = 0.1$)	0.2	6,019	6,019	6,019	657
($D = 0.01$)	0.02	59,999	59,999	59,997	6,583

systems such as the second-order oscillator. However, a caveat has to be stated here—*the effect of integration method has not been considered.* The results for the orbiting body in Table 1 were obtaining using a trapezoidal method for both DEVS and DTSS integration. The results presented in Table 3 were obtained using the simple Euler method for both. There are many varieties of integration methods for differential equation systems with arrays of parameter settings and accuracies. Thus, we have to be cautious with respect to the stronger conjecture concerning DEVS as a better integration approach than conventional integration methods in conventional uniprocessor simulation. It may well be that conventional methods are preferred for small differential equation systems on isolated sequential processors or even multiprocessors with shared memory. However, as the size of the system increases and also the number of processors with message passing required for inter-processor communication, it appears that DEVS quantization has distinct message reduction advantages for the same accuracy.

The developments so far suggest that we can refine our conjecture into a restricted and strong from:

Conjecture (Restricted)
The message passing efficiency of a quantized DEVS simulation of differential equation systems is never less than that of counterpart quantized DTSS to achieve the same accuracy.

Conjecture (Strong)
The efficiency (both message passing and execution time) of a quantized DEVS simulation of differential equation systems is never less than that of counterpart conventional integration methods to achieve the same accuracy.

The efficiency of quantized DEVS relative to the alternative approaches increases with the following factors:

- *Order of the differential equation system,* i.e., with increasing numbers of integrators the frequency of occurrence of simultaneity is diminished.
- *Temporal heterogeneity of the network,* i.e., the dispersion in the derivative values (interestingly, a class of such systems are called stiff systems in the literature and are hard to solve with conventional methods—are they easier to solve with DEVS?)
- *Connectivity of the network,* i.e., with the fraction of other integrators influenced by an imminent integrator. In the extreme of a fully disconnected network (a not very interesting case!), the only cost (internal transitions) of conventional approaches is that due to less than full simultaneity. As the connectivity of the network increases, there is a greater penalty for the communication required for unneeded state updating.

Further research is needed to establish the correctness of the conjectures. Especially, as indicated, the effect of integration method on the comparison must be investigated for the strong conjecture.

Exercise: Consider quantization-based DEVS simulation of the second-order oscillator with positive and negative damping, respectively. Predict which model will have the largest efficiency.◆

16.6 Summary

This chapter argued that distributed simulation requires expansion of the concept of simulation complexity to include measures of communication among nodes. We showed that discrete event, rather than traditional, approaches are better at reducing such complexity while enabling accurate representations of continuous systems. To do this we developed the theoretical foundation for the quantized systems and used this foundation to show how the DEVS representation can provide more efficient simulation at lower error cost than the traditional integration methods of differential equation systems, especially in a distributed simulation context. This forms the basis for the DEVS Bus, a distributed simulation framework for multi-formalism modeling.

16.7 Sources

DEVS representation of piecewise constant systems was first described in Ref. [9] and further developed in refs. [7, 10–13]. Discrete time methods for real-time distributed simulation were developed by Howe [3,4] and Laffitte [5]. Dead reckoning plays a major role in distributed interactive simulation [1,2,6].

1. Bassiouni, M. A., *et al.*, "Performance and Reliability Analysis of Relevance Filtering for Scalable Distributed Interactive Simulation." *ACM Trans. on Model, and Comp. Sim.* (*TOMACS*) **7**(3), 293–331 (1997).
2. Goel, S. G., and K. D. Morris. "Dead Reckoning for Aircraft in DIS." Presented at AIAA Flight Simulation Technologies Conference, South Carolina, 1992.
3. Howe, R. M., "Dynamic Accuracy of the State Transition Method in Simulating Linear Systems." *Trans. of SCS* **5**(1), 27–41 (1988).
4. Howe, R. M., "The Use of Mixed Integration Algorithms in State Space." *Trans. of SCS* **7**(1), 45–66 (1990).
5. Laffitte, J., and R. M. Howe, "Interfacing Fast and Slow Subsystems in the Real-Time Simulation of Dynamic Systems." *Trans. of SCS* **14**(3), 115–126 (1997).
6. Lin, K. C., and D. E. Schab. "The Performance Assessment of Dead Reckoning Algorithms in DIS." In SCSC, 1994.
7. Praehofer, H., and B. P. Zeigler, "On the Expressibility of Discrete Event Specified Systems." In *Computer Aided Systems Theory, CAST, Lecture Notes in Computer Science.* Springer Verlag, Ottawa, 1996, p. 65–80.
8. Samir, S., and M. D. S. Soliman, *Continuous and Discrete Signals and Systems.* Prentice Hall, Englewood Cliffs, NJ, 1997.
9. Zeigler, B. P., *Multifaceted Modeling and Discrete Event Simulation.* Academic Press, London, 1984.
10. Zeigler, B. P., "DEVS Representation of Dynamical Systems: Event-based Intelligent Control." In *Proc. IEEE,* 1989.
11. Zeigler, B. P. and D. Kim. "Orders of Magnitude Speedup with DEVS Representation and High-Performance Computation." Presented at Enabling Technology for Simulation Science, SPIE AeoroSense 97, Orlando, FL, 1997.
12. Zeigler, B. P., and Y. Moon, "DEVS Representation and Aggregation of Spatially Distributed Systems: Speed versus Error Tradeoffs." *Trans. of SCS* **13**(5), 179–190 (1996).
13. Zeigler, B. P., *et al.*, "DEVS Approximation of Infiltration Using Genetic Algorithm Optimization of a Fuzzy System." *Journal of Math. and Comp. Model.* **23,** 215–228 (1996).

16.8 Problems

Fast/Slow System Decomposition

Often components are coupled together that have quite distinct rates of change. For example, when water flows through a river bed its bank may erode, but the erosion may be measured in inches/year while the water flows at rate of gallons/minute. Thus, the average derivative input to the fast system may be one or more orders of magnitude higher than that to the slow system.

This means that many outputs from the fast system have very little effect on the state and time advances of a quantized DEVS integrator for the slow system. Show that if the fast system outputs are all equal, the output message rate of the slow DEVS is not affected by the rapid arrival of input events, but there may be many needless state and time advance recalculations. Thus, efficiency can be improved by using an input quantizer for the slow system to cut down the input arrival rate. The input sensitivity in this case can be related to modeler's error tolerance (T) in the average time advance, τ_{avg}. Derive the formula for the input quantum size shown in Fig. 19. (Hint: Relate a change in time advance to a change in input x using elementary calculus.)

Consider a bank erosion example where on the average it takes 1 year to produce a change of 1 inch in erosion. Suppose we can tolerate being off by a month in the time for a 1 inch change to occur. Let the output quantizer for the water (fast) integrator be such that it produces outputs every minute on the average and the average output value (in/yr) is $1/K$ times the input value

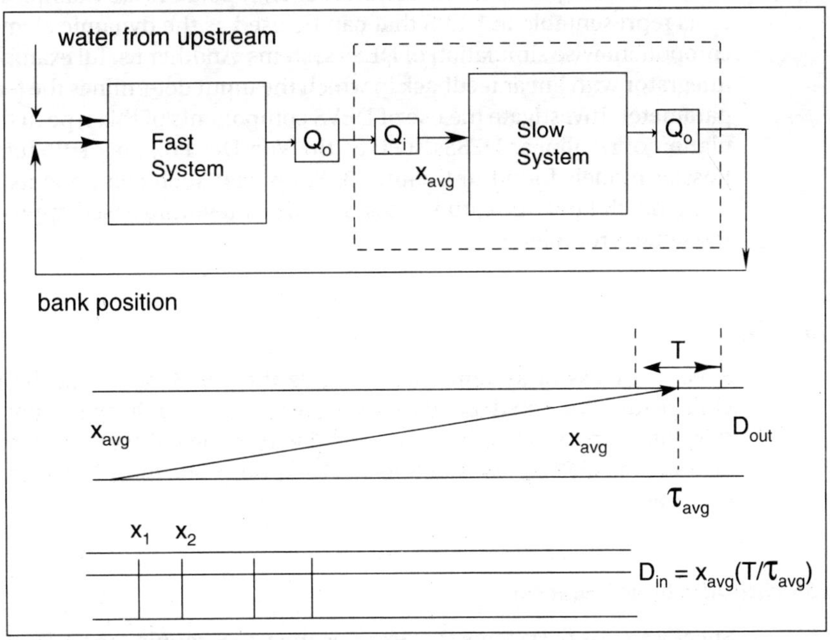

Figure 19

(gal/min), where K is large. Let's add a second output quantizer to the fast system that is tuned to the sensitivity of the slow system. If the fast system output value remains constant, how many messages and updates in the slow system are saved? Suppose that the every year there are winter and summer flow rates that are constant for 5 months each while there is a linear transition from one rate to the other during the transition months. Characterize the message flow from fast to slow system and the savings in messages and updates.

Consider feedback from slow to fast system. For example, a change in river bed position will affect the flow of water through it. Is an input quantizer needed for this feedback? If so, show how to get its quantum size.

Dead Reckoning (Second-order Extrapolators)

Dead reckoning employed in distributed interactive simulation [1] employs second-order extrapolation. Here, position, velocity, and acceleration (p,v,a) are used to predict positions at regular time steps following the arrival of an input (p,v,a) vector. Formulate a quantized version of such an extrapolator where output positions are generated at quantum boundary crossings instead of at fixed time steps. Write the DEVS representation for such a quantized extrapolator. Discuss the efficiency advantages and error trade-offs as compared to the conventional approach.

Exponential Systems

Quantized integrators and second-order extrapolators are examples of systems representable in DEVS that can be used as the dynamic elements in component wise simulation of DESS systems. Another useful example is an integrator with linear feedback in which the input determines the feedback parameter. Investigate the use of DEVS components of this type in the simulation of nonlinear DESSs such as the Van Der Pol, Lotka–Volterra, and Rossler models found in Chapter 3. Show that such components enable using much larger quantum sizes than the integrator-based approach for the same error tolerance.

DESS with Delay

Specify a class of systems that extends the DESS such that the rate of change function can depend on the state transmitted through a pure delay (Fig. 20). Can this class be represented within the DEV&DESS formalism? Within the DEVS formalism? Specify the appropriate morphism concept in each case.

DAEs: DESS with Algebraic Equations

Specify a class of systems that extends the DESS coupled models such that algebraic cycles are allowed, provided that unique solutions result. Can this

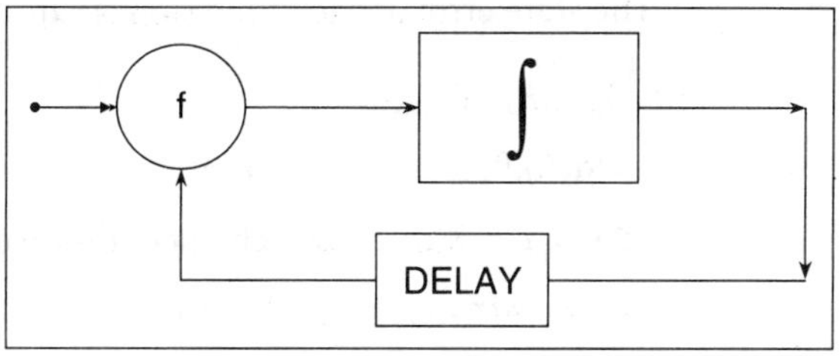

Figure 20 DESS with delay.

class be represented within the DEV&DESS formalism? Within the DEVS formalism? Specify the appropriate morphism concept in each case.

Quantization Error

The errors introduced by discrete time sampling of continuous signals are well known [8]. Quantization errors are less easily characterized since, unlike sampling, quantization is a nonlinear operation with respect to the frequency domain. The application of signal processing error theory to systems is complicated by the closed loop feedback effects—the signal itself is not a given, but the result of a fixed-point solution (see Appendix 1). Nevertheless, some insights might be obtained by applying known results of signal processing theory. Investigate the problems that can arise in coupled models with components having different integration rates and quantization sizes, and including nonlinearities in their I/O functions.[5]

Appendix 1 Closed Loop DTSS Simulation

In Fig. 3, let $\delta_R(q,t)$ be the resultant closed loop transition function and let β_q be the output trajectory when starting in state q. Then $\beta_q(t) = \lambda(\delta_R(q,t))$. The feedback of output to input then is expressed by $\delta_R(q,t) = \delta_S(q, \beta_{q,t>})$.

Exercise: Using the preceding relations, show that the possible feedback input segments are segments β_q that satisfy the fixed-point equation

$$\beta_q(t) = \lambda(\delta_S(q, \beta_{q,t>})). \blacklozenge$$

In closed loop, we use the DTSS component transition function for state q with input x, where $x = \lambda(q)$ because of the feedback. Thus, the transition function of the DTSS simulation becomes

$$\delta_{DTSS}(q,h) = \delta_S(q, \lambda(q)_{h>}).$$

We will show that the identity mapping is an approximate isomorphism between R and DR.

[5]Thanks to Duncan Clark for suggesting this problem.

The state error at each time step is expressed as

$$\|\delta_R(q,h) - \delta_{DTSS}(q,h)\|$$
$$= \|\delta_S(q,\beta_{q,h>}) - \delta_S(q,\lambda(q)_{h>})\|$$
$$\le k\|\beta_{q,h>} - \lambda(q)_{h>}\| \text{ (Lipschitz condition on input)}$$
$$= k\,h\,max_{t\varepsilon<0,h>}\|\beta_{q,h>}(t) - \lambda(q)_{h>}(t)\| \text{ (definition of trajectory norm)}$$
$$\le k\,h\,max_{t\varepsilon<0,h>}\|\lambda(\delta_S(q,\beta_{q,h}) - \lambda(q)\| \text{ (above exercise)}$$
$$\le k\kappa\,h\,max_h\|\delta_S(q,\beta_{q,h})) - q\| \text{ (norm preservation of } \lambda)$$
$$\le k\kappa\,h\,m\,h \text{ (condition 1).}$$

Thus, the upper bound on the introduced error at each time step is

$$\varepsilon_{max} = kM\,h^2 \text{ (where } M = m\kappa).$$

The amplification of the state error is obtained as the difference in states at the next time step:

$$\|\delta_{DTSS}(q,h) - \delta_{DTSS}(q',h)\|$$
$$= \|\delta_S(q,\lambda(q)_{h>})) - \delta_S(q',\lambda(q')_{h>})\|$$

$$= \|\delta_S(q,\lambda(q)_{h>}) - \delta_S(q,\lambda(q')_{h>})$$
$$+ \delta_S(q,\lambda(q')_{h>}) - \delta_S(q',\lambda(q')_{h>})\| \quad \text{(adding and subtracting } \delta_S(q,\lambda(q')_{h>}))$$
$$\le \|\delta_S(q,\lambda(q)_{h>}) - \delta_S(q,\lambda(q')_{h>})\| + \|\delta_S(q,\lambda(q')_{h>}) - \delta_S(q',\lambda(q')_{h>})\|$$
$$\le k\,h\,\|\lambda(q) - \lambda(q')\| + (1+\alpha h)\|q - q'\| \quad \text{(Lipschitz condition on input and}$$

open loop amplification)

$$\le k\,h\,\kappa\|q - q'\| + (1+\alpha h)\|q - q'\| \text{ (output norm preservation)}$$
$$\le ((1 + hK\kappa + \alpha h)\|q - q'\|$$
$$\le (1 + Kh)\|q - q'\| \quad \text{(where } K = hk\kappa + \alpha).$$

Since we can make Kh as small as desired, we use the error propagation approach of Chapter 14 (for the case where $a = 1 + b/N$). The error after N steps, for large enough N, is

$$e_N \le N\varepsilon_{max}.$$

For a fixed interval T, the number of steps is T/h and the error bound becomes

$$e_T \le kMTh,$$

which goes to zero as h goes to zero. This has the same form as the open loop case. However, here the input growth parameter M is derived as a product of the output and change parameters, $M = m\kappa$.

Appendix 2 Uniformly Segmentable Input Sets

We now characterize uniformly segmentable input sets. We say that a *BCS* input segment ω is *finitely oscillatory* if its derivative function ω′ has at most a finite set of points at which it vanishes $\left(\frac{d}{dt}\omega(t)=0\right)$.

The set of points mentioned just now are maxima, minima, or inflection points. The restriction to a finite set of such points does not permit an oscillation with infinite frequency as input—which is reasonable; there are too many events to simulate with a DEVS! The first case to examine is where this set is empty. In this case, we have the following lemma.

Lemma

A BCS segment ω for which the magnitude of the derivative function is bounded from below is uniformly segmentable.

Proof: Bounding from below implies there no points of vanishing derivative (no maxima, minima or inflection points) and we have $Max > Min > 0$ such that

$$Min < \left\|\frac{d}{dt}\omega(t)\right\| < Max$$

for all t in the domain of ω.

Consider any quantization. It is easy to show that it has a finite set of boundary crossings. Consider any two successive boundary crossings. By time invariance, we can take these instants to be 0 and $\tau > 0$. Consider the segment it represents, $\omega_{\tau>}$.

Now since $\omega_{\tau>}(0)$ and $\omega_{\tau>}(\tau)$ are on boundaries, there are two cases: (1) $\omega_{\tau>}(0) = \omega_{\tau>}(\tau)$ and (2) $|\omega_{\tau>}(0) - \omega_{\tau>}(\tau)| = D$. The mean value theorem of calculus states that

$$\omega_{\tau>}(\tau) - \omega_{\tau>}(0) = \tau \times \frac{d}{dt}\omega(t) \text{ for some t in the interval } (0,\tau).$$

But for case (1), we have $\frac{d}{dt}\omega(t) = 0$, contradicting the assumption that the derivative does not vanish.

Thus we have only case (2), and for it the length of the segment τ can be determined from

$$\tau \times \frac{d}{dt}\omega(t) = D.$$

Using the upper and lower bounds on the derivative of ω, we have that

$$D/Max = \tau_{min} \le \tau \le \tau_{max} = D/Min,$$

where *Min* and *Max* are as given above.

Remark. The *Min* and *Max* terms in the error expression of Section 16.3.2 are now interpretable as the lower and upper bounds on the magnitude of the derivative of the input segment. The ratio *Max/Min* in the error expression (recall $k = 1$),

$$e_T \leq D\,T\,Max/Min,$$

is a measure of the variability of the input. The greater this variability, the smaller the quantum size needs to be keep the error below a desired tolerance.

Now we are ready to apply the lemma to a BCS set with a nonempty set of points of vanishing derivative.

Theorem

The integrator with a BCS input segment set is an exactly quantizable system.

Proof (sketch):

As illustrated in Fig. A1, given any segment, choose a small enough quantum D that isolates each point of vanishing derivative in the interior of its own generator segment. By continuing to reduce D, we can retain the isolation of these points as well as reduce the error introduced in the finite set of isolating segments as small as we like. Now use this quantization as the starting D_0 in Theorem 5. The set of intervals that remain after removing the isolating segments all satisfy the conditions of the lemma. Thus, we can reduce the error as much as we like in these segments as well.

Exercise: Provide a complete proof. This requires examining the error dependence of the segments enclosing the vanishing derivative points on D in detail.◆

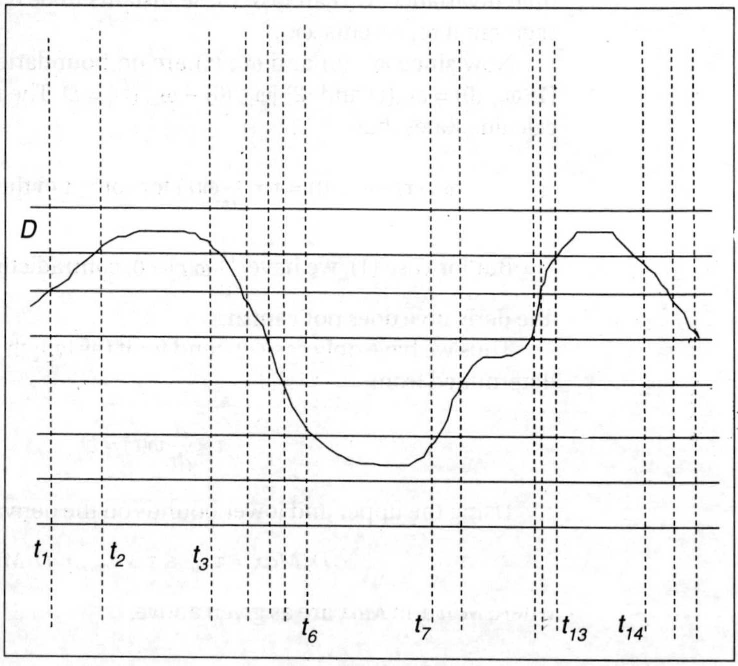

Figure A1 A bounded continuous smooth input segment with four points of vanishing derivatives.

Appendix 3 Exact Simulation by DEVS

Figure A2 shows how we can construct the morphism to demonstrate showing exact simulation of the internal system by the DEVS system. Recall that input quantizer produced a piecewise constant segment. We introduce a mapping g that translates piecewise constant segments into corresponding DEVS segments. Its definition is straightforward,

$$g(\hat{x}_{t1>}\ \hat{x}_{t2>} \ldots\ \hat{x}_{tn}) = \hat{x}_{t1>}\ \hat{x}_{t2>} \ldots \hat{x}_{tn},$$

where $\hat{x}_{t>}$ on the left is a constant segment and on the right is a DEVS generator segment starting with the constant as its event.

The morphism requires that (1) when the system is started in state q and given an input segment ω, its ending state corresponds to that of the DEVS system started in state $(q,\omega(0),0)$ with the input $g\ (Q_{x1}(\omega))$, and (2) that the output segments produced by each system agree modulo the g mapping, i.e., they are the same except that one is piecewise constant and the other is discrete event in nature.

The proof proceeds by using the iterative system approach (Chapter 5). We need only examine the generator segments and show that the homomorphism requirements hold for them.

Exercise: Define the map $h(q,x,e) = \Delta(q,x_{e>})$ that places the DEVS system states in correspondence with those of the internal system. For any generator segment, show that (1) this mapping is preserved under corresponding input segments applied to the two systems, and (2) starting in corresponding states, the systems produce the same output generator segments, modulo the g map.◆

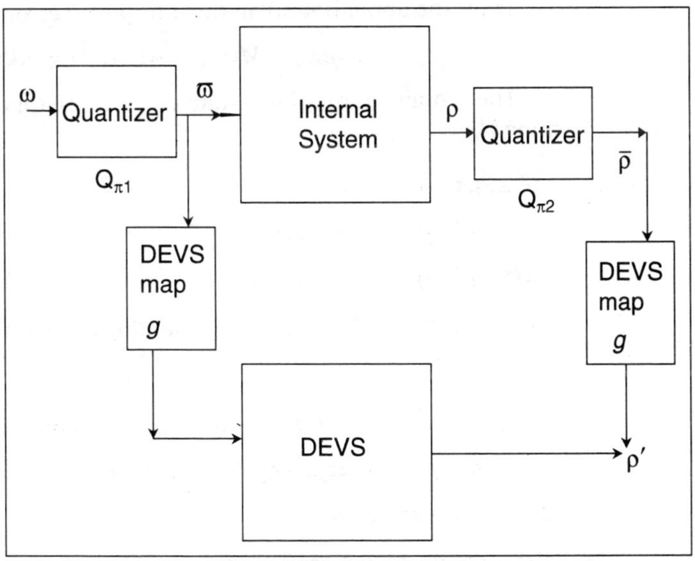

Figure A2 DEVS simulation of quantized system.

Appendix 4 Closed Loop Quantized Simulation

To prove Theorem 9 we will show that the identity mapping is an approximate isomorphism between R and QR.

Using property 1, the spacing between boundary crossings of the resultant quantized system can be bounded as follows:

Let q be on a boundary. Then we have the subsequent trajectory described by

$$\delta_{QR}(q,t) = \delta_S(q,\lambda(q)_{t>}).$$

A next boundary crossing occurs in time τ where

$$\delta_{QR}(q,\tau) = q \pm D,$$

i.e., $\delta_S(q, \lambda(q)_{\tau>}) = q \pm D$ or $D = \| \delta_S(q, \lambda(q)_{\tau>}) - q \|$.

From property 1a (small excursion behavior), we have $D \leq m\tau$, i.e., $\tau_{\min} = D/m$.

Also, directly from property 1b, we have $\tau_{\max} = D/M$.

The state error at each boundary crossing (output event, hence also input) is expressed as

$$\begin{aligned}
&\left\|\delta_R(q,\tau) - \delta_{QR}(q,\tau)\right\| \\
&= \left\|\delta_S(q,\beta_{R,q_{\tau>}}) - \delta_S(q,\lambda(q)_{\tau>}\right\| \\
&\leq k\tau \left\|\beta_{R,q,\tau>}(\tau) - \lambda(q)_{\tau>}(\tau))\right\| \text{ (Lipschitz condition on input)} \\
&\leq k\tau \left\|\lambda(\delta_S(q,\beta_{R,q\tau>})) - \lambda(q))\right\| \text{ (definition of trajectory endpoints)} \\
&\leq k\kappa\tau \left\|\delta_S(q,\beta_{R,q\tau>}) - q)\right\| \text{ (norm preservation of } \lambda) \\
&\leq k\kappa\tau\ m\tau \text{ (small excursion behavior)}.
\end{aligned}$$

Thus, the upper bound on the introduced error over an interval T is

$$\varepsilon_{max} = M\tau_{max}^2 \quad \text{(where } M = mk\kappa).$$

The amplification of the state error at the quantized system is determined by

$$\begin{aligned}
&\left\|\delta_{QR}(q,\tau) - \delta_{QR}(q',\tau)\right\| \\
&= \left\|\delta_S(q,\lambda(q)_{\tau>}) - \delta_S(q',\lambda(q')_{\tau>})\right\| \\
&= \left\|\delta_S(q,\lambda(q)_{\tau>}) - \delta_S(q',\lambda(q')_{\tau>})\right. \\
&\left. + \delta_S(q,\lambda(q')_{\tau>}) - \delta_S(q',\lambda(q')_{\tau>})\right\| \quad \text{(adding and subtracting } \delta_S(q,\lambda(q')_{\tau>}))
\end{aligned}$$

$$\begin{aligned}
&\leq k\tau\left\|\lambda(q) - \lambda(q')\right\| + (1+\alpha\tau)\left\|q-q'\right\| \text{ (Lipschitz conditions on input and state} \\
&\leq k\tau\kappa\left\|q-q'\right\| + (1+\alpha\tau\left\|q-q'\right\| \text{ (output norm preservation)} \\
&\leq (1+\tau k\kappa + \alpha\tau)\left\|q-q'\right\| \\
&\leq (1+K\tau)\left\|q-q'\right\| \text{ (where } K = k\kappa + \alpha).
\end{aligned}$$

Using the error propagation approach of Section 1.6 (for the case where $a = 1 + b/N$), the error after n steps, for large enough n, is

$$e_n \leq nM\tau_{max}^2.$$

For a fixed interval T, the number of steps is less than T/τ_{min}, and the error bound becomes

$$\begin{aligned} e_T &\leq (T/\tau_{min})M\tau_{max}^2 \\ &= MT\tau_{max}^2/\tau_{min}. \end{aligned}$$

Since $\tau_{max} = D/M$ and $\tau_{min} = D/m$, we have

$$e_T \leq DTm^2/M^2.$$

Thus, the error can be made as small as desired by making D as small as necessary. This proves the Theorem 9.

IV

System Design and Modeling and Simulation Environments

17

DEVS-Based Design Methodology

In view of the DEVS Bus concepts, we can consider DEVS to be not just a simulation formalism, but also a strong candidate for a more general computational formalism to support systems design. To do so, it would have to support, or allow embedding of, other formalisms that are more tuned to analysis and design. In this part of the book, we consider DEVS within an "end-to-end" systems design environment from this point of view. Systems design involves modeling, simulation, and analysis of candidate systems. To design a software system, such as a real-time controller, a discrete event model for the required system may be developed and simulated to verify operational correctness as well as to evaluate the performance of the modeled system. During such a design phase, more than one model for the designed system may be developed and evaluated to select the most attractive one for implementation. Implementation may be viewed as a transformation from the selected model to executable program code and is known to be an error-prone process.

In this chapter, we present a DEVS-based design methodology as a unified framework for developing discrete event systems. The framework provides an approach to modeling discrete event systems in which logical analysis, performance evaluation, and implementation can be performed—all within the DEVS formalism. Within this framework, implementation need no longer be an error-prone transformation of a model to executable program code. Instead, the DEVS model used in the designed phase itself becomes an implementation that runs in real time on a real-time simulation engine. The framework is applicable to development of various discrete event subsystems or algorithms within larger discrete event systems such as communication networks, manufacturing systems, and computer systems.

17.1 Methodology Overview

Figure 1 shows a unified framework for design and implementation of discrete event systems. As shown in the figure, the DEVS formalism is the core of the framework on which all phases of design, analysis, and implementation are theoretically based. The DEVS formalism provides a general, theoretical basis for solving various problems, but other formalisms may address distinctive design issues in a more efficient manner. For example, a DEVS model, or any other simulation-based model, for that matter, developed for performance evaluation would typically contain timing with associated probability distri-

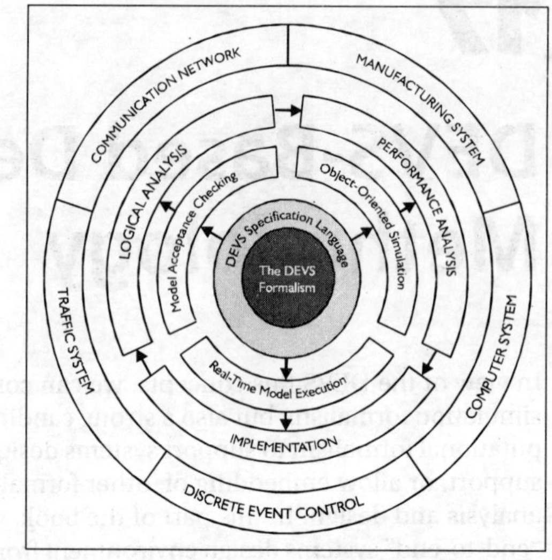

Figure 1 DEVS methodology for system development.

butions. However, an untimed model is more amenable to logical analysis. In general, models developed for logical analysis typically reside at higher levels of abstraction than their performance-oriented counterparts.

Transitioning between design, simulation, and implementation models is often performed manually and is a major hurdle to a seamless design process. To help bridge these gaps in the DEVS design methodology we introduce a general language for defining DEVS models. The DEVS definition language is phrased at a sufficiently abstract level so as to provide a basis to develop a standard model for various application areas based on the DEVS formalism. The objective is that a model specified by the DEVS definition language can be used for all phases of systems development within our methodology, i.e., logical analysis, performance evaluation, and implementation. Of course, different design phases may require additional information that cannot be expressed in the DEVS definition language. For example, performance evaluation requires sojourn times between states that are specified by the time advance function in the DEVS formalism.

Logical analysis within the methodology is a model verification phase. It employs a dual specification approach in which two specifications for a discrete event model are used: an *operational* specification and an *assertional* specification. Model verification becomes an acceptance checking process in which the operational specification (expressed in DEVS definition language) is checked against an assertional specification specified in a temporal logic language (Fig. 2). These languages will be developed in the ensuing sections. Performance evaluation employs object-oriented simulation of hierarchical DEVS models. Unlike conventional software development, the implementation phase is no longer a manual transformation of models into executable program code. Instead, the developed DEVS models remain unchanged and are implementations that are executed in exactly the same way as the transformed program code. Of course, execution of the models in such a manner requires a model execution engine. The engine

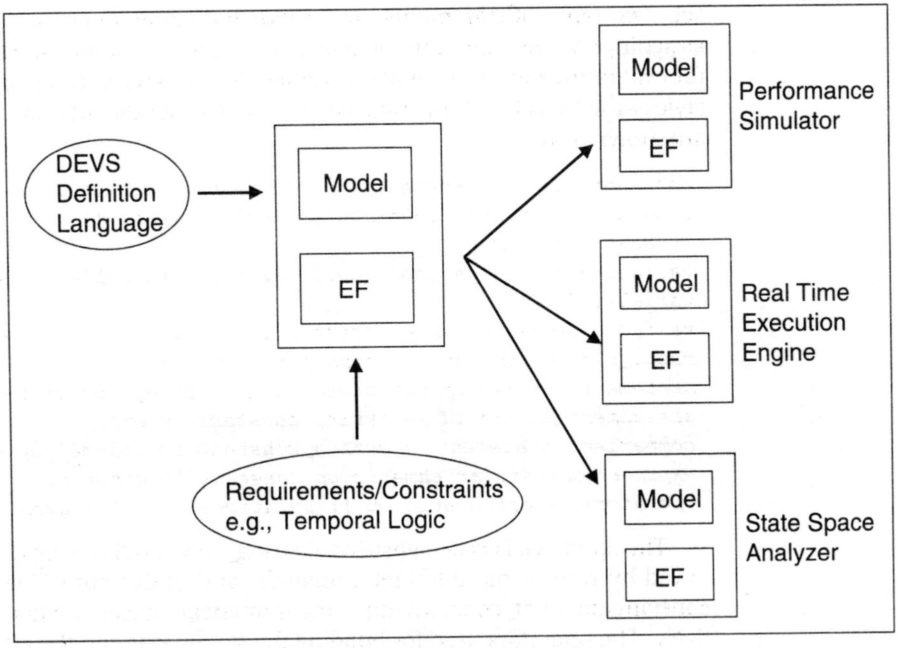

Figure 2 Model verification. Ef = Experimental Frame.

within the methodology can be developed either as a language compiler or as an operating system class library.

17.2 DEVS Definition Language

The DEVS definition language preserves the modeling semantics provided by the DEVS formalism. There is a one-to-one correspondence between the elements in the formalism and the statements in the DEVS definition language. A set of keywords and grammar rules are defined to allow direct descriptions of DEVS models. The DEVS definition language consists of two sections following the overall model declaration: an atomic model definition section and a coupled model definition section.

```
begin description
  overall model declaration → overall model: model_name
  atomic model definition section → atomic_model_definition
    || atomic_model_definition_section
  coupled model definition section → coupled_model_definition
    || coupled_model_definition_section
end description
```

The DEVS definition language provides three types of constants: string constant, integer constant, and float constant. The constants are used in the declaration section of the atomic and coupled models for specifying the input/output event list, the range set of a variable, and the components list. A variable is defined by concatenating the variable name and its range value set. Two types of statements are provided: an assignment statement for assigning a value of an expression to a variable and a comparison statement for evaluating logical truth of a variable. The Backus Normal Form (BNF) style grammar rules of constant list, variable list, statements, and operators are shown next.

```
constant_list → constant; || constant; constant_list
constant → string_constant || integer_constant
|| float_constant
variable_list → variable_declaration || variable_declaration
variable_list
variable_declaration → variable IN {range_set};
range_set → constant || constant, range_set
statements → assignment_statement || comparison_statement
assignment_statement → string_constant := expr
comparison_statement → string_constant relational_op expr
expr → constant arithmetic_op constant || constant
operators → arithmetic_op || relational_op || logical_op
```

The language is case-sensitive. A string_constant is a single letter followed by zero or more letters, numerals, and underscore. The integer_ constant and float_constant imply the numerical integer and float, respectively. The operators used for building the statements and the expressions are as follows: the arithmetic operators(+, –, *, /), the relational operators(=, >, >=, <, <=, <>) and the logical operators (||, &&, ~ for logical AND, OR, NOT). Comments are bounded by /* and */ as in the C language or started with the // symbol as in C++. Comments cannot be nested. The following identifiers are reserved keywords:

```
assertional   assertions   atomic        components      condition
coupled       coupling     description   end             external
float         function     global        in              initial
input         inputs       integer       interactional   internal
model         output       outputs       overall         phase
definition    state        transition    variables
```

17.2.1 Atomic DEVS Definition

The following language is developed for classic DEVS; a similar language can be developed for parallel DEVS. The atomic model definition consists of a *name*, a *set declaration* section, an *initial state* declaration section, and a *function* declaration section.

```
atomic model model_name
  set declaration section
  initial state declaration section
  function declaration section
end model_name
```

The *set declaration section* defines the three sets of the formalism: the *input event* set, the *output event* set, and the *sequential state* set of an atomic DEVS. The DEVS definition language also provides the *phase* concept. A *phase* is defined as a representative state for a set of states that can be grouped according to the semantics of a model. If the *phase* is defined in the *set declaration section,* it should be accompanied by the definition of the phase transition in the *function declaration section.* The *initial state declaration section* defines the initial condition of the atomic DEVS. The *function declaration section* defines three characteristic functions: the internal transition function, the external transition function, and the output function. In the atomic model definition, the time advance function is unspecified. So a model regards the time advance value as an arbitrary value. The time advance function is further elaborated in the performance evaluation and implementation phases of Fig. 1.

Table 1 summarizes the available statements of the atomic DEVS definition language for assigning the elements of the atomic DEVS formalism.

The general format of an atomic DEVS definition is:

```
atomic model model_name
  inports: input ports list;
  outports: output ports list;
  state variables:
    state variable list;
  phase:
    phase definition list;
  initial condition:
    state value assignment list;
  internal transition:
    internal state transition list;
  external transition:
    external state transition list;
  output function:
    output function list;
end model name
```

The input and output port lists are defined by the *constant_lists.* The state variable list is defined by the *variable_list.* The syntax for the declaration of a state variable is "*var_name* in {*range set*}". This specifies the fact that the state variable *var_name* has the range value set *range set.* For exam-

Table 1 Statements of Definition Language

DEVS formalism	DEVS definition language
X	Input events list
Y	Output events list
S	State variable list
	Initial condition definition
	Phase definition
δ_{int}	Internal state/phase transition list
δ_{ext}	External state/phase transition list
λ	Output function list
ta	Unspecified

ple, for a state variable *queue*, whose type is integer, the definition of the variable is given as "*queue* in { *INTEGER* }". The initial state should be defined for the evaluation of a model and it is given as a list of *assignment_statements* separated by a semicolon. For example, if the state variables *queue* and *status* have the initial values empty and free, then the initial state is given as *queue* = 0; *status* = *free*;. The general form of the internal state transition function is given as "*current_state* => *next_state*". The external state transition function is defined as "*current_state* * *input_event* => *next_state*". The *current_state* and the *next_state* are expressed as a Boolean expression that should be given as a conjunctive normal form. Suppose that s_0 = (*queue* = 0, *status* = *free*) and s_1 = (*queue* = 1, *status* = *busy*). Then these states are expressed as (*queue* = 0 && *status* = *free*) and (*queue* = 1 && *status* = *busy*). The internal state transition from s_0 to s_1 is defined as (*queue* = 0 && *status* = *free*) => (*queue* = 1 && *status* = *busy*). If the state transition from s_0 to s_1 occurs by receiving an input event *req*, this is defined as (*queue* = 0 && *status* = *free*) * *req* => (*queue* = 1 &&*status* = *busy*). The output function is defined as "*current_state* => output_event". The BNF style grammar rules for defining the characteristic functions are shown below.

```
state_tran_list → state_tran; || state_tran; state_tran_list
state_tran → internal_tran || external_tran
internal_tran → state_cond => state_cond;
external_tran → state_cond * string_constant => state_cond;
state_cond → boolean_expr
boolean_expr → conjunctive_expr || conjunctive_expr ||
  (logical OR) boolean_expr
conjunctive_expr → statements || statements && (logical AND)
  conjunctive_expr
output_function → state_cond => string_constant
```

17.2.2 The Coupled DEVS Definition

The coupled model definition consists of a *name* followed by two declaration sections, a *component* declaration section and a *coupling* declaration section.

```
coupled model model_name
  component declaration section
  coupling declaration section
end model_name
```

The *component declaration section* defines only the component model set that constitutes a coupled model. The other two element sets in the formalism, the input event set and the output event set, are unspecified. This information is explicitly included in the definition of the component models and the coupling schemes. The *coupling declaration section* defines the connections between the coupled model itself and its component models: (I) the external input coupling specifies connections from input ports of the coupled model to input ports of the component models, (ii) the external output coupling specifies connections from output ports of the component models to output ports of the coupled model, and (iii) the internal coupling specifies connections between output ports of the component models and input ports of other components. The general format of coupled DEVS definition is as follows:

```
coupled model model_name
  components: component model type list
  internal coupling:
    internal coupling list
  external input coupling:
    external input coupling list
  external output coupling:
    external output coupling list
end model_name
```

The component model list is defined as a list of model type definitions separated by a semicolon. The syntax for the model type definition is "*component_model model_name*". This statement creates an instance of a predefined component *component_model* whose name is defined by the *model_name.* If a coupled model has two identical component models "*BUF buf1; BUF buf2;*", then two models *buf1* and *buf2* are instantiated from the predefined atomic model BUF. The reserved symbol "→" means the coupling between components. The general format of coupling is "*from_model.port_name to_model.port_name*". The BNF style grammar rules for defining the coupling list and the component list are shown below.

```
component_type_def → component_var || component_var
  component_type_def
component_var → string_constant string_constant;
coupling_list → coupling_assignment || coupling_assignment
  coupling_list
coupling_assignment → dotted_string_const dotted_string_const;
dotted_string_const → string_constant.string_constant
```

17.2.3 Example: Generator–Buffer–Processor Model

As a simple example, consider DEVS modeling of a simple job processing system that consists of generator, buffer, and processor. The generator runs autonomously, that is, it generates jobs periodically according to the predefined time interval. The buffer acts as a synchronizer controlling flows of jobs that are sent to the processor. The processor performs the received job. The buffer increments the queue size whenever it receives a job. The DEVS model for the system GEN-BUF-PROC is shown in Fig. 3. Using the model description explained in a previous section, the GEN-BUF-PROC model is specified as follows:

```
Components: GEN, BUF, PROC
Atomic Component GEN
  State Variables:
    status with range {ACTIVE}
  Atomic Operations:
    A1: Generates jobs repeatedly after a predefined time
    interval
```

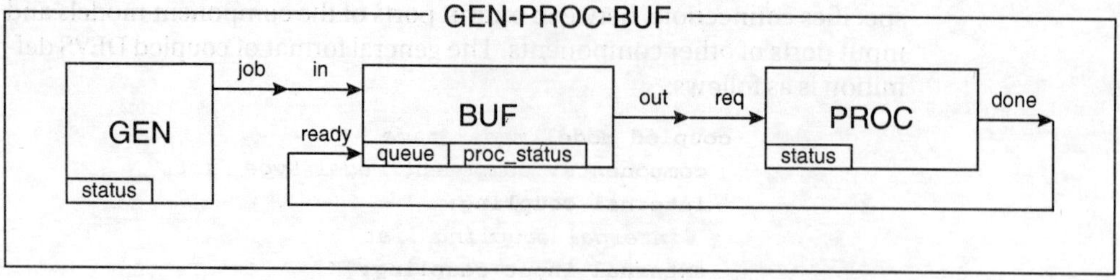

Figure 3 GEN-BUF-PROC DEVS model.

```
Atomic Component BUF
  State Variables:
    queue with range numerical INTEGER
    proc_status with range {FREE, BUSY}
  Atomic Operations:
    A2: Sends a job whenever the processing of the job sent
      previously ends.
    A3: Decreases the queue size whenever it sends a job.
Atomic Component PROC
  State Variables:
    status with range {FREE, BUSY}
  Atomic Operations:
    A4: Processes a job in a predefined time.
Interactive Operation
  Components GEN and BUF:
    A5: BUF increases the queue size whenever GEN generates
      a job.
  Components BUF and PROC:
    A6: BUF and PROC run synchronously.
  Global Operations
    A7: If BUF receives a request signal from PROC, it should
      send a job if the queue is not empty.
    A8: A generated job should be processed eventually.
```

To specify the operational behavior of the model using the DEVS formalism, we develop DEVS transition diagrams for each atomic model that are shown in Fig. 4. In the state diagram, a solid line arc represents an external transition with an input event on the arc; a dotted line arc represents an internal transition with an output event on the arc. Interpretation of the solid line arc is that a model transits a state to another state with the received input event(?in). On the other hand, the dotted line arc means that a model generates an output event(!out) first and then transits its state internally.

We now translate the DEVS transition diagram in Fig. 4 to DEVS definition language for each atomic model as follows.

```
atomic model GEN
  inports: { };
  outports: job;
  state variables:
```

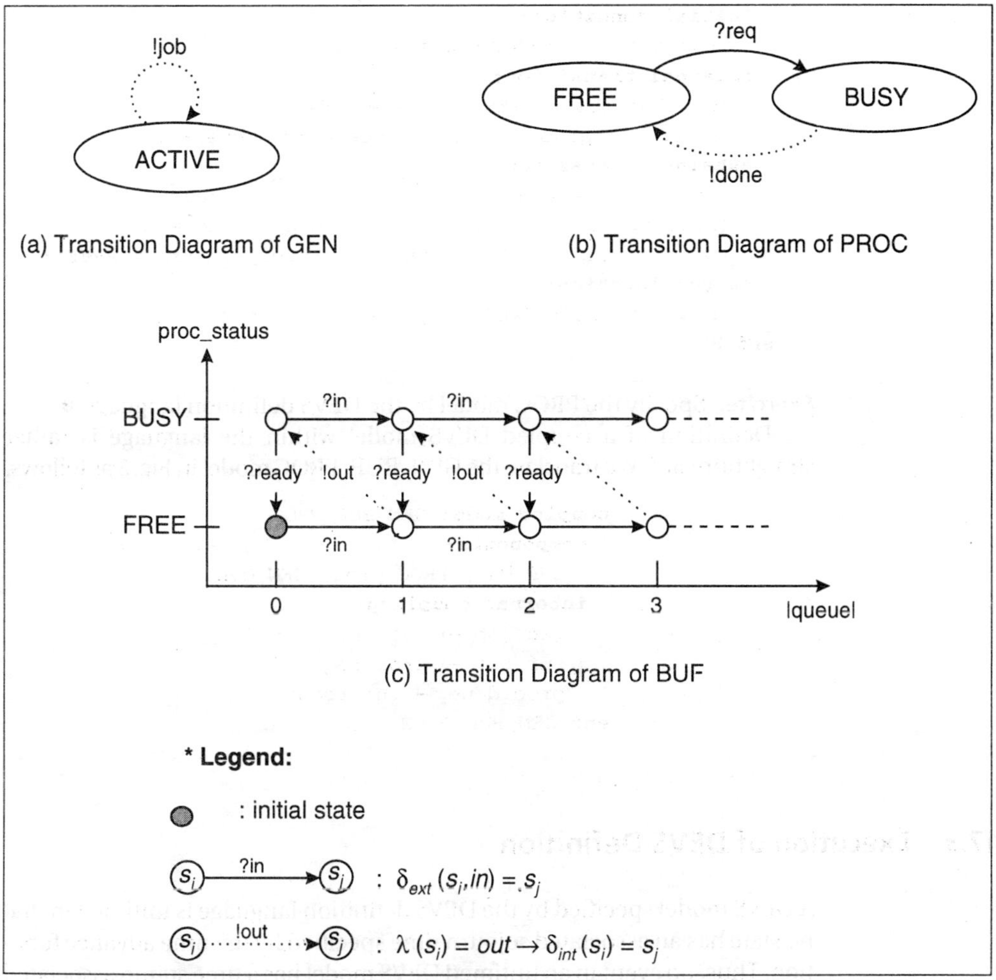

Figure 4 DEVS transition diagram of GEN, PROC, and BUF models.

```
    status in {ACTIVE};
  initial condition:
    status := FREE;
  internal transition:
    (status = ACTIVE) ⇒ (status := ACTIVE);
  external transition: { };
  output function:
    (status = ACTIVE) ⇒ job;
end GEN

Atomic model BUF
  inports: in; ready;
  outports: out;
  state variables:
    proc_status in {FREE, BUSY};
    queue in {integer};
```

```
initial condition:
  proc_status := FREE; queue := 0;
internal transition:
  (proc_status = FREE && queue > 0)
  ⇒ (proc_status := BUSY && queue := queue - 1);
external transition:
  (proc_status = FREE) * in ⇒ (queue := queue + 1);
  (proc_status = BUSY) * in ⇒ (queue := queue + 1);
  (proc_status = BUSY) * ready ⇒ (proc_status := FREE);
output function:
  (proc_status = FREE && queue > 0) ⇒ out;
end BUF
```

Exercise: Specify the PROC model by the DEVS definition language.◆

Definition of a coupled DEVS model within the language is rather straightforward. We translate the GEN_BUF_PROC model in Fig. 3 as follows.

```
coupled model GEN_BUF_PROC
  components:
    BUF buf; PROC proc; GEN gen;
  internal coupling:
    gen.job → buf.in;
    buf.out → proc.req;
    proc.done → buf.ready;
end GEN_BUF_PROC
```

17.3 Execution of DEVS Definition

A DEVS model specified by the DEVS definition language is untimed in that no state has an associated sojourn time specified by the time advance function. Thus, no event in an untimed DEVS model has a time stamp associated with it. However, the definition should be executable, i.e., simulated to generate dynamics of untimed DEVS models. We call such an execution environment a *model execution* engine to differentiate it from a discrete event simulation environment for timed DEVS models. Since no time stamp is associated with an event, the model execution engine considers all possible sequences of events as valid. Thus, a state trajectory of an untimed DEVS model includes all possible sequences of states, including any state sequence generated from a corresponding timed DEVS model. In this sense, unspecified time advance is a generalization of specified time advance. We now show that the model execution engine performs concurrent execution of a set of untimed DEVS models that generates all possible state sequences generated from timed DEVS models.

To illustrate concurrent execution of two untimed DEVS models, we construct a composite untimed DEVS model. An input (output) events set of the composite model is obtained by set union of two input (output) events set of the two models. A composite state set is constructed by the crossproduct of the state sets of the two models. A composite state transition is obtained by considering concurrent state transitions of each model. Once a composite untimed DEVS model is obtained, the execution engine considers all possible sequences of events as valid in the composite state transition.

Figure 5 shows a composite state transition diagram of two untimed DEVS models GEN and PROC (Fig. 4). The composite state transition diagram can be generated by a nondeterministic traversal process illustrated as follows. Assume that PROC is in the BUSY state and GEN is in ACTIVE. Then, two possible events, stimulatión of the output ports, *job* and *done,* can occur. The order of occurrence depends on time advance values at GEN and PROC. The engine selects an event from those possible. If it selects the event *job,* then the composite state remains the same. Again, one of the possible events, *job* and *done,* is selected. If *done* is selected, then the composite state transits to the state (PROC=FREE & GEN=ACTIVE). At the new state, there are two possible events, the output event *job* and the input event *req,* to be considered. Note that *req* is an input port of PROC that is connected to the output port out of BUF. In this case, the order of occurrence depends on the time advance values at GEN and BUF. Again, the execution engine nondeterministically selects one of the two events. In this way, the execution engine can generate the transition structure of all possible sequences of states (events) for each atomic model as well as the overall composite model.

Exercise: Construct an untimed DEVS model for the GEN-BUF-PROC Model.◆

DEVS support of hierarchical modular construction provides a powerful modeling semantics. However, it also causes a deep search path whenever the execution engine examines the transition conditions of atomic models included in different coupled models. Thus, a hierarchical model is *flattened* before it is analyzed (Chapter 5).

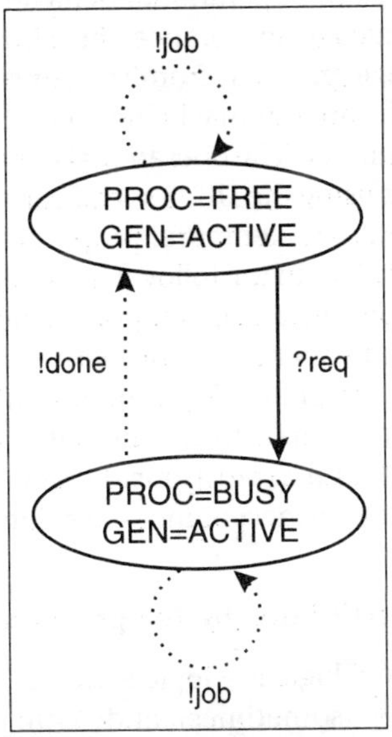

Figure 5 Composite state transition of GEN and PROC.

17.4 Logical Analysis: Model Verification

The real system, the conceptual model, and the operational model are three types of entities involved in modeling and simulation. The conceptual model is built through a collection of assumptions on system components and the interaction between components, which involves some degree of abstraction and/or simplification of systems operations. The operational model is the computer program that implements the conceptual model. Model verification is the process of assessing the correctness of the operational model with respect to the conceptual model. Most methods suggested in verification are the same ones used in debugging a computer program. One common method is to instrument a counter to the code and print it at appropriate time. Another method is predicting a valid range of output statistics and careful evaluation of the statistics for various run lengths to detect mistakes in model logic and data misdefinition. These approaches are basically nonautomatic procedures.

The DEVS-based design methodology employs a framework for automatic verification of discrete event models using a dual specification approach. The approach employs two specifications for a discrete event model: an *operational specification* for the behavior of a model and an *assertional specification* for its temporal properties. The DEVS formalism is employed for the operational specification, and temporal logic(TL) is used for the assertional specification. A model's verification is based on a language acceptance checking mechanism for which TL constitutes a language grammar and DEVS models act as string generators.

Figure 6 shows the overall structure for the proposed verification framework. The approach first specifies a model by using two specification methods. One specifies the conceptual model in terms of temporal properties and the other specifies operational behaviors for the operational model. Then, it checks the operational behaviors against temporal properties by using the language acceptance checking method. To be specific, we construct a language grammar from the temporal property while enumerating strings from the operational behaviors, which can be either accepted or rejected to the grammar. The operational behaviors are specified by the untimed DEVS models using the DEVS specification language, which was explained in Section 17.2. The temporal properties are specified by a TL language that we shall explain in the following section. The TL language specifies the conceptual model in a set of temporal logic (TL) formulas, each of which is an assertion on an operational property of the modeled system. To construct the TL grammar from the TL formulas, the decomposition process transforms the TL expressions into an automaton by applying a set of decomposition rules for temporal expressions. Finally, the automaton is used in the language parser for the acceptance checking phase.

17.4.1 Assertional Specification by Temporal Logic

Temporal logic is a logic extended with temporal operators, $\Box$ (always), $\bigcirc$ (next), $\Diamond$ (sometimes), and $\cup$ (until), to describe temporal information. It has proven to be well suited for expressing temporal properties. A set of tem-

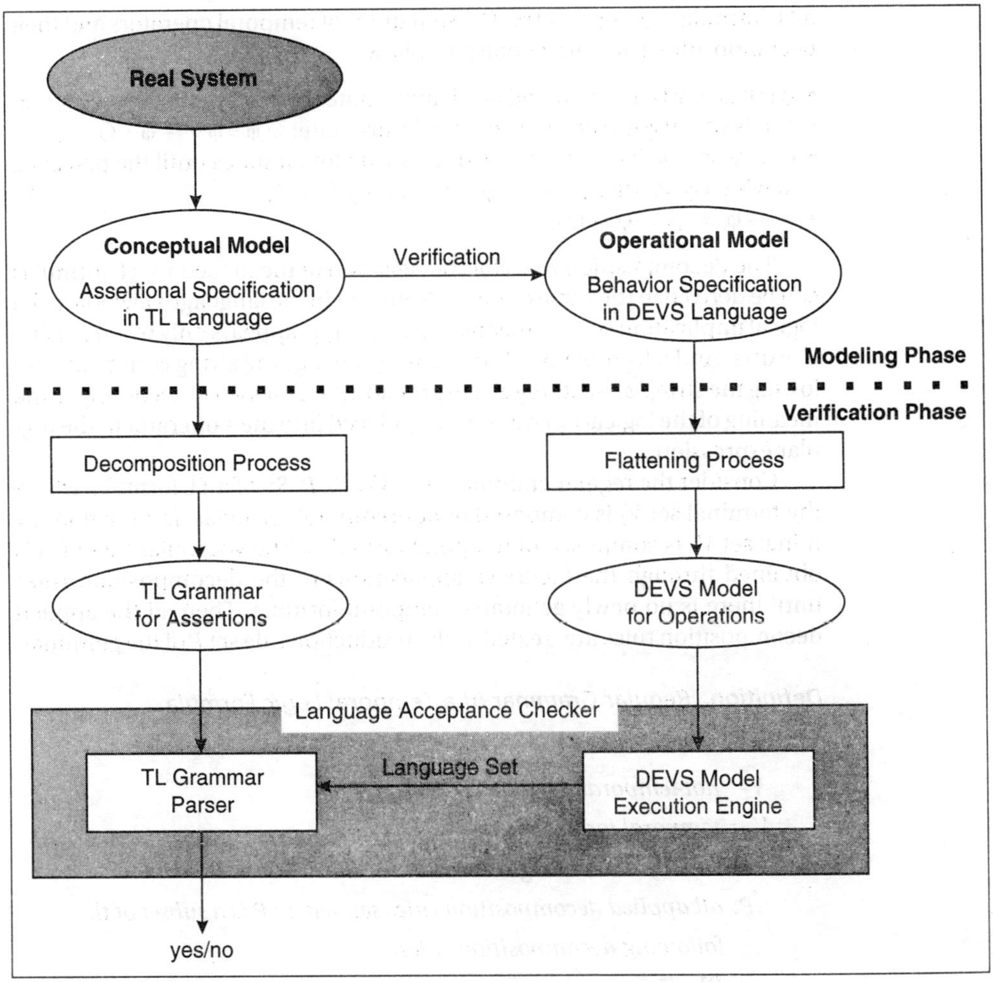

Figure 6 Model verification framework using dual specification.

poral formulas, $\phi = \{\varphi_1, \varphi_2, \ldots . \varphi_i\}$, specifies a temporal property, i.e., the timing precedence between entities of a system. A temporal formula φ_1 presents a sequence $\sigma = (s_1, s_2, \ldots, s_i, \ldots)$ of states, where each state consists of atomic propositions that are true in that time. TL formulas specify conceptual operations of an operational untimed DEVS model. Suppose that the formulas use state variables and I/O events of the operational DEVS model. Then the state sequences of the formulas become the desired state trajectory of the operational DEVS model.

Let us describe the decomposition process for building the temporal logic grammar and define the finite automaton for that grammar. From the definition of the temporal logic operators, a TL formula with only one temporal operator can be decomposed into two formulas. The first one is a nontemporal formula that contains no temporal operator, and the second one is a temporal formula that contains a temporal operator. The two formulas are connected by the next operator (O). The decomposition result of a TL formula is $\varphi \rightarrow \varphi_{nt} \wedge O\, \varphi_t$. The semantics of temporal operators and their decomposition rules are defined as follows.

- φ is true if φ is true now and in all future states of that sequence: $\varphi = \varphi \wedge O\, \varphi$.
- $\Diamond\, \varphi$ is true if φ is true now and in a future state: $\Diamond\, \varphi = \varphi \vee (-\, \varphi \wedge O \Diamond \varphi)$.
- $\varphi_1 \cup \varphi_2$ is true if φ_2 is true now or φ_1 is true for all states until the first state at which φ_2 is true: $\varphi_1 \cup \varphi_2 = \varphi_2 \vee (\varphi_1 \wedge O\, (\varphi_1 \cup \varphi_2))$.
- $\varphi_1 \rightarrow \varphi_2 = -\varphi_1 \vee (\varphi_1 \wedge O\, \varphi_2)$.

The decomposition rules for the negation of the preceding TL formulas can be derived in the same manner. Note that in the language viewpoint, the logical implication $\varphi_1 \rightarrow \varphi_2$ means that a string φ_2 appears only when a string φ_1 exists. And a formula $\varphi_1 \wedge O\, \varphi_2$ is interpreted as the string φ_2 appears following the string φ_1, so its regular expression becomes $\varphi_1\, \varphi_2$. According to the meaning of the logical operator $\vee$ it is replaced into the + operator in the regular expression.

Consider the regular grammar $G = <V_N, V_T, P, S>$ of a TL formula, where the terminal set V_T is composed of nontemporal formulas and the nonterminal set V_N is composed of temporal formulas. The vocabulary set of G is obtained through the recursive applications of the decomposition rules until there is no newly generated temporal formula. Then all the applied decomposition rules are treated as the production rule set P of the grammar.

Definition. *Regular Grammar of a Temporal Logic Formula*

$$G = <V_N, V_T, P, S>$$

V_T: *not-temporal formulas set*

V_N: *temporal formulas set*

S: *start symbol, i.e., given TL formula*

P: *all applied decomposition rules set, where P is a subset of the following decomposition rules:*

$P1$: $\Box\, \varphi \Rightarrow \varphi\, \Box\, \varphi$

$P2$: $\Diamond\, \varphi \Rightarrow \varphi^{+} \quad \varphi(\Diamond\, \varphi)$

$P3$: $\varphi_1 \cup \varphi_2 \Rightarrow \varphi_2 + \varphi_1 \left(\varphi_1 \cup \varphi_2\right)$

$P4$: $\neg\, \varphi \Rightarrow \varphi + \varphi\left(\neg\, \varphi\right)$

$P5$: $\neg \Diamond\, \varphi \Rightarrow \neg\, \varphi\left(\neg \Diamond\, \varphi\right)$

$P6$: $\neg\left(\varphi_1 \cup \varphi_2\right) \Rightarrow \neg\, \varphi_1\, \varphi_2 + \neg\, \varphi_2\left(\neg\left(\varphi_1 \cup \varphi_2\right)\right)$

$P7$: $\varphi_1 \rightarrow \varphi_2 \Rightarrow \neg\, \varphi_1 + \varphi_1 \varphi_2$

The decomposition process to build a grammar for a TL formula is as follows:

1. Set the given TL formula to the start symbol S.
2. Apply a decomposition rule to the TL formula. Add the applied decomposition rule to the production rule set if it is used for the first time.
3. If a new nontemporal formula is in the decomposition result, add it to the terminal set V_T.

4. If a new temporal formula is in the decomposition result, add it to the terminal set V_N and go to step 2.
5. If a new temporal formula does not appear, then terminate.

Example 17.3.1

The decomposition rules are exemplified in the following example.

(a) $\varphi : \varphi = init \rightarrow \Box(\neg deadlock)$

(i) $S \leftarrow \varphi$

(ii) apply P7: $\varphi = \neg init + init(\Box(\neg deadlock))$

$- V_T \leftarrow \{init, \neg init\}$

$- V_N \leftarrow \{\Box(\neg deadlock)\}$

$- P \leftarrow \{S \Rightarrow \neg init, S \Rightarrow init(\Box(\neg deadlock))\}$

(iii) apply P1: $\Box(\neg deadlock) = \neg deadlock \,\Box\, (\neg deadlock)$

$- V_T \leftarrow V_T \cup \{\neg deadlock\}$

$- P \leftarrow P \cup \{\Box(\neg deadlock) \Rightarrow \neg deadlock \,\Box\, (\neg deadlock)\}$

(b) $\Diamond\, \varphi : \varphi = send \rightarrow \Diamond\, rcv$

(i) $S \leftarrow \varphi$

(ii) apply P7: $\varphi = \neg\, send + send \,\Diamond\, rcv$

$- V_T \leftarrow \{send, \neg send\}$

$- V_N \leftarrow \{\Diamond\, rcv\}$

$- P \leftarrow \{S \Rightarrow \neg send, S \Rightarrow send \,\Diamond\, rcv\}$

(iii) apply P2: $\Diamond\, rcv = rcv + \neg\, rcv(\Diamond rcv)$

$- V_T \leftarrow V_T \cup \{rcv, \neg\, rcv\}$

$- P \leftarrow P \cup \{\Diamond rcv \Rightarrow rcv, \Diamond rcv \Rightarrow \neg\, rcv \,\Diamond\, rcv\}$

(c) $\varphi_1 \cup \varphi_2 := send \rightarrow (send \cup rcv)$

(i) $S = \varphi$

(ii) apply P7: $\varphi = \neg\, send + send(send \cup rcv)$

$- V_T \leftarrow \{send, \neg send\}$

$- V_N \leftarrow \{send \cup rcv\}$

$- P \leftarrow \{S \Rightarrow send, S \Rightarrow \neg send(send \cup rcv)\}$

(iii) apply P3: $send \cup rcv = rcv + send \,\neg\, rcv(send \cup rcv)$

$- V_T \leftarrow V_T \cup \{rcv, send \,\neg\, rcv\}$

$- P \leftarrow P \cup \{send \cup rcv, \Rightarrow rcv, send \cup rcv \Rightarrow send \neg rcv(send \cup rcv)\}$

(d) $\neg\Box\varphi : \varphi = send \rightarrow \neg\Box(\neg\, rcv)$

(i) $S = \varphi$

(ii) apply P7: $\varphi = \neg\, send + send(\neg(\neg\, rcv))$

$-V_T \leftarrow \{\neg send, send\}$

$-V_N \leftarrow \{\neg(\neg\, rcv)\}$

$-P \leftarrow \{S \Rightarrow send, S \Rightarrow send(\neg(\neg\, rcv))\}$

(iii) apply P4: $\neg\Box(\neg\, rcv) = rcv + rcv(\neg\ (\neg\, rcv))$

$-V_T \leftarrow V_T \cup \{rcv, \neg\, rcv\}$

$-P \leftarrow P \cup \{\neg\Box(\neg\, rcv) \Rightarrow \neg rcv(\neg\Box(\neg\, rcv)). -\Box(\neg\, rcv) \Rightarrow rcv\}$

(e) $\neg \Diamond\ \varphi : \varphi = init \rightarrow -\Diamond\ (deadlock)$

(i) $S = \varphi$

(ii) apply P7: $\varphi = \neg\, init + init(-\Diamond\ (deadlock))$

$-V_T \leftarrow \{init, \neg init\}$

$-V_N \leftarrow \{\neg \Diamond (deadlock)\}$

$-P \leftarrow \{S \Rightarrow \neg init, S \Rightarrow init(-\Diamond\ (deadlock))\}$

(iii) apply P5: $\neg \Diamond\ (deadlock) = \neg\ deadlock(\neg \Diamond\ deadlock)$

$V_T \leftarrow V_T \cup \{\neg\ deadlock\}$

$P \leftarrow P \cup \{\neg \Diamond\ (deadlock) \Rightarrow \neg\ deadlock\ (\neg \Diamond\ deadlock)\}$

The language $L(G) = \{\omega \mid S^{P*} \Rightarrow \omega, \omega \in V_T^*\}$ is generated from the temporal logic grammar G. Here, x^* denotes the concatenation closure of a set X. It is defined as $x^* = \cup_{i=0}^{\omega} x^i$, where $x^i = xx^{i-1}$ and $x^0 \in x$. Since G is regular, a finite automaton M that generates the same language $L(M) = \{x \mid \delta(q_0, x) \in F, x \in \Sigma^*\}$ can be defined as follows.

Definition

Finite automaton M of the TL grammar G:

$$M := <Q, \Sigma, \delta, q_0, F>$$

$$\begin{aligned} Q&: \textit{finite states set} \\ \Sigma&: \textit{finite input symbols set} \\ \delta&: \textit{transition function} \\ q_0&: \textit{initial state}, q_0 \in Q \\ F&: \textit{final states set}, F \subseteq Q, \end{aligned}$$

with the following constraints:

$$\begin{aligned} &Q: V_N \cup \{f\}, \textit{where } f \textit{ is newly defined final state, i.e, } f \in F \\ &\Sigma: \textit{set of } V_T \textit{ of TL Grammar} \\ &\delta: Q \times \Sigma \rightarrow Q \\ &q_0: \textit{start symbol } S \textit{ of TL Grammar}. \end{aligned}$$

From the preceding definition, we know that the tuples of the regular grammar G and of the finite automaton M are in one-to-one correspondence. The nonterminals set V_N of G, together with the final state set f, corresponds to the set of states Q. The terminals set V_T of G is mapped onto the input symbol set Σ of M. The start symbol S of G becomes the initial state q_0 of M. If the production rule is $A \rightarrow aB$ the transition function becomes $\delta\,(A,a) = B$. If the production rule is $A \rightarrow a$ the transition function becomes $\delta\,(A,a) = f$. If a temporal formula follows the *always operator* ($\Box$), this means a model always satisfies the property that is specified by the TL formula. In this case, we consider the finite automaton have an ε-movement to the initial state from the final state. So we treat the final state as the initial state. The final states set F of M is defined as $\{S, f\}$ by the consideration of ε-movement.

Example 17.3.2

The finite automata for the TL grammar obtained in Example 17.3.1b is defined as follows:

- State set $Q = \{S, \Diamond, rcv, f\}$
- $\Sigma = \{send, \neg send, rcv, \neg rcv\}$
- Initial state $q_0 = S$
- Final state set $F = \{f\}$
- Transition function is defined as

$$\delta(S, \neg send) = f$$
$$\delta(S, send) = \Diamond\, rcv$$
$$\delta(\Diamond\, rcv, rcv) = f$$
$$\delta(\Diamond\, rcv, \neg\, rcv) = \Diamond rcv$$

17.4.2 TL Specification Language

We next provide a language in which temporal logic assertions can be stated. This *assertional specification* is composed of three parts: *atomic assertions, interactional assertions,* and *global assertions.* The specification is developed in a hierarchical form. It begins with consideration of the autonomous operations for each atomic component (*atomic assertion*). Then, an assertion for the interactive operations between each coupled component pair is given (*interactional assertion*). Finally, an assertion for the overall operations is given (*global assertion*).

Each such assertion is developed as a set of temporal logic formulas that represents the conceptual operations as the sequences of states. The basic elements such as identifier, constant, keywords, and grammar rules of an expression that constitute the TL specification language are the same as in the DEVS definition language. It also adopts reserved keywords, **Always, Sometimes, Next,** and **Until,** for representing temporal operators $\Box$, $\Diamond$, $\bigcirc$, and $\cup$, respectively. The general format of the assertional specification is:

```
assertional specification
  components: components list
  atomic assertions: atomic assertions list
```

```
interactional assertions: interactional assertions list
global assertions: global assertions list
end specification
```

The BNF style grammar rules for the assertions list are shown below.

```
assertion_list, → assertion || assertion assertion_list
assertion → assertion_name temporal_op temporal_formula
          || assertion_name temporal_formula
assertion_name → string_constant || dotted_string_const
temporal_op → ALWAYS || SOMETIMES || UNTIL || NEXT
temporal_formula → non_temporal_formula →
   temporal_formula
      || non_temporal_formula
      || binary_temporal_formula
      || unary_temporal_formula
non_temporal_formula → boolean_expr
unary_temporal_formula → temporal_op non_temporal_formula
binary_temporal_formula → non_temporal_formula temporal_op
  non_temporal_formula
```

The assertion is transformed into the finite automaton form for the automated verification by the decomposition process. The decomposed finite automaton consists of four sections following the assertion name definition: an initial state definition, a final state set definition, a component list definition, and a state transition definition section. The syntax for the definition of a state transition is "*current_state* ⇒ *next_state* ? *condition*". This means a state transition from *current_state* to *next_state* occurs when the *condition* is satisfied. The *condition* is a logical connection of Boolean expressions. The general format of the decomposed finite automaton is:

```
assertion assertion_name
  components: component list definition
  initial state: state definition
  final state: state definition
  state transitions: state transition list definition
end assertion_name
```

Example 17.4.1

The state variable *proc_status* of BUF in the GEN-BUF-PROC model represents the status of PROC. If PROC finishes the processing, *proc_status* changes to FREE. And if BUF sends a job to PROC, *proc_status* becomes BUSY. So the atomic operation A2 in Section 17.2.3 is specified like this temporal logic assertion "Sending_Op: *proc_status = FREE* → ◇ *proc_status = BUSY*". The specification for this formula is given as follows.

```
assertional specification
  components: PROC processor
atomic assertions: Sending_Op: Always((proc_status = FREE)
                         → Sometimes (proc_status = BUSY))
end specification
```

The specification for the decomposition result of the formula is shown below, wherein we abbreviate the temporal formula ◇ (*proc_status* = BUSY) as BUSY_STATUS for convenience.

```
assertion Sending_Op
  components: PROC processor;
  initial state: S;
  final state: S;
  state transitions:
    S ⇒ S ? ~ (proc_status = FREE);
    S ⇒ BUSY_STATUS ? (proc_status = FREE);
    BUSY_STATUS ⇒ S ? (proc_status = BUSY);
    BUSY_STATUS ⇒ BUSY_STATUS ? ~ (proc_status = BUSY);
end Sending_Op
```

17.5 Model Verification by Language Acceptance Checking

The language acceptance checker determines whether the operational specification satisfies the assertional specification. If a language set defined by temporal logic formulas contains a language set generated from the untimed DEVS model, the language acceptance checker concludes that the developed model satisfies the desired properties. The language acceptance checker consists of the untimed DEVS model execution engine, the temporal logic grammar parser, and the language acceptance checker. The TL grammar parser controls the transition of a TL finite automaton by examining the language set generated from the DEVS execution engine. The language acceptance checker examines the containment between the language of the DEVS model and the language of the TL grammar. This is done by memorizing the global state transitions for an overall DEVS model to check whether the transition is closed.

If a model has a state trajectory $S_0,S_1,S_3,S_4,S_3,S_4, \ldots$, then a sentence $\omega = s_0 s_1 (s_3 s_4)^*$ can be generated from the model. Generally, a model can have various state trajectories. So we can define a language *L(M)* for the DEVS model as a set of all possible state trajectories:

$$L(M) = \left\{\omega \middle| S_0^{\delta^*} \Rightarrow \omega, \omega \in S^*\right\}.$$

We can also define a language for the grammar *G* of the temporal logic formula. The language for *G* is defined as

$$L(G) = \left\{\omega \middle| S^{P^*} \Rightarrow \omega, \omega \in V_T^*\right\}.$$

A sentence ω of *L(G)* consists of non-temporal logic formulas that represent a status of the DEVS models. Thus, there exist logical containments between sentences of the languages *L(G)* and *L(M)*. We now examine whether the language *L(G)* of TL formulas contains the language *L(M)* of the DEVS model. If *L(G)* contains *L(M)*, then the behaviors of the DEVS model satisfy the desired properties.

The language acceptance checking process is a tree traversal with backtracking as follows:

1. Start with the initial state of the DEVS model and of the finite automaton.
2. Find the set of all possible next states from the DEVS model. Then, select a state from the set that satisfies the transition condition of the finite automaton. If there exists a satisfied transition condition, then transit to the next state. If none of the generated next states satisfies any transition conditions in the finite automaton, then this current global state is a deadlock state. In this situation, both the DEVS model and the finite automaton backtrack to the previous state.
3. Repeat the generation of the global states of the DEVS model and the finite automaton until the generated global state trajectories are closed.

Consider the global operation A7 in Section 17.2.3. The temporal property of this operation is specified as: (BUF.queue = $n > 0 \wedge$ PROC.status = FREE) $\rightarrow \Diamond$ (BUF.queue = $n-1 \wedge$ PROC.status = BUSY). By applying the decomposition process to this formula, the finite automaton as shown in Figure 7a is obtained. The possible reachable state set of the GEN-PROC-BUF model is shown in Figure 7b. In the state diagram, we abbreviate the global state ((BUF. queue = v1, BUF.proc_status = v2), PROC.status = v3, GEN.status = v4) as ((v1, v2), v3, v4). A concurrent operation of sending and receiving a job in the GEN-PROC-BUF model causes a transition from the initial state ((0, F), F, A) to the next state ((1, F), F, A). Then the model sends a string ((BUF.queue = 1 $\wedge$ BUF. proc_status = FREE) PROC. status = FREE $\wedge$ GEN.status = ACTIVE) to the finite automaton. The finite automaton has two alternative transitions at the initial state S0. However, the received string satisfies only the condition of the transition S0 $\wedge$ S1. So the global state of the DEVS model and the TL finite automaton moves to [((1,F), F, A), S1]. In the same manner, the computation of state transition between the model and the finite automaton is

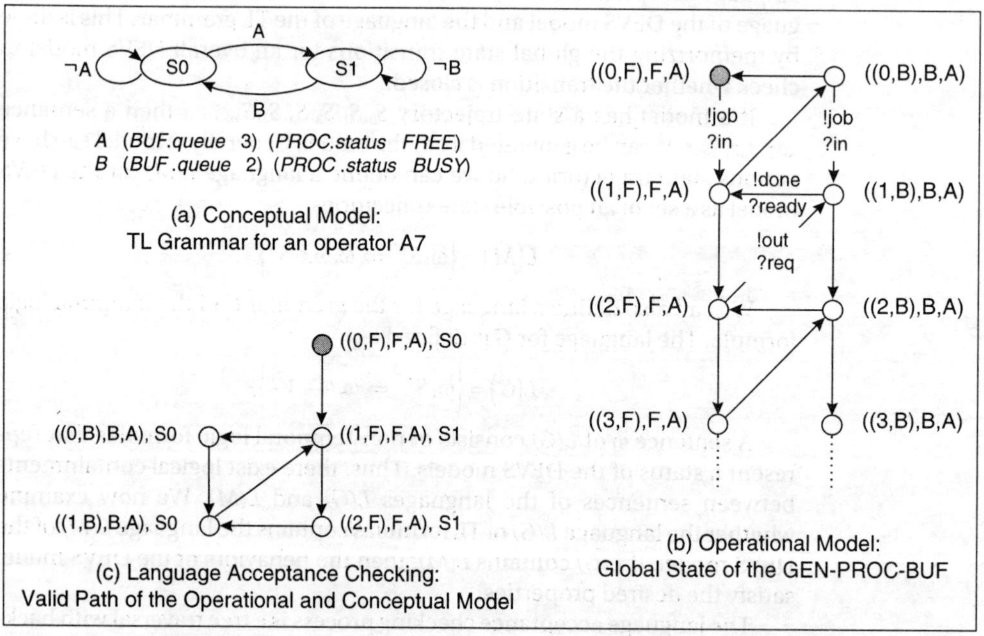

Figure 7 The language acceptance checking for the GEN-BUF-PROC.

continued until the global state trajectory is closed. Figure 7c shows the state transition results for the language acceptance checking.

17.6 Performance Evaluation

Performance evaluation can be done by simulation of DEVS models. To measure time-related performance, such as delay time and throughput, requires timed DEVS models in which sojourn time between states for each atomic DEVS model is specified. Thus, time-related information should be added to specification of untimed DEVS models for simulation-based performance evaluation. Such information includes time advance function for atomic DEVS models and select function for coupled DEVS models. Once a timed DEVS model is constructed, simulation of such a model is performed by using simulators explained in Chapter 8.

Simulation-based-performance measurement requires careful design of the experimental frame (Chapter 2). Design of the experimental frame is objective-driven, i.e., different design objectives require different experimental frames. More specifically, a set of design objectives is transformed into a set of performance indices. Then, an experimental frame is designed such that the desired performance indices are measured by simulation. Thus, simulation-based design is an iterative process in which a model is simulated with a set of different experimental frames, or a set of candidate models is simulated with an experimental frame, until a desired design is found.

An experimental frame basically consists of three models: a model for generating inputs to the model under study, a model for collecting output data from the model, and a model for controlling the simulation run. We call these three models a generator, an acceptor, and a transducer, respectively (Chapter 2). The three models are analogous, in their functions, to a signal generator, an oscilloscope, and a spectrum analyzer, respectively, in an electronic circuit experiment. The generator model is often called an input model and characterizes the statistical distribution of data to be generated. However, the statistical characterization needs to be validated against meaningful data collected from a real system. Likewise, data collected from an acceptor needs to be analyzed statistically to conclude a meaningful result.

17.7 Implementation: DEVS Model Execution

Unlike conventional software development, the implementation phase is no longer a transformation of DEVS models into executable program code. Instead, the developed DEVS models remain unchanged and are themselves implementations that are executed just like the transformed program code. Of course, execution of the models in such a manner requires a model execution engine or environment. The engine within the methodology can be developed either as a language compiler form or as an OS-like library.

Figure 8 shows comparison between conventional and DEVS-based implementation methods. As shown in the figure, the DEVS-based implementation requires no code transformation, since it provides a DEVS

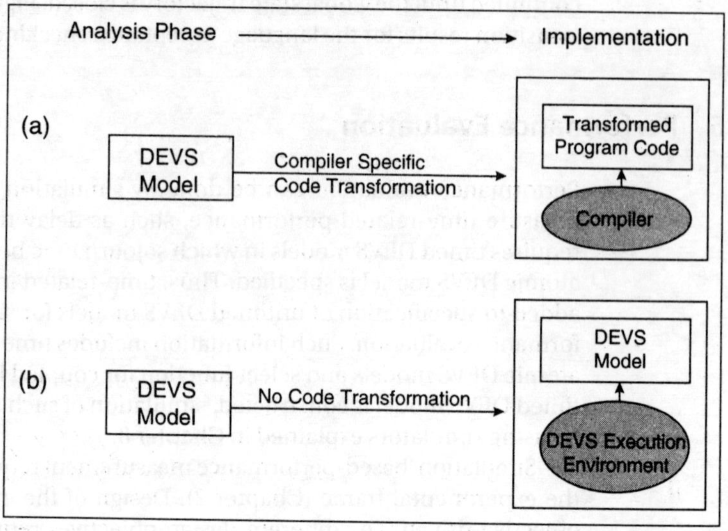

Figure 8 Systems development methods (a) Conventional implementation, (b) DEVS-based implementation.

execution environment. An executable DEVS model is specified by the real-time DEVS formalism discussed in Chapter 10. Recall that specification of a real-time DEVS requires an activity associated with each state. The activity is a function, which is executed during an internal state transition. In this sense, each activity can be thought of as an implementation of the internal state transition. In other words, if the activity is abstracted to an internal transition, this presupposes that its details are not required in the logical analysis and performance evaluation phases. Consequently, any function that is required in the real system is implemented either (1) as an activity in the real-time DEVS formalism or (2) as an atomic or coupled model with a set of activities under its control. Since each atomic model has a set of activities, an overall coupled model has a set of activities running concurrently.

Although an executable DEVS model is specified by the real-time DEVS formalism, the time advance function defined for the formalism cannot be used for the executable DEVS. This is because an executable DEVS model actually executes a function, i.e., an activity, during internal transition, whose execution time may not be known in advance. Thus, event synchronization in the model execution environment may not be the same as in the real-time DEVS simulator, which uses the time advance information for event scheduling.

The model execution environment is designed such that a set of activities during internal transitions for atomic models runs concurrently while it handles an external event generated from an atomic model as an interrupt to an activity. Thus, an activity is interrupted by an external event and resumed after executing the external event. Multiple threads, which are supported by a real-time operating system, may be used to emulate such control of concurrent processes. Thus, the execution control of the model execution environment is done by a set of threads. There are different ways to associate threads to

DEVS models to execute DEVS models in real time. One way is that a thread is associated with each atomic model for internal transition, while only one thread is used for external events for a set of atomic models. Another way is that two threads are associated with each atomic model, one for execution of an activity during internal transition and the other for external event handling.

17.8 Summary

This chapter has presented and "end-to-end" systems design methodology based on the DEVS formalism. The methodology incorporates logical analysis and automated implementation in addition to simulation. Although the framework is quite general, the aspects considered here were restricted to temporal logic analysis and to the real-time software domain. Since, as discussed in Chapter 9, there are many formalisms for discrete event systems analysis, and many design domains, what we have presented represents only one possibility for such a design methodology. Many variations can be expected on the same theme. Speaking of variations, the next chapter considers how to organize and generate alternative model structures in a systems design methodology.

17.9 Sources

The role of systems-theory based modeling in computer-aided systems design is discussed in Ref. [6]. Employing the DEVS formulation as a computational basis for systems theory-based modeling is advocated in Refs. [8,9]. The DEVS-based methodology presented here is based on Refs. [2–4] and temporal logic [2,5]. As another alternative, Schulz [7] presents an integrated systems design environment, employing DEVSJAVA, and incorporating model specification in Statecharts (Chapter 9).

1. Gotzhein, R., "Temporal Logic and Applications—A Tutorial." *Computer Networks and ISDN Systems* **24,** 1992.
2. Hong, K. P., "DEVS-Based Framework for Logical and Performance Analysis of Discrete Event Systems," Ph.D. Thesis, Dept. of EE, KAIST, 1996.
3. Hong, K. P., and T. G. Kim, "The DEVS Formalism: A Framework for Logical Analysis and Performance Evaluation for Discrete Event Systems," *Proceedings of AIS,* pp. 170–175, 1994, Gainsville, FL.
4. Hong, K. P., and T. G. Kim, "A Framework for Verifying Discrete Event Models Within a DEVS-Based Development Methodology," *Trans. of SCS* **13** (1), 19–34 (1996).
5. Manna, Z., and A. Pnueli, *The Temporal Logic of Reactive and Concurrent Systems.* Springer Verlag, Berlin, 1991.
6. Pichler, F., and H. Schwaertzel, Eds. *CAST (Computer Aided System Theory) Methods in Modelling.* Springer-Verlag, Berlin, 1992.
7. Schulz, S., J. W. Rozenblit, M. Mrva, and K. Buchenrieder, "Model-Based Codesign." *IEEE Computer* **31** (8), 60–74 (1998).

8. Zeigler, B. P., H. Praehofer, and J. W. Rozenblit, "Integrating System Formalisms: How Object Orientation Supports CAST for Intelligent Systems Design." *J. Sys. Engineering* **3,** 209–219 (1993).

9. Zeigler, B. P., T. G. Kim, H. Praehofer, and H. Song., "DEVS Framework for Modelling, Simulation, Analysis, and Design of Hybrid Systems." In *Hybrid II, Lecture Notes in CS,* P. Antsaklis and A. Nerode, Ed. Springer-Verlag, Berlin, 1996, pp. 529–551.

18

System Entity Structure/ Model Base Framework

Simulation-based systems design employs a plan–generate–evaluate process. The *plan* phase organizes all the models of design alternatives within the chosen system boundary and design objectives. The *generate* phase synthesizes a candidate design model intended to meet the set of design objectives. Finally, the *evaluate* phase evaluates behavior and/or performance of the generated model through simulation using an appropriate experimental frame derived from the design objectives. The overall design cycle repeats the generation and evaluation phases until an acceptable design is found.

How can we organize a family of alternative models from which a candidate model can be selected, generated, and evaluated? This chapter presents the systems entity structure/model base (SES/MB) framework for such an organization. The idea is as follows. Let us first extract the hierarchical composition structures of hierarchical, modular models (Chapter 7) from their implementations. Then we save the structures and the implementations separately in organized libraries. Figure 1 shows the basic idea in which libraries for model structures and model implementations are called *system entity structure base* and *model base,* respectively. Our goal is to be able to synthesize a simulation model by traversing a model hierarchical structure, retrieving component implementations and coupling them together. As will be seen later in this chapter, a system entity structure represents not a single model structure, but a family of model structures from which a candidate structure called a *pruned entity structure* can be selected. Thus, the system entity structure/model base framework supports the plan–generate–evaluate process in systems design.

18.1 Model Base Management by System Entity Structure

A *model base* is an organized library of models that may be either atomic or coupled. Models can be saved in the model base for later retrieval. Models so retrieved may be reused to create more complex models. Thus, the model base approach will improve the productivity of the modeling subtask in the overall systems design process.

Figure 2 shows an approach to model base management that relies on the concept of system entity structure to be explained in the next section. The behaviors of primitive components of a real world system are specified by atomic models and saved in the model base (Fig. 2a). The structural knowledge of the system is represented as a system entity structure (Fig. 2b)

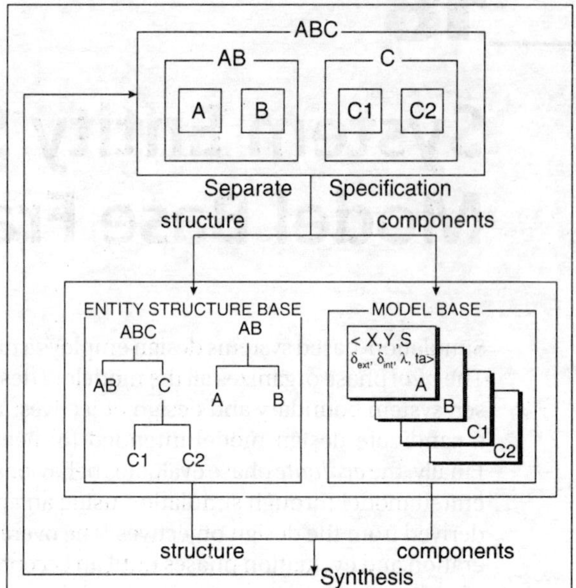

Figure 1 System entity structure/model base concept.

by means of an operation called *entity structuring*. The entity structure, here, serves as a compact representation for organizing all possible hierarchical composition structures of the system. This separation of model composition structures from their behaviors may reduce the modeling complexity of real-world systems. Moreover, such separation allows designers to easily construct candidate models with different structures while using the same components. To construct a desired simulation model to meet design objectives, the *pruning* operation is used to reduce the SES to a pruned entity structure, PES (Fig. 2c). This pruned entity structure can be transformed into a composition tree (Fig. 2d) and eventually synthesized into a simulation model (Fig. 2e) by combining it with models in the model base. Such models are evaluated via simulation to determine superior solutions to the design objectives.

18.2 System Entity Structure

The system entity structure formalism is a structural knowledge representation scheme that systematically organizes a family of possible structures of a system. Such a family characterizes decomposition, coupling, and taxonomic relationships among entities. An *entity* represents a real-world object. The decomposition of an entity concerns how it may be broken down into subentities. As discussed in Chapters 2 and 7, coupling specifications tell how subentities may be coupled together to reconstitute the entity. The *taxonomic* relationship concerns admissible variants of an entity.

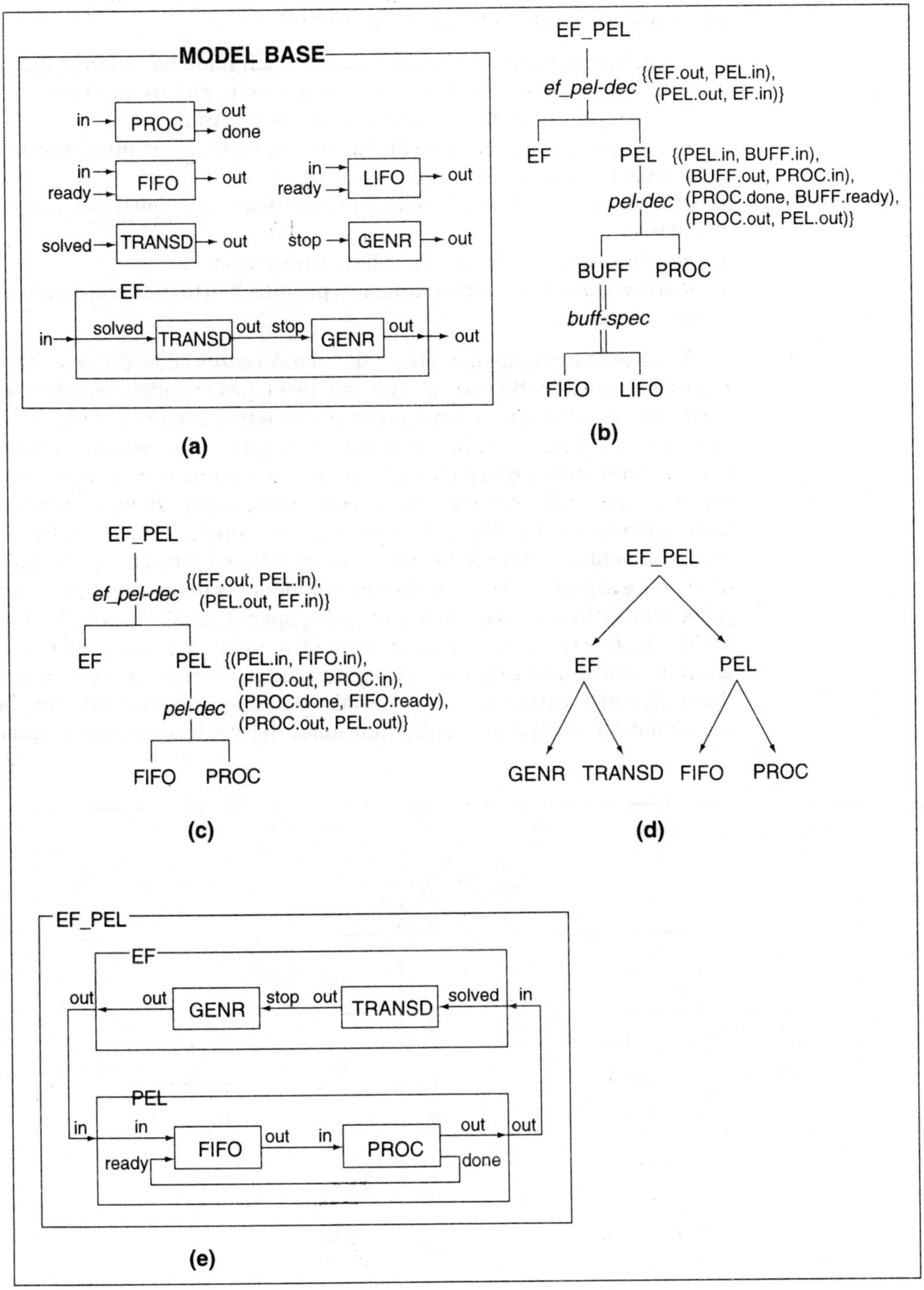

Figure 2 Model base management scheme. (a) Model base, (b) system entity structure (SES), (c) pruned entity structure (PES), (d) composition tree, (e) synthesized model.

As shown in Fig. 3, an SES is represented as a labeled tree with attached attributes that satisfies the following axioms:

1. Alternating *entity aspect/specialization:* Each node has a mode that is either *entity* or *specialization* such that a node and its successors are always opposite modes; the mode of the root is entity.
2. *Uniformity:* Any two nodes with the same names have identical attached variable types and isomorphic subtrees.
3. *Strict hierarchy:* No label appears more than once down any path of the tree.
4. *Valid brothers:* No two brothers have the same label.
5. *Attached variables:* No two variable types attached to the same item have the same name.

There are three types of nodes in the tree. An *entity* node, e.g., *A* in Fig. 3, represents a real-world object. There are two types of entity, namely *composite* entity and *atomic* entity. A composite entity is defined in terms of other entities (which may be either atomic or composite), while an atomic entity cannot broken down into subentities. Each entity may have attached *variables.* It may also have several aspects and/or specializations. An *aspect* node, such as *A-dec* in Fig. 3, is connected by a single vertical line from a composite entity. It represents one decomposition of the entity. The children of the aspect are entities, distinct components of the decomposition. Associated with each aspect is a *coupling* specification. A *specialization* node, e.g., *B-spec* in Fig. 3, is connected by a double vertical line from an entity. It defines the taxonomy of the entity and represents the way in which the entity can be categorized into specialized entities. *Selection rules* may be associated with each specialization and guide the way in which a specialized

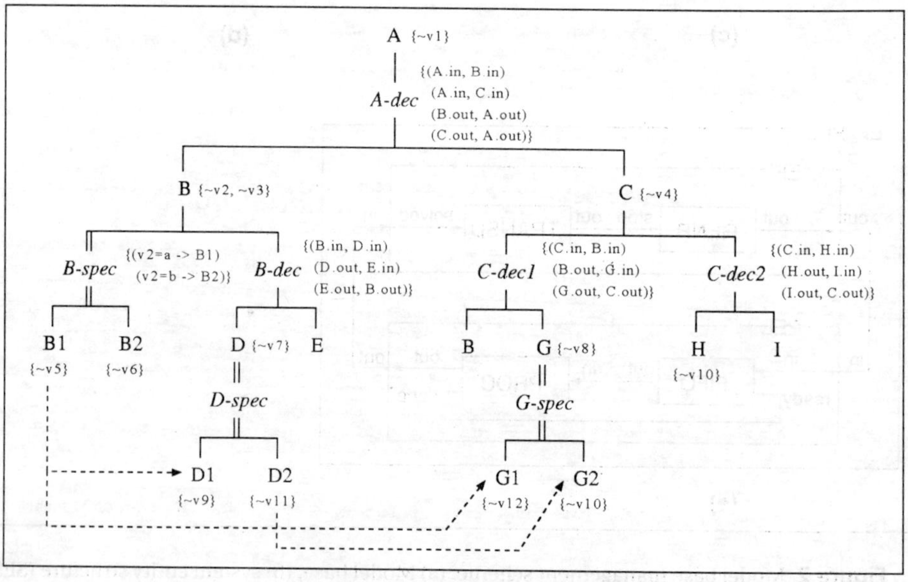

Figure 3 A system entity structure.

entity is selected in the pruning process. A *selection constraint*, depicted as dotted arrow from an entity to other entities in Fig. 3, means that not all entities may be selected independently. Once a specialized entity is chosen from a specialization, some specialized entities in other specializations associated with the specialization are also selected. The dotted arrows from *B*1 to *D*1 and *G*1 in Fig. 3 enforces the following selection constraints: "If entity *B*1 is selected from specialization *B-spec* then select entity *D*1 from specialization *D-spec* and entity *G*1 from specialization *G-spec*."

18.3 System Entity Structure/Model Base (SES/MB) Framework

As we explained in a previous section, the SES/MB framework is a powerful means to support the plan–generate–evaluate paradigm in systems design. Within the framework, entity structures organize models in model base. Thus, modeling activity within the framework consists of three subactivities: specification of model composition structure, specification of model behavior, and synthesis of a simulation model.

Figure 4 shows a modeling and simulation methodology based on the framework in the process of iterative systems design. In the figure, the generation phase consists of two subphases: *pruning* and *model synthesis*. The structure specification and/or the behavior specification may already exist in the entity structure base and/or model base. However, if the structure

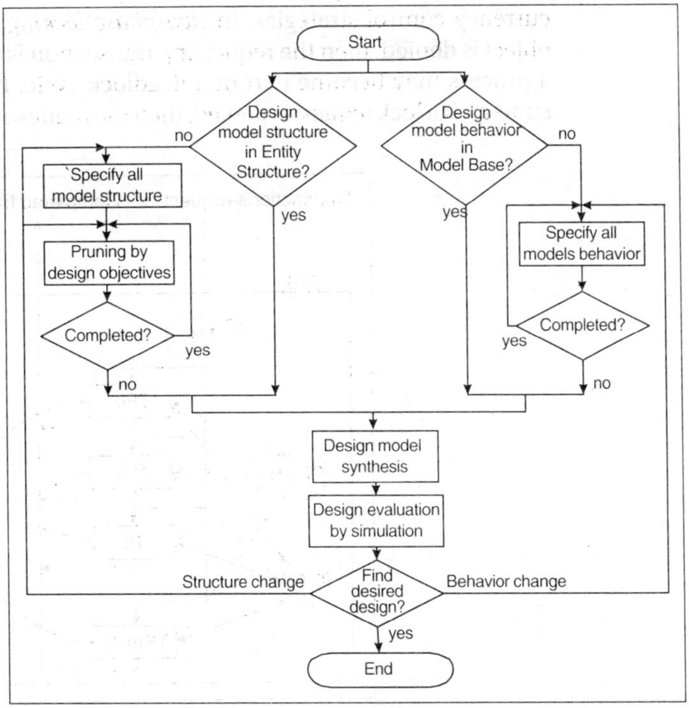

Figure 4 Design methodology using SES/MB framework.

specification is not in the entity structure base, we need to specify it by building an entity structure that represents a family of possible model structures. Likewise, if the desired model components are not in the model base, we need to develop them and store them in the model base for later use. In the pruning phase, we select a substructure by pruning the SES with respect to design objectives. A simulation model is automatically synthesized from such a pruned entity structure. Simulation experiments may require changes of structure and/or behavior of the design model. The pruning–synthesis–evaluation process is repeated until a desired design is found. Once simulation experiments are completed, the designer can save structure and behavior specifications in the system entity structure base and the model base, respectively, for later use.

18.4 Example: Design of a Transaction Processing System

Let us exemplify the SES/MB framework with the design of a transaction processing system. As outlined in Fig. 5, the transaction manager *TM* assigns transactions requested by users to transaction processes. Each transaction process *TP* model represents a particular way of processing a transaction. Once assigned a transaction, it works on it until the transaction is completed or aborted. *CPU* and *DISKS* are resources that can be used when the transactions are executed. *CPU* actually executes the operations of transactions, and *DISKS* are used to store databases. The concurrency control *CC* shares the resources among the transaction processes. There are three kinds of concurrency control strategies. In *two-phase locking*, if a lock request on an object is denied, then the requesting transaction is blocked. In this strategy, a process may become part of a deadlock cycle. In the *immediate-restart* strategy, if a lock request is denied, then the requesting transaction is aborted

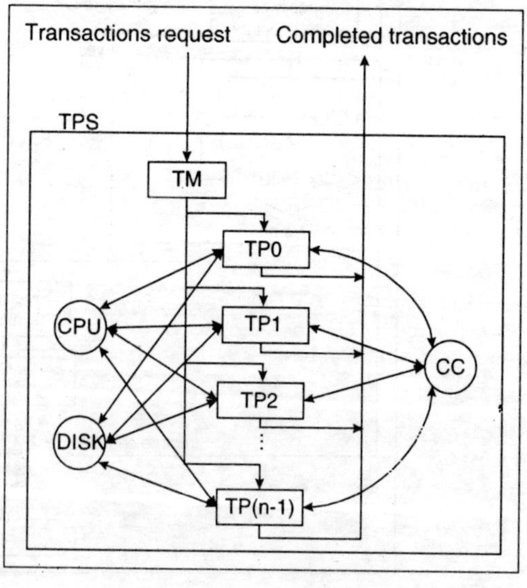

Figure 5 TPS overview.

and restarted. In the *optimistic* strategy, transactions are allowed to execute unhindered and are validated only after they have reached their commit points. Notice that the two-phase and optimistic strategies have counterparts in the distributed simulation protocols discussed in Chapter 11.

18.4.1 System Entity Structure

Let's assume that the primitive models of the TPS are already developed and stored in the model base. From these models, a configuration expert can construct the SES, which organizes possible architectures of the TPS and its performance evaluation module. The root entity *TPS_EXP* is the top-level entity to evaluate a TPS architecture. It is composed of transaction processing system (*TPS*) and experimental frame (*EF*). *TPS* is composed of *TM* for transaction manager, *TP* for transaction processes, *CC* for concurrency control, *CPU*, and *DISKS*. Using the *cc-spec*, the *CC* can be implemented with the two-phase locking (*Lock*), the immediate-restart (*Restart*), or the optimistic (*Optimistic*) algorithms. *CPU* is actually composed of *Buff*, which stores the operations of transactions, and *Proc*, which actually executes the operations. The *Buff* may be classified into two specialized types (*FIFO*, *LIFO*) under the specialization *buff-spec*. The *Proc* is also classified into high-performance processor (*Hproc*) and low-performance one (*Lproc*). The *TP* can be composed of several transaction processes from 1 (*TP1*) to 16 (*TP16*). The *DISKS* may be configured with either one disk (*disks-dec1*) or two disks (*disks-dec2*). Each disk also has a buffer. There are several attributes, such as variables and couplings, attached to entities and aspects.

18.4.2 Model Base

As shown in Fig. 2a, the model base is an organized library for component models in modular form. Such component models can be either atomic or coupled models specified in the DEVS formalism. Since the entity structure of Fig. 6 manages the component models in the model base, there is a correspondence between entity names and model names. A simple correspondence is that names of node entities are identical to names of the corresponding models in the model base. In this case, names of atomic models in the model base are labels of leaf nodes of type entity in the SES. Care must be taken with coupled models, if any, in the model base, since they represent already pruned structures. Thus, the name of a coupled model also labels a corresponding entity in the SES that has children nodes of aspect type—but there is no specialization type on any path from the node down to the leaves.

18.4.3 Pruning and Model Synthesis

Once the TPS_EXP entity structure has been constructed, a designer can explore alternative transaction processing architectures using the pruning operation. Many alternatives may be extracted from the SES. Among the alternatives, the most interesting ones arise from the CC and TP specializations. Consider the following design objective:

> *Find an optimal number of transaction processes and a best concurrency control algorithm that give both high throughput and low response time.*

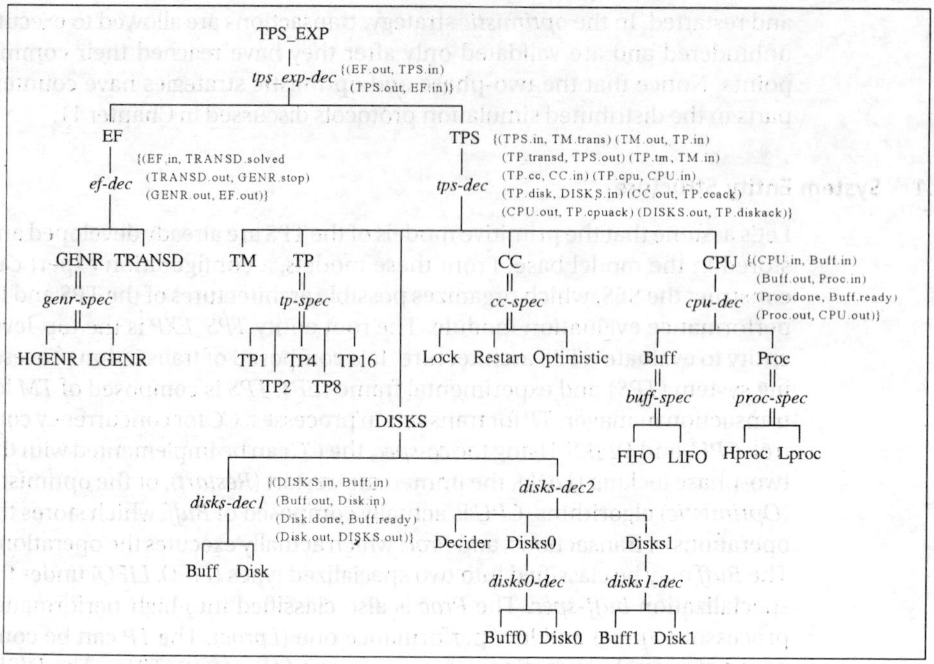

Figure 6 SES for TPS and its experimental frame.

The design objective requires us to construct several kind of simulation models, each with a different algorithm for concurrency control and with a different number of transaction processes. The number of transaction processes puts a limit on the number of transactions allowed to be active at any time. Table 1 shows an example of the pruning choices consistent with the design objective. It selects the *TP8* for the *TP* specialization, the *Lock* for the *CC* specialization, and so on.

A configuration expert who constructed the TPS entity structure may also provide some facilities to help users generate good alternatives by constraining the pruning process as mentioned earlier. Figure 7 shows an example pruned entity structure. A simulation model can be synthesized by retrieving component models from the model base, which correspond to entities in the PES from the model base. Figure 8 shows the synthesized model TPS_EXP from PES of Fig. 7.

18.4.4 Performance Evaluation

Once a simulation model is synthesized, performance evaluation can be carried out via simulation experiments. Performance indices to be measured in the experimental frame should be derived from the design objectives (Chapter 2). Recall that our design objective was to find the optimal number of transaction processes and a best concurrency control algorithm for both high throughput and fast response time. Thus, our performance indices are

Table 1 Pruning Specifications

Entity	Selection	Input
TP	tp-spec ?	TP8
CC	cc-spec ?	Lock
Proc	proc-spec ?	Hproc
Buff	buff-spec ?	FIFO
DISKS	aspect ?	disks-decl
GENR	genr-spec ?	HGENR

throughput and response time. These will be measured for different concurrency control strategies as a function of number of concurrent transaction processes. The model TRANSD (transducer) within the experimental frame is already designed to measure such indices. The simulation model in Fig. 8 is used to evaluate the lock concurrency control strategy with a maximum of eight transaction processes. For each alternative concurrency control strategy, we provide a pruning specification of the form shown in Table 1. Each such specification generates a corresponding PES, which automatically synthesizes an alternative simulation model for performance

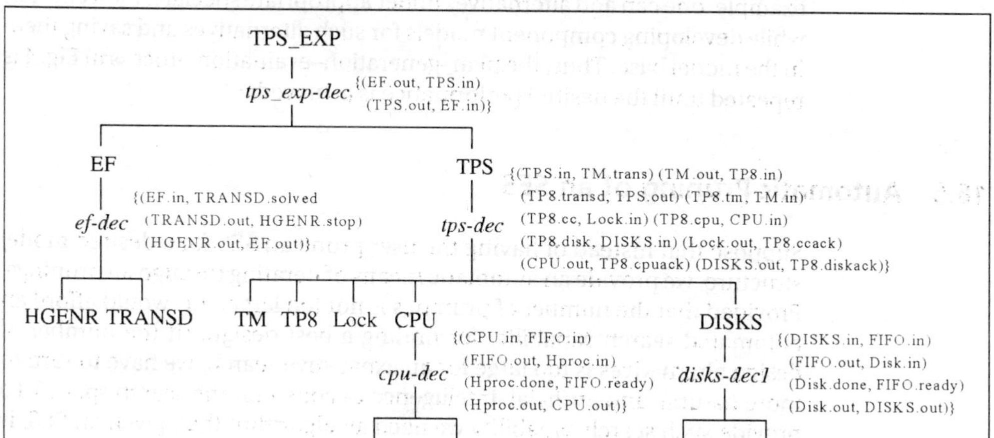

Figure 7 TPS pruned entity structure.

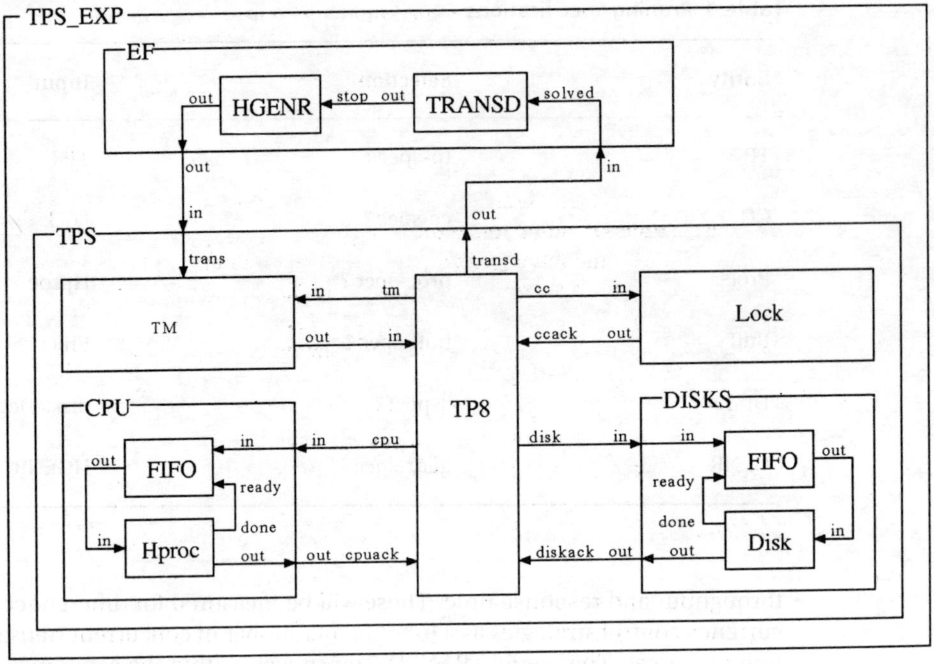

Figure 8 Synthesized simulation model for TPS evaluation.

evaluation. The pruning–synthesis–evaluation process is repeated until an optimal number of transaction processes and a best concurrency control strategy are found. If however, the process fails to achieve the desired performance, the designer must return to extend or modify the SES/MB. For example, one can add alternatives under appropriate specialization entities, while developing component models for such alternatives and saving them in the model base. Thus, the plan–generation–evaluation process in Fig. 4 is repeated until the desired performance is achieved.

18.5 Automatic Pruning of an SES

Suppose that instead of having the user prune an SES for a desired model structure, we provide an automatic means of iterating through all prunings. Provided that the number of prunings is not too large, this would afford an automated search capability for finding a best design. (If the number of design alternatives is too large for an exhaustive search, we have to turn to more natural, and artificial, intelligence to constrain the search space.) To provide such search capability we need an algorithm that, given an SES, is capable of computing its total number of prunings and iterating through them one at a time, each time synthesizing the associated hierarchical simulation model from the model base and evaluating it. In the following we describe a design for such an algorithm.

Recall that an SES is built recursively with alternating specializations and decompositions. Likewise, the number of alternative prunings can be enumerated and generated recursively. An nCounter (discussed in Chapter 4) is used to iterate through the number of alternatives (n) at each specialization. A multicounter, which is a serial composition (Chapter 5) of nCounters, iterates through all alternatives under a decomposition by stepping its component nCounters through these alternatives one at a time. The number of alternatives under a decomposition is the *product* of the alternatives under its entities. For example, there are nCounters for each of the subtrees under *E1, E2,* and *E3* under *E-dec* in Fig. 9. The multicounter under *E-dec* cycles through a total of $N1 \times N2 \times N3$ alternatives. The number of alternatives under a specialization is the *sum* of those under its entities. For example, the number under *E2-spec* is *S1+S2+S3.* This recursion stops when leaf entities are encountered. The number of alternatives represented by a leaf entity is just 1 (itself). Finally, the number of prunings of the SES is the number of alternatives under the root node.

***Exercise*:** Recall the design the nCounter as a parameterized atomic model in Chapter 5. Design the multicounter as parameterized coupled model with nCounter components. Write the formal algorithm that assigns nCounters and multicounters to nodes in the SES. Design an iteration control that steps the root nCounter through its cycle, thereby stepping each of the counters in the SES through their cycles.◆

18.6 Summary

We have discussed the System Entity Structure/Model Base methodology for organizing model families and storing and reusing model components. The SES supports combinatorally, and automatically, generating alternative model candidates in a plan–generate–evaluate methodology for systems

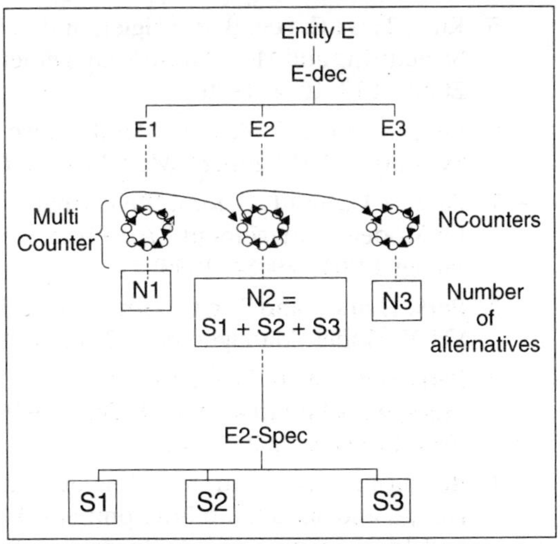

Figure 9 Enumerating SES prunings.

design. Here, planning involves developing an SES/MB for an applications domain, generating is done by automatically synthesizing simulation models from pruned entity structures, and evaluating is accomplished through simulation of the candidate designs. When the combinatorics grow too large, more intelligence, natural and artificial, needs to be brought in to make headway. Collaboration is an essential way to make this happen, as we discuss next.

18.7 Sources

The system entity structure concepts were first presented in Zeigler [12]. Subsequently, Rozenblit [10] extended and implemented these concepts in a knowledge based design environment. The combined SES/MB methodology originated with Kim [5] and Zeigler [13]. Subsequent formalizations and implementations were developed in Luh [6] and Park [7, 9]. Automatic SES pruning is discussed in Couretas [4]. Applications of the SES/MB methodology to various domains are given in Refs. [1–3,8,11,14]. The SES/MB framework is implemented in DEVSJAVA, available on the Web from www.acims.arizona.edu

1. Chi, S. D., J. Lee, and Y. Kim, "Using the SES/MB Framework to Analyze Traffic Flow." *Trans. of SCS* **14**(4), 211–221 (1997).
2. Cho, T. H., and B. P. Zeigler, "Simulation of Intelligent Hierarchical Flexible Manufacturing." *IEEE Trans. Syst. Man Cyber.* **27**(1), 116–125 (1997).
3. Cho, T. H., B. P. Zeigler, and J. W. Rozenblit, "A Knowledge Based Simulation Environment for Hierarchical Flexible Manufacturing." *IEEE Trans. Sys. Man & Cyber.—Part A: Systems and Humans* **26**(1), 81–91 (1996).
4. Couretas, J., "System Entity Structure Alternatives Enumeration Environment (SEAS)," Ph.D. Thesis, Dept of ECE, University of Arizona, 1998.
5. Kim., T. G., C. Lee, B. P. Zeigler, and E. R. Christensen, "System Entity Structuring and Model Base Management," *IEEE Trans. Sys. Man Cyber.* **20**(5), 1013–1024 (1990).
6. Luh, C., and B. P. Zeigler, "Model Base Management for Multifaceted Systems." *ACM Trans. on Modeling and Comp. Sim* **1**(3), 195–218 (1991).
7. Park, H. C., and T. G. Kim, "Relational Algebraic System Entity Structure for Models Management," *IEE Proceedings Computer and Digital Technology* **143**(1), 49–54 (1996).
8. Park, Hyu C., and Tag G. Kim, "A Relational Algebraic Framework for VHDL Models Management," *Trans. of SCS* **15,** (2), 43–55 (1998).
9. Park, H. C., W. B. Lee, and T. G. Kim, "RASES: A Database Supported Framework for Structured Model Base Management." *Simulation Practice and Theory* **5,** 289–313 (1997).
10. Rozenblit, J. W., J. Hu, B. P. Zeigler, and T. G. Kim, "Knowledge-Based Design and Simulation Environment (KBDSE): Foundational Concepts and Implementation," *J. Operations Research Society* **41**(6), 475–489 (1990).

11. Sevinc, S., and B. P. Zeigler, "Entity Structure Based Design Methodology: Application to LAN Protocol Design," *IEEE Trans. on System Engineering* **14**(3), 375–383 (1988).
12. Zeigler, B. P., *Multifacetted Modelling and Discrete Event Simulation.* Academic Press, London, 1984.
13. Zeigler, B. P., *Object-Oriented Simulation with Hierarchical, Modular Models: Intelligent Agents and Endomorphic Systems.* Academic Press, San Diego, 1990.
14. Zeigler, B. P., M. Young, and S. Vahie, "Successive Approximation in Multifacetted Modelling Methodology: Human Performance Models." *Trans. of the SCS* **14**(1), 25–36 (1997).

19

Collaboration and the Future

We all know that we can get much farther ahead by collaborating with others than by working alone. Why, then, is it so hard to do? In modeling and simulation, partial knowledge about a system may be held by many people and it is difficult to unify such partial views into a more unified whole. Partial views are inherent in many aspects of modern life, among them the breakdown of knowledge into disciplines, the physical separation of work environments from each other, and the specialization of tasks and reporting structures.

Collaboration can take place in conventional meetings (same time/same place), synchronously (same time/different places), or asynchronously (different times/different places). A wide range of multimedia technologies can be invoked to provide capabilities such as whiteboarding, voice, and video teleconferencing in order to promote rich and natural interactions among remote users. Although various modeling and simulation tools can support people who work together to build models and execute simulations, their support for collaboration of this sophistication level is ad hoc and limited.

In this concluding chapter, we look into the future where modeling and simulation environments will support extensive and productive collaboration among the different and varied people who construct models, execute simulations, and interpret the results. We will provide an architecture for such environments that serves a secondary purpose—it provides an organized summary of the concepts developed in the book.

19.1 An Architecture for M&S

Figure 1 shows a conceptual layered architecture that is intended to provide a framework for implementing comprehensive collaborative environments for M&S (Modeling and Simulation). First we outline the layers:

- The *Network Layer* contains the actual computers (including workstations and high-performance systems) and the connecting networks (both LAN and WAN, their hardware and software) that do the work of supporting all aspects of the M&S lifecycle.
- The *Simulation Layer* is the software that executes the models to generate their behavior (the essence of simulation). Included in this layer are the protocols of Chapters 8 and 11 that provide the basis for distributed simulation (which are standardized in the High Level Architecture (HLA)). Also included are database management systems and software systems to

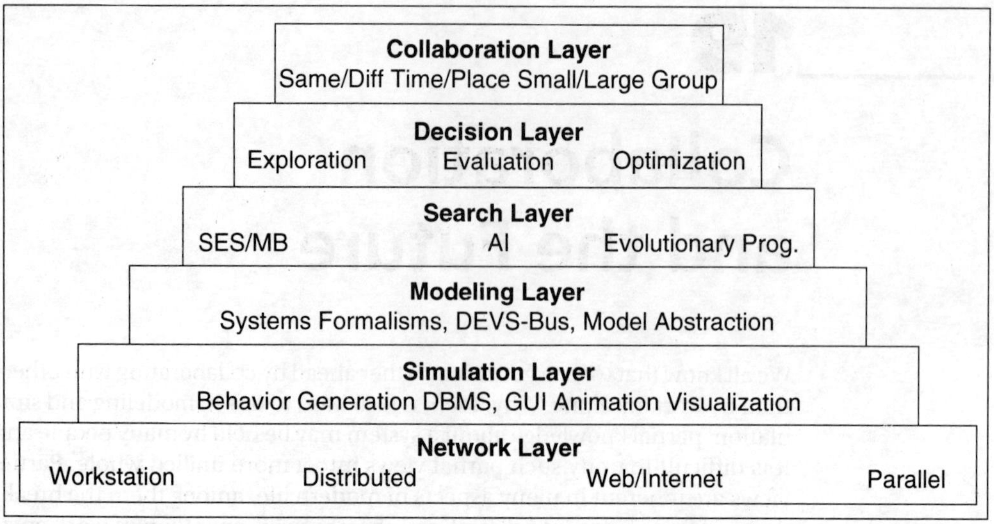

Figure 1 Architecture for modeling and simulation.

support control of simulation executions, visualization, and animation of the generated behaviors.

- The *Modeling Layer* supports the development of models in formalisms that are independent of any given simulation layer implementation. The HLA just mentioned also provides object-oriented templates for model description aimed at supporting confederations of globally dispersed models. However, beyond this, the formalisms for model dynamics, whether continuous, discrete or discrete event in nature (Chapters 6, 7, 9, and 10) are also included in this layer. Model construction and especially, the key processes of model abstraction (Chapters 13 and 14) and the DEVS-Bus representation (Chapters 15 and 16) are also included.
- The *Search Layer* supports the investigation of large families of alternative models, whether in the form of spaces set up by parameters (Chapter 13) or more powerful means of specifying alternative model structures provided by the SES/MB methodology (Chapter 18). Artificial intelligence and simulated natural intelligence (evolutionary programming) may be brought in to help deal with combinatorial explosions occasioned by powerful model synthesizing capabilities.
- The *Decision Layer* applies the capability to search and simulate large model sets to real problem domains to support explorations, "what-if" investigations, training exercises and optimizations. The DEVS-based design methodology of Chapter 17 is an example of work at this layer.
- The *Collaboration Layer* enables people with partial knowledge about a system, whether based on discipline, location, task, or responsibility specialization, to bring to bear individual perspectives and contributions to achieve an overall M&S goal.

One primary issue that must be addressed in developing collaborative environments is what form of collaboration is best suited to which activities in M&S and under what circumstances. We take a brief stab at this sort of question next.

19.2 How Does Collaboration Support M&S?

M&S comprises a complex and multifaceted set of activities, many of which require the joint efforts of diverse, geographically dispersed participants. Rather than attempt to characterize the applicability of collaboration support to the whole gamut of M&S activities, we will concentrate on two types of activities that are germane to current concerns.

19.2.1 Model Construction

The first example, *model construction,* considers creating a model from scratch. As illustrated in skeletal form in Fig. 2, some main phases of this process involve *clarifying objectives* of model development, *collecting data* whether in the form of knowledge of how things work or in numerical observed data of rates and other such parameters, *model building* per se, and *model validation.*

19.2.2 Model Composition

The second example is that of *model composition,* as sketched in Fig. 3. Here, rather than building a model from scratch, it is cobbled together from models resident in a repository. This is the paradigm underlying the HLA and is intended to save time and effort by facilitating high levels of model and simulation reuse.

19.2.3 Supporting M&S with Collaboration Environments

Figure 4 illustrates how modes of collaboration—conventional meetings, synchronous and asynchronous forms of work—might apply to model construction. Figure 5 presents a similar assignment for model composition.

To justify these assignments, consider that it is very hard to get people to agree on common objectives in building a model. Perhaps the only way to do that is to bring them together in one room and try to hammer out agreement through seemingly endless discussions. Several meetings of this sort might be required. However, once objectives are settled, much of the work can be done independently and at one's own site, using one's own resources. For example, collecting data or searching for available model components might be done in such an asynchronous fashion. At some

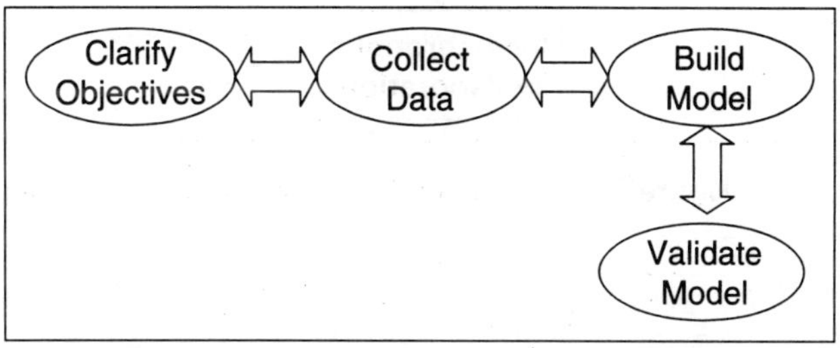

Figure 2 Sketch of model construction use case.

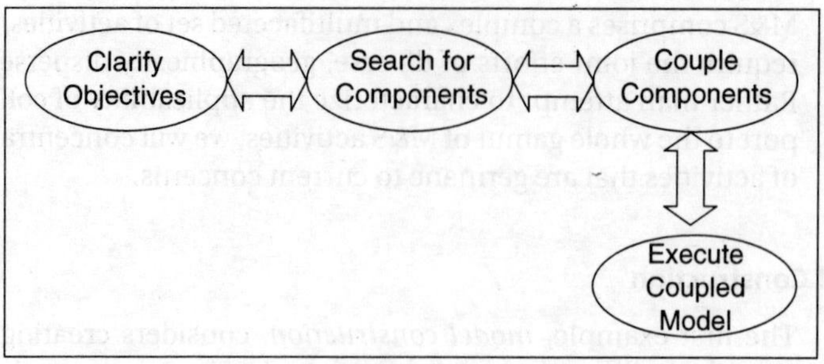

Figure 3 Sketch of model composition use case.

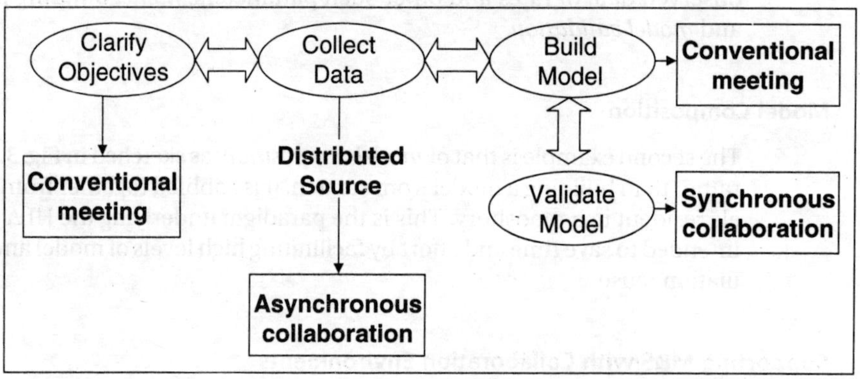

Figure 4 Model construction with assigned collaboration modes.

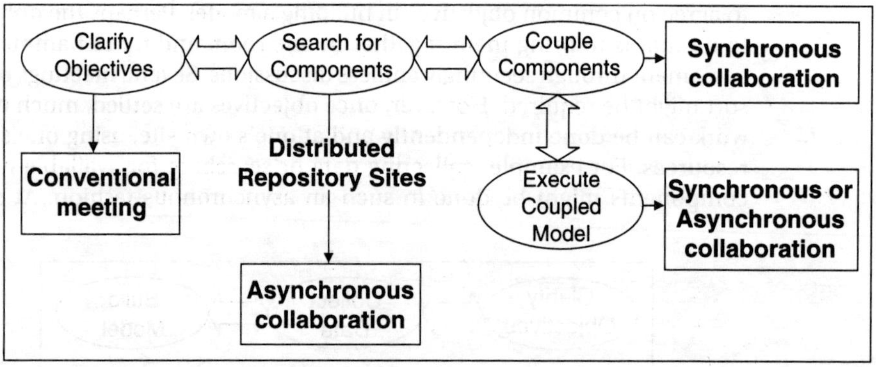

Figure 5 Model composition with assigned collaboration modes.

point, it may be advisable to bring all participants together at the same time, although not necessarily at one place. This form of asynchronous meeting, such as a video teleconference, might be the best way to coordinate activities requiring rich interaction, for example, coupling of model components at dispersed sites to form a distributed simulation.

19.3 Summary

We have discussed an architecture for support of collaborative M&S. The architecture of layers organizes the concepts and activities discussed in this book and enables us to examine some issues that emerge when considering how to develop support for collaboration in M&S. These can be outlined as follows:

- What are the benefits of collaboration, specifically in the context of M&S?
- Distinguishing between asynchronous and synchronous collaboration modes, which activities in M&S are amenable to support by one or another of these means? On what set of criteria should such choices be made?
- How can a collaborative architecture, expressed at the logical design level, be implemented in current and foreseeable hardware and software platforms?
- How does the choice of M&S activities to be supported and the assignment of collaboration modes to them affect the design?
- How can M&S itself be used to study alternative implementation designs of the collaboration architecture?
- Can such an environment be "boot-strapped" into existence—using a rudimentary implementation to design successively more capable ones?

It is too early to give definitive answers to these questions and others like them. We hope that this brief presentation, and this book, have brought to light some new possibilities for support of collaborative M&S, and indeed, new vistas for the enterprise of M&S itself.

19.4 Sources

1. Sarjoughian, H., and S. Vahie, "Group Enabled DEVS Model Construction Methodology for Distributed Organizations." Presented at Enabling Technology for Simulation Science, SPIE AeoroSense 97, Orlando, FL., 1997.
2. Sarjoughian, H. S., James Nutaro, and B. P. Zeigler, "Collaborative DEVS Modeler." Presented at SCS Western Multi-Conference, Web-based Modeling and Simulation, San Diego, 1999.
3. Zeigler, B. P., H. S. Sarjoughian, and S. Vahie, "An Architecture for Collaborative Modeling and Simulation." Presented at 11th European Simulation Multiconference, Istanbul, Turkey, 1997.

Index

Numbers followed by the letter f indicate figures; numbers followed by the letter t indicate tables.

D

E

N

O